HOUSE OF LORDS

Science and Technology Committee

1st Report of Session 2005-06

Ageing: Scientific Aspects

Volume II: Evidence

Ordered to be printed 05 July 2005 and published 21 July 2005

Published by the Authority of the House of Lords

London : The Stationery Office Limited
£30.50

HL Paper 20-II

CONTENTS

Written Evidence

The Committee's Report drawing on this oral and written evidence is
published as a separate volume, HL Paper 20-I.

Minutes of Evidence

TAKEN BEFORE THE SCIENCE AND TECHNOLOGY COMMITTEE

TUESDAY 12 OCTOBER 2004

Present   Emerton, B   Soulsby of Swaffham Prior, L

Finlay of Llandaff, B   Sutherland of Houndwood, L (Chairman)

Hilton of Eggarton   Turnberg, L

May of Oxford, L   Walmsley, B

Mitchell, L

Murphy, B

Memorandum by the British Geriatrics Society[1]

INTRODUCTION

The British Geriatrics Society welcomes the decision of the House of Lords Select Committee on Science and Technology to hold an Inquiry into the Scientific Aspects of Ageing. It is also grateful for the opportunity to present evidence. Both of the areas of investigation have direct relevance to the core work of the Society—the promotion of the health of older people. The study of the biological processes of ageing will lead to a greater understanding of the mechanisms of ageing thus unlocking potential areas for therapeutic advance in the prevention and treatment of diseases of later life. Technology and design have the potential to revolutionise diagnosis and therapy and, by enabling improvements in the built environment, improve the quality of life of older people, particularly those whose independence is threatened by physical or mental health disabilities.

THE BRITISH GERIATRICS SOCIETY

The Society is the only learned society in the United Kingdom for doctors practising geriatric medicine. The 2,000 members are consultants and registrars in geriatric medicine, the psychiatry of old age, public health medicine, general practitioners, and scientists engaged in the research of age-related disease.

It was founded in 1947 for "the relief of suffering and distress amongst the aged and infirm by the improvement of standards of medical care for such persons, the holding of meetings and the publication and distribution of the results of such research".

Geriatric Medicine (Geriatrics) "is that branch of general medicine concerned with the clinical, preventive, remedial and social aspects of illness in older people. Their high morbidity rates, different patterns of disease presentation, slower response to treatment and requirements for social support call for special medical skills". The purpose is to restore an ill and disabled person to a level of maximum ability and wherever possible return the person to an independent life at home. Although principally concerned with secondary care there is a growing partnership between the Society and primary care reflecting changes in which services for older people are provided.

The Society undertakes its work through its Standing Committees, its Biannual Scientific Meetings, its journal "Age and Ageing", its Regional Branches, its Special Interest groups and through its partnerships within the United Kingdom and abroad. Two years ago it established National Councils to relate to the devolved Health Departments in the separate countries of the United Kingdom.

Earlier this year the Academic and Research Committee of the Society published a research strategy, which can be located on the BGS website at: http://tinyurl.com/65cen, that includes an ongoing programme of activity for the development of research themes, capacity and delivery. This submission has been developed from that Strategy and from the work that has flowed from it.

---

[1] See also supplementary evidence, p 335.

THE SOCIETY'S ACADEMIC AND RESEARCH STRATEGY

A thriving research culture in ageing and clinical geriatric medicine is of key importance to the future care of older patients. Academic medicine in general and academic geriatric medicine in particular are experiencing difficult times for a variety of reasons not least the squeeze in higher education funding and the rush to attempt to enhance research assessment ratings for the next research assessment exercise. The focus of the NHS on short-term targets and continuing under funding of research by the NHS (< 1 per cent total expenditure) has also contributed to increased difficulties in maintaining active research programmes in geriatric medicine in many universities. It is only necessary to look at the evidence base underlying those medical specialties without significant academic activity to understand the likely long-term detrimental effects of a loss of research activity within the specialty. In keeping with many other specialties, there are vacant chairs of geriatrics (eg Birmingham, Liverpool, London and Oxford) and senior lectureship posts in geriatric medicine. There is a trend to disestablish academic departments. Whilst loss of departments in itself is not a problem, loss of posts in academic geriatric medicine will have far reaching negative effects on both teaching and research and in providing role models for the researchers of tomorrow. Cross disciplinary institutes of ageing research have been established (eg Newcastle, Keele). These provide an ideal opportunity for clinical, basic and social scientists to work collaboratively. Chairs in Geriatric Medicine have also been established in some of the new Medical Schools (eg Warwick, Keele, Brighton/Sussex and Leeds/Bradford). However, given the huge clinical challenge posed by the health care needs of older people, the Society believes that there is a convincing case that academic geriatric medicine should be represented in all medical schools.

IDENTIFICATION AND SUPPORT OF POTENTIAL INDEPENDENT RESEARCHERS

It is crucial that the "supply" of young researchers is increased and that they are supported. The Society believes that research experience within Specialist Registrar training should be seen as the "norm" and not the exception. Without being directly exposed to a research environment it is impossible to identify, with any certainty, those that will flourish and become the future leaders of academic geriatric medicine. The Society is contributing towards this process in a number of ways:

— Research methodology workshops have been established jointly with Help the Aged/Research into Ageing.

— Successful "Meet the Researchers" sessions are held at the Society's national meetings.

— Success in research by Specialist registrars is being spotlighted in the Society's Newsletter.

— The Society's funds are used to provide start-up grants for registrars and to fund travel expenses to visit centres of research excellence.

— The Dhole bequest to the Society is being used to fund a Training Fellowship (jointly with Help the Aged/Research into Ageing).

These initiatives complement the Training Fellowships offered by the MRC and medical charities. Targeting of this type of award for "ageing" researchers rather than those involved in "disease-specific" research may be one way of giving a message to younger researchers and to the Heads of Medical Schools that the study of ageing is a priority area.

IDENTIFICATION OF EVIDENCE GAPS

One consistent obstacle to effective clinical practice is the paucity of robust evidence on the effectiveness of therapeutic interventions in the oldest old (those aged 80 and over). This section of the population is the one growing the fastest and yet it has been systematically excluded from clinical trials either because of specific age restrictions or because the presence of co-morbid conditions or concomitant medication are exclusion criteria. In the absence of evidence the production of clinical guidelines and the involvement of the patient in decision-making is made more difficult. The risk in clinical practice is in balancing the use of treatments that may be at best ineffective and at worst potentially dangerous with adopting an ageist and nihilistic approach to disease in later life.

The Society is working with its Special Interest Groups in identifying clinical areas where there are evidence gaps. These are then being fed into the Health Technology Assessment process. This process is not yet completed but both delirium and frailty are common, important conditions with major adverse outcomes that seem ideal for cross-disciplinary study involving basic scientists, clinicians and social scientists and which have potential for the beneficial application of new technologies.

Other potential areas identified by this process include:

— Primary prevention of disease in the very old.

— Pulmonary rehabilitation in later life.

— Management of anxiety and depression associated with physical illness.

— The management of chronic disease in care homes.

— Complementary therapies in later life.

— The development of strategies for enhancing the quality of prescribing to older patients at home, in hospitals and in care homes.

An important general area for development is the promotion of clinical trials that include the oldest old. These individuals are going to make up the majority of patients that present to geriatricians in the next 10–20 years.

External Links

The Society seeks to strengthen its links with other research-focused organisations. It was instrumental in establishing the European Union Geriatric Medicine Society which has as one of its aims the bringing together of researchers from the enlarging community. There are also good links with the American Geriatrics Society. In the UK, close collaboration exists with Research into Ageing with two members of the BGS Academic and Research Committee serving on the former's Research Advisory Committee. It is recognised that collaboration between the three learned societies of gerontology has not been as productive as it could have been and the process of revitalisation of the British Combined Committee for Gerontology has started.

The Status of Academic Geriatric Medicine

A review of the status of Geriatric Medicine was undertaken in 2002, which can be found on the BGS website at: http://www.bgs.org.uk/publications/acadmedicine.htm To quote from that review "The major deficit in academic Geriatric Medicine now is in the infrastructure. There is not a large body of senior lecturers committed to an academic career, pursuing research of a high standard and preparing themselves to be the academic leaders of the profession in the future. Hence when chairs become vacant, there are often no suitable applicants and sometimes no applicants at all. Research activity in academic Geriatric Medicine is under-performing. It is notable that a significant number of research reports on areas relevant to Geriatric Medicine are published by researchers working in other fields. Geriatric Medicine is the single biggest medical specialty and is broadening the scope of its activities. The opportunities for research in ageing, age related disease and the care of elderly people are enormous and increasingly research funders are keen to support such research. It is essential that the specialty has a strong teaching and research base and that the brightest young doctors in the specialty are attracted to academic careers".

Conclusions

The Research Assessment Exercise with its financial implications for research performance has caused universities to appoint only those with who have strong research records and research potential. There is a comparative lack of appropriate research training opportunities and infrastructure in Geriatric Medicine and it will need a culture change on all sides if this is to change.

It is recognised that smaller specialties such as geriatric medicine, if they do not build up very large research teams of their own will have to collaborate with others and to some extent risk losing their identity as Geriatric Medicine Departments. Solutions will vary from institution to institution and might include inter-disciplinary groupings focusing on ageing or groups investigating the specific problems of older people within a disease-specific department.

It is likely that proposals to shorten the period of training before physicians can reach specialist status will further dilute exposure to research. The establishment of specific training opportunities through fellowship schemes may to some extent counter-balance this.

The threat to existing academic geriatric medicine groupings in teaching hospitals gives a signal that medicine of later life is less important and will deny exposure of geriatric medicine researchers to medical students and to young doctors in the formative stage of their career.

The British Geriatrics Society is striving to develop the status and standing of research from its own resources and by partnership with like-minded organisations. The role of the research establishment in this process is also of crucial importance.

September 2004

12 October 2004

Memorandum by the British Society of Gerontology[2]

The British Society of Gerontology seeks to promote the understanding of human ageing and later life through research and communication. It has a remit to foster the application of this knowledge to the improvement of quality of life in old age. The Society welcomes the opportunity to submit evidence to the House of Lords Select Committee on Science and Technology Sub-Committee's review of Scientific Aspects of Ageing.

1. INTER-DISCIPLINARY PERSPECTIVES

As a general point, the Society would wish to highlight the importance of linking biological perspectives on ageing with other disciplinary approaches—in particular those coming from within the orbit of social science. Exploring links across disciplines is essential in the context of appreciating the way in which ageing is shaped by the movement of individuals and groups across the life course. Understanding ageing from a *life course perspective* has become an important theme within social gerontology. Here, ageing individuals and cohorts are examined as one phase of the entire lifetime and seen as shaped by historical, social, economic and environmental factors that occur at earlier ages. The key elements of this approach are that: *(1) ageing occurs from birth to death; (2) that ageing involves social, psychological and biological processes; and (3) that experiences in old age are influenced by membership of a particular birth cohort.* The value of this perspective is to show how biological, sociological and related processes interlink to influence change in later life. Further development of this perspective (still under-explored in the British context) is essential if "prospects for healthy and active life expectancy" are to be improved. This will almost certainly require interventions earlier in the life course to influence resources and lifestyles relevant to a secure old age.[3]

The above approach is especially important given the role of inequalities related to social class, gender and ethnicity in influencing active life expectancy.[4] From a sociological perspective, this can be expressed in terms of the way which inequality (in respect of money, health and status) increases with the passage of time. The idea of "cumulative advantage/disadvantage" experienced by individuals over the life course has been supported by data from longitudinal studies that provide evidence of greater inequality and variability with increasing age. The idea that age peers become *more dissimilar* from each other is a major finding from social science research, one which underlines the need for interventions to address inequalities throughout the life course.[5]

A greater research effort is required in respect of earlier prevention of chronic illness in old age. Achieving this will, however, require bringing together a number of disciplines to establish the range of causal influences that might promote healthy ageing. Understanding the latter as "socially produced and constructed" in equal measure to the influence of biological factors is an essential starting point. From a sociological perspective, the following are important research areas that justify further exploration and refinement:

— The development of approaches to "quality of life" which challenge the view of ageing as a time of decline and dependency.[6]

— Research in the broad field of family and personal relationships that demonstrates on the one side the centrality of family life for the majority of older people; on the other side, the importance of access to friends and leisure associates in sustaining morale and autonomy in old age.[7]

— Evidence for the significant influence of ethnic status in determining quality of life and active life expectancy. Ethnic *inequalities* are likely to be at their greatest in the case of older people, with the greatest disadvantage experienced by elderly Pakistanis and Bangladeshis.[8]

[2] See also supplementary evidence, p 335.

[3] A summary of life course perspectives can be found in Concepts and Theories of Aging: Beyond Microfication in Social Science Approaches. In Binstock, R and George, L Handbook of Aging and the Social Sciences (5th edition), pp 3–21. San Diego: Academic Press.

[4] *See,* Marmot, M G (2000) Do Inequalities Matter? In Daniels, N, Kennedy, B and Kawachi, I (eds) Is Inequality Bad for our Health? Boston: Beacon Press.

[5] This area is developed in Dannefer, D (2003) Cumulative Advantage/Disadvantage and the Life Course: Cross-Fertilizing Age and Social Science Theory Journal of Gerontology Vol 58B (6) S327–S337.

[6] The volume edited by Alan Walker, with papers from the ESRC Growing Older Programme illustrates this point. Walker, A and Hennessy, C (eds) (2004) Growing Older: Quality of Life in Old Age. Maidenhead: Open University Press.

[7] Phillipson, C, Bernard, M, Phillips, J and Ogg, J (2001) *The Family and Community Life of Older People: Social Support and Social Networks in Three Urban Areas.* London: Routledge.

[8] Nazroo, J (2001) Ethnicity, Class and Health. London: Policy Studies Institute. Nazroo, J (2004) Ethnic Disparities in Ageing Health: What Can We Learn from the United Kingdom? In Anderson, N, Bulatao, R and Cohen, B (eds), Critical Perspectives on Racial and Ethnic Differentials in Health in Later Life. Washington DC: National Academy Press (in press). Nazroo, J (2003) The Structuring of Ethnic Inequalities in Health: Economic Position, Racial Discrimination and Racism. American Journal of Public Health, 93 (2), pp 277–84. In Walker, A and Hennessy, C (eds) (2004) Growing Older: Quality of Life in Old Age. Maidenhead: Open University Press.

— Institutional forces associated with ageism. These have been widely documented but require further examination, notably in areas such as employment and access to health and social services.[9]

— Problems associated with social exclusion. A substantial minority of older people come under the heading of the "socially excluded" experiencing multiple forms of deprivation associated with poverty and limited participation in key areas of social and cultural life.[10]

— Research on the importance of the physical environment in daily life. The broad field of "environmental gerontology" has emerged as a promising field of enquiry. Research is needed examining, for example, how attachment to particular places (such as home and locality) may play a significant role in maintaining a sense of self and identity in old age.[11] The scope of environmental gerontology might also cover issues relating to the impact of urbanisation and changes to city life on experiences in old age. The majority of people now live in urban centres and considering how these can accommodate and support ageing populations is an important issue for social science research.

2. TECHNOLOGY AND DESIGN

The Society takes the view that technology and design has a crucial role in improving the quality of life in older age. This has been a neglected area for research although projects funded through the EPSRC have pointed to the potential for innovative work. Relevant areas that assist with extending active life include:

— *Electronic assistive technology*. This has considerable potential for improving the quality of life for people with a disability. Evidence produced by the British Society of Rehabilitation Medicine suggests that the provision of communication aids is patchy and "somewhat of a lottery".[12] Findings also suggest that the supply of environmental control equipment and resources are inadequate, irrespective of the fact that these services were devolved to local authorities in 1995.

— *Promoting mobility*. People with disabilities often remain highly restricted in their ability to move around urban as well as rural environments. There is an urgent need to support research examining safe, affordable, all-weather mobility for people with different types of disability, with particular reference to issues relating to transport and road design.

— *Technology in the home*. Improved application and use of technology is especially vital in the home. Some research is available examining the effectiveness and value of housing adaptations[13] but there is considerable potential for further work. Existing technologies could certainly be used to a greater extent to benefit older people. Technology has a major role to play in improving the quality of life of people experiencing cognitive impairment. Such technologies should be made available to older people regardless of individual characteristics, such as social class, gender or ethnic origin. The role of design is also crucial and there is a strong case for encouraging leaders in design to take more interest in supporting innovation and best practice to improve quality of life in old age.

3. RESEARCH CAPACITY AND CO-ORDINATION

The Society takes the view that a major expansion in research into ageing is now underway, supported by greater awareness (illustrated by the work of the House of Lords Sub-Committee) of the social and scientific implications of ageing populations. Nonetheless, major issues are apparent in respect of securing good quality research which will prove of benefit to the lives of older people. Some major concerns identified by the Society include the following:

— *Research capacity*. The demand for skilled and committed researchers in gerontology will be substantially increased in the context of dedicated funding, notably through initiatives such as the Cross-Council Research Programme on Ageing, projects developed through the work of the leading charities, and research collaborations across Europe. There is considerable concern, however, whether sufficient researchers are available to meet the potential demand. There are relatively few

[9] For evidence in the field of employment see Taylor, P (2004) A "New Deal" for Older Workers in the United Kingdom? In Maltby, T, de Vroom, B, Mirabile, M L and Øverbye, E (eds), Ageing and the Transition to Retirement. Aldershot: Ashgate Publishing. For evidence on health and social care see Scharf, T and Phillipson, C (2004) The Impact of Government Policy Among Older People. London: ODPM.

[10] Scharf, T, Phillipson, C, Smith A E and Kingston, P (2002) Growing Older in Socially Deprived Areas: Social Exclusion in Later Life. London: Help the Aged.

[11] Kellaher, L (2000) A Choice Well Made: Mutuality as a Governing Principle in Residential Care. London: Centre for Policy on Ageing. In Walker, A and Hennessy, C (eds) (2004) Growing Older: Quality of Life in Old Age. Maidenhead: Open University Press.

[12] *See* www.bsrm.co.uk

[13] Making Research Count is one such example. See www.making-research-count.org.uk/

centres of gerontology able to give systematic attention to training the next generation of researchers. Many junior researchers are lost to the field having completed a particular project. The "career ladder" for research has never been strong, but its limitations are especially apparent given the need to expand work in high priority areas. Solutions to these problems do exist. The Research Councils and some charities (such as the Nuffield Foundation) are promoting post-doctoral fellowships and general fellowships targeted at junior researchers. These offer an opportunity for expanding the number of researchers and for promoting greater security for the profession. We would strongly encourage the expansion of this route as a relatively "low cost" option for maintaining research capacity. Attention must also be given to the need to increase the number of students studying age-related issues at a doctoral-level. Some research on historic trends in the number of doctorates awarded in ageing across the different disciplines would be useful—data on the supply of trained researchers is limited, especially when related to monitoring changes in particular disciplines.

— *Research co-ordination*. This remains relatively limited in the case of research into ageing. In part this reflects the relatively recent surge in initiatives—with most large and medium-size funders now identifying ageing as a priority area. The growth of interest is encouraging; it needs, however, to be managed in a way that encourages collaboration wherever possible. The Society has welcomed the creation of the UK National Collaboration on Ageing Research, which seeks to stimulate multi-disciplinary research. However, new mechanisms for ensuring agreement and understanding of changing research needs in the field of ageing are urgently required.

— *Research topics and priorities*. A new approach is needed in respect of identifying future research issues and priorities. Current research is too often driven by the needs (important though they are) of the current generation of older people and the problems facing those responsible for the delivery of services. Fresh thinking is urgently needed as to the new questions that will surface as, for example, the "baby boom" generation move into retirement and eventually late old age. Similarly, family change associated with high rates of divorce, lower rates of marriage and declining family size, all raise challenging issues in respect of influencing patterns of adjustment to later life. The changing sociological and demographic context of ageing needs translating into new topics for the next generation of research.

— *Improving research dissemination*. Translating research findings into policy and practice remains of variable quality. The major funders have influenced improvements in this area, urging researchers to establish close links with different kinds of users—from older people to service providers. Some forums have been established which connect researchers to those organising health and social care services. Charitable bodies such as Age Concern and Help the Aged have also played a significant role in facilitating knowledge transfer. But as the amount of research grows—both nationally and internationally—a systematic approach to research dissemination will be vital. One suggestion might be to establish a centre specifically focusing on disseminating research findings, through mechanisms such as: fact sheets, conferences and seminars, and systematic literature reviews. Such a centre could also play a useful role in exploring links across disciplines in the utilisation of research findings.

October 2004

Memorandum by the British Society For Research On Ageing[14]

PREFACE

The British Society for Research On Ageing (BSRA) is pleased to be given the opportunity to provide written evidence to this inquiry. Established in 1943, the BSRA was the first learned society to be concerned specifically with the scientific study of biological ageing and was the forerunner of the many national gerontological societies now established throughout the world. The BSRA promotes research to understand the causes and effects of the ageing process, and provides a forum for the discussion of the latest scientific theories and data. Our membership comprises more than 120 scientists from Europe, Asia and North America and includes some of the most respected figures in biological ageing research. Drawing on their expertise our Society is well placed to provide the latest information on the biological aspects of this inquiry. Please note that we have contributed (together with our partner organisations) to the report supplied by the Biosciences Federation. Our independent evidence expands on some of the issues touched upon in that submission.

---

[14] See also supplementary evidence, p 335.

Executive Summary

Research has established that ageing is a normal biological process that increases the frailty of otherwise healthy organisms. Ageing compromises a creature's ability to cope with physiological stress producing an increased likelihood of long-term sickness and death. Until the 1980s, although our understanding of *why* ageing happened advanced rapidly, research into the mechanisms controlling *how* the process occurred was a question essentially beyond the power of the science of the day to solve. However, in the 1990s a series of scientific breakthroughs and technical innovations rendered the ageing process "attackable" and accordingly it became the focus of serious UK research efforts. These new UK research programmes produced a series of breakthroughs. Some of these can be translated into new treatments for our elderly population in the near future and others have established the theoretical groundwork for advanced therapies. However, all is not well. Biological ageing research in the UK currently lacks a secure funding future, an effective national strategy and a working co-ordination framework. The long-term sustainability of our national research programmes is thus threatened. We argue that urgent action must be taken if our ability to deliver real quality of life benefits to the elderly population is not to be compromised.

The Biological Processes of Ageing

Biological ageing research in the UK is at a crucial point. The country has developed an outstandingly strong research community in an extremely short period of time. That community has delivered fundamental knowledge about the ageing human body and is now poised to turn that knowledge into practical benefits for elderly people. However it can only achieve its promise if the levels of funding committed by sponsors are significantly increased. It is important to appreciate that dedicated research into the biology of the ageing process is a relatively new area of scientific endeavour. Until quite recently a prevalent view among a significant section of the medical community was that there was no such thing as an "ageing process" only the sum of symptoms of the diseases from which the older person suffered. Reasonably enough, that which does not exist was not considered a pressing topic for study. The study of ageing became synonymous with the study of age-related degenerative disease.

However this view of later human life eventually became scientifically untenable. A series of physiological studies demonstrated striking differences between the *healthy* tissues and organ systems of the elderly and those of the young. Put simply, old tissue, even when perfectly healthy is more frail than its youthful counterpart and more prone to failure. Ageing is thus an independent but potent risk factor for the development of many diseases and imposes serious quality of life deficits in its own right. The relationship of the ageing process to disease is akin to that between a worn part and a broken part.

Thus, as a result of disordered function at the cell and tissue levels, ageing produces increased organismal frailty. However it is clear that many of the degenerative effects of the process could potentially be ameliorated through appropriate dietary, environmental or pharmaceutical interventions. This strongly suggests that the development of healthcare systems that will result in long healthy lives and quick deaths is a realistic option for the UK.

Promising Avenues of Biological Research

The following areas of research are a small sample of the most promising areas of study. They have been selected because they are particularly illustrative for the other areas of inquiry for which evidence is being sought. Much of the research which has *made* these areas promising has been carried out in UK labs as a direct consequence of the decision of the Research Councils (especially BBSRC) to become sponsors of gerontological research following the 1994–95 identification of the ageing population as a Foresight priority area by the Health & Life Sciences panel. Promising areas include:

— *Study of the insulin-IGF axis.* Cross species studies of the type recommended in Foresight have shown that animals carrying mutations in this biological pathway have significantly increased healthy lifespans. This is true of fruit flies, nematode worms and laboratory mice. The challenge in the years to come is to understand the ways in which this pathway determines lifespan and how it could be utilised to improve human well being with age.

— *Replicative senescence.* Foresight recognised the importance of the study of cellular ageing. Patients with a rare genetic disease, Werner's syndrome, show the accelerated development of most of the classical age-related diseases. This disease is now known to be caused by the premature accumulation of "senescent" cells. Future research in this area will focus on determining the scale of the contribution that such cells make to normal ageing and developing treatments aimed at preventing their degenerative effects.

— *Ageing of the immune system.* Foresight emphasised the importance not just of understanding ageing, but of applying that knowledge to the development of new therapies. Nowhere is this more promising than in the study of the ageing immune system, known as immunosenescence. A decline in immune function impacts on the ability of the body to fight infection, respond optimally to vaccinations and detect and delete cancerous cells. UK research has demonstrated that a loss of the ability to produce new T cells is a significant cause of the failure of the immune system in each of these areas. It has been shown that the decline in T cell production can be prevented in several types of elderly mammal by treatment with the hormone interleukin7. The immune system is also influenced by hormones and the production of one of these, dehydroepiandrosterone (DHEA), declines significantly with age. DHEA helps to counteract the negative effects of stress hormones on the immune system, and the reduced DHEA levels seen in the elderly appear to contribute to their vulnerability to infection immediately following serious physical or emotional trauma (eg hip fractures or bereavement). DHEA may offer a cheap and safe therapy to reduce illness in the elderly following hip-fracture or loss of a loved one. Such therapies would not have been envisaged if research effort had been focused solely on identifying treatments for age-related disease.

— *Ageing of muscle.* Skeletal muscle declines during normal healthy ageing, such that muscles are considerably smaller and weaker. In a similar manner, osteoporosis is almost universal in very old age, and is a major cause of morbidity and mortality in the elderly of both sexes. The effects of loss of muscle and bone during normal ageing are interlinked. Loss of muscle results in instability and this frequently leads to a fall. These falls are more likely to lead to bone fracture, which can result in permanent immobility and a need for residential care. UK research has demonstrated that acute or longer-term exercise regimes are beneficial in slowing or reversing the rate of muscle or bone loss. Further work is required to optimise this effect and develop advice for the elderly on healthy exercise regimes.

— *Ageing of the gut.* The importance of the gut to human health is often underestimated, it is the largest organ in the body and plays a role in defence against pathogens as well as the absorption of nutrients from food. The elderly are at high risk of malnutrition and there is evidence to suggest that normal physiological changes of the GI tract (such as loss of taste sensation, disregulation of hormonal appetite control, loss of absorptive function, reduced gut motility) could contribute to this. Since the luminal contents of the gut appear to have a large effect on gut function, and can easily be changed, there is a real possibility that simple interventions (such as probiotics) could improve the health of the elderly.

How Will this Research Benefit Older People?

Virtually all ageing research will eventually benefit older people through interventions designed to increase their healthy (rather than maximum) lifespans, combat age-related frailty and enhance independence. These interventions may include healthy life-style advice such as that already given to the elderly concerning the benefit of regular exercise and a diet high in fibre, (measures that will, respectively, boost the ageing immune and musculoskeletal systems and help to maintain a healthy gut in the face of the age-related decline in gut function). However they are also likely to include novel interventions as described above for interleukin-7 and DHEA. Such research may also identify common interventions that could protect against the age-related damage to several systems. For example it has been established that normal ageing is accompanied by the development of a more "inflamed status" in the body, so-called "inflammaging". The chronic inflammation caused by ageing is a major risk factor for several key age-related diseases such as Alzheimer's, cancer, cataract, heart attack and stroke. This may indicate that a simple intervention such as low dose aspirin or non-steroidal anti-inflammatory drugs could protect against these diseases, particularly in those people who show the inflammatory risk phenotype early on. Improved understanding of the ageing process may also lead to the development of technologies to screen for early markers of age-related disease, allowing for early prophylactic intervention. For example recent studies in to the ageing of the lens of the eye in humans have unexpectedly detected a protein (amyloid) that is normally linked with Alzheimer's disease. This protein can be detected in the lens of the eye by a simple eye examination, allowing early diagnosis.

Has Ageing Research Shown Differences Between the Sexes and Between Ethnic Groups?

Biological ageing research as a serious venture in the UK is very new and it might perhaps have been over-optimistic to identify sex and ethnic differences in the ageing process. However, intriguing observations have already begun to shed light on these areas. A UK research group have demonstrated that the immune system ages differently in men and women. The key organ responsible for the output of new T cells is the thymus. This organ progressively atrophies over the life course but the rate of this atrophy is significantly faster in men than women. This appears to correlate with the increased rates of death from infection seen in elderly men compared to elderly women and the increased frequency of autoimmune diseases seen in elderly women compared to elderly men. A second example relates to the ageing musculoskeletal system. Bone is lost at a rate of 0.2–0.5 per cent per year and muscle strength falls by 1–2 per cent per year in both men and women after the age of 40–45 years. However, both muscle and bone are preserved by oestrogen. For example, bone loss is accelerated to 2–5 per cent per year immediately before and for up to 10 years post-menopause. This research indicates the need to identify sex specific strategies designed to ensure healthy ageing.

Ethnicity, environment and cultural practice are difficult to separate but all clearly influence ageing. This influence may be exerted in many ways but diet and social exclusion appear to be major factors. Many factors can influence the diet of an elderly person: access to shops can be restricted if they do not drive and public transport is limited; low income may also influence their choice of food tending towards a high calorie diet low in protein, fresh fruit and vegetables; the fact that a significant proportion of people over 65 in the UK do not have their own teeth can also limit their food choice, leading to an avoidance of fruit and meat. Considering social environment, the current retirement age of 65 can have a significant impact upon the elderly. Most social research supports the advantages of an active life-style with good social involvement as positive health factors. These observations are supported by scientific data showing that stress has a negative impact upon immunity and enforced retirement of a healthy 65 year old can increase stress due to low self-esteem, loss of a structured life and reduced social interaction. These could easily be counteracted by raising the upper limit to the working age or by encouraging voluntary work amongst the elderly.

How Effectively is Research Co-Ordinated Between the Public, Private and Charitable Sectors (Including Internationally)

Biological ageing research can and must be effectively co-ordinated if we are to ensure that research in the life sciences continues to diversify to include normal human ageing. Co-ordination is also required to ensure interaction between life scientists, clinicians and social scientists and to allow communication of data to policy-makers influencing clinical and social practice. The current impact of UK biological ageing research on public policy is minimal. UK research on ageing does not comprise a vast portfolio at present, but if we are to develop and progress then co-ordination will be a necessity. Effective co-ordination can only be achieved if we define *what* is to be co-ordinated and *why* and if funds are provided to carry out the required research. Thus some advice is offered.

At the national level co-ordination activities between the Government sponsors fall into two distinct types (i) translational co-ordination aimed at passing discoveries made under the remit of one Research Council *to* those of another and (ii) activities designed to ensure that interdisciplinary research that bridges the remits of two councils is adequately assessed. Translating breakthroughs funded by BBSRC into MRC sponsored clinical research would be a good example of the first type of co-ordination (nothing like this currently exists); supporting linkages between EPSRC & BBSRC funded research (eg through the recently approved SPARC programme) is an example of the second. Effective national co-ordination also requires interaction with the charity sector. Effective linkage of Government sponsored research to the charity sector requires the recognition by Government that (i) Charities are in the main mission (disease) focused and thus only a small proportion of generic ageing research will be of immediate value to any given organisation (ii) that even an interested Charity has only limited funds available for research. Activity aimed at spreading knowledge of a sponsor's research portfolio and rationale for the adoption of that portfolio is simple, cheap and effective.

The National Collaboration on Ageing Research (NCAR) was funded over five years to try and co-ordinate ageing research in the biological and social sciences, but was in the opinion of the BSRA executive largely unsuccessful. We would suggest that the BBSRC with its knowledge of research council remits and working practices and an established record of identifying, funding and co-ordinating research on the biology of ageing would be a suitable body to co-ordinate ageing research at national level. BBSRC would also be able to communicate key outcomes of this research to government in order to inform health and social policy.

Maximising the UK's return on international co-ordination requires the recognition of three tenets:

(i) effective *national* co-ordination must be in place. The US has addressed this problem by setting up a National Institute of Aging (NIA) and while this may not be practical in the UK, a virtual institute achieved through tight national co-ordination, research workshops and proper resources, may achieve the same end.

(ii) an integrated national strategy for ageing research must be developed and its importance communicated to the research community.

(iii) the international situation is itself highly dynamic with regard to UK opportunities, necessitating an opportunistic approach. It is probably fair to say that the UK has not obtained full value from EU funding instruments directed at research on ageing. This is likely to reflect the low level of involvement of the UK research community in ageing research, which may in turn be a result of the low regard with which such research is held within the UK (see below).

HAVE THE CORRECT PRIORITIES BEEN IDENTIFIED? ARE THERE GAPS IN RESEARCH? IS THERE SUFFICIENT RESEARCH CAPABILITY IN THE UK?

Within biological gerontology the areas selected for support under the BBSRC Science of Ageing (SAGE) and Experimental Research on Ageing (ERA) special initiatives captured much that biology has to offer in meeting the challenge posed by an ageing population. These areas were:

SAGE

— Cellular senescence, mechanisms of tissue damage and breakdown.
— Biochemistry of stress, repair and the accumulation of damage.
— Ageing in biological systems, particularly neuroscience and immunology.
— The ageing population demography and evolution.

ERA

— The genetics of normal ageing.
— Interventions in ageing processes.
— Model systems for ageing research.
— Low priority for areas supported under SAGE.

Life science research in the UK is strong, but the proportion of scientists actively involved in addressing biological ageing in their own discipline is small. Gerontology is considered by many as a fringe subject of little academic merit. BBSRC recognised these problems and a key objective of both SAGE and ERA was to expand the number of scientists involved in ageing research by recruiting established scientists in to gerontology, allowing the funding panels to award grants to researchers with no previous track record in gerontology but who submitted high quality proposals addressing the key priority areas of the two initiatives. This was a high risk strategy that paid off. A total of 48 awards were made under these initiatives and over 200 applications were received. Areas that were under-represented were ageing population demography and studies of the ageing gut, these are areas that still need to be developed.

Ten of the principal investigators in SAGE maintained their interest in biological ageing research, gaining grants under ERA. Others have gained funding via charities or the BBSRC's main responsive mode panels. Unfortunately, a special initiative mode of support for ageing renders the sustained delivery of research into one area over a period of more than three years very difficult. This could potentially allow gaps in UK research to develop a few years after they were "plugged". Thus the capacity to conduct national ageing research in all the promising areas cannot be grown and sustained through this type of funding instrument. This is a serious threat to biological ageing research capacity.

At first glance funding for ageing research seems unparsimonious. It appears to combine ample opportunity for current project support with the potential to close research gaps, translate research into practice and accommodate new research priorities as they develop. For example (from Oct 2001–Sept 2002) the Wellcome Trust spent £13.1 million on UK medical research projects it considers relevant to ageing. However it seems to the BSRA that the "ageing research" portfolio of Wellcome (and some other research sponsors) consists almost exclusively of research aimed at understanding age-related degenerative disease. An examination of the

2001–02 Wellcome portfolio by the BSRA executive was able to identify only one project designed to study normal ageing (a small project on muscle). The remainder of the support was dedicated to specific age-related diseases. The reason for this apparent mismatch between the intent and action of some funders appears to be a simple misunderstanding of what ageing is. It appears that many funding decisions are still informed by a model of human late life that assumes that ageing either does not exist or cannot be fruitfully studied. Seen from this perspective research on disease alone is sufficient. The BSRA does not argue for a redirection of resources away from the study of age-related degenerative disease, or that such research portfolios lack either relevance or quality. We simply point out that having a strong research programme on age-related disease is not a substitute for an adequate biological ageing research programme.

Some charity funders have broad portfolios that strike a good balance between research on the ageing process and research on the diseases of old age, a strategy similar to that recommended by Foresight at the national level. Research Into Ageing, for example, funds research into the biology of ageing, stroke and circulation, exercise and falls and incontinence among other areas. The problem for an NGO with such an ambitious portfolio is a simple lack of funds to support all the high quality applications it receives. For example, in the last two completed grant rounds RIA *shortlisted* projects with a total value of £8.3 million and were only able to support £1.4 million. Of this only about 20 per cent was on the basic biology of ageing. Overall the level of funds available for basic ageing research in the charity sector is limited particularly in comparison with the $26 million budget available each year to the two major US Charities (the Ellison Medical Foundation and the American Foundation for Aging Research). There is essentially no industrial support for basic ageing research in the UK.

An obvious question is, how much research capacity and funding for biological ageing research do we need in the UK? Here the example of the USA is informative. The demographic challenges faced by the UK and USA are very similar. To meet them the largest US sponsor of biological ageing research (NIA) deploys a current annual budget of $50 million (which has increased from $10 million 10 years ago). The current NIA budget is four times the current per capita annual expenditure on biological ageing research in the UK and represents the continuation of a period of sustained investment in US ageing research capacity totalling hundreds of millions of dollars. In contrast the BBSRC SAGE programme has completed, the ERA programme will complete in less than 18 months and investment in biological ageing research from other Government sponsors is currently negligible. With regard to the biology of ageing, a sensible immediate goal for the UK would be to match the per capita expenditure seen in the USA. Matched per capita funding would require an extra annual investment of £5 million per annum, which would support an active UK research community of about 40–60 groups working in all the areas supported under SAGE and ERA. £5 million per annum would probably represent the most funding the biological gerontology community could immediately absorb without sacrificing research quality.

In conclusion, the cross-council nature of ageing research and the need for both interdisciplinary and translational funding streams urgently warrants a major cross-council investment in biological ageing research through the next spending review. Many past examples exist where additional funding through government spending reviews have increased the capacity and the competitiveness of the UK (eg in genomics, e-Science) so redressing the current "capacity gap" is likely to be both successful and beneficial to the UK and Europe. Our national research situation should also be reassessed every five years to identify developing areas and gaps in the research portfolio.

October 2004

Examination of Witnesses

Witnesses: PROFESSOR JANET LORD and DR RICHARD FARAGHER, British Society for Research on Ageing; PROFESSOR CHRISTOPHER PHILLIPSON, British Society of Gerontology; and PROFESSOR PETER CROME, British Geriatrics Society, examined.

Q1 *Chairman:* May I say welcome and many thanks for taking time to come to visit us, but also for the effort that clearly your organisations have put into submitting evidence. What you have submitted has been much appreciated and will help inform our thinking. You are our first witnesses before the Committee and that in many ways is very appropriate. Can I warn you also that the proceedings are being recorded orally and indeed being broadcast orally, should anyone be out there listening, so any asides that you mutter may well be picked up! That being said, members of the Committee all have name tags in front of them, as do you, and I thought we might start—and there is a whole range of questions we might want to ask—by asking you to go across the table introducing yourselves and perhaps saying very briefly something about the group you represent and the kinds of aims and objectives the group has, and how they relate to our primary concern which is scientific aspects of ageing. That sounds a lot but just initially briefly to say what the particular focus of your group is and open up the discussion in that way. Do you want to start?

Professor Phillipson: My name is Chris Phillipson and I am President of the British Society of Gerontology. The Society has around 500 members. They are sociologists, social scientists, behavioural scientists. I think historically from its development in the early 1970s the Society has been particularly concerned to try and develop social and behavioural science, which I think had been relatively under-developed historically in terms of British gerontology, so that has been a crucial role. I think it is also true to say of the Society that it is a mix of academics, but practitioners as well, so in terms of trying to link academic research findings into practice there is quite a strong focus and that is reflected particularly in the annual conferences.

Professor Crome: I am Peter Crome, President-Elect of the British Geriatric Society. The Society itself was founded in 1947 for the "health of the aged", as the tag line goes. It is predominantly a medical society although in recent years its membership has been opened up to para-medical staff, nursing staff and some social scientists as well. We have about 2,000 members, the majority of whom are working as practising geriatricians at either consultant or registrar grade in the National Health Service, but we have a member mix from other medical disciplines as well. Our work is done through a variety of committees, through our scientific meetings, through our journal *Age and Ageing*. As I said, the majority of our members are not academic but we have a separate academic structure with an academic research committee who have recently produced an academic strategy which has determined the basis of the submission I made to your Lordships.

Professor Lord: Janet Lord, the chair of the British Society for Research on Ageing. The Society was formed in 1943 and has approximately 120 members at the moment, the majority of whom are academic scientists. We have a few medical practitioners in there. Their disciplines are really very broad so we have biologists, epidemiologists, nurses, dentists, a very broad range. Our primary aims are really to promote research into the causes and the effects of the ageing process, not just in humans but in a range of species to try to identify common traits. We are also interested in trying to identify means for counteracting these processes. We achieve our aims through the publication of research in our journal *Mechanisms of Ageing and Development*. We have an annual scientific meeting which promotes

networking amongst our members and the spread of knowledge in this area.

Dr Faragher: I am Dr Richard Faragher and I am a cell biologist with an interest in ageing. I was the Treasurer of the British Society for Research on Ageing until recently. I am appearing as an assistant to Professor Lord. I would echo much of what Professor Lord has said. I would also point out that one of the goals of our Society is to facilitate public education about the basic biology of ageing and to that end we have also undertaken to engage in a variety of public understanding of science activities. Many of our members also undertake appearances on television, radio and other media in order to try and broaden the knowledge of the biology of ageing throughout the community.

Q2 *Chairman:* In that work can I just ask is the main response you get from the young or the not-so-young? In other words, whom are you educating?

Dr Faragher: I have found it has varied. If you attend, for example, the British Association Festival of Science meetings you will see that there is a wide age range focusing on the older age group, I think largely because they have time. However if, in fact, you undertake, as some of our members have, activities such as Café Scientifique you can find a much younger age group who have come to listen to an entertaining talk being performed about ageing and have a pleasant evening with wine and nibbles.

Chairman: That sounds very civilised. One of the things we have discovered is that there are clearly other debates going on and meetings, and people will come and go so I will ask Lord Soulsby to ask the next question because he may have to leave as he is speaking in one of the debates going on at the moment.

Q3 *Lord Soulsby of Swaffham Prior:* I wonder if you could encapsulate what each of your societies contributes to ageing and research in ageing? If you could give the highlights and then I will probe a little further once you have done that, but if you could start off in that way.

Professor Phillipson: I guess in terms of our society there is quite a range of research. In a way it is difficult but if I were going to give a sound-bite it is making the argument that ageing is a socially constructed process which is influenced by a range of social factors—somebody's class position, their gender, their ethnicity—and understanding how that influences biological and other processes is an extremely important task to be done. I think that phrase "social construction of ageing" is one that has been extremely important in being explored by the society and, equally, I think the society has argued very strongly, individual members have, that there is something more to ageing than decline, there is something more to ageing than dependency as a product of biological processes, and we argue very strongly that dependency in later life is something that is as least as much produced by social processes such as poverty, life-long inequality, and so on, as by biological processes, or at least an interaction between the two. That would be a summary of the core principle of the research.

Professor Crome: As far as the British Geriatrics Society is concerned I think you can divide it into two aspects about what the society does in terms of research, one of which is the promotion of research among its members through research grants, fellowships, et cetera, and the second is its relationship between the academic aspect of the society and the clinical aspect of the society, which is to do with the promotion of best practice and evidence-based practice, the production of guidelines, and the interaction with government and other policy makers identifying areas of deficiency and trying to get them to incorporate evidence-based practices into government policies for the development of health services.

Professor Lord: As we said, we are a small society and we do not fund research ourselves, but via our annual scientific meeting we do promote dissemination of the knowledge of the various members from various disciplines and our members are interested in the biological process of ageing itself, to try to find out if we can prevent the mechanisms that increase frailty of humans as they age rather than treating disease once that has set in. Can we prevent frailty, can we extend healthy lifespan, which is fine, but can we also compress morbidity, what can we do about that, that is one of our key driving aims.

Q4 *Lord Soulsby of Swaffham Prior:* Your three organisations get together and discuss the progress made in research on a regular basis, do you?

Professor Lord: We do not actually. There was a meeting—this is prior to my time and I am an immunologist by training so I am very interested in infection in the elderly and I came into the ageing research field through the actions of the BBSRC trying to bring scientists who were not previously working on ageing—apparently in 1996 of the three societies but since then there has been not too much activity. We feel that might be because the societies themselves perhaps do not want to work in a talking shop, we want something to do, so we have not met too often, but perhaps that is because we have not got any key objective to try and aim at, something to get our teeth into. We have not met too frequently I am afraid.

Q5 *Lord Soulsby of Swaffham Prior:* With due respect, it would seem to me it might be useful periodically for the three bodies who are taking a clinical, a social science and a basic research aspect to ageing to get together to see what progress there is.

Dr Faragher: I would agree. We have had for a number of years a small contact group that works across the societies. One of the things which I think all the societies identified was that although there was a mechanism in place by which discussions could take place, the level of substantive activity that was actually there for that body to get its teeth into at the time it was set up was quite limited. We feel—and I think I speak for all the members of the society—that one area that we seek actively or will seek actively to collaborate on is to directly inform policy because this is an area into which all of us can input our strengths and an area in which all our members have an interest.

Q6 *Lord Soulsby of Swaffham Prior:* Just one final question and that is when one is conducting research, whatever area it might be, what is the main source of your funding? Is it the Wellcome Trust, for example?

Professor Phillipson: In the case of social science and behavioural science it is a very wide range actually. The research councils are extremely important such as the Economic and Social Research Council, but equally there are a lot of charities who also fund social scientific research on ageing. Can I just add a rider to the discussion about work across the societies. I think if you look at a corporate level that is true, there is a problem there, but I think it is important to say that many individual members of all our societies would contribute to inter-disciplinary and multi-disciplinary gatherings and conferences where different members of other professional bodies and other professional groups are there, so I think there is more mixing than sometimes does go on but less at a corporate level than is desirable.

Chairman: I think Baroness Hilton might want to come in on this one.

Q7 *Baroness Hilton of Eggardon:* The logical question to ask you all I think is why do you need three separate societies? I know you are looking at different aspects of ageing and have different historical set-ups and so on, but it does seem to me it would be much more coherent and perhaps productive if you were all operating together rather than separately.

Professor Phillipson: If you look at the States, for example, it has a Gerontological Society, but even within that society there are very strong sub-divisions and even though they have that kind of society, equally there are separate societies to represent different disciplines. My own view is that it is absolutely essential, because the different disciplines have important philosophical, intellectual and scientific agendas to address. They are not equal in terms of their funding, history, and methodological tools, if you like, and I think they have to develop a confidence to engage with other disciplines and to have their own particular body to do that. From my own point of view I think you do need to have these different societies, they do have different objectives, but equally we need to improve the forums, the mechanisms by which they come together, I would agree with that.

Baroness Hilton of Eggardon: I did wonder whether it is because the medical profession tends to see itself as a class apart that the rest of you have had to put yourselves—

Lord Turnberg: Never! Never!

Q8 *Baroness Hilton of Eggardon:* You were talking about self-confidence and status and it is always the medical profession which has self-confidence and status and the other organisations perhaps felt obliged to have separate organisations to maintain themselves. No?

Professor Crome: If I could say something from our point of view. I think one of our differences is that a good chunk of our work is related specifically to being a doctor, training as a doctor and continuing in practice as a doctor, and I think that would require a medical section of an enlarged British organisation. I know from other countries where they do not have this division that what has actually happened is that the medical section has developed and in some cases has split off and I would have thought there was a good chance that that type of thing could have happened in Britain as well. It is an historical accident, if you like, why there are three separate societies in this country.

Dr Faragher: I think we would echo what Professor Phillipson and Professor Crome have said. One of the things that we can see when we have contacts with the other two societies is the difference of expectation of our respective memberships about what the society should be delivering, even in things as trivial as for example an annual meeting. Should it have a forum in which all discuss equally, should it be a series of plenary lectures at which the newest data are given, should it be a symposium at which good practice is disseminated. Those three sets of expectations are difficult to marry within one organisation

Q9 *Chairman:* What would you think if I had four representatives from the research councils sitting in front of me and they gave roughly the same set of answers? Things really are different in our corner because I would have thought one of the messages that you all present is the need for inter-activity, and

if it is good enough for research councils I suppose we are asking whether it is good enough for you as well.

Professor Phillipson: Research councils expect two things now, do they not, they expect very good disciplinary research which we are concerned to promote but they now expect inter-disciplinarity which we are equally concerned to promote. The latter of course is a much more recent ambition and is something which is testing all of us and I think nobody has a clear solution as to how good inter-disciplinarity can be pursued particularly as it is not encouraged by the research assessment exercise which drives all of us, frankly, in terms of achieving certain things for our universities, so I think they would not be surprised at our answers.

Dr Faragher: I think we see inter-disciplinarity as very much the roof on the house on which the supporting walls are provided by either the research councils through the provision of funding or the societies through the provision of academic exercise. It is important but it is not essential and it cannot substitute for focused activity.

Chairman: Can I ask Lord Turnberg to pick up the questions.

Q10 *Lord Turnberg:* If I could just comment very briefly on your responses. There are other professional societies which do combine research and clinical aspects reasonably successfully and they work rather well so they are good models, and at the very least I suspect developing common policies in the areas of common interest which you obviously have. It might not be a bad thing. However, my question is a much more general one. As you know, this Committee is interested in the scientific aspects of ageing not simply because we are curious, not simply for personal reasons, but because we believe that scientific developments in ageing are occurring at a great pace, as you are obviously aware, and we are interested in seeing whether we should harness those to inform public policy and government policy so that is where we are coming from. So in view of that what are your current priorities in your individual societies, which might help us in our particular roles?

Professor Lord: I will start at our end from the BSRA's point of view reiterating what we provide in our written statement. We see these really rapidly developing areas which can make a real impact on the health of the elderly population, such as immunosenescence or the declining immune system as you age. There is a potential in really quite a short term of five to 10 years that developments which have been funded under BBSRC in the Science of Ageing and ERA initiatives have really shown the way forward that we could prevent infections in elderly people. So that is one area we see as a priority. Another one that is a little further away again would be the area of molecular genetics so the insulin-IGF axis which is essentially how you handle food and your metabolic rate. That is potentially open to manipulation. And then a longer term challenge is this idea of senescence, the build-up of senescent cells, whether that can be again harnessed and manipulated. Also we have put in the written evidence that looking at the musculo-skeletal system, muscle-wasting with age and osteoporosis, is something we would see as a priority where we have got real information that has arisen out of the research that should be translated.

Q11 *Lord Turnberg:* You talked about immunosenescence. Are you suggesting that we will be able to manipulate that?

Professor Lord: Yes, the evidence coming from several UK labs is that this decline in your immune function can be overcome, so for example one thing we know that happens as we age is that we have an altered stress response. You may think that is nothing to do with the immune system but the way you respond to stress if you have an increased stress response is you suppress your immune system and we know that this is something that happens with age and gradually your response to stress does increase and the problem there is that you reduce the output of a hormone called DHEA as you age. That can be replaced in the diet very simply so it could be that, not in general but in times of stress, or it could be after a fall, perhaps a hip fracture, or after a bereavement—and we know these are two times when the elderly are very susceptible to infection—that at those times for a short period a very simple DHEA dietary intervention could reduce morbidity and mortality in that group, so that is something that is very achievable.

Dr Faragher: What we should perhaps stress as well is that we are talking about very substantial negative indicators. I believe, Professor Lord, that the death rate from infection in the elderly following a hip fracture is approximately 50 per cent in three to six months.

Professor Lord: That is in the winter period. If you look annually year-wide that percentage is still 25 per cent. It is quite horrific. And these are previously healthy people.

Dr Faragher: We are anxious as a society to capture these new developments and make sure that they make it to people who really need them. We think these hearings will offer a great opportunity for policy to evolve that will let us do that.

Q12 *Lord Turnberg:* I can see that these are potential mechanisms of getting into some of the problems that occur during ageing to influence the ageing process and the response, but I am not quite clear how you

see that feeding into policy decisions. What should be done in relation to that?

Professor Lord: You could see a direct change perhaps in policy in the NHS and how we deal with people with a hip fracture. I think that is quite simple. Bringing in the social side and dealing with bereavement would then be quite different. You would need to have a different policy there of how you would handle someone dealing with a bereavement. In another area, if we look at the musculo-skeletal system, again there is data that is coming out of basic research and the benefits of a particular level of exercise for the elderly to try and slow down the muscle loss. You can see that that again could be something that would come into more of a social health visitor-type situation so that might involve policy there.

Q13 *Lord Turnberg:* That is very helpful. Professor Crome?

Professor Crome: I think our society's priorities follow on in a way from that in that we believe our greatest deficiency at the moment is the relative paucity of suitably qualified academics to oversee the translation of new interventions into the clinic and produce results which could then be translated into treatment protocols and guidelines. We have gone in recent years from a situation where most medical schools had chairs or senior lecturers in geriatric medicine to a situation where there are an awful lot of vacant chairs. We do not have a large group of senior lecturers ready to take over the leadership roles nor do we have a large number of people currently undertaking research training so they would be ready to take on roles in 10 or 15 years' time. I think we consider that is a relatively big problem given that the geriatricians will be the people who will be largely responsible for carrying out these interventions in practice.

Q14 *Lord Turnberg:* How many professors of geriatric medicine are there?

Professor Crome: I was counting them on the train. They were not all on the train!

Q15 *Chairman:* While you were on the train you were counting them!

Professor Crome: I think it depends who you count as a professor of geriatrics and who you do not but we think about 22 at the moment. For example, in the five London medical schools very soon there will only be two professors and then Birmingham—one could go on and on.

Q16 *Lord Turnberg:* You have concentrated very hard on the clinical delivery of care.

Professor Crome: Yes.

Q17 *Lord Turnberg:* But I have a sense that it is not going to be clinical delivery of care that is going to be the sole factor which we have to take into account in advances in research into results of ageing. Do you have a comment on the non-medical?

Professor Crome: Sure. We have got to ensure that the whole of the societal delivery of this activity is in place. This means dealing with issues like age discrimination of which, although officially it is against Government policy, we see example after example. We now have "working-age services" as a way of saying, not for the elderly and, as I said, the general priority needs to be increased.

Q18 *Baroness Finlay of Llandaff:* Following on from your comments about wanting to have an influence, we were wondering what interaction you have with Government departments and whether they are receptive to your views, and whether you feel that there is a good link between science and policy? Perhaps we could focus initially on the Government departments and ones that you link with and whether you are heard.

Professor Phillipson: I think the interaction certainly between social science and behavioural research in government departments has improved quite considerably over the last five to 10 years and clearly there are a range of departments that are very concerned about ageing issues. To give one example that I have been involved with, I have been closely involved with the Social Exclusion Unit which hitherto has not been taking up ageing issues as part of its remit, and we have been arguing that with them and have done some research with them and they are taking on board ageing and the isolation of some groups of older people as one of their agendas, so I think there is responsiveness there. Of course our role is quite clear. The agenda here is shaped by politics of course and today the crisis is pensions, next week it will be elderly abuse, and the week after it will be residential care. I think it is very important for our kinds of societies to present the evidence and say, "Well, yes, some of those things may be going on but there is an alternative view and this is the evidence." I think you have to have a dual role there. We do respond to calls for research from the Department for Work and Pensions, Department of Health, whatever it is, but I think we also have a role in terms of putting forward other views in what is a political debate. There is a political construction of ageing issues, a crisis of ageing so-called. I do not subscribe to that view but it is important to put forward scientific arguments as to why that view may be limited. So I think there is a dual role that we are playing.

Professor Crome: I guess the British Geriatrics Society's main interaction would be with the Department of Health and I guess the overall response about the quality of that interaction would be mixed. For example, the National Service Framework for older people is very much in our minds as the main policy directive for health in England and although it does not cover now the devolved administrations of the United Kingdom it is the same general principles, and in the run-up to that we advanced the cause of providing services based on strong evidence and some of those were taken on board, for example, the very clear guidance about fall services and services for stroke patients, which is based to quite a large extent on work conducted by members of our society. On the other hand, in some areas such as intermediate care there is very much less evidence and there is a lot of resistance to our view that research in this area should be funded not at the same time as the policy, preferably before the policy comes out, but at least within a short time afterwards. If I can give an example which we would probably use as a classic example which applies to the previous Government. Next year at the British Geriatrics Society we will have the evaluation of the over-75 health checks presented to us 15 years after they were introduced. There was a five-year battle to get funding, perhaps even longer, and now of course the agenda has moved on. So I guess the answer is mixed. We do have a member of our society as the director of the older persons' programme and he is a member of our policy committee and it is a close relationship at that level.

Professor Lord: For the BSRA our main interactions at the moment are with the BBSRC where we have been consulted on the Science of Ageing and the ERA programme, so we feel that is quite appropriate. We were also involved in the past with the OST via the Foresight Ageing Population Panel and we had members on that. We have had interactions with ESRC as well, so our main interactions at the moment are with the research councils. As far as anything else we feel that we have had very little engagement with government departments and we feel this is something for the future we would like to improve. We feel that we have got a valuable contribution to make. Following on from Professor Phillipson's point about social exclusion, if we think about the area of work and pensions certainly a lot of the data we have got about the basic biology of ageing would say that the more a person stays within social interaction, whether it is work or whether it is promoting volunteering, the more active they are in the community would again reduce their stress levels and again reduce their immuno-suppression, and keeping active would again promote a reduction in the loss of muscle, et cetera, et cetera. So we feel that

12 October 2004 Professor Janet Lord, Dr Richard Faragher,
Professor Christopher Phillipson and Professor Peter Crome

we have a valuable contribution to make there. We are certainly not consulted there at the moment.

Dr Faragher: Those interactions which we have had with government have been positive. We feel we have a role to play in offering good scientific advice that will increase the options of policy makers but what also we would like to stress is that we have always seen ourselves as an advice bureau rather than a pressure group, as it were, so we have waited to be asked rather than put ourselves forward. To an extent this is changing. There are some programmes active in the research councils where there is an active attempt to engage with Government and tell people what we are actually doing, so in that sense hopefully what will happen is that our profile as a society will be much higher in following years.

Q19 *Baroness Finlay of Llandaff:* It just strikes me as you are talking that as a Government department it has got different groups to go to and simplicity is all. My background is in palliative medicine and there was a very strong message "we want one place to go to talk to, not all these different hospices beating a path to our door", which was completely understandable. I just wonder whether the different scenarios of reception you are outlining may be because you are taking a more reactive position and perhaps the geriatricians are taking a more proactive role, but that there may be a real need for Government departments so they could come with any question to a single point and get filtered through. I do not know what your comments are.

Professor Phillipson: It is difficult to have a single point. Again there are different objectives which the societies clearly have and the members of the societies have so I am not sure absolutely how effective that would be. The issue is that there are a whole variety of objectives and agendas of course which different government departments have as well so I think it is quite difficult. I think, though, we should improve as much as possible the effectiveness of the relationship we have with departments, that is clear.

Q20 *Baroness Finlay of Llandaff:* I do not wish to put words in your mouth but it sounds as if sometimes the science is not always informing policy.

Dr Faragher: I think it depends on which types of policy you are talking about. For example, *Winning the Generation Game* I think could have had some additional options with a greater input of scientific advice. That I think is very clear. How in fact we manage to close that divide I am unsure because I think what we would stress from biology is that we are in an unusually advantageous position and we only reached this very recently. We could tell you why the ageing process happened. We could not offer much in the way of substantial, real, concrete

opportunities to achieve compression of morbidity. I think that has changed and I think it has changed quite dramatically over the last 10 years.

Professor Phillipson: Winning the Generation Game is a very good example of where sometimes research gives unpalatable news because what that promoted was the view that if you kept working that would be good for your health. Unfortunately, there is no research evidence for that. It was asserted in the *Generation Game* as a research fact but there is no evidence for that at all. The Government does want at the present time researchers to line up and say, "If we encourage people to go on working that will give them extra years." Whatever my biology colleagues say there is no sound evidence for that whatsoever. This is some of the problems where just feeding into policy I think it is quite difficult at times.

Professor Lord: Following on from that, this is where this translational work is required. We know the effect of stress as far as biology is concerned. We know that being involved in work and social interaction should reduce stress but, as Christopher says, we need that evidence, that link is not there yet.

Q21 *Baroness Finlay of Llandaff:* What about the link to the more technological aspects of lifestyle? How much research is going on there in terms of research into the links with technology coming in and informing policy?

Dr Faragher: It is my hope that the Committee will be seeking submissions from Professor Peter Lansley of the EQUAL programme at the EPSRC. I have some knowledge of that area through a collaborative programme the EPSRC and BBSRC are developing called SPARC (Strategic Provision of Ageing Research Capacity). It is clear to me from the documents that I have read that that has taken the user focus approach to the development of assisted technologies and best practice to a very high level, and I am sure that what you will hear from Peter will be good news and evidence that you can really start off with a research council focused programme and end up with things that do go into practice and do go into policy.

Q22 *Baroness Walmsley:* Could you say whether there any key policy decisions that you think Government should make either to improve the organisation of research in the UK or to implement the results of that research in a way that would improve the quality of life of older people? I would ask you not just to limit yourself to the departments that have already been mentioned—the Department of Health, the Social Exclusion Unit and the DWP. There are lots of other departments which might also be relevant such as the Office of the Deputy Prime Minister, Transport, Education, Culture, Media and

Sport, you name it, so please do not restrict yourselves at all in your answers.

Professor Phillipson: Are you asking if there is one single thing that—

Q23 *Baroness Walmsley:* Start with one and see how far we go!

Professor Phillipson: I think if you asked most people concerned with ageing research (and I do not know whether you wanted to come on to this) research capacity is an issue and I think most societies are concerned about the fact that clearly there is the potential and actuality of increased funding for ageing research on the one side but the problem with research capacity on the other. This is a great concern, the fact that we do not have a clear ladder for researchers to go through and that people are lost, having been trained on particular projects. This is a waste of human capital which we really cannot afford to go on with. There are relatively few centres of gerontology of whatever kind, whether it is biological, sociological or psychological in the country, so there are problems anyway in terms of infrastructure and training people within the context of centres like that. So I think that the Government does have a role in raising questions about where is the next generation of researchers going to come from who will provide some of the answers that committees like this say are needed because it is very fragmented at the present time, it is serendipitous in terms of how people's careers develop outside a limited number of centres, and I do think that is grossly inadequate in terms of meeting the challenge that is clearly there, however you define it. I do not know if that is quite getting at your question but there is clearly a role and some departments are responding. As you mentioned the ODPM, the ODPM is a very interesting example where they have collaborative studentships with the Economic and Social Research Council and possibly other research councils, I do not know, on particular areas. I think that is very exciting especially as the ODPM and ESRC have 20 studentships on particular themes scattered in different universities on issues about transport, I think was one, urban deprivation was another. For a relatively small resource you can really kick on with research. However, then there is the issue of what happens to those people when they have done their doctorates and will there be enough post-doctorate opportunities around. I think that is incredibly important to develop research.

Q24 *Baroness Walmsley:* Before we move on to anybody else can I just probe a point there. Do you think that one main centre of excellence would help this issue of career pathways being absent?

Professor Phillipson: No, personally I think we should not go down that road. A number of centres exist and we should be encouraging those to develop in different ways but I am not a great fan of single centres of excellence, no.

Q25 *Baroness Walmsley:* Thank you very much. Professor Crome?

Professor Crome: Taking up the same thing, I think the issues apply equally for medical graduates who are seeking to undertake research. We have a lot of pressures from people not to do research. Government policy is to expand the number of consultancies as rapidly as possible. If you want to undertake research it will extend your training no matter what way you look at it and at the end of it there may not be a job for you or a job that you would want. So I think clear signals coming from government through the various agencies that this is something that the medical schools should be supporting and they need to develop the appropriate assessment processes which would allow that to happen and would not penalise medical schools for investing in this area. If, for example, at the next research assessment exercise those medical schools which have geriatric medicines submissions do not do very well, the reaction to that is that we will see a further decline in academic geriatric medicine and inter-disciplinarity.

Q26 *Baroness Walmsley:* Are we losing a lot of people overseas?

Professor Crome: No, I do not think that is the case. Of course the issues that I am talking about are not unique to geriatric medicine. Obviously I am here to talk about geriatric medicine but they apply to other medical and surgical disciplines as well.

Q27 *Chairman:* What about research in the NHS, do not consultants do research from time to time?

Professor Crome: Consultants do research from time to time, that is quite correct, and of course we have a big funding stream from the NHS R&D Directorate, and so far that has not been threatened. My own personal research component of my salary comes from that source but we are threatened from time to time that we may be subject to the same assessment process and of course in planning where we invest our NHS R&D money we are concerned of course at having to deal with the consequences of any reduction in funding from that route.

Q28 *Chairman:* But just to clarify in my own mind, are you suggesting that the NHS money is perhaps more likely to move towards departments of geriatric medicine than university money? Is that a difference between the two? That is really the question.

12 October 2004 **Professor Janet Lord, Dr Richard Faragher,
Professor Christopher Phillipson and Professor Peter Crome**

Professor Crome: I do not think I have the knowledge to answer that question as directly as that. We treat both of those sources of funding with equal priority and with equal rigour as to where the expenditure goes.

Q29 *Chairman:* It is just I hear where all the barriers are in the university world and it usually goes back to the R&D. Whether right or wrong, that is where a lot of it ends up. What is the position?

Professor Crome: What I can tell you—and I can only speak for our local organisation—is that the funding that we have got from what we call the Culyer money has not kept pace with inflation so that in turn translates into not being able to replace people as and when they leave and retire, so that is a negative aspect. There is some positive that has come out of it. As a new medical school we have had capital funding and an increase in revenue funding and some of that for the first time has gone into ageing research in our local area. I think this is a deficit of our society. I guess as well that we do not have a good idea of where the NHS R&D money goes within geriatric medicine departments.

Dr Faragher: With regard, my Lord Chairman, to Baroness Walmsley's questions with regard to key policy objectives, we as a society would refer you again to our written evidence but we would take this opportunity to restate that we consider that if the quality of life of the elderly population is to be improved the decision to set up goal-orientated translational funding streams is going to be essential, otherwise the ability to promote progress in research into real practices is going to be lost. In terms of overall funding we would restate the need to achieve parity at least of per capita funding with the States. Within biology of ageing we think that this is a figure of several million pounds per year, not tens of millions of pounds, and we would also say in terms of policy the original remits given to research councils under Technology Foresight are broadly correct. We would welcome a co-ordinated national strategy from above but not if it blurs responsibility for delivery of progress. We would also, I guess, echo again our feeling that inter-disciplinary research between councils designed to pick up stuff that may fall between two remits is useful. That is distinct from the inter-disciplinary research required for a translational programme. You need a different set of players and you need a different set of objectives.

Q30 *Chairman:* Thank you. Have you noticed a difference over the last couple of years among the research councils in the way in which they are working together?

Dr Faragher: I think with BBSRC and EPSRC in the last couple of years the difference has been very marked. Those are the only two councils I can personally speak of. There is a real willingness to get something done. The attitude of both those councils to ageing research has been extremely positive. That has been the most obvious change for us in the last five to six years, just how positive BBSRC in particular have been in promoting R&D on ageing. There is a willingness to work within the council so it is positive.

Professor Lord: I think the outcome there has been very positive. They met the challenge of Foresight as far as research capacity. We have got a very good life sciences base in the UK but very few of those life scientists are interested in working on ageing. It is seen as a peripheral subject and I think if we can overcome that it would be useful. The BBSRC has made real strides there saying, "Come on, move into ageing, it is interesting, there is money for it", and that really has started to build up a base in the last five years.

Q31 *Lord Turnberg:* Just briefly, listening to you talk about what is required, it sounded very much like the answer to your prayers might be the development of a gerontology or ageing or geriatric research network like the Cancer Research Network that was set up and funded by cancer research and by a variety of other sources. A number of other research networks have been set up recently with new money through the R&D initiative which are acting as foci so that they can develop centres of expertise around the country. This would be just one or two or perhaps half a dozen major centres with networks in the community using a variety of inputs. Do you think a policy in which you all got together and tried to aim for that would be helpful?

Dr Faragher: In terms of overall policy we need to recognise that in terms of biology at least the level of research capacity is probably adequate. The recent Help the Aged request for large-scale projects demonstrated that there is not a lack of capacity within the UK if the funding streams are made available. I think in terms—

Q32 *Lord Turnberg:* I was thinking about getting a funding stream. That is what this would entitle you to. It is only a suggestion and you might think about it.

Dr Faragher: I do not think any of us here are sufficiently familiar with the mechanism to comment. I do not know.

Professor Crome: I think within geriatric medicine and the remit of the work of the British Geriatric Society that may be a useful way forward. We have not

discussed it outside our own group and of course there are—
Lord Turnberg: I do not want to delay the questioning.
Chairman: It is an interesting question that we leave with you and ourselves. Baroness Murphy?

Q33 *Baroness Murphy:* I am going to ask you to go even further ahead in terms of following on from Lord Turnberg's earlier questions. What do you think are the most exciting emerging opportunities for research in your particular areas of expertise? First of all, over the next five to 10 years and then looking ahead? This is really asking you to be very imaginative. If we were suddenly to give you a great deal of research money and it was going to go on for the next 25 years (we can all dream!) what would be the most promising areas?
Dr Faragher: I think what we would say on that is please do not give us a great deal of research money immediately, give us a modest amount of research money for a long time. Again we would refer to our written evidence. We at the BSRA genuinely feel that within five years the developments in senescence, the DHEA supplementation to block infection and interleukin 7 treatment to improve T cell output have real clinical potential and real legs. They need to be translated now. In the medium term I think we would see developments in the musculo-skeletal systems trying to protect old muscle and trying to regenerate old bone as the hot area. I think moving on to that we would see attempts to remove senescent or aged cells through regenerative medicine on the one hand and on the other hand to try and understand how it is that this insulin IGS access appears to play a controlling role in lifespan in a wide variety of species as the most important thing. That is a long way away. Once you appear to have a process that occurs across all species you need to find out how it is doing it and once you know how it is doing it you can start to produce beneficial effects based on that knowledge. That is the blue sky stuff for us I think.
Professor Crome: If I could go on I guess to two or three points. Again taking up the point that has already been made, the prevention and treatment of frailty is, I think, a big area in which we should make progress in the next 10 years. I guess perhaps it is shorter than 10 years. We also hope that we will increase the evidence base of the effectiveness of the interventions in the over 80s. There really are very few conditions for which we have a good evidence base of what treatments are required in people over the age of 80 and these are the largest group that are growing, particularly those who have co-morbidity because they are always excluded from any clinical trials even if over 80s are allowed in. The third area I guess is the question of primary prevention of disease

in very old people. That is people who want to know how to maintain vigour and health in people who have reached their 80s without obvious disease, what to tell them about diet and alcohol and all these other things. I think if there was investment in trying to answer those questions now we should have the results of those by then.
Professor Phillipson: I think from the point of view of social and behavioural sciences the shorter term time period is about trying to better understand diversity. I think one of the biggest problems in the debate about ageing is that it compresses the range of behaviours, lifestyles and characteristics of older people and that is still a problem. The diversity of the population is huge and it will get wider with each cohort and that will make generalisations difficult. To some extent I would urge caution against the aspirations of my biological colleagues here in that sense because I think that diversity will create considerable issues in terms of the kind of interventions we will make and the successes of some of those interventions. We will still have that social diversity that will create issues. I think that leads into the long-term issue because the longer term goal has to be earlier interventions which can give greater equality about the expectations that people will achieve quality of life in old age. The big challenge for our Society is that there is vast inequality in that regard, an extraordinary level of inequality, both in terms of your likelihood of reaching old age but certainly in terms of the quality of life which you have in old age, and you cannot resolve that when people are in old age. I think the challenge, which is an interdisciplinary challenge, is to intervene earlier in the life course and tackle those things which mean that people age badly instead of ageing well. I think that is the challenge which is not being tackled at the present time, clearly not being tackled, but is really the most profound one we face.

Q34 *Baroness Murphy:* Can I pick up on the issue of capacity, which you mentioned earlier, and research capacity. I am not clear whether the impact, for example, that we know the RAE has had on the departments of geriatric medicine, has had an equally harsh impact on social and technological gerontology.
Professor Phillipson: There are not that very many of those so it is difficult to measure the impact. Social gerontology is a relatively small academic animal, as it were, so I think it is limited. I do not think it has necessarily discouraged it. I think the factors which promote social gerontology, or encourage or discourage it, are probably unrelated to the RAE as such, but, given that it is a relatively small area of work, clearly where there are problems with developing research careers and so on, then

obviously it is affected by that to a very great extent. I think that is shared by all the professions, all the academic sub-disciplines and disciplines to some extent that have an interest in ageing.

Q35 *Baroness Murphy:* Can I ask a very harsh question just to pick up on that. Is it that gerontological research, and particularly in medical gerontology, has not been very good across the country as a whole that it has not done very well in the RAE? I am asking remembering that I am an academic gerontologist. Is that the issue? Is it not very good?

Professor Crome: I think in terms of what we have achieved to improve the health of older people I would judge it as being successful. I have already mentioned work on stroke and work on falls which was led by geriatricians which has saved lives, if you want to put it as crudely as that, and which is on a par with that which comes from other countries. Also, I would comment that our European colleagues are very keen to publish their results in *Age and Ageing* because they judge the UK geriatric medicine research to be the leader. If you compare it with the United States, obviously they are much bigger in America and I guess that is the country that we would regard as the leading country for geriatric medicine research in the world at the present time.

Q36 *Lord Turnberg:* Is it not that geriatrics is good for the patients but not necessarily good for the RAE?

Professor Crome: So it would appear, yes.

Chairman: Lord Mitchell, do you want to pick up on the comparisons with overseas that we have been hinting at?

Q37 *Lord Mitchell:* Yes, I do. I always like asking this sort of question because I like to feel that this is a global community, especially in the scientific area, and to know what is happening there. I would like to know what your various societies have done to develop links with complementary organisations in other countries. You have spoken about how internationally competitive we are but I wonder if you could expand upon that.

Professor Crome: The British Geriatrics Society has been very active in recent years in establishing links with colleagues and sister organisations in Europe and led development of the European Union Geriatric Medicines Society. Its initial president was from the United Kingdom, the academic director was from the United Kingdom and the present secretary is from the United Kingdom. We now have expanded membership to include not only the European Union but countries that are not in the European Union. Also, on a regular basis we have dialogues with our colleagues in America and

Canada with a view to try to support the development of links between the two countries in terms of exchange fellowships and that type of activity. That is what we have done on the international scene. As an indicator of the standing of UK geriatric medicine, I guess one would say that selecting people from the UK to lead it indicates a level of trust in the standing of where we are, both in terms of the service developments, academic research and our role in training across the broad areas of activity.

Professor Lord: As far as the BSRA is concerned, we are also active members of the IAG so we are in dialogue with them and they are currently helping us to set up a young members' section to try to boost awareness amongst PhD students and young post-doctoral workers about normal ageing processes and it is an interesting field. We are working closely also with the American Ageing Association, who have very similar interests to ours, to try to get joint workshops going, so again that is something that is on our agenda at the moment. Also, we are pursuing similar links with Japan who have a very active biology of ageing research community. As far as biology of ageing, although the UK has done a burst, a sprint, in the last five years, the standard is very high. An example there was the ability of a group in Liverpool, for example, to get funding from the NIH. They got substantial funding for their muscle work. There is another group in London that has almost £5 million from the Wellcome Trust to look at genetics across species to identify genes that extend longevity. There is yet another group, who are members, who have had substantial EU funding. I think the international standing of biological ageing research from the UK is high. If you look at the publications from the members, it must amount to hundreds of papers in good journals. Coming back to a previous point, this perception of geriatrics as being a peripheral subject really is a misconception and, again, I think we need to educate people that it is a subject that is on the up and is academically challenging.

Dr Faragher: One thing that I think we should also emphasise is that the most exciting developments, the ones that we have chosen to outline to you today, that really have a chance of making a difference to the lives of ordinary elderly people have come about from UK labs as a result of UK money and UK will to do something. In that sense, I think we are small but perfectly formed compared to the United States.

Professor Phillipson: I think the only thing I would add to that is that what I have noticed over the last five to 10 years is far more collaborations between researchers in my Society, but in other societies as well, concerned with ageing in European and international projects generally. I think this is extremely encouraging. Equally, at prestige international conferences, interventions and papers, symposia organised by researchers from my Society are very common. I come back to one of the questions earlier about the quality of research, which I would agree is patchy, I think at the good end, at the prestige end, at the end which is well regarded by international bodies, there is quite a lot of it and probably we perform above our weight in many respects.

Q38 *Baroness Emerton:* If you imagine that in 10 years' time you were to look back at the achievements of your societies in terms of various objectives and priorities for scientific aspects of ageing, bearing in mind that we have been talking about what is happening now this afternoon, what would you regard as evidence of success?

Professor Phillipson: Gosh! I think that is enormously difficult. I am going to give a rather prosaic answer to that in two parts. One is that in terms of the disciplines, the various disciplines, that are represented within our society which go all the way from, say, social anthropology, economics to psychology, one success indicator might be better representation of all of those disciplines. There are virtually no social anthropologists studying ageing at the present time. I do not know how much that matters but, on the whole, I think it is disappointing that there are not very many interested. There are a few but not very many interested. I think one measure is that you do need a broader spread and more people in the different disciplines represented. Certainly the other factor is that we do have properly established, in my case, social and behavioural gerontology centres which are providing greater coherence, infrastructure and support to ageing research. I think it is still too much of an amateur occupation in the sense that it is too often done by people who are relatively isolated: certainly in the social and behavioural sciences, but I think that is less true for some of my colleagues. You will not have advances in scientific research with people relatively isolated. That is clear from the Research Councils, that is clear from everybody. I think making gains, that will be a success indicator. I suppose the third, if there is a third, is that we will not have research initiatives on ageing because ageing as an area will be embedded in the research process.

Q39 *Baroness Emerton:* Yes.

Professor Crome: Perhaps I have three points to make. The first one is that on the level of our Society it would be seen as the place to come to for medical advice on aspects of the health of older people, from everybody: from government; from older people themselves and from their families; all sections of society. The second in terms of our present strategy is to see that delivered and the most obvious example would be thriving groups, departments of geriatric medicine inter-related with other disciplines in a larger number of medical schools than is presently the case. The third area, I guess, has to be that this effort would be translated into beneficial effects for older people in terms of their health and welfare.

Professor Lord: From the BSRA, echoing what Professor Phillipson said, we would also like to see that the good work done by the special initiatives is continued. We have already got this nice base there but if that funding does not continue it may well wither, so in 10 years' time we would like to see an established core of somewhere between 30 and 60 research groups in the UK working on ageing, that would certainly be an outcome for us, and that ageing is seen as a priority across the Research Councils. Again, following on from Professor Crome's point, as biologists interested in the ageing process we would like to see some of the exciting findings that we have got now translated through into the clinic. That is two things that we would look for.

Dr Faragher: I would echo the aspiration of the Society to see a real shift in quality of life for the frail and elderly as a result of our efforts. We would also like to see enhanced participation from other components of the life science base and linkages in place between the physical science and the biological science that are actually producing some useful fruit. We are starting down that route now. I feel as if I am stressing this continuously, but this is a unique time in the history of ageing research in the UK and we would like to see Society members used in an advisory capacity on the largest scale thought necessary by government to show that we can have science informing policy.

Q40 *Baroness Walmsley:* Could I just follow up a point Professor Lord made. You mentioned that you would like to see between 30 and 60 research groups but what level of increment is that? How many are there now?

Dr Faragher: That figure is based on being able to maintain all of the research groups that were active under the science of ageing programme at BBSRC and the experimental research programme at BBSRC active concurrently. At the moment, within BBSRC I believe there are about 28 to 30 active groups that would see themselves as gerontologists. One point to stress is that the more resource that is available, the more groups will be drawn into doing this kind of stuff. I believe BBSRC identified approximately 90 active researchers who could make the shift into ageing. It is rather like running a tractor factory. You ask how many tractors you can make and you will make as many tractors as the market will bear. If there is a lot of money for tractors, people who currently make cars will consider retooling, but if you are making tractors and half of them are unsold the inclination to shift is not there.

Q41 *Lord Turnberg:* I just want to put a last point to you. It is pretty obvious that everyone is living longer, and we are going to have older and older people through the efforts of science and society at large. The message that we seem to be getting is that not only are we going to live longer but live more healthily, that is we are not going to prolong periods of ill-health, we are prolonging healthy life and that message is coming through to us. The implication of that is that we are going to have a larger proportion of the population who are elderly, and who are not only elderly but well, and can contribute; that is we are going to have a large number of people who are less a burden but more a resource, and I am not sure that society has caught up with that.

Professor Phillipson: I do not agree with that. There are two sections of your argument that I do not agree with. Whether everybody will be healthier in the future is unclear. I think new cohorts potentially will bring in new types of disability and I think we need more investigation of that. As far as our Society is concerned, the big emphasis over the past 10 years has been to try to push the argument very hard that in some senses it is true that old people are a major resource but they are already committing themselves as a resource through their activities in the community, with their families. I think one of the big mistakes that the debate has made is to imply that old people are dependent in some way whereas I think all of the sociological evidence, if you like, is that they are active providers within the community already. I think the societies have been quite strong on providing that message, however I think it is interpreted through a filter of institutional ageism that makes its reception quite difficult at times and I think that has been a problem. Of course, it is now in the interests of government to accept that older people are a resource and that is very encouraging. I think that is a good element but the motives are perhaps rather mixed.

Dr Faragher: What we would probably like to see, speaking personally, is a change in the way society views ageing such that people are thought of more in terms of their biological age rather than their chronological age. All scientific data shows you that the trajectories of ageing vary quite widely between different individuals and yet what tends to happen is that we compartmentalise people into discrete age groups. There are very fit 75 year olds and very unfit 55 year olds. I think the question of whether somebody is fit to continue working, for example, could be looked at informatively within the context of their own individual biology and by and large associated with how well they are holding up.

Q42 *Baroness Finlay of Llandaff:* This is a supplementary specifically to Professor Crome. I am wondering whether there is a need for the medical speciality of geriatric medicine to separate out issues specifically related to medical aspects of ageing versus general medical care of a population that has an older age numerically and if that may help develop the pure academic expertise. The other question that is linked to that, going back to your comment on the RAE and the shortage of academics, is whether there is an urgent need for the assessment to recognise that clinical academics should only count as 0.5 because half of them are busy doing non-academic clinical and the other half is the academic bit, and to count them as if they were laboratory researchers, puts a pressure on them that will drive them all away.

Professor Crome: I think that latter comment that you make is a fair one. As far as the first point of your question is concerned, I think it is the case that geriatric medicine as a *speciality* is refocusing, if I can put it like that, on to a special involvement with the frailest and most vulnerable of older people and allowing the *speciality* services to deal and treat patients who just happen to be old. I think that is a real change that has occurred, and is occurring, over the last five years. There has been perhaps a swing one way but now it is swinging the other.

Chairman: May I thank you very warmly for the time that you have given us generously this afternoon, for the written evidence that you have submitted, they were all very interesting pieces. If, as a result of this discussion, there are any points that you feel you would want to clarify in your written evidence then please do, but fairly soon I must say. Do please feel that you can amend or extend any written material that you have sent. Thank you very much indeed.

TUESDAY 26 OCTOBER 2004

Present	Drayson, L	Murphy, B
	Emerton, B	Soulsby of Swaffham Prior, L
	Finlay of Llandaff, B	Sutherland of Houndwood, L (Chairman)
	Hilton of Eggardon, B	Turnberg, L
	Oxburgh, L	Walmsley, B

Memorandum by the National Osteoporosis Society

1. INTRODUCTION

1.1 The National Osteoporosis Society (NOS) welcomes the opportunity to provide evidence to the committee on the scientific aspects of ageing.

1.2 The Society's evidence concentrates on the impact that osteoporosis and osteoporotic fractures have upon older people. We suggest areas of research that could be beneficial in preventing osteoporotic fracture and therefore improving the quality of later life.

2. ABOUT THE NOS

2.1 The NOS is the only national charity dedicated to improving the diagnosis, prevention and treatment of osteoporosis and osteoporotic fractures. Osteoporosis is a common condition that is most prevalent in the over 50s, particularly amongst post-menopausal women.

2.2 The NOS aims to:

— offer support to people with or at high-risk of osteoporosis, their families and carers;

— raise awareness of osteoporosis and bone health amongst people of all ages;

— raise funds for research into osteoporosis to increase understanding of the condition, improve treatment options and patient care; and

— work in partnership with health care professionals to facilitate greater understanding of the needs of people with osteoporosis and to promote the implementation of effective healthcare services.

3. OSTEOPOROSIS AND ITS EFFECTS

3.1 Osteoporosis is described as a progressive, systemic skeletal disease that is characterised by low bone mass, skeletal fragility and susceptibility to fracture. Osteoporotic fractures affect at least one in three women and one in 12 men over the age of 50 and may result in pain, disability, dependence, reduced quality of life as well as reduced life expectancy.

3.2 Osteoporotic fractures result in significant costs to health and social care services. The combined social care and acute costs for treating the 80,000 + osteoporotic hip fractures that occur annually in the UK amount to over £1.7 billion. Each year hip fractures block a large proportion of orthopaedic beds. These figures are expected to rise as a consequence of increased life expectancy and the growth in the ageing population.

3.3 Bone mass increases during early life, reaching a peak at about age 30 years and decreasing in later life. As women have smaller skeletons and lose bone mineral density (BMD) rapidly after the menopause due to oestrogen deficiency, they are at a greater risk of developing osteoporosis than men.

3.4 The commonest osteoporotic fractures are of the vertebrae (spine), proximal femur (hip) and distal radius (wrist). Other sites include the pelvis, ribs, proximal humerus and distal femur. It is fractures, rather than osteoporosis per se, that cause individuals to suffer severe pain, disability, significant reductions in quality of life and premature death. Regardless of the type of fracture, those who sustain one fracture are at a significantly increased risk of sustaining further fractures.

3.5 The large majority of hip fractures occur during a fall, whilst the majority of vertebral fractures are triggered by everyday activities such as bending or lifting what would typically be thought of as "light objects".

3.6 Osteoporotic fracture affects a person's ability to carry out even the most basic of daily activities such as walking, eating, dressing and bathing, as well as the more active tasks of cooking, shopping, housework and travelling. These can have a devastating impact on an older person's quality of life, often resulting in isolation and disengagement from social and community activities. These can also result in low self-esteem and feelings of being burdensome.

3.7 Osteoporotic fracture often results in a loss of independence; amongst those who have sustained a hip fracture 50 per cent require some form of long term nursing care. However, 80 per cent of women who have sustained a fracture have admitted that they would rather be dead than admitted to a nursing home.

4. WHAT ARE THE PROMISING AVENUES FOR RESEARCH? HOW WILL SUCH RESEARCH BENEFIT OLDER PEOPLE AND DELAY THE ONSET OF LONG-TERM ILLNESSES AND DISABILITIES?

4.1 Over the last decade, there have been substantial advances in our understanding of the causes of osteoporosis, and in the availability of diagnostic aids and treatments aimed at reducing its health impact. For example, it is now clear that thinning of the bones starts immediately after the menopause in women, and is in one sense part of the normal ageing process. In addition, it is recognised that as well as the speed of bone loss, the likelihood that a given individual will develop osteoporosis depends on how strong a skeleton they developed earlier in life.

4.2 Therefore, there are two different types of opportunity to reduce or delay the adverse impact of osteoporosis on health in the elderly:

(i) preventive measures designed to maximise skeletal strength in early life; and

(ii) therapies which aim to prevent or even reverse bone loss in later life.

Both will benefit older people by preventing or minimising the impact of osteoporosis in later life, however, it is the former which is the most relevant for this inquiry.

4.3 Some people are genetically predisposed to developing osteoporosis, but it is clear that the impact of this process can be mitigated by our lifestyle choices earlier in life. Lifestyle factors can influence the amount of bone you invest in your bone "bank" during your youth and how much you save in later life. We already know that following a diet which is well-balanced and enriched with calcium; taking regular weight-bearing exercise; avoiding excessive smoking and drinking can all help towards building and maintaining a healthy skeleton and improve an individual's chances of not developing osteoporosis later in life.

4.4 However, there is still much more we need to understand about the condition if we are to mitigate the substantial impact on both the individual and society. We need to expend much more energy into research and understanding the effects that various factors can have on the development of the skeleton and osteoporotic fracture risk.

4.5 Awareness and understanding of osteoporosis and ways to prevent fracture are still low amongst the general population and even health professionals. More effort is required from Government, the NHS, schools and all other stakeholders to help younger people to take good care of their bones, to enable them to enjoy an active and fulfilling later life. For example, ensuring that children engage in adequate amounts of exercise and eat nutritious meals whilst within the school gates and at home could have an enormous impact on the future older population.

4.6 Although the Government has been active in developing policy on osteoporosis in recent years, much of the focus has been on people who already have osteoporosis, have fractured or who are at high risk, eg Standard Six of the National Service Framework for Older People and the various pieces of guidance that are being developed by the National Institute for Clinical Excellence (NICE). Although these initiatives are crucial for current patients and those who are and will be at risk from osteoporosis, they do not address the root cause of the condition. In particular, the NICE clinical guideline, which looks at the overall clinical management of osteoporosis, only looks at prevention amongst those who are already at risk. The guideline has expressly omitted from its remit, "population-wide primary prevention strategies in the general population not considered to be at high risk for the condition . . . For example, this might include health promotion activities within schools."

4.7 The UK holds an international leadership role in population-based research studies aimed at identifying causes of osteoporosis. For example, the Southampton group has led the world in terms of understanding the childhood origins of many diseases including osteoporosis, and in Bristol, the Avon Longitudinal Study of Parents and Children (ALSPAC), which consists of approximately 10,000 children, provides a cohort which is uniquely placed to examine the role of factors such as diet and exercise in childhood, in causing osteoporosis in later life.

4.8 These lines of research should attract strategic funding and be of interest to both the Government and the NHS, since many of the factors, which predispose to osteoporosis, such as lack of exercise, are likely to be the focus of prevention strategies which may play an important role in determining other health outcomes in older people, such as cardiovascular disease and arthritis.

4.9 A further promising area of research is in examining the relationship between the effect of a given environmental risk factor on bone development, and genetic predisposition, since there is an increasing realisation that environmental influences are likely to have greatest impact in individuals with specific genetic risk factors. As well as requiring large cohorts to detect these gene-environmental interactions (such as ALSPAC) these studies also depend on knowledge of underlying molecular pathways which regulate bone cell activity that are likely to be affected by these interactions, and the availability of technology to identify genetic variations in large cohorts in a cost effective manner.

4.10 Osteoporosis research is now in a strong position to pursue this line of research, since recent advances in bone biology have identified many of the mechanisms which regulate bone cell activity and are likely to be altered in osteoporosis, and high throughput genotyping techniques have been developed, enabling screening of large populations for a wide range of genetic risk factors at relatively low cost.

5. How Effectively is Research Co-ordinated in the Public Private and Charitable Sectors (Including Internationally)? Have the Correct Priorities been Identified? Are there any Gaps in Research? Is there Sufficient Research Capability in the UK? Is the Research being used to Inform Policy?

5.1 In the UK, a wide range of public, private and charitable sectors have invested in osteoporosis research, including the National Osteoporosis Society. A diverse range of research programmes have been supported, including drug trials, health services research, epidemiology studies and laboratory-based research. International Conferences, which include all of the major stakeholders in the field, are held on a regular basis. Furthermore, research is shared amongst the osteoporosis community through publications and charitable organisations such as our own.

5.2 The pharmaceutical industry funds an increasing amount of osteoporosis-related research in the UK, with a focus on the use of licensed drug therapies in older patients who have already developed, or are at high risk from, osteoporosis.

5.3 Despite the large number of bodies involved in osteoporosis research in the UK, the combined total of research funding available for research into osteoporosis from public or charitable funds is relatively small, and there is little attempt to prioritise what type of research should be supported. In particular, there seems little or no strategic investment intended to identify relatively simple population-based preventive measures, as described above, which are likely to be more cost effective than approaches based on treating the disease with clinical and therapeutic interventions, once the patient has developed the disease. This is a message that appears to have filtered through in areas such as Coronary Heart Disease and diabetes, however the link has not yet been sufficiently made with osteoporosis.

6. Recommendations

6.1 The prevalence and burden of osteoporosis and osteoporotic fracture on both patients and the NHS suggests that the prevention of osteoporosis should be a health priority for the Government and the health service. As well as ensuring that older people with osteoporosis receive excellent treatment and support from health and social care services, the NOS believes that the Government should seek to engage in wider population based prevention programmes which would benefit future generations.

6.2 Population wide strategies might include increased physical activity and increased calcium intake for promoting optimum bone health throughout life.

6.3 NICE often makes recommendations for research as part of the guidance it develops. However, we understand that there is no onus on any organisation to undertake the research that is recommended. With the osteoporosis clinical guideline, NICE did not tackle the population-based prevention strategies mainly because the overall evidence base is not comprehensive enough, making the guideline a difficult and unwieldy piece of work. It would be useful, when these sorts of difficulties are encountered, if recommendations for research could be made at an appropriate stage and are at least prioritised when decisions are made about funding, and perhaps commissioned, by bodies such as the Medical Research Council and the Department of Health.

6.4 There is also a concern about what happens to research once it has been completed. Organisations such as the NOS endeavour to spread best practice and advise patients and the general population about lifestyle messages. However, as we have seen with the public health work around smoking and CHD, a great deal of political/national will is necessary in order to bring about change. Notably, however, the effects of such a campaign for CHD can be appreciated almost immediately, unfortunately the same cannot be said for a condition such as osteoporosis. Damage occurs over a long period of time and cannot always be rectified by lifestyle changes at a later stage in life, although these can be helpful. Benefits from these sorts of initiatives for osteoporosis might only be realised some fifty years later and therefore, it is often difficult to obtain political/national support for these sorts of projects for osteoporosis when the Government of the day cannot hope to reap the benefits.

6.5 How this problem can be addressed is difficult. The continued devolution and growing independence of the NHS can mean that bodies such as NICE can provide advice and leadership without too much political interference. However, funding will remain an issue and whilst there are competing priorities in the health service quick, immediate wins will always attract the lion's share of the funding. Unless funding can be apportioned to an independent body to work on these sorts of long-term public health projects, population-based prevention of osteoporosis is unlikely to happen in the near future.

October 2004

Examination of Witnesses

Witnesses: PROFESSOR GRAHAM RUSSELL, Norman Collisson Professor of Musculoskeletal Science, Oxford University and PROFESSOR CYRUS COOPER, Professor of Rheumatology, University of Southampton (on behalf of the National Osteoporosis Society and the Arthritis Research Campaign), examined.

Q43 Chairman: May I welcome you both very warmly? I think you know something of the remit of our Committee. I shall not go round the table, but name tags are in front of all of us. We have a number of questions we want to raise and if there are matters you think we should have raised but have not, please indicate. Equally, if after the session, you have perhaps second thoughts, we should very much welcome any additional written comment. May I thank Professor Cooper particularly for the evidence that he and his colleagues in the National Osteoporosis Society have sent to us; that has been read with great interest and has formed part of the background to our discussions today. The other thing I should tell you is that this is being recorded and indeed may be broadcast on one of the remote channels. That being said, may I start with a fairly general question? We are focusing clearly on bones and muscles today particularly. As some of us know more than others, the ageing process does affect these very directly and we are conscious of that. I just wondered whether you would like to talk, very briefly, each of you, about your own research in this area and how that research is facing questions about the impact of these problems on the quality of life, of an increasingly ageing population, because we do want to tie it to quality of life. Are there issues that are now being pursued quite vigorously in this country and well, or are there key issues that in fact are not being as adequately treated as they might be

perhaps for want of staff or funds? That is a very general starting point. Who would like to begin?
Professor Cooper: My Lord Chairman, Members of the Select Committee, good afternoon. Just by way of background: I am a rheumatologist by clinical discipline and an epidemiologist by research discipline and I direct the MRC's epidemiology resource centre at the University of Southampton. So my particular research remit is to map out the health impact of these chronic musculoskeletal disorders, to characterise their patterns of occurrence, their individual risk factors and develop means of preventing them, both in the general population and in individuals at the highest risk. My focus is on osteoporosis, but we also have research programmes in osteoarthritis and soft tissue rheumatic disorders. The particular hallmark of our current programme of research, and it is interesting that you should start with this question given that it was decided at an MRC board about three days ago—

Q44 Chairman: We are perspicacious on this Committee.
Professor Cooper:—but my particular focus of interest is prevention throughout the life course, commencing *in utero*, then through infancy, childhood and into middle and late adulthood.
Professor Russell: Lord Chairman, my background is as a chemist and bio-chemist, then I qualified in medicine at the time when you did not have to be a

specialist, so I embrace a bit of rheumatology, endocrinology, general medicine and so on. My current position is perhaps symbolic of what we are talking about today because I am director of the Institute of Musculoskeletal Sciences; that nomenclature is actually coming into public use, particularly within universities and also within the Health Service, much more than previously. Our particular group comprises people, mainly clinicians and scientists, who are working especially in genetics. There is a genetic basis underlying most of the disorders that we are talking about, particularly osteoarthritis, rheumatoid arthritis, many of the other forms of arthritis, osteoporosis, but most of these are not single gene disorders; they are very complex genetic disorders with many factors contributing. It is against that background that the epidemiology that Professor Cooper does impacts on the genetic substrate. We have strong interests in cell biology including stem cell biology. I am embedded within an orthopaedic hospital and one of the things that we see, particularly within our setting, is the coming together of rheumatology and orthopaedics as a natural alliance, which is perhaps somewhat new and is going to be very important in the future for the management of musculoskeletal disorders. My particular research interest is in pharmacology of bone and joint diseases. I was responsible largely for the development of the bisphosphonate drugs which are now the major drugs used in osteoporosis and we continue to be interested in new drugs, both ones which block tissue destruction as well as drugs which build new tissue, particularly bone and cartilage. This is a very, very active area and there have been some really exciting advances in the last 10 years or so. We have therapies now for diseases that we did not have 10 years ago, so I hope we can get over a little bit of that excitement to you as well.

Q45 *Chairman:* I am sure that would be appreciated very much. May I just put a question to each of you before handing over the discussion to others? Each of you is involved in particular research groupings, the Institute and the Epidemiology Unit, which has been fairly long-term based in Southampton. May I ask about that and also about the Institute? Is that a fairly recent creation and if so, how did it come about? Was it identifying a particular problem or was it an academic with ambition? A bit of both doubtless, but one of the questions we want to face up to is how you tackle the issues. Are we putting enough direction into the research effort in the country in general?

Professor Cooper: The origins of the Resource Centre and Epidemiology Unit prior to it were largely based around the MRC's philosophy of direct intramural funding going to individual high quality scientists. So its founder director was Donald

Acheson and it was founded in 1979. Five years into its existence, about 1984, David Barker took it over and led it until his retirements in 2003; thereafter I have taken it on into its new form. That particular role of intramural funding within the MRC is just one small part of a much wider network of funding, say musculoskeletal disorders of ageing, which needs to be put in place, so that the activity can be well coordinated.

Professor Russell: Ours is a wonderful example of foresight and luck. Our institute building was built with private donations, money raised by the hospital appeal actually under the directorship of Lord Tebbit and the people who work in the building are funded by the usual sources, Arthritis Research Campaign, Wellcome Trust, MRC and so on. The building has been adopted by the university, so we run it as a typical research institute, but were it not for some private money, including some grateful-patient money, the project would not have got off the ground. It was a long-held dream by the orthopaedic community, at the Nuffield Orthopaedic Centre in Oxford, that they would build a research building and it has finally come about. We opened two and a half years ago.

Q46 *Chairman:* So there was intention within the health community but also, as it turns out, you were able to harness some funding from outside.

Professor Russell: Yes. It is interesting that universities in general, perhaps partly as a result of research assessment exercises, which happen every few years, as you know, have increasingly recognised musculoskeletal groupings, where they are strong within the university. There are at least five in this country which specifically speak to having a musculoskeletal grouping within their research portfolio: Newcastle is one, Southampton is another, Oxford and there are two others.

Q47 *Baroness Finlay of Llandaff:* Everybody experiences ageing in their bones, in their joints, in their muscles and so on, and then there is another group who suffer because of the ageing processes and because of things that have happened where these processes seem to be accelerated. Do you think it is helpful to have a division between the so-called normal ageing processes and those where things seem to be particularly advanced? I wonder whether you could talk about the disadvantages as well of trying to draw some line to determine the way that one would manage conditions.

Professor Cooper: At its theoretical level, that remains a question across all sorts of different systems. But if one were to take the two big specific examples in the rheumatological arena, osteoporosis and osteoarthritis, the answer looks pretty clear: that there is a continuously distributed risk variable, so bone mineral density, the thickness of the cartilage of the joint. As one moves along the distribution of that variable, which is changing with age, one finds an increasing risk of the likelihood of the adverse health event: the fracture for osteoporosis, the joint pain, disability and arthroplasty for osteoarthritis. So the original approaches to definition have just picked the threshold on that distribution at which it was felt by the body politic that the risk of disease became unacceptably high and set the definition at that point. As we become more sophisticated about our capacity to predict the outcome, we are moving away from definitions that focus on the process measure, the bone density, the thickness of the cartilage and thinking about means whereby we can actually estimate the individual's likelihood of a bad outcome. Blood pressure and stroke is a very easy to identify with example of this. Rather than say "You, the patient, have hypertension therefore we must treat you with an anti-hypertensive", we are moving towards saying "You, the patient, have an X per cent likelihood of a stroke over the next 10 years. You have an X per cent likelihood of a fracture over the next 10 years". You can get there by a variety of routes. When that reaches a particular level of unacceptability and we have an intervention and that intervention is cost-effective, we can justify treatment. That move in our field is just happening now. The WHO are just redefining osteoporosis, for example, in those new probabilistic terms from the old definition, which was just like blood pressure, where you said "Your bone density is below some threshold, you have got the disease". Now, if I may just continue, the burden, however you define it for musculoskeletal disorders, is very well characterised. I do not think that the burden of these disorders is really at issue. Just some examples from our two charities and from the research in our constituencies: the prevalence of musculoskeletal disorders in all adults is 25 per cent, the second most frequent cause of medical consultation after psychiatric disorder, and 25 per cent of the total costs of illness in Europe. If we go to the three big age-related disorders, they are osteoporosis, osteoarthritis and gout. Rheumatoid arthritis, which is the commonest inflammatory arthritis, goes up with age but just a little bit less steeply. We know that seven million adults in the UK have arthritis with long-term health problems; we know that two million people visit their GP every year with osteoarthritis; we know that 4.4 million people have x-ray evidence of osteoarthritis from large population surveys. Likewise, we know the numbers that suffer from rheumatoid arthritis and gout and we know the frequencies of osteoporotic fracture. What is rather more important is the move towards targeting of our newer developed measures to those

at the highest risk in a kind of societally cost-effective way that the current research and public health challenge.

Professor Russell: I do not have much to add to that, but I think if we talk about ageing and musculoskeletal diseases, I would remind you of this road sign which actually says it without words. That pictures shows osteoporosis, with a bent back, the walking stick and the implied frailty. We were not meant to bring hand-outs.

Q48 *Lord Turnberg:* I was fascinated by the data and the new analyses. May I turn to priorities and challenges in the research and where you see you need to focus within the research community? What are your priorities and what are the challenges?

Professor Russell: In all three of the areas, if we say we are talking about osteoarthritis and osteoporosis as examples of joint and bone diseases and muscle disease, with muscle wasting in the elderly, sarcopoenia, as it is called, in all of those, we need to understand causes better. With the development particularly of basic biology and genetics, we are getting new leads almost on a monthly basis. If I take the bone area for example, within the last two or three years at least three or four genes have been discovered which have major influences on bone development and bone mass in the elderly; all of which could lead, first of all to an improved understanding of the disease and, secondly, to targets for developing new therapies. So concentrating on the basic biology and applying the new knowledge from genetics will be a priority both within the commercial sector as well as the academic sector over the next few years for sure.

Q49 *Lord Turnberg:* You mentioned that these diseases are polygenic and you are unlikely to pick up a gene, apart from in very rare cases I imagine. How is that going to follow through in terms of what one can do for patients? Are you going to be able to predict those at risk from a complex array of genetic information and will this be better, for example, than scans?

Professor Russell: We have some examples already, for example in the arthritis area, of working out what the inflammatory mediators were, with tumour necrosis factor being the mediator and the anti-tumour necrosis factor antibody, which is now expensive, being probably the best treatment for rheumatoid arthritis. So there are examples where understanding the biology has led extremely quickly to new therapies. There are examples now within the bone field, and maybe I could quote a very similar one, where the development of bone destroying cells, the osteoclasts, is now recognised to be controlled by a cytokine system which involves something called RANK ligand and if you develop antibodies to this and give them as biologic therapies—it has already been done—you can block bone destruction for nine months after a single injection of antibody. This system was discovered within the last four years and the therapeutic antibody is already in clinical trial. It is actually a somewhat hazardous business predicting where we are going to be even five years from now, let alone 10 or 15. I think those of us in the field are just very excited by the rate of progress and the fact that new things are coming along all the time. Meanwhile, we have the challenge of actually doing the best with what we already have. If we take the osteoporosis example, it is estimated at the moment that maybe only 10 per cent of patients at high risk of fracture actually get any preventative treatment at all and that includes peoples on steroids, for example, who almost universally should be given some form of protective therapy. One of our challenges in the less intellectual end is just the sheer problem of identification of patients and delivery which comes back to healthcare systems.

Q50 *Lord Turnberg:* Applying what we already know has a long way to go.
Professor Russell: Yes.

Q51 *Lord Turnberg:* Professor Cooper, you spoke about the need for lifelong preventative measures. Where is that taking us?
Professor Cooper: In terms of osteoporosis first and then the bigger research agenda that osteoarthritis represents, for osteoporosis we now have epidemiological evidence and animal studies that suggest that intrauterine and early post-natal characteristics in the environment of the mother and the trajectory of the skeletal growth of the offspring are intimately linked. For example, maternal smoking, poor maternal nutrition, very high maternal exercise are linked to the capacity to transport calcium across the placenta and the foetus and subsequently infant's capacity to grow.

Q52 *Lord Turnberg:* Did you say high maternal exercise?
Professor Cooper: Yes. It appears from a cohort study in this country and one in the States that very high physical activity of the Mum in late pregnancy perhaps leads to inability of her skeleton to release calcium and maintain the maternal-foetal gradient. However, that is then supplemented through childhood and adolescence, another critical period during which the bones that you have grown have to be filled out with trabecular and cortical components of adequate density. There is then the whole period of consolidation in young adulthood, the menopausal years and the involutional decline. The kind of health policy approaches to prevention

require delineating the environmental perturbations at each of those stages of the life course, working out how those might be amplified by the experience that has gone on before and then determining in controlled trials. So one example that would be relevant to this discussion might be, say, supplementing pregnant women who are deficient in vitamin D with vitamin D to see whether in a randomised controlled trial it alters the minimalisation of the offspring. So that programme of research will help to fill in the blanks through the life course, so that we can retard fractures in future generations.

Q53 *Lord Turnberg:* That sounds like a very long-term research programme lasting a lifetime.
Professor Cooper: But it starts with immediacy: exercise in the elderly, calcium and vitamin D malnutrition in the elderly will have relatively rapid dividends. Moving backwards though, as has been the story in osteoporosis, might lead to intervention arenas at different times. In osteoarthritis I think that almost the whole of that life-course agenda, with the exception of the adulthood risk factors, obesity, joint injury, joint shape and so on, remains an important area for research.

Q54 *Baroness Emerton:* It is very interesting to hear about the research but may I just ask you to what extent your priorities are recognised by the government departments? Do you feel that there is a good link between science and policy in government in the field of musculoskeletal ageing? In what respects perhaps do you think the links might be improved in relation perhaps to more focus on prevention rather than cure?
Professor Cooper: Thank you for that. I believe that we are beginning to recognise that this is an important problem and there are exciting initiatives, but they are relatively, in my humble opinion, unconnected at the moment. We do not have a national service framework for musculoskeletal disease, we have launched a national clinical research network emphasising the critical role of translational research, taking knowledge to patient care and disease prevention in the population, we have emphasised that, but we have not got a co-ordinating centre nominated for musculoskeletal disease within the first five of John Reid's priorities; we hope in the field that it will follow. We have the National Institute of Clinical Excellence and they have pronounced on secondary prevention of osteoporosis, but the process through which that has happened has been a relatively painful one, indeed, just in the last couple of weeks, one of the appeals against their ruling has happened. I think that in the arena of policy and its impact on research, there are certainly initiatives which can be undertaken. There are also initiatives within the funding of

research which can be brought to bear on that policy. For example, the research councils do not, to our knowledge, have a particularly co-ordinated approach to musculoskeletal disease between, say, the BBSRC, MRC let alone bringing in the Wellcome Trust and the charities. Our opening, on how MRC intramural funding is designated, sort of speaks to the focus on individual achievement which I hold great store by, but sometimes that leads to a move away from considering the relevance of that whole area as a priority and building up areas that are originally Cinderella in their impact. Lastly, the involvement of the charities in that alliance is also something which is just in its infancy. At the ARC I chair a clinical trials committee which represents a link between that charity and an MRC clinical trials unit. But it was very much bottom-up and that same sort of process for translational research could be top down between the councils, the major charities and the NHS research and development directorate.

Q55 Baroness Emerton: So, really what you are saying is that you would really like to see a little more speed in connecting with the government to get into the national framework.
Professor Cooper: Indeed

Q56 Chairman: Do you have any suggestions about how that could be brought about?
Professor Cooper: I would not deign to offer them here.

Q57 Chairman: If you would like to send them to us in a brown envelope afterwards, it might be quite useful.
Professor Russell: May I just add that the universities also have a role to play here, as we have mentioned already, the fact that several of the universities are recognising musculoskeletal diseases as an entity, that, where they are strong in this interest, they are prepared to invest more in terms of staffing resources and so on. I think the other thing that we can do is to look to what is happening elsewhere in Europe and particularly in the United States. To the best of our knowledge, in the United States, there are six divisions of the National Institutes of Health (NIH) which have an interest in musculoskeletal diseases in one form or another, including a National Institute of Aging, there is an institute NIAMS, which has musculoskeletal diseases as its major remit. Even those that are somewhat peripheral, for example, imaging and application of physical sciences to medicine, have a strong interest in imaging as an important future topic in seeing how joints work, how muscles work and indeed how the skeleton works.

Q58 Baroness Murphy: I was going to ask you about the possibility of developing links with other disciplines related to ageing, particularly aspects of biological ageing, brain ageing, immune system ageing and so on as a starter. Is that possible, indeed is it being done and where do you see it going?
Professor Cooper: My own view of that is that age-related processes and disorders are still quite silo-based within systems and do not really transcend that to biological gerontology, which is about those processes across systems. Even when you do very rudimentary research into whether age-related processes, which by definition go with chronological age, cluster together in individuals, you find that the evidence base for or against that is not really as good as one might wish. For example, some limited studies have suggested that structural age-related characteristics, cataract, muscle, bone, skin, go one way whereas the neurological, cognitive, macular, auditory, might cluster together but be out of sync with the first group. That is just an example of the kind of information that we are going to need to work out whether the ubiquitous mechanism to look for, for ageing in all systems, is a target worthy of serious pursuit. In order to kick-start that, I definitely agree that having some kind of cross-system approach to ageing would facilitate it. I simply hesitate to make a pronouncement on the answer, because it may that there are certain system-specific aspects of change with age which actually provide the important targets for prevention and treatment.
Professor Russell: We may see some really good examples of multi-system effects from things that dominate in one system rather than another. I am thinking, for example, of oestrogen where the post-menopausal decline in oestrogen certainly affects the skeleton but actually affects a lot of other bodily functions as well, cardiovascular, brain and so on. This is obviously quite a controversial area, but it leads very quickly once again into therapeutics where the idea of designing oestrogen-like drugs which have the good effects of oestrogens and weed out the bad effects is something that several big pharmaceutical companies are involved in. Another linking theme would be vitamin D, which, although we always think of it as a calcium hormone and as a bone hormone and in fact a big public health problem in this country because all of us get deficient every winter, clearly affects other systems: it affects the immune system, it probably has a link to cancer if we believe some of the recent data and so on. There are common themes in physiology that link between different systems and every now and again we find examples where the disciplines come together. The ageing of the intestine for example, which I see cropping up in one of the submissions, affects our field too. If you have an aged gut, you respond less well to vitamin D.

Q59 *Baroness Murphy:* Could I follow up on that and this is a matter of your perception about the way you sit in relation to research into ageing? We have had evidence from the British Society of Gerontology, the British Society for Research on Ageing and the British Geriatric Society. Where do you sit in terms of where you see yourself in relation to those organisations?

Professor Cooper: I certainly see the work that we do as completely overlapping with the remit of those organisations; indeed, I am the welcome recipient of funding for example from research into ageing. However, I do believe that cross-fertilisation of scientific ideas particularly between the biological gerontology arena and what we do within system-based research would really enhance the efforts of both. Across the three organisations that you spoke of, as an outsider if you like from rheumatology, as my professional affiliation is the British Society for Rheumatology, I sense that at the British Geriatric Society, where I have presented on occasion, there is a deficiency in considerations of the research findings and sort of key advances of biological gerontology. There is a kind of management of care of the elderly professional society, there is biological gerontology as a field and we are in the system-based arenas, which have overlap with both because of the diseases we cover. Some kind of unity at least around the sort of research priorities and policy initiatives must be helpful.

Professor Russell: I think professionally, we all work in groups and the crossing over between groups is something that is quite difficult to achieve, but certainly worthwhile achieving. I can give you an excellent example, now living within an orthopaedic community, of the traditional problems of orthopaedic communities being separate from medical communities and in those places where rheumatology and orthopaedics have come together, patients who get fractures actually get labelled as having osteoporosis, if it is appropriate, because people start to talk to each other. Probably the most fruitful area for us to identify patients at high risk is for the medical people to link up with the surgeons and spot it. It is a tiny example but in fact the British Orthopaedic Association produced a blue book on osteoporosis and fractures which has transformed practice within trauma clinics as a result.

Q60 *Lord Turnberg:* We are talking about collaboration, co-operation and co-ordination of effort between different groups. I gain the impression that the funders do not necessarily come together. You mentioned that there are five major musculoskeletal set-ups in the UK. Do you collaborate across the five and how does that work? Does that form a network of interests?

Professor Cooper: There is certainly collaboration. Professor Russell mentioned Aberdeen, Southampton, Sheffield, Oxford and Newcastle and I can actually think of co-authored work between our groups just offhand.

Q61 *Lord Turnberg:* So that works.

Professor Cooper: That works. I think at the level of funder, there is plenty of scope for encouraged collaboration. The arthritis research campaign, as an example, is an £18 million a year research funder and with a lot of the diseases which we have been talking about, for example inflammatory arthritis 46 per cent, bone disease 17 per cent, connective tissue 12 per cent, osteoarthritis 11 per cent, I am sure the extent to which that funding goes outside of rheumatology and orthopaedics and the extent to which biological gerontology principles might be applied to these particular disorders is more limited than it ought to be. Likewise, those of us who are researching these disorders would not routinely view age-related charities as being the primary sources of funding. At the level of co-ordination of funding and research strategy, there is room for improvement. At the level of knowing what different groups around the country do, I think actually there is rather more interchange.

Q62 *Lord Drayson:* Would you say that that was a particularly UK-based problem? Do you see that taking place in other research areas in the United States or do you think they have a more integrated approach to the research?

Professor Cooper: Although, I think it is more marked in this country, I do feel that if one looks at say the US centres, where there are GRECs, Geriatric Research and Education Centres, the extent to which they take on what we would call musculoskeletal or rheumatic disease research is relatively limited and NIAMs and NIA tend to fund grants, project grants, programme grants, RO1 is the nomenclature for this. They tend to fund groups that are within their own constituency. I see symptoms of it, even in the North American system. I completely agree with Professor Russell that the very fact there is an Institute of Ageing to cover some of these system-based approaches is extremely helpful to avoid that kind of direction of funding in a pre-specified manner. There is still overlap to be gained, even over there.

Q63 *Chairman:* Presumably the less funding there is, the more important it is that we do actually look round the system and make sure that, as far as possible, we cover. The USA is a very rich country, perhaps a bit more serendipity is possible there because a lot more money is being spent and most of the gaps will be covered. It that a fair assessment?

Professor Cooper: Yes; absolutely.

Q64 *Baroness Finlay of Llandaff:* May I ask about Europe? You have addressed this country and the US, but what about within the European groupings.
Professor Russell: There are other frameworks which allow for co-ordination across Europe which have been successfully used in our area. One is the EVOS study of vertebral fractures throughout Europe which Professor Cooper was a member of. So there are examples. There has been a European call to action in osteoporosis, which is more of a political agenda, but for raising awareness of diseases, the European initiatives are being effective.
Professor Cooper: There have been osteoporosis initiatives in Framework 5, there is one on male osteoporosis in Framework 6 and there are groups that have obtained funding for osteoarthritis research within each of those frameworks. Again, I think that they have arisen from the system based sort of groupings, rather than been brought together through different perspectives on ageing in musculoskeletal tissues.

Q65 *Lord Soulsby of Swaffham Prior:* We have been talking largely about government or government sponsored research, what about the private sector in ageing of the musculoskeletal system, either as a whole or in the context of particular diseases? Is there a priority by the pharmaceutical or healthcare or lifestyle industries to attend to ageing, signs of ageing? If there is, what is the focus? Is it on cure or is it on prevention?
Professor Russell: I think the pharmaceutical industry, if we start with that, is particularly effective at identifying potential markets; if we are talking about the commercial sector, that is actually what drives it. So we do have a problem that drugs tend not to get developed for rare diseases, but some of our diseases like osteoporosis have certainly been a major focus for most of the big pharma companies throughout the world. Something like eight-plus therapies have been introduced in the last 10 years; there is approximately a new treatment for osteoporosis coming every year at the moment and that is set to continue as far as we can see. So innovation and introduction of new drugs, which very quickly become commercially successful in spite of not being given to all the eligible patients, is certainly a feature of the osteoporosis area. Osteoarthritis, on the other hand, has been somewhat disappointing because some of the most promising biological leads have turned out not to have borne fruit. There is a particular example of enzymes, called metalloproteinases, which destroy connective tissues and many companies try to develop very selective inhibitors of these enzymes and enzyme inhibitors are used as drugs in other areas, ACE inhibitors and so

on. So far this has been very disappointing with no new drugs emerging despite 15 years or so of experience. Some of the companies are waking up to the muscle side, sarcopoenia, and realising that if you can improve muscle mass in the elderly, you actually also help the skeleton; you diminish frailty, reduce falls and so on if you can produce effective therapies. That is an area of fairly active research at the moment too. The answer is that the companies certainly recognise the need. The other commercial sector which I come across quite a lot is that which deals with implants and devices, particularly in the orthopaedic area, and there is a lot of interest in developing ever-improved implants. Clearly as the population gets older, you have your joint replacement at a relatively younger age compared with your lifespan, so the longevity of the joint replacement becomes just as important as the lifespan of the patient. There is an increasing problem of having to replace these and understanding the basis for them failing in patients. There is also a lot of emphasis on tissue repair and fracture repair and a lot of interest in tissue engineering and implants in orthopaedics and in the use of growth factors and so on applied topically to improve fracture repair. The commercial sector is doing what it does best: spotting potential commercial opportunities and looking to develop the science around that.

Q66 *Lord Soulsby of Swaffham Prior:* But it is a profitable area to get into in terms of research.
Professor Russell: Musculoskeletal diseases, because of their prevalence, are certainly a profitable area for commercial development.
Professor Cooper: And the fatalism of 20 years ago for osteoporosis has been transformed by how you measure it and what you can do about it. For osteoarthritis we are one step behind and so we need still to learn the cell-cell gene environment interactions which result in cartilage loss and sub-chondral bone action and I feel that will undoubtedly lead to as exciting innovations. With sarcopoenia, we are one step further behind again and we are still at the bio-marker development, relationship between muscle and frailty and ill health, but the relevance to metabolic disease, diabetes, insulin resistance, to cardiovascular disease, to psychological well-being, as well as to osteoporosis and osteoarthritis make it a really important target. I actually see this as no reason why, just as the commonest metabolic bone disorder has gone, as an intellectual discovery problem, osteoarthritis and sarcopoenia cannot be legitimate followers of it.

Q67 *Lord Soulsby of Swaffham Prior:* I presume that the development of a new drug, let us call it in the broad sense, takes about as long as any other development, eight to 10 years or something. Is that so with ageing?

Professor Cooper: Maybe longer.

Q68 *Lord Soulsby of Swaffham Prior:* And $100 million, shall we say?

Professor Russell: That would be inexpensive for some of our drugs. We have to be careful about quoting figures, but the one which is banded around is $500 million to develop an osteoporosis drug. You have to be expecting considerable commercial success to make it worthwhile as a company to do it. This is partly because you have to do trials of 10,000 to 20,000 people, both for safety reasons and also for efficacy reasons, because the endpoint now is that it is no longer sufficient just to show an increase in the amount of bone you have: you have to demonstrate that you reduce fractures and by today's standards that has to include hip fractures if you want a commercially successful drug. It automatically demands trials, with large numbers studied over at least two to three years, preferably with a long-term follow-up after that. So you can see why it becomes very expensive to do it.

Q69 *Lord Soulsby of Swaffham Prior:* That in a way is the crux of my question. With such massive expenditure and such a long development time, is it still an attractive thing to do?

Professor Russell: It can be attractive to do and there are some examples already of being able to fast-track development; some of these antibody approaches to novel mediators have a much shorter route to being approvable and used in patients than some of our traditional small molecule drugs.

Q70 *Chairman:* A very quick supplementary on one point you made there about clinical trials and the size of the trials is clearly very important. Is this the point at which different skills from different experts must be brought to bear to read what the outcomes are, just because it is the unintended consequences which you cannot predict which cause the real difficulties in clinical trials?

Professor Cooper: Yes and that applies differentially to the different disorders we are talking about here. Even in osteoporosis you need radiologists, medical physicists, cell biologists, biochemists and orthopaedic surgeons as well as trial designers and statisticians to generate an adequate clinical trial network. With osteoarthritis and sarcopoenia we are still at the stage of developing the intermediary bio-markers, the imaging, the biochemical measures of cartilage and bone turnover which apply to osteoarthritis; with sarcopoenia the imaging is really in its infancy, the extent to which you can use ultrasound and magnetic resonance, enzymatic measures of muscle function and so on. Although at

different stages, the design of those intervention studies undoubtedly needs to bring together multidisciplinary teams and of these groups of disorders that has clearly been done best in osteoporosis and the inflammatory arthropathies. The TNF-alpha story is a wonderful one of a 20-year bench to bedside progression in a snapshot of living memory.

Q71 *Baroness Finlay of Llandaff:* In the trials arena, when you were talking about the large numbers, is there any recognition of sub-groups within that who have greater loss of bone density at the neck of femur versus another group who have greater loss of bone density in the vertebral bodies? Are the trials actually looking at those as separate sub-populations in terms of accruing data or have the trials to date always put them all in?

Professor Cooper: Generally speaking it is not so much site-specific rates of bone loss which are the issue, vertebra versus hip: it is much more whether it is secondary or primary prevention. It is much more that a previous fracture increases your risk of a future fracture so much, by two to threefold at least, even at a given bone density, that the trial base has been one which takes people with a fracture, randomises them to treatment or control and follows them forward. The inference is then: what is the impact in a fracture-naïve group which represents that elderly population, the primary prevention one? Most of the phase 3 trials are secondary preventive, but some of them are coming along which are primary preventive too and that is very exciting.

Q72 *Lord Oxburgh:* I found your answers very illuminating and helpful. The sort of impression I get is that, given the extraordinary complexity of the human physiology and the way it changes over time and the extraordinary advances in scientific medical understanding, as you pointed out earlier "siloisation" has almost become inevitable. This is not unique to medicine of course. If one looks at the object of our inquiry, which is fundamentally driven by the recognition first of all that we perhaps for the first time have a group which we can call the young-old and that our generation is doing things which our parents probably stopped doing 10 or 15 years earlier and that in the overall population this group is going to become a larger and more significant group, against that background I get a feeling that research across the systems affecting this group is a little bit haphazard and depends on individual initiatives of the kind which some of you have described and perhaps on a few relatively small charities which actually have this as their named objective. Would that be a fair description?

Professor Cooper: I would not want it to be viewed as a disparaging description of what goes on. If the connotation to it is that with limited means we do the best we can, but that the skills which are required for individual investigators are necessarily so specialised in each system that it is an inevitability of the way we do it, then sure, that is a description of how things are at the moment. I do not feel that there is, however, any kind of structural unwillingness to engage in the collaborative work. Take disposable soma for example, a more overarching view of biological ageing, which impacts upon the research that many of us do: where it does, we recognise it and can build those collaborations. The question is how to attract more combined private and public sector resource and target it effectively to build up those cross-system collaborations. I view it as an exciting challenge rather than a rather depressing perspective on where we are now. That is my view.

Q73 *Lord Oxburgh:* I have to confess that there was a disparaging implication in my remark. Let me put it another way. Do you feel that there is any group or body within the UK addressing what must be seen as a national health problem? What you describe is a system which can flourish from a series of individual initiatives by co-operative and wise individuals, but that does not necessarily add up to a tackling of the relevant problems in what one might describe as the national priority. In my experience medical scientists are no different from any other set of scientists: they tackle problems which are interesting and which they think are solvable. They may not be the highest priority as far as the national health is concerned.
Professor Cooper: That is absolutely correct and I personally feel that the societies I represent here would welcome participation in some kind of unifying or umbrella structural development to facilitate that.

Q74 *Lord Oxburgh:* If there were such an initiative, what would be the organisation to provide the umbrella to promote it? Would it be the NHS? Would it be the research councils? Would it be the charities?
Professor Cooper: My view is that it must be multi-stakeholder. In my view, to be effective it needs to represent the research fraternities themselves, the principal funders, the councils and the charities, and the governmental processes which are going to oversee the introduction of that research into practice, the NHS. I see no escape, if one is going to bite that bullet, from trying to get it together as a multi-stakeholder.

Q75 *Lord Oxburgh:* It sounds awfully like a national programme, does it not, with funding?

Professor Cooper: Well . . .

Q76 *Lord Oxburgh:* May I go on from that a little bit and invite you to do something you will not want to do, which is to gaze into a crystal ball. You have talked about what we may expect over the next few years, the immediate possibilities. Where can we expect to be in 10 or 15 years' time in very broad terms? I should like both of you to answer this.
Professor Russell: That is a tough question. Just to follow up on the earlier conversation, there are encouraging trends in terms of disciplines coming together, which was not happening 10 years' ago and it is happening now. There is absolutely no doubt that you would do more by giving something a name and calling it an initiative but still putting specific funding against it. Professor Cooper is the epidemiologist, so he should probably give you the figures. If you are talking about 20 or 30 years from now, the number of people affected by the diseases we have been talking about will be significantly greater, perhaps twofold greater, even within that time span. So if we want to reduce the burden of disease we have to have interventions which have a very substantial impact, not just at the individual level but at a population level. There is no prospect of doing that if we are still only accomplishing what we are accomplishing now. For example, in osteoporosis, if we only treat 10 per cent of the eligible population with drugs which reduce fractures by 50 per cent, the best we can expect is a five per cent reduction in overall fracture rates which will be immeasurable; you probably would not be able to see it. The challenges are undoubtedly there and maybe we should be looking for those things which have even greater impact and for the healthy old the impact of good nutrition, exercise and all those things certainly should not be overlooked. The use of very affordable but very effective treatment is specifically going to be a very important thing to be able to do: reducing falls in the elderly, for example, which we have not really talked about, even removing pets from the house or flexes from the carpets and things like that, very simple measures, can be made to have an impact. This is certainly something which has a very broad number of requirements in order to accomplish something significant. It is not always very expensive to do it and some of them are relatively simple public health messages.

Q77 *Lord Oxburgh:* May I just pursue that for a moment? What you are saying is that you do not see a particular Holy Grail in your area which a lot of people are trying to achieve and which may be achieved in 10 or 15 years.
Professor Russell: We should probably partition that answer into some of the disease areas we have been talking about. In the osteoporosis area we know what

the challenges are rather well in terms of treating those people we need to treat, and identifying them. We have effective therapies but we need more effective therapies. Some of the new treatments which are coming along can probably reduce fracture rates by more than 50 per cent, maybe up to 90 per cent. These types of developments are potentially capable of having an enormous impact if appropriately delivered. In osteoarthritis it is more complex because we do not have the interventions, apart perhaps from the orthopaedic interventions when total joint failure has occurred; that can give you a long span of good quality life if you have a joint replacement, for example, at an appropriate time. The sarcopoenia frailty story, though it may not be fair to lump those two together, is further off in some ways.

Professor Cooper: I suppose in terms of the technology foresight and what are going to be the 10- to 15-year timeframe movements, we really have to take on board some of the innovations in physical sciences, in engineering, computing. I see great scope for e-science, web-based research. I see scope for nano-technology in this area. I see scope for stem cell biology influencing tissue engineering and replacement of cartilage. The problem with that is that as an historian of medical research, ever since the year dot with monoclonal antibodies and then the human genome, each new technology can be viewed as the answer to it. Of course, from what I have said, I clearly do not view it as some kind of answer, some kind of Holy Grail in your terms. I do think that there are really exciting ways of looking at the pathogenesis of disease afforded by these new technologies and by the post-genome proteomic revolution which will highlight new therapeutic targets, alter our understanding of how different systems weave together. A very simple example is: why should a statin affect bone? Well, it does. Now we know how. Can we get a statin to the bone? We never thought about that five years ago. That kind of example can be multiplied up many times and I do see important challenges for the high risk and therapeutic end of the research agenda. As always, it is following that up at the policy end: what can you do in the general population? Is there a robust evidence base with clinical trials and so on? As I mentioned earlier, I think that movement throughout the life course represents a really important way of consolidating that evidence base. I do think there is quite a big research challenge on both the high risk and population ends

Q78 *Baroness Walmsley:* I should like to ask you to turn your attention in a moment to assistive technologies and you have already begun to touch on that. Before I do, it is clear to me from what you have said that, with the greater understanding of the

biology of these diseases, a great deal can be done in terms of prevention. I just want to ask you, looking over the next 10 to 15 years, what you think are the barriers to the implementation of what we know about what can be done in terms of prevention, because that could reduce very much the need for therapeutic intervention in the future.

Professor Cooper: I have always been clear in my view of the number one barrier to any of this and that is the squandering of our human resource in clinical research. I believe that if we genuinely want to take innovation and put it into the health policy and therapeutic arena, we need the people who can cross that divide. We have not really been able to preserve our competitiveness in doing that or, at least, we have done so swimming against the tide, if you want to look at it with a benevolent eye. To me, our clinical, academic and translational research infrastructure is really creaking. If we are serious about doing this, rather than having innovation which is then exported for the translational component, then we are going to have to act on that rather soon. There are many testimonies to that: the royal colleges, the academies of medical science, the ABPI. You can look at different sectors. To me that is the problem we need to address first and foremost. We need to recruit our best minds to do innovative translational research. Once we achieve that, there is then developing an adequate skill mix for these new technologies and bringing them to the medical questions at hand and there is a challenge in that too. If we do not have the first, we will not achieve the second at all.

Q79 *Baroness Walmsley:* When we have all those things—
Professor Cooper: If we do.

Q80 *Baroness Walmsley:* —preventive treatments really require a great deal of co-operation from patient or somebody who does not yet consider him or herself to be a patient. Do you see any barriers perhaps in terms of scientific education and understanding to such levels of co-operation?

Professor Cooper: If we are talking about lifestyle modification as a very simple example of this kind of intervention, that in itself has become a science. How do you persuade individuals to change their diet? How do you reduce adiposity, excessive thinness, at different stages in the life course? How do you manipulate physical activity levels to be at that optimum rather than over or under? All of those in themselves are subjects to study and they bring in sociological, psychological, behavioural and physiotherapeutic, occupational therapeutic skills which are just beginning to be marshalled in university departments? Academic departments which are already competitive, of allied health professional research, are just beginning to grow.

With a continuation of that trend, we will be actually rather strong in that area.

Q81 *Baroness Walmsley:* Back to the original point I wanted to ask you about. We have heard a lot about therapeutic interventions. While we are waiting for all those to work assistive technologies are going to be very important. Perhaps you could both look into your crystal ball and tell us what you think are going to be the most exciting areas in terms of assistive technologies in the next 10 to 15 years.
Professor Russell: We are struggling a little bit with "assistive technologies" as to what is meant by that.

Q82 *Baroness Walmsley:* I know Professor Cooper mentioned things like implants and joints and all that kind of thing. We had in mind more external things, things which would compensate the individual in terms of his or her lifestyle for the shortcomings of his or her own body.
Professor Cooper: A very simple example in osteoporotic fracture would be that, say, one in three women over the age of 65 will fall in a year but only one in 100 of those will have a fracture. When you look at the risk factors for that fracture, it is direct trauma to the skeletal site involved in the fall. Rather than focusing on all falls, which of course is laudable, just rather difficult to stop, energy is focused on what falls will end in a fracture. That has led to the development of mechanical devices, hip protectors, which are supposed to dissipate the energy which is sustained when a person falls over and makes contact on the floor with their hip. That is an example of the development of an assistive technology which may, if it is made more acceptable and people comply with it—your earlier question—alter and there are certainly two or three controlled trials, one in *The Lancet*, one in *The New England Journal of Medicine* suggesting that these sorts of devices might reduce the incidence of hip fracture amongst the elderly, particularly the institutionalised elderly. That is an example of the kind of development one needs to see more of in osteoarthritis for a long time at the knee. We know that the alignment of the femur and the tibia are associated with different bio-mechanics to the part of the cartilage which suffers in knee osteoarthritis. By altering that, using devices in footwear and using assistive locomotive devices, sticks and so on, patella taping is another example of alteration of the joint, that by doing that one can alter pain, but there is still an issue as to whether one can alter long-term structural integrity of the joint. There is an almost evidence-free arena of research which can be engaged in to evaluate in a controlled manner all these sorts of interventions and they can be at the level of policy. Do speech therapy, occupational therapy, physiotherapy, manipulative treatment, acupuncture, complementary and alternative medicines work or do they not in formal randomised control settings? They can be at the level of much more localised things such as injections and intra-articular cartilage derivatives, so-called hyaluronic acid and so on. I just see this as a very open research agenda rather than one in which we have built up a big knowledge base.
Professor Russell: There are advances in the surgical aspects coming on all the time and some of the tissue replacement type of procedures are coming in quite rapidly. The problem is how to evaluate them. There is a specific procedure for vertebral fractures which is called vertebroplasty or kyphoplasty where you actually refill the vertebral body with foreign material or with a balloon to re-inflate the vertebra as a one-step surgical procedure, for example. That is something which requires evaluation which is potentially capable of producing a good result.

Q83 *Chairman:* I guess that has come a long way from the picture you held up where the very primitive assistive technology was a walking stick.
Professor Russell: It still works.

Q84 *Lord Drayson:* Do you feel that the research councils are giving enough emphasis to diseases of ageing, in particular musculoskeletal disorders?
Professor Russell: The answer from our perspective would be probably not. There have been some specific initiatives through the BBSRC for the Sage programme, which paid very good dividends, but with all these initiatives the rate of funding of even high quality grants is still quite low. Coming back to this general theme of funding of research, all of us who sit on research panels are faced every time with the fact that we should like to fund three to five times more of the grants we see before us than there is money for. There is a lot of activity out there to create good research projects which will answer important questions and the charities and research councils do not have enough money to do this. Certainly the research councils are in difficulties in keeping going what they have in place, let alone taking on new initiatives.

Q85 *Lord Drayson:* Just to clarify my question a little bit, given that the research councils have a certain amount of money to invest in research, do you think that the balance is right between other areas of research and research into the diseases of ageing? Is there any ageism in terms of the way research councils are looking at this?
Professor Cooper: I am employed by a research council and I spend my time researching diseases of ageing. In a way it is rather difficult for me to speak on that in a completely dispassionate way. If one were to take the Medical Research Council and the BBSRC and look at the apportionment to diseases which are

associated with chronological ageing, the allocation of resource still comes through a system-based route rather than through a more cognizant ageing disease route. However, if one were to tot it all up with neuro-sciences, with the clinical physiology and systems within medicine boards, one would probably find that quite a lot of resource goes in. Likewise with the BBSRC. It comes back to co-ordination of that for strategic goals, rather than perhaps, given that there is a small cake, arguing that too little of it goes to age-related disease.

Q86 *Lord Drayson:* In an earlier answer you mentioned that what was really needed was this partnership funding between the private and the public sector. Could you give us some sense of what barriers you believe are preventing more of this happening?

Professor Cooper: It is difficult. I shall try to give a very brief answer to that. I feel that if there is a private and public genuine partnership towards moving science forwards, as I believe there is in our area, then the whole issue of the conflicting of interest of investigators, because of sources of funding and tightness of research that they are doing, becomes a very problematic one. I should like a world in which the fact that I was able to resource a particular area of my work directly from industry and still be able to offer insights into policy could be done in an arena where the straitjacketing of conflicts of interest were able at least to be set aside. The way in which policy is determined at the moment and the way in which private/public partnerships and resourcing impact on that perception is such that it is quite a difficult path to tread, though I believe I manage to tread that path. For those who are involved in the organisation of the charities at the National Osteoporosis Society and

the ARC the extent to which it can truly develop into a privately funded and public partnership is an issue which vexes all of us involved in that administration.

Professor Russell: One of the things which has perhaps lapsed in recent years is some of these partnership arrangements between industry and the research councils which used to exist, for example, for research studentships, the so-called CASE studentships, those types of schemes which are now unusual, if there are any left at all. I can recall many examples of people who held positions of that sort as students where they worked in industry and worked in universities as part of their PhD project who came out very well and had very successful careers afterwards and came out to be creative scientists. It is a missed opportunity for those types of relatively inexpensive investments in young people to have disappeared; it is a shame.

Q87 *Chairman:* The time we allotted for this discussion is well nigh up and I do know that you have to be in other places very shortly; I appreciate your coming at the time that you did. Are there any points you want to add, where you felt we had not covered the ground in the way you had hoped we might? Of course the option of writing to us afterwards is there and you will have a copy of the transcript. Do you want to add anything?

Professor Cooper: Not from my point of view.

Professor Russell: Thank you for your time. If you have questions you want to put to us, it would be good to hear them.

Q88 *Chairman:* E-mail works and is alive and well.

Professor Russell: It works very well.

Chairman: Thank you very much indeed; it was much appreciated. You will see in due course what good use we make of this. Thank you.

TUESDAY 2 NOVEMBER 2004

Present	Drayson, L	Mitchell, L
	Emerton, B	Murphy, B
	Finlay of Llandaff, B	Soulsby of Swaffham Prior, L
	Hilton of Eggardon, B	Sutherland of Houndwood, L (Chairman)
	May of Oxford, L	Turnberg, L

Examination of Witnesses

Witnesses: Professor John Mathers, University of Newcastle (on behalf of the British Nutrition Foundation), Dr Frans van der Ouderaa, Vice President, Corporate Research, Unilever plc and Professor Elizabeth Kay, Manchester University (on behalf of the British Dental Association), examined.

Q89 Chairman: May I welcome you very warmly indeed to this Committee. As you know the topic is the scientific aspects of ageing. What we would like to do is to give you the chance to say the sorts of things you want to say but equally we will do that significantly by asking questions and we will move around the table quite a bit. If you feel there is any point where we have not been pressing where we ought to have pressed and you want to add or extend the question, please feel free to do so. Equally if after the session you wanted to amplify any point or send any further information in or comment in in writing or e-mail we would be very happy to receive that. The members of the Committee round the table have name tags in front of them so I will not take time to go round. I suspect you know Professor Kirkwood who is our scientific adviser. The first question, a fairly general starting point and an opportunity for each of you perhaps to introduce one of the main themes that you might wish to push, has to do with the effect of nutrition on health throughout one's life, and I wondered if you would like to expand a little bit on what particular aspects of nutrition you consider especially important with regard to its impact on the ageing process. For example, supposing you were to be weighing it against genetic factors, is it 100/0 or 50/50? Do you have any estimate on that with which you can help the Committee?

Professor Mathers: Nutrition can affect the function of cells and tissues at any stage in life and I think we are looking at ageing as part of a continuum. It is difficult to put a precise figure on what contribution a single factor might make. Clearly if you look at something like length of life, nutrition makes a contribution as does genetics and I think the best estimates are that genetics contributes about 25 per cent of the variability in longevity so non-genetic factors make up the rest of it. Nutrition and other aspects of lifestyle will contribute to that.

Professor Kay: Nutrition has a double effect with oral health and we are very grateful that oral health is being included in the remit of this Committee; very grateful indeed. First of all, life time nutrition affects how your oral health turns out when you are elderly and it is mostly exposure to sugar and exposure to fluoride that will affect the amount of dental decay that you end up with. The amount of dental decay you end up with will affect whether you have teeth in your elderly years and at that point, when you have lost a significant number of teeth, it then affects what you are able to eat. Specifically it reduces the amount of vitamin C that people consume and the amount of fruit and vegetables they consume, and all the knock-on effects that that might have.

Dr van der Ouderaa: Nutrition is obviously a very important factor in the context of people's ageing trajectories and everybody has a trajectory which is defined by genes, by lifestyle, by behaviour and by the environment. As Professor Mathers indicated, about 25 per cent of people's ageing trajectory is in principle defined by the genes. However, that is malleable and it is dependent on lifestyle and nutritional behaviour. There is very strong data from epidemiology and in particular the excellent EPIC-Norfolk study by the University of Cambridge which shows that high fruit and vegetable nutrition reduced the prevalence of disease by up to 50 per cent for cardiovascular disease and a similar percentage for mortality in the period of eight years that the two studies were done. There is a similar study done by the EU called the Senega Study which was done in the 1990's which shows that the combination of lifestyle and nutrition for an optimum nutrition and lifestyle person versus a non-optimum lifestyle nutrition makes about an eight to nine year difference. So you can extend healthy ageing by the right lifestyle and the right nutrition by that sort of period, which is over life quite a significant number. However, on the other extreme, if you have someone who chain smokes, has a sedentary life and has high stress shift work, then a couple of pieces of broccoli and two oranges are not going to save this person. You have to look at all these things in the context of the whole picture of lifestyle and environment.

Q90 Chairman: Can I ask a supplementary that has two elements to it? One is, generally, how strong is the evidence that you would bring to bear on the nutritional impact? But a particular aspect of that, it was stressed that ageing is an extensive process and it may well start on day one of one's life, what about the evidence of early nutrition and childhood nutrition which is not easily available for those reaching mature years?

Professor Mathers: That is a very interesting area and there is very active research going on at the moment. There is a lot of evidence that early life nutrition— that is nutrition in the womb as well as nutrition in the first year of life—can affect diseases of middle age and later life and that evidence is really quite strong. However, it does not preclude the effect of nutrition at later stages and I think we should be concerned with nutrition from conception all the way through.

Dr van der Ouderaa: There is brilliant work done by Professor Barker at Southampton which states that even before conception, at the time of conception and the whole life of the foetus and then infancy, that period is extremely important from a nutrition point of view. Malnutrition at that stage will relate to higher rates of diabetes, blood pressure and cardiovascular disease in later life. In low birth weight babies the growth trajectory in infancy is extremely important to change the perspective so if a low birth weight baby grows very quickly the chances of getting a disease in later life of a coronary or vascular nature are much higher than in the low birth weight baby who gains weight very slowly. The environmental factors are extremely important and the nutrition in this particular case, at the very early age is extremely important and is well documented by British groups.

Q91 *Chairman:* Longitudinal evidence is available on this because clearly if we were to see the whole cycle you are talking about events of 70 or 80 years ago.

Professor Mathers: That is really part of the problem with this hypothesis, that most of what we have are cross-sectional data. We have data on birth weights or weights at age one and so forth and then we have information on people in middle age or later. The data that follow individuals from birth all the way through are rather sparse and in fact most of them are being conducted in India by the Southampton Group and they have some very nice studies there following people from birth and looking at their nutrition. Currently with MRC funding they have undertaken a nutrition intervention study in that setting.

Professor Kay: In terms of oral health the evidence is extremely strong, that what you eat and your exposure to sugar throughout life affects your oral health. That is not randomised controlled trial data obviously, it is ecological data but it certainly meets the criteria of the causality, and that is the nature of the disease.

Q92 *Lord Drayson:* What is the role of the food industry in addressing the links between nutrition and healthy ageing? How much interest is there in developing functional foods, for example? Or foods particularly targeted at the more elderly section of the population?

Dr van der Ouderaa: This is a very complex area. In the first instance because it is not very clear what precisely the market is so we have done a fair amount of market research and there is a great deal of difference between people of 50 to 65, 65 to 75 and 75 to 90 from a needs point of view but also from a communication point of view. One of the most important things for us as a company is to understand how you communicate with people who are older, because the one thing you do not want to tell them and they do not want to hear from you is that they are elderly people. Then we have done as a company a fair amount of research on functional foods which is quite successful and one of the key examples is, for instance, the recent addition of phytosterols to margarines and to yoghurts which in principle gives a 10 per cent lowering of cholesterol levels. It does not sound much but in actual fact it is quite a significant effect. If you were to apply this to the whole of the British population between 30 and 74 you would have a 10 year time scale reduction of cardiovascular death by a quarter of a million people. The key thing that one needs to understand about foods is that since the whole population takes foods every day, the effect of small effects of the foods— which are smaller effects than from drugs—is, on a population basis, quite a big effect. Another important thing is to make sure that we take out the negatives so, for instance, our company has taken the lead in removal of trans-fatty acids from saturated fat and reducing saturated fat per se which again is a cardiovascular benefit measure. As an industry and as a company in particular we are also busy reducing the salt levels. That is a little bit tricky because if you do it too quickly that affects the acceptability of products and then there is no point in it. There is a fair amount of work in the context of the oxidative damage theory of ageing; we are looking into the effect of flavonols and anti-oxidants. There is evidence, for instance from the EPIC Study, that high levels of fruit and vegetables have this quite extensive benefit. How to communicate this to the population is quite a difficult issue which I do not think the industry as a whole has cracked yet.

Professor Mathers: From the perspective of academic research there has been a lot of interest in potential benefits of functional foods and one of the things that has troubled people is getting real evidence of efficacy alongside evidence of safety. I think that is coming and it may be stimulated by EU legislation around food labelling which I understand is on its way. But related to that is an issue around inequalities because in all probability such foods are likely to be more expensive than the standard foods so the people who are likely to benefit are the people who are least in need, perhaps, of those special foods.

Q93 *Lord Turnberg:* There has been quite a lot of interest in folic acid supplementation in the belief that it reduces the incidences of coronary artery disease. What is your view on this?

Professor Mathers: The best evidence of course of folic acid is in the prevention of neural tube defects, and that is where there are really good randomised controlled trials. There is supportive evidence for the idea that folic might protect against cardiovascular disease but the trials are not yet finished; there are trials on the way to try to prove that. There is no doubt that raised homocysteine concentrations is an independent risk factor for heart disease and folate may lower homocysteine and therefore lower risk of CVD. However, until we have the RCT trials finished we will not know.

Dr van der Ouderaa: There is quite interesting data from the Nun's Study from the Mid-West United States carried out by Professor David Snowdon that there is a relationship between folic acid in the serum and dementia risk. You could post-rationalise this from the point of view that folic acid reduces homocysteine in people who have a specific genetic permutation in the folate reductase enzyme and because of the lowering of the cardiovascular risk you get the additional dementia risk. This is found in nuns of relatively high age, of 95-plus.

Q94 *Lord May of Oxford:* I have a question which is inherent in the question we are asking—what is the role of the food industry in addressing the links between nutrition?—Not wishing to be cynical, I would have thought that the role of the food industry was selling food and that would explain the fact that it is relatively hard (although it is slowly changing) to get low salt versions of various things on the grounds that people on the whole are more inclined to buy things with salt in them. I would like to go back more to the root of the question and ask you to what extent do you feel the food industry should be held responsible for having a degree of interest in healthy foods as distinct from simply selling it?

Dr van der Ouderaa: I think we have a great responsibility to help with the health of the nation. In Unilever this goes back to William Hesketh Lever in the 1890's—he was a salesman of bars of soap—saying that his vision was to contribute to the health of the people and I think that vision is still within the company. In the first instance our role is precisely as you say, to make sure that we give people safe, healthy foods from a microbiological point of view

and foods that are nutritious so that you avoid deficiencies, in particular vitamin deficiencies.

Q95 *Lord May of Oxford:* The majority of things on the supermarket shelves have added salt. That is not done for nutritional reasons surely. It may, in fact, be anti-nutritional reasons; it is done for other reasons. I am not even criticising it necessarily because your aim is to sell the things people want to buy which are not necessarily the same things that are healthy. I would have thought it was possible to defend the view that because the food industry—demonstrably, in my view—does not take a primary responsibility in delivering nutritious food, you really have to defend the indefensible or say that it is not true at all.

Dr van der Ouderaa: The food industry as a whole is trying to lower salt levels; I am not sure if I am defending the indefensible but I do think they have a responsibility.

Professor Kay: Could I just add that exactly the same argument applies to sugar.

Professor Mathers: From my perspective I do think that the food industry does need to do more about reducing salt intakes. There are just some practical issues about how to do it.

Q96 *Lord Soulsby of Swaffham Prior:* What is the role of the British Dental Association and of oral health practitioners and related industries in this issue?

Professor Kay: The British Dental Association is the professional association and trade union of dentists in this country. Amongst its missions is promoting the oral health of the population, hence our presence here. We are not a research organisation but we do link, as far as we can, with oral health promoting industries who sell products that promote oral health. We link with them as much as we can in order to try to raise the profile of oral health. Unfortunately, although it has such a profound effect on the psycho-social welfare—particularly of the elderly who have poor oral health—it tends to be a poor relation in terms of the notice the public take and the research funding.

Q97 *Lord Soulsby of Swaffham Prior:* I can anticipate that you do not undertake research but do you promote it? Do you made representations to government to say that this is an area that must be looked into and areas like that?

Professor Kay: The BDA are very strongly supportive of evidence-based practice because obviously the advice we can give to our members is as a results of the research that is going on. We also like to take that the other way, in that we feel quite profoundly that it is the actual carers of people—the people who are trying to deal with the very difficult problems in the very elderly population and their dentition—who should be leading the research agendas. So it is their questions, the difficulties that they face, that should be telling us where we ought to be going with the research that is going on out there.

Q98 *Lord Soulsby of Swaffham Prior:* Is there any burning question that the British Dental Association has that the Government should do something about?

Professor Kay: Last year we published a report on Oral Healthcare for Older People which may be of interest to this Committee because it is one the key policy issues that we are interested in. Please stop me if I am going too deeply into this but there is a big issue at the moment because the very elderly come from a population in whom, around 1948, it was common to have all your teeth removed at the age of 20, 25 or when you got married. So we have a population of very elderly who have worn dentures for 50 or so years and they are technically extremely difficult to treat because the bone resorbs and it is very difficult to provide dentures. The next cohort is a highly diseased population that have had a lot of dentistry available to them so they have very highly restored mouths, and very complex restorative problems towards the end of life. The difficulty with that group is that we have to keep restoring those dentitions because at 75, 80 and 85 you simply cannot adapt to suddenly have no teeth and using a denture. At 21 you can do it, but it is a very, very difficult problem for the elderly. We have a cohort coming up who are going to need quite intensive restorative care to keep them going into old age.

Q99 *Chairman:* Does the Association have any evidence one way or the other on whether the evident shortage of dentists in certain parts of the country who will provide effectively free health care is causing a disproportionate problem for old people because on the whole they are poorer—whatever bracket of income—than their younger peers so is this a special problem?

Professor Kay: The older elderly—if I can call them that—have had dentures for a long time. That goes with negative attitudes towards oral health and if you have no teeth you do not feel the need for dentistry. They are very typically non-attenders because they have no perceived need. You can accept that as, "Oh, good, we don't have to provide treatment for them" or feel that this is a very vulnerable group who need to be looked after. There are risks of oral cancer et cetera so they should be screened, but by nature of their age and mobility they would find probably find access to a dentist difficult. Their treatment costs would not be high. The next group—the next cohort down, if you like—the pre-elderly or the young old,

their treatment costs are likely to be high as they go into old age, probably beyond a state pension.

Q100 *Chairman:* So they will have special problems if all the dentists in the area are basically private practices.

Professor Kay: Yes.

Q101 *Baroness Finlay of Llandaff:* That leads us on to a question I have which relates to the current trends in oral health and how they affect nutrition. Looking at it from eating being very complex it does not just mean that you have to have an intact mouth but it is the whole digestive system as well that needs to be in good condition.

Professor Kay: That goes without question, but I think the mouth and teeth have a specific role in terms of eating not just being a function; it is also a very large part of the psycho-social well being, and it is known that people who have embarrassment with their teeth then their nutrition suffers from that. They do not like eating in front of people.

Q102 *Baroness Finlay of Llandaff:* I have to declare an interest here. I have a specific interest in Canada in the terminally ill. I was wondering if there was any research going on outside of that area into some of the communication problems that arise for people with bad oral care as well, socialising, part of being socially integrated and being able then to eat socially and how that affects nutrition.

Professor Kay: There has been a great deal of research—specially in Canada actually—that has looked at the impact of oral health on quality of life, specifically in the elderly. There is no question that the number of teeth that you have impacts on your psycho-social well-being. There are a lot of studies that show that throughout the world.

Dr van der Ouderaa: There is also data from the United States that the level of dental plaque and sub-gingival plaque are proportionate to the risks of cardiomyopathy and cardiovascular complications. If people have sufficient dexterity to clean well they will have less risk of these sorts of infections of the heart valve.

Q103 *Baroness Finlay of Llandaff:* Is there a direct link between the plaque and the disease or is it because those who do not clean well tend to be more depressed and have all the other lifestyle factors that put them at risk?

Dr van der Ouderaa: If you have a lot of sub-gingival plaque then there is probably also a permeability of the epidemia that leads to direct bacterial infection.

Professor Kay: I am aware of that data but there is also another study that has looked at edentulous people—as in they do not have plaque—that has shown that their cardiac risk is the same as people with plaque.

Chairman: So you cannot solve a cardiovascular problem by having no teeth.

Q104 *Baroness Murphy:* In the area of oral health and whether or not you have dentures depends, rather like nutrition, on your life time habits and your individual behaviour and clearly that is going to have a big impact on how ageing affects you. You have been very good at telling us about that. However, I do not see any evidence that there is much public awareness of the impact of oral health in later life. Although we have many messages about nutrition we do not get much aimed at middle-aged people or younger people about looking after their teeth or how to hang on to their own teeth into later life. Is that something you could talk to us about?

Professor Kay: Yes. I think that is partly because the research is relatively recent, so the recognition of the enormity of the impact has only fairly recently come to light. I think the other problem is that although the face is such a huge part of your psycho-social well-being people do not recognise it until they lose it and therefore oral health has not been recognised as a huge quality of life issue. You have this history of people replacing their teeth with plastic teeth and assuming that would be all right and we are only just understanding that that has quite a profound impact particularly towards the end of life.

Q105 *Baroness Murphy:* What do you think could be done or should be done to engage the public in this debate? It is remarkable how much has been done for children and parents in convincing parents that they should pay to have their children's teeth straightened—whether wise or not, but probably wise—but what should we be looking to do?

Professor Kay: That is an issue I have been battling with most of my professional life, how do we persuade people about it? I think the answer is that we, as a profession and professions in general, have to stop telling people what is good for them because we believe it to be good for them and try harder to understand why it is important to them and, if I can use the term, sell the messages on the basis of: this is of profound interest to you, your family and your own personal life.

Q106 *Baroness Murphy:* I have a question now for all of you about nutrition, how much in later life—and particularly later old age—does the age-related loss of taste and smell impact upon nutrition? That is an issue we have not covered but seems to be clinically quite important for some people.

Professor Mathers: It is a very important area. The best evidence of links between nutrition and taste perception is through the effect of zinc. There are some nice examples of where people are zinc deficient and they cannot taste things, they do not taste normally, and so on. I am not aware of good nutrition data from very old people on what factors affect taste perception in that particular group; most of this work has been done on younger people. In general I think it is a potential problem. It is exacerbated of course by the fact that many older people are taking drugs of one kind or another which also affect taste.

Dr van der Ouderaa: I have done a study on this subject specifically a few months ago and there is very, very little data. Also people seem to lose their sensory faculties relatively late in life so it may only be a problem aged 75-plus and that is a sort of forgotten population almost in research terms. We are planning to do a big review of this in December. This is an area where a lot of research needs to be done.

Q107 *Lord Drayson:* Do we take from that in a sense that there is ageism in terms of a lack of interest in that population? Given that the over-85's is the fastest growing segment within the population, why is there not more research being done?

Dr van der Ouderaa: I have asked that question of a lot of eminent researchers in the academic field and they say there is no real funding for it. A lot of funding in the context of ageing research is given for age related diseases and not for how to live healthily for longer. The research interests are into cancer, cardiovascular disease, dementia but not in quality of life issues like sensory perception and sensory faculties. It is just a question of priorities and if you are a researcher interested in senses you probably do not get through the competition at the research level which is extremely high and get it funded. It is just a question of priorities. Because it is so difficult to get funding people are not going to put proposals in because they put proposals in in the areas where they can get funding.

Q108 *Baroness Finlay of Llandaff:* How much evidence is there behind dental hygienist intervention and how much nutritional advice is there? Quite often they are telling people to cut down on fruit because of the acid content of fruit and so on, but that flies in the face of some of the nutritional advice which one is given typically.

Professor Kay: The traditional role of the hygienist was concentrating more on gum disease, periodontal disease, than on decay. Therefore the concentration is almost solely on oral hygiene and things that will not damage the gums. That is changing with the evolution of a more team approach in dentistry and there are a greater number of dental therapists where a much more holistic preventative pattern is emerging. The evidence that giving dietary advice to patients in the dental chair has an effect is not strong. There is a little pilot evidence from a colleague of Professor Mathers showing that when you are fitting a denture if you explain very carefully and give nutritional advice to the elderly person who is receiving the dentures about how it may affect them—fruit and vegetable and vitamin C intake—you can make quite dramatic changes in their food intake. That is just pilot evidence; it is certainly something that needs to be explored.

Professor Mathers: Can I add to that that I think there is a resource issue here that very few dental schools have nutrition experts on the staff. It has not been traditional to have that and I think it might help to build this team work that my colleague referred to.

Q109 *Baroness Hilton of Eggardon:* You mentioned the role of diet in relation to tooth decay but not in relation to gum disease. I was wondering whether anything was known about what aspects of nutrition produced gum disease rather than the effects of having it and losing teeth and not being able to eat properly.

Professor Kay: It is the plaque in the mouth that causes the gum disease and it is the plaque that plays a role in dental decay as well. There is some evidence that the higher your sugar intake as well as causing decay it affects the micro-biology of the plaque basically, making it stickier, so it is harder to get rid of and it builds up more quickly. There is a link but it is not quite as direct as with sugar and decay.

Q110 *Baroness Hilton of Eggardon:* Is there anything people could do in a preventive way in terms of nutrition?

Professor Kay: Reduce sugar intake is the evidence based message. We used to say that an apple a day or a carrot a day, but there is no evidence that detersive types of food help clean the mouth in any effective way.

Q111 *Baroness Hilton of Eggardon:* I have a more general question now, if I may go onto that, about what you see as being your highest priorities in terms of improving nutrition and what are your particular scientific challenges which you see in the way of improving the nation's nutritional health.

Professor Mathers: This is a huge topic and I think there are a number of different aspects to it. There is one fundamental area and that is understanding nutritional needs of people as they get older. In the UK we have what are known as Dietary Reference Values which describe the nutritional needs of different population groups. The last publication in that area was in 1991 and it has not been revised since then. The evidence base for nutritional needs of older people was very thin then and I suspect it is still rather patchy. That is an area which I think needs some attention. It would fall into the remit of the Scientific Advisory Committee on Nutrition and I understand they are going to revise the DRVs at some point but I am not sure when. The other area is around understanding the biology of ageing and understanding how the normal homeostatic mechanisms are disrupted as we get older and the extent to which nutrition can help us buffer those changes. That introduces a very large area of biology which has been largely unexplored and I think that is a fundamental area I would like to see work done in.

Professor Kay: Could I have four priorities? In terms of nutrition in oral health there are two things: one is, decrease sugar intake and have the optimum level of fluoride intake. I think the other two priorities are to determine how this very vulnerable elderly population (with very poor oral health which does affect their nutrition) can access and be persuaded to access affordable oral care. I think there is one other issue that we have not touched upon. Because of this cohort effect in people's oral health, we need to take very great care that we are continuing to train an oral care profession who are adequately and suitably trained to deal with these issues because they are going to be different for each generation of dentists.

Dr van der Ouderaa: I think I have seven priorities. I think we need to build a holistic picture of how nutrition and lifestyle together improve ageing outcomes. This is to do with metabolic circulation. If ageing is to do with regulation of the metabolism, how can we prevent metabolic dysregulation due to overweight, due to the wrong nutrition, due to the lack of physical activity and so on? Then I think there is a lot of mileage in understanding the genetics of longevity and using the genetics of centenarians, for instance, to come up with new solutions on how to prevent age related conditions in people who do not have these genes. There is some evidence, for instance, that the metabolism of fatty acids of centenarians is more effective. For instance, after a meal the concentrations of LDL cholesterol are brought down quicker. If we can by nutritional measures mimic what the genes do in centenarians then that would be a step forward. I think we also need to have bio-markers for healthy ageing to allow people to self-assess. Then I think we need to learn more about studies for behavioural change because if people want to live longer healthier they will have to change behaviours. We need to understand how to communicate that to people.

2 November 2004   Professor John Mathers, Dr Frans van der Ouderaa
and Professor Elizabeth Kay

Q112 Lord Turnberg: We have spoken about nutrition but not about appetite and the two must go together. What about research into appetite as we age? Is there much going on in that field?

Professor Mathers: I suspect rather little. Much of the work on appetite has been concerned with appetite in relation to energy balance because of the problems of obesity. There is a great deal of work in that area of appetite but I am not aware of anything being done on appetite and ageing.

Dr van der Ouderaa: I searched for this for two days and I found two papers, so there is very little done. There is a huge amount of appetite research done to understand defective appetite and weight gain in the general population but that is not geared to the older population. There is also evidence that people of 75 and older lose weight rather than gain weight.

Q113 Lord May of Oxford: This might be a more futurist question and I preface it by a parenthetic remark that the person who coined that word was an obese character called Herman Khan 40 years ago who published a book which listed the 50 major research priorities for the future. A pill to control appetite was ranked number four and safe, effective contraception was in the twenties which has permanently imperilled my respect for anything futuristic. Against that background, can I ask you, looking more broadly and basically at your nutrition and teeth, within your period looking five or 10 years ahead, what would you see as possible areas of scientific research on ageing that ought to be pursued? And even looking beyond that, setting aside the question of whether the Research Council would smile on them or not, what are the things you think are specific research agendas in the medium term and the longer time we might be thinking about?

Professor Kay: From the BDA's point of view what I think is the most crucial thing is some joined up thinking. There are relatively few people with expertise in this tiny area so what I think we need are longitudinal studies whereby we are sure that not only general health variables data are collected but oral health data and nutritional data. I am not sure that we have actually got all the causal links necessarily in the right direction. We do not understand enough as yet and we need to collaborate, possibly internationally, so that we have the relevant expertise to join up all the areas that hinge on nutrition and the elderly together.

Dr van der Ouderaa: For me a very important parameter is to have accurate bio-markers that look at people's ageing trajectories. We all have a lifetime of professional work and ageing studies generally last so long because the end bio-marker is mortality and you cannot race these things. We need some very good measures that relate as to whether certain interventions actual improve or do not improve your trajectory. We have some of these markers—blood pressure, cholesterol, HDL-/LDL- levels—but we need much better metabolic markers from modern techniques that help us to find new interventions on a much shorter timescale than a 50 year timescale.

Professor Mathers: On a cellular level what we describe as ageing is a result of damage to cell macro-molecules. I think we need to try to understand that process of damage accumulation and defence against damage and how nutrition can modulate it. I think that will require an inter-disciplinary approach which we have not had in the past and it requires some large scale biology.

Q114 Lord May of Oxford: I am ignorant of this, but my impression is that the big, half-million cohort genetic study that the MRC and Wellcome are planning, does that have a very deliberate component of following nutrition or is it just looking at the medical history in relation to genotypes? If not, it is quite a specific thing that one might wish to recommend. There is a similar study about to get underway in China too, governed by a much more rational set of rules and informed consent than we have in this country.

Dr van der Ouderaa: I think that is very important, but there are limitations from a financial point of view which constrain the degree of information being obtained in the study. I do not think that the nutritional information is going to be guaranteed to be sufficiently detailed to be of the highest value. Interestingly Professor Cole in Cambridge has probably developed the best nutritional measures for big population studies so the ways of doing it are actually known.

Professor Mathers: The parallels with EPIC that Dr van de Ouderaa has already referred to are quite striking. They are cross-European studies and have excellent measures of dietary exposure.

Q115 Lord Mitchell: Could we now turn to Government and Government relations with what you do? First of all, to what extent are your priorities recognised by Government departments? Secondly, do you think there is a good link between science and policy in Government in the field of nutritional or oral health and its impacts on ageing? In what respects could more be done to develop such links and what benefits do you think might result? Could I also ask you just to look at the issue that always comes up, that is relationships between Government departments and them not speaking to each other?

Professor Mathers: I think DH has the primary responsibility in the area of nutritional health but I had a look at their website at the weekend and if you put "nutrition" into the website it does not come up as a heading which I think is rather striking; nor does "ageing" interestingly. So the two things we are discussing here this afternoon do not appear as major headings in the Department of Health. We are eagerly awaiting the Public Health White Paper and I hope that that will address some of these issues but the omens are not particularly strong. More broadly, of course the Government does put an enormous amount of money into ageing research and I think the Research Councils would argue that it is tens of millions of pounds per year but it is not clear that very much of that is spent on the interface between nutrition and ageing. I think that is an area which has been poorly funded up to now.

Professor Kay: There is a national service framework for older people. Unfortunately it pays very little attention to the impact of oral health on the quality of life of the elderly.

Chairman: Can I just halt for a moment because a division has been called and there may be some who have to go or want to go or have good reason to go, in which case perhaps we can just pause for a few minutes.

The Committee suspended from 4.25 pm to 4.36 pm for a division in the house

Q116 *Chairman:* I think we should resume now. The two still to come back will catch up with us. Professor Kay, you were answering Lord Mitchell's question.

Professor Kay: I was talking about the national service framework where oral health does not really feature. Of course, primary care trusts refer to that framework to drive what they do, to decide what to pay for, and while oral health is not there you are certainly not going to get implementation of it on the ground for the elderly population. There are a lot of health issues which may not be within the national framework.

Q117 *Baroness Emerton:* Following on the departments' issue, do you think that the Research Councils and the Department of Health and other research funding organisations really give appropriate recognition to the importance of ageing in general and to nutritional and oral health aspects of ageing in particular? I think you have answered some of those already. If not, what actions might remedy the situation?

Professor Kay: The short answer is, no, I do not think they do.

Q118 *Baroness Emerton:* What are the actions which you think might remedy this situation?

Professor Kay: I will let my colleagues speak, I think.

Professor Mathers: Let me start with something about the research community because I think that is part of the problem. The research community who are interested in this area are rather small and fragmented and, by and large, poorly funded. I think this is an area where something should be done to stimulate that community. The very basic work on the ageing process is funded, if you like, at the cellular level. When you get to the whole person that is where it begins to fall down; I think that is where we need considerably more effort. The BBSRC has the Healthy Organism as part of its portfolio of work and they have just instituted a strategy panel to look at diet within that Healthy Organism umbrella and will be looking at ageing as part of that process.

Dr van der Ouderaa: I am a board member of the Medical Research Council so I know the situation there from the inside. Ageing is one of the 10 priorities of the Medical Research Council but the translation of councils' intention to what is happening on the ground does not seem very strong so the boards look at proposals on the basis of scientific merit and not on the basis of social merit. I think maybe something should be done to fine tune a little bit because this is a very important area for society. There are very few young researchers who are interested in doing this because there is no funding. There should be new instruments that encourage people to come with proposals and I concur with Professor Mathers that it is particularly important to work on new models where you can look at model ageing units and not go too much to animal experiments where there is also a difficulty. In the United States there is the National Institute of Aging. Maybe to have a single focus in this country from the research councils for ageing research would be extremely valuable.

Q119 *Baroness Emerton:* Do I take it from what you are saying that you would recommend that this Committee makes some recommendation on the basis of taking forward research?

Dr van der Ouderaa: Absolutely.

Professor Mathers: It might be creating a national centre which would be a focus for this kind of research and would help to raise the profile.

Baroness Emerton: Perhaps, Lord Chairman, we could ask them to put forward a recommendation.

Chairman: Please do.

Q120 *Baroness Finlay of Llandaff:* I would like to follow up on the research because it strikes me that pharmaceutical industries actually do have money going into drug development but the testing of the effect on saliva production does not seem to be a routine question that is asked, particularly in drugs which are aimed at the elderly, and yet there is a lot of dry mouth in the elderly.

Professor Kay: That is one of the huge impacts on the elderly. The usual polypharmacy—where they are taking a number of drugs which can interact with the drugs that a dentist might use and also the normal auto-immune problems in ageing and then dry mouth caused by drugs—has the most dramatic impact on the mouth and can cause a fairly healthy dentition very rapidly to become a very painful and difficult one in a person who is already unwell. Of course they should be looking at it.

Q121 *Baroness Finlay of Llandaff:* I just wonder where we should be recommending it and it is a question that general reviews should be asking and looking at papers and drugs coming through.

Professor Kay: As I say, you can see people's teeth dissolve in their mouths in front of your eyes, almost. It is terrible.

Q122 *Lord Soulsby of Swaffham Prior:* A phrase that keeps occurring when one is discussing ageing and aged people is quality of life. What work or research if any has been done on the psychological or psychiatric side to study quality of life to try to understand it more from the point of view of the aged individual, because younger people are quite ready to say that the quality of life of that individual is very poor, but how does one define that? Is there some qualification or definition which is helpful?

Professor Kay: I would like to think that oral health research has possibly stolen a march on some of our medical colleagues on this because we have recognised for some time that you cannot separate the mouth from the person or the body from the person and the only point of worrying about dental disease and dental problems is because it belongs to an individual person. There have been a large number of cross-sectional studies—and they are cross-sectional studies mostly—that have measured function in terms of whether they can actually eat and what they can eat, but also social embarrassment, worry and concern and their general feeling about what limitations oral health—in our case—puts on them. I am not so familiar with research in other areas, but those measures are available.

Professor Mathers: There is some work going on in the area of cognitive decline and trying to understand how you might ameliorate that with nutritional interventions. It is a very young science and part of the problem there is that there have not been very good instruments for measuring cognitive function serially over relatively short time periods. Although it is beginning—the Foods Standards Agency is funding a little bit of work in that area—it is still a very young science.

Dr van der Ouderaa: I think it is a vital point you are making. Happiness is the differential between the sort of quality of life you have and the expectation you have of it at a single time point. There has been relatively little research done on this and part of the happiness is to do with the state of your health and whether the state of your health is much worse than you expect it to be. The other one is obviously to do with the psycho-social status. I think the only people who have a sustained research programme in this area are the McCarter Foundation in the United States. A number of groups in different states in the United States have a sustained research programme and the effect of SES and social status on health. I do not think there is anything like it in this country.

Professor Kay: Could I just say that I have done some work on that myself through general dental practitioners and if you would be interested to receive the papers I would be delighted to send them.

Chairman: Yes, that would be useful.

Q123 *Lord Turnberg:* There is a very good set of studies relating social status to health done by Michael Marmot in his book "The Status Syndrome". My question comes back to what you suggested in response to Lord May, Dr van der Ouderaa, about bio markers. You quoted a number that we have, like cholesterol, LDL-/HDL- and blood pressure, but they are risk factors rather than bio markers. The question that has been taxing us is whether old age is simply the accumulation of ill health of a variety of types or is there a process of ageing? How does the whole business of nutrition and oral health have an impact on the ageing process as against the accumulation of diseases?

Dr van der Ouderaa: I think it is helpful to discriminate between age related diseases and ageing as separate processes from a communication point of view. I think a lot of the etiological factors are actually quite similar, and so the etiological factors for dementia go from overweight and metabolic dysregulation to diabetes to cardiovascular disease to dementia. If you do not become overweight, if you do not get diabetes, then the risk of dementia is maybe ten per cent off the risk of you getting it. It is very important to understand these etiological steps because that will then help you to come up with intervention strategies. In the context of ageing we can improve the repair of the small challenges of day to day life. For instance if you apply sunscreen every day versus walking in the sun without sunscreen, your facial skin will age much faster. It is about understanding where we can make these relatively small steps. A number of small steps in a concerted way have quite a big effect on the ageing process as a whole.

Q124 *Lord Turnberg:* I am not absolutely convinced by the argument that you are distinguishing between prevention of an illness as against prolonging the ageing process. In both the instances you describe they were both related to preventing the development of an illness rather than helping the ageing process. What I really want to know is what interventions might actually improve the ageing process or inhibit the ageing process per se and are there studies in relation to this?

Professor Mathers: I tend to think of the ageing process as a process in which our ability to cope with perturbations of the norm become more and more difficult. The ability to maintain homeostasis, if you like, becomes more difficult so we need to be able to defend that state and ageing is a way in which we begin to lose that ability. If we think of the kinds of damage that are causing that—damage to genes and damage to other cell macro-molecules—then dietary factors which will help to prevent that damage or help to repair the processes—DNA repair systems—are very important. There is now some evidence that nutrition will enhance DNA repair process.

Q125 *Lord Turnberg:* What sort of nutrition?

Professor Mathers: Individual micro-nutrients. Most of this work has of course been done at cellular level. We do not know very much about how well it works at the whole person level, but at least it is pointing us in that direction which might be helpful.

Professor Kay: In terms of oral health there is little question that it is the accumulation of diseases across the lifetime plus the accumulation of treatments across the lifetime that lands you up in a certain place when you are older. However, what I would say is because of the huge social class differences in the same cohorts there must be some interventions to do with lifestyle that would bring the people at the lower levels up to the same as their peers.

Dr van der Ouderaa: We have constructed in our programme a sort of triangle of successive measures for healthy ageing and it starts with smoking cessation and emotional well-being, so having a stress level that you can cope with.

Q126 *Lord Turnberg:* How do you do that, I would be very interested to know?

Dr van der Ouderaa: The second is avoiding overweight and having enough physical activity. The third layer is about having the right macro-nutrients so the right balance of fat versus carbohydrates versus protein adding predominantly poly-unsaturated fatty acids in the fatty acids component; not having too many easily fermentable carbohydrates and then, as Professor Mathers points out, micro-nutrients and anti-oxidant vitamins, flavanols, isoflavols.

Q127 *Lord Turnberg:* Do you have evidence for all of those?

Dr van der Ouderaa: Indications and evidence.

Q128 *Baroness Finlay of Llandaff:* Nutrition receives a great deal of attention from the public in terms of cookery advice and issues around food safety, diet regimes for weight control and body image and so on, and now the promotion of herbal and complementary or alternative therapies, but I was just wondering to what extent there is scope to include the nutritional impact on ageing in public discussion of such issues. Rather than a quick fix, should we be looking at a much longer term view and a view in terms of nutrition and its affect on the ageing process and maintaining a homeostasis which Professor Mathers referred to?

Professor Mathers: Perhaps I could start by saying that we will not know until we try; we need to try to stimulate that debate. If we are going to do it I think we need to start from some kind of evidence base so we need to have something to say to people that will be helpful. That brings us back to not knowing enough about nutrition and older people. But I suspect that some of the messages will not change; we will still want people to eat more fruit and vegetables, we will want them perhaps to reduce their fat intake and reduce the salt intake and so on. At that level it is fairly straightforward. It is the more subtle things which we are trying to draw out that we do not yet have the evidence for. You mentioned body image. I do not think people give up on body image just because they are getting a little bit older; I think it will be important all the way through life and people, as they get older, want to age well. People talk now about silver surfers, people who are at an age when they have the luxury of the time to do things they might not have done early in life and they want to be well enough to do that. I understand they are very interested in websites and television programmes and so on which address nutritional issues, food issues, at least.

Professor Kay: In dentistry, based on very good evidence, we have been trying to persuade people to eat differently for the sake of their health for many, many years. I, myself, did a review of the evidence of how well it worked and it is lacking. It is very, very difficult to change what people do, let alone what they eat. However, I guess—and this relates back to something I said earlier—that because people are interested in all the issues that you said, that rather than try and persuade them that they want to be interested in it because it is healthy for you or because we think it is a good idea, we can utilise that interest to encourage people to behave in ways that will benefit their health, but they may not see that they are doing it necessarily for that reason.

Q129 *Baroness Finlay of Llandaff:* Has there been a comprehensive epidemiological study looking at the micro-nutrient status across a population of people who are particularly elderly and comparing that to their functional status and perhaps one of their perceived quality of life measures?

Professor Kay: The others will know more than me but the American Veteran Study has looked at that, I believe.

Professor Mathers: In the UK the NDNS—the National Diet and Nutrition Surveys—is the body which undertakes these kinds of surveys and they have published reports (1998 was the most recent one) dealing with older people. That provides information on nutritional intake and nutritional status.

Q130 *Baroness Finlay of Llandaff:* In terms of?

Professor Mathers: Some blood markers, the sort of things that Frans was speaking about earlier. What they do not include, as I understand it, is the sort of functional things you were referring to.

Q131 *Chairman:* Can I just extend the range of the question a little bit. We live increasingly in this country in a multi-ethnic and multi-cultural society and of course that intersects very closely with lifestyle and not least nutrition. I just wonder how that is affecting—or how it ought to affect—the structure of research projects and research objectives.

Professor Mathers: That is an extremely important area and it is one that has not been addressed by the National Surveys. It is not been included to any extent at all in them. We know relatively little at that level, but the evidence that we do have suggests that the impact of nutrition on quality of life in terms of expectation of disease differs with ethnic groups so we do need to know a little bit about individual groups.

Q132 *Chairman:* Are you saying that there is not much of this information around.

Dr van der Ouderaa: There is some very interesting information from the state of Singapore where in one generation people have come from rural to fully urban and if you then compare three ethnic groups—the Chinese, the Indian and the Malays—then in an urbanised environment, a high stress environment, not a lot of physical activity and different nutrition, it looks like the Asian Indians become diabetic about 15 years before the Chinese and about 10 years before the Malays. There are quite strong ethnic influences

on changes in an environment against genes that have been developing over 20,000 years without urbanisation.

Q133 *Baroness Finlay of Llandaff:* Can I just ask, as well as food type nutritional intake, have these looked separately at fluid type intakes in terms of adequate hydration in elderly people because elderly people are often slightly dehydrated a lot of the time.

Professor Mathers: I am not aware that there is any systematic collection of information of that kind.

Q134 *Lord Soulsby of Swaffham Prior:* This may sound like a flippant question but it is not meant to be flippant. We are bombarded on the television by food programmes and eating and cooking programmes, do you think that they do an adequate job from the point of view of nutrition for the ageing person or could they do better? Could they have a better message for older people who might be living by themselves and doing their own cooking and things like that?

Dr van der Ouderaa: I am not convinced that they are doing a very good job. There was a programme about a month ago by the BBC on vitamins and from a scientific point of view I thought it was a sensational and quite a poor programme, because they tried to imply that higher intakes of RDAs and vitamins was a bad thing and it was argued on a few people who took high doses of vitamin A—which is clearly not the right thing to do—but then all the other vitamins were tarred with the same brush. Certainly for elderly people whose intake is not optimal and by availability through improper chewing is not optimal. I think a lot more could be done. The point I was going to make is that there is no single population group. We need to look at the population and what is coming out of our consumer studies that there are different people who are differently engaged with investing intellectual time and money into buying better food for the longer term.

Professor Kay: I am afraid I do not cook and I do not watch television so I cannot answer your question.

Chairman: Can I thank you very much indeed. It has been a very helpful session in a critical area that was perhaps under-emphasised. You have got from the discussion a sense of the range of issues that we are grappling with and if, as a result of that, you have further thoughts, do not hesitate to let us know. At best our report can inform Government policy and perhaps influence it. That is our intention so this is your opportunity if you want to contribute further. Thank you very much indeed.

TUESDAY 9 NOVEMBER 2004

Present	Finlay of Llandaff, B	Soulsby of Swaffham Prior, L
	Hilton of Eggardon, B	Sutherland of Houndwood, L (Chairman)
	Mitchell, L	Turnberg, L
	Murphy, B	Walmsley, B
	Oxburgh, L	

Memorandum by the Department of Health

1. INTRODUCTION

1.1 The Department welcomes the opportunity provided by the Science and Technology Committee inquiry to set out its policy and describe its role in promoting the science and technology that will help older people live healthier and more independent lives. This memorandum describes the nature and form of our contribution, the research and development context in which it is set, and the network of other government departments, research bodies, and voluntary and private sector interests with whom we work.

1.2 The Government has a 10-year strategy and programme of action, underpinned by research, for providing better services and promoting better health for older people (*NHS Plan and the National Service Framework for Older People*).

2. DEPARTMENT OF HEALTH RESEARCH AND DEVELOPMENT OVERVIEW

Research in the NHS

2.1 The budget for NHS research and development is over £600 million in 2004–05, of which £480 million is allocated to NHS providers. Some 75 per cent of the money from these allocations meets the service costs to the NHS of research funded by research councils and charities.

The National Research and Development Programme

2.2 The main parts of the national R&D programme are:

— Health Technology Assessment;

— Service Delivery and Organisation;

— New and Emerging Applications of Technology.

2.3 Each of the three programmes has commissioned work of relevance to the scientific aspects of ageing (see paragraphs 5.2 to 5.6 below). They are supported by a further three cross-cutting programmes on methodology, research capacity and public involvement.

The Policy Research Programme (PRP)

2.4 The Policy Research Programme aims to underpin policy development by commissioning high quality research-based evidence. Its remit extends across the full range of the Department's responsibilities, including health and social care services, healthy living and well-being, disease prevention, the role of the environment in health, the organisation of the NHS and strategies for treating particular diseases and conditions. Significant programmes of research designed to promote healthy and active life expectancy of older people are underway or planned (see paragraph 5.1 below).

UK Clinical Research Collaboration and Clinical Research Networks

2.5 The UK Clinical Research Collaboration was established in April 2004. The Collaboration is a partnership between government, the charity sector, the private sector, and the public. Its broad aim is to improve national health, increase national wealth, and enrich world knowledge by harnessing the clinical research potential of the NHS. The Collaboration will oversee the translation of scientific advances into patient care and promote the growth in research activity, infrastructure and capacity needed to achieve this.

2.6 The Department of Health funding to support this growth—£25 million in each of the next four years from 2004–05—will be invested in the first instance in research networks covering mental health (a core component of the National Institute for Mental Health), children's medicines, diabetes, Alzheimer's disease, and stroke. These networks will be modelled on the successful Cancer Research Network set up in 2001. Alzheimer's disease and stroke disproportionately affect older people: the networks will significantly further our ability to understand and deal with these disabling diseases of old age.

Genetics Research

2.7 The Department, with the Department of Trade and Industry, is investing £15 million to support the development of five genetics knowledge parks (GKPs) in England. The aim of the Parks is to foster collaboration between scientists, health professionals and the commercial sector so as to transfer the benefit derived from genetics to support and improve human health and well-being. Several of the GKPs focus on areas of relevance to the Inquiry. The Northern GKP examines genetic damage over the life course, the London IDEAS Park will examine the provision of genetic information to a multi-ethnic population and the Oxford GKP specialises in many of the diseases associated with ageing, including cancer and neurological and neuropathological conditions.

2.8 In addition, the Department, the Wellcome Trust and the Medical Research Council are providing an initial £61 million to support the development of the UK Biobank. This project aims to obtain comprehensive data on the combined effects of genotype, life-style and environmental exposure to assess the risk of developing the common multi-factorial diseases of later life.

3. THE ROLE OF SCIENCE AND TECHNOLOGY

3.1 The Sub-Committee has invited information on two areas of central relevance to the promotion of healthy and active life expectancy: the biological process of ageing, including the link between this process and wider social-economic factors, and the application of research in technology and design. Details of work of relevance to each area are provided below.

Assistive technologies including electronic technologies

3.2 Assistive technology has, for some time, provided a means of enabling elderly and disabled people to live independently in their own homes. New electronic technologies increase this potential. The Department's information strategy "*Information for Health*" encourages the use of Information and Communications Technologies (ICTs) in the NHS to deliver service benefit for citizens, patients, professionals and employees in a cost-effective manner. It identifies telemedicine and telecare as priorities for further research, both to improve the evidence-base relating to cost-effectiveness, and as options to be considered routinely in all Health Improvement Plans.

3.3 Horizon scanning reviews of both telemedicine and telecare were commissioned in 1997 and 1998 and informed a developing research agenda within the Department. This built upon earlier involvement in European research programmes (*Technology Initiative for Disabled and Elderly People,* and *Advanced Informatics in Medicine*) and was closely linked to policy making in a number of areas, including the potential for the technologies to support elderly and disabled people. In 2000 the Department commissioned a report on *The Use of ICTs in Assistive Technology.*

3.4 A report on *Research and Development Work Relating to Assistive Technology* is prepared annually for Parliament under Section 22 of the Chronically Sick and Disabled Persons Act 1970. The report is funded by the Department of Health and prepared by the Foundation for Assistive Technology whose database of research projects is used both to highlight gaps and identify funding sources. Other influential publications are the Audit Commission's *Fully Equipped* reports in 2000 and 2002 and, this year, *Older People— Independence and Well-being* and its sub-report on assistive technology (Audit Commission, February 2004). The latter helped support the case which led to the Spending Review funding for the preventive technologies grant.

3.5 The 2004 Spending Review led to the announcement of £80 million funding for a social services' preventive technologies grant from April 2006 to extend the benefits of new electronic technologies. In August 2004 the Department formed an Electronic Technologies Policy Collaborative to develop, with stakeholders, policy on the use of the grant.

New Opportunities for Service Development

3.6 Modern, responsive electronic community alarm-type devices offer the potential for older people to stay in control of their lives for longer and reduce the risk of untoward events. Technologies for the remote monitoring of health conditions could also, in time, share the same infrastructure as care-orientated technologies. Technical advances mean that the devices are easy to install and are relatively unobtrusive and provide a comprehensive service including:

— safety and security monitoring;

— physiological and activity monitoring;

— care-related information.

3.7 As well as the improvements in quality of life, technological advances can deliver efficiency gains to health and social care systems by reducing "just-in-case" admissions of older people to hospital and residential care. Other areas of potential policy impact include:

— admission avoidance and timely discharge;

— falls prevention strategies;

— saving lives through more reliable fire/smoke detection for older people;

— timely information to inform people's care package reviews;

— improving quality of life and reducing care costs for people with long term conditions and with strokes;

— better monitoring of people with chronic obstructive pulmonary disease (COPD) and diabetes which can alert to changes in condition and significantly reduce out-patient attendances.

3.8 Further research is being planned that will evaluate some of these developments to provide more evidence in relation to the most cost-effective approaches. Some of the more sophisticated electronic technology options will be studied further within a wider programme of research currently being developed to investigate *technological support for chronic disease management, for self-care and for healthy living.* The Department is discussing with the Engineering and Physical Sciences Research Council and Economic and Social Research Council their interest in joint research in this area.

4. HEALTHY AND ACTIVE AGEING

4.1 The Department commissions a wide range of research designed to improve the prospects of healthy and active life expectancy of older people. Ministers have given priority to research on the medical conditions most associated with ageing, such as heart disease, stroke, cancer and mental illness. Strategic reviews of research in these areas were undertaken in 2001–02. The *NHS Improvement Plan* restates the commitment to reduce mortality rates in these areas and to improve the quality of life for those experiencing them.

4.2 Extensive research was commissioned and used to inform the development of the *National Service Framework for Older People* (2001). The NSF aims to deliver improvements in the quality of older people's lives, with key targets on stroke, mortality, support for complex needs and enabling people with long-term needs to remain at home. Major programmes of research on age-related disease, on the better management of long-term conditions and on the tacking of continuing heath inequalities will underpin the implementation of the NSF.

4.3 In developing its research agenda, the Department has worked actively with other government departments and across commercial and not-for-profit sectors, including service user and carer organisations. Collaborations include the Funders' Forum on Research on Ageing and Older People set up by the Department. This brings together major UK funders in ageing research to exchange information about research priorities and to identify research areas that would benefit from a joint approach.

4.4 Active links have also been established with consortia led by other bodies, such as the UK Research Councils' National Collaboration on Ageing Research (NCAR), the Engineering and Physical Sciences Research Council funded research network on Extending Quality of Life (EQUAL), and the Economic and Social Research Council's "Growing Older" research programme and its successor "The New Dynamics of Ageing". The Department is considering buying in to the national longitudinal study of health and disability currently being developed by the DWP.

4.5 The Department is a founder member of the Cardiovascular Research Funders' Forum which includes the major research funders (UK Health Departments, MRC, British Heart Foundation, Wellcome, Diabetes UK and industry). Following an international workshop on future research directions in heart failure, in 2002, the Department and the British Heart Foundation jointly funded £1.5 million research in this area. The workshop also focused on advances on stem cell research and the Department is closely following progress in this field.

4.6 International collaboration has also included the European Forum on Population Ageing Research that aims to influence national and European research priorities. The Department is the major funder, with the US National Institute for Aging and a consortium of other government departments, of the English Longitudinal Study of Ageing. This investigates the links between health and wider socio-economic factors, improving our ability to plan for the consequences of ageing on income and health.

5. COMMISSIONED RESEARCH

The Policy Research Programme (PRP)

5.1 PRP research on promoting healthy and active life expectancy for older people can be grouped in two broad areas. The first is the biological processes of ageing, where there are two main strands:

(a) investigation of the cause, prevention and impact of diseases that specifically affect people in older age. Studies have been undertaken on cancer screening, the links between health and iron deficiency, the biological effects of the cold and the efficacy of influenza vaccination. Research in dementia ranges from specialised studies of atypical dementias related to CJD to studies of the quality of life of people with dementia, including collaborative work with the MRC on the "natural history" of cognitive decline and dementia.

(b) the influence of inequalities on morbidity and mortality. Studies have looked at socio-demographic factors and healthy life expectancy and at indicators to assess health inequalities. Gender-specific data are collected via the National Women's Heart and Health study and the British Regional Heart Study (men) and the impact of race/ethnic inequality on cancer survival, in stroke patients and in influenza vaccination coverage has been investigated.

The second area is promoting active and healthy ageing which also comprises two central strands:

(a) ways to prevent or reduce dependency and extend the quality of life of older people. Reviews have been undertaken on dietary behaviour and major new initiatives on Living Arrangements for Older People and accidental injury are being planned. Work on the use of Information Communication Technologies (ICTs) has included web-based cancer information, the influence of age, sex, ethnicity and social isolation on the use of ICTs and the computerised review of long-term prescribing.

(b) research designed to increase understanding of the changing nature and needs of the ageing population. This includes work on the experience of long-term carers and on the development of measures for assessing quality of life. Ongoing research utilises computer-simulated models to predict future levels of demand and risk and idata from national longitudinal studies to explore the relationship between ageing, disability and dependency over time.

The Health Technology Assessment Programme (HTA)

5.2 The HTA programme assesses the clinical effectiveness and cost-effectiveness of interventions used by those working in the NHS to promote health, prevent and treat disease, and improve rehabilitation and long-term care. It seeks to provide all of those making decisions in the NHS with high quality information on costs, effectiveness and the broader impact of health care.

5.3 The HTA portfolio of work related to the health and well being of older people includes some 67 studies. These include 25 published in the recent past (including three primary research studies and 22 systematic reviews) and 42 ongoing (including 27 primary research studies and 15 systematic reviews). A number of the systematic reviews inform National Institute for Clinical Excellence decision making. Details can be found on the HTA website (www.hta.nhsweb.nhs.uk).

The Service Delivery and Organisation Programme (SDO)

5.4 The SDO is a national research programme set up to consolidate and develop the evidence base on the organisation, management and delivery of health care services.

5.5 Since its establishment in 2000, the SDO programme has commissioned much research of relevance to older people, including work on continuity of care, self-assessment of care needs, and the needs of carers. Specific projects addressing the needs of older people have looked at discharge arrangements, rehabilitation, and particular conditions including fractures, constipation and chronic knee pain. The SDO website is at www.sdo.lshtm.ac.uk.

The New and Emerging Applications of Technology Programme (NEAT)

5.6 The main aim of the New and Emerging Applications of Technology Programme (NEAT) is to promote and support, through applied research, the use of new or emerging technologies to develop health care products and interventions to enhance the quality, efficiency and effectiveness of health and social care. Current research of particular relevance to older people includes work around rehabilitation following hip fracture. The NEAT website is at www.neatprogramme.org.uk.

The Health Technology Devices Programme (HTD)

5.7 Led by the Department, the Health Technology Devices Programme is a new funding scheme supporting the research into innovative healthcare technologies needed to develop new medical devices. Around £15 million of government funding will be available throughout the programme to support collaborative R&D projects involving industry, universities and the NHS. Public investment is matched by industry. As well as medical devices, the programme covers healthcare devices for use in the community and the home. Current projects of particular relevance to older people include the development of a knee reciprocal walking orthosis and a stair climber aid.

Research in NHS Trusts

5.8 Significant programmes of work are being undertaken by the NHS Trusts on the biological process of ageing and on the development and application of technology and design. A 2003–04 analysis of NHS R&D activity shows 99 studies in the "older people" priority area. Numerical distribution across the main diseases linked with ageing reveals the following activity pattern (number of studies):

mental health (21)	rheumatology/musculoskeletal (18)
cancer (21)	neurological (11)
diabetes (19)	cardiovascular (6)
respiratory disease (5)	stroke (3)

Details of this work can be found on the National Research Register http://www.nrr.nhs.uk

5.9 Many Trusts have grouped together with local Universities to form collaborative research groups. Oxford R&D consortium, for example, has groups on neuroscience, cardiovascular disease, cancer and diabetes. Other consortia have developed programmes of work specifically related to older people. Examples include:

— *Royal Liverpool and Bridegreen University Hospital NHS Trust* has a programme on Ageing and Older People's Health, including influenza immunisation, falls, heart failure, Parkinson's disease, dietary supplements, diabetes and the impact of stress on the cells;

— *Sheffield Teaching Hospitals Trust's* Older People programme comprises studies on screening for hip fractures and diabetes, orthopaedics and rehabilitation.

— *Hammersmith Hospitals NHS Trust's* Care of the Elderly programme includes research on hypertension, electronic bed and char monitors, vascular disease in diabetes, the link between androgen and arterial stiffness, late life depression and screening for depression.

— *Barts and London NHS Trust's* The Health of Older People has work on male osteoporosis, faecal incontinence in women, chronic obstructive pulmonary disease, arthritis/rheumatoid arthritis, mastication and chewing patterns, joint inflammation, osteoarticular disease, ocular hypertension, vitamins and hip fractures, Parkinson's disease, rectal prolapse and carers' perception of compassion from nursing staff;

— *The Kings Consortium's* Improving the Health Care of Older People programme is examining walking stability, impact of growth hormone/testosterone on well-being, genetic and nutritional factors influencing eye disease, genes and ageing, prevention of falls, hypertension, use of hip protectors to reduce fractures, impact of lifestyle advice, recovery from/prevention of stroke and immunogenetics.

September 2004

Memorandum by the Department for Transport

INTRODUCTION

It is clear from research around the world that mobility and travel are very important in enabling older people to maintain active and healthy lives. Mobility is often described as the key to independence. For older people this can mean being able to visit family, friends and leisure facilities as well as continuing to be self-sufficient in day-to-day living.

Planning for an ageing society involves looking at a wide range of policies and services from the perspective of older users. The Department for Transport's audit of older people's transport needs[1] showed that the concerns of older people are similar to those of other transport users. In some cases, however, the combination of dependence on public transport, low income and mobility difficulties exacerbates problems to the point that transport becomes a major limiting factor in an older person's ability to access services and facilities, such as food shops and to continue to live independently. There is evidence that older people who do not have access to healthy and affordable food are likely to have a poor diet[2]. Loss of mobility can also have a profound psychological impact in terms of isolation and loss of independence, which can lead to depression.

Older people who are drivers want to continue to drive for as long as possible but many may have to give it up because of declining health or financial constraints. It is therefore important to look at alternatives that are accessible, safe, affordable and available. There is a large body of research looking at issues of older transport users and there is significant international co-operation in this field. This memorandum draws on recommendations made by an OECD report on ageing and transport[3], work done by the USA Transportation Research Board and a number of European Commission projects. However, the major source of evidence is the Department for Transport itself including the Driving and Vehicle Licensing Agency (DVLA) and the Highways Agency (HA).

The memorandum looks in detail at evidence relating to older motorists and also touches on the Department's work in improving mobility for older pedestrians and public transport users.

DRIVER LICENSING AND FITNESS TO DRIVE

Current UK licensing legislation allows a driver without a disability to be issued a Group 1 (ordinary) licence valid until the age of 70 years with renewals three yearly thereafter. Group 2 (vocational) licences are renewed on an annual basis from the age of 65 years. The choice of these age criteria is somewhat arbitrary but recognises the need to balance cost against benefit, bearing in mind that drivers have a duty to report medical conditions during the tenure of a licence.

Amongst the most common problems experienced by older drivers is a loss of motor function, for example caused by joint stiffness, particularly in the neck, and slowness of movement which can cause difficulties with observations at junctions and during parking manoeuvres, and safe operation of the car controls.

Reduced visual functions are also common as part of the ageing process. These may include reduced acuity, difficulty adapting to darkness, or recovering from glare. In addition, any reduced visual field from disease processes means that the quality of information gained from the environment may be inadequate, increasing the probability of errors and misjudgements.

Age-related decline in cognitive functions such as attention, anticipation, executive functioning and information processing means that older drivers tend to have difficulty in dealing with complex traffic situations and reduced capacity to respond quickly and flexibly to changing traffic situations. These processes of normal ageing may be exacerbated by medical conditions, which are more common in old age—eg

---

[1] Older People, their Transport Needs and Requirements, published DTLR 2001.

[2] Making the Connections: Final Report on Transport & Social Exclusion, SEU 2003.

[3] Ageing and Transport: Mobility needs and safety issues, published by OECD 2001.

dementia, stroke, Parkinson's Disease. In addition, the use of medications may create additional problems for driving. Detailed information can be obtained in the DfT report, Older Drivers, Illness and Medication.[4]

Relicensing for Group 1 licence holders is based on self-declaration whereas Group 2 renewals require a medical examination in addition to the medical declaration. Licensing decisions are based on guidance given by medical panels covering specialist areas, eg neurology, psychiatry, and vision. At present only one medical panel, psychiatry, includes an "old age" specialist. American guidelines suggest that all medical panels should include someone with an interest in ageing[5] although there is no evidence to show that this would necessarily alter the current recommendations of the panels in any way.

ACCIDENT INVOLVEMENT

In spite of the decline in function associated with normal ageing and the preponderance of medical conditions with the potential to impact on driving amongst older people, research internationally (including the UK) shows little increase in the incidence of road traffic accidents. However, older drivers are disproportionately involved in fatal or serious accidents rather than ones in which someone is only slightly injured. This is now generally believed to be due to the increased frailty of the older population. Older motorists are frailer than their younger counterparts and are therefore more likely to die as a result of an accident.[6]

Accident statistics also demonstrate that older drivers are involved in different types of accident than their younger counterparts. Accidents involving older drivers are more likely to happen at junctions, particularly when crossing oncoming traffic and while parking or reversing. They are less likely to be involved in risk-taking behaviour resulting in accidents.

Evidence suggests that the older drivers compensate for reduced functional abilities by modifying driving behaviour eg by avoiding driving in the dark, in rush hour conditions, by driving only in familiar areas and by avoiding motorways. This is acknowledged in some countries by the use of restricted driving licences eg restricted to daylight hours only, to within a certain radius from the driver's home, to avoid motorway driving etc. which is allowed for in the European Driving Licence Directive[7]. The Department is looking at experience from other countries including how to decide what restrictions would be required and how to enforce the restrictions. Among our concerns are reports that many older drivers fatally injured in car accidents demonstrate signs of dementia, the likely clinical effect of which is to reduce insight and the likelihood of modifying behaviour in response to driving difficulties experienced[8].

DRIVER ASSESSMENT

With the increasing average age of the population and longer life expectancy it is likely that there will be an increase in the incidence of neurodegenerative disorders such as Alzheimer's and Parkinson's Disease and of a variety of disorders likely to lead to more locomotor problems. In addition, increasing amounts of medication to counteract these conditions may also have an impact on driving.

Much research worldwide has looked at the development of screening tools to aid licensing authorities in making decisions about medical fitness to drive. However, results have been inconsistent. Screening tools have been measured either against accident rates, which may not reflect driving ability due to the compensatory strategies of older drivers, or because of avoidance behaviour of other drivers[9], or against driving tests, which vary between studies. The current European Commission part-funded projects, CONSENSUS[10] and AGILE[11], aim to define common assessment criteria, methods and tools for the practical "fitness to drive" assessment of disabled and older drivers respectively.

[4] Older drivers, illness and medication, Road Safety Research Report No 39, published by DfT 2003.

[5] Physician's Guide to Assessing and Counselling Older Drivers published jointly by the American Medical Association (AMA) and the National Highway Traffic Safety Administration (NHTSA). Report published 2003.

[6] Older drivers: a literature review, Road Safety Research Report No. 25, published by DTLR 2000.

[7] Commission Directive 2000/56/EC on driving licences, Annex 1.

[8] Johansson K. Older Automobile Drivers: Medical Aspects. Doctoral Dissertation, Karolinska Institute Stockholm, published 1997.

[9] Withaar F, Aspects of Attention in Older Drivers, Doctoral Dissertation, Groningen University, published 2000.

[10] CONSENSUS—Promoting a Consensus of Opinion in assessing driving ability of People with Special Needs (PSN) through common methodologies and normative tools. EU project funded by IST, due for completion Oct 2004.

[11] AGILE—Aged people Integration, mobility, safety and quality of Life Enhancement through driving. EU project funded by DG-TREN, due for completion April 2005.

While the DVLA relies on information from drivers and their doctors to aid the decision making process, where in doubt, they value the practical assessment of fitness to drive offered by the Forum of Mobility Centres[12]. The practical assessment process makes recommendations for adaptive technology which may enable the older driver to prolong driving wherever possible, and helps in the decision to stop driving where safety is a concern. The demonstrable face-validity of the assessment means that the decision to withdraw the driving licence may be more acceptable to the driver. In addition to referrals from DVLA, many disabled and older people seek the advice of mobility centres either independently or on the advice of GPs. The Department for Transport has provided funding to increase the level of service provided by these driver assessment services but there are insufficient at present to meet the needs of the changing demographics of the population[13].

In 2002 68 per cent of men aged over 70 were driving licence holders—an increase over the 59 per cent who held a licence a decade ago. In the same period the percentage of women aged over 70 holding driving licences increased from 17 per cent to 28 per cent. Projections suggest that by the years 2020 to 2025, 78 per cent of men and 58 per cent of women over 70 will be licence holders.

USE OF TECHNOLOGY

Because driving is so critical to maintaining personal independence it is important to prolong the safe driving period for older drivers. People with reduced motor function may be enabled to continue to drive through the use of adaptive technology eg additional mirrors for better vision at junctions and while parking, power assisted steering, automatic transmission.

In addition, vehicle technology is going through a rapid expansion and some of the driver assist systems (ADAS) and in-vehicle information systems (IVIS) currently being developed have the potential to aid the older driver. Through extensive research, the Department has developed a Code of Practice, Design Guidelines and a checklist for system assessment to promote production of "safer" IVIS[14]. The development of these good practice guidelines used volunteers spanning the age group between 35 and 55. OECD recommends that older drivers should be included in future trial populations, as they are becoming an increasing proportion of the driving population. Japan is one of the countries to take this on board and many of their studies on information and assist systems include an older driver population.

Driver assist systems are now being developed to aid such tasks as speed adaptation, gap acceptance at junctions, lane merging, parking and reversing. The AGILE project has suggested that driver assist systems most beneficial to older drivers are those which address the areas where older drivers have difficulties (junctions, parking, reversing etc). Previous work carried out in EC funded projects such as TELAID[15] and EDDIT[16], has shown that navigation systems not only assist older drivers to drive further, but also enable them to do so with more confidence even when the navigational system has been removed. Research is required to ensure that the use of driver assist systems does not actually increase the accident rate, eg through over-reliance on the systems or through distraction.

New technology is also being used to improve occupant protection within the vehicle, eg through the use of seat belt pre-tensioners and airbags. Traditional systems have involved rapid deployment with relatively high force which has given some cause for concern. Recently, more intelligent systems have been introduced which sense the position of the car occupant. Current research through the project BOSCOS (Bone Scanning for Occupant Safety)[17] is looking at the likely effect of reduced bone density on injury risk with the aim of tuning the car restraint system to maintain the optimum effectiveness without causing excessive loading on the bodies of the more vulnerable individuals. This may help to reduce the fatality level of older drivers.

[12] The Forum of Mobility Centres is an accredited network of organisations which aims to help elderly and disabled people achieve independent mobility as drivers, passengers and wheelchair users. The 12 English centres are funded by the Department for Transport.

[13] The Provision of outdoor mobility services for older and disabled people in the UK, unpublished report commissioned by Department for Transport.

[14] Guide to in-vehicle information systems—DD 235:1996—BSi Draft For Development.

[15] TELAID—TELematic Applications for the Integration of Drivers with special needs, EU funded project report published 1995.

[16] EDDIT—Elderly and Disabled Drivers Information Telematics. EU funded project report published 1993.

[17] BOSCOS—Bone Scanning for Occupant Safety—is a co-operative project involving Cranfield University and a number of vehicle and component manufacturers, partially sponsored by the Department for Transport under the FORESIGHT programme.

[18] Presentations in Your Safe Mobility Conference held in Brussels, October 2003.

[19] Influencing driver behaviour to improve junction safety. TRL report PR/SE/253/2001, commissioned by Highways Agency, 2001.

DRIVER TRAINING

Because of the rapid changes in vehicle technology, and the declining skills of older drivers, it has been suggested by the European Commission, supported by many agencies[18] that opportunities be made for life-long learning in driving. The Highways Agency looked at training to influence driver behaviour at junctions[19]. For older drivers, this focussed on the need to be more aware of increasing vulnerability in accidents and on right turn accidents. It was felt that this could be a useful measure to reduce risk nationally, rather than the more local benefits of re-designing junctions.

The Department has commissioned work to look at the advice services available for older drivers[20] and has identified several local authority schemes that provide a valuable service in maintaining the safe mobility of older drivers. However, there has been no evaluation yet of these services or of their potential effect in reducing accident risk. The Forum of Mobility Centres also has a role in providing advice and information on adaptive devices, which may assist in driving.

The Department also promotes driving as a lifelong skill. It is seeking new ways in which older drivers can refresh their driving skills, including greater take up of the Driving Standards Agency's "Arrive Alive Classic" scheme which provides a programme of presentations for drivers aged 55 and over with a particular focus on the retired age group.

ROAD DESIGN

The Highways Agency commissioned research to investigate whether road design should be influenced by the type of drivers using particular roads. However the research concluded that the existing design parameters, which have been determined to cater safely for the majority of typical drivers, also have sufficient factors of safety included within them to allow for the minority of drivers who have inferior skills. Other recommendations for consideration proposed by the USA Transportation Research Board[21] include better road signs, improved lighting at junctions, more appropriate timing at signal controlled junctions and reduction of intersection skew angles. These measures must be economically effective as well as effective in increasing the safety of road users.

DRIVING CESSATION

While driving remains the preferred mode of transport for many older people, there usually comes a stage when it is no longer possible. Research by the Automobile Association on when and why people give up driving[22] shows that it tends to be for financial or health reasons. People who keep driving for longer tend to be from a slightly higher socio-economic group and to live in suburban or rural areas. The main health reasons for ceasing driving were related to vision. One of the main concerns for older people was the loss of mobility associated with driving cessation. It is therefore important to improve the alternatives available for older people. The Department is currently undertaking research[23] looking at the issues facing older people giving up driving.

THE PEDESTRIAN ENVIRONMENT

One of the difficulties associated with stopping driving is that older people are also at risk as pedestrians. The Department has carried out an extensive review of literature looking at pedestrian safety[24]. There is a higher rate of fatality among older pedestrians than young pedestrians, again due to the increased frailty of the older person. Accidents are mainly attributable to crossing roads, particularly at complex junctions, and to trips and slips on the pavement. Reduced motor function makes it difficult to observe traffic when crossing roads, and slower walking pace means more time is required to cross. Reduced vision causes difficulty in detecting/ locating vehicles or other hazards, especially in darkness. There is little research to show the impact of cognitive impairment on pedestrian accidents.

---

[18] Presentations in Your Safe Mobility Conference held in Brussels, October 2003.

[19] Influencing driver behaviour to improve junction safety. TRL report PR/SE/253/2001, commissioned by Highways Agency, 2001.

[20] UG394 Review of driving advice / assessment services for older drivers—due for completion February 2005.

[21] Guidance for Implementation of the AASHTO Strategic Highway Safety Plan: Volume 9: A Guide for Reducing Collisions Involving Older Drivers, published by the Transportation Research Board 2004.

[22] When and Why Older Drivers Give up Driving, published by AA Foundation for Road Safety Research 1996.

[23] UG535—MIU Research Project: Investigation of the Issues for Older People Giving up Driving.

[24] Older Pedestrians: A Critical Review of the Literature, Road Safety Research Report No. 37, published by DfT 2004.

Recommendations from the Department's research were to support older people as drivers and to improve quality of access to public transport. Interventions to make the road environment safer include vehicle speed reduction, provision of signal controlled crossings—particularly the puffin crossing which senses pedestrians on the crossing, improved quality of walking surfaces, increased traffic signal timing, and education of other road users.

Safety cameras have benefited all road users, particularly in urban areas where they have targeted high casualty locations. They have led to a significant reduction in numbers of people killed and seriously injured across a broad spectrum of the population, including older people.

The Department is also encouraging local authorities to design and manage their road space with all users in mind. Home Zones are residential areas designed with streets to be places for people, instead of just thoroughfares for motor traffic. The aim is to change the way that streets are used in order to improve the quality of life for local residents, including older people. In a Home Zone, the streets will become the focus of community life and early experience of completed schemes in existing residential areas suggests that they have often led to a stronger, more vibrant and diverse community.

For people with walking difficulties, buggies and pavement vehicles (class II and III vehicles) may provide a viable alternative for increased mobility. Legislation covering these vehicles is currently being reviewed in a research project commissioned by the Department[25]. This is looking at a range of issues including licensing, insurance and training for the use of these vehicles. The OECD report on new transportation technology for older people also recommended that national governments should be more open to innovation in personal mobility solutions.

PUBLIC TRANSPORT

The Department's report on the transport needs and requirements of older people addresses issues of accessibility, safety, affordability and availability. Accessibility issues, such as the physical difficulties associated with boarding and alighting buses and trains are being addressed through implementation of accessibility regulations under the Disability Discrimination Act 1995[26]. For example by the end of 2003 a third of buses met the accessibility requirements of the Disability Discrimination Act with a much higher proportion doing so in major urban centres.

The Department's research shows that those older people who have never been drivers are much more mobile in old age than those who have had to give up driving. One major cause is lack of familiarity with how public transport works. The way in which transport information is produced and made available to older people is a key factor.

Improving safety of older people includes improving the perceived safety, eg through reducing the fear of crime. Isolated stops and badly lit waiting areas can lead to a feeling of insecurity. The Department has a programme of work to help transport operators and local authorities identify and address personal security concerns through better design and maintenance of facilities.

There is evidence that availability of concessionary fares for older people also encourages public transport use.

Door to door transport services, often provided by voluntary and community transport schemes are essential for many older and disabled people unable to access or use other forms of transport. The Department supports the Community Transport Association and encourages local authorities to work closely with voluntary transport providers in addressing the needs of people who are socially excluded. The Department is currently researching the role of community transport in reducing levels of social exclusion.[27]

The Department's Urban and Rural Bus Challenge schemes support innovative and/or unconventional solutions to the problems of public transport provision. Over 400 hundred schemes have been supported. A number of the projects involve community transport and have particular emphasis on meeting the transport needs of older and disabled people.

September 2004

---

[25] UG460—MIU Research Project: Review of Class II and Class III Invalid Carriages.

[26] The Public Service Vehicles Accessibility Regulations 2000 (No 1970) and the Rail Vehicle Accessibility Regulations 1998 (no 2456).

[27] UG536 MU Research Project Using Community Transport to Reduce Social Exclusion.

Memorandum by the Department of Trade and Industry

INTRODUCTION

The Department welcomes this inquiry. Several areas within the Department of Trade and Industry (DTI) have a specific interest in the science of ageing, either as direct or indirect funders of research or as users of research. This paper sets out the involvement of each of these areas.

OFFICE OF SCIENCE AND TECHNOLOGY (OST)

Research Councils

1. The Office of Science and Technology funds research through the Research Councils who have established a Cross-council Co-ordination Committee on Ageing Research to facilitating greater interdisciplinary collaboration. The Research Councils and Research Council funded UK National Collaboration on Ageing Research (NCAR) are both submitting evidence to this enquiry and therefore not included in this report.

Foresight

2. As part of the drive to increase UK exploitation of science OST's Foresight programme provides challenging visions of the future, to ensure effective strategies now. It does this by providing a core of skills in science-based futures projects and unequalled access to leaders in government, business and science (see www.foresight.gov.uk for more details). The current round of Foresight—launched in April 2002—operates through a fluid, rolling programme that looks at three or four areas at any one time. Before 2002, Foresight operated through a number of Panels, covering business sectors or key issues such as the Ageing Population.

3. The Foresight Ageing Population Panel operated between 1999 and 2001. Its objectives were to:

— raise awareness across all Foresight sectors—business, government, education and training, voluntary organisations—about population ageing, the issues that it raises, and its potential impact on markets and economic and social structures over the next 20 to 30 years;

— assess the main social and economic effects, identify potential market opportunities and lay out the scope for technology to improve the quality of life for all in an ageing population;

— collaborate with other Foresight Panels and encourage them to take on board the implications of the Age Shift in their work;

— work with other government departments, and encourage them to take account of the issues raised by population ageing in developing policy, regulation and legislation;

— assess the roles of research, education, training and skills in this wide context.

4. These overall objectives do not focus significantly on science—this panel formed part of the wider Foresight programme at that time which looked at broader socioeconomic issues. Five task forces were also established, one of which examined applications of Information and Communication Technologies (ICT). Reports are available on the Foresight website (see above).

5. Although Panel's work as such ceased at on the publication of "The Age Shift—priorities for action" in December 2000, the work it started has been carried on by other organisations. For example, the Royal Society for the Encouragement of Arts, Manufactures & Commerce (RSA) used much of the Panel's work in promoting user-centred design in their Student Design Awards competition.

6. Three members of Ageing Population Panel Task Forces are now partners in Population Ageing Associates, an independent team of professionals with experience in all areas of the ageing field—from direct care to management, gerontology to policy, marketing to research. They bring a multidisciplinary perspective to the task of helping organisations seek, identify and implement effective and appropriate strategies for preparing for, and benefiting from the "Age Shift". See their website at http://www.populationageing.co.uk/index.htm

7. HM Treasury used the Foresight Healthcare and Ageing Population reports, and that of their joint task force as source documents in their study of the future costs of healthcare. This report, "Securing our Future Health: taking a long-term view" is now available at http://www.hm-treasury.gov.uk/wanless

8. On 6 March 2001 Lord Sainsbury, Minister for Science and Innovation, spoke for the Government in a House of Lords debate on the Government's response to the Ageing Population Panel's (see www.parliament.the-stationery-office.co.uk/pa/ld200001/ldhansrd/vo010306/text/10306-15.htm£10306-15—head0 for details).

EUROPEAN FRAMEWORK PROGRAMME

9. Research on ageing which has been highlighted by the European Commission as a priority area for funding through the EU Sixth Framework Programme (FP6) is identified as one of 16 sub-sections of Thematic Priority One—Life Sciences, Genomics and Biotechnology for Health.

10. Seven topics under the Ageing and Human Development sub-section were identified under the first two calls for proposals for Thematic Priority resulting in the award of €29.2 million to four projects. The work programme for the third call for proposals for Thematic Priority One, which closes in November 2004, identifies a further five topics in the Ageing and Human Development sub-section.

11. In addition to projects funded within the sub-section there are also a number of topics elsewhere in Thematic Priority One with relevance to research on ageing, many at the fundamental level but some of more direct relevance. For instance around €24.8 million has been awarded to three projects on neurodegenerative diseases such as Alzheimer's and Parkinson's disease; and a further €27 million has been awarded for three projects involving research on autoimmune diseases including arthritis.

12. Finally the Commission also supports research on ageing elsewhere in the Framework Programme. €2.4 million was recently awarded under the new ERA-NET scheme, which supports the co-ordination of national programmes. ERA-AGE the European Research Area in AGEing research, is led by the UK National Centre of Ageing Research (NCAR) and aims to co-ordinate the activities of national funders of research on ageing through a systematic process of mapping activity, identifying and sharing good practice, and defining common objectives and mechanisms.

LINK COLLABORATIVE RESEARCH

13. Government support for research partnerships between UK companies and universities/other research base organisations can be offered through the LINK Collaborative Research scheme. Research, which is pre-commercial or strategic, is funded by Research Councils and Government Departments at up to 50 per cent, with the balance of support being provided by the participating companies (see www.ost.gov.uk/link for more details). There are several LINK Collaborative Research programmes that are relevant to the ageing population these are:

LINK Integrated Approaches to Healthy Ageing

14. This MRC-led programme aimed to improve understanding of the psychological, physiological and social factors affecting good or ill health in old age. Also to develop new ways of supporting healthy ageing, independent living and the prevention, management and rehabilitation of disorders affecting the elderly. A total of 12 projects were funded. Most are studies of Alzheimer's and other neurodegenerative conditions. Other projects are focused on incontinence, cancer and infections. MRC funding of projects is some £3 million, which, as in all LINK projects, is at least matched by the participating companies. The programme was announced in 1995 and closed in 2000.

LINK Health Technology Devices

15. This Department of Health-led programme follows on from MedLINK (see below). It focuses on medical devices for tissue engineering and trauma care, new or improved technology for current medical devices, novel IT which enables a significant improvement in the performance of healthcare technologies, and social care devices. Ten projects are currently being supported. They include three aimed at the development of: a knee reciprocal walking orthosis; Raman endoscope for cancer detection; and a stair climber aid.

MedLINK

16. This Department of Health-led programme focused on support of research projects with potential to lead on to new and improved medical devices for diagnosis, prevention, monitoring and treatment of illness or injury. A total of 48 projects received Government support of £15 million. They included three aimed at: a small diameter vascular graft; improved product for incontinence; and a smart inactivity detector.

LINK MEDICAL IMPLANTS

17. This DTI-led programme, which was open for five years in the 1990s, was aimed at the use of novel materials in the provision of medical implants with increased lifetimes. Government funding of £5 million was made available for 19 projects which included three aimed at: improvements to prosthetic hip implants; a stent to relieve bladder flow obstruction; and a prototype mechanical heart valve.

LINK Applied Genomics

18. This DTI/ BBSRC/ MRC programme, which closed to bids this year, is aimed at accelerating the exploitation of genomic knowledge by UK companies, thus increasing their competitiveness in this key area, and enhancing healthcare delivery. Total Government funding of £21 million is currently supporting 17 projects, with the final few project grants to be awarded shortly. Current projects which focus on the applications of genomics and proteomics to medical problems and the development of underpinning technology include research which it is hoped will result in new therapeutics for Alzheimer's, cancer and wound healing.

Foresight LINK Award projects

19. A "New Urological Technologies" project, led by North Bristol NHS Trust, has the ultimate aim of producing a state-of-the-art urine collection system to assist patients suffering from intractable urinary incontinence. FLA funding £1.2 million.

20. A "Millennium Homes" project, led by Brunel University, and completed in 2003, was to research the use of computers and sensors in homes for elderly people with reduced abilities. The aim was to enable an increased number of them to live independently and safely in their own homes. FLA funding £0.4 million."

DTI TECHNOLOGY STRATEGY

21. DTI is currently implementing a Technology Strategy and Technology Programme to support research and development and the sharing of knowledge in technology areas critical to the growth of the UK economy. Future technology priorities will be identified by a Technology Strategy Board comprising mainly senior business leaders, The Technology Programme is being delivered through support for collaborative research and development and Knowledge Transfer Networks in these key priority areas.

22. Stem cell technology, which will underpin new therapy areas such as replacement of cells lost in neurodegenerative conditions, was one of the technology areas covered in the second call of the Technology Programme in April 2004. Proposals were invited for collaborative research and for a Knowledge Transfer Network in Stem Cell Technology to accelerate technology transfer and improve partnering opportunities in this area. The final awards will be announced in November 2004.

23. Technologies for healthcare are being considered for future support, recognising that ageing is a key driver in this area.

EMPLOYMENT RELATIONS

24. There have been three consultations so far exploring the way forward in implementing the age strand of the European Employment Directive. Towards Equality and Diversity in 2001 explored the issue of age discrimination in the workplace, and The Way Ahead subsequently considered some broad approaches to discrimination legislation. Age Matters in 2003 was devoted solely to proposals for age legislation, including the extent to which we should use the Directive's power to allow differences of treatment in certain limited circumstances.

25. Our intention has been to ensure individuals know what new rights they will have, employers and other covered by the legislation know about their new responsibilities, and we need to know what people think about our proposals. We are reviewing the responses we have to the Age Matters consultation and are on course to have legislation making age discrimination in employment and vocational training unlawful in place from October 2006.

26. In formulating its proposals associated with older workers and with age discrimination, we have used and continue to use official statistics, Department of Work and Pensions (DWP) research, specially commissioned DTI research, academic papers and papers produced by national and international organisations.

27. Official statistics from sources such as the Office for National Statistics, the Government Actuaries Department and the Small Business Service are used in developing the Department's understanding of the employment of older people, including retirement, and in particular in the preparation of the Regulatory Impact Assessments on forthcoming age discrimination legislation. Papers from academia and organisations such as the OECD, the European Commission and the Joseph Rowntree Foundation have also been used.

28. Furthermore, the DTI has made extensive use of research commissioned by other government departments. Research used from the DWP includes DWP Research Report 200—*Factors affecting the labour market participation of older workers* and DWP Research Report 182—*Working after State Pension Age: Quantitative Analysis.*

29. The DTI has equally made use of the Cabinet Office publication *Winning the Generation Game* and material from the last pre-budget report.

30. Where there has been a need to explore a particular issues surrounding older workers and age discrimination in depth the DTI has commissioned its own research, including *Retirement age in the UK: a review of the literature,* by Pamela Meadows, and *Age Matters: a review of existing survey evidence,* by Peter Unwin. The former summarises the literature on when and why people retire, and the effect of age on productivity. The latter outlines age-related findings from the main national surveys, set in the context of latest academic research, which cover age-related issues such as employment, training, recruitment, equal opportunities policies, pensions and retirement. This will be used as a baseline for evaluation purposes. Both have also been used extensively in preparing the Regulatory Impact Assessments referred to above, as well as in other papers developing policy on age discrimination.

DTI, Energy and the Ageing Population

UK Fuel Poverty Strategy of November 2001

31. The goal of the Government and the Devolved Administrations, set out in the UK Fuel Poverty Strategy of November 2001, is to seek an end to the problem of fuel poverty. In particular, England, Wales and Northern Ireland will seek an end to the blight of fuel poverty for vulnerable households by 2010, which includes those containing an elderly person. This goal is behind one of DTI's PSA targets to "eliminate fuel poverty in vulnerable households in England by 2010 in line with the Government's Fuel Poverty Strategy objective".

32. There is no specific research DTI has carried out to see how the ageing of the population will impact upon fuel poverty, but many of the fuel poverty alleviation schemes have a focus on the elderly. The main scheme for alleviating fuel poverty, Warm Front, which is administered by Defra, has grants of up to £2,500 available to householders who are over 60 and receive an income-related benefit. The grant provides insulation measures and, for those who do not have an existing heating system, a central heating system for the main living areas of the household. The health sector also plays a role in fuel poverty alleviation in that at the strategic level fuel poverty is incorporated into National Service Frameworks which set national standards to support implementation at the local level and establish performance measures.

33. In terms of analytical work underlying DTI's fuel poverty work, we carry out analysis of the English House Condition Survey conducted by ODPM in order to determine the number of households who are in fuel poverty. The most recent year for which data was available from the survey in 2001 and for that year we did present information by household composition (available at http://www.dti.gov.uk/energy/consumers/ fuel—poverty/england2001analysis.pdf). This showed that 7.6 per cent of pensioner couple households were in fuel poverty and 22.2 per cent of single pensioner households were in fuel poverty in England. This compares to 8.4 per cent of all households. We also publish a suite of statistical indicators on fuel poverty (available at http://www.dti.gov.uk/energy/consumers/fuel—poverty/monitoringindicators2004.pdf). Among the suite of fuel poverty indicators, there are a number of statistics relating to pensioners, but these are sourced from other Government departments.

The Cost of Energy

34. Since 1996, the introduction of competition in the domestic gas and electricity markets has provided customers, including pensioner households, with access to a range of lower-cost tariffs. It has also led to the introduction of a new range of tariffs some of them are specifically geared towards the needs of pensioner households.

35. DTI is concerned that, in a period where energy prices, which have been historically low, are rising, disadvantaged and potentially vulnerable customers should minimise their energy costs by accessing the best deals. We are, therefore, working with the industry regulator, OFGEM, and the statutory consumer body, Energywatch, to encourage poorer customers to access the competitive market and to make use of the lower-cost methods of paying bills (chiefly direct debit).

36. The Design and Demonstration Unit, a team of private sector secondees based in DTI and designing and delivering projects in support of Energy White Paper objectives, is developing a number of pathfinder projects, using existing and new technologies, to assist deprived households, including pensioner households, on a community basis.

September 2004

Examination of Witnesses

Witnesses: PROFESSOR SALLY DAVIES, Director of Research and Development, MS SUSAN LONSDALE, Acting Branch Head, Research and Development Policy Research Programme, and MR CRAIG MUIR, Director, Older People and Disability Division, Department of Health; and MR PAUL WILLIAMS, Director of the Research Councils Directorate, Office of Science and Technology; examined.

Q135 *Chairman:* May I say, welcome to the four on the panel and their significant supporting cast, and to members of the public. I think you know the basis of our inquiry, which is to produce a report, we hope, towards the early summer next year but that remains to be seen. I shall not go round the table introducing members of the Committee but names are in front of them and you too are labelled. I remind you that this is recorded and may well be broadcast, so if you mutter things into the microphone they will be heard by any who feel brave enough to listen when it is broadcast. Thank you very much for coming. You represent two Departments. We have just received this report, *Better Health in Old Age*, but literally just received it, and we will be interested to read it and perhaps get back, if necessary, to Professor Philp, who takes full responsibility for it, I would assume. As you know, we had a day seminar in September and unfortunately there was not anybody from the Department who was able to be there, but that meant that we had quite a good briefing and there were other departments represented who could help us in preparing for the discussion. We will go round the table with our questions. We have a number of questions that have come up, I suspect none of them will surprise you, but we will be very interested to hear what you have to say. Can I add that if at the end of the session you feel there are things on which you would like to elaborate, or if there are issues that have not properly been aired that you would like to comment on, please feel free to write fairly promptly or e-mail to the clerk of the Committee, Michael Collon. That being said, welcome again. It is much appreciated your taking time. Just to start and, in a sense, to give you the opportunity to introduce yourselves and your priorities, can I remind you of something you clearly know, that life expectancy is rising, and the figure we have in front of us is one year for each five years that pass, and we have all seen the demographic charts and the number of older people there will be in the community. I want to ask of each of the two Departments what impact is this having on what you are aiming to do and what you are actually doing, and in particular, granted the nature of our inquiry, the ways in which you will commission and use research from other groups round the country? Because that will be a significant focus of our report, what kind of research ought to be stimulated and perhaps encouraged, and we would be interested to hear your priorities and the kinds of use you would make of the research you see coming down the line? As you speak, please, would you introduce yourselves?

Professor Davies: As you know, I am the R&D Director at the Department of Health. I suppose I would like to start by saying that the reason we know that life expectancy is increasing is because of research that we have commissioned jointly with other government departments. Of equal interest, it is not only the increase in life expectancy but the increase in healthy life expectancy, which is not increasing at the same rate. One of our concerns from the Department of Health is the gender differences, which you will know about, and this increasing period of life where there will be ill-health and how we may improve healthcare and maintain health. In general, our research policy, or our research strategy, from the Department of Health, as you will have seen in the National Service Framework for Older People and the report you have in front of you today, builds on checking where we are with that, and the longer version has elements about research. We aim to have research underpinning our policies and our services so there is a sound basis to build on those, and they are around supporting independence of people, around improving their health and their healthcare, so we will be able to give you examples of research and research programmes that we have funded.

Perhaps it is also useful to say that I started only on September 1, so in preparing for this presentation to you I have had an opportunity, which I might not otherwise have had, to review our portfolio, and we have got a good story to tell across a broad range of areas. It is clear that our ministers have given priority to diseases that matter in old age, cancer, cardiovascular disease and diabetes, that we are increasing our work in those areas, but there is a significant amount of work funded by ourselves alone, in partnership and by our colleagues, the major research funders, around the more social care end and the social areas, that we can explore with you if that would be helpful.

Q136 Chairman: When you refer to your colleagues, the major research workers, is that a pretty broad band or is it a group who are formally attached to the Department?

Professor Davies: We fund two main programmes, the NHS R&D programme and our Policy Research Programme, but major funders, when I talk like that I include the research councils, from whom you have had a submission, and of course the charities, who play a big role. You will be aware, it was announced in the Budget speech, that we are bringing all of that together under the UK clinical research collaboration to try to increase co-ordination across clinical research generally. We define clinical research very broadly, so it is not just patients and beds, it is about public health, interventions to promote health and everything. One of our proposals, though we have yet to activate it, as I have only just started, is to bring the Cardiovascular Research Funders' Forum under the UKCRC as we are already bringing other research funders' fora under that, in order to increase collaboration and cross-agency research funding.

Q137 Chairman: Thank you. We will come back on this, I am sure, but would either of your colleagues like to take up the story, and introduce yourself at the same time?

Ms Lonsdale: I am Susan Lonsdale and I am the Acting Head of the Policy Research Programme. Apropos of your question about who does the research, we do not do very much research in house, although we do some economic analytical work, but we commission research very widely, often through competitive tender, which means we can actually draw on the entire science base across the land, as it were. In addition to that, we fund specific research units in the universities, so we have a very broad range of people that we get to do our research.

Mr Muir: I am Craig Muir. I am Deputy Director of Care Services in the Department of Health. I think my response to the question is that demography is absolutely fundamental to the whole of the

Department of Health's Strategy for Older People and for many of the individual initiatives within it. The Older People's Strategy focuses on promoting independence and choice, rooting out age discrimination, promoting dignity and respect and early access to joined-up services across health and social care and more widely. The sense behind that is to promote independence, to stop people losing their independence, to help people regain their independence, so that their healthy, active life can continue for longer. That is better for the individual but also it is a better way of making sure that people stay healthy for longer and need services later and less, and that is partly because of the evidence base, also it is because we know what older people want, from the evidence base. The National Service Framework for Older People is the expression of that overall Strategy for Older People. It was published in 2001 and it was the first ever set of standards and milestones and concrete proposals for older people across the whole of the health and social care system. It was based very closely on the evidence base, and each of the recommendations and proposals was cross-referenced to the evidence base, giving an indication of the strength of that evidence base as well. We have used a very broad range of research in developing the overall strategy and we will continue to commission research. I think, in a sense, my priority in the short term is commissioning evaluations of the specific initiatives that we have introduced, like intermediate care and work to reduce the number of delayed discharges and the sorts of proposals that are coming to fruition as a result of the National Service Framework.

Q138 Chairman: Do you want to comment, from the OST, at this point, and then maybe we will come back? What are the links like between the sorts of research for which, in the end, ultimately you are responsible and, say, the Department, which you are sitting alongside?

Mr Williams: I am Paul Williams. I am Director of the Research Councils Directorate in OST. Our role is slightly more distant. We have a responsibility given to us by the Treasury to ensure the overall health of the science and engineering base in the UK and to promote knowledge transfer from that base, both in terms of the commercial sector and its impact on policy use in the UK. Of course, we do not fund research directly, apart from a very small amount which is related directly to those particular aspects. Our role then is to allocate funding to research councils to set priorities within an iterative approach and having regard to the priorities of other funders in the number of mechanisms for co-ordinating that. In the case of MRC and the other Research Councils, we know that they have a very close relationship with the Department of Health, and that is the level at which the scientific priorities would be set. Then the Director General of the Medical Research Council, in conjunction with our ministers, will have to take a view on how much resource he wishes to allocate to each council. We are just entering the process of doing that for the period 2005–08, and we expect to have the outcome in about February.

Q139 *Lord Turnberg:* I want to follow up some of Professor Davies' responses. I have two specific questions. I think you said that we are expecting a longer period of ill-health prior to death because people are living longer. The evidence we have been getting suggests that is not quite the case, that actually people live longer, healthier lives and the time between getting ill and dying, that is, getting so ill that you cannot really survive without strong support, that period is not lengthening. That is one question. The other relates to your response to the question of what research is going on, and I know that this is a difficult area because there is an awful lot of research going on, in heart disease, cancer, and the like, and all of that will have an impact on the elderly. What we seem to be getting is that there is not a lot of effort being made in the research community towards the elderly and things that the R&D initiative should be doing for ageing people, as against for specific diseases. The elderly gain, of course, from all of that but is there some more focus that can be given, do you think, to this area?

Professor Davies: My Lord, clearly we can give you the source for the data that we have about increasing life expectancy and healthy life expectancy, but the data that I have been given in preparation for today does show that life expectancy is increasing faster than healthy life expectancy, therefore the gap is widening.

Q140 *Lord Turnberg:* Is that dependency; because there is a difference between being required to take medicaments to maintain a reasonable state of health and dependency?

Ms Lonsdale: The data that we have got is looking at healthy life expectancy which is simply disability-free life expectancy. I think there is quite a lot of data about in relation to healthy life expectancy, but the Office of National Statistics is monitoring healthy life expectancy based on, as I understand it, Census data and survey data. That is not ideal, because what one really wants to do is look at longitudinal data to be able to get a real sense of healthy life expectancy. The most recent figures, in July, showed that, for instance, for men, life expectancy was 75.7 and healthy life expectancy was 67, and the gap for women, in fact, was slightly greater. The picture that we think we are getting is that everybody is going to live longer, men

are going to be less healthy and women in particular are going to have lives of more disability. I think also that picture probably can change quite rapidly, depending on what happens in medical science, and of course that may change.

Professor Davies: We are also funding currently the English longitudinal study of over 11,000 older people, tracking changes in their health over a period of time; it is cross-government and national institutes of health and the state's funding. If I go then to the second part of my Lord's question, it is quite difficult to get a handle on specifically what is spent on ageing. If you think first of our NHS funding going to Trusts, £467 million, there are in there 99 programmes highlighted specifically as working in ageing. Six overall programmes costing £39.4 million are in ageing and they cover things from basic science to nutritional additives, mastication, protection of hip joints, so issues going from the very biomedical right through to supporting people in healthier life. Meanwhile, 22 per cent of the studies funded by our Health Technology Assessment programme are in ageing. Examples are the EVAR study, which is a study of prosthesis as opposed to open aneurism repair, studies about different ways of treating pressure sores, studies about different ways of treating leg ulcers. There are significant tranches of work. Neurological deficit has been highlighted as an issue for older people. We spend now over £1 million a year from the Policy Research Programme on stroke, with the Stroke Registry. We will have a stroke network looking at that. We have trebled our spending on dementia, it is reaching a quarter of a million pounds a year, but that is from a very low start. We have other programmes, such as a cross-departmental programme of £1.75 million about living arrangements for older people. We have a Policy Research Unit in personal social services. It is quite difficult to get an absolute handle on exactly how much we are spending, but, as I said in my first statement, on reviewing the portfolio there is a lot aimed specifically at the elderly and ageing as well as a lot of other work in diseases that are more prevalent. A large grant has been given to local councils for digital hearing-aids; we are evaluating the roll-out of that. Several other areas where we are evaluating services for older people as well are coming in.

Q141 *Lord Oxburgh:* Professor Davies, you have described a great deal of expenditure, a great many activities. I have to say, the impression we get from reading an awful lot of the submissions that we have is of a great deal of work going on, but a great deal of isolated pockets here and there, an enormous amount of activity. I wonder if there is any group, a senior, experienced group, probably within your

Department, that actually sits down and reviews the national scene, reviews what you are doing internally, reviews what the various charities are doing, looking at what the research councils are doing and which says, "Look, we've really got to cover this spectrum, and here there are gaps where things ought to be going on," and effectively takes a strategic view? Clearly, you cannot direct the charities to do something, you cannot direct the research councils to do things, but, in a sense, when it comes to something like this, you are the funder and strategist of last resort and you are the people, if it is upstream research, who probably have to talk to people in OST about this. Does such a body exist, does it look at all that you are doing and confirm that you are spending the money the right way, and that indeed there are not higher priority gaps which ought to be covered?
Professor Davies: There are a number of bodies in the Department for the National Sercice Framework and its implementation, and now the long-term conditions of NSF, which we hope to publish next spring. We have done that about our own work, and the research that is out there and the needs, and the research councils work across with each other. I think the body that you are talking about is the funders' fora. Through the UKCRC, we are taking the opportunity to try to make all of the funders' fora— and this is no exception, the one for ageing—make more effective the model that has worked, which I am sure, my Lord, you are aware of, the National Cancer Research Institute. That really has shown that, by bringing together the charities, the research councils, the Department of Health and everyone, they can map what the gaps are and be strategic. I think we could do more in this field, and by bringing the funders' fora under the UKCRC I am signalling that I propose to do more in this field.

Q142 *Lord Soulsby of Swaffham Prior:* Part of my question has been asked already by Lord Oxburgh, but I was going to ask how do you rank British research into ageing in general internationally? The science citation international indices are one of the measures of these. How do we rank with other major nations, like the USA and Germany and France, etc?
Professor Davies: My Lord Soulsby, I would be telling a lie if I said I knew. I would have to go back and check it and we would be bedevilled by the problem that I have in presenting the full range of what we do, how do we decide what falls into this area and what does not? However, I would say that the work that is funded is of high quality, both by the research councils and by us, so the issue is not of quality. I think we manage from ourselves a fair degree of focus on areas that are not biomedical, leaving that for the research councils, but there is a fair question, which I think my Lord Oxburgh was getting at and you are

hinting at, are we covering the spectrum effectively enough? Until we make the funders' fora work really effectively and map it, it will not be something that I can truly answer.

Q143 *Chairman:* Is there a specific funders' forum on the issue of ageing and a separate one on cancer, and so on, is that what you are implying?
Professor Davies: There is. The one on cancer has been a great success. The one on cardiovascular disease is really beginning to work. We have work to do on the one on ageing.

Q144 *Chairman:* It has been in existence but it is going to increase its pace of activity, is it?
Professor Davies: I am expecting to put in some effort.

Q145 *Lord Turnberg:* It has only just formed, the ageing one, has it not?
Ms Lonsdale: No. It was formed probably three years ago now.
Lord Turnberg: It has been very quiescent.

Q146 *Lord Oxburgh:* Who organises it, convenes it and sees that it continues to exist?
Ms Lonsdale: The secretariat for it is the Medical Research Council, and up until Professor Davies took on her role it was chaired by Professor Sir John Pattison, the previous Director of Research and Development. I think it is a more complicated funders' forum than some of the others because it covers a very wide spectrum of research. We have membership from the BBSRC, the basic biological side of research, all the way through to some fairly small charitable organisations which fund research but are concerned with a very different kind of research.

Q147 *Lord Soulsby of Swaffham Prior:* Research into the scientific aspects of ageing is relatively new and even professionals within the medical, biological and social sciences, at least we have found, have only limited awareness of the current knowledge and often it is not co-ordinated. What is the department doing to keep itself informed of this research and to disseminate the relevant knowledge to its staff and agencies and indeed to co-ordinate it?
Professor Davies: We have a variety of mechanisms for scanning what is going on and harnessing and reviewing the evidence, and the last time we undertook a major exercise was for the National Service Framework. It is updated, and as new policies are developed we have to look at whether they have the research basis for it. If they do, we have to supply it, if they do not, we have to commission it and then we have to evaluate the policies as they roll out. We have to commission new research if it is lacking,

where it is needed, or persuade others to. Of course, the czar, the National Clinical Director in this field can play a major role because of their specialist links into the research base. Again, it could be a role which could be played out more effectively by the funders' forum, if we can rejuvenate and re-energise it, but there are a number of ways, through the Cochrane collaboration library, the Campbell collaboration, and everything, where evidence is collected together and disseminated.

Q148 Lord Soulsby of Swaffham Prior: I presume that, as with any other research, there is not sufficient funding to cover all that you would want to do. If that is so, do you have a notional age period when this research starts to drop off, in terms of being undertaken? We have heard a figure of 75, where after 75 it might not be as urgent to do research as before 75. Would you agree with that?

Professor Davies: My Lord, I could not agree to that, as I get older and older.

Q149 Chairman: I think we are on common ground here.

Professor Davies: Moreover, we have a policy around non-ageism, if you see what I mean, and diversity relating to ethnicity and gender. In fact, it is a concern of ours that trials should be open to people of all ages, and we have examples where specifically we have reviewed and evaluated services in older people, for instance, breast cancer screening and the take-up by decade, so we have gone from 75 upwards. Clearly, my personal belief, and I know that this is a departmental value, is very anti-ageing, in every sense, as a matter of fact.

Ms Lonsdale: We have a very strong research governance framework as well, in which discriminating against people on the basis of age and race, and so on, is very strongly proscribed. I think if we had a research proposal come in which had an age limit we would look at that to see whether there was a reasonable reason for having an age limit, but we would not wish to encourage that unless there was a very good scientific reason for it.

Q150 Chairman: Does that apply to drug trials, clinical trials?

Professor Davies: That is exactly the point I was making earlier, that we believe they should be open to all ages. There is an issue about medicines in children, which is separate from today's discussion.

Ms Lonsdale: I was referring to the research that we commission and fund.

Q151 Lord Oxburgh: If one follows this a little, is there a comparably developed geriatric medical community, if you like, the mirror image of the paediatric medical fraternity at the other end of the life span? Is that community as well developed, and, if it is not, ought it to be?

Professor Davies: My Lord, that is a very interesting question. My reflection, unprepared, is that actually paediatric research is in dire straights in this country, more so than geriatric research. That is not to say that we do not need to do more work in geriatrics. What you are raising is a very interesting issue that we have not yet picked up in a programmatic way, which is that as we get older we handle drugs differently, which is the mirror image of handling drugs differently in children and polypharmacy. On the other hand, we have funded projects about polypharmacy, so I think we have a better story in geriatrics than child health.

Q152 Baroness Murphy: I think I would be right, from your response, Professor Davies, and Mr Muir's particularly, remembering your response to Lord Sutherland's first question, that the Department of Health's express formulated goals for age-related disability and disease is the National Service Framework?

Professor Davies: Yes.

Mr Muir: Yes. Certainly that is the key one, if I may, and that was published in 2001 and it covered health and social care. It did cover both health and social care but there was a major announcement in 2002 by the then Secretary of State, Alan Milburn, in the context of the Spending Review 2002, which set out new Public Service Agreements for older people, focusing specifically on an attempt to shift away from residential care towards intensive home care for people who needed intensive support. It added in also specific targets for rapid access to assessment and to services following assessment and that was associated with announcements about funding as well, which I can talk about if it would be helpful.

Q153 Baroness Murphy: I would be interested in talking about the funding relative to, for example, the explicit goals set for the NSF in cancer and cardiac services, both the funding and also whether or not there were explicit targets set for local NHS bodies to achieve, in the same way there were for other National Service Frameworks?

Mr Muir: There has been an evolution in terms of the National Service Frameworks over time and, in a sense, the older people's NSF was in the middle of that development. Certainly there is a series of specific milestones, like the introduction of integrated stroke services, numbers of people treated for intermediate care, integrated falls services, protocols for dementia, there is a range of things, rooting out age discrimination, which we were talking about in a slightly different context a moment ago. There is a whole range of specific milestones there. As I added in specifically the Public Service Agreements, there are very specific targets for shifting the balance towards intensive home care rather than residential care, very, very challenging targets for speed of access to assessment, with, I think it is, 40 per cent to be assessed within two weeks of first contact and 100 per cent within six weeks. That is a dramatic change from the existing performance, in terms of assessment, and there are similar targets for treatment.

Q154 Baroness Murphy: Could I just follow up on that. As you are monitoring that, does that indicate that has been a success?

Mr Muir: The PSA targets are not yet complete. In terms of the National Service Framework targets, the document that you mentioned at the beginning, Professor Philp's report on *Better Health in Old Age* is a round-up of progress since the National Service Framework was introduced, and it does show a very strong improvement in a whole range of things. Also it shows areas where there is still a little way further to go, but the overall picture is one of dramatic increases, for example, the number of integrated stroke units increased from 45 per cent to 90 per cent. There is a whole range. The number of people receiving intermediate treatment increased to 330,000 from just over 100,000, I think, over the period, so a quite substantial improvement. Of course, in terms of the NHS, there was an unprecedented five-year settlement of over seven per cent real terms' increases for the NHS as a whole, and since, for example, older people take up 66 per cent of acute sector services, they are the principal beneficiaries of that. The 2002 Spending Review announcement that I mentioned announced six per cent per year average increases in real terms for older people's services over three years, with at the end of the period an extra £1 billion a year being spent on older people's services.

Q155 Baroness Murphy: Just a final one, in connection with that. Were older people themselves involved in formulating the National Service Framework?

Mr Muir: Absolutely. It was a very fundamental part of the arrangements, older people and also stakeholder groups. I think the Department of Health was one of the first departments to adopt an approach to policy development which involved all stakeholders at a very early stage, at the very earliest stage, and the National Service Framework was developed by Professor Ian Philp. There was a group of stakeholders, including Help the Aged, Age Concern and the British Geriatrics Society, a whole range of health and social care professionals, the Stroke Association, a whole range of professionals. That group, which developed the National Service Framework, was chaired jointly by a colleague of mine from the Department of Health and Professor Philp, who went on to become the National Director for Older People's Services, but then was a Professor of Geriatrics in Sheffield. There was an Older People's Reference Group which worked in parallel with the working group for the National Service Framework. I was not around at that time but I am told the input of the Older People's Reference Group was very significant in framing the overall themes and aims of the National Service Framework, in particular the very strong aim to root out age discrimination across health and social care, which we talked about in a different context earlier on. Also the focus on respecting the dignity of older people, because that is right in itself but also because it empowers older people, and if you listen and respect older people you are much more likely to get right the support that they need.

Q156 Baroness Walmsley: In the Department's view, is there sufficient capacity within the Health Service to address the needs of an ageing population, and what steps are you taking to make provision for future needs in this direction? Also, could I ask about your own headquarters. I understand there is no one individual or group with responsibility for this issue. Is that a deliberate decision or simply do you not have the capacity or the relevant expertise?

Professor Davies: Let me dissect this out so we address it effectively for you, my Lord. The first would be about capacity in the Service, and clearly we fund quite a lot of research to review capacity in the Service. Michael Goldacre's work about medical careers. King's College about nursing careers. Two million pounds of research at the moment being commissioned collecting basic information on the social care workforce, about three-quarters of a million people, of whom three-quarters are not in the health and social care sector, they are in the independent and private voluntary sector, many of them care assistants and not professionally qualified. We do research to look at the workforce, and I will ask my colleague to address the workforce and the policy issues from the centre.

Mr Muir: By all means. I am struggling just slightly with the end of the question, in a way, that we have not got an individual responsible for this. I am not quite sure what 'this' was?

Q157 Baroness Walmsley: I am referring really to your response to our invitation to the seminar, when you said that you would not be sending anyone because "there is no one single person or group within the Department of Health with responsibility for this, and the other option of sending a delegation does not seem right." That is what stimulated the question.

Professor Davies: May I pick this up. It would have been most appropriate had I personally gone to this, and I apologise that I did not come. It was not brought to my attention because we were changing Director. Because this is the Science and Technology Committee, it would naturally fall to me, recruiting whoever was needed. I think there was a misunderstanding, for which again I apologise, about quite the role of that seminar and whether it was R&D or whether it spread across R&D and policy, and hence that response. We are quite clear about which are our bits and how we work together and we believe that we work very effectively together.

Q158 *Baroness Walmsley:* Maybe you can go back to the capacity. Do you want to say more about that?

Mr Muir: In part, obviously, it follows on from the discussion on resources, to some extent, and making sure that older people's services get their fair share of resources across the board in health and social care. We have set challenging targets, both in the NHS Plan and in the National Service Framework for Older People and the Public Service Agreement, particularly in relation to social care. The challenges are very great indeed that we face in meeting those targets, and part of that will be through getting enough good, well-trained staff, and clearly there is an issue about capacity, given the demographic change. It is partly about resources, it is partly about the workforce itself, it is partly also about prevention, about taking action to reduce the need for intensive services, it is about giving people the right care in the right place at the right time. It has been demonstrated by the effort to reduce delayed discharges and to ensure that people are treated in the right place, which generally is at home, wherever possible, and therefore not taking up more expensive resources, and less effective resources, in hospitals. Partly it is about exploring alternatives, in a way supporting dependency, or, alternatively, promoting independence, and there is a whole range of things, like promoting expert patient programmes, which is part of the Department's approach to improving self care by individuals, and also the use of technologies. In terms of the workforce itself, there is an awful lot of activity going on, of course, across the NHS in general. The numbers of nurses and doctors are going up, but if we think of the number of 'old age' psychiatrists they have increased by nearly 70 per cent over the last few years. We have got lots of work going on in dealing with long-term conditions, which affect everybody but particularly older people, and the pilots of introducing community matrons, to make sure that high-risk people are identified early

and given targeted support so that they get the right support, at home generally rather than having emergency admissions to hospital. Social care staff has been increasing, there has been a four per cent increase in council field-work staff, and we have been running from the Department major recruitment campaigns for professionally-qualified social workers but also for social care staff. We have been developing with TOPSS, the Training Organisation for Personal Social Services, for example, new types of worker with different skill mixes, and we have given £6 million worth of support from the Department of Health for that. So a whole range of things going on specifically on the workforce front. In terms of technology and assistive technology, there are a lot of things which councils and the NHS have been doing, as part of their existing proposals, to develop assistive technology in telecare, telemedicine, which ranges from having voices to remind people to shut the door, if they are developing dementia, for example, and they tend to leave the door open, to light switches which come on automatically in the middle of the night, if somebody gets up, to prevent falls, sensors to detect when the fridge door has not been opened for a few days, to alert people that there is absence of movement in the house, all those sorts of things, to reduce the demand for services. Again, as part of the Spending Review this year, the Chancellor announced £80 million more over two years for assistive technology, to promote the use of this assistive technology to promote independence but also to reduce reliance on heavy-end services. The NHS Direct Helpline is both an instance of new technology and a way of supporting independence and reducing reliance on formal services, doctors and nurses or face-to-face services, and self-care advice has been provided to more than 30 per cent of patients. There is a new pharmacy contract to support self care, for example, as well. There is a whole range of things we are doing to increase the number and flexibility and effectiveness of the workforce, to provide the resources necessary to introduce alternatives to support independence rather than dependence, and to work differently in the future.

Q159 *Baroness Walmsley:* If I may, my Lord Chairman, I have just two follow-up questions there. One is, you talked a lot about reducing the need for the capacity about which we are talking; how do you anticipate that being a success? To what extent do you anticipate that being successful in stemming the tide of the need for greater capacity?

Mr Muir: I do not think it will reduce the need; it will stop the need going up as quickly as otherwise it might have done. There is some evidence that we have been successful in some of the things that we have done already to suggest that it is not just a pipe dream. For example, the work that we have done on delayed discharges has reduced the number of delayed discharges by 60 per cent since September 2001, and that saved about a million hospital bed days, and that equals eight general hospitals. There is evidence that some of the things we have done already have increased the overall capacity by reducing demand in parts of the system. Wanting to be helpful, I wanted to say also that, in terms of the discussions over resources in the Spending Review, we do take account of the epidemiology, and the predictions for spending take account of increasingly older people and the statistical link with increasing morbidity.

Q160 *Baroness Walmsley:* The other little question was that you talked about three-quarters of the workforce not being part of public service at all but being within the private sector, and an awful lot of them are relatively low-skilled people who get their skills improved through the further education sector, which is often described as the Cinderella of the education sector. I wonder if you could say anything about how you are encouraging those people to upskill and how you are helping to forge links with the further education sector so that training is delivered effectively to the right people?

Mr Muir: Essentially, on this, we work largely through TOPSS, the Training Organisation for Personal Social Services in England, and also through strategic health authorities, who have responsibility for the local workforce development across health and social care. There are also things like the National Minimum Standards that require a certain percentage of staff to have National Vocational Qualifications, which applies across the board, whether services are provided in the private sector or the independent sector, the voluntary sector or provided directly by councils. DoH Workforce Development Grants, which are fed through to councils but with the intention that they should be spent across the whole of the social care workforce, by next year will be three times higher than they were in 2002 and 2003. There has been a lot going on in that field.

Q161 *Lord Mitchell:* I suspect that much of my question has been answered, but we will have a bash, and let me just go through it and perhaps a couple of points need to be highlighted. Age is used sometimes within the Health Service as a criterion for determining access to treatment. What is your position on this? I think you have discussed this but you may want to make just a few more points on it. Is the practice monitored by the Department, and you have referred to that as well? Finally, is evidence

required in cases where such criteria are applied, and we have not addressed that?

Mr Muir: On service issues, certainly I am very happy to deal with that. As I said before, the National Service Framework has got a very strong commitment to rooting out age discrimination throughout the health and social care system. One of the specific targets in the National Service Framework was for strategic health authorities to review all their written policies to identify any which had an age-based part to them. To be fair to the NHS and social care, there were relatively few of those, and it was clear that where there were any of those left they had to be justified objectively. As I say, there were very few to start with and many of those that were found were simply dropped and any that were remaining had to have an objective justification. At a very early stage the National Service Framework target to address written policies which were age-discriminatory was addressed. There is a much bigger question about unwritten policies and a culture of age discrimination, which I think the National Director for Older People's Services and the National Service Framework accept is fairly widespread in society, and that is reflected in health and social care. The National Service Framework recommends also that local health and social care systems monitor treatments for major illnesses by age group, for those of 65 and over, 75 and over, 85 and over. The Department itself has done quite a lot of work to support the work by local health systems, for example, by producing a benchmarking tool which enables you to compare quickly and easily your performances in a local health system in giving access to particular kinds of treatments with other health systems which are comparable, to see whether you are in line with them or higher or lower than them, to allow you to ask questions. It is not necessarily the case that if you are out of line you are wrong, but it allows you to ask some difficult questions. We commissioned the King's Fund Centre to do some work on producing toolkits for local councils and NHS bodies to audit themselves, an audit tool, in terms of age discrimination, and with the King's Fund Centre organised regional conferences and networks in order to promote good practice in the field. I think it is probably true to say that things are getting better. I think population-based activities and screening are probably the area where you are most likely to be able to find a theoretical justification for some age-based cut-off point. Even in that area breast screening, for example, now includes women over 65, which previously it had not done, so even in that one area where you can see that there might be different cost-benefit analysis that has changed. Older people more generally, I think, are the beneficiaries of the huge investment in the NHS, with, for example, coronary artery bypass grafts increasing for over-65 year olds by 16 per cent over the last two or three years, 75 and over by 32 per cent, and 85 and over by 65 per cent, when overall for coronary artery bypass grafts for other age groups they have been steady, not increasing at all. There is a very strong push in the National Service Framework to root out age discrimination, a lot of activity to try to address it, some success, but I suspect still quite a long way to go to overcome age discrimination which is unwritten.

Q162 *Baroness Finlay of Llandaff:* You have told us a lot about what is being done and what is being rolled out, and in both acute and chronic conditions people who are older, sadly, still wait longer and there is a morbidity associated with that wait. We were wondering whether the cost of this wait has been assessed by the Department and balanced against the benefits for earlier intervention, and particularly whether there has been a health economics model in the Health Service's research arena to look at the cost of this inherent delayed ageism to which Mr Muir has been referring?

Professor Davies: We are not aware of an economic analysis, but I would say not only has significant money been going in, aimed particularly at the older age group, but of course the targets that have been biting in the NHS benefit everyone, so that by the new year more than 90 per cent of people attending A&Es will be seen within four hours, no operations will wait longer than nine months and that is moving to a six-month target. Then by 2008 we have got a target, and if we keep hitting them, as we are doing, then this is a realistic one, of 18 weeks from presentation to starting treatment. While these are targets aimed at our whole population, they have their same impact in the elderly, and perhaps even better in the elderly, if they were the ones which had been left longer then they have to come within the targets, so there may be a disproportionate benefit for the elderly. Perhaps I could make a personal reflection. As I look back over my medical career, I think there was significant ageism when I was a medical student and a young doctor, not intentionally, just that was the way society was. Whereas when I go and do my regular clinics in my hospital I feel that life has changed in the NHS and I do think that we have made progress not only policy-wise and on targets but there is a different feel about it.

Mr Muir: I am not sure I want to add a great deal to what Professor Davies has said, but reflecting on four-hour waits in A&E it still sounds like quite a long time. We were talking about international comparisons earlier on, that actually now is the best in the world, routinely to treat people within four hours, and it is the Secretary of State's ambition to

work so that waiting times and waiting lists no longer become an issue in the NHS, so that people simply do not talk about it any more so that it is not an issue for anyone. There is still a long way to go but progress so far has been pretty good and, as Professor Davies said, older people, being the major users of the Health Service, will be the biggest beneficiaries of that change.

Q163 *Baroness Finlay of Llandaff:* I think behind this perhaps is the thought that, if you have a health economics model, that can be incredibly powerful evidence to bring about change. There was some very good work on hospital mattresses some years ago, showing just how awful hospital bed mattresses were and the cost of pressure sores from them. Actually the change to prevent those pressure sores has been really cost-effective, and it was to ask whether there is that philosophy behind it of actually looking at the benefit the whole time of what might appear at first sight, to commissioners particularly, to be an expensive option but is not?

Professor Davies: I think I would say that would be one way of doing it, but because there is such a thrust to targets we are using a different lever, but it is a very helpful lever.

Mr Muir: In other fields we use very much economic analysis, on the balance of care model, for example, and we used a lot of economic modelling and operational research techniques in developing reimbursement proposals to address delayed discharges.

Lord Turnberg: It sounds like there is an awful lot of good work going on, and all to the good, of course, but I wonder if I can provoke you a bit, because not everything is fantastic. There are an awful lot of gaps. I wonder if I can ask you to talk to us—anyone— about the gaps that you see, that you need to plug, in which more work is needed? Because we are getting a lot of information from other groups which point to the problems. You are pointing to the solutions you have put in place, fantastic, but where do you see you need to put in more effort?

Q164 *Chairman:* Has anyone seen a gap recently?

Professor Davies: From the research perspective, I think that we could, and ideally should, be doing more on the social care side, the assistive technologies, healthy life, out there. It may well be we need more on the basic science of ageing. I will leave that for the MRC to debate with you. From our perspective, were we to have the money, we could and should do more about health services research, better healthcare for the elderly, things like mattresses, ulcers, issues that matter to the elderly. We did a big project on laxatives; very important. This whole area of social care, independence, assistive technology, from the research perspective, is not as well-funded as I feel would benefit, but again there would be a capacity issue. It is one thing signalling an area as needing research, it is another not only finding the funds to do that, because there is always competition for prioritisation, but developing the workforce to address these areas, which would take time as well.

Mr Muir: Can I add that I think the direction of travel of the Department of Health policy, and indeed Government policy as a whole, is quite clear, towards promoting independence. The Local Government Association and the Association of Directors of Social Services talk about a triangle of care, with the most dependent people at the top and the general population at the bottom and needing different kinds of approaches with, at the top, intensive interventions, at the bottom, community-based systems with a continuing upwards and downwards triangle of care. They want to see the triangle of care inverted so that most effort goes into the people who at the moment are fit and healthy, and we want to keep them that way, the direction of Government policy is in that direction. Much more needs to be done before we get there and, as ever, with preventive approaches, it is very difficult to put the money up front to get a benefit in a number of years' time. I think the research evidence, in relation to the middle band, shows that investing in people who are potentially about to tip over into a higher level of dependency or to need hospital care, an investment at that level, can produce clear cost benefits, and the research shows that quite well. There is much less evidence about primary prevention. It is not that the evidence is not there, it is that there is not a lot of evidence of that, and it would be good to see more evidence to give the economic arguments for people to make that investment up front, but we are working on that as well. As I say, the general direction of policy is clearly in that direction. Another of the Spending Review announcements was for demonstration prevention pilots in this middle band to demonstrate what the research evidence shows, which is that you can invest in preventing people spilling over into a higher level of dependency and keeping more independence, and that is both better for the individual and saves more expensive resources in hospitals and elsewhere.

Q165 *Baroness Finlay of Llandaff:* Very quickly, looking at service delivery, I wonder if there is any research looking at the economics of running things like outpatient clinics in a completely different way, in the evenings or at the weekends, so that other family members who are working can bring people, because elderly people find the mornings particularly difficult to get to places?

Ms Lonsdale: We have got a fair amount of research which is looking at service delivery. Whenever we have a new policy, like booked admissions or new treatment centres, we evaluate these to see how they are working, so there is a certain amount of research being done. I think there is a much bigger problem, which actually is partly a response to the question about what gaps there are. That kind of research, and we have commissioned it and we have commissioned research looking at re-engineering of hospitals and reorganising hospitals as well, is very difficult to do. I think one of the gaps we have got is actually a methodological gap, because what we are trying to do is look at complex, if one wants to call them complex, interventions and try to isolate what aspects are the things which are having the effect, or having the good or the bad outcome, which is key. That is very difficult and it is an issue of science and methodology, I think.

Q166 *Baroness Hilton of Eggardon:* If I can pick up the theme of cost-benefit and preventive measures, and so on, some of those lie within other departments of Government, and I am thinking about things like decent housing, fuel poverty, as well as nutrition and exercise, and so on. I wonder how influential you feel you are, in respect of other departments, in persuading them that there will be certainly economic benefits in some preventive measures? Some of them will be expensive, like having decently-insulated houses and ensuring that people have enough heating to heat themselves, but obviously, from a cost-benefit point of view and preventing health problems further down the line, very important.

Professor Davies: As you must know, the Department of Work and Pensions champions the older people's issues across Government. They have a formal Cabinet Sub-Committee on Older People, which they established in 2001, and a senior-level Older People's Strategy Development Group, which they set up earlier this year, so, through colleagues, we have an input into that. We have an input also, through our Policy Research Programme, across other government departments about public health, and actually a lot of what you are talking about I would not label up as geriatrics or elderly but I would talk about public health. We do co-fund with other departments work in the public health field, and there will be new tranches of work funded following the publication of the White Paper.

Chairman: We have not covered a lot of ground with the OST. I apologise for that. I should say also that we have got two sessions coming up later with research councils and other major research funding bodies and, if possible, it might be very good if someone from the OST came to at least one of those sessions. As you see, your colleagues in the

Department of Health have preoccupied us, for obvious and good reasons, with the interesting evidence that they had to give. I think we ought to stop now because we have another group waiting outside, and I do not want to keep them too long, from another government department. I thank you all very much and I do urge you to consider what ground we have covered and whether supplementary comment and evidence from, clearly, your very ample briefs might be of use to us. Thank you very much indeed.

Examination of Witnesses

Witnesses: Ms ANN FRYE, Head of the Mobility and Inclusion Unit, Ms YVONNE BROWN, Research Manager, Mobility Advice and Vehicle Information Service, and Ms JAN BROCK, Head of the Drivers' Policy Group, Driver and Vehicle Licensing Agency (DVLA), Department for Transport, examined.

Q167 *Chairman:* May I welcome you to the Committee table. Thank you very much for giving time, some of which clearly you have given already, but we hope to make the most of the time available to us. You have heard the Committee in action. We welcome your input, in prospect and in written form, and as you answer the questions initially perhaps you might introduce yourselves and say what your particular role is in the Department. Can I start with a fairly general question, of the sort that I put to your colleagues from the Department of Health. Granted the way in which life expectancy is changing and the speed at which that is happening, how is that, or is it, affecting the priorities set by your own Department, both for policy in practice but also for the kind of research which you either commission or are looking for and the way in which that research feeds into your own policy-making?

Ms Frye: I am Ann Frye, Head of the Mobility and Inclusion Unit at the Department, which is responsible for policy and service delivery across a wide range of social policy transport issues, including older people. The Department for Transport regards the ageing of the population as an enormously important priority. The White Paper that we published just a few months back recognised the impact of the demographic changes and the need for that to be reflected in the way that transport policy is developing. Perhaps I could run through a range of the issues that we are addressing. One of the key factors from a mobility point of view is that there is a very clear correlation between age and disability; two-thirds of disabled people are over pensionable age. One of our main planks of policy and delivery at the moment is implementing the transport provisions of the Disability Discrimination Act, which progressively are requiring not just wheelchair access to buses and trains but also things like colour contrast, non-slip surfaces, better hand-holds, bell-pushes you can ring before you get to your feet and lose your balance, very simple, practical things, which are being rolled out now across the transport industry and have a huge impact on the ability of older people to travel. We have addressed also the issue of cost and there is now a national minimum half-fare concession across England, for concessionary fares, and indeed more generous schemes in Scotland, Wales and Northern Ireland. We are looking also at the role of voluntary and community transport, because many older people, particularly outside the cities, are very dependent on voluntary transport, which may be something as unco-ordinated, if you like, as a volunteer car scheme involving neighbours, it may be a much bigger scheme. We have looked at the way in which legislation in the past has constrained the way that those services develop and we have tackled some of that. We are looking at the way that those services are funded and delivered. We have looked in particular at the role of voluntary and community transport in getting older people to healthcare, which has been one of the huge issues because of the withdrawal of non-emergency ambulance transport, in many cases. One of the keys there has been to work with the Ambulance Service and with the clinicians to try to make better sense of the way that appointments are given, so that somebody in their eighties who lives 50 miles from the hospital is not given an appointment at nine o'clock in the morning, if the only way they can get there is being got up at five and driven by a volunteer, so trying to get transport into part of the healthcare equation, if you like. We are looking in a public transport sense very much at information. We are very much aware that information at the moment is not very good on a lot of public transport. It is fine if you are an experienced public transport user; if you are not, it is quite difficult. One of the things we have found from the research we have done, talking to older people about their transport needs, is that those who have never been drivers are much more mobile in old age than those who have been drivers all their lives, and the reasons are fairly obvious. What we need to do is look at the way that transport information is delivered so that the ageing baby-boomers, and I am certainly one of them, can be persuaded out of our cars and to understand how to get onto the bus network, or whatever it might be. That is a very big issue and we have got schemes, like

Transport Direct and 'traveline', which are now rolling out those kinds of systems. We are also looking at the way that public transport is planned and delivered and we are just implementing accessibility planning, which is part of the local transport planning process. That will require local authorities to do a very thorough audit of the nature of their population and to analyse where there are people without access to public transport, what is the age profile, what are the needs, and to bring forward a very comprehensive plan on how they are going to deliver those needs. We will then be both funding them on the basis of what they tell us but also monitoring how effective that is. That was one of the big recommendations that came from a recent Social Exclusion Unit report on transport, and we are following that through with a lot of other departments who also have a part to play, Health, and so on. Land use planning also is crucial and we have got the legacy of generations where hospitals and shopping centres were built out of town, and again those without access to private cars often find it very difficult to get about. Working with colleagues in the Office of the Deputy Prime Minister, we are looking at what we can do to improve land use planning, which obviously is not a quick fix, but at least if you can stop making the same mistakes you have got some issues there. We are looking at personal security, because again our research shows that older people are disproportionately very much frightened when they use public transport, both waiting at bus stops and travelling on buses and trains, so we have got a whole programme working with transport providers, trying to improve both the actual and perceived levels of safety on the transport system. Also, of course, we are looking very much at drivers, and we are very keen that older people stay driving as long as they possibly can. We have set up and are funding a network of mobility centres around the country, who offer advice and assessment to disabled drivers and to older drivers. We have got a range of schemes, for example, through our Driving Standards Agency, working with groups of older people to try to encourage people to recognise issues like failing eyesight, and so on, and to take steps to ensure that they can continue to drive safely. We are then looking also at what we can do better to fill the gaps when people do have to stop driving, because very often people go on rather longer than they should because they cannot see an alternative. So, rather than just saying to somebody, "You need to stop," if we can say, "but here are the kinds of schemes and initiatives which you might find bridge the gap," I think we will be much better placed to deal with that. I think, my Lord Chairman, those are the main policy initiatives. Perhaps my colleagues could comment.

Ms Brown: I am Yvonne Brown. I am one of the Research Managers within the Mobility and Inclusion Unit. My specific area of responsibility is developing a research programme for disabled and older motorists, so any motorist, that is, looking at driver and passenger issues. I am working in the Department's own Mobility and Driving Assessment Centre, the Mobility Advice and Vehicle Information Service. We are involved in assessing disabled and older drivers, in giving them advice on what adaptations are available and providing a general information service to the public for people with mobility impairment. I am hoping to be able to give you some information on the research that we are involved in but also the research other divisions within the Department for Transport are involved in.

Ms Brock: I am Jan Brock and I am from the Driver and Vehicle Licensing Agency and responsible for the drivers' policy, which includes medical licensing as well. Just to put it in context a little bit, DVLA has 38 million drivers' records, 2.5 million are drivers over 70. In 2002–03, we had about 140,000 cases involving drivers over 70, and, of those, 6,000 drivers lost their licences. In working within the Agency and within the Department we aim to be able, as far as possible, to allow drivers to retain their licences, provided it supports road safety benefit for them and for others. Within the Agency, we have a major programme of work on at the moment, which is to replace the whole of the driver licensing system. We are upgrading our technology which will support the electronic systems of the future, which will allow people to apply for their driving licences from their own homes. Hopefully, we would be able to provide a lot more information for them through web accesses in terms of what is generally available. In addition to that, bearing in mind we have got only 2.5 million over-70s in 2004, we are expecting by 2010, 2015, that the problems will have increased quite a bit, so it is important that we get the data we need to be able to manage that increasing population as it goes forward. As part of the work we are doing with replacing our system, we are going to do a lot more work in terms of better data collection and better data analysis so that we can pinpoint the vulnerable areas and where we need to do more work. One major issue that we have got on now is that we are going to do a fundamental review of the driver licensing medical policy. Because drivers are expected to notify medical condition at application and during the currency of their licence, and because of the costs, which are involved and because of the changes which are going on in the next couple of years, we think it is important that we evaluate the system that we have got at the moment to decide whether it is the best system for going forward.

Q168 *Chairman:* Thank you. Can I go back to the very impressive range of activities which Ann Frye outlined, just to take a very practical example, does all of that inform the process of awarding rail franchises, for example? How do you feed down to a very important decision of that kind the range of understanding you have of the needs of older people? For example, do you expect those proposing that they take over a rail franchise and bidding for it to have part of their proposal dealing with how they will cater for the groups you mentioned, or do you specify it and say, "Well, these are the kinds of things we would like to see someone who is awarded this franchise do"? Just to take this specific issue.

Ms Frye: The rail companies are required, as part of the franchise process, to produce a rather oddly-named 'disabled persons' protection policy', how it got that name I do not know. In that, they would be expected to set out what they were doing specifically on disability, but in a transport sense it is mobility and the physical accessibility of the system, so it is very relevant to older people. That policy has to be assessed and approved by the Disabled Persons' Transport Advisory Committee, who are our statutory advisers, who again have a specific role with older people as well as disabled people in that sense. That process rolls forward, and it gives us a way of both checking what their policies are from the outset but also monitoring against delivery.

Q169 *Chairman:* And indeed steering the rail system towards an adequate railway?

Ms Frye: Yes.

Q170 *Baroness Finlay of Llandaff:* I think my questions have been partly answered by particularly Ann Frye and Jan Brock. As the population ages, the number of older drivers is going to increase, but really it is about what research is being done to inform the planning process, and it might be helpful if you could tell us about any specifically independent research, over and above the project work which you have both described so thoroughly?

Ms Brown: There are four main areas in the Department which are involved in research, some of them very specifically for older people and looking at safety issues and at improving the mobility of older people. Under safety, it is looking at the driver, looking at the vehicle and also looking at the road infrastructure itself. Road Safety Division had a large programme looking at disabled driver issues. They had a large project looking at older drivers and their thoughts on licensing, would they like to be screened, looking at how they would be able to self-regulate. They have looked at older drivers and illness and medication and looked at how medication affects driving performance for older drivers, and they have produced guidelines based on that. At the moment they are looking at the attitudes of healthcare professionals, because they realise it is important that older people are given the correct information to enable them to make decisions about whether to

continue driving or not, and they are proposing doing some further work, although the specifications for that research are still to be done.

Chairman: We have not heard the bell, but I am afraid there is a division coming up and some Members will have to go and vote in that, and indeed will do so, which means, if you can hang on, it will be at least eight minutes before we can resume.

The Committee suspended from 5.05 pm to 5.13 pm for a division in the House.

Chairman: I wonder, Lord Mitchell, if you want to pick up any themes?

Q171 *Lord Mitchell:* The question I would like to ask is about the increasing amount of people who cannot and do not drive. First of all, is it an increasing amount, as a percentage? You mentioned some numbers before, but I did not quite hear them so perhaps you could address those, and what research is being done and what practical steps are being taken to build the necessary extra capacity within public transport systems, which is a very key question?

Ms Brock: If I just run through the numbers from a driving licence perspective and then Yvonne takes over on research. Basically, we have got 2.5 million drivers who are over 70 on our records at the moment.

Q172 *Lord Mitchell:* How would that compare with, say, ten years ago? Is that an increasing number or a decreasing number, do you know?

Ms Brock: I think it is much about the same, to be honest. We do not seem to see much of a change coming up before about 2010, which is why we need to do a lot more analysis of our data to find out. Of those, we have about 140,000 which are drivers over 70 which were involved in a medical condition, whether they notified that themselves, whether it may have been notified by a relative, by the police or by their GP. Out of that 140,000, 6,000 lost their licences, so, as you can see, it is quite a small proportion of that number and of the overall population, in that respect.

Ms Frye: Perhaps just to give a gloss on that, I think one of the issues currently is that a lot of women in their seventies and eighties have never been drivers and we are seeing quite a strong change coming through, with the number of women, not very long hence, being equal with the number of men holding licences, so in the next generation of older people there will be as many women as there are men drivers. What we have got at the moment is a lot of older women who are perhaps widowed and have never driven and therefore are having real mobility problems, particularly if they have retired to rural communities, and so on, so there is a particular issue there.

Q173 *Lord Mitchell:* Can I ask a question on that. When first I got my own driving licence I saw that it expired in 2013, which caused me some degree of mirth, and it is getting perilously close now. I just wonder, is there a cut-off point at all? I should know that, but is there?

Ms Brock: When we centralised driver licensing, which was about 30 years ago now, I do not know if you recall, when the local authorities used to issue licences they were generally every three years. We decided to see whether we could issue licences for longer and it was felt that until 70 was a reasonable time for medical conditions, and all the rest of it, getting that balance between cost-effectiveness for the driver, for the organisation, in terms of processing the driving licences, so we set the age at 70. At 70, what you need to do now is make an application for a licence where you will be asked a series of health questions, and providing you have not got any problems with your health then you will be issued with a three-year licence. I am glad to say that in 2004 we did away with the fee for renewing licences at 70, because prior to that there was a fee involved.

Ms Frye: My mother is 91 and still driving. You asked about extra capacity. Actually I do not think we have got a capacity problem with public transport, not least because the majority of older people do not want to travel at peak times, they want to travel during the rest of the day when generally there is capacity. I think the issue is much more to do with the nature of public transport and with encouraging people to understand it and to use it, as I touched on earlier. One of the pieces of work we are doing is looking at what encourages or provokes older drivers to stop driving and what more we could be doing to help them understand the alternatives, so that rather than becoming isolated and house-bound they are able to move into public transport, taxis, community transport, and so on. We have got quite a big piece of work looking at that, also, as I mentioned earlier, looking much more at flexible transport services, at the kinds of services that can deviate from main routes, that can go to people's houses, can go into remote villages. We have simplified the legislation to make it possible to register those services so you do not have to run a fixed bus from point A to point B, which in rural communities can be of little use, you can have a much more flexible service that identifies people who are in need because they have not got access to private transport. Those sorts of initiatives, I think, are what are enabling us to deliver, and increasingly will enable us to deliver, the sorts of services that people need. In summary, it is not the capacity, it is the type of transport, I think, that is the real issue there.

Q174 *Lord Soulsby of Swaffham Prior:* I never cease to be amazed at the new developments in transport which make driving a car or some sort of vehicle a lot easier than ever it used to be. Do you commission studies or research on vehicles for older people to make them easier? One thing might be automatic transmission, but that is so common now you never worry about it, things of that nature which would make older people more comfortable driving in them?

Ms Brown: The Mobility and Inclusion Unit has quite a large research programme looking at the issues of disabled people in general and older people specifically. Part of that is looking at modifications for vehicles which could make driving easier for older people with impairment, and it is looking at ensuring, or improving, the safety and the various aspects of those vehicles and the adaptation. We are looking also at a general data-gathering project at the moment, which is looking at the numbers of people using cars, so drivers and passengers, who have mobility difficulties, whether it is due to age or due to disability, really just to try to provide information on the numbers of people out there. Then we can give information to vehicle manufacturers when they are designing vehicles to try to improve access for older people and to the car adaptation industry so that they know what type of market they have got when they are doing things like, say, for example, swivel seats, and things like that, and also to our policy-makers within the Department so that we can know what size of a population we are dealing with.

Ms Frye: Often it is getting in and out of the car that is the bigger problem for older people rather than actually driving it, and the way that cars are designed can make it quite difficult. Climbing over the sill which has been built in for accident protection actually can form quite a barrier. Getting the car manufacturers again to recognise the demographics and look at the buying power of more and more older people who do want to go on buying new cars is, I think, beginning to come through in the developments that we are seeing.

Ms Brown: In addition to that, the Transport, Technology and Standards Division in the Department are doing quite a lot of work on improving the secondary safety issues for older people, or for people in general. For instance, they are looking at things like bone density scanning, to see if sensors can be fitted in the car so that, as well as looking at the weight and the position of the person in the car, air-bags and restraint systems can accommodate them based on things like bone density, which should help the safety of older people. They are doing a lot of work on more intelligent seat restraints and obviously there are smart air-bags and things. There is a lot of work looking at those types of issues within the Department which will benefit the older person. There is also a lot of new technology coming in, vehicles which potentially could help older drivers, and what we are trying to do is encourage people developing the technology and people researching the technology to include older drivers in any samples who are trying out for research purposes.

Q175 *Lord Turnberg:* You have talked about the statistics on old people who have had their licences removed. How does that compare with other age groups? Is it a similar proportion or is it that more have their licence withdrawn in the older groups?

Ms Brock: We dealt with about 400,000 cases involving medical condition in 2002–03 and there were 22,000 in total where we had to remove the licence, so this was about a third of that. I guess, proportionately, it is slightly higher. A number of these would probably be vision cases and cognitive impairment, where again maybe the individual does not have insight into the fact that they can no longer drive safely. Those are two of the areas where we have the most difficulty with the older driver.

Q176 *Lord Turnberg:* Thank you. That is very helpful. There is an awful lot of research going on, it is fascinating stuff. I wonder whether we might have access to the results of the research that has been going on in this field and whether we might have a list of the sorts of these and of the results of the research which has been completed?

Ms Frye: Quite a lot is on the Department's website but we can supply you with a list of ongoing work as well as completed work.

Chairman: That would be useful.

Q177 *Baroness Walmsley:* My question follows on quite nicely from what Lord Turnberg was just asking, in two respects actually. It is about the link between the results of research and the practical implementation of strategies to help older people keep on driving safely, and perhaps I could use a particular example to illustrate what obviously has general application. I was also taken by the numbers that you quoted, Ms Brock, about the number of older people who had to have their licence removed, and it occurred to me that one of the reasons may be that there are road design strategies and signage design strategies which might help older people. What I am wondering is, once you have established through research that improvements could be made and what sorts of improvements could be made, how do you ensure within the Department that feeds through to the practical implementation of that sort of thing on the ground?

Ms Frye: We are working through our Highways Agency, who are looking at exactly the issue you have described, at whether design of things like junctions could be made easier for older people to cope with,

because we know, in terms of accidents, that most accidents involving older people tend to be turning out of junctions, and so on. The research tends to have shown that actually you can improve junction design, and so on, to a certain extent for the general driving population, but that there is also benefit in training and running refresher programmes for older drivers, to make sure that they are up to speed with modern traffic conditions, and so on, so it is a combination of the two. The way we make it work is through a combination of research that we do centrally and that our agencies do and that gets turned then into practical application either directly by the Highways Agency, in that case, or through local authorities who manage the more local road network.

Q178 *Baroness Walmsley:* Do you have a joint committee which works on that?

Ms Frye: We do not have a formal committee but we work very closely together in a collaborative sense, and, because my unit co-ordinates everything to do with older people, all the work that is going on will feed into that. Either we will suggest that it is an area which might be looked at, or they will come to us saying "We're looking at this." We put forward research programmes on an annual basis and we compare notes and make sure that the areas we are researching are compatible and are moving forward in the same direction. We have a very strong policy that the output from all our research needs to be practical guidance for dissemination. We are not very keen on academic tomes which sit on shelves, so there is a strong preponderance in favour of putting something out into the field so it can be taken on board.

Ms Brown: Most of the divisions within the Department do have twice-yearly meetings. Road Safety and the Transport, Technology and Standards Division organise a meeting twice a year for all the relevant agencies of the Department and scientists who are doing research for them. Other relevant organisations meet to advise on the research and to look at how the research should be taken forward into policy, so Highways Agency would be involved in that. When it comes to the driver side of things, we have our own consultative committee as well, so we try to work with each other that way.

Chairman: Can I say, thank you very much. For various reasons, we have run a little over time and we thank you for your patience. Just to urge the point once again that if there are further matters, not least the account of ongoing research that Lord Turnberg was asking about, that you could let us have in writing or by e-mail, that would be very helpful. Thank you very much indeed.

WEDNESDAY 24 NOVEMBER 2004

Present	Oxburgh, L	Turnberg, L
	Sutherland of Houndwood, L (Chairman)	Walmsley, B

Memorandum by the Centre for Usable Home Technology (CUHTec) and the Joseph Rowntree Foundation

1. This evidence is presented on behalf of CUHTec and the Joseph Rowntree Foundation. CUHTec is a joint initiative between the University of York and the Joseph Rowntree Foundation. CUHTec has the objective of harnessing world class research expertise in Psychology, Computer Science and Electronics at York University to articulate user requirements for the next generation of home technologies.

2. The case to be made here is that there is a poor understanding of how to improve the quality of life of older people, in particular, that engineers and designers lack a clear specification of what older people really want technology to do for them.

3. The design of information and communication technology for the home is driven more by technological opportunity than by user needs, largely because these needs are poorly articulated. Research is needed to express, in ways useful for designers and engineers, what older people really want. This requires an interdisciplinary approach: applying psychological and sociological techniques to elicit the needs and wishes of older people in some specific area of design, and then, engineering approaches to translate this understanding into a form that is useful to people who make domestic technologies.

4. EXAMPLE 1—LINKING OLDER PEOPLE BY PHONE

Age Concern has identified loneliness and isolation as a serious problems facing many older people today [1]. Charities such as Community Network and the RNIB are using telephone conference switches to join together groups of older people into a single telephone conversation. Research studying these pioneering schemes examined precisely why people find this experience so valuable [2]. The data suggested ways in which new developments in domestic communication technology (eg, 3G mobile phones and broadband connected PCs) could be used to combat loneliness in the older population.

5. EXAMPLE 2—ACCESS TO ONLINE SERVICES VIA VOLUNTEERS

The inability to shop for food is a serious problem for many older people who wish to live independently in the community. A detailed ethnographic study of older people's needs and wishes in this area also identified shopping as an important and greatly valued opportunity for social contact. Thus this research suggested that, for many older people, the strategy of providing internet access to online shopping via specially adapted PCs, for example, would not fulfil their real needs. We have developed, with Age Concern York, a service where volunteers are coupled with one or two older people who they ring up, chat to them and then do their online shopping for them. Net Neighbours York is supported by a secure internet database that makes the volunteers job easy and pleasant. We are adapting engineering methods from Computer Science to ensure that the service is dependable.

6. The above examples show that scientific methods from Psychology, Sociology and Computer Science can be used to address so called "soft" problems in the design of the technology. There are many other areas where this sort of research is needed to improve the quality of life of older people.

7. The EPSRC EQUAL programme is one of the few publicly funded research initiatives addressing human factors in the design of technology for older people. Work has been carried out in other programmes such as PACCIT (ESRC, EPSRC, DTI). These limited resources have been spread rather thinly so that projects that start with a quest to find out what older people want, rather than an assumption of what they will get, are relatively rare.

8. In short, there are existing technologies, particularly communication technologies, that could be used to benefit older people, that are not being used to good effect as engineers do not understand what older people want of them. Publicly funded research in this area is piecemeal and is not seen as a priority. The larger and more enlightened companies providing domestic technologies understand that they need a better understanding of their customers but do not know where to get it.

9. One solution would be to set up a research institute, funded by industry and government, that will champion the need to have a clear specification of what older people really want as a preliminary to all design innovation. In the last year, CUHTec has made a small step in this direction but with very limited funds. Major resources are needed to provide the inspiration and leadership needed to change the often rather paternalistic attitudes to the design of technology for older people that currently prevail in much of industry and the research community.

10. References

[1] Age Concern (2002) *Concerned About Ageing? The needs of older people: key issues and evidence.* London, Age Concern England.

[2] Reed, DJ and Monk, AF (2004) Using familiar technologies in unfamiliar ways and learning from the old about the new. *Universal Access in the Information Society*, 3, 114–121.

September 2004

Memorandum by Kevin Doughty and Gareth Williams

PRACTICAL SOLUTIONS FOR THE INTEGRATION OF COMMUNITY ALARMS, ASSISTIVE TECHNOLOGIES AND TELECARE

TECHNOLOGY IN HEALTHCARE

ABSTRACT

The use of telecare with appropriate domiciliary care packages may provide the means to manage many of the risks associated with the increasing number of older people who wish to continue to live independently in their own homes. Those who become especially frail or disabled can also retain their independence and quality of life if their homes are made "smart". This paper discusses range of services that are available, or under development, for the prototype "MIDAS" telecare system, which enable traditional community alarm, telecare and assistive technologies to be used in an integrated and hence intelligent fashion. A range of services that allow autonomous operation within the home (and hence increase the perceived independence of a client by decreasing the reliance on a response centre operator) known as "HAMISH" may be used to offer a wider range of cost-effective services of relevance to both the individual, and to society, in different types of home environment including dispersed housing and new sheltered housing schemes.

INTRODUCTION

The proportion of older people within society during the next fifty years will increase significantly (Khaw, 1999; ONS, 1999). A more noteworthy statistic perhaps is the number of disability free years that we are now likely to live. The Disability Adjusted Life Expectancy (DALE) is used by the World Health Organisation (WHO) as a measure of quantifying the healthy life expectancy of an individual. In the UK, for example, the DALE is approximately 69.7 years for males and 73.7 years for females; this compares with an actual life expectancy of 75 and 80 years respectively indicating a significant period of disability, usually towards the end of life, the so-called "compression of morbidity" (WHO, 2000). The DALE and the proportion of older people in society may increase further if health promotion succeeds in changing the diets and life-styles of people so that diseases such as stroke, osteoporosis and diabetes are either defeated or better managed leading to fewer cases of chronic disability.

Future improvements in health are likely to have little impact on the millions of Westerners who have already spent the greater part of their lives smoking, eating foods full of animal fats while using motor cars to restrict exercise. However, due to advances in medicine, many more people will survive the effects of cardio-vascular disease and cancer but may then proceed to suffer from a number of disabilities and chronic ailments that will challenge their independence. Social changes, including divorce and geographically dispersed extended families, will leave many living alone without the support of informal carers. Unfortunately, a falling birth-rate will compound this problem by reducing the pool of formal carers that are available (Khaw, 1999). This may have an adverse effect on an already stretched healthcare system.

Successive governments in the UK, and elsewhere, have assumed that shortages in human and financial resources within the healthcare system may be overcome through a process of modernisation and integration. In the UK, the NHS Plan (DoH, 2000) and the information strategy for the NHS (Department of Health, NHS Executive, 1998) detail the governments intention to re-engineer the healthcare system with increasing use of information and communication technologies (ICT). Similarly, a shift of emphasis from the expensive and regulated world of institutional care (ie hospitals) into the more flexible setting of primary care (generally the home environment) is likely to result in a reduction of overall costs and gains in consumer satisfaction (Brownell, et al, 1999). This may be achieved by moving many healthcare facilities from secondary into primary care, allowing hospitals to become treatment and specialist advice centres. Such changes may be possible if there is an increase in the adoption of electronic health and patient records (EPR) and an advanced telecommunications infrastructure to distribute information and knowledge such that expertise is shared throughout the entire healthcare enterprise. NHS Direct is one example of how such innovations may empower individuals to access healthcare information from the comfort of their own homes on a 24 hour basis (www.nhsdirect.nhs.uk). In the community it removes the distinctions between housing types (nursing homes, residential homes, dispersed housing, sheltered housing etc) so that home care services may be offered to everyone.

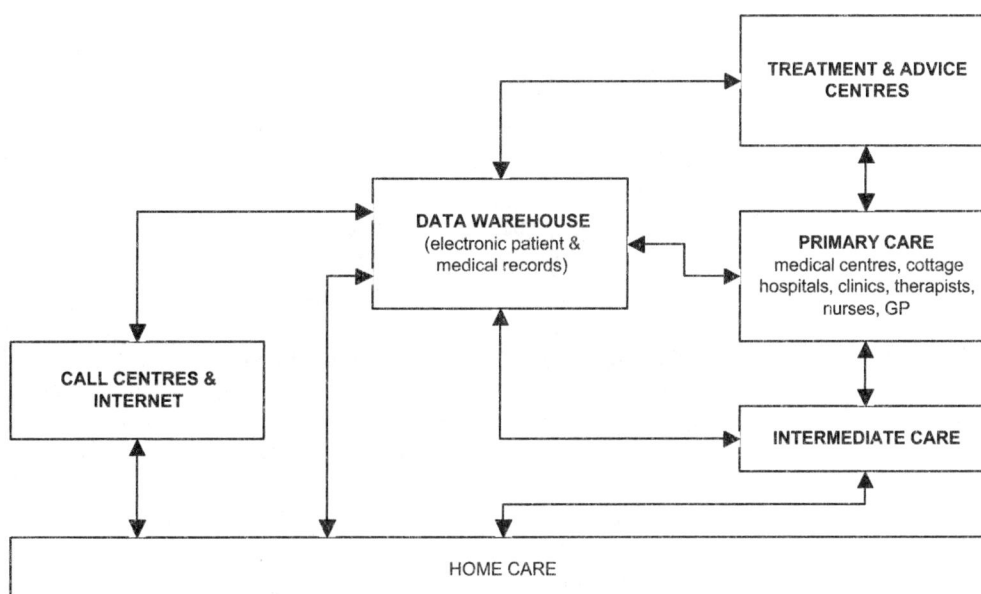

Figure 1. New Healthcare Structure.

A possible arrangement for a new "Continuum of Care" is shown in Figure 1. The old pyramid structure is replaced by a more flexible one, which includes a "data warehouse" where electronic patient and health records may be kept so that they are accessible to the relevant health professionals, irrespective of their location. Figure 1 illustrates the data warehouse as a separate entity, but in reality it may be distributed throughout the enterprise. Reliable and secure access to this information might be via the NHSNet, an NHS-wide computer network, giving patients improved diagnosis, information and referral. By 2002, all GP practices should be connected to NHSNet and by 2004, 75 per cent of hospitals and 50 per cent of primary and community trusts should have implemented EPR systems (DoH, 2000). The structure also includes an intermediate care facility which may be used for intensive rehabilitation enabling patients to be prepared for returning home after being hospitalised following illness, accident or surgery. It may be apparent that these facilities need to be provided with a high level of input from the various professions allied to medicine. It is occupational therapists, speech therapists and physiotherapists, amongst others, who are likely to have the correct skills to assess the needs of patients and ensure that no culture of dependency is allowed to develop. Figure 1 is an example of how information and communication technologies in union with medical informatics can influence healthcare processes by enabling the provision of remote care services ie telehealth. The application of telehealth technologies may be split into 2 groups, that we choose to distinguish as follows:

1. Telemedicine—remote consultations, diagnosis and opinions between medical professionals (in their surgeries and in hospitals), ie a business to business service (b2b) in e-commerce terminology; and

2. Telecare—remote healthcare monitoring and support for patients/clients (business to customer services—b2c).

It is, of course, telecare services which are of greatest relevance to the patient, client or resident in any community setting (including intermediate care facilities). In practice, there are several different types of telecare as described by the groups shown in Table 1. These reflect the unique situation in the UK where many different agencies have responsibility for delivering or commissioning care. These include formal care agencies but also many of the bigger or more forward-looking social landlords (eg Anchor Trust, Hanover, Fold and Touchstone) who provide an increasing level of care especially in the newer Extra Care (or Very) sheltered housing schemes. It is perhaps inevitable that there will be a future role for a new inter-agency based generic home-care worker who is trained in such a way as to be capable of interfacing between the social and medical care needs of the client-base. This is one of the reasons why potentially innovative telecare devices and systems designed for markets in other countries may not be appropriate in this context.

Table 1

TELECARE SERVICES

Telecare Group	Description of Service	Examples
Social telecare	Automatic notification of accidents or risky behaviour	Fall detection; night wandering; failure to return to bed at night
Environmental telecare	Detection of abnormal and/or dangerous living conditions	Detection of fires, poisonous or explosive gases, flooding or low temperatures
Personal telecare	Assistance in managing the body's natural functions	Warning of wet incontinence pads; reminding of the need to turn over in bed
Therapeutic telecare	Distant teaching or re-learning of activities	Development of physical and occupational skills by telephone or through internet
Nursing telecare	Remote advice and help with specific symptoms	Advice on medication, pain management, wound dressing and symptoms, tele-triage
Medical telecare	Remote analysis of and response to physiological measurements	Management of acute conditions eg asthma and coronary disease as well as chronic conditions such as hypertension
Educational telecare	Access to approved databases of health-related information and relevant care networks	Provide on-line access to health promotion material; background information on subjects such as: diabetes, dementia, stroke, hypertension, etc.; the sharing of experiences using newsgroups

QUALITY OF LIFE

One of the major drivers for changing the pattern of care is to provide consumer choice and, thus, to improve the quality of life (QoL) of thousands of older people whose lifestyles are adversely affected by premature admission to institutional care. This is so often a "knee-jerk" reaction to an accident (eg a fall) or to a change of personal circumstances such as the death of a spouse (and hence informal carer) that alternatives aren't always considered in the rush to provide adequate care, especially when healthcare professionals perform risk management exercises.

There is a great body of work that aims to better define the meaning of the quality of life of an individual (Bowling, 1998; Guggenmoos-Holzmann, et al, 1995). This qualitative term is difficult to quantify due to the complex relationship between the objective and subjective variables that contrive to affect the perceived quality of life or well-being of an individual. Many workers have attempted to measure the QoL of an individual using a variety of quantitative techniques or instruments (Guggenmoos-Holzmann, et al, 1995). However, few seem to take a holistic view and there are significant differences in emphasis between measures prepared by psychologists, doctors and social workers. Thus, the whole subject tends to remain highly subjective; we may conclude that every individual is different; it is impossible to prescribe universal courses of action to improve QoL.

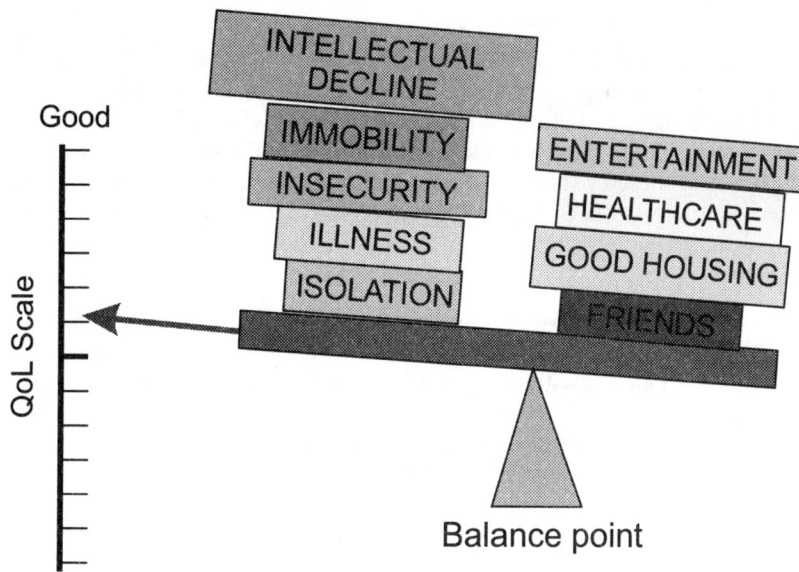

Figure 2. Factors that affect quality of life.

Figure 2 shows a crude representation of how certain factors (such as ill-health and social isolation) act to depress QoL while good housing, social interaction and entertainment tend to increase it. In the case of the elderly, many of the negative factors are caused by what are sometimes referred to as the "Big I's of old age" (Bennett & Ebrahim, 1995). These negative factors have been expanded and collated with other positive factors that act to counter-balance their effects in Table 2.

Table 2

THE BIG I's FOR OLDER PEOPLE

Positive	*Negative*
Independence	Isolation
	Insecurity
Interests	Immobility
	Instability
Information	Intellectual decline
	Illness
Inclusion	Insensitivity
	Intrusion
Interaction	Incontinence
	Iatrogenesis
	Inability
	Insanity

There can be little doubt that the negative factors are a harmful influence, though the extent to which they each impact an individual may depend on that person's previous lifestyle and history. In the above model, this can be included by shifting the balance point in the horizontal plane. The relevance (and interdependence) of the negative factors vary to an even greater extent between individuals. Independence is particularly a matter of choice as some people may happily give up some independence in order to share in facilities for food preparation and dining. Inclusion may be necessary to overcome ageist agendas. However, some older people expect to be treated differently on account of their age. Positive age discrimination already applies in transport (bus passes, rail cards etc.), winter fuel allowances (£200 per household in 2000–01) and for television licences (free for over-75s). There can be no doubt that many older people would like to see this extended to healthcare services even though 70% or more of total healthcare spending is consumed on this group and a general improvement in the NHS would benefit the elderly the most.

There is far less difference of opinion on the importance of information, interests in providing a good quality of life. Many older people are frustrated by their inability to take advantage of services which provide easy access to both either through financial limitations, or geographical disparities (the problem of providing services in a rural setting) or through failing faculties such as eye-sight and hearing. The perceived safety of an individual is also an important aspect that may affect the level of stress experienced and hence influence their perceived QoL. It would therefore appear to be something of a priority to use technology to facilitate all of these needs, where possible.

THE HOME ENVIRONMENT

The elderly population of the UK is currently housed in a variety of dwellings, many of which are old and unsuited to their needs and capabilities. For example, the British preference for two storey homes (and many Victorian and Edwardian town houses with three or four levels), together with a desire "to stay put" when the house becomes too big when families disperse, results in problems when an older person is no longer able to climb the stairs without great effort and discomfort. The high price of houses and of land, especially in the South East of England, leads to a low renewal rate for housing. Thus, opportunities for providing the latest innovations are quite limited.

There are, however, a number of purpose-built developments by private developers, local authorities and housing associations/charities wishing to offer older clients the choice of single-level accommodation perhaps within a complex of homes where such clusters might lead to a mini-"care village" or sheltered housing complex. The size, and cost, of these homes might vary considerably from a bed-sitter arrangement through to a bungalow with several bedrooms, garden and garage. Many sheltered housing schemes remain popular despite the fact that they were built up to 40 years ago. Some of them, however, are difficult to let because they are in areas which might no longer be desirable for residential development. Nevertheless, they offer a platform on which high quality domiciliary care can be provided.

Such schemes may be suitable for adaptation to include new technologies, especially those which allow for easy electronic communications between neighbours—as in a "wired community" or "virtual neighbourhood" (Doughty et al, 1996). It would then seem relatively straightforward to extend such homes to be telecare compatible. This is a challenge that is worthwhile especially if the residents are to include frailer individuals in the future. Indeed, in those sheltered housing schemes where the provision of "extra-care" is intended to replace existing residential homes, it may be difficult to imagine successful and efficient operation without incorporating a suitable level of telecare.

It is reported that only some 500,000 of the UK's retired population of over 10 million live in sheltered housing (www.shelteredhousing.org). The vast majority are dispersed within the community where they are unlikely to benefit from dedicated intercom and alarm facilities. Yet, it would seem that a great many older people would be prepared to accept a certain level of technological intervention, discomfort or a lack of facilities if it allowed them to remain in their own homes rather than move into more institutional care. This is borne out by research undertaken during the Royal Commission on the Long Term Care of the Elderly (Stationery Office, 1999) and from work undertaken during Age Concern's Debate of the Age. One study reported that 82% of respondents indicated that they would prefer to remain in their homes even if they were unable to manage tasks of daily living without help (Jarvis et al, 1998). Their independence may be more relevant to their quality of life than is often assumed by healthcare professionals assessing their needs.

24 November 2004

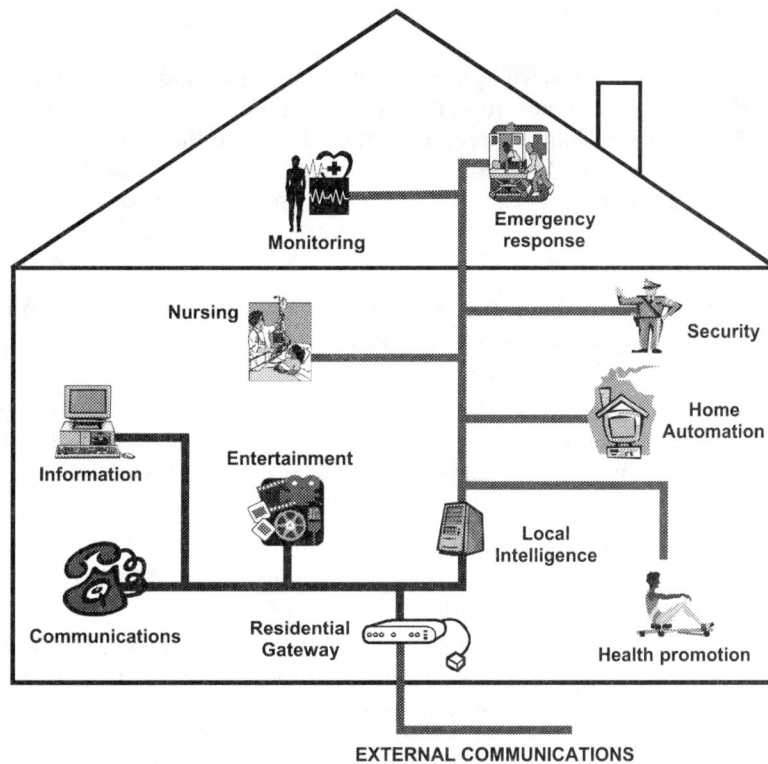

Figure 3. e-care enabled home.

The opportunity then exists to support older and/or disabled people in their own homes through a combination of traditional domiciliary care, new and old assistive devices and information and communication technologies that may deliver a wide range of services. Figure 3 shows a house which can receive these services, including security, entertainment, health promotion, local information and news through internal and external networks. In combination, they must create an environment which promotes the individual's independence in a manner which minimises (but cannot eliminate) risk. This home may be described as electronically enabled for care services—"e-care ready". It may receive these services whenever the resident requires them, thus empowering the client to select the care services that he or she requires. This can, however, lead to isolation and a slow response to problems unless the processes are monitored from afar ie "tel-e-care". The "WISE" home described above (Well-being, Information, Safety and Entertainment) uses technology to support independence. In this respect, it might seem like the smart homes that have been discussed by housing experts for a decade or more, except that other smart homes tend to be built to the specifications of the designer and architect which may not include a high level of telecare. However, they are worthy of further discussion.

SMART HOMES

There appear to be at least four types of smart home that have been proposed over the past 10 years, appealing to specific user groups:

1. *The automated home*

This is the "high-tech" environment designed with the busy young executive in mind. It allows automation, push-button remote control of many appliances and remote access (including virtual presence) through telecommunications.

2. *The green home*

This controls lights, heating and ventilation to make the most efficient use of energy (which may well come from renewable sources close to the home). It is likely to appeal to environmentalists who wish to optimise their use of energy.

3. *The assistive home*

This allows the resident to control the use of appliances, the doors and windows from any point in the home. This may share many of the features of the automated home but is designed to satisfy the needs of people with disabilities including those in wheelchairs. It requires attention also to the built environment to ensure that there is adequate access and support for people with various physical impairments. If the principles of universal design are applied properly to such homes then they are often referred to as "barrier-free".

4. *The safe home*

This provides security from intruders and features services to prevent accidents either in the environment or to the individual. People suffering from confusion or those in the early stages of dementias, such as Alzheimer's Disease would benefit from such a home.

A fifth type—which could be termed "a health home"—may also appear in order to support "Hospital at Home" initiatives. However, it may be difficult to see the features that may be needed in advance without knowing the medical problem. There are few suitable definitions of smart homes but we would propose that a smart home is:

> "A home that contains an abundance of sensor, actuator, control, communication, information and machine intelligence technologies to facilitate user, automatic or remote control or enhancement of the environment, lifestyle and well-being of its inhabitant."

This definition's emphasis on technology must be correct and is certainly consistent with user expectation; the relative importance of each technology has, however, tended to be governed by commercial pressures and practical issues associated with the built environment rather than on a holistic assessment of the client's needs. It is then hardly surprising that standards have been slow to materialise and even slower to be accepted especially with regard to communications between devices in the home. A smart home system therefore consists of the following components:

1. *Sensors*

They should provide information about the status of the home and its inhabitant(s) and, ideally, automatic detection of specific emergencies. In most designs, these have tended to be environmental and security devices in order to exploit developments in the buildings control and burglar alarm industries.

2. *Actuators*

This covers all responsive devices but especially switched units such as electrical door and window openers, and lights. More sophisticated medical devices such as infusion pumps might also appear under this heading. These tend to be the most expensive part of the system and are therefore selected as appropriate to the individual client.

3. *Interfaces*

These are the mechanisms by which the client controls and monitors the status of the local environment. They are normally centralised control units or remote control hand-sets, perhaps with custom user interfaces to accommodate people with special needs.

4. *Internal communications*

Devices need to communicate with each other (and with any local intelligence or control unit) in some way. Remote control devices usually use radio or infra-red wireless communication. However, the more general approach has been through a hard-wired bus as this can be installed during construction of the house. Some control-type instructions can be relayed using simple codes but other data such as in the case of video, will require a wide-bandwidth. The search for a common standard has probably held back smart homes take-up more than any other technological problem. The arrival of low-cost, reliable wireless systems, especially those based on UHF radio, may revolutionise short-range in-house communications. Blue-tooth is a standard which has already been adopted by many companies throughout the world and is likely to become the standard in the future when price, range and availability become reasonable (www.bluetooth.com). However Blue-tooth is a medium-access technology only (ie it enables two or more devices to communicate via wireless links)— further confusion reigns as regards which application level protocols (ie the meaning of the messages that are transmitted) will establish themselves as the de-facto standard.

5. *Local Intelligence Unit*

The purpose of a smart home is to allow devices to be connected in such a way as to enable intelligent operation. This intelligence is often rule-based in the form of "production rules" (eg "If room temperature is low" THEN "turn up heater") although other forms of artificial intelligence such as fuzzy logic or neural networks may be applied also. This intelligence may be distributed throughout the home and/or be located centrally and is needed to process data and make decisions based on the various sensor and human inputs. The LIU is effectively the focal point of the smart home through which most communications, internal and external, are channelled. In the case of the MIDAS system, the LIU is referred to as the CareStation.

6. *External Communications*

These may be either into a private network (hard-wired or radio) or into the Public Switched Telephone Network (PSTN) either directly through a land-line link or through a cell-phone. The type of link required should be sufficient to provide the bandwidth necessary for all the services required. Simple information requires little bandwidth and can be transmitted through a standard telephone line. However, moving images and fast access to the internet require more specialised approaches ranging from ISDN through to cable networks who are keen to promote Voiceover-IP services. New digital communication technologies are also becoming available including Digital Subscriber Line (x-DSL) services such as A-DSL (Asymmetrical DSL) and eventually V-DSL (Very High Speed DSL) which use standard telephone wires and offer more options and bandwidth (into and out of the home). Finally third generation mobile telephones should not be overlooked as a possible wireless communications technique (and hence ideal for temporary installations).

If used within the context of telecare, then we would argue that it also needs a seventh, remote component, namely a response system. This is an essential component when telecare is introduced and the importance of remote monitoring is recognised. In smart homes to be developed for either rehabilitation or for assessment purposes, the role of the care responder becomes fundamental (see later).

Although older people have often been described as those who would make the most apt residents for smart homes, efforts to design a house using technological aids specifically for their use have in the main centred on one-off "new-build" showcase installations with often inappropriate (though sometimes impressive) specialised and hence expensive technology on display. Perhaps this is because the needs of older people vary so much that there could be no such thing as a universally acceptable design. It is just as likely that most older people would describe themselves as generally well (though suffering from various chronic but medically controlled conditions) and so it might be difficult for them to justify relocating into a smart house.

There would appear to be an obvious need for a method of converting any home into a smart home. If this can be done quickly (in a day or two) and economically (for less than £5,000) then this would seem to meet the requirements of both potential users and the providers of such a service. In practical terms, this means a modular approach which allows the exact mix of facilities to be set at a local level (Williams et al, 1998). It intuitively requires also that the level of support can be increased (or decreased) as the need arises. This is entirely consistent with the approach to telecare provision provided by our advanced second generation prototype system, MIDAS (Modular Intelligent Domiciliary Alarm System) (Doughty et al, 1999) which can already provide a number of smart home features.

EXTENDED FIRST-GENERATION TELECARE

In the short-term, the difficulties involved with introducing smart home technologies into sheltered housing schemes and dispersed housing in particular can, to a certain extent, be overcome through the use of existing community alarm systems. Community alarm systems offer a mature and well-trusted method of providing a suitable response to people in need based on a care telephone and may be considered as the first-generation of telecare (Doughty et al, 1996). They are in use in over one and quarter million homes in the UK and are controlled by about 300 monitoring and response call centres. Despite their success, they have a number of short-falls as listed in Table 3. These limitations are essentially related to the "active" nature of the alarm-generation mechanism, ie the client must either press a button or pull a cord if they are in need of help.

It may be evident that the solution to this problem is a shift to "passive" techniques in the form of automatic sensing devices. Community alarm care phones generally have very limited computational processing capabilities and hence cannot provide any system intelligence, however, modern care-phones have enough sophistication to accommodate the introduction of many new event-based telecare services. This is possible by placing any necessary intelligence into the sensors themselves, which then communicate the required information to the community alarm response centres via the care phone. The nature of the services that can be delivered using such a hybrid extended first-generation approach is limited to event-based services (such as alarms or alerts) because community alarm systems do not, as yet, support the transmission of actual data within the home. Community alarm protocols can however provide unambiguous interpretation of these event-based messages at the community alarm call centre, enabling rapid and appropriate responses and interventions to be made.

Table 3

FAILURES AND LIMITATIONS OF SIMPLE COMMUNITY ALARM SYSTEMS

Limitation	Example
Client may not realise that there is a problem	Impairment of senses such as hearing problem
Client may be physically unable to activate alarm	Unconscious or weak due to fall or illness
The alarm trigger may not be accessible	Pull cord in wrong place or pendant out of reach
The client is unclear as to what constitutes a genuine emergency	Reluctance to disturb staff (especially at night)
Client denial time	Pretending that a problem will go away on its own

As an example, a smart bed monitor may provide an alarm if a client has left their bed during the night and has not returned within a specified period. This could mean that they have experienced a fall. The same device might send a different alarm call if the client leaves bed on more than, perhaps, six occasions during a single night. This might indicate illness (eg a stomach bug) and may need a different form of response. This system can be extended further, if required, to assist in fall prevention by automatically and gradually increasing the brightness of a bedside lamp upon detecting the client getting out of bed at night. Figure 4 illustrates the set-up required and details the main elements of the smart bed occupancy sensor. The "intelligence" required to determine alert and alarm conditions is situated within the bed monitoring unit itself, which then transmits the appropriate alarm message to the care phone.

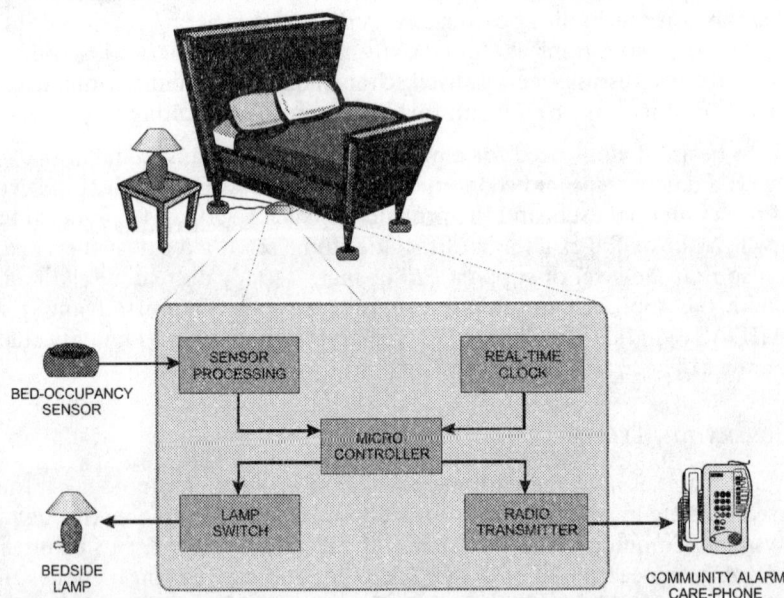

Figure 4. An example of extended first-generation telecare that exhibits 'intelligent' behaviour (BELINDA).

Table 4 lists a number of smart devices that are under development, available for use in pilot studies, or have already been launched as commercial products. They represent part of the "family" of TIH's extended first-generation telecare devices (ie compatible with community alarm systems) and represent examples of social, environmental and personal telecare. To this range should be added some new nursing and physiological telecare devices which can provide early warnings of medical conditions of relevance to people with chronic illnesses. These may be relevant to those suffering from asthma, bronchitis, Chronic Obstructive Pulmonary Disease (COPD), angina, high blood pressure and diabetes.

Thus, in the short-term at least, it is almost certainly more cost-effective to incorporate new telecare services onto the existing platform of the community alarm system using automated 'smart' sensors. This has many advantages, not least the fact that much of the infrastructure required in client's homes (ie a telephone line and a care phone) are already well-established and may already be installed in the homes of clients who are most likely to benefit from extended first-generation services. The use of the community alarm platform has the added bonus of client familiarity with the technology and a trust in its ability, along with the response call centre to respond to any needs.

Table 4

SMART TELECARE DEVICE POSSIBILITIES

Device Name	*Application*
FRED	A client-worn fall alarm device
BRENDA	Monitors bed usage for abnormal activities, such as unusual absence at night
BELINDA	As BRENDA but with the capability of controlling a bedside lamp
BERT	A medication compliance aid that provides appropriate reminders and alarms
FLORA	A flood alarm that detects excessive amounts of water on the floor
HETTIE	Warns of low or very high room temperatures
ESME	Provides early warning of wet sheets or incontinence pad
PAM	Reminds client or carer of need to move or change orientation to avoid bed sores

However, even though extended first-generation systems offer a quick and convenient method of providing telecare type services as soon as possible, there is limit to the range of services that can be offered. In particular, the motivation for moving to a second-generation telecare system is the desire to:

1. Be able to detect problems *before* they become the emergencies that the first generation sensors will detect, ie provide a range of preventative services; and

2. Be able to act in "real-time" on information presented to the system.

These present more of a challenge because a far greater knowledge of the home environment, the individual and his or her habits are required. In addition, to complicate matters, in order to protect the privacy of the client and hence avoid any "Big Brother" comparisons, this should be achieved with minimum intrusion and, hence, without cameras or other imaging devices such as pyrolectric vidicons.

SECOND GENERATION TELECARE

A comprehensive analysis of the requirements of future-generation telecare systems has been undertaken and has resulted in a sophisticated model detailing the advanced services, information infrastructure, system architecture and intelligence, device functionality, and safety implications required to meet the present and future telecare needs of both clients and carers. The details of this academic model, referred to as the "CarerNet" model have been discussed elsewhere (Doughty & Williams, 1998). This model has influenced the design of MIDAS (Modular Intelligent Domiciliary Alarm System), TIH's prototype realisation of a second-generation telecare system, Figure 5 (Doughty et al, 1999).

24 November 2004

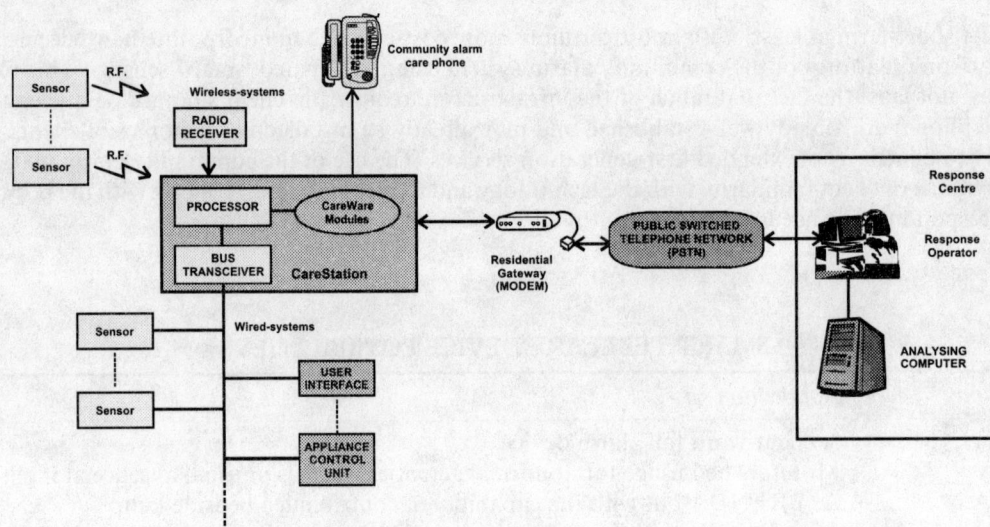

Figure 5. Block diagram of MIDAS system.

MIDAS employs the principle of modularity in providing services that can be introduced and configured adaptively to meet the changing needs of clients. These intelligent services (referred to as CareWare) allow the nature of the overall system to be tailored to the specific needs of a particular client. Five classes of sensor may be required in order to perform the preventative (and hence predictive) form of telecare: activity, event, environmental, utility and physiological. Indeed, the sensors may not be useful in isolation; information on sequence, timing and the presence of carers or other people within the home are necessary in order to convert raw data into genuine knowledge. It is for this reason that there needs to be significant local intelligence within the home. Such intelligence requires considerable computer power and resident software. These are provided in the Care Station which collects and collates all the data from the sensors.

Table 5 summarises the important points in selecting the set of sensors. It may be evident that a poor or inadequate choice will lead to anomalous results and further problems when trying to derive quantitative values for activity, mobility or other indices. It may also be clear that assessments may only be valid if all the parameters of interest are being measured.

Table 5
SELECTION OF SENSORS FOR SYSTEM

Sensors	Comments
Small number (3 or 4 only per home)	Low cost
	Incomplete data set
	Anomalous interpretations
	Poor potential for analysis
Large number (> 25 device per home)	High cost
	Potential for cross-talk and transmission error
	Duplication of results
	Unnecessary intrusion
	Data smog
Inappropriate device selection (eg pressure mats and "dumb" PIR's)	Low cost
	Poor reliability and sensitivity
	Wrong data collected
	Transmission errors
	High number of transmissions
	Anomalous assessments
Smart sensors (purpose-designed	Less intrusion
	Better quality data
	Reliable transmission
	Allows reliable analysis

The sensors used in MIDAS are tailored to particular applications. Generally, a number of sensors are integrated into a single package in order to provide self-checking but also to minimise installation time. They include a core set of devices to monitor movement and environmental parameters. The MIDAS sensors can transmit data using a proprietary protocol either on a wired network or using radio telemetry. The former is installed using category 5 wiring which has the advantage of offering the means to provide power to all the sensors from a central source, thus saving on battery use and replacement. The latter approach provides more flexibility and is particularly useful for rapid installation and removal especially when an assessment of lifestyle is required within a person's home. A hybrid arrangement is also possible. The data collected by the Care Station is time-stamped and entered into a data-base for analysis.

Examples of second-generation devices available from TIH are: MAVIS monitors room activity, temperature and humidity and is used in every room; KATIE provides an indication of the number of times that a kettle is switched on (or effectively any device that is plugged into it). It is one of a series of devices which monitor the use of specific appliances. Once events are presented to the CareStation, it must decide on the urgency of the information and subsequently which CareWare modules are affected. The nature of the services provided by CareWare can be segregated into "real-time" and "retrospective".

Real-Time CareWare

These modules require a "real-time" response or action and cannot therefore be run in a remote monitoring centre. They are based on a number of logic rules and sophisticated algorithms that have been developed specifically for telecare applications. For example, SIAN is a sophisticated automatic intruder alarm which monitors the home day and night. It is aware of the occupancy of the home at all times and does not therefore need to be set or switched off by a resident on entry or before exit. DANIEL is a module which monitors events and data to ensure the general safety of the client. For instance, one of the algorithms embedded within DANIEL monitors the relationship between room temperature and humidity in the kitchen to distinguish between environmental variations caused by cooking and of those caused by a pan that has boiled dry, which represents a hazardous risk of burn situation. DANIEL also looks for a failure to respond in any way to the telephone or to the door bell, which may be viewed as a problem; indeed, it might be reasonable to expect a client to open the door within, say, two minutes of the bell being rung. However, if the client's mobility deteriorates then this time should be increased accordingly. This is possible because the real-time CareWare modules are able to adapt to changes in normal behaviour during the duration of the monitoring.

Retrospective Care Ware

The MIDAS data-base can be processed to separate the various types of data according to room or parameter. Thus, the correct management of the heating may be confirmed or the activity profile of the client may be displayed on a daily, weekly or monthly basis. In this way, trends or significant alterations to the normal pattern of events may be easily seen by the appropriate carer. In practice, these analyses may not be needed on anything other than an irregular basis. In other words, it is only those CareWare elements that are deemed to be relevant and necessary that would be applied. More generally, they would be activated according to a scheme negotiated and agreed with the client and that it would only be exceptions to regular occurrences that would be worthy of reporting. Preliminary CareWare modules could be used to screen for abnormal events, which subsequently trigger more advanced analysis at the response centre. This approach allows the level of telecare to be increased or decreased very easily as the need changes. A selection of retrospective CareWare modules under development are listed in Table 6.

Table 6

RETROSPECTIVE CAREWARE MODULES

Name	Application
SEAN	Uses risk factors and other data to predict problems
BEN	Assesses lifestyle parameters
NORMA	Continuous measure of ADL
SID	Used to measure social interaction
COLIN	Monitors confusion of client
MAT	Measures mobility quantitatively
ARCHIE	Compares care episodes with "golden standard"

Name	Application
WANDA	Combination of measures to give Quality of Life
ELVIS	Detects incidence of elderly abuse

As an example, consider the activity profiles of two very different individuals over a period of 24 hours are shown in Figure 7. The upper trace is that of a 79 year old widower. His general activity level is quite low with obvious peaks around meal times and before going to bed. He also gets up once during the night (to go to the bathroom). On the other hand, the lower trace is for a heavily pregnant young woman who is experiencing discomfort and difficulty sleeping. The differences in lifestyles are plain to see but neither should be construed as being unusual. However, significant deviations from these "normal" profiles might well be indicative of some change in circumstances. In an older person, this is often the first indication of some underlying problems and is worthy of investigation.

ARCHIE may be of particular relevance to commissioners of care especially when one considers that an estimated 46 per cent of home care is sourced from external care providers (Thompson, 1999). ARCHIE enables the quality of care provided to be assessed by the interpretation of monitored parameters and by logging the arrival and departure of carers as they enter and leave a premises. This is achieved by monitoring the punctuality of a carer for pre-arranged visits or the response time if responding to an alarm call; how long the carer stays per visit; the total number of visits; and the type of care provided in each visit. The latter may be achieved by comparing monitored events with a-priori information regarding the care package of the client. Thus, a "care episode" may be separated into a number of essential steps which may be identified by the local intelligent system which can be compared with an ideal sequence in order to produce a quality approval index. For example, if the carer is responsible for bathing the client then it is possible to monitor the flow of water into a bath, the temperature of the water and to detect the length of time for which the bathroom is occupied. Thus whilst not strictly monitoring the quality of the care provided to the client, it does offer a technique of monitoring the quantity, type and punctuality of care that may be of use for auditing purposes, especially where external care agencies are used.

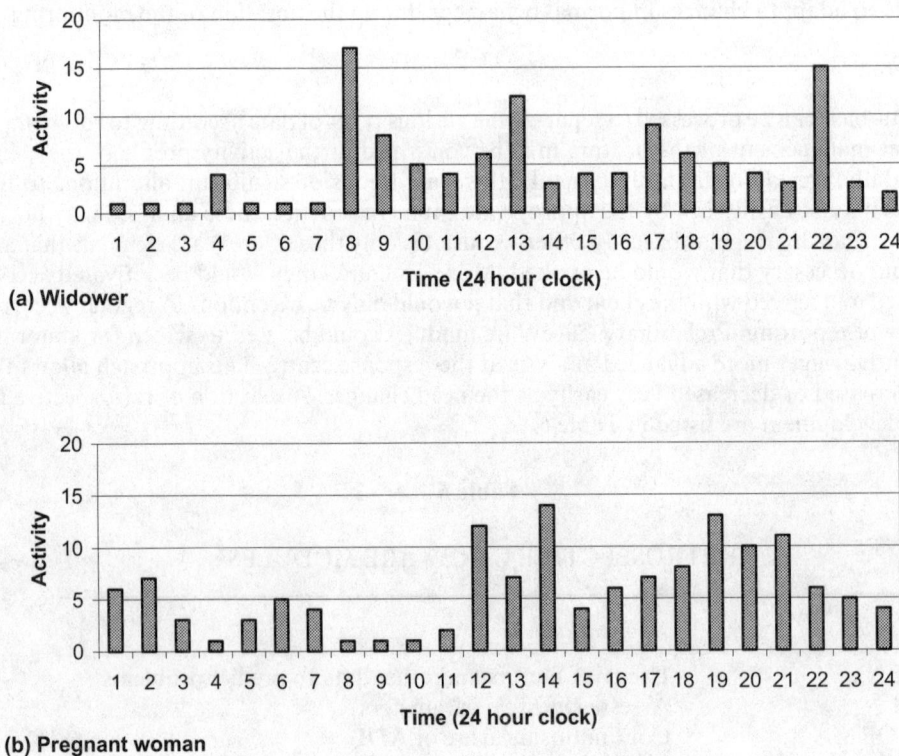

(a) Widower

(b) Pregnant woman

Figure 7. A comparison of the activities of (a) 79 year-old widower & (b) 26 year old pregnant woman.

HAMISH (HOME AUTOMATION—MIDAS IN SMART HOUSING)

Although the compatibility of MIDAS with community alarm telephones provides an emergency link to the response call centre, there will be times when an action should be performed immediately, or information and advice should be made available to the client. HAMISH is an extension of MIDAS whereby the nature of the services are extended from mainly monitoring to include the ability to perform actions locally without the response centre being in the feedback loop. As an example, if a flood is detected in the bathroom, then ideally the system should automatically turn off the water supply to the bath and inform the client. Likewise, if the front door is left open, then the client should be alerted to this fact and be given the opportunity of rectifying the situation before a carer is called out unnecessarily. In order to achieve this level of local control, it is necessary to remove the need, at least initially, for the human intelligence in the care feedback loop. This involves closing the loop of care within the home by using local intelligence to control local parameters.

Figure 8 illustrates the control loop required to control the flow of water into the bath using community alarm systems and extended first-generation telecare systems. The human operator in the loop, introduces an unnecessary delay as they are unable to directly control the flow of water into the bath; hence, all that they are able to do is inform the client that the bath is overflowing. The hazardous situation may then be rectified, providing of course that the client is able to turn off the bath-water (why is it overflowing in the first place?). Alternatively, if the response operator is unable to contact the client or the client is unable to turn off the water supply, then a carer must be called out, which could take several minutes or several 10's of minutes, depending on the carer's location in relation to the client's premises. A much better solution involves the arrangement of Figure 9.

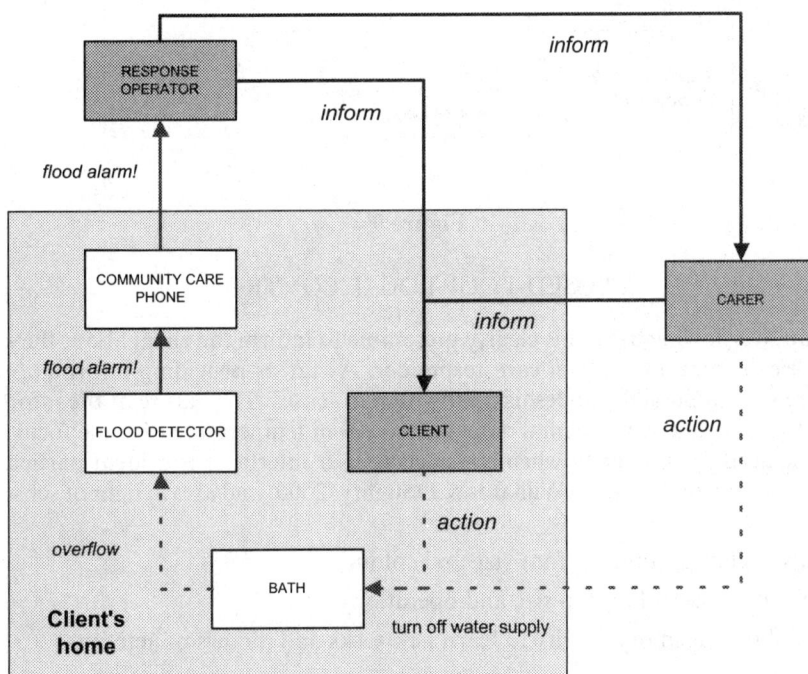

Figure 8. 'Human in the loop' control.

Figure 9 illustrates that for certain events, the CareStation can take responsibility for performing the critical action. It will still inform the response centre who can request a carer to call if necessary, but by automatically performing the critical action of turning off the water supply, in this case, it has limited the damage and hence controlled a potentially hazardous situation much faster than if a carer had to come round to turn it off.

There are many other situations in which the control of local parameters by the CareStation would be advantageous. For instance, people with dementia have been associated with an increased risk of an accident caused by the use of gas appliances because of their short-term memory impairment. The problem is compounded by the fact that elderly people have an increased likelihood of suffering from some form of olfactory impairment (anosmia or hyposmia) (Doty, 1979). Often the individual is unaware of their impaired capacity for smell, and this can be especially true of people suffering from Alzheimer's disease (Nordin et al, 1995).

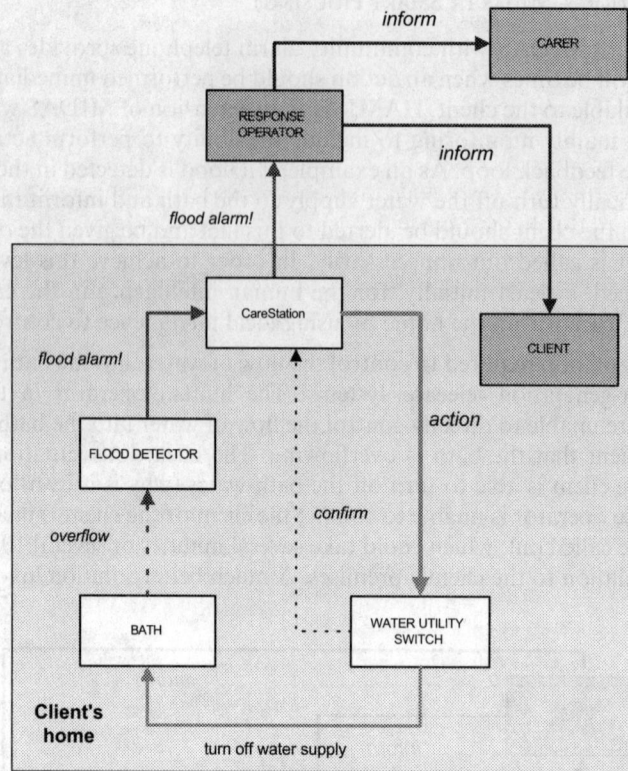

Figure 9

CLOSED-LOOP LOCAL CONTROL

In many cases, eg an overflowing bath, it is clearly preferable to inform the client about the situation without having to rely on a call from an external care responder. As far as providing information to the client is concerned, there are several possible modes using the human senses. The nature of the information might be an alarm, a reminder, general environmental data such as room temperature or some form of cue to refer to a control panel. The need for simplicity when considering user interfaces is evident particularly if incorrect actions impact on the safety of the client (Williams & Doughty, 2000) and also in light of sensory impairments, including:

1. Visual acuity (lighting, contrast, font-size and colour).

2. Manual dexterity (control/button size and operation).

3. Cognitive ability—(memory, ability to learn new tasks and models of activity).

Models of activity refer to the sequence of events that are necessary to undertake or accomplish a given task, eg making a telephone call, setting the video recorder, or setting some parameter in a smart home environment. In general, wherever possible, the direct interaction of the client with the system should be minimal; but where it is desirable for the client to have control over system events, the sequence of commands and the user-interface presented should be as consistent as possible for each task. Failing memory should be supported by appropriate reminder mechanisms that are triggered using appropriate sensory cue's. However, some techniques are more practical than others, for instance, although there is no doubting the power of the sense of smell to rekindle memories, there is some doubt as to the feasibility of relying on it in a telecare setting. For example, the use of taste and/or smell to stimulate the minds of older people suffering from confusion (perhaps to remind a person with Alzheimer's that it is time to eat) may seem innovative and appealing until one considers that many older people lose selectivity and sensitivity in these areas (see above). In any case, it may just lead to even greater confusion on the part of the client.

Sound and sight then become the primary communication channels and need to be optimised again to take into account hearing and visual impairments. Hearing impairment is very common amongst the elderly, with approximately half of over 75 year olds experiencing some form of auditory problem (ONS, 2000). In addition, approximately one million people are registered blind or partially sighted in the UK; 66 per cent of these are over the age of 75; 97 per cent of all people aged 65 + wear glasses or contact lenses, however 22 per cent of this age-group still report having difficulty with their eyesight even after using corrective measures (ONS, 1996). A means of obtaining the attention of a client (and perhaps directing them to their main means of information and control) may also be achieved by using a tactile vibration-alert system (like those used in many pagers and mobile phones).

Table 7 lists a range of HAMISH modules that run on the CareStation and provide a service directly to the client (ie without a need to go through a response centre). They include reminder systems, lost-item locators (especially useful for people with dementia who frequently misplace items such as door-keys and pension books) and a drug compliance monitor that can raise an alert if compliance is sufficiently poor to be of concern.

Table 7

HAMISH REMINDER SYSTEMS

Name	Application
MARIA	Helps improve compliance with drugs regime
EDITH	Provides a warning of open windows and heaters left on
BESSIE	Provides a safety and security check
LIL	Indicates where items have been left
DORIS	Displays time and day information (for people with dementia)

Although many of these are intended for use by those suffering from confusion, they may benefit anyone who might otherwise become anxious at night or when they have left their homes. For simple low-cost systems, the use of an audible alert signal and a flashing light emitting diode (LED) next to a fixed message may be adequate, depending on the potential for confusing the client. For optimum operation, however, there would ideally need to be a display screen at a number of locations throughout the home; or alternatively, the individual could carry a device similar to that of a pager. Options for the display unit include liquid crystal displays (LCD's) which are available with touch screen facilities and hence can be used as an input device also. This technology has been implemented in several high-end "learning" remote control handsets for controlling the growing plethora of entertainment devices found in the modem home. Alternatively use can be made of a standard television set, the price of which have tumbled over the past few years. In the future, genuine flat-screen television will appear at reasonable prices, this will allow the sets to be mounted at convenient locations on the walls of the home.

CONCLUSIONS

A number of innovative and smart devices have been developed in order to enable current community alarm systems to be expanded to provide more advanced care services than at present. These represent the easiest route to incorporating telecare into the home-care packages of clients. However, in order to provide even more levels of telecare, a genuine second generation telecare system is required. MIDAS is the realisation of a model of integrated care in which technology plays a leading role. It allows any individual to achieve a greater level of independence provided that their homes have been made "e-care ready" through the installation of appropriate communications, sensors, actuators, and intelligence. We anticipate the first applications of MIDAS to be in assessment units, possibly in the new step-down or intermediate care facilities that are being introduced to enable older people to be discharged from acute hospital units into a safety-net of rehabilitation to prepare them for independence at home. The perceived risks to living alone may be determined from MIDAS and this will be instrumental in selecting the level of telecare (and the specific services and assistive devices) that should be provided as part of the domiciliary care package. Data recorded by MIDAS can be archived and used in case reviews to demonstrate the effectiveness of rehabilitation and to provide evidence of a client's ability to cope with appropriate support. HAMISH modules may be appropriate for clients who require a higher level of immediate care, often where there are significant risks to be managed if they are to remain at home successfully, thus retaining their independence.

Memorandum by the Tunstall Group Ltd

BACKGROUND

1. As a company with direct contact on a daily basis with older people, we are aware of the impact of new and improved healthcare provision, including the use of new medicines and medical interventions. However, one of the most important influences on the wellbeing and quality of life of individuals has been the increasing use of supportive technology to minimise risk and provide reassurance, so that individuals can participate fully in society and reduce their need for more costly interventions.

TUNSTALL GROUP LTD

2. Tunstall is the world leader in telecare. Telecare is the use of sensors and alarms that enable the elderly, frail, at risk and those with chronic conditions to live safely and securely in their home for as long as possible. We are a British company based in Yorkshire employing over 650 people in the UK and 750 in total. Most of our products are manufactured at our Yorkshire facility where we have invested in modern electronic manufacturing plant. We have subsidiaries in Germany, Holland, Belgium, Canada, Australia and New Zealand and operate through distributors in many other regions of the world including the United States. We export some 30 per cent of our production. We annually spend approximately 5 per cent of our sales revenue on Research and Development, employing around 50 people in this area. We work with the Housing, Social Services and Health sectors to design innovative assistive technology for older people, enabling them to live independently in their own homes. There are approximately two million telecare and social alarm systems deployed worldwide of which 1.5 million are in the UK.

INTRODUCTION

3. This submission is about the use of technology and not about scientific developments relating to the healthcare of individuals. It is about using technology to minimise the impact of the ageing process and to promote the independence of individuals.

THE SCALE OF THE PROBLEM

The demographics of the increasingly elderly population in the UK and other countries are well documented. There are however a number of points to emphasise:

— The number of very elderly people is increasing disproportionately to the general increase. Whilst the population of people aged 65 or over in the UK is forecast to increase from 9.4 million in 2002 to 12.8 million in 2022, a 36 per cent increase, the population of people 85 or over is forecast to increase by 66 per cent over the same period.

— Whilst people are living longer they are not generally more healthy and have to live with chronic conditions for longer than in previous generations.

— Conditions such as Dementia are age-related but the age of onset is not increasing in conjunction with the increase in average age. Hence 30 per cent of people over 90 suffer from some form of dementia and that was the case 50 years ago as well. The difference is that the proportion of people over 90 is many times greater than it was 50 years. Hence the number of people with dementia is increasing rapidly and is expected to double to 1.5 million by 2050.

— The number of people with chronic conditions is increasing rapidly with some 17 million such conditions recorded. The reality is that whilst some of this growth is in the younger population due to Type 2 Obesity Based Diabetes most of it is in the elderly population suffering one of more chronic conditions.

— The number of deaths from MRSA and other Hospital Related infections is also increasing rapidly. Whilst the incidence of infection is spread across all age groups, the deaths are mainly concentrated in the elderly.

Hence the demands on acute and residential resources made by the elderly population is increasing at an unmanageable rate and a new model of care that keeps them out of hospitals and residential homes is essential.

EXISTING TECHNOLOGIES

4. The first generation of social alarms were largely developed to enable local authorities and some early housing associations to offer an alternative to residential care, which in turn was expanded following the 1948 legislation aimed at closing the former workhouses and long-stay hospitals. The concept later moved from traditional sheltered housing to dispersed housing, both in group schemes and more recently general housing in the community. The sole purpose of this early technology was to provide residents with the ability to call for help if it was needed, as well as offering reassurance to the individual and their family and/or carers. The development of "voice" systems extended the benefits of such schemes. There are now over 1.5 million people benefiting from this type of technology in the UK, monitored by 280 call centres operated by local authorities, housing associations and some private organisations, including this company.

5. These policies were undoubtedly successful, and there was a very clear shift both in national policy and at a local level away from institutionalised forms of care to solutions which enabled older people to maintain their independence. However, all too often the shortcomings of such systems became evident, with huge pressures being put on wardens and managers of such services when an older person's needs could not be met using existing technology. One of the key differences between the systems we are currently describing and those we mention in the next paragraph is that they all depend on a proactive action by the recipient of the service to initiate a response. Traditionally many of these systems were non voice based, and it was only in the last 20 years that systems increasingly became voice based, with the recipient being able to talk to a person if there was a problem.

NEW TECHNOLOGY

6. The current and second generation technology now increasingly being used is different in a number of aspects:

— Systems do not rely on the users pressing a button to call for help.

— They are wireless based and therefore are easy to install (and remove).

— They are non-intrusive (they generally exclude any kind of camera so the user is able to control "visitors" to his/her home in the normal way).

— The equipment can generally differentiate between emergencies and false alarms.

— They cover a much wider range of risks including both environmental and physical conditions (eg escaping gas, inactivity or the health of the individual).

— The systems can contain a large amount of personal and service detail which enables decisions made in an emergency to be based on a greater knowledge of the overall circumstances of the individual (eg the doctor called to an emergency during the night or the call centre operator know that a carer will arrive shortly).

— The equipment does not require the recipient to move to a specific property and so can remain in the house and community she/he is familiar with.

— The system can provide a record of the delivery of services to an individual including the ability to generate charging systems/invoices in a cost effective way.

— The technology allows the rationalisation of call/support systems to offer "best value".

— The technology has the support of all the political parties.

OUTCOMES FROM THE USE OF NEW TECHNOLOGY

7. The following outcomes arise from the deployment of this technology:

— Allows choice by the individual.

— Avoids the need for more investment in housing which has a limited usage.

— Reduces demand on more expensive residential and hospital care facilities. We estimate that at least 10 per cent of acute beds and 25 per cent of residential beds could be freed up by the systematic deployment of telecare in the home.

— Allows earlier discharge from hospital, or reduces the need for admission.

— Allows early detection of problems eg falls.

— Enables independence to be maintained.

— Provides protection against intrusion (which studies have shown can accelerate death in older people).

— Enables "risk" to be managed.

— Reduces the pressure on carers and provides reassurance to both the individual and the support network.

— Promotes greater efficiency in the delivery of primary healthcare and home care.

— By requiring agencies to work together improves the overall delivery of services at a local level.

— Prolong the lives of the elderly and frail.

To summarise, systematically deployed, telecare can significantly cut the cost and at the same time improve the quality of healthcare delivery.

THIRD GENERATION TECHNOLOGY—THE WAY FORWARD

8. The next generation of technology takes the evident advantages current systems are offering a stage further. By monitoring the pattern of behaviour of the individual in a non-intrusive way, future systems will be able to predict problems so that crises can be avoided. For example, by monitoring usage of the kitchen, the bathroom etc. changes in the activity of the individual can be noted and action taken so that the need for more intensive and costly interventions are not necessary. Already it is possible to measure some health indicators such as blood sugar levels, with no action taken if the level is within set parameters, but action remotely triggered where a problem is perceived.

RESEARCH EVIDENCE AND POLICY DEVELOPMENT

9. In recent years a growing body of evidence of the benefits of the use of technology in the care and support of ageing people has become available (see the recent Audit Commission report on assistive technology and telecare). Until recently national policy has been lacking and departmental responsibility confusing. This is evidenced by the slow realisation at a local level for the need for the various statutory bodies to work more closely together. Whilst national policy is coming together, as witnessed by the Chancellor's July announcements in the Comprehensive Spending Review, actual guidance to local authorities and health trusts remains uncoordinated. Funding streams do not reflect responsibilities or financial benefits so that it is a slow process in convincing these bodies of the benefits of using technology to promote the wellbeing of older people.

The big challenge is that whilst there is still a need to develop even greater use of this type of technology to promote the social and health wellbeing of older people, the dissemination of existing knowledge and research finding must be more widely adopted.

RECOMMENDATIONS

10. We recommend that:

— Mainstream deployment of telecare should be firmly embedded in national policy for older people. There should be clear central direction and guidance to local authorities and health trusts should be co-ordinated. Local authorities and the NHS should work closely together within a whole systems framework to encourage investment. Resources for training and consultancy in telecare should be made available to spread best practice and communicate the evidence emerging from existing and future projects.

— Research funding should be made available further to develop and pilot the third generation of technology described above, particularly in relation to lifestyle monitoring with emphasis on prediction, prevention and early detection so as to prolong active and healthy independent living.

23 September 2004

Examination of Witnesses

Witnesses: PROFESSOR ANDREW MONK, Professor of Psychology, University of York, MR PETER WRIGHT, Department of Computer Science, MR SURESH MANANDHAR, Natural Language Processing, PROFESSOR JOHN ROBINSON, Department of Electronics, University of York; and MR KEVIN ALDERSON, Business Development Director, Tunstall Group, examined.

Q179 *Chairman:* Since we are now approaching as near formal as we are likely to be today, can I say firstly thank you very much indeed, it has been a fascinating trip so far and we are very much looking forward to you amplifying your written evidence, which we found very helpful, and at the same time raising some questions of our own. We are on the record because this is technically a public meeting. I think that has been declared somewhere, because, if it has not, we will have to disregard your evidence, you understand! The point of this Committee is that we have no legislative powers or anything of that sort but the House of Lords Select Committee on Science and Technology, which Lord Oxburgh chairs, each year takes a couple or so topics and explores them in some depth and produces a report which we would hope to do on this topic some time in the late spring/early summer. I am afraid it depends on the timing of the General Election because we cannot meet when the House is in recess, as there are all sorts of quaint rules of that kind. We hope that the report will have some impact and possibly some real influence, but it is an opportunity for us to raise issues in this area to which the Government are bound to reply because the report will eventually come before the House of Lords and there will be a Government response. That is where our leverage comes in. We are very interested in a whole range of topics. There are two main scientific areas, one involving assistive technologies and the other is very much the bio-medical area. We are looking at some of the questions we have just been raising in terms of whether or not the research provision is sufficiently wide and comprehensive, the problems of multi-disciplinary work, and whether or not—and there never are adequate funds, we all know that—there are enough funds for what might or ought be done, so all of that is part of the scenario. However, we are here for a specific reason to discuss the work that you are doing. Again, I would say that we appreciate that very much. I will just ask my colleagues very briefly to say who we are and then as you make your presentations. For the record it would be helpful if you introduce yourselves and if any particular slides are verbally described. Do not worry about that too much because you have got several memories here that are still working! My name is Stewart Sutherland and I am chairing this Sub-Committee.

Baroness Walmsley: I am Joan Walmsley, member of the Committee.

Lord Turnberg: Leslie Turnberg. I am an ex-academic physician.

Lord Oxburgh: Ron Oxburgh, member of the Committee.

Q180 *Chairman:* I think you know Tom Kirkwood who is our Scientific Adviser. Now over to you. We will come in with questions and, as I say, if you say who you are for the record that would be helpful.

Professor Monk: I am Andrew Monk. We saw it as our task to present to you the scientific developments that are needed, as we understand it, from our particular point of view in order to support people who wish to live independently. So what kind of technologies can we provide and what is the science that is needed to make that effective? What I thought would be quite a good format—and we have got just 90 minutes—would be if the four of us, so myself, Peter Wright, John Robinson and Suresh Manandhar do a very brief presentation of ten or 12 minutes and use that to get some discussion going. We will possibly steal some of the time from John and Suresh because I think the major issues you are interested in are more the stuff Peter and I are saying, although equally interesting. So that is the plan. Obviously we are very interested also to understand the way that you are thinking. I understand that you have had quite a lot of deliberations already so we would be very interested to see whether what we are saying meshes at all with what you are thinking now having gathered quite a lot of information.

Q181 *Chairman:* I should say on that that we have taken a lot of evidence but we have not spent a lot of time discussing it yet, that is to come, and most of the evidence has been in the bio-medical science. You are first up on the assisted front.

Professor Monk: That is a good position to be in. I thought I would take you through the tour of the home that we did this morning and talk about the different technologies under the following headings. First, to talk a bit about monitoring technology. This in general is technology that picks up the pieces when things go wrong. It is not actually doing anything specifically for you, compared with the kind of technologies like the sink which are assisting you with your activities. I also want to talk briefly about advice for people with cognitive problems as symbolised by the fridge, and also communications and leisure. On monitoring technology, as you saw, the way that this works is that there are a number of sensors, pull cords and personal triggers. We saw the fall detector. I do not know whether I mentioned the bogus call button

24 November 2004   Professor Andrew Monk, Mr Peter Wright, Mr Suresh Manandhar, Professor John Robinson and Mr Kevin Alderson

to both groups. The idea here is that if you are worried about somebody who is at the door you can press this and it will trigger the care phone and if that is fairly near the front door, which it would be if you had a bogus caller button, the call centre can hear what is going on, they can record what is going on, so as to give somebody confidence about what is going on. I think I described the bed occupancy detector to everybody and the various other detectors. The key element in all of this is the call centre and how that is organised. The technology for getting to the call centre is one thing but the key thing for the success of this kind of system is what happens when the call arrives at the call centre, what can be done, and the way that this is programmed into the system and acted upon. So it is very much a socio-technical system. Designing this is designing a whole way of working, not just different bits of technology. Kevin Doughty—and I had hoped he could be here but he was not able to come in the end—has been doing a lot of work recently on lifestyle monitoring. These are his slides. You can tell because the graphics have suddenly got fancier! The idea of lifestyle monitoring is you have a number of detectors around the house, so you might have movement detectors in different rooms, you might have a sensor on the toilet, on the stove, and so on, so you know when people are using them. You would have a number of detectors around the front door so you could tell whether people were in or out, whether they are in bed, whether they are in the chair, and so on. On the basis of that data, which is collected by a computer somewhere, you can start to draw inferences about what the person is doing. Here is an example of raw data which was obtained from a real client in an intermediate care facility. What the top graph shows is the activity, the number of events in a time period in the four different rooms in this dwelling. You can see that between the hours of midnight and six or seven o'clock there is not much activity going on whereas in the daytime there is a lot of activity going on. You can tell the difference between day and night. You can see a little activity at four o'clock. The trace underneath shows temperature and humidity (I think that is in the kitchen), light level (I do not know which room that was in), sound level and water use. You can measure water use fairly easily just by sticking a microphone on a pipe. You see a blip at four o'clock in the morning when somebody had a call of nature. That is the raw data but what Kevin has been working on is ways of putting together this raw data to look at trends. So here for example is a mobility index which is a weighted index from all the different sensors. You can see that there is some kind of decline going on. There is a little dip around 15 May and what he has been doing is looking at ways of setting thresholds for alerts. So you might say this trend here looks like it is a downward trend, it hits some threshold here—

Q182 *Lord Oxburgh:* This is for one person?

Professor Monk: This is for one person. If you have got a two-person household it gets more complicated. At that point you might want to alert the call centre and perhaps somebody would organise an extra care package of some kind. You have different levels of alert. Here is a similar aggregated index, this time showing activity at night, and that peak around 18 June corresponds to a urinary tract infection, so again you might start to be able to detect problems remotely. So that is what they call lifestyle monitoring. Some people call it second generation telecare. I think it raises a lot of issues that we might discuss in a moment. Just going back to the simpler technologies that you saw in the home. The main issues, I think, are socio-technical issues. The science that needs to be done is to apply the techniques that Peter will be talking about in a moment from human factors and social science basically to understand what would make these things attractive to people and what things we can do with these systems. One of the major problems is that people tend to get this technology very late on when it is hard for them to adjust to what it is doing and to understand what it is doing, when they absolutely desperately need it. The two barriers to getting it in are getting it to do various things that could be useful to them other than just detecting falls and medical emergencies, and the other thing is you see quite a lot of resistance from older people because it is stigmatising. I think that phone looks quite attractive but I know people who just do not want something like that in the house that says something about them. These are problems that are solvable but they require research. It can be quite generally applicable research. I think there is a need for, if you like, management and economic theory to understand the business models that make these systems work. Some people have got successful ones and some people have not, and understanding that is pretty critical. In terms of developing the technology, as you said, most of the technology you have seen today in the monitoring technology is not rocket science. It is quite a long way short of rocket science. When that technology improves it will still be using the basic existing science, but, nevertheless, I think looking ahead, particularly when we start thinking about lifestyle monitoring-type things, second generation telecare, that natural language processing and computer vision will be essential. Natural language processing is getting the thing to talk to you. I do not know whether you have had evidence from Heinz Wolfe and the Millennium Homes people, as were, but they are working very much on that kind of approach so that the house talks to you, it has little conversations with you when it thinks there is something wrong. We think that is the way it has to go if you start doing this monitoring, so

24 November 2004   Professor Andrew Monk, Mr Peter Wright, Mr Suresh Manandhar, Professor John Robinson and Mr Kevin Alderson

developments in science which allow us to have computers to talk to people and computers that see what people are doing. A problem with the detectors that you have to wear is that people are not always wearing them and there is so much you can do now with a camera and processing which would be much more effective. I will gallop through this and then we can go back, if that is okay. As I pointed out, in the responsive home we have got very little assistance with activities in daily living. That is basically to do with the fabric of the building. Very commonly used assistive technology would be the door entry systems, something that gives you a view of who is at the door and allows you to let them in or not let them in as you want to. Environmental control—I guess that is what most people think of as "smart" homes, a button you can press and it switches on the telly remotely or a button you can press and it switches on the light. Possum make a large range of this sort of equipment and you can control the television, lights, the heating and so on. It generally goes under the buzz word of "environmental control". There is a variety of switches you can use to do this. The thing on the left is a zapper on which you press a button like you would to control a television and we have all got that. The thing on the right is a suck and blow switch so somebody whose only motor responses they could make would be to suck or blow would control these things. Hoists—very, very important. Those are all assistive technologies for people with mobility problems. There are also technologies for people with sensory problems so that is a text phone marketed by BT for people who cannot hear. That is a phone that they can use and it has a whole service to add to that. For people with cognitive problems my favourite is— and I think I am going to get one of these—this thing on the right which is a thing that Roger Orpwood at the Bath Institute of Medical Engineering has built. You attach a tag to all the things you lose like your glasses and your keys and so on and you have this thing by the front door and if you go out and cannot find your keys you look for the picture of the key and you press it and it beeps until you find them. There are all sorts of things you can do there. In terms of the scientific advances needed with this class of technology it is not something I know very much about. What I can say from talking to housing associations and social services and so on is the problem, as they see it, is the expense. If you have got to have a motor, you have got to have a power supply, if you have got to have a power supply you have got large maintenance and installation problems. I guess the developments that are going to improve this will be material sciences of one kind and another, as new developments come along. The next category is advice for people with cognitive problems. I think there are enormous possibilities

here by drawing on existing science, that is to say adapting and working with it. For example, there are very good, well-developed models of human memory that psychologists have developed over the years. That is a top-level scheme of one such thing. There are also large numbers of people out there characterising different kinds of pathologies in terms of this memory model. Somebody can come along and say that top box in early dementia is pretty well spared but that middle box is completely done in whereas the bottom box might be middle affected or whatever. If we combine that kind of knowledge with a detailed theory of human memory, a detailed mapping from that on to a particular pathology and then combine that with an analysis of a task—for example, making a cup of tea, what are the cognitive demands when you are making a cup of tea, the planning, you need water and to remember what you have done and so on—we can produce that kind of thing. If you put these three things together, you can make quite strong predictions about where the problems are going to occur for particular patients, someone with a particular pathology, and how you can prevent the problems or how you can assist them. I think that is something that we will see more and more of in the future. It depends very much on new developments and on natural language processing and computer vision as well as applying these existing technologies in psychology. We looked at communication. The two-button phone and the notice board on TV, the screen saver. Again, there is an enormous amount of theory about mediated human to human communication psychology and human factors. I myself spent about ten years studying why video conferencing with a picture of just a head and shoulder shot of somebody does not do anything for you at all and what kinds of video images might be more useful. There is lots of theory out there. It needs to be adapted, it needs to be applied to the problem of solving the loneliness and isolation experienced by many older people. There are so many opportunities there that really need to be attacked. Then finally, leisure. Somebody was saying today, "Is the end of my life going to be spent playing dominos?" (Or even worse, for me, watching Coronation Street, although I do not want to insult anybody who is a Coronation Street fan here.) What can we do? There are all these people out there devoting enormous amounts of energy to understanding what teenagers and young adult males can do with computers to entertain themselves, but the "silver surfers", or whatever you want to call them, are out there as well. Go out there and design something that is fun for me. We here have been very much in the forefront of scientific studies of fun, trying to understand leisure, and scientific studies of the leisure use of technology. I have to keep saying to people (some people do not understand it) that it is a perfectly reasonable thing to do. People think, "Fun, er, enjoyment? You want public money for that? Whatever next?" The conclusion is that there are many opportunities for technology to improve the quality of life of older people, but to exploit them effectively we have got to understand what people want and then put it into a form where engineers and designers can use it. That is an important thing. There is a summary of the things that I covered and we can use that as a prompt.

Q183 *Chairman:* Thank you very much. If it is possible to let us have a disk with the slides on that would be useful.
Professor Monk: That can be done.

Q184 *Chairman:* Do you want to do the other presentations now and then have the discussion?
Professor Monk: It is up to you.

Q185 *Chairman:* You know what is coming, we do not. So long as we ensure that we have time because I am sure the questions are already stacking up. We really want to have a good half an hour's discussion.
Professor Monk: I do not think anybody else will be as long-winded as I was.

Q186 *Chairman:* Let us get on with it rather than discussing it.
Mr Wright: My name is Peter Wright. My background is cognitive science and psychology although I work in the Computer Science Department. I am one of the rare examples of inter-disciplinary crossover, I suppose. Andrew has been emphasising near-term technology, what we can do now and so on. I want to think a little bit about future-term technology but I do not want to give you a technological "Futurama" type vision. I want to make one point really which is unless we have sensitive research which is about understanding users' needs and involving users in design then inevitably the technology will be technology led and will not fit users' needs. As I said, in Europe and with the DTI there is a big research initiative in the area of what is called intelligent ambient technologies. What is meant by that is the idea that computers will disappear and that there will not be a box under your table. Instead, the processing power will be embedded in the fabric of the house or clothes or whatever. That has very interesting possibilities in terms of ageing communities and truly responsive homes. It also has interesting problems to do with understanding how we could possibly interact with those. That is what meant on this slide by the idea "ambient technology embedded". Another concept is that technologies will be context-aware which means

the systems which have disappeared into the built environment will know who is in them and where those people are. And that again provides a tremendous amount of potential in terms of assistive technologies. They might also be personalised so that we can tailor the services offered by such systems to individuals since we know where they are, we know what time of day it is, we know through quality of life monitoring what kinds of things they might be doing at this time, and you can make certain intelligent inferences about what individuals needs are. Of course in terms of lifestyle monitoring if we know the identity of people in the house we can deal with the problem you alluded to. At the moment the only lifestyle monitoring you can do is if you live in the house on your own. Thus there are various things there. The other concepts are that they will be adaptive, they will change both in terms of hours and days but also over years potentially, and they will be anticipatory. Anticipatory means that based on this lifestyle monitoring, systems will be able to predict your needs and so on. Instead of thinking about interacting with a terminal like this we might think about the concept of interaction with spaces. You walk into a room with John's image sensing analysis or other techniques and you will be able to interact with the system as you move around the space and by moving around the space you will be communicating through the system. There may be smart materials in this. Lots of advances in nanotechnology mean that we will be able to produce intelligent wallpaper, wallpaper that is sensitive to touch, so instead of having a keyboard you could gesture out the square on the wall and use that to inter-act with the system. Equally, you could have a large interactive display or a small mobile phone from which a display can be echoed on a large display. All of this however requires quite a lot of intelligent image analysis, intelligent handwriting analysis, and intelligent natural language. There is a need though in this future armour for user-centred design. We are all incredibly familiar with the opposite to that which is a design-led design. This is the creeping futurism, as Donald Norman refers to, that you find on your home VHS recorder or the next generation of mobile phones. The original version of Microsoft Word had about 20 functions on it, now they have released it with 380, hardly any of which are used. That is a model of development and that is not a user-led type of thing, it is a designer-led type of thing. Typically if designers are not informed by user studies then they design for people like themselves. That is okay a lot of the time, but when you are thinking about ageing communities there are not many people over 35 in Microsoft, let alone over 60. User-centred design is the thing here at York. Certainly Andrew and I are specialists in that and this is what we have done over

24 November 2004   Professor Andrew Monk, Mr Peter Wright, Mr Suresh Manandhar, Professor John Robinson and Mr Kevin Alderson

the last 15 or 18 years. This is the most recent application to ageing but it is an application of principles which have been developed elsewhere which are about involving users in the design. It is about the empirical measurement of interaction activities in the context of the user. The bottom line of this presentation shows that it is going to be essential to getting the right kind of technology ten or 15 years down the line. The great slogan of user-centred design is "know your user". We have theories, methods and techniques for doing many types of user study. In the old days it was simply a question of knowing what people's physical capabilities were and psychological capabilities were. Now we are being challenged to find out what people's social needs are and what the risks and hazards associated with their lives are. In order to do this intelligent quality of life monitoring we have got to understand what their behaviour patterns are, what their social and cultural dispositions are and what their routines of daily living are. That takes us out of the narrow range of psychological research into a more inter-disciplinary field of research where we are working with sociologists, psychologists, arts people, humanities, researchers all sorts of radical multi-disciplinary groups. We even have to start thinking about people's experiences with technology, what is people's understanding of a home as opposed to a house? How is trust established and built up? How do people identify with technology? What governs whether or not they appropriate a technology or reject a technology? In terms of sources of information about users the bottom line of this pyramid is about building the models and representations of users you bring into design as proxy models. You can think about that as formal scientific simulation or more informal representations of users through various techniques which have been developed. We can do laboratory-based studies whereby we get people into laboratories and look at how they interact with technologies. And we can do real-life empirical studies which are the kinds of things we have been talking about and emphasising earlier today. As you move into the home in particular, these kinds of real-life studies are difficult to do but essential. At the top of the pyramid is what we were talking about earlier. I refer to it there as co-design, the idea that users and designers work together to establish design, either through involvement in the design process itself or the idea of building technology which can be adapted and adopted by users after its release. Ten years ago Andrew and I would have said the key thing you have got to think about in design is useability, how to make things easy to use, easy to learn and easy to remember, and that is still true today. You have also got to think about different things now such as what

the users' experience of this kind of technology is. Whether or not a person accepts a piece of technology is a much richer kind of question than whether or not it is useable. That is because we live with technology and we use technology to say things about ourselves. It is as much about self-expression and identity and quality of life. A fall detector can be a tremendously useful and useable thing but if people feel that is saying something about them as a disabled person that may dissuade them from using it. How do we make this technology acceptable? The modern ubiquitous ambient technologies are moving into these small, wearable devices, technology that you can wear in your clothes. One simple question is, why can a fall detector not be a piece of jewellery? So there is a great need for research in this broader area of users' experience of technology and the factors which make it acceptable and allow people to appropriate it. So near term the research agenda is to do with things that Andrew has talked about. Long term we have to think about what technological potentials there are ten or 15 years down the line. We will have a new generation of users with new capabilities because these are the young people of today or people like us. We need long-term studies of user patterns and the way in which user patterns change as we grow older. We need more sophisticated models and measurements and new technologies around the idea of adaptivity and responsivity, not just studies of how people interact with larger keyboards and all the rest of it. Of course inevitably this kind of concept of a house as an intelligent place leads us to principles of security, access, control, public and private space, where data is going, what principles are we going to install as design principles about who has that access and how that data is used. Finally, involving users in design.

Q187 *Chairman:* Thank you very much. We are picking up speed. Keep it going!
Mr Manandhar: My name is Suresh Manandhar and my background is artificial intelligence, specifically computational language, also known as natural language processing. I am a lecturer in computer science. What I want to discuss today is some applications of natural language technology in a smart form and the potential of how that technology might be useable for older people. The first idea is the idea about embedded digital assistance. The idea is that what we want to have is natural language understanding ability in everyday devices. So we want to make this so that people can interact with everyday devices like a phone or a washing machine or a microwave in plain natural language. We want this technology to be always on and always available. So the challenge here is really to be able to bring this technology down into a small device with very limited

24 November 2004   Professor Andrew Monk, Mr Peter Wright, Mr Suresh Manandhar,
Professor John Robinson and Mr Kevin Alderson

computing power. The project that I am currently working on, which is called the Ubiquitous Digital Assistant Project, is being funded by the DTI and we have been working towards this goal of building such a platform. So the question might be how is this feasible? Is this technology rocket science? Is this *Star Trek*? Can we have this technology? One answer is that we have already deployed such technology in First Direct. This was a pilot system that we ran for about a year and this was doubled up by a company called Lexicle which I am involved in. We produced a "smart" mortgage adviser called CARA to which you can ask questions in plain language. Since we did not have voice recognition you needed to type in your question and she will give you advice on smart mortgage products. The point about this is that this technology is already there in a certain sense. The aim of the exercise we are doing is to make that technology available in small devices. One reason we think that might be feasible is that the functionality of a small device is very limited so the range of natural language understanding that a small device requires is also going to be bounded by its functionality because a device only needs to answer questions that it knows about. If you scoped a problem that way you could perhaps make this technology available and also bring it down into a small device. The idea is that in a networked home what we want to be able to do is to access any service from any device in the home. If the devices are networked themselves then it is not essential to ask the right device. The device itself will channel that question to the right device and hopefully you will get an answer. That is the kind of idea we are working towards and we believe that a natural language interface will reduce dependence, for example, on carers in the home and on tele-care services, making older people more independent. The scientific challenge is that natural language processing technology needs to be significantly improved and obviously that is part of the research goal that we are working towards in order to bring it to devices in the home. Also, more importantly, we need to again make this technology acceptable to people. We need to understand human-to-human dialogues and human-to-computer dialogues better so we need to put the research from computational linguistics and psychology and take that research and put that into our natural language interfaces. The other application that I see is something that Andrew also mentioned earlier in that we want to apply or bring in natural language interfaces to monitoring devices in the home. For example, Andrew mentioned if you had a computer vision system we would not need to attach fall detectors on the body; we could just use a cheap web camera and use computer vision software to recognise if somebody has fallen. A system might be smart enough, for example, to detect that a bed is a bed and you are allowed to lie down or fall down on the bed as opposed to the floor and so on. So here the idea is that you could use a virtual agent, like the fridge demonstrator you have seen which is part of the project that I am working on, as an interface to act as a go-between between the emergency services. For example, the agent could say, "It looks like you have fallen. If you do not move in the next 30 seconds I am going to ring the emergency services," and you could monitor the person's movement and based on that react accordingly. Also something that Andrew mentioned earlier about passive monitoring of health and lifestyle where we could again use AI techniques to do that more efficiently. Also door entry systems related to passive monitoring, bed occupancy, and so on. Here I believe that by combining the techniques of computer vision and natural language processing we can make this kind of technology available and also make it affordable and cheap to build a business case for it. Obviously with decreasing hardware costs and decreasing sensor costs such as webcam this could truly be affordable.

Q188 *Lord Turnberg:* What sort of timescale do you put on that?
Mr Manandhar: For the whole thing?

Q189 *Lord Turnberg:* Sure, why not?
Mr Manandhar: For the computer vision side I am not an expert on it, my expertise is purely on natural language processing. Certainly for the natural language side of things we already have a working system. The question is how adaptable that kind of system is and how well we can understand the daily chores of people.

Q190 *Lord Turnberg:* Ten years, five years?
Mr Manandhar: I would say somewhere in between.
Mr Wright: There is computer vision and voice recognition as well.
Professor Robinson: Yes, I think the two sides are quite related because in computer vision in constrained environments we are doing increasingly clever things. That is also true in computational linguistics. The range of signals that one can deal with is the next significant advance that is required so that being able to be speaker-independent in spite of the washing machine being on is akin to being able to sense a posture of the body despite some bizarre lighting condition. Both of those are very tough problems and they are the next big thing that is required. Therefore ten years may be pessimistic or it may be optimistic.
Mr Manandhar: I think the central point here is context awareness. It is a context aware environment because we can put in sensors and the system knows this is a table, this is a meeting room, and so on, and

we can use that context awareness to greatly reduce the computational tasks or make that computational task easier. That is the point that we are trying to take advantage of.

Mr Wright: Classically you can constrain interpretation of multiple mode of input, so if you know where someone is or who that someone is in a particular place then you have a better understanding of what is being said.

Mr Manandhar: Nobody has begun working on this area but the point is, for example, if a natural language system knows where a particular sentence has been spoken and in the context it is spoken, for example by using a computer vision system, then we can reduce the disambiguation problem.

Q191 *Chairman:* Context and language are inter-dependent?

Mr Manandhar: Absolutely, yes.

Mr Wright: Again that is an issue in getting that kind of inter-disciplinary research applied to a particular problem that both parties can work.

Mr Manandhar: Another scenario would be, for example, a language-driven interface to your entertainment system, so if you imagine a Sky Plus-type system where you want to have voice-driven access to your TV schedule or voice-driven recording of your programmes. Some systems already do that. They try to automatically learn your recording preferences and so on. This is something we can in some senses already do so the technology is kind of already there to make this happen. This shows some statistics on the ageing population so in 1999—

Q192 *Chairman:* I think we are fairly well up on that one, it comes up every time.

Mr Manandhar: Basically the average population is ageing quite a lot and the question is who is going to look after us? The Japanese are very keen on building robotic companions. For example, here is a picture of one that is available right now. In contrast, I also think we can use natural language technology to build virtual companions so we can have virtual companions that can engage in social chat or offer helpful advice. For example, the advice could be something that could be driven by scientific data, for example from passive monitoring systems, which is coupled with analysis of health and so on.

Mr Wright: You could have someone nagging at you in the morning saying, "Eat more Special K"?

Mr Manandhar: That is the last point. I currently have a PhD student working on persuasive dialogue. The idea is how a dialogue system could engage a user and try to alter the user's behavioural pattern slightly in a regular way so that the person has a healthier lifestyle.

Q193 *Lord Oxburgh:* Why should this be restricted to old people?

Mr Manandhar: The system we are building is not just for older people. However, to do this we need to understand human-to-human dialogues and the notions that Peter also mentioned earlier, for example notions of trust—how to make systems more believable, more trustworthy from the point of view of the user, and what other kind of language games that people play for example to make this happen. We need a better understanding of the role of social chitchat. People use chitchat, for example, to make themselves more friendly to the other person. If we design a system we need to ensure that that familiarity is somehow shown by the system. Again, we need to understand mechanisms for persuasion in dialogue, which is something I mentioned just now. Also a lot of human communication is non-verbal so if you want to design virtual personalities then you need to ensure that these virtual personalities also produce gestures in the most natural way to make it more acceptable by humans. We need to understand models of human gestures and gain a better understanding. It is interesting because here recently I have done a project where we have tried to characterise the gestures of Meg Ryan in *Sleepless in Seattle*. So we have done a complete model marked up of all the gestures and we are trying to see if we can automatically model her gestures. I will pass on to John.

Q194 *Chairman:* We are running out of discussion time.

Professor Robinson: Indeed, so rather than giving my presentation may I hand round a sheet and spend three minutes taking you through it. I am conscious that we really need to get back to the earlier material because that is perhaps closer to your interests. As has been said, I am John Robinson and I represent a researcher in computer vision. I suppose I have two simple points to make. The first is that while the 40 years of research in computer vision has seen many advances in terms of object recognition and in terms of characterising 3D scenes and so on, in the current research emphasis the key problem to solve is the one that I expressed a moment or two ago, which is to do with generality in hostile environments. Britain is very well placed in computer vision. I have given praise to some of our competitors there. I imagine some other universities would disagree with Surrey and Oxford but they are extremely strong teams and we have a lot of other good teams, including York, in the UK. The fact that there is a technology lead in this country is an opportunity to capitalise on this. Once the generality problems are solved there are many opportunities both for monitoring in terms of interpreting people's postures and movement and the monitoring of appliances and so on as well, and for interaction in terms of being able to gesture towards objects, and maybe have a control projected onto your hand and say what you want done with that object and it is done. So the first thing then is with this solution of the generality problem, which is the key focus of computer vision now, there is the possibility of instrumenting people without putting physical devices on them, instrumenting objects without having physical devices in them, and using vision as we can also use sound. The second thing to say is that of course the adoption of this kind of technology is much more invasive perhaps than those that people are already having social problems with because computer vision systems take pictures and they involve networked cameras. There are issues of trust in respect of the technology. Ideas concerned with systems, whether wholly automatic or ones into which people can tap, being able to observe you about your daily life. That is definitely something we want to do research on here because it is exactly this inter-section of the psychological, sociological, anthropological and the technical where we think that the big issues are going to be. The last part there outlines one or two of those research questions and useability is part of that, too.

Q195 *Chairman:* That was very, very helpful and very precise. Thank you very much, we will take this sheet with us. I will launch straight in. I have got two questions, neither of which you need answer now but I would be interested in your reactions. One is, could any of the fall technology be adapted to deal with some of the problems of elder abuse, because that is a growing issue in the provision of care as increasingly care is provided (although family members can be just as bad) by folks who are outside the family as well. That is the first one. There follows the next question because if it were possible to do that you might be able to make some inroads into child abuse in the same way. That is my second question. How much of this is distinctive to the needs of older people and at which stage does it get distinctive as you go down the road of application? If you have any reactions now, fine, but if not then—
Mr Wright: My immediate reaction to the first question is child abuse would be very difficult with fall detector technology because children are going to spend all their time jumping off trees and hanging upside down and so on, so it would not really give you a technological answer. I could not proffer an answer on the first one because I suppose it would depend what form that physical abuse took, but I could certainly see that potentially there might be possibilities there, certainly with the kind of what we

are calling second generation lifestyle monitoring and image analysis.

Q196 *Chairman:* Direct monitoring?
Mr Wright: Yes, but it would be interesting to think about that and give you a more considered response.
Professor Robinson: I think it is difficult because it is in the interests of the abuser to thwart any monitoring system. In a general sense hands-off monitoring systems such as vision, for example, do have an advantage in being less obviously easy to remove and so on, but even so they obviously have to be thwartable for legitimate reasons.

Q197 *Chairman:* Basically monitoring various forms of body trauma and you would then begin to be clearer what is causing that trauma. If it was all happening at two in the morning you would begin to worry about the night staff, to be blunt.
Professor Monk: The care-phone call centre technology is already being used for household violence cases. I think Tunstall make a portable unit, and a social worker can take it and put it in a pendant and if they feel violence is being committed they can press it. Of course, that does not quite solve—

Q198 *Chairman:* It is an entirely different range of problems. I will leave it with you. I do not want to push the issue.
Mr Wright: Another thought is that we have been doing some theoretical conceptual work around wearable, wireless cameras that are outward facing. We are talking about crime prevention and this camera is an always-on monitoring camera. It is not looking in so it is not that same sense of privacy invasion as looking out. The Microsoft Research Lab in Cambridge are doing work in that area.

Q199 *Lord Oxburgh:* First a factual question: what sort of ratio of number of individuals in call centres do you need to handle a particular number of households or individuals under surveillance?
Mr Alderson: I do not actually think there is any particular limit. The biggest ones have 50,000 or 60,000 people connected to them; the smallest ones have 1,000 to 2,000, and we believe that the right level is round about 30,000 in a locality.

Q200 *Lord Oxburgh:* But how many individuals do you need to look after the 30,000?
Mr Alderson: I misunderstood. We have a 30,000 call centre and we have eight.

Q201 *Lord Oxburgh:* Thank you. The second question is much more general. Most technology fails some of the time and you are going to have people use your technology who have very little in the way of recourse and who are likely to panic if it does not work because of the degree of dependency that they have developed on it. How much thought do you give or has been given to failing modes and failing safe?

Professor Monk: That is certainly something that we have been pursuing here at York. We have been adapting methods from safety critical systems in computer science that have been previously applied to things like flight decks and control rooms to monitoring technologies and assistive technologies, trying to think how you would use those kinds of methods in that situation. In terms of how much actually goes on out there now in those companies I do not really know.

Q202 *Lord Oxburgh:* Because it is the system analysis that you need to look at.

Professor Monk: That is exactly what we are doing. There is a joint project with Lancaster University and they took a slightly different tack.

Mr Wright: It is part of the SRC-funded multi-centre research collaboration called DIRC (Dependability Interdisciplinary Research Collaboration) and there are a number of activities around the issues of dependability in these sorts of systems. There are case studies in air traffic control and aviation flight decks. One activity Andrew and I have been involved in is looking at issues of dependability in domestic settings, but I suspect, although I would not like to swear to it, that it is not something that many producers or manufacturers currently think about too carefully because it is not a heavily regulated kind of area.

Q203 *Lord Oxburgh:* Finally, whose responsibility do you see it as being to actually bring this to market or not, to turn it into useful devices that are produced?

Professor Robinson: What is the "it" in that question? Who is responsible to bring "it"?

Q204 *Lord Oxburgh:* The technologies that you are developing. You are having great fun academically working with splendid research problems but they do not magically transmute into useful gadgets that will go into people's houses. That requires development and investment. How are you looking after that?

Mr Wright: We are probably not currently in any big sense, but one key feature of the Centre for Useable Home Technology is the collaboration with manufacturers, through our partners Hewlett Packard, Tunstall and Microsoft Research Labs. We are encouraging them to become involved precisely because that would be, at least in our limited context at the moment, a path to market, but of course beyond the kinds of concepts that we are working with, there are all sorts of considerations that would

affect that when you are working with competitors. There may be other ways of providing more motivation and more impetus for industrial partners to develop products further.

Mr Manandhar: What I would like to say is that, first of all, we are scientists and if we want to make this technology available in the home we have to carry out our research in such a way that it is marketable and it is commercialised. For example, the project that I am involved in has the goal to bring natural language processing into a small device. Clearly that is a commercial goal because without that that technology would never appear in the market place. So I think that is the first thing—that we need to have goals which will ensure that the project has got some commercial success. Secondly, what we should try to do is collaborate with investors to see the feasibility and get their input into that research work.

Mr Wright: Of course the third thing you have experience of, Suresh, is spin-off companies.

Mr Manandhar: Yes, spin-off companies. For example, the First Direct web site I showed you and CARA the smart mortgage adviser—that was a spin-off company which I was involved in. It is a York University spin-off company.

Q205 *Baroness Walmsley:* This intelligent environment system obviously requires programming specifically for a particular user and that is where they work best, when they are adapted to a particular person's needs and lifestyle. Clearly they are complex and they require considerable understanding and technical skills in setting them up and then re-setting them up when the customer goes on to the "great rest home in the sky" and somebody else lives in the house. Do you anticipate difficulty in finding enough of the right trained people to do this sort of work? What about the workforce that is going to be needed to actually get these things up and running to serve the older community of the future?

Professor Monk: I will let my colleagues answer that specific question. I am not sure it is a problem because most of the systems learn for themselves. You put them in learning mode and they learn about the way you behave and then they can detect. However, I think there is a big problem with training. If you want to put in a new washing machine you can get a plumber. If you want to put in a new lighting system you get an electrician. Where do you get your smart home technology fitter from? With monitoring technology that is very easy. You Velcro them or Sellotape them to the wall, effectively. As things get more sophisticated and more assistive there is a problem there but maybe that is a problem that solves itself when you get a sufficient number of people doing it. I do not know. That is a very interesting question. Is it true that these systems typically would learn from themselves?

Professor Robinson: Well, there is a useability question for the configuration phases. I suppose one could say that you may need professionals or you may need someone with perhaps a basic level of competence in computer-type applications. I am not sure. We really do not know enough about the deployment in a widespread way.

Mr Wright: You have done some studies. One of the issues we are recognising is a kind of through life/ through service issue so that installation is not without its tremendous difficulties. We have done studies, as indeed have Harvard, where we are looking at the problem of getting these systems on line and then, similarly, maintaining them, which is a real problem. I guess that is almost as much a question about the business model or the commercial model that you would employ to make this technology sustainable as much as a research question.

Q206 *Baroness Walmsley:* They need to be installer friendly as well as user-friendly, do they not?

Professor Monk: I think manufacturers are very aware of that.

Q207 *Lord Turnberg:* I have two questions. I am quite conscious of the fact that we are going to be writing a report which we hope will advance the field of research into ageing and promote those activities. I am trying to pull out from what you are telling us what is still needed and I am not quite clear what the rate-limiting steps in progress in your fields are. Is it money? I am sure the answer to that is yes. Would it make the difference between ten years and five years if you had lots more money in the field? That is one thing. Is it lack of ideas or is it lack of materials or technology? Or is it applying much of what we have got and therefore lack of commercial involvement and investment? Or is it all of these? That is one thing. I will come to my other question in a moment.

Mr Wright: Do you want us to respond to that one? My personal view is that it would be great if there were the means by which in some kind of long-term collaboration people like material scientists could come together with usability specialists, focused around a specific problem or a population. In the problem of ageing, the material scientist would go off and build their high-capacity network or their large screen displays, which will be great. We will go along saying, "You need to be user-centred and we really know what the users' needs are in this community." And never the twain shall meet apart from an occasional two-year project employing an RA. Whereas if there was some infrastructure that allowed people who had the vision to come together

to produce some kind of agenda or programme to focus on a particular problem, that would be an interesting step forward.

Q208 *Lord Turnberg:* To bring material scientists in or engage them in the exercise?

Mr Wright: Yes, and the builders and also, to bring architects into discussions about digital technologies.

Q209 *Lord Turnberg:* What stops you doing that now?

Mr Wright: It may be a shortage of vision on my part but the way in which I would do that now is with a three or four-year EPSRC-funded project involving a few architects or whatever and employing a few RAs while I carried on doing teaching and so on. What I am thinking is something more infrastructural, a think-tank kind of thing that would allow people to take a step back and be more reflective.

Professor Monk: One of the things that we wanted to do with the responsive home was to get a group of people together all working on the same problem so they start to inform each other. I think an of institute of some kind would be—

Q210 *Lord Turnberg:* In York?

Professor Monk: Of course!

Mr Wright: A think-tank.

Q211 *Baroness Walmsley:* A real one, not virtual one.

Professor Robinson: If I could make a remark on behalf of my colleagues—and they may want to disown it after I have made it—in my earlier career I have been involved with human-computer interaction professionals quite a lot, but they have tended to be cognitive psychologists whereas the group here are social psychologists, coming out of projects like the Net Neighbours project where these issues of sociability and enjoyment and quality of life are paramount. The difficulty, of course, is that they are hard to get a handle on compared with how efficient it is to use a particular interface and yet questions of loneliness and enabling half a generation down to support the generation so that as everyone moves through the system there is a technology-supported network of care and community seem to me to be very important. It is a philosophy of looking at these technologies as sociable technologies that really do need stimulus and support. That is on their behalf. On my behalf I would say we have a world lead in a particular area of technology and I think there ought to be a lot more money put into computer vision. I am sure my colleagues think the same.

Q212 *Lord Turnberg:* I have got my second question in a moment but go on.

24 November 2004 Professor Andrew Monk, Mr Peter Wright, Mr Suresh Manandhar, Professor John Robinson and Mr Kevin Alderson

Mr Manandhar: I just wanted to add perhaps a more concrete proposal which is perhaps government could make a specific call to help build this kind of technology and more research into this kind of technology.

Professor Monk: A single Institute for Technology for Independent Living. We said earlier that it was easy to do interdisciplinary research. It is not really. What happens is that we do fall between cracks. The latest thing that a colleague of John's in electronics and I put to the EPSRC got rave reviews from the human factors group but the electronics people hated it. With computer science and psychology there is now a community of people so it is easy but if we suddenly want to bring in architects it would be really hard. If you had an institute where you could do that—

Mr Manandhar: The point I am making is the Government could give a push to initiating this.

Q213 *Lord Turnberg:* My second question is what you have been describing is "all-singing, all-dancing" for everyone. It seemed to me that this is great for the future and it is going to tell everyone where everyone is everywhere in the house and it is going to tell us what they are doing, but I start as a mere clinician from the point of view of the patients or elderly people at home and think about what it is that they need. Do all of them need all of that? Some of them cannot see very well so they need something to help with their vision. Some of them cannot hear very well so they need something for that. Some of them lack mobility or dexterity and some of them just feel lonely. Maybe there are other things as well, they may be incontinent and a whole lot of other things. I cannot quite see how we get what you are describing to the patients or the people. What you are talking about is new technology which will come but there is an awful lot of existing technology which is not being applied. That is why I think the question about engaging with the commercial side to develop and to produce what is already known for those specific areas of need is important. Do you think in those sorts of terms?

Mr Wright: I would like to clarify what I think your point is relative to what we have seen today. Obviously the Tunstall technology and the fall detectors are there and there is a market now.

Q214 *Lord Turnberg:* Again we are talking about fall detectors. I would like fall preventors.

Mr Wright: Yes, okay. I think my response to your question is about the position that I put forward to do with two things really. The first is that you really need to start with users rather than start with technology and work up from there, and then to say

that the technologists need to be working towards a concept of open systems, systems that are flexible enough to meet different types of needs, so if we were looking at how you would do this in real life and real practice, a care manager would go into a home and be able to assess the needs against some kind of criteria and that could be mapped on to technology tool kits. You could say, well, if this person has these kinds of visual disabilities, or has problems with speech impediments, then the way we need to think about the support is adapting the systems to respond in this way. So the two parts for me are an open systems kind of approach to the development of the technology plus a user needs led service which provides the requirements.

Q215 *Chairman:* That is partly why I asked the question of how much of this is distinctive to the needs of older people because the bigger the market the better the likelihood. I am going to ask another question. I do not mind leaving it on the table but I would like a reply in due course. Earlier on before the formal session one or two of us were talking about housing regulations and since you are in the business of homes is there anything you would like to suggest to us that we can think about in relation to building regulations that we might press the Government on because if we put this stuff in early the cost is minimal but if we want to adapt houses later it is much more expensive. If there is anything that could realistically be put forward as a housing regs matter then that would be useful.

Mr Wright: I am sure the answer is that there are things but I would not like to say just right now what those are. The whole of the ten year or 15 year concept rests on the idea of inter-operability and networking and so on.

Chairman: There is no guarantee they will pay any attention to us.

Q216 *Lord Oxburgh:* To take that a little further bit further. When I think of my own experience, when my mother was very old I wanted to install a lever tap which she could operate easily but she said, "No, people will think I am getting old"! There is no reason why taps of that design should not be general and some architectural tap designs are positively user-unfriendly.

Chairman: Baroness Walmsley has another question.

Q217 *Baroness Walmsley:* It is just following on a little further from your point about the mass market. We were talking earlier about some devices which had actually been developed for one thing and then were found to be very useful for something else, like audio cassettes came out of newspapers for the blind and central locking on cars out of something else. Is there any kind of think-tank that actually looks at some of these technologies and says what else could that be used for, because that is going to develop your mass market and that will then bring the cost down for installing it for helping elderly people? Is there any mechanism at all for that kind of thing?

Mr Wright: I do not know whether there is a think-tank. What we are talking about here is a concept which is not a York concept, it is bigger than that, it is inclusive design and the whole concept of inclusive design. I do not know whether there is a think-tank that thinks in that kind of way. There are tons of examples of these kinds of things and some of the things you buy off the shelves in B&Q are developed for older people. There are design centres like the Helen Hamlyn Research Institute who have spearheaded this movement of inclusive design and run competitions every year.

Professor Monk: I think the design centres do have things of this kind.

Mr Wright: It would be really useful to talk to those people because you are absolutely right, in discussions we have had with Joseph Rowntree as well, although there are specific, unique and particular needs both of populations at the demographic level but also at individual level, there are also many things where that population can serve as a forcing function for other issues—child abuse which we have already mentioned and all sorts of other things.

Q218 *Lord Oxburgh:* One of the technologies that is going to become pervasive and therefore very cheap, which we were talking about informally before, is RFID. I think that it would be incredibly useful if groups like yours looked at this technology and its application to what you are going to do because you know that that technology is going to be cheap and there is a lot that you can do with it, it seems to me, in the context that you are working in.

Professor Monk: That is a very good point.

Lord Oxburgh: In fact, that is what the military are doing in a sense because they cannot afford to develop new technologies of their own. They are taking pervasive, off-the-shelf technologies and adapting them to their needs.

Q219 *Chairman:* This is the last question and it requires just a yes or no answer because we must stop now. Do you belong to the British Society of Gerontology or are you in touch with any of the groups that are coming at the issue of the needs of the elderly? Do you participate in their conferences?

Mr Wright: Do want to speak to that, Andrew?

Q220 *Chairman:* All it needs is a yes or no.

Professor Monk: No really, but it is something that we need to do.

Mr Wright: It is certainly the plan for the next year's activity within CUHTec to begin to get partnerships with those kinds of organisations, and that is one of the deficiencies that we recognise in our work.

Q221 *Chairman:* Because we see a lot of big cottage industries, people doing things, and it is how do we join it together, and there are some societies that set out to do this.

Professor Monk: What society would you recommend?

Q222 *Chairman:* The society that includes psychology as part of its remit is the British Society of Gerontology. Thank you again very much. It has been a very helpful session. If you have written comments on any of the matters we have covered today or even on reflection you think, "Gosh, I wish I had said that ..."

Professor Monk: Send it to you and you will circulate it?

Chairman: E-mail is helpful because it can be passed straight on to us because that is how we operate. Thank you once again.

Supplementary evidence by Professor Andrew Monk, Director, CUHTec

1. *Could this (existing) technology be used to prevent or detect elder or child abuse?*

Existing technology could be used to call for help—though this is probably not what you have in mind. The technology has to be easy to override. So it is also easy to thwart. Conventional video surveillance is probably the best bet for detecting abuse. Again the social circumstances will probably make this difficult.

2. *What is the ratio of call centre operators and response units to clients (or dwellings)?*

A social alarm system for 5,000 users will typically have two operators at night and four plus a supervisor in the day time.

3. *What measures are taken to prevent failure?*

There are standards for social alarms and codes of practice (see appended list Kevin Alderson sent me after the meeting, these are the ones Tunstall work to). I have also attached a paper we wrote on the topic suggesting there is a need for a further standard akin, but not identical to the Medical Devices Directive.

4. *Is there a labour force that could install this stuff?*

This is a problem that researchers and developers need to take more note of. The usability question extends to designing the configuration to be installed and maintenance too.

5. *What are the rate limiting steps to getting the research done?*

I don't think we have anything to add to what we said at the time: funding for interdisciplinary work; motivating industry to take a user-centred approach.

6. *Whose responsibility is it to get new developments in this area to market?*

Manufacturers really, there may also be a role for the big customers (eg, ICES) in specifying what is required.

7. *Not everyone needs everything. How do you decide who gets what?*

This is a valid topic for research, that is, procedures for (i) assuring that people who pay for their own assistive technology get what they need, and (ii) allocating equipment according to need. The latter is more political and complicated by the SS/NHS integration problem that the joint assessment procedures and so on are intended to address.

8. *Are there implications for housing regulations?*

The problem with specifying infrastructure for home ICTs is that technology changes so fast. For example, people have suggested wiring standards which are now largely redundant with new wireless protocols.

December 2004

TUESDAY 7 DECEMBER 2004

Present   Drayson, L   Murphy, B
            Finlay of Llandaff, B   Soulsby of Swaffham Prior, L
            Hilton of Eggardon, B   Sutherland of Houndwood, L
            May of Oxford, L   (Chairman)
            Mitchell, L   Walmsley, B

Memorandum submitted by the International Longevity Centre

FOREWORD

— The ILC-UK is not a specialist body dealing with research or outcomes created by assistive technology (AT). Our comments will therefore largely attempt to reinforce the relevance of such technologies as a cross-generational issue which impacts on the majority of us, not just older people who are direct recipients of care. We hope that this will provide a useful additional contribution to the Committee.

— Nonetheless it is evident technological developments hold much promise. These can range from high tech applications in healthcare to improved systems of communication and appliance design for older people without specific disabilities. This submission addresses a middle ground concerning the potential of technology for people with varying degrees of impairment and disability (often related to the diseases associated with ageing) who, in consequence, need varying levels of care and support.

THE ILC-UK

The objectives of ILC-UK are:

— to ensure that decision makers in the public, private and voluntary sectors understand the implications of the demographic changes brought about by an ageing population;

— to encourage planners in all sectors to factor these changes into their thinking;

— to promote public awareness that the issues raised will affect people of every age, in many aspects of their lives, including education, work and leisure.

THE CONTEXT OF AN AGEING SOCIETY AND CARE-GIVING

Caring forms a vital part of the fabric and character of Britain today, and affects most people directly or indirectly. It is important to understand this if we are to grasp the high relevance that assistive technologies could have to an ageing society.

— One in eight people in Britain is now a carer—close to 6 million people.[1]

— Some 855,000 carers already provide informal care for more than 50 hours a week. Their care duties shape the nature of their day-to-day contribution to society.[2]

— Twenty-two percent of households in Greater London report a member of the household with a long-term condition which restricted their day-to-day functional ability.[3]

[1] General Household Survey, 1998.
[2] 1999 Carers' Strategy, HM Government.
[3] Carter, S, 1997

— Families are the bedrock of informal care provision. It is important to note that the structure of families is changing and that this will impact on patterns of care provision:[4]

    — Wider intergenerational spacing is creating 40–50 year olds "in the middle"; people expected to juggle work and care for young and older family members at the same time.

    — Divorce and separation rates are very high leading to new partnerships and caring roles.

    — Voluntary childlessness may leave many older people without access to a immediate family carer.

    — Despite these changes there is little evidence that emotional ties between existing relatives are lessening. As patterns of employment and residency take individuals increasingly further afield from their place of origin, visits in person will most likely become less frequent. Interestingly, however, contact via communication technologies remains high between relatives and may become increasingly central to inter-family relationships.

    — It has been estimated that there may be as many as 51,000 young carers throughout the United Kingdom looking after their ill, elderly or disabled relatives.[5] These younger carers are more likely to be able to make full use of care systems which use ICT.

The nature of disability is changing in line with patterns of demographic ageing:

— Morbidity and mortality from infectious diseases is largely on the decrease over the long-term (AIDS and other STDs excepted) as the technology needed to cure these conditions has been developed and applied.

— Illness and disability in later life is driven increasingly by more stubborn and complex "degenerative" medical conditions, often poorly understood and frequently unavoidable. These will take medicine a considerably longer amount of time and resources to remedy.[6]

— This creates long-term conditions such as type II diabetes, asthma, arthritis and perhaps most importantly, brain failure through Alzheimers, which can cause a high level of impairment of life.

— There are now thought to be 17 million people in the UK living with one long-term condition or another. This trend seems likely to increase in future, and the likely progress of brain-disease in future has been likened to that of an epidemic.[7]

RELEVANCE AND SCOPE OF TECHNOLOGY

Given that there is ample evidence of need for innovative solutions both today and tomorrow, it follows that technology can deliver real results in terms of service provision, return on investment and the promotion of independence:

— The Audit Commission reported that:

The potential of technology to support independence in later life is enormous . . . With better access to higher education, information sources like the internet . . . people want more say in how their health and social needs are met. In addition, massive advances in information management, technology and science . . . are rapidly converging to create exciting new ways to improve public services.[8]

— Sixty percent of carers look after someone with a physical disability, 7 per cent with a mental disability and 15 per cent with both a physical and mental disability.[9] These figures underline the importance of AT in shaping their care workload.

— Three-fifths of all carers receive no regular visitor support services at all and free local authority services and benefits are on the decline. Carers' needs are currently only being met patchily in spite of many improvements in their rights to support introduced by the Government.[10]

[4] Dr Sarah Harper, ILC-UK "Who Cares?" Seminar, London, Feb 2004.

[5] Carer's National Assocation website, Sept 2004.

[6] Prof Jay Olshansky, ILC-UK/BSPS Conference "Data Needs in an Ageing Society", London, April 2004.

[7] Dr Clive Bowman, BUPA, ILC-UK "Who Cares?" Seminar Feb 2004.

[8] Audit Commission, "Assistive Technology; Independence and Well-being 4", p2, London 2004.

[9] Carer's National Association website, Sept 2004.

[10] Higherground website, Sept 200.4

THE POTENTIAL OF AT IN THE WORKPLACE

AT is also of high relevance to areas outside those of the immediate concerns of older people's care needs. In employment, greater research is needed to see how AT could boost older people's workforce participation:

— Technology could play a much needed role in helping older workers. Nearly 2.8 million people between 50 and the state pension age are not in work, less than a third of which is voluntary.[11] Of the 2.8 million, around 1 million receive incapacity benefit, a good indication that assistive technologies might prove effective at increasing workforce participation rates given their relevance to disability.[12]

— Early exclusion from the labour force is a terrible waste of human capital. Those who are retired or excluded from the workforce are particularly at risk from the mental and physical deterioration that can result from inactivity and under-stimulation,[13] further exacerbating their care and health needs in later life.

— Of the 1.5 million working age carers not in employment, around 60 per cent resigned in order to care—with the resultant loss of expertise to industry, and loss of income, status and independence for the carer.[14]

— The UK Government must be more receptive to the potential that AT holds in the workplace. The UK is already tied into key objectives in this area including the Stockholm and Barcelona targets from 2001 and 2002 to boost older people's workforce participation rates in the 55–64 age group by 50 per cent by 2010, and the ambitious target of raising the average age of retirement by five years by 2010. The UK will also bring legislation to ban age discrimination in the workplace from 2006. Several studies of how workers can be helped to stay longer in physically demanding jobs have been carried out through ergonomic improvements, for example by the European Foundation for the Improvement of Living and Working Conditions, located in Dublin.[15]

— However, while numerous research studies and official reports have considered the issue of the ageing of the labour force and the health and well-being of older workers, the workplace factors associated with this and the role that technology could play in facilitating these conditions have not been much considered in the UK context.[16]

— Some employers in the UK are currently leading the field in piloting innovative technologies which they hope will benefit their own employees who are care-givers, creating a workforce freed of some of the care burdens which might interfere with their workload.

INCLUSIVE DESIGN FOR OLDER PEOPLE

— As 20 per cent of our population is already over 60, and this will grow to around 30 per cent by 2031[17] there should an ample market to justify inclusive design.

— It is important to appreciate that disabilities can be exacerbated by a failure to design products or environments inclusively. Any given person has the same potential to be excluded from a product by its design, but mainstream differences in physical conditions or characteristics are rarely discriminated against.

— Over the past 20 years, considerable advances have been made in the field of extending quality of life through better and more inclusive design. The importance of bringing disabled people into the mainstream of society is increasingly recognised, and is resulting in new legislation impacting on the major world economies. In the USA, the concept of "Barrier-Free" design was developed in response to the demands of the disability movement which led to robust legislation from 1973 to 1990. However, most companies and their designers are struggling to fully understand and meet these new requirements.[18]

[11] Prime Minister's Strategy Unit website, "Winning the generation game" March 2002.

[12] "Improving the life chances of disabled people", Prime Minister's Strategy Unit, June 2004.

[13] BBC Website, Sept 2004.

[14] Higherground website, Sept 2004.

[15] "Ageing in Europe", European Foundation for the Improvement of Living and Working Conditions, 2004.

[16] Taylor, P & Clarkson, J, Redesigning industry for an ageing society, Outline Research Proposal Summary, Cambridge University, (Ongoing.)

[17] GAD website Sept 2004.

[18] Taylor, P & Clarkson, J (as above).

— Research has shown that while many companies in the UK and elsewhere agree with the principles of designing inclusively, they consider that it is impractical for them to do so. The common reasons cited include: insufficient financial resources or time; inadequate access to users; inexperience in dealing directly with users; and, most frequently, commissioners of the design not asking for it.[19]

— The Government therefore needs to ensure that it is working in partnership with organisations from all sectors working in the field, and that it encourages them, perhaps through incentives, to tap into this key market.

TECHNOLOGY IN THE HOME

Independence

— Ideally, all new houses should be built to an inclusive design. If this were to be a general requirement, the initial cost would not be excessive. However the UK has many old houses and older people tend to live in the oldest among them.

— Study after study shows that older people wish to remain independent within their home for as long as possible and that this is key to the definition of quality of life:

"Home" has a range of meanings for older people, extending beyond being a physical environment. It is the place where they conduct the majority of their social lives and it gives them a social identity. The cumulative effects of ageing, together with environmental barriers, can mean that older people spend increasing amounts of time within their own homes.[20]

— The most effective assistive technologies are likely to be those that maintain an older person's sense of dignity, independence and social status, and also help them cope with some of the social challenges of social isolation and immobility in old age.

— As the ability to live at home tends to be compromised when declining physical or mental ability transforms a suitable environment into an unsafe one, it therefore follows that assistive technologies can help prolong the period of "self-reliance."[21]

— It is the subject of much speculation that tomorrow's older people, the "baby boomer" generation will wish to take more responsibility for themselves in later life. It is expected that products and practices which support independence, provide information, and assist decision-making will be particularly popular.

— It is possible that videophones and internet resources may encourage well-travelled "boomers" to live, as many already do, in warmer climates abroad. However these older migrants may not have considered the importance of adequate care plans if and when they become frail.

— There is evidence that modern technology can help maintain older people's sense of independence and self-worth through their interaction with health and social services. Healthcare is not in the remit of the Committee's call for evidence but there is much potential in the interaction of home technology and the NHS Single Assessment Process (SAP), itself a product of merging services. In summary, SAP stipulates care and health outcomes which are tailored as closely as possible to an individual's requirements.[22] Key to this is the storage and handling of patient information, and many localities are advocating that the patient themselves keeps their records, or a copy of them, in response to this challenge.

— The logical conclusion of SAP is a system where the patient, where possible, is central to ascertaining their health and care needs. Anecdotal evidence is that the empowerment of being more involved in your care decisions has considerable psychological benefits.[23] IT appliances like "memory sticks" which could allow the older person to store their social care and medical records on one small computer insert could be popular. Another imaginative AT solution could be to educate older people to become more involved in their healthcare without leaving the house, performing low-level tasks such as taking their own blood pressure, measuring their heart rate, or measuring cholesterol measurements themselves, the results of which could be fed electronically to websites which highlight

[19] Milner 2001.

[20] "Joseph Rowntree Foundation, *The importance of "low level" preventive services to older people*" July 1998.

[21] Case Study "Millennium Homes": *Technology helps elderly people with reduced abilities to stay in their own*, Office of Science and Technology Website, Sept 2004.

[22] *SAP Question and Answer*, Department of Health (DH) website, Sept 2004.

[23] Interview with Seamus Breen, Change Agent Team, DH, Sept 2004.

anomalies to the attention of skilled staff. A pilot project is currently looking at using ICT to help assess a diabetic's blood sugar levels remotely.[24] If properly monitored, and used appropriately to complement existing services rather than to replace them, such technologies have great potential to augment self-worth and confidence amongst older people.

Telecare

— We understand that BT's Research and Venturing Unit have already contributed to the Committee regarding the development of 2nd and 3rd generation "telecare" systems.

— To recap, "telecare" is the use of ICT to provide or assist care at a distance. This could range from a videophone conversation with a relative to "pervasive" technologies which report events to an external carer. These can now go beyond the simple "alarm buttons" of 1st generation systems; 2nd generation telecare can alert a care-giver some distance away of potential anomalies, such as the front door being open at 3am, or a lack of movement in the house in the morning. These can be particularly useful in providing peace of mind for carers of mild to moderately impaired dementia sufferers, a particularly stressful care duty, as well as reminding the care recipient to perform daily tasks such as taking medicine, or turning off the oven.

— With third generation telecare we have the opportunity to not only to improve the efficiency of the carer but to also to "intelligently" monitor the effectiveness of the care and possibly the overall well-being of the client, currently the aim of the DTI funded care in the community centre run by BT.[25] A report by Dr. Andrew Sixsmith, Social Gerentologist and advisor to BT, found that this technology was indeed fairly robust and had flagged up patterns of deterioration in the care recipient's behavior[26] (eg not leaving the house, not using the oven enough, or a decreasing frequency of moving between rooms.)

— Integrating Community Equipment Services (ICES) report that:

Telecare is set to play a key role in maintaining people at home through building their confidence and independence as part of a community care package. This is good news for older people particularly. It is also good news for carers.[27]

— So far these systems appear to have been successful, and they provide a range of opportunities for Government to take up. Coupled with some of the trends described above, such as the importance modern society appears to place on maintaining family ties despite increasing physical distance between members, these offer great potential for reducing care-burdens and increasing well-being.

— Fourth generation telecare holds out the prospect of a home-based system providing the older person with information. Coupled with measure such as self-assessment for minor medical tasks described above, the older person could feel significantly empowered in day-to-day life.

— A major problem with the development of various forms of technological support has been the imbalance between the enthusiasm of technology developers and the often overwhelming difficulty in finding service commissioners prepared to invest. Furthermore, budgetary restraints often mean new technologies have to be viewed as substitutes to existing services whereas logically their role may be best seen as additional options that over time refine and improve the use of hands on care services.[28]

— The greatest burden on care resources now and increasingly in the future is the loss of personal competence through varying degrees of brain failure. Tagging remains controversial and public policy and sentiment are limiting the adoption of AT that could enhance the independence and safety of individuals.[29] However, if it is ethically sound to search for people when they "go missing" then, surely it is proper to do so with the help of tagging and tracking technologies. With so many dementia sufferers locked away for fear of coming to harm, the potential to increase quality of life is large. Simple policy guidance could make such approaches valued options for citizens.

[24] Vodaphone Foundation website, Sept 2004.

[25] Interview with Steven Brown, BT Research and Venturing Unit, Sept 2004.

[26] Sixsmith A: *An evaluation of and intelligent home monitoring system.* Journal of Telemedicine and Telecare 2000.

[27] ICES Website November 2003

[28] Dr Clive Bowman, BUPA, Sept 2004.

[29] *See* BMJ 2002; 325:847–848, "*Electronic tagging of people with dementia who wander*" 19 October 2002.

INFORMATION NEEDS FOR AN AGEING SOCIETY:

— Projecting and identifying future needs scenarios from past trends via statistical technologies is a crucial part of our technological, scientific and institutional readiness for an ageing society.

— To illustrate the point a Joseph Rowntree Foundation study noted an interesting example of lack of needs projection:

There is increasing recognition among policy-makers and practitioners of the value of low level preventative services in promoting quality of life and social engagement, and enabling older people to care for themselves and to maintain their homes, delaying any need for more intensive and costly services. Yet social services departments may be reluctant or unable to divert resources to promote quality of life and social engagement as ends in themselves without clear evidence of cost-effectiveness.[30]

— This issue of funding could presumably be addressed if the balance of immediate cost to future economy could be satisfactorily assessed and there was a greater clarity regarding personal entitlements. In this case, therefore, a lack of information and relevant methodology is hindering the provision of low-level services to numerous older people, and therefore also impacting on their prospects of healthy life expectancy. New micro-simulation techniques which differ from conventional demography are reported to offer useful opportunities for population modeling,[31] underlying the importance of research in this area.

— It is the opinion of the ILC-UK that there is a major lack of local and ward level data for local authorities and regional planning bodies to base their strategic planning objectives on. The Office for National Statistics, the General Register Office Scotland, the National Assembly for Wales and the Northern Ireland Statistics and the Research Agency all carry out, from time to time, local authority level population projections. However, these are rather sporadic in production. The last for England were based on 1996 base populations and lack the fine granularity of detail to project technology potential. Better ways of encouraging integration and uniformity between survey data need to be developed.[32]

— The Department of Health currently envisages the Electronic Care Records Service being in operation from 2007–08. This will be crucial to the success of initiatives such as the Single Care Assessment Process. Although admittedly in the realm of healthcare, outside the remit of this enquiry, these records are a considerable opportunity to ensure that social resources can be allocated in a preventative fashion and the relevant assistive technologies applied to prolong a good quality of life and delay the onset of physical and mental deterioration. The ILC considers that the adoption of a single assessment tool would make the process of assessment much more conducive to information management.

— One of the issues that the ILC-UK has encountered is that social workers are often reported to be too busy to participate fully in research projects for care. Given the blossoming possibilities that IT is offering developers, this could be a major problem. One solution may be to provide local authorities with extra funding to ensure experienced care workers can take part in research. However the goal must be to put modern communication technology at the heart of care and not merely investigated as a peripheral parallel activity.

CHALLENGES TO POLICY-MAKERS

— There is a good case for better national co-ordination of research. The UK does not have a national ageing body such as the National Institute on Aging (NIA) in the USA. The NIA:

". . . leads a broad scientific effort to understand the nature of aging and to extend the healthy, active years of life. Since 1974 it has provided leadership in aging research, training, health information dissemination, and other programs relevant to aging and older people. It trains and develops highly skilled research scientists and develops and maintains state-of-the-art resources to accelerate research progress. It disseminates information and communicates with the public and interested groups on health and research advances and on new directions for research."[33]

[30] *The importance of "low level"* preventive services to older people, Joseph Rowntree Foundation July 1998.

[31] Interview with Professor Phil Rees, School of Geography, Leeds University, Aug 2004.

[32] Professor Phil Rees (as above)

[33] NIA website September 2004.

In the absence of such an organisation, research bodies in the UK often find themselves in competition with each other although this has improved since the creation of the Research Councils, for example the Engineering and Physical Sciences Research Council's (EPSRC) EQUAL programme. Policy-makers must ask themselves if the UK would be better off with a single NIA-style body on ageing.

— Is policy taking research in the direction that older disabled people want? The evidence is that it is to some extent, but could be much more closely orientated to demand "on the ground".[34] The high cost of care services to the elderly disabled reinforces how important it is to get effective, efficient research looking at the many alternative possibilities and solutions that technology offers.

— It is important to tackle a culture which treats the elderly disabled as an "add-ons" to the mainstream.[35]

We must remember they are part of our society, and an unfortunately greatly wasted resource. Their health and ability to contribute to society affect us all. Research in this area is a priority.

— The challenge to policy makers and providers of assistive technologies is how to respond appropriately to the ever inflating demands of an ageing society, balancing the benefit of introducing preventative strategies with the increased cost that this will accrue.[36] For example, AT which encourages increased workforce participation would balance the initial outlay against three major likely cost reductions for the public purse: a lower or delayed incidence of mental degeneration, lower rates of benefit take-up and better pension provision.

September 2004

Memorandum by Professor Anthea Tinker and Dr Claudine McCreedie, King's College London

THE APPLICATION OF RESEARCH IN TECHNOLOGY AND DESIGN TO IMPROVE THE QUALITY OF LIFE OF OLDER PEOPLE

The House of Lords Select Committee on Science and Technology are inquiring into the scientific aspects of ageing. They wish to know how science and technology can help improve people's prospects of healthy and active life expectancy, and whether Government policy is in place to achieve this.

1. GENERAL POINTS

1.1 In answering the points below we would advise caution against generalisations. In particular it is stated in the brief that half the population over 65 had a long-term illness or disability. This figure is based on self-reported illness and hides differences between:

— men and women who have different physical and mental problems in old age;

— younger old (65–80) and older old (80 +);

— ethnic variations which include cultural and physical differences;

— those with severe mental problems such as dementia where technology presents different problems including ethical ones.

1.2 There are also likely to be cohort differences and there should be no presumption that the next generation of older people will have the same needs and/or experience or lack of experience in using technology as the current one.

1.3 Our specific focus is Assistive Technology (AT), which we originally defined for our research for the Royal Commission on Long Term Care (Tinker *et al*, 1999). This embraces a wide range of products from simple portable items like walking sticks to fixed housing adaptations, and increasingly embraces applications of electronics and ICT (Information and Communications Technology).

---

[34] *Improving the life chances of disabled people*, Prime Minister's Strategy Office, June 2004.

[35] Prime Minister's Strategy Office, June 2004.

[36] *Supporting Independence with Assistive Technology*, Integrating Community Equipment Services, 2003.

2. EXISTING AND NEW TECHNOLOGIES WHICH COULD BE USED TO A GREATER EXTENT TO BENEFIT OLDER PEOPLE

2.1 Our research (including KCL/Reading, 2004 and Tinker *et al*, 2001) supports others (eg Grundy, 1999) in showing clearly:

1. how AT can help preserve independence and improve the quality of life of older people both in their own homes and in care homes;

2. that there is a good deal of unmet need particularly for housing adaptations and notably for level access showers.

In one of the few pieces of research that compared two groups of older people (in the USA), one with extensive and one with minimum AT, the health care costs of those with extensive AT were approximately half that of the group with minimum AT (Mann *et al*, 1999). Our research (KCL/Reading, 2004) brings out clearly that a good deal can be done to help older people remain in their homes by introducing AT, but that the cost of doing so will not only relate to the extent of their need, but also to the type of housing they occupy in terms of building construction.

2.2 Labour saving domestic equipment (eg dishwashers, washing machines) benefit older people as much as other groups. Microwave ovens assist with meals. Automatic (robotic) vacuum cleaners and lawn mowers that operate without someone to guide them have the potential to save time and energy. The whole development of "smart housing" (defined as "a dwelling incorporating a communications network that connects the key electrical appliances and services, and allows them to be remotely controlled, monitored or accessed" (Porteus, 2004), needs demystifying. Small motors and sensors positioned round the home can do a number of things automatically such as opening and closing curtains, turning on and off lights and raising and lowering sinks and cupboards. Within the home "'smart" or "intelligent" devices can include beds that track sleep patterns, chairs that monitor breathing and heart rate and fridges with a camera inside so that the contents can be scanned for a computer.

2.3 Personal alarms and emergency response telephones are relatively low cost and could be provided more widely. Research shows that the most useful are personal ones, which can be worn on the body. One problem is that they are often not worn. Fixed alarms such as those on walls or hanging in bathrooms are of limited value if people cannot reach them.

2.4 Mobile phones are another technology increasingly in use. The current generation of older old people are less likely to own a mobile phone than the younger generation and more likely to keep it for emergency use. However, in our view they could be used to a greater extent, and we are currently part of a research team considering the possible benefits to older people of using mobile phones for locating services and way-finding. Mobile phones are mainstream technology and therefore less likely to have the stigma, which is sometimes attached to other means of communication such as a community alarm. Mobile phones can benefit not only people who live alone, or are alone for part of the day, but may have particular benefits for older people in care homes. In the latter personal phones may not be provided, or are in public parts of the building where there is a lack of privacy. Text messages can remind people about, for example, their medical appointments or when to take medication.

2.5 Sensors and electronic devices. The rapid growth of relatively inexpensive electronic devices (eg smoke alarms, carbon monoxide detectors, window and door openers, passive infra-red lighting) has also opened up a new group of products that older people might also value but may have difficulty in accessing

2.6 Toilets. "Smart loos"—which are more prevalent in both Switzerland and the Far East—have great potential. These range from mainstream ones which combine the functions of a bidet and a wc. They spray hot water and soap on to the bottom and then hot air dries the skin (thus eliminating in some circumstances the need for a carer to come in and toilet someone). More complex ones monitor blood pressure, urine, etc via the seat of a toilet.

2.7 The Internet is increasingly used by older people both as a source of information and for contacting others via email. Income is at least as important as age in determining computer use and this is a good example of how pensioner income is key to accessing much technology. For those who do not have access to computers a more widespread production of simple booklets and information sheets on where to get information about AT (such as the ones produced by Age Concern) would be helpful.

2.8 New technologies are likely to prove of great importance in the realm of health care. These are often referred to under the umbrella term of telemedicine and telecare. This has been defined as: "the practice of medical care using interactive audiovisual and data communications—this includes the delivery of medical care, diagnosis, consultation and treatment, as well as health education and the transfer of medical data" (WHO quoted by Porteus, 2004). In summary it involves both the delivery of health care and the exchange of information. They include devices so that health can be monitored either from a distance (eg blood pressure) or at home through the use of a device, which older people operate themselves.

2.9 The use of televisions for people to interact with a professional is also of importance especially in rural areas where it is more difficult to access services. In these cases the older person can seek advice and even be photographed (for example if the problem is the skin) by putting part of the body by a camera. These methods are also of importance to professionals so that, for example, a nurse or doctor can seek specialist help from a hospital. Innovative projects in County Durham, for example, are beginning to try out these new ideas with older people in more remote areas.

2.10 The use of sensors to detect falls and changes in people's routines such as failure to flush the toilet in the morning or to get out of bed are more controversial, as is the use of electronic tagging of people with dementia, and pose ethical problems.

2.11 The increased use of new technologies can suddenly creep up on individuals and policy makers. In our research on the adaptability of the housing stock (KCL/Reading, 2004), the use of scooters generated problems of access and storage that were difficult to address within the constraints of a good deal of the housing stock.

3. THE FOUR QUESTIONS WHICH ARE OF CONCERN TO THE COMMITTEE.

3.1.a. How effectively is research co-ordinated in the public, private and charitable sectors (including internationally)?

The main attempt in the UK to co-ordinate research in technology and design to improve the quality of life of older people has been the EPSRC EQUAL research initiative (approximately £3.5 million research funding) which flowed from Foresight—a Department of Trade and Industry initiative that followed the 1993 White Paper on Realising our Potential. Although the ESRC initiated a research programme on quality of life under EQUAL (the Growing Older programme), no proposals were funded that addressed the technology and design agenda. EPSRC stipulated that all research funded under the EQUAL initiative had to involve users and required partnerships between different academic disciplines and outside organisations. Our own research has involved collaborations with rehabilitation engineers, building surveyors and occupational therapists as well as with users in local Age Concern branches, the University of the Third Age, and with local authorities and a spread of housing associations. The National Forum to co-ordinate UK Ageing Research has been slow to get off the ground, and the call for research proposals under The New Dynamics of Ageing programme is currently still awaited. It will be interesting to see what priority this gives to research on technology and design.

3.2 At the level of networking and dissemination, the winding-up of AgeNet at the end of the 1990s was unfortunate. However, the EPSRC Equal Research Network (www.equal.ac.uk) has, on a small scale, been very successful. The Foundation for Assistive Technology (funded by the Department of Health) runs an extensive database on all AT research and disseminates a valuable free annual publication detailing this research (FAST, 2004). Internationally an attempt was made five years ago by the International Society of Gerontechnology to list all the relevant research on assistive technology but it proved too difficult. However, their biannual conferences are a good means of exchanging information

3.3.b. *Have the correct priorities been identified? Are there any gaps in research? and is there sufficient research capability in the UK?*

Despite laudable attempts to give priority to research partnerships and user-centred research, an inspection of the projects funded, particularly at European level, but to some extent nationally, suggests that research is still dominated by funding for "high-tech" proposals and the ideas of academics who have to keep a close eye on their research ratings as measured by original articles in academic journals. Competition for research funding is intense and drives the type of research that is funded. Thus there is little academic kudos in reviewing and bringing together research done by other people. In terms of publication, the kinds of journals that matter for the Research Assessment Exercise are invariably specialised, are largely interested in "original" work and—rightly—address high academic standards. But one unintended consequence is that academics get very little credit, if any, for trying to disseminate their work, or other people's, to senior managers or practitioners. Research funding also frequently does not allow sufficient time for this process however much it is regarded as desirable in principle. Overall, the widespread dissemination of research findings takes second place to the demands to secure new research funding.

3.4 There will always be a need for cutting edge research, and research that concentrates on the needs of the minority of people with severe disabilities. However, there is also a need for more research on:

(i) Products. This is the kind of work that is done admirably by RICAbility, the research based consumer organisation that tests products especially for older and disabled people. RICAbility have to raise funds for each product they examine and currently, for example, have been unable to raise funds to examine stair-lifts, although these are constantly being advertised and bought by older people, often without adequate advice as to what is appropriate. RICAbility and Age Concern England were instrumental in researching recently the issue of doorstep selling, leading to initiatives by the Office of Fair Trading.

(ii) Information. A priority is to encourage older people, their families and professionals to seek advice about technology and, where appropriate, to use it. We have a small grant from the Helen Hamlyn Foundation to address this important issue of information—"Improving the provision of information on assistive technology to older people".

(iii) Users. Despite the valuable stress on users in the EPSRC funded research, there is still a need for small-scale research that begins with the user. The possible spin-off from this is shown by a small one-year project that we worked on (funded by the EPSRC, £45k). Older people, whom we recruited for the research, came up with the idea of a device to assist them with climbing stairs (McCreadie *et al*, 2002). An elementary prototype was developed with the help of a research student and tried out with volunteers. This is now the subject of a three-way partnership between KCL, a commercial partner and the Department of Health.

(iv) ICT. Given the increasing use of the Internet and the issues arising in terms of access for older people, very largely related to income, research on the best ways of involving older people and teaching them about computers would be useful.

(v) Costs. Research is needed which assesses the business case for AT. For example it is claimed (without a great deal of evidence) that among other things it empowers users, makes better use of staff, delays or reduces admission to residential care and reduces the number of hospital inpatient stays/outpatient attendances. There is need for much more research on the acceptability, reliability and costs of all the various kinds of AT especially the latest electronic devices.

(vi) Evaluation. It would be valuable to fund research that evaluated over a ten year period what research has been funded both nationally and at a European level in technology and design, what the outputs have been and who has been influenced by the research.

(vii) Design issues. Assistive Technology is invariably "medicalised" in design with consequent stigma attached to it. There is need to bring it into the mainstream of provision. Some manufacturers are now realising the commercial advantages of a simple universal design (Harkin and Huber, 2003) and much valuable work is being done at the Royal College of Art. If good design for all was the norm it would help everyone and not just older people. For example well written instructions (perhaps divided into basic information and then more detailed for those who need it), clear markings on AT such as mobile phones and video recorders (large enough to be read without peering), would be valuable for the whole population. The design of mobile phones needs to accommodate some of the issues facing older people such as poorer vision and dexterity. Community alarms, while used by a very large number of older people, are still designed in an unimaginative way, relying on the ubiquitous white plastic so beloved in medical equipment design, and dominant in the design of grab rails, bathroom rails and raised toilet seats.

4.1.d. *Is the research being used to inform policy?*

How far research informs policy is difficult to answer. At central government level, technology spans a number of different departments eg ODPM, DH, DTI. The Audit Commission is influential in picking up on relevant research. An analysis of policy developments (Tinker, 2003) showed greater awareness of AT but there is still a good deal of confusion and lack of integration between the various AT sectors. The Foundation for Assistive Technology (FAST, 2004) argue that there is a lack of clear standards, guidelines and legislation for AT. The Integrated Community Equipment Service is an important policy development. Integration between health, social care and housing is essential. Addressing the needs of older people in all tenures is important. A valuable policy initiative in Nottingham City exemplifies desirable policy: this is the Preventive Adaptations Scheme, whereby all older people in the City can apply for very basic adaptations, such as smoke alarms and grab rails, which are supplied without charge.

We would add a fifth question:

5.1.e. *What are some of the problems in doing research on this topic?*

Research in this field has to be multidisciplinary. Social scientists can find out the problems and possible solutions from older people but it is often others, such as rehabilitation engineers and architects, who have to solve them. Despite the praiseworthy research initiatives such as the EPSRC EQUAL one on quality of life it is not easy to obtain funding for these kinds of projects. In addition it is very time consuming and therefore more expensive to work in a multidisciplinary way (Tinker and McCreadie, 2004).

5. Conclusions

6.1 We would like to see:

— the greater involvement of older people at all stages of research (Tinker *et al*, 2003);

— steps taken to build modules on good design for all in engineering and architecture courses with much greater emphasis on the needs of older people, and their diversity, but without an excessive emphasis on dependency and frailty;

— more information to be available for professionals and families about the advantages and disadvantages of different types of AT;

— more research on the cost effectiveness of technology;

— encouragement to the market to produce well designed and user-friendly products.

6.2 All of these would involve research in showing good practice.

30 September 2004

Memorandum by The Royal Academy of Engineering

1. Biological Aspects of Ageing

1.1 *What are the promising avenues for research?*

1.1.1 *Some of the most promising avenues for research lie in developing diagnostic tests which enable the individual to maintain checks on their own health status or to enable cheap and efficient regular screening programmes to be established. A significant burden could be removed from the health service by individuals carrying out basic monitoring of their own health in the home on, say, a daily basis. Technology already exists which allows the monitoring of blood pressure, ECG, respiration etc using simple to operate devices and software. This allows the logging of information which is then sent in compressed form to, for example, the GP's surgery. The software detects deviations from the normal pattern of results; hence there is no need for the GP or nurse to monitor each trace. In the case of hospital based scanning and analytical tests, potential developments to increase accuracy and reduce the price of such tests would be a great advantage. Any such improvements in the accuracy of the techniques would apply not only to the ageing population and could facilitate routine sampling that leads to early diagnosis of debilitating diseases.*

1.1.2 Current research strands which will potentially offer interesting future developments and are important to note are:

(a) The sensor specialist company e2v Technologies has entered into a partnership with Brunel University for image sensing technology. There will be projects for six PhD research students and additional staff and this work will commence in October 2004.

(b) A Cambridge-based firm, Astron Clinica, has recently produced a product, SIAscope (Spectrophotometric Intracutaneous Analysis) which uses visible light in a scanning process to detect melanomas. In parallel the Biomedical Optics Research laboratories at University College London is using infrared tomography to analyse the oxygenation state of tissue in the brain.

(c) Teraview of Cambridge is developing analytical methods to detect Basal cell carcinoma using terahertz radiation.

1.1.3 All of the technologies quoted above would assist in speeding up the identification of physical or biological change associated with the onset of disease and could be carried out at high speed and low cost needing fewer people, trained to a lesser degree to operate the equipment. Present imaging techniques require a high degree of training and the time taken for scans varies depending on the type of and complexity of the requirements.

1.1.4 The vast majority of the elderly fall into two categories, those are that are physically able but mentally impaired, and the reverse. There is therefore, a need to carry out research on how domestic devices can be modified to meet these requirements. If carried out properly for those people with only physical problems, these modifications could be of benefit to the whole of society.

1.1.5 There is also great promise in harnessing the benefits of communications and remote monitoring systems to enable greater independence for the elderly citizen. A recent DTI Foresight study on the Exploitation of the Electromagnetic Spectrum showed how mobile communications and remote sensing technology could open up the opportunities for early and/or remote healthcare monitoring. In addition to this, the development of communications media which compensate for reduced ability to hear or to write (text to speech/speech to text) could enable an older person to continue to take part in mainstream society with minimal external assistance.

1.2 *How will such research benefit older people and delay the onset of long-term illnesses and disabilities?*

1.2.1 Early diagnosis can be vital in improving the effectiveness of the treatment of many life threatening conditions. The detection of changes in blood and tissue in the early stages can often lead to arresting or preventing further onset of disease. In order that early diagnostic tests are carried out regularly it is essential that an education process be established to make so that older people aware that they need these check-ups. Swift identification of developing conditions will avoid complex treatments later on.

1.2.2 Technological developments will benefit older people by increasing their available lifestyle choices for a greater number of years. Technology can extend the period of independent living and also allow the delivery of medical care and support at home. This has important consequences for lessening the burden placed on the NHS to provide hospital based care.

1.3 *What are the consequences of the biological differences between the sexes, different social backgrounds and ethnic groups within the UK?*

1.3.1 Women have a greater life expectancy than men and are therefore more likely to need to access services for longer and more likely, in cultures where the nuclear family unit prevails, to live alone following the death of a spouse. In cultures where living in extended family units are more common, there is a greater likelihood of the effects of the death of a spouse being alleviated to a certain degree by the support of younger family members. Although the older members of the family can rely on the support of the relatives, the family as a whole may need support to adapt their lifestyle in order to accommodate the needs of an older person within the family unit.

1.3.2 As the population of the UK ages, it becomes more important to change the perception of "elderly" as a unique condition needing specific age-related developments—the effects of ageing must be thought about within the whole range of human conditions. It is not correct to consider people today on the basis of their biological age. Some people in their late 70s are physically and mentally more active than others in their 50s. Many vital consumer goods could be redesigned to meet a wide range of users without compromising their performance or making them less suitable for "able-bodied" people

1.3.3 It must also be noted that any study of age must remain mindful of both the genetic issues (nature) as well as the influence of life-style and society (nurture) on seniority and the ageing process. The two shaping forces must be considered in unison, as they are inseparable, in order to create a valid picture of the impact of ageing—not merely biology alone.

2. The Application of Research in Technology and Design

2.1 Employing existing technologies to give greater benefit to older people

2.1.1 There is a great deal that can be done to develop existing technologies for the benefit of older people. For the purposes of this response, we have considered where technology can help in four particular life aspects:

2.1.1. a. Facilitating living in, and maintaining one's own home and garden

For an older person, having to leave their home is, in any event, a cruel loss of independence; it can also be seriously disorientating. Simple measures could be employed to allow the long-term use of the family home, well into old age. These could include: houses built with flexible internal layouts to allow bedrooms to be moved to the ground floor level; a centralised vacuum cleaner with localised points in every room; high-level sockets; standardised plugs and taps; improved cooking aids and domestic cooking devices utilising "fail-safe" sensor technology which automatically turn off electricity or gas supplies should a saucepan boil dry; household appliances and furniture made lighter or at least easier to move; higher-level flower beds, and increased developments of robotic lawn mowers would assist in maintaining an independent existence. In addition to this, electronic and IT-based security systems could monitor safety devices (for example, for detecting falls or for monitoring respiration and blood circulation during sleep). IT is also able to provide healthcare monitoring facilities from home, reducing the need to travel to a doctor's surgery or hospital.

2.1.1. b. Facilitating a continuing intellectual life

Lifelong learning opportunities to develop new interests or extend existing ones would encourage individuals to remain active. The situation when retirement at 65 no longer means the withdrawal of an individual from the majority group in society will require maintaining and prolonging the intellectual capability of the person as this is vital to promoting good mental health. Computing software designed specifically for the needs of the elderly could help to maintain active engagement with the developing world, as well as helping the individual to remain mentally alert. For the elderly who are not mentally impaired there is a great need and often desire to keep up with modern technology such as web technology, mobile phones etc. For the young and middle aged this technology is incorporated into their lives through peer group usage at work, university etc. This is often not the case with the elderly because they do not tend to mix so often with groups using these devices. It is therefore important to carry out research as to how to access and provide easily understandable information.

2.1.1. c. Enabling mobility

Continued development of mechanical/mechatronic aids will help people with mobility problems—for example, better wheelchair designs which can tackle steps or improved walking aids.

2.1.1. d. Enabling communication

As previously discussed, the loss of hearing, speech or writing ability can be overcome by adapting current remote user hardware and software devices for people with hearing/speech problems (text to speech, speech to text). Indeed the current development of haptics (the science of applying tactile sensation to human interaction with computers and computer driven devices) in the automotive industry may also provide useful offshoots for replacing a defective sense of sight or sound.

2.2 The development of new, possibly specialised technologies

2.2.1 New and specialised technologies for assisting the elderly will come from the development in materials, microsystems and ultra-precision engineering. Science and engineering will need to produce longer lasting artificial joints and possibly new artificial organs (for example, portable kidney machines) as well as other surgical, medical and healthcare devices. Equipment using sonar, laser beams and even global positioning satellites have been developed to aid partially sighted people to live independently, but there is scope for improvement. In addition, miniaturisation of electronics, wearable electronics and monitors, and biocompatible electronics that can be implanted will help frail elderly people to be monitored remotely. This will permit them to remain in their own homes and allow doctors to monitor how they are coping and to assess what the medical issues really are.

2.2.2 In addition to the development of technologies, there is a need to improve the training of designers and engineers to include incorporation of feedback from the potential user from both psychological and physical/ medical viewpoints into product design. This must have a much greater role than is evident today.

3. OVERARCHING CONSIDERATIONS

3.1 *How effectively is research co-ordinated in the public, private and charitable sectors (including internationally)?*

3.1.1 Private and public research has been reasonably co-ordinated and the charitable sector has been closely involved in the human factors aspects. However the UK has not generally been good at cross-Research Council funding. There is also a concern that if we do not take action soon to co-ordinate our research, we could find ourselves missing out on a lucrative share in the fast growing market of the provision of the medical care solutions for the ageing population. This market has the potential to be extremely beneficial to the UK economy.

3.1.2 Collective collaboration between organisations having religious, ethical or philosophical connections often only starts from a common interest in a particular field. There is no automatic, nationwide coordination or research strategy to address issues—except in some rare and specific cases which are of such public interest, eg cloning, where collaboration is identified to address a high profile story.

3.2 *Have the correct priorities been identified? Are there any gaps in research?*

3.2.1 With respect to the financial impact of technological advances, further research is needed into the economic trade-offs between providing better independent care for older people through technology and the savings this can create in care home accommodation or hospitalisation.

3.2.2 It is noted that there is a lack of a national research strategy which underpins the specialist work undertaken in specific areas. The priorities may have been identified by the researchers in each field but it is doubtful whether true priorities of nationwide concern often apply to the overall research scenario. This need not be the case.

3.3 *Is there sufficient research capability in the UK?*

3.3.1 It may well be the case that there is not sufficient research capability at this moment for all of the topics of concern. The current health care system tends towards filling gaps, and responding to a crisis as it arises. Meanwhile the private sector has the luxury of dealing with issues where there is an identified need and budget available to address it with a solution.

3.4 *Is the research being used to inform policy?*

3.4.1 The research carried out in the UK seems to be by well-informed groups that have identified a need and are being funded by those organisations that have also identified the need, but there is a lack of a co-ordinated national policy.

3.4.2 We would like to see a move in policy towards founding a nationwide programme which promotes an automatic health review at 60. This review could provide the basis for regular monitoring—carried out both by healthcare professionals and by self assessment—throughout the rest of the person's life.

3.4.3 Changes in policy should also reflect the need for better use of the intellect of older people. The payback of better long-term health care would be that useful members of society could be saved from early onset of debilitating diseases and therefore keep in better health for professional activity beyond the age of 65.

3.4.4 In the long term, the UK government should look to reforming policy outside that which currently directly connects with the scientific aspects of ageing. Implementing long term policy to discourage obesity and smoking; encouraging health self-awareness; and the provision of better access to primary care across the entire demographic spread of the population of the UK should ensure that the older generation of the future are better prepared for their extended life.

October 2004

Examination of Witnesses

Witnesses: BARONESS GREENGROSS, a Member of the House, Chief Executive Officer of International Longevity Centre UK, former Director General of Age Concern England; PROFESSOR ANTHEA TINKER, Professor of Social Gerontology, King's College London; DR ROGER ORPWOOD, Deputy Director, Bath Institute of Medical Engineering; and PROFESSOR GARTH JOHNSON, Professor of Rehabilitation Engineering, University of Newcastle (on behalf of the Royal Academy of Engineering), examined.

Q223 *Chairman:* May I say welcome. We very much appreciate your interest in the work that we are carrying out on the scientific aspects of ageing. Thank you also for the written evidence which you have either produced and authored yourself or caused someone else to write and send in. It has been very helpful to have that. If after this session there are any points that you feel would be useful to expand on in writing or by e-mail, that would be very helpful indeed as well. There may be matters that you feel on reflection we did not cover thoroughly. The members of the Committee all have labels in front of them and in addition to the Members we have Tom Kirkwood, who I am sure you know is the Specialist Adviser, and Michael Collon, the Clerk with whom you have been liaising over this particular session. Can I remind you that this is being recorded and may be broadcast so the microphones are now live. We would like to put a series of questions to you and as I do that perhaps on the first one, which will be fairly general, you might each want to introduce yourself and say something about the particular areas of responsibility or interest which you have. We have to stop by five and I am afraid there may be divisions downstairs because there is quite an important Bill going. That being said, I want to start by asking you a question about how we set the context for the areas of interest which you represent. There are two main areas that the report will focus on. There are many we could have chosen but we have had to be reasonably focused. One is very much in the biomedical area, those scientific aspects of ageing, and the second is in the area of assistive technology and the ways in which that can make independent life more extensive or increase the quality of independent life, and that is what we are focusing on today. In thinking about this second area some have suggested to us that the right way to think about it perhaps is that biological ageing is

a gradual but intrinsic loss of adaptability, how you adapt to, in this case, the environment and context in which you live. That is one way of us trying to focus and ask questions but there may be an alternative framework and you may have a completely different perspective on where our questions should be generated and the kind of focus that we ought to have. I would like you to react to that. Shall we give priority to Baroness Greengross, our colleague downstairs, in answering this question and then just move across the table.

Baroness Greengross: Thank you very much, my Lord. I think it is quite a useful way of thinking about ageing and it is useful in a number of ways. It is rather about physical adaptability rather than the brain, which is a different question, and I think going back to the physical side it is very often that we create barriers or we do not adapt the environment ourselves so that people can overcome those increasing difficulties that come through the loss of adaptability. I always work on the basis that if we design something and somebody cannot use it, then the fault is in the design not in the person, and that implies that if you have got an environment with your wall sockets at floor level or where you have to rummage around on all fours to get the kitchen drawer open to get out a pot or a pan, then the design is wrong. It is not your fault and it is not because you cannot adapt; it is because it was not designed to cope with a more lifelong approach to living. In terms of mental adaptability, very often the way that we approach new ideas is that if older people build very carefully—and I am looking at Baroness Murphy here who knows this very well—on the knowledge that they have and they can use that to gain new insights and new ways of coping with life, then they do very, very well, surprisingly well in many people's view, but we have to design that learning procedure so that people can use their adaptation skills to the best possible outcome and that is really up to everybody else who is doing it. Older people can learn new tricks; it is the wrong way round to say they cannot.

Q224 *Chairman:* Thank you very much. Do you want to move across the table and again introduce yourself?

Professor Tinker: I am Anthea Tinker, Professor of Social Gerontology at King's College London. I think it is one way of looking at it but I think it hides the wide differences that there are. It is still a focus on disability and I think the point of the question in age-related frailty or disability is that it is inferred that one does get more disabled with age. Of course for some people that is true but disability, as you know, can strike at any age and chronological age is not always a very good marker, as Professor Kirkwood knows. The other thing is if we are thinking about environment it does not just include the physical environment, there are all sorts of other environments. I think social attitudes should be included in this and they may be just as important as what happens physically.

Professor Johnson: I am Garth Johnson, Professor of Rehabilitation Engineering at the University of Newcastle, and I am representing the Royal Academy of Engineering today. When I hear about pieces of equipment that older or indeed disabled people find difficult to operate, my first feeling is that this is engineering design that does not work. There has been a lot of talk in the engineering design community for a long time about "design for all" but I have a suspicion that a large number of the things that might be developed and designed with older people in mind are actually things that many younger people would also love to have. One of the examples that I used to cite—and this is now out of date—is I would have liked in my car a cassette player where I could just throw the cassette into a basket and it would play and so I did not have to line it up. Thinking not of older people but of children with cerebral palsy for instance, who may have severe hand movement problems, that would be a dream for them. There are lot of examples here where the things that we all want if they are done well are then much more suited to people who may have handicaps or disabilities resulting from age or illness.

Q225 *Chairman:* Thank you. Dr Orpwood?

Dr Orpwood: I am Dr Roger Orpwood from the Bath Institute of Medical Engineering. We are a design and development group attached to the University of Bath with a strong interest in assistive technology across the board, but with a major focus on looking at older people and people with cognitive problems. I guess I share the views that other

members of the panel have expressed. There is a need for design to encompass something that represents a kind of familiarity on the part of the user of that equipment. If they, for whatever reason, have developed inabilities to cope with various aspects of their environment and there is a design issue at stake here in trying to generate something which can enable them to deal more effectively with their environment, then I think building on things that are familiar is a very important rule of thumb to use. I think that becomes even more important when you start to look at issues of cognitive disabilities where people find it very hard indeed to adapt to change, and the need then to build on what is familiar to them is extremely important.

Chairman: Thank you very much indeed. I wonder if we could just move the questioning on a bit and Lord May will pick up the next point.

Q226 *Lord May of Oxford:* I wonder if you could give some further examples of the major impacts of the environmental aspects of ageing. I wonder how strong the evidence base is and do you think it is a subject that gets enough attention, both in its positive and negative aspects, in the research community?

Professor Tinker: I think that one needs to separate the outside and the inside environment. There are quite different problems for people getting outside, such as uneven pavements and so on, compared with inside, where if you ask older people, as we have in some of our research studies, where we have started with asking older people, you find that major problems are to do with getting upstairs, getting in and out of bed, and so on. I think you do need to divide the two. Your second question concerns how strong is the evidence base. There is plenty of evidence on problems and you can get that from national surveys and you can get that from asking individual older people, but there are far fewer solutions which involve older people themselves. Later on I could give you some examples of how we have involved older people in starting with their problem, thinking about a solution, and then testing out the solution. You may want to come back to that.

Professor Johnson: There are some extraordinary gaps in knowledge at a very basic engineering level. 90 per cent of the users of wheelchairs do not propel their own wheelchairs, they have them propelled for them by relatives (frequently older relatives) yet the published literature on the problems of manoeuvring attendant-propelled wheelchairs is incredibly weak and there is very little known about the bio-mechanical problems associated with propelling and manoeuvring in small spaces. They are some really very, very simple engineering questions. It is interesting because if you look at self-propelled wheelchairs in which the user population tends to be much younger, there is a mass of literature about the subtleties of how you position wheels for propulsion and turning corners and so on. So there are gross mismatches in knowledge between these two groups of people.

Q227 *Lord May of Oxford:* I must say my own personal impression is that for example the reaction to real and perceived hazards of people in the preparing of food is to devise caps that are put on things that require a great deal of physical strength, not to say ingenuity and mental agility to get off, in the thought that this will foil people. It is a matter of mystery to me why somebody has not approached that particular seemingly trivial problem.

Baroness Greengross: Perhaps if I could come in I would say that we make many mistakes and some of them are actually in saying that we are designing things for older people. For example, in transport the way good public transport is designed to be useable by disabled people of any age or pregnant women with children or indeed buggies and prams means that that serves a huge number of people if you just have step buses and easy access and so on. So we have to start thinking about universal design and we can make dreadful mistakes. To quote one example, some years ago when I was in the House of Commons meeting a Minister of Social Security, he was from Wales and his eyes filled with tears when we got on to talking about housing in the Valleys in Wales. The reason was that the local authority started "enveloping" all the rows of houses in the Valleys because they thought, how wonderful, these would be great for older people. His mum was in one and she was imprisoned on the first floor of this house which had become sheltered housing. She could not move because she was a heavy woman and these were little houses and nobody had realised that these were totally unsuitable for older people. We had to organise strong, young men to carry her out once a month to have lunch down the road. That sort of thing happens because we have a very narrow view and we do not try it out, as Anthea has said, on older people themselves, who really know what works and what does not. We imprison somebody in something we think is good for them rather than testing it out.

Q228 *Baroness Murphy:* Chairman, do you think it would be good for me to come in with my question at this time because it is so pertinent to what Sally and Anthea have said. You have mentioned the importance of involving older people in design and that was going to be my question; that so often they

are not. I wondered if you could both give us some more examples of good practice in that area and tell us what difference it has made.

Professor Tinker: I have given an example attached to the evidence of a poster, if you want to look at it later. One particular project was about mobility and we started by asking older people what their needs were. Instead of just asking them as I might ask you and you would say in an embarrassed way "going down stairs" we actually produced playing cards for them which we knew from scientific research showed the major problems. Different groups were asked then to put down three playing cards showing what they thought were the main problems, and top of the list with all of them when we put them together was climbing stairs. So then we had engineering students who got together with the research team and we asked what sort of climbing aid they would want and you will see the picture on the poster. The researchers, the engineers and the students (because it is important that we were educating students as well about the needs of older people) went away and designed a very, very simple stair climbing aid which you could go up and down stairs with. They re-designed it in wood, took it back to the group, they tried it, they made their comments, it was then designed and it is now a prototype and it is being patented, so here is one success story.

Q229 *Baroness Murphy:* Great.

Dr Orpwood: Could I add to that. I think it is an important point really that we need to involve older people in the whole process. It is not just a matter of doing surveys and using questionnaires and focus groups to try and get some idea of what the issues are from the perspective of the older user, it is also important to engage them in the development process itself so that their understanding, and indeed their actual physical interaction with the things that you are developing is part of the development process. Their understanding is used to guide the way that a device evolves during the design process. I think that is so crucial because there are so many aspects of the factors that impact on design which are very difficult to pick out just from surveys and questionnaires. A lot of them will not even be obvious to the user themselves until they have tried out an early prototype and said this is no good for whatever reason they had not anticipated before this process.

Professor Tinker: Could I just add one sentence to that. Too many people think they can try out a product on older people, if in fact they do that, but it is the stages before that that are so crucial.

Q230 *Baroness Finlay of Llandaff:* I really wanted to follow on from Lord May's question but related to medication labelling and medication containers, and this habit of sticking a label which is difficult to read over bold print that is on a packet which is actually easier to read. What comment do you have about what we should be doing about that labelling of medication and containers?

Baroness Greengross: I think there are some quite good containers. I have seen some rather nice American ones and I think we have got a few here which tell you what you take every day of the week. It is fairly obvious that you have got to have large print because most of us have eye impairment as we get older, it is not the minority, it is like hearing impairment, and not to take that into account is just silly. We know about the quantities of unuseable medication that are found in people's homes just because they do not know or they get muddled.

Q231 *Baroness Finlay of Llandaff:* I wonder if you have got any data on the number of drug errors that are occurring because of patients getting in a muddle, either being unable to open their container or muddling up the containers because they cannot read these little brown bottles and packets?

Professor Tinker: I do not personally, although I chaired a conference last month at which a pharmacist was talking about this and he said in care homes this was certainly a problem and that staff, too, would give the wrong medication because either the label had come off or they could not read it. It is part of a scenario of things being too small. You need simple buttons and large letters on everything, I would think.

Q232 *Baroness Walmsley:* The environment experienced by people of every age comprises many different elements, including the home, support services, local amenities, transport, education, leisure facilities, and of course in the case of some people the workplace. I know Baroness Greengross is particularly interested in issues related to older people carrying on working if they want to. The problem is that responsibility for all these ingredients is very fragmented, so the question is what opportunities are there for cost-effective integration of effort in relation to all these different environments in enabling people to cope with them and how might those initiatives be best developed?

Baroness Greengross: Well, the Department of Work and Pensions has an initiative to encourage older workers into the labour market. It has not been as successful as those for young workers and it has not had nearly as much attention or indeed money given to it. However, you could start there. I think Government needs to take note, and are for other reasons taking note, of the fact that if we cannot encourage more people to stay longer at work then financially this is going to be very difficult for the country. I think between the Treasury and the DWP there should be enough interest and I think there is quite a lot now to encourage, by whatever means, more people through incentives of one sort or another to stay on in the workplace or to come back if they have left for some reason. There are other things that can be done. There is a European Centre for Work and Society which I mentioned in our evidence and they have done quite a lot of work on the ergonomics of the workplace, and indeed colleagues here would know more about it than me. You can, in fact, increase significantly the number of years that, say, a nurse can stay and work if you do your studies really well, and the same in factories and assembly units. It is just a question of realising that if you can keep people in good shape so that they do not get bad backs and they do not become disabled unnecessarily, and you have financial incentives as well, many people will stay on in the workplace. We lose a lot of people onto disability benefits of one sort or another because they do suffer in the workplace physically or indeed through stress, and so there is a lot that the Government needs to take a lead on but I think employers as well, and I think one of the ways forward is to work a lot with employers. The big ones like BT for example are doing a huge amount to encourage older people, particularly older carers, to stay in the workplace by giving them much more flexible conditions. There are some lovely schemes. There is a beautiful one that BT have introduced. They can use the phone for the person they are caring for to be reassured that everything is alright. They can come in and out at times to suit them. It is the same I think with older workers and particularly disabled people. The majority of disabilities being acquired means that the majority of disabled people are older, so older people in the workplace need to have much more time spent on them to make sure that that environment is conducive to them staying on and not having to go because they just cannot cope, and that is where, Baroness Warmsley, what you were saying about transport, hours, being able to get there, being able to get home, being able to get out to look after somebody you are caring for, et cetera, is very, very important. We all have to recognise that this is a priority for the economy and for society as a whole.

Q233 *Chairman:* Do others want to come in on this one?

Professor Tinker: May I just ask through you were you specifically asking about older workers or was your question directed to co-ordination in general?

Q234 *Baroness Walmsley:* Co-ordination in general. I simply added workplace to the other list of environments which are so many and varied.

Professor Tinker: If you are talking specifically about assistive technologies here, there is, as we all know, considerable evidence that there is not enough co-ordination, either nationally or locally. If you are thinking about assistive technology the key is to think about the home first. That is what we are really concerned about and keeping older people in their own homes which is where 95 per cent live and I do not think there is any simple answer. You can say put everything into one organisation, give it all to health or social services, but research shows that even in one organisation it does not necessarily happen. So I think you have got to have a variety of tactics. In a particular area it may suit very well to have something in the primary care trust. In another area social services may be doing it extremely well. However, a lot of it, sadly, comes down to either personalities (and that is shown in research) or money, and so one way is to have something like ring-fencing of a grant or something like the Integrated Community Equipment Services. This is a very interesting initiative, not evaluated yet, where you do have a body that is responsible for co-ordinating the assistive technology and trying to produce best practice for other parts of the country.

Q235 *Baroness Walmsley:* If I can just follow up. Are we looking through the wrong end of the telescope here? Should we be looking at the older person themselves and starting from there rather than looking at the various organisations that can do something and saying how can they work better. If we should be looking individually at the older person or the person whose abilities are waning, how can that be done? Should there be funding following each individual? How do you think it should be done?

Professor Tinker: I do not think it is realistic to have funding for every individual. I think it is what is appropriate for a particular situation. I do not think you can generalise. The example I gave was of a particular problem and we wanted to try and solve it to produce some kind of device, and we used that approach. For something else you may want to get people together in another environment. You may want to have a structured questionnaire whereby you ask 1,000 people. You may want to just interview three or four people or you can work through organisations. I honestly do not think there is one simple answer. You are absolutely right, in my view, that we start with the older person and the problem with research is how do you get at people who will not come forward, the people who do not

belong to any pressure group, the people who do not go to Age Concern. They are the ones that you have to find some way of getting them in the framework and saying, "What do you need? What do you want?" Our experience—and we did research on people who are 85 and over—is often it is the very simple, inexpensive things that they want at the end of the day.

Q236 *Chairman:* Just to supplement the issue, one way is to ask the older person and then you get a catalogue of needs and wants and that is very important, but I suppose partly the question is how do you trigger a response because that comes potentially from many different sources. Maybe that is just reality and we have to accept that, but in other areas what you might say is X is responsible for making sure at least that there is a response to the need and it is X's job, whoever it is, to analyse these needs as they come through and trigger action because clearly one of the things that one finds is that the older person themselves does not know to whom you go.

Professor Tinker: But that is the value of the single assessment process which the Department of Health has brought in. I think that can be, if it is done properly and involves the older person really from the very beginning, an excellent way of achieving it.

Baroness Greengross: I am also not sure from the beginning of your question whether you are talking about older workers who may be quite elderly in years chronologically but who are actually a huge resource to the country, potentially greater than we know because so much is wasted because they do not get jobs and because we do not use perhaps assistive technology or any technology enough to make sure that they get the opportunity to work and because there is lots of prejudice against them.

Q237 *Baroness Walmsley:* I added the workplace to the list of the other environments because I think it is important that we do not see all older people as house-bound, dependent and needing a lot of assistance because there are a lot of older people who with just a little bit of help can carry on being economically active and healthy and mentally active as well.

Baroness Greengross: The vast majority. You have to remember when we get to septuagenarians the vast majority are relatively all right. We are not even talking about septuagenarians, we are talking about people of 50 and over here, the ones who are not getting to work when they possibly would very much like to. The vast majority, even when you think about dementia which is a huge problem, are not suffering from dementia. We get this terrible picture of despair really and it is just not true.

Q238 *Lord Soulsby of Swaffham Prior:* My question is to do with the older end rather than the younger end but with the increasingly ageing population there are a number of institutions that are set up to deal with the aged and the ageing. Often these are called retirement homes or something similar. How do you perceive the balance between the public and private institutions in this area? Are they equally good or do they vary enormously in delivering the improved environment that we are talking about?

Dr Orpwood: I suppose in looking at my own particular area of interest in terms of supportive environments, using technology to provide some kind of support for the occupants of a sheltered housing scheme, say, in the way that you described, a lot of the initiative and excitement seems to be coming from private initiatives, supported also by an interest from industry. There is no doubt about it. Clearly industry sees there being quite a burgeoning market here for this kind of technology. If the evidence were there they would all be jumping on the bandwagon without any doubt whatsoever. The liaison between private companies and particularly sheltered housing schemes run by housing associations seems to be quite an exciting environment in which some of this technology is evolving and being pushed forward. It will only go so far of course but a lot of initiatives seem to be coming from those kinds of liaisons.

Professor Tinker: I would say, as you hinted at the end, that there is not a simple answer, there is good and bad. If you are talking specifically about retirement housing there are very good and very poor examples in the public and private sectors. I would hate all the emphasis to be on the private because I do think we are tending to run down social housing philosophically and in all sorts of ways and it does meet a tremendous need. Do not let's forget the voluntary sector, for example housing associations, because there are excellent examples there. Of course, retirement housing is only one example and research that I have done shows that there is still a proportion of people who go into that form of housing who do not want to go there and could have stayed in their own home had they got the appropriate assistive technology and of course care as well, some sort of support, so I do not think it is the answer to everything, however good it is.

Lord Soulsby of Swaffham Prior: You answered the question I was about to follow up as a supplementary.

Chairman: Alpha double plus is the answer.

Q239 *Lord Soulsby of Swaffham Prior:* There are some people, let's put it that way, whom one meets who are quite unhappy in sheltered housing. Their normal lives have been taken from them and the things that they like to have around them such as a companion animal are not allowed, and they feel that terribly. One or two people that I have talked to feel that their life has come to an end and they are eking out life because of the strict regulations. That does not apply to them all but one wonders what can be done to make the lives of some of these people a lot more pleasant.

Professor Tinker: I think research is showing most of the major providers that there are these problems. I did a study some years ago of difficult-to-let sheltered housing. Some people said, "Surely this wonderful new form of housing cannot be difficult to let?" but it was, for all sorts of reasons. The people you have described may be unhappy because of the rules like no pets, but they may also be unhappy because of poor design of assistive technology like shared bathrooms and the mad places that people put sheltered housing developments in. We looked at sheltered housing that was in a red light area, another in a converted church, which is fine, trendy, loft living, wonderful for younger people but the older people felt it was very spooky, and another in little villages where people had no links at all. I think both the design of the building and the design of where it is placed has something to do with it as well as what you have mentioned about the rules and regulations.

Baroness Greengross: I think that the whole of this depends on the design and the range of services that is available because the age that people go into some sort of retirement housing has changed enormously. At one stage about 25 to 30 years ago anybody over 65 was considered too old to go into sheltered housing and now the average age of going in is getting nearer to 75 or 80. When you go into some sort of retirement accommodation at that age you really do need to have more services available as and when you need them than the category one sheltered housing (which used to be the norm) provides, and that is getting out of date. Really we have to think in terms of bringing services to people in retirement housing. It has to be a mix between public and private and voluntary because of the value of housing in this country. So many of us have a home that we own and we think that is very important, and wherever people live in this country (almost without exception) the value of that has gone up enormously in value, so it would be silly to think that the public sector could provide all the retirement housing needed. However, I would like to see us get away from the thought that everything that is provided for older people is exclusively for older people because there are many younger people who would love to go into a serviced flat and people who are single—and there are many more single people living in flats now—who would like services, and it would be great if we could get away from having to block people together because of their birthdays and think about the sort of services that single people very often need if they are living in a block where they want private space but they do have requirements for some space where people can get together and meet or have a meal or get a bit of shopping if they are in a rural area. These need not be age restricted. As for this thing about animals, if you go to France you are allowed to take an animal. If the animal is a nuisance then other people will make the usual complaint and it would have to be sorted out. We can change that rule. It is just ridiculous and awful to say you cannot take your pet. We can change that. It is just a question of encouraging the people who need to sell or rent or find tenants for their sheltered housing to make these attractive to people who want to go in. It is marketing really.

Q240 *Lord Soulsby of Swaffham Prior:* Just one final thing, my Lord Chairman. The sort of housing that I think is very good—and I wonder how many there are in this country and whether they are private or delivered by local authorities—are those where you start off self-catering in an environment and then as you get older and less able you gradually are brought in and you are fed every day and maybe even washed every day depending on your capability, but it is phased in over a period of years. I know that this is common in the United States of America. Is it common in this country?
Professor Tinker: There are a few retirement communities with a limited amount of research on them and what limited research there is shows that people do not tend to move. What they would much prefer would be to have the services brought to them, which you may not be able to do at the extreme when somebody really needs nursing home care. But it is fairly untested in this country and I do not think we can compare with the States where they have much more restrictive rules such as when you reach a certain level of disability you will be discharged, and of course a number of them have gone bankrupt so I am not sure we ought to look to the States for an example. We have only got a few. The Joseph Rowntree one in York is a very famous one but has only been in existence for a short time and it is for older people with pretty high incomes.
Baroness Greengross: There is a charity called Extra Care which is in the Midlands and the North and they provide what we could call social housing with continuing care really, so that you can get more care as your needs become greater, if they do. They are quite an interesting newcomer to the market, I

think, and there are a few retirement communities like the York one being established now and there are plenty of those on the continent of Europe with different models. I think we can learn a lot from continuing care.

Q241 *Baroness Hilton of Eggardon:* I was relieved to hear what you said about pets because we had an earlier witness who said that elderly people should not have cats because they were a trip hazard and they might fall over them. We have been talking about house design, have we not, at some length and I am wondering whether having Building Regulations which require houses to have doorways wide enough for wheelchairs and grip handles and things like that should be an automatic part of the design of new houses? Would that be viable or too expensive?
Professor Johnson: I saw this question last night and it was intriguing me because our university, and I am sure all others, have just been subjected to quite major structural alterations because of the new requirements for people with disabilities, and I wonder whether that is the appropriate way forward. It sounds appealing in one way, but I wonder whether there is a danger of an over-prescriptive solution which might be overkill. It somehow seems to me to lack the user pull which I always want to see in these matters. The whole of assistive technology suffers greatly from a lot of technology push and insufficient user pull and I wondered whether there was another example of that, whether somehow we can create demand at the other end so that these things get done where appropriate rather than through legislation.
Professor Tinker: The lifetime homes part of Building Regulations is excellent because it does create a design which means that you can stay in your home for the whole of your life but it is not going to help most older people because they are in existing homes and the real problem there is how do you look at their existing home. On your subject of cats I have just come back from the Gerontological Society of America where there was a very high-powered symposium on assistive technology, and what did we have but a robot cat which has been designed quite seriously for people with dementia because it reacts exactly the same except it does not have its claws out and it does not attack you. The researchers said that this was very calming for people with dementia. It is an example of assistive technology I have not seen before. I stroked it; I did not like it.

Q242 *Baroness Hilton of Eggardon:* Not real enough?

Professor Tinker: No, I do not like cats!

Baroness Greengross: I think we have to remember as well that very often lonely elderly people have nobody they touch or who touches them at all for months on end and if they have something with fur that is the only sensual feeling of something that reacts to them that they experience and it is terribly, terribly important.

Chairman: Perhaps we could improve our cat breeding and move over into the biological side of things and selective genetics. We select animals for all sorts of other purposes; why not this. We will move on. Lord Mitchell?

Q243 *Lord Mitchell:* One of the issues that exercises this Select Committee is the relationship between universities and all sorts of institutions and the transfer of technology and sometimes as in this case the transfer of research. The research tends to be based in the university sector. I just wanted to know the extent to which the applied initiatives that come out of that are taken on by central and local government? Just to go a little further, do you feel there is sufficient dialogue to ensure the research is being done in the right areas?

Professor Johnson: This is a complex issue. Certainly the traditional university engineering research model is of central funding from research councils, very frequently accompanied either by industrial money or else industrial participation of one kind or another. In the assistive technology business that is almost impossible to achieve. If you look at the industry itself, it is highly fragmented and consists of large numbers of very small companies who have small profit margins and little manpower and find it very, very difficult, even if they are interested, to get closely involved in that kind of way. At the other end they are not able to provide the major market pull that again is familiar to research engineers in universities when they launch into partnerships with industry, so there are some particular difficulties there. Whether it is possible in some way to cluster companies around research projects I do not know. There are obviously then problems of competition and so on. It is a major difficulty that we face. I am embroiled just as we speak actually in such a problem in a major European project where the same problems exist on the continent of Europe as well as here.

Professor Tinker: The problem is we have different objectives and the universities' objectives are for high-quality research where we are all trying with the research assessment exercise to produce international articles, as you well know, and no sooner do we finish one project than we are onto getting money for the next one. So it is very, very difficult to spend time disseminating information and having links with industry. With the best will in the world a lot of us try it, but we are constrained by what we are required to do in a university.

Q244 *Chairman:* In fact, one of the ways in which we might try to have influence is by suggesting if we think policies could be redirected in some way or another that might be taken on board by the Government. For example, some of the research councils, indeed some of the funding councils have proof of concept money where the intention is precisely to bring research nearer the position where it could create a product and be marketed in some way, and it is the balance of research spend and how that relates to policy which is one of the questions we are interested in which, is why we are asking the question.

Baroness Greengross: May I come in there, not from the university end, but I have been a judge with the Royal College of Art and the Helen Hamlyn Foundation and also the Royal Society of Arts where there were some very excellent designs—and these are all post-graduate students so some of them are already producing products which are manufactured—these awards are excellent but very often they stop at the design stage. I remember one whole range of Helen Hamlyn beautifully engineered products that were too expensive and they never got into the mass market but recently that has got a bit better. I am an addict of Homebase and I remember recently going into Homebase and seeing tools and tool boxes of tools which are all designed with very clever handles which are excellent for people with arthritis or any other impediment. These are now very cheap indeed. There is another whole range of kitchen utensils which, as I say, are easy to hold, very carefully designed kitchen tools. They were designed here but they were taken up by an American manufacturer and it seems to me that if somehow the Select Committee could influence the take-up of these very excellent designs by manufacturers to put these on to the general market that would be so helpful because a lot of them would really transform people's lives. They stay in the university or they stay as good ideas. We know we are bad at that switch from one to the other in this country. They are brilliant ideas but they do not always get into the market-place.

Dr Orpwood: There is the element of development here. So much work that goes on with the universities will be very innovative in looking at new ideas and concepts, but the gap between that and commercial product is enormous and the money for that has got to come from somewhere, usually from the industrial sector. A lot of research programmes, as you know, will encourage manufacturers to become involved in the work right from the word go so that there is more integration between the research activities and the commercial product at the end of the day, but if that is not done, there is no doubt about it, people like ourselves do struggle enormously to take really good ideas where you can demonstrate the effectiveness in what you are trying to achieve with a smallish number of individuals who have been involved in some sort of evaluation programme. From there to go through all the processes that are required to make a product economically viable is a long drawn out and quite expensive process. As much resource is needed to do that as to get to that point in first place.

Q245 *Baroness Finlay of Llandaff:* My question really follows on from that. To a certain extent you have spoken about a worrying gap between innovation and translation. What about collaboration between universities themselves and collaboration between universities and the NHS sector where many older people are ending up as the patient population?
Professor Tinker: One of the problems is that we are in competition with one another. I think one interesting way forward is more and more of the research council grants are now given for collaborative work. For example, in our last big study of assistive technology and how it can enable people to stay in their own homes we did in collaboration with the University of Reading where they have surveyors and occupational therapists so it is a joint King's/Reading project. I think more and more research councils are giving money to consortia. This sounds wonderful in theory but it does require a lot of time and you have to decide where are you going to meet and how often. With e-mail and internet you could say it is easy but it is not, you do need to meet face-to-face and, of course, there is this element of competition. One way it is an advantage, if you talk about the NHS, is if a university has a medical school and a hospital with it. That is easier and we have found it quite easy to work with our medical school and our hospital, but it is a problem, I think, of competition.
Professor Johnson: I think perhaps the engineering community does not see it in quite the same way. We are perhaps more used to sharing facilities and sharing skills with other universities. It is not something we find too difficult. Working with the NHS at the university hospital level can be fairly easy on a personal basis but finding collaborative funding with the NHS is not always easy. In the assistive technology area for instance the NHS does not see it as a priority. Collaboration with social services in my experience is exceedingly difficult in that there is not perceived to be a working pattern

that has ever been established in this sort of area. That is something that could work fruitfully, I believe.

Q246 *Baroness Finlay of Llandaff:* Are there blocks by ethics committees in terms of the non-medically qualified group having access to the patient population?
Professor Johnson: Not in our experience.
Professor Tinker: I chair the King's Ethics Committee. There may be problems partly to do with insurance. If you have got a project that has both patients and people who are the control group who are not patients there can be problems there but Lord Warner, as you probably know, is chairing a committee which is looking at ethics committees, and I have just done a national survey of university ethics committees. I think people are beginning to realise that people have got to overcome these barriers and ethics committees have got to get their own act together.

Q247 *Baroness Finlay of Llandaff:* What would be your solution or recommendation as a way of bringing these different sectors together such as the universities and social services, such as getting rid of the competitive element between universities and the NHS, and so on?
Professor Tinker: You could say in an ideal world everybody would be nicer to one another but we are constrained by different formulae. I think money tells. If there is a pot of money for anything—and Baroness Murphy knows this in her field—if there is money for people in health to get together, they will get together and I think that is one way forward. You can talk to people about getting together. The other way of course is to have somebody charismatic who will carry everyone with them, but you cannot legislate for that.

Q248 *Baroness Finlay of Llandaff:* No, but funding to collaboratives?
Professor Tinker: I think that funding is absolutely crucial. One problem here is if it is short term. If it is a pilot project what do you do at the end of it and the money runs out and you have got lots of disappointed clients? That is a real dilemma.

Q249 *Chairman:* Can I just ask as a supplementary, is the European Union a useful source, because certainly in the various research Directives they simply stipulate that you must have a university from the South as well as those which are more successful in the North? Whether the collaboration is real is another matter and I think that would have to be looked at but they do stipulate and provide significant sums of money for partnerships.

Professor Johnson: The associated management overheads are enormous. That is the price that you pay.

Q250 *Chairman:* Value for money in other words.
Professor Tinker: It takes an awful lots of work to get these projects off the ground and I would hazard a guess—and I cannot reveal what happens in King's obviously—that most of them make a loss. You do it for the prestige saying you have got a new project but they are very time consuming and very expensive to do.
Baroness Greengross: However, they do necessarily produce collaboration because in order to qualify you have to have at least three countries of the Union getting together to do that properly so from that point of view they force people to collaborate.
Professor Tinker: We have found it is much better to get an individual collaborator. For example, this project I have talked about putting assistive technology into people's existing homes, it is a very big project that has finished. We collaborated with the Netherlands because we thought they were very similar. One of the things we found there on assistive technology is something that nobody had seen in this country. You probably know that in the Netherlands they have got these very steep, winding staircases which nobody here would ever think of putting a stair lift in and, lo and behold, they were there and we came back and reported to our 10 partners (we were working with five housing associations and five local authorities) and within two or three weeks one local authority had installed 30. This was just an example of what you can learn where you know that there is someone who is working in a similar area to you with a similar population, so I think there is more mileage in identifying your partners rather than going in for a big project.

Q251 *Baroness Walmsley:* Can I just follow up on the idea of partnership. If various institutions work together in collaboration, say, for an EU project which may not be terribly profitable for them and may not come to anything, at the end of it, do any of you have any experience of the fact that they have got to know each other and each other's abilities within that collaboration which means that they then go on to do other things together?
Professor Johnson: It is an interesting remark. I am just coming towards the end of an EU project with two other partners. We are having active dialogue about how we can fund future things that do not involve the EU framework!

Q252 *Baroness Walmsley:* Yes, that is what I had in mind!

Professor Tinker: At the end of some projects you wish you had never met the people and got involved and certainly would not want to work with them again!
Chairman: You do not have to go to Europe to meet that problem!

Q253 *Lord Drayson:* I would like to probe some of the points you have made about the lack of commercial take-up of some of the ideas which you feel would be highly useful based on assistive technology. You have said that there is a huge demand and that elderly people have a great amount to give to society if they are assisted in this way, so why are not more commercial organisations seeing this as an opportunity for them to develop products to fulfil this need? What is the mismatch here?
Baroness Greengross: Can I come in on one sector which has seen a market, which is the motor car manufacturing sector. Cars now are designed—and nobody says this because everybody wants to think of themselves as very youthful when they buy a car, particularly, if I may say so, men wanting sporty cars—

Q254 *Chairman:* You may say so!
Baroness Greengross: But if you look at the design of modern cars which have wider doors, bigger dashboards, larger signals and they are higher with more headroom and easier to get in and out of because of all of that, they are designed for the people who are actually buying the cars who are older people on the whole—50 plus and many of them women—so they are designed quite differently from the way they used to be. There are all sorts of reasons given for that about aerodynamics but I think it is, in fact, who buys them. This is just not quoted in the sales pitch because, as I say, people like to think of a car as being very much for giving a young image. So the market is determining this and I am sure with things I was mentioning like household equipment and kitchen tools this is changing. It is just very slow and that is because of this huge built-in reluctance to think about ageing and older people in a positive way. It takes a long time for those prejudices to disappear but they are gradually disappearing because the market now is no longer a youth market, it is an older people's market.

Q255 *Chairman:* Given that you have said that older people are not involved enough in the development and design of those products, do you think there is a need to encourage the older generation to get more involved in starting companies and being entrepreneurs to fulfil this market need? Have you done any work to look at what works in developing government policy to encourage that?

Professor Tinker: It is certainly an interesting idea because one research project in housing in the North used older people as researchers and at the end of it these researchers formed a company and they are now hiring themselves out. I think the answer to your first question is, it is a source of amazement to me that industry is still stuck in this disability mode. Everything is white plastic. How come they do not see that older people want good design, whether it is Marks & Spencer's classic design or whatever it is? I just cannot understand why they still have this image. Maybe it is the fault of gerontologists like me who do not say enough about what ageing is and talk more about the normal rather than disability, but somebody is going to make a fortune when they do realise that there is this big market for good design.

Q256 *Baroness Hilton of Eggardon:* Why does it cost more to have coloured things than to have white things or for grey filing cabinets to be cheaper than coloured filing cabinets? It is a total mystery to me.

Baroness Greengross: I do not know the figures, Lady Hilton. Actually, I think a lot of entrepreneurs and start-up businesses are in fact older entrepreneurs. They are not always young.

Q257 *Lord Drayson:* The older ones are certainly more successful.

Baroness Greengross: Yes, exactly, and much less of a risk.

Professor Johnson: It is part of the design-for-all argument again, though, is it not? Baroness Greengross's example of the motor car is the perfect design-for-all example. We all want motor cars that suit us, whether we are 95 or 25, and if a designer can make one that suits us all then there is the greatest profit to be made, but when you come to the more specialist piece of equipment that becomes much more difficult and that is when you start to see the fragmentation of the industry.

Q258 *Baroness Murphy:* I wonder if you would agree with me that part of the difficulty, and I have had many conversations with people about this, is that the Mothercare revolution has not been repeated for older people, with special facilities where people can go for aids not actually labelled as for older people, but with those aids and assistive technology where you can actually find it all together in one place. Why do you think that has not taken off? Might it be because often things are sold through chemists and places that have surgical connotations?

Baroness Greengross: Boots are now doing it much more. All we need to do is speed this up. It is happening. You can get in Boots now walking aids, continence aids, all sorts of things that used to be hidden behind somewhere that nobody would dare speak about, and it is all changing. It is just slow.
Chairman: But you want to get them out of Boots into the shop next door?

Q259 *Baroness Murphy:* Yes, I want them in Homebase. We have not got them on the high street where you can go in and you have got technology for life.

Dr Orpwood: It depends very much on the technology, I think, and technology for people who have a disability is pretty specialised and the market for that device is really quite small. There is clearly a wide variety of products that are going to be much more general in their applicability instead of items that companies like Boots would be attracted to. To come back to the original point that was made about the issue of trying to persuade manufacturers to take these products up, if you talk to manufacturers about a new device that has just been shown to be effective, inevitably their calculations are going to revolve around what market type is perceived as being available for that particular product. That is quite difficult to do at that stage until quite a number of items have been out and have been used and the applicability of that device to a variety of different disabilities has been established. Even for items where on the surface you would say that there must be an enormous market for these sorts of things, items that are going to be appropriate for the elderly population in general, a lot of companies get quite nervous until there is some evidence base that this stuff really is doing the sort of job that the designers are saying it can achieve. That takes quite a while to establish. Manufacturers, certainly in my experience, have been very nervous about taking things on until there is a real demonstration that the market is there, and that does take time.

Q260 *Lord Mitchell:* As an ancient entrepreneur let me comment on that. I think that it is all a question of disposable income, and in some ways the 70 and 80-year olds are the last of an era of a whole section of the population that have not typically had a large amount of disposable income. I may be wrong on this but that is my instinct on that. I think that the baby boomers are moving towards that with more disposable income. I think that is going to change dramatically because manufacturers respond to markets, they respond to opportunities, and if there is a segment there that has a lot of money to spend they will react very quickly. I am just interested whether in the United States, where presumably people in that segment have got more money to spend, there are more products available for people in that area. I do not know the answer but I just wonder.

Baroness Greengross: I do not think there are. I think we know all about that. I do not think there are more. You get now wheelie shoppers and things because more people use them. You do get those things in our shops now and you are right, that the baby boomers are in the new market, the mass market and that this is only a question of us trying to hurry up the process of it happening.

Dr Orpwood: There is a kind of acceptance of technology by the baby boomer generation which was not there for their predecessors. They are much more accepting of pieces of technology to support their daily activities rather than personal care from another individual.

Baroness Finlay of Llandaff: As you were talking I was wondering whether we are just a disability averse society rather than a gadgets-for-living society. Perhaps there is a fundamental shift that needs to happen in attitude towards living rather than disability equals decline equals heading towards death, a perception which there is in the life of so many people, in order to get the entrepreneur to pick up the marketing. Perhaps gadgets-for-living might be the next Mothercare.

Q261 *Baroness Walmsley:* Going back to what you were saying earlier, why are the manufacturers of these aids so much more sensitive to the need for a mass market and evidence before they try anything out than, for example, the food retailing industry? There is not a big market for pickled walnuts but you can still get them in Sainsbury's. The food manufacturers are constantly trying new products. If they work they keep them and if they do not, unfortunately for those of us who happen to like them, they discontinue them. Why is it? What is the difference?

Professor Johnson: They do not have to invest in R&D. There is no research for pickled walnuts.

Lord Soulsby of Swaffham Prior: There jolly well is. I do it myself.

Q262 *Baroness Walmsley:* There are many products that you see launched and then they disappear and the food technologists will have developed those products, so it is not a matter of there not having been any R&D behind them, but they are floated and if they do not work they disappear, and if they do work you see them carry on on the shelves. I am not clear about why there is such a difference between the manufacturers, or potential manufacturers, of some of these aids for living, or

gadgets-for-living, to use Baroness Finlay's phrase, which I think she is going to patent, and the food retailers.

Professor Johnson: The final market size in that case is important. If your pickled walnuts really are a success you may sell them to 10 million people quite easily, but if you produce some modified wheelchair device which is better for manoeuvring in bathrooms, you will probably only sell perhaps a thousand or a few thousand.

Q263 *Baroness Walmsley:* But I bet you make a lot more profit on your wheelchair than you will on a jar of pickled walnuts.

Professor Johnson: I do not know that that is true, because there tends to be a monopoly of purchasers who hold prices down.

Q264 *Baroness Walmsley:* Ah; that might be a point.

Professor Tinker: Also, the baby boomer generation will be much more used to labour-saving devices and if we market them that way, as labour-saving, these sensors and things which come under assistive technology, alarms and so on, they will be much more acceptable. Just think about the acceptability of a mobile phone now, which has transformed the lives of some people, for example, in residential care homes who now can make a phone call in privacy; they do not have to go to the open hall to talk their daughter or whatever. I think it is partly a generation thing which may hopefully change.

Dr Orpwood: Also, there is an awful lot of very small companies in the whole assistive technology field. If you go to the major shows and exhibitions that these companies put on you get a large number of companies which are two or three or four-men bands making a living out of one or two products. For them, to introduce something fairly novel is a major investment and if it does fail it is something which is going to have a major impact on their business. Okay; there are other companies around who are much larger and who are able to take those kinds of risks more easily, but yes, the point you make is a valid one about why they are more risk averse than some sectors.

Q265 *Lord Drayson:* It sounds to me, listening to you, that this has all the hallmarks of a market that is in the very early stages of development, with small companies and a highly fragmented market. It is because the market does not yet understand the opportunity. As my noble friend remarked, as the baby boomer generation comes through this will change quite quickly. I want to pick up your point about how we can accelerate this process given that a lot of these products take a long time and a lot of money to develop. Is there an effective trade association, do you think, representing companies that focus on this market?

Baroness Greengross: I have to say I am not quite sure what market it is we are talking about, because we have now shifted to talking about disability and if you take everybody with a disability as well as the older person, it is already a huge market. For example, in wheelchair technology I have seen some wonderful examples of lightweight wheelchairs made in Japan, but I do not know how aggressively those are marketed over here. I just do not know.

Q266 *Lord Drayson:* I am specifically focused on the market defined by the impact of ageing, and so technology investment into the environment and into products which assist people as they get through the ageing process. Is there an effective trade association of companies who are looking to develop products and services which addresses that market?

Professor Tinker: There is an association, for example, for alarm manufacturers. That is an example where they have responded to the market and in particular one very large one I will not say has got a monopoly but has got very extensive coverage.

Professor Johnson: The Foundation for Assistive Technology is a charitable organisation which essentially promotes the use of and attempts to promote research and development in assistive technology. It manages on a tiny budget and employs about two people at the moment. I work with them. The British Health Trades Association does not seem to be terribly effective as I see it in promoting the whole industry. Those are the two organisations which appear to represent the industry.

Q267 *Chairman:* I would guess that one of the issues relates to what the banks will lend money on, and they are much more reluctant to lend money to a small three-person company with no assets behind them than they are to, say, one of the big multiple superstores. Since the banks are now in fact much more interested in care homes for the elderly one gets the impression that there is a change in perception and even the banks are realising that there is a major market here because they are funding all sorts of things, but it has not got through to the assistive technology end. Maybe that is one of the points we might pick up, that the awareness of the banks here would make a difference in terms of who can borrow money to develop a product. One last theme that has already been touched on and keeps coming up and we are interested in your comments on is the extent to which the work in

which you are engaged and have knowledge of is dealing with the problems once they have come up and they are seen as difficulties for individuals with forms of disability or what-have-you, as distinct from saying that there is actually a wholeness of life which can be continued for a much longer period and some of the focus of our energies and of the groups you represent could go in that direction. Is there a development taking place there or is it very much, "There is a problem. Let us see if we can solve it"?

Dr Orpwood: A lot of the work that is coming in, looking at things like tele-care and smart homes, for example, has been very much focused on looking at systems which can provide security and safety within a given environment. That is fine and there are obviously issues there that need addressing, and a lot of evidence is starting to accrue as to the effectiveness of this technology. As you suggest in your comment, if you have got people in a given environment where they are nice and safe and secure they are not going to stick the cooker on and leave the gas pouring out; somebody is going to sort that out, but there is much more to their lives than just being safe and sound and secure in that situation. I think that is recognised more and more by people involved in that area of technology and there are programmes under way, and we are involved in one ourselves, looking at what aspects of quality of life, issues which older people themselves are commenting on as being crucial to their sense of having some quality of life, can be influenced through the use of new technology and new design. I am sure the potential is enormous. Our own programme has got an enormous great list of about 73 different devices that all seem to impact on quality of life, and this was for people with dementia so we are looking at quite a small sector of the elderly population.

Q268 *Chairman:* Could you give us some examples of the potential products?

Dr Orpwood: The particular work I am talking about started very much as a quality of life survey, so it was looking at people with dementia, trying to see from discussions with them, with focus groups and with their carers what kinds of issues underpin their quality of life. A whole range of things came out, such as social isolation, a sense of not being in control of their lives. We pulled this lot up and we were keen to encourage all the social sciences who were not doing that work not to think about technology but just try to pull down the ideas that these people were suggesting. That was a wonderful starting point for people like Professor Johnson and myself to engage researchers in to explore ways in which new technology can have an impact in this area. Some of the ideas may sound slightly wacky but once you get involved in exploring their potential and working with people to see what impact it is having, then some of them do not seem quite so stupid. For example, in the area of trying to reduce social isolation there was some very nice work done in York looking at the impact of phone conferencing on older people, trying to give them a sense of being engaged with the local community and having a chat through phone conferencing. Actually, phone conferencing is not easy to do. You have got no eye contact, you have got no means of knowing who is about to talk or whatever, and yet people got enormous satisfaction out of that to the extent of knowing it was coming up and dressing up because they knew they were going to get their conference call in a moment.

Q269 *Chairman:* You do not do this in your dressing gown. Some of us saw a little bit of that a couple of weeks ago in New York. There is one very specific thing and I would be interested to know if there is any background research being done on this. I am thinking of people with dementia that is beginning to come on. One of the big things, especially if they are not 65, but equally if they are over 65, is, "Can I continue in any form of employment?". Is there any accessible source to which an employer can go—and I know of cases where this has been done on a one-to-one basis—and say, "X clearly has the following profile. I am told that Y, Z and A will happen to X. What kind of work pattern could I reasonably expect if I were to keep this individual in the company?". As I say, I know of examples where that has been done but I do not see a lot of evidence of support which can be given so that the employer can make knowledgeable judgements about that.

Dr Orpwood: There are two sides to that. One is the advice of people who have an understanding of dementia and its progression and the impact it is going to have on their capabilities, and there are organisations around which can provide that kind of support. The other is access to some understanding of what support equipment there might be around, for example, if somebody has got a developing memory problem some kind of reminder type of device which can enable them to flag up that at half three something has not happened. Quite often these things are stuck on notepads and somebody will write down, "Half three you have got a visitor", or whatever. All the device does is make a noise so that it reminds them to think about something that is coming up. There is quite a lot of equipment like that around. One area that certainly hits you quite loudly, working with people with dementia, is that there is no

collective source of information about that kind of product, there really is not. The various databases that have been set up go quite quickly out of date. We have had some discussions with a number of the marketing companies in the assistive technology area to say, "Look: there is an enormous market here. There are hundreds of products that could be applicable to people with dementia. Why do we not pull them together into some sort of catalogue?". I think we are getting some success but it is amazingly hard work to try and show them that there is a market for this kind of equipment. People do not seem to see that there is a link between dementia and supportive technology and that there is an enormous amount that can be done with fairly simple pieces of equipment.

Q270 *Chairman:* There is an assumption that it is all or nothing, which it is not, in fact.
Dr Orpwood: Absolutely.

Q271 *Baroness Finlay of Llandaff:* Going back to my question about universities, do you think that the RMU, as it has now been re-formatted, is going to help at all or hinder?
Professor Tinker: You may know more about this than I do but I do not think the format has changed all that dramatically. It is still going to be your four international peer reviewed articles and the amount of research that you brought in and your international reputation. Obviously, there are things to be said for that but I am not sure it is going to help people like us who are desperate to spend time disseminating and doing more research with unsexy subjects. A lot of the things are very mundane. I am sure you are looking at the extreme of assistive technology and all the wonderful new gadgets and so on, but the reality for many older people is how do you get the funding for basic adaptations, level access showers and so on, and how do you get people to know about them? It is very basic stuff and people like me do not have the resources to go round the country talking about this.
Baroness Greengross: That is the key to this, that is where the integration needs to take place, whether it is the primary care trust or whoever has to take responsibility under the label of continuing care or whatever it is. Somebody has got to bring those things together because assistive technology is only one bit. I think we said in our evidence that there are 17 million people now with some sort of chronic condition, long term condition, and these people are not just to be thrown in the rubbish bin. There is a lot they can do but it needs to be brought together so that the research that is being done is not just wasted because it is not put to good practice. If you

as the committee could influence that it would be wonderful. I am sure you can.

Chairman: I am sure if we can we will think it is wonderful as well. I thank you very much for what has been a very interesting session. I will just repeat

my request that if there are points that you think you could have developed further do let us have a response as soon as possible, because we hope to begin to pull ideas together early in the new year. Thank you very much.

Supplementary evidence by Professor Anthea Tinker

The Chairman kindly invited a "follow-up" letter. There are four points arising from their Lordships' questions that I would like to respond further to.

1. Following Lord May's question there is currently no way of knowing in any detail, or with any accuracy, about people's ownership of the full range of Assistive Technology and, more particularly, how this is changing over time. We made suggestions for the inclusion of some pertinent questions in the new English Longitudinal Study of Ageing, but unfortunately they were turned down. I wonder if their Lordships might suggest that a more detailed survey of Assistive Technology is included every five years, perhaps in the General Household Survey.

2. Baroness Walmsley Q236 rightly emphasised the importance of starting with older people, and I understood the Chairman to say that, if older people were asked what they would like, there would be a "catalogue of responses". Currently, the evidence suggests that older people are modest in their requests and address what they experience as a need. This may, of course, change with cohort, but our recent research suggests the cost-effectiveness potential of making Assistive Technology more accessible. As was pointed out, this is crucially a problem of information and I venture to suggest that the report might include a recommendation about investment by government in information about all kinds of Assistive Technology. I understand, from research that we are doing at the moment, that we are the only European country that does not provide a free information service relating to Assistive Technology. The Disabled Living Foundation, the main national information provider in this area, have to charge users—who are professionals, rather than the public—for their service.

3. Lord Mitchell Q260 made a very significant point in relation to the disposable income of older people. Current forecasts suggest that, given existing policies, the current inequalities in pensioner income will widen and that pensioner poverty will increase. It would be most valuable if your report could flag up the fundamental connections between income in old age, and people's ability to make choices about how they adapt effectively to their environment.

4. Finally, in response to Lord Drayson Q253 I would like to re-iterate the point in our evidence about the importance of a small organisation like RicAbility, who provide excellent information provision on a range of Assistive Technology. I will post a recent leaflet just in case this has not come to your Lordships' attention. It would be most helpful, I believe, if your report could highlight the good work that RicAbility do in the context of very limited resources.

December 2004

Supplementary letter from Dr Roger Orpwood

Thank you for the offer of receiving further comment following the oral evidence provided at the Committee meeting at the House of Lords on Tuesday 7 December. I thought the meeting covered a large number of points but there are a couple of further issues I would like to take this opportunity to raise.

TELECARE

There is a lot of interest in Telecare at the moment to support older people in their own homes, and generous imminent funding from the government to enable local authorities to explore its potential. Evidence about the effectiveness of Telecare is only just starting to be available and although it is encouraging, limitations are being uncovered. Its effectiveness is only as good as the network of carers who can be contacted by call centres to deal with problems that are highlighted by the sensors in people's homes. Responses are inevitably going to take some time. If a bathroom flood sensor detects water on the floor it can be some time before the call centre is alerted, and for them to contact a carer, and for the carer to come round to turn off the taps.

Technology that is currently being developed, that rather more accurately carries the "smart home" label, provides a home with the ability to act in an autonomous fashion. A smart home installation would detect that the water level in the bath had reached a high level and would itself turn off the taps and provide the user with a reassuring message. In other words the house itself would deal with the problem. All the issues being tackled by Telecare can also be supported through autonomous smart home technology. Call centres are only contacted in emergencies, support does not rely on carers being contactable and able to help, and the user does not have the sense of being "monitored" and people being sent around. They are much more empowered by such autonomous dwellings. Smart home technology is at the stage Telecare was 3–4 years ago, and has been shown to be effective even for people with dementia. Some manufacturers (eg Huntleigh Healthcare) are investing in it and much research is currently underway. As a longer-term solution such installations are likely to be far preferable to Telecare, but as mature commercial products they are still a few years away.

DESIGNERS

In the list of questions you provided, one of them related to the age of designers and their preconceptions. It is true most designers are going to be at the younger end of the age spectrum. However those involved in work with a strong ergonomic element, such as assistive devices for elderly people, are usually encouraged to use design methodologies that involve the end user quite intimately in the design process. In this way the user's priorities and observations guide the way that designs develop, and the designer is just providing the design skill rather than reflecting on their own experiences. Not all do this however, and work in North America particularly is often more technologically led. Initiatives such as the EPSRC EQUAL programme where it was mandatory for applicants to involve user groups are a good step in the right direction. Encouraging the involvement of actual users would be even better.

Such design approaches are quite common in academic or healthservice-related design work but not necessarily in the commercial world. A good example is the design of mobile phones. They have much potential for supporting older people, including those with dementia. Being able to contact a relative or friend if you are uncertain of your whereabouts would be very valuable. But mobiles are very confusing for a lot of elderly people. They are designed for the teens and 20 year olds, with complicated user interfaces and small buttons. A phone with one or two buttons only, and no screen, would be great for someone with dementia. The phone companies could easily do this but they are not interested in the older market. They design for people who see mobiles as fashion items to be regularly replaced, and who run up big phone bills. There are many examples of such approaches by commercial manufacturers. Some incentives to encourage them to look at the needs of the older market would be so valuable.

December 2004

TUESDAY 14 DECEMBER 2004

Present	Hilton of Eggardon, B	Soulsby of Swaffham Prior, L
	May of Oxford, L	Sutherland of Houndwood, L
	Mitchell, L	(Chairman)
	Murphy, B	Turnberg, L
	Oxburgh, L	Walmsley, B

Memorandum by The Stroke Association

The Stroke Association has been the major funder of research into all aspects of stroke illness and its care including prevention. The Association has a major concern for the prevention of disability through the primary prevention of strokes and transient ischaemic attacks (TIAs), improvements in the early management of stroke illness (the creation of stroke units) and the effective rehabilitation both immediately after the acute episode and in the longer term. The Association is concerned to assist patients achieve independence through adjustment to disability and effective rehabilitation. The case is compelling:

— Suffering a stroke increases the chances of disability more markedly than any other condition.

— Stroke is a more powerful cause of disability than musculo-skeletal and other chronic disorders.

— Stroke has a greater disability impact than other chronic diseases.

— Stroke causes a greater range of disabilities than any other condition.

— A quarter of a million people suffer with long-term severe disability due to stroke in the UK.

The conclusions from the research conducted for the Association informs the care of all older people with disability[1] and for this reason and because stroke services are covered by standard 5 of the National Service Framework for Older People it has been appropriate for the Stroke Association to serve as a member of the Funders' Forum.

THE BIOLOGICAL PROCESSES OF AGEING

— What are promising avenues for research? How will such research benefit older people and delay the onset of long-term illnesses and disabilities?

Derek Wanless has focussed on the importance of life style factors in the development and progress of chronic illness. Older people stand to be major beneficiaries of the change in emphasis that Wanless recommends. Whereas the benefits have been identified effective strategies for bringing about these benefits have not been defined.

The report from the Academy of Medical Sciences "Restoring neurological function: putting the neurosciences to work in neurorehabilitation" prepared by Professors Ray Tallis and Richard Frackowiak identifies the opportunities which research in to rehabilitation presents.

— Differences between the sexes, and between different social and ethnic groups in the UK.

---

[1] Adamson J, Beswick A, Ebrahim S. Stroke and Disability. Journal of Cardiovascular Diseases. In press.

Although there is a social gradient for stroke as for coronary heart disease this is not presently afforded a high priority. On the other hand Professor Hugh Markus (St George's Hospital, research supported by the Stroke Association) reporting on his research concludes: "Individuals of African and African Caribbean descent living in the United Kingdom and the United States have a markedly increased risk of stroke compared with white individuals. In a recent population stroke registry study in London, UK, African Caribbeans had a doubling of stroke incidence compared with that of whites. This increased incidence remains after adjustment for cardiovascular risk factors and socioeconomic status. The reasons for this increase in stroke risk are uncertain, although the increase in risk could be related to differences in the prevalence of cardiovascular risk factors or susceptibility to them, reduced access to or utilization of medical care, uncontrolled for socioeconomic factors (including associated environmental factors), and/or differing genetic predispositions."

Professor Markus's study reached the conclusion that—more advanced deleterious changes in the wall of the carotid arteries (atheroma) occur in UK African Caribbeans even after controlling for conventional risk factors. There are highly significant ethnic differences in the distribution of many potential cerebrovascular candidate genes. Although those examined did not explain the ethnic differences in extent of damage to the carotid arteries, other genetic predispositions or environmental exposures could account for these differences[2].

— How effectively is research co-ordinated in the public, private and charitable sectors (including internationally)?

— Have the correct priorities been identified? Are there any gaps in research?

The Funders' Forum for Research in Ageing and Older People has identified priorities for research in its field and gaps. The list is included here because it is relevant but it will have been discussed in greater detail in a submission from the MRC.

— the psychology of ageing, disability and dependence;

— the economic and social implications, behaviour and aspirations of an ageing population;

— technologies and design to help people maintain independence and autonomy and their effects on older people;

— technologies for the detection, prediction, diagnosis and treatment of age related disease, and the effects of these technologies on older people;

— the molecular and cellular changes associated with basic biological processes of cell death, senescence and physiological ageing;

— the causes of, and influences on age related diseases and disability;

— prevention of breakdown in health and loss of independence in old age and of specific diseases and conditions which cause these;

— treatment of disease and breakdown in health in older people;

— rehabilitation strategies to improve and maintain function and restore independence; and

— the delivery of effective and efficient health and social care for old and frail people.

DISCUSSION OF THESE TOPICS IN THE FFRAOP BUSINESS PLANNING GROUP LED TO THESE CONCLUSIONS: (SEPTEMBER 2003)

"High quality research in basic sciences in relation to ageing, and research in the epidemiology, causes, prevention and treatment of disease in old age should continue to be supported. Research which is of particular relevance to ageing should be identified and categorised.

What is relatively sparse is multi-disciplinary research into the causes, prevention, and rehabilitation of multi-factorial breakdown of independence in old age. Research in ageing and older people requires a new strategy."

[2] Markus H, Kapozsta Z, Ditrich R, Wolfe C, Ali N, Powell J, Mendell M, Cullinane M. Increased Common Carotid Intima-Media Thickness in UK African Caribbeans and its Relation to Chronic Inflammation and Vascular Candidate Gene Polmorphisms. Stroke 2001; 32: 2465–2471.

Co-ordination

Research has depended upon support from a number of relatively small medical research charities faced with a set of research priorities, which has inhibited collaboration on more ambitious research.

The Research Councils point to a considerable amount of research funded by them which is taking place in many of the common diseases of adults as well as older people. They point to a considerable amount of basic research being undertaken in the biological, social and behavioural sciences, some of which may be specifically directed at ageing and some of the rest will have implications for ageing. Close examination of the previous research strategies suggests that the issues specific to the needs of older people have been neglected.

These are very Similar to the Recommendations Proposed by The NHS Strategic Review on Ageing and Age-Associated Disability, which Reported in June 1999. Progress has been very Disappointing

— Is there sufficient research capability in the UK?

— Is the research being used to inform policy?

Definitely Not . . .

The Stroke Association has placed a high priority upon the building of the research capacity in physiotherapy, occupational therapy, speech and language therapy and nursing. It has offered a small number of research bursaries annually for 10 years. The Association welcomes recent initiatives made by the DoH.

The Application of Research in Technology and Design to Improve the Quality of Life of Older People, including:

— Existing technologies which could be used to a greater extent to benefit older people.

— The development of new technologies.

Research in this area consists of pilot projects and the design of exciting prototypes only. Funding is required to expand these pilot studies into extensive trials.

September 2004

Examination of Witnesses

Witnesses: Professor Peter Fentem, Chairman of the the Research Committees, The Stroke Association, Professor Peter Weissberg, Medical Director of the British Heart Foundation, and Professor Kennedy Lees, Professor of Cerebrovascular Medicine, University of Glasgow, examined.

Q272 *Chairman:* Good afternoon, and welcome. My name is Sutherland and I am chairing the Sub-Committee of this Select Committee. My colleagues all have nameplates in front of them, so I shall not go round the table; we would rather use our time talking to you and hearing what you have to say. Just two points: first, thank you very much for the written evidence that has come in. I know that some of you have been directly, and all of you indirectly, involved in that. The written evidence is immensely important to us. That leads me to say that if, after this session, there are points that you would like to amplify that you feel we have not done full justice to, please feel free to communicate directly by e-mail or letter any further material that you think we should have. Lastly, I now must point out that we will be recorded and it may go out on air at some point—perhaps some lonely hour of the early morning—so anything you say will be heard by a larger group than now sitting round the table. Can I kick off with a fairly general question, then, and then we will go round the

table asking our questions. As you respond, if you could just remind us who you are, partly for the oral record, and what organisation you represent that would be helpful. Clearly, cardiovascular is our central theme today. As your written evidence, and indeed as our other understanding, makes us well aware, it has a huge impact on the lives of many people but, particularly, older people. I wonder if you would like to talk just a little bit about the extent of this impact and how it affects more than the initial trauma situation but, perhaps, the social aspects of life: quality of life, economic aspects of life and what the impact of this form of illness is. If you would then say just very briefly (and we will come back to this in detail) what are the main areas of research that you think are or should be pursued as a result of this.

Professor Fentem: My Lord Chairman, I am Peter Fentem, I am a trustee of the Stroke Association and I was the Stroke Association's first Professor of Stroke Medicine appointed in 1992, and I left my post in 1997. It is perhaps relevant that before that I was

14 December 2004   Professor Peter Fentem, Professor Peter Weissberg
and Professor Kennedy Lees

Professor of Physiology in Nottingham and my special interest was in the physiology of older people, particular cardiovascular function. On the particular question, clearly there are the figures available regarding mortality and so on, and there is no doubt that many people die of stroke—about, perhaps, 125,000 people in this country have a stroke and of those something like 70,000 people die each year. I think, perhaps, as a preliminary to this session, I could just quote what Professor Ian Philp said recently (perhaps he said it to you): "Having a stroke is one of the more alarming and devastating things that can happen to a person, and will happen to a quarter of us over the age of 45", always provided, as it were, we have a reasonable expectation of reaching the age of 85. Twenty years ago nothing could be done with stroke, there was a rather nihilistic attitude to management, but now things are very different. I think that is quite a good way of introducing things. I have mentioned mortality, but mortality underestimates the burden of stroke both for the individual who has the stroke and for the nation, and that I think is the important thing. The important characteristic of stroke is that it leads to disability. We talk about 125,000 having strokes but, of course, quite a number survive a stroke albeit with quite serious disability. So out there there are about a quarter-of-a-million people who have disability as a consequence of their stroke. That, of course, as I say, is a disaster for the quality of life of many of them but, also, of course, is exceedingly expensive for the country that looks after them.

Q273 *Chairman:* Is there any estimate of how much?
Professor Fentem: Two point three billion pounds, or 6 per cent of the national spend, approximately, when it was last estimated.

Q274 *Lord Mitchell:* Six per cent of the national spend—on?
Professor Fentem: On health and social care. The impact on quality of life, of course, is because of the range of disabilities; the outward, visible signs are that people suffer from problems with their mobility and with their ability to reach and so on, but there are others—sight, hearing, incontinence and, of course, difficulties in communication. There are some quite subtle cognitive impairments which interfere with social interaction. Skipping on, perhaps, to the question that you wanted me to deal with, I think it would suffice, at the moment, if I say that I think the possible areas for research are to do with acute care, with both primary and secondary prevention, with rehabilitation, with the delivery of long-term care (and I think this is where stroke has many things in common with the care that is required by many different groups of frail old people) and then there is

the management of stroke in primary care, that we really have not touched on.

Q275 *Chairman:* Where do you draw the line between primary and secondary prevention?
Professor Fentem: Primary being preventing a stroke ever happening, and secondary prevention being to prevent people having a recurrence.
Professor Weissberg: I am Peter Weissberg, I am currently the Medical Director of the British Heart Foundation, having just taken over that post two weeks ago, so I am not really familiar with the workings of the British Heart Foundation yet. Up until that time I was the British Heart Foundation's Professor of Cardiovascular Medicine at the University of Cambridge and a practising clinical cardiologist. My main research interest has been vascular disease, and that is what I feel I should speak about. Put in a nutshell, certainly the heart and, to a large extent, the brain are remarkably resilient organs and they are well capable of doing their job for eight decades or more, providing they have a decent vascular system and a decent blood supply. Virtually all of the mortality and morbidity that we see, either prematurely or of this age group, is as a direct or indirect consequence of a problem with vascular supply to that organ, and that is usually due to atherosclerosis which causes coronary arteries and causes heart attack. As you will all be aware, the incidence of heart attack, as we know it, is falling in the under-65s, but of course that means it is rising in the over-65s and it leaves behind the myocardial equivalent of a stroke, which is damaged tissue, and that is heart failure. Heart failure is a rapidly growing problem in the elderly, particularly as we get better at salvaging patients from what would have been a fatal heart attack, because we cannot prevent them having myocardial damage, very often, and, as a consequence of that, they accumulate more myocardial damage as time goes on and end up in the clinical syndrome of heart failure. It is estimated that there are about 900,000 people in the UK with heart failure, at the moment, and a not commonly recognised statistic is that the mortality from that for about 40 per cent is one year, and it is a very miserable year. The prognosis for heart patients is considerably worse. If we follow exactly the same track that Peter has been following, the estimated cost at the moment for people over the age of 65 to be treated for heart failure in the NHS is £625 million a year. So it is enormous morbidity and enormous cost. If it affects the cerebral arteries then stroke is a consequence and that has just been covered, although it affects the peripheral arteries as well—the arteries to the legs and to the kidneys—and that leads to renal failure, it leads to gangrene and it leads to the inability to

walk, and maybe to blindness. So the major focus, I think, in terms of research has necessarily to be on the prevention of that vascular disease in middle age, because it is certainly my belief that if we could prevent the development of atherosclerosis in middle age then the consequences of vascular disease would be very much less in the elderly, and they would die of other things, in effect, because the organs involved are pretty robust. In terms of where I see research going, we have made pretty good headway, actually, in terms of understanding the biology of atherosclerosis and tackling it in middle age through lipid-lowering drugs, ace inhibitors—all drugs which have been shown in clinical trials to reduce the progression of vascular disease and the outcome of vascular disease. I think what we have to turn our attention to is accepting that we are not going to be able to prevent these problems and learn how to repair the organs that are affected. Whilst that once upon a time might have appeared rather science-fictional, I think with the advent of stem cell research it becomes not science reality yet but it certainly becomes plausible (and probably more plausible in the heart than in the brain) that one might be able to use cells, either embryonic stem cells, although they have their problems, or perhaps more realistically bone marrow derived or circulating stem cells (these are cells taken from that person and re-infused back into their heart). There is good scientific evidence, at least, that some of these cells can adopt the characteristics of a heart cell and, in effect, repair an organ which was traditionally thought of as being unrepairable. That is, in fact, the biggest problem. The reason why cardiac and cerebral disease is such a problem is that neither organ has the capacity to regenerate or repair, unlike the liver for instance, so that once damaged it remains damaged and probably goes downhill thereafter. So the scientific focus at the cellular and molecular biological level now is understanding the cellular processes that might allow one to induce repair in those organs. I have applications sitting on my desk at the moment for clinical trials in stem cells for heart attack patients, and I think that does offer some promise for salvage, if you like, of the heart and, therefore, downstream effects for the elderly.

Q276 *Baroness Walmsley:* Professor Weissberg, you said that when the heart tissue is damaged, it tends to go downhill after. Is there potential for stem cell therapy to actually prevent that further degeneration?

Professor Weissberg: There are two reasons why it goes downhill thereafter. One is that there may be further vascular events. We are all familiar with the major heart attack that strikes somebody down in the street

and is a very major event—and likewise with stroke—but what we are less familiar with is the fact that all the time most of us are having micro-infarcts ("infarct" is the term used for death of tissue); that is, little bits of the tissue in the heart and brain being picked off as a consequence of this vascular disease throughout life, and that accumulates. That is one reason why the heart may continue deteriorating. The other reason is that if you effectively wipe out a third or a quarter of the heart the other three-quarters can cope for a limited period of time before it starts to fail, and that is why it tends to be cumulative.

Professor Lees: Kennedy Lees, I am Professor of Cerebrovascular Medicine at the University of Glasgow. My main work is as a clinician and clinical triallist in stroke, and I am interested very much in both the prevention and treatment of acute stroke. I do not disagree with anything my colleagues have said. I think the enormity of the expenditure on stroke, particularly, is absolutely massive. I do not think we can prevent all strokes. I think one of three things is going to get most of us: it is either going to be cancer, heart disease or stroke. We can delay this, I think, and that is a useful thing to do, but eventually one of those is going to get us. One of the things that really worries me and my colleagues is that stroke does carry a very similar prognosis if not a worse prognosis than most forms of cancer, in terms of mortality—the survival time—and also in terms of the disability. It is just as devastating to be left unable to communicate or unable to be independent as it is to realise that you are slipping downhill from cancer. However, we spend about 1 per cent on stroke research of what we spend on cancer research in this country. It is not just in this country, this does apply internationally, but we are particularly bad on that. It is a tiny proportion, and yet there are clearly things that we can do. The one area on which I absolutely agree with Professor Weissberg is that we must work on prevention and work on repair. The other area we can work on is dealing with the condition as it happens, because if you fail to prevent there is no point in sitting there for the first few hours after a stroke is happening and watching it develop to its full extent and then starting the rehabilitation process, because there are things you can do in that interim. So if it is an ischaemic stroke, a stroke that is caused by a lack of blood supply, where the brain tissue is dying from this lack of blood supply, we should be trying to restore the blood supply, and there is very good evidence—proof—that treatment with thrombolytic drugs can restore the blood supply and can make a difference—not in everybody but if there is a Number Needing to Treat of eight—that is, for every eight patients treated, one extra complete recovery will occur—that is really a very powerful treatment, far more powerful in stroke than it is in myocardial infarcts.

Q277 *Chairman:* Can I ask within what time period does it have an effect?

Professor Lees: That is the point. There is a three-hour time window in which the drugs are licensed, at the moment, but there is pretty good evidence that they could work much later. One of the areas of research that we desperately need to look at is extending that time window. There is very good reason to think that we can extend it; in many other countries they have access to imaging—that is MRI scans or CT perfusion scans—which will allow us to detect salvageable tissue still there at later times and allow us to direct treatment to the patients in whom that treatment would be beneficial. We, unfortunately, in this country have virtually no centre that can provide that sort of imaging quickly; there are only half-a-dozen centres in the country that are really using the drugs regularly and really getting access to this imaging, which is not particularly high-tech; these are scanners that are available in most hospitals but we do not have access for our stroke patients. I think that is an area that we could definitely be working on.

Q278 *Baroness Hilton of Eggardon:* You have already begun to address what you would like to do about the problems. I wonder whether you would like to develop that further and tell us what your priorities are and what you see as being the chief scientific challenges within each of your disciplines or organisations. Are you addressing different aspects of these problems or are you all addressing the same priorities?

Professor Fentem: We are different organisations, of course, with a quite different remit. I think it is worth just saying a little bit more about acute care because acute care is high on the Stroke Associations' agenda. Although there are probably only a limited number of patients who after a stroke can benefit from thrombolycis—ie, clot-busters—nevertheless, I think the particular problem that we need to address and which, I am sure, Kennedy Lees would explain further, is that the mortality in this country in the first 30 days after a stroke is about 30 per cent, on average. There are problems because elsewhere in the world we are not always comparing like with like but the 30-day mortality in Canada is between 11 and 15 per cent. Those are a lot of deaths, and on the present evidence it would appear that it depends on the admission of patients to stroke units and the detailed care within those units. We do not know which components, at this stage, are producing this effect but one thing that we suspect is important is the imaging. The point I would like to make is that this, of course, would lead to changes in the way the ambulance service transports patients, because you would need to get rapid admission to hospital, and it is not only a matter of the scanners but where you put them; in Canada the scanners are in A&E, and the interpretation of the scan is undertaken by people either on site or on the end of a telephone link to a computer. So that is one area that we feel needs to be explored in detail. I suppose this will come up somewhere in the meeting, but this is where the opportunities will present when the National Stroke Clinical Research Network is formed, and this is an important opportunity, not only for stroke, of course, but for some of the conditions. In the case of prevention, certainly for patients in the younger age groups we think that prevention is feasible and the research area that we think is important is the question of what is the package and how do you deliver it? In South London, St Thomas's, Guy's and Kings have one of our programme grants and are looking at that particular question in the incidence of secondary prevention. It is no use identifying the fact that high blood pressure after stroke matters if you do not decide to do something about it, and clearly there are many, many patients who are not getting attention to their continuing problems after they have had their first stroke. Rehabilitation I mentioned as one of the other areas, and of course possibly your attention will have already been drawn to Professors Tallis and Frackowiaks' report on putting the neurosciences to work, and that covers many of the issues which are important in relation to rehabilitation. We must understand the rehabilitation, we must understand what works and what does not work, and we must stop providing token rehabilitation. If you, by any chance, have had a chance to look at the National Audit Office report *The Way to go Home*, you will have seen that many hospitals were only providing 10 minutes of physiotherapy a day to many of their patients. It just so happens that stroke is used as a marker for that study but the approach to rehabilitation goes right across the needs,of older people whose independence is threatened. Then, of course, there is the question of continuing care, community care. Again, we feel we have to challenge adequately the current wisdom which is that you can have six weeks' physiotherapy after your stroke on the assumption that that is the end of the improvement that can be achieved. Yet those units which are being brave enough now to re-introduce physiotherapy to people who are obviously deteriorating have shown that it works. I hope that gives a flavour of some of the issues that the Stroke Association thinks are important.

Q279 *Lord May of Oxford:* I had a specific question, going back to your comparison with Canada (and you did qualify it by saying you were not comparing like with like) but I am curious: it does seem to me there is a difference between keeping people alive and the quality of the life that you keep them alive for. I would ask, as it were, of the 30 people that die in Britain versus the 15 that die in Canada in the first 30 days, what is the quality of that surviving life of the 15 who survive in Canada? Is this a measure of the more heroic attempt to keep more people alive in some form of life in North America, or is it really something that is more operational?

Professor Lees: May I respond to that? It definitely is not just keeping people alive who would otherwise be left disabled. If you look at the figures for the recovery as well, you will see that countries like Germany and Canada have a far higher proportion of patients making a good recovery. One of the extremely disturbing facts is that in this early period of acute care if you do not provide good care then somebody who could well make a good recovery can be left disabled unnecessarily or die unnecessarily. So I think it is extremely important to recognise that this is a measure of overall care, but we can move everybody up one or two stages and get many more people back home and functioning normally.

Q280 Lord May of Oxford: So, from the point of view of the NHS budget, comparing the cost of looking after people who could have been in much better shape if they had had better care, you are suggesting that, even in purely brutal cost-effective terms, it is better to spend more money on this?

Professor Lees: Let us look at the numbers. The use of statins to prevent stroke may cost about £20,000 to prevent one stroke; to treat a stroke when it has occurred—one, average stroke patient's time spent in hospital, looking at the hospital cost—is maybe £10,000 to £15,000. To give acute treatment with something like thrombolysis, at £400 for one patient's treatment (you need to treat around eight to get the benefits), it is £3,000 or £4,000. So you are saving money by getting in there early and doing as much as you can. I am not saying that is all you need to do—

Q281 Lord May of Oxford: That is not the only consideration, but it is interesting way of looking at it.

Professor Lees: And it certainly will not work for everybody, but this is a very important, very cost-effective argument.

Q282 Chairman: While you have the floor, do you want to continue on the priorities in scientific channels?

Professor Lees: I think the priority is to apply what we have already learned. We have learnt a lot about prevention, and we still have people out there in the pubs and clubs smoking—and perhaps that will change shortly—but there is a very powerful thing that we could do to help reduce or delay stroke and heart disease. It will help other conditions as well. We have learnt about acute treatment, we have learnt that stroke unit care does make a difference but we have not yet worked out how to get everybody into these units; we have learnt that we can examine stroke and tell: "Is it ischaemic or haemorrhagic?" In fact, there are indications that both can be treated by different mechanisms early, but we are not yet applying that. We have learnt that by using imaging we can discover much more about the mechanisms that are going on and, therefore, we can discover whether some of the mechanisms that seem to work in animal experimentation could be useful for stroke—whether these do apply and, therefore, we could target our research and our treatments better in that. However, we have huge barriers to research, and stroke particularly. Barriers include the fact that stroke is a heterogeneous disease and that by the time somebody has a stroke they are already reasonably old and they may well have other conditions. These other conditions and the variation in care they get make an enormous difference to the outcome, so we need very large trials; trials of thousands of patients to give us an answer. There are barriers to running multi-centre trials, particularly in the UK. A research assessment exercise measures us as academic clinicians on our individual contribution to authorship of papers, our contribution to the grants that we get, and only one or two people can get credits for that but we need hundreds of people all round the country contributing work to these trials. They get no credits for that so they are disadvantaged as soon as they take part. Hospital managers are not encouraged; there is no incentive for them to put patients into trials because it tends to be more expensive to put patients into trials; they have to spend a bit more time with the patient and a bit more on imaging costs, so there is disadvantage there. We need to start giving ourselves incentives to take part in this sort of research.

Q283 Baroness Walmsley: You talked about the multi-centre trials. Do the people in all the different centres have to deal with their local ethics committee? So have we got multiple ethics committees as well, or is it done in one place?

Professor Lees: Let me declare a conflict of interest here. I chair the Multi-Centre Ethics Committee for Scotland—the one that deals with Adults With Incapacity. There is no question that we have simplified the ethics procedure, to some extent, but we have done it at the cost of increasing the amount of bureaucracy in many other ways: the forms that have to be filled in now run to some 60 pages. This is partly due to the Central Office for Resrach Ethics Committees, the organisation that has taken over the running of the ethics system. We have a very cumbersome form-filling process and we have to go through the R&D departments in individual hospitals, whereas before perhaps they were not involved. We have all the European Clinical Trials Directive mandates on the numbers of forms that have to be filled, and if it is an academic study you still need to have huge organisation there to be able to report what we call serious adverse events—which, in most cases for a stroke trial, are things that would happen anyway to the patient—nothing to do with the treatment we are researching but all to do with the complications that arise anyway. So we have an enormous bureaucracy which is not all of our own doing in the UK (some of it is thrust on us by Europe), but we have applied it in a way that makes life very difficult. There are very many people who would be interested in multi-centre research who are now saying, "I just do not have the resources to do this. It is too complicated".

Q284 *Baroness Walmsley:* Is it done differently in England?

Professor Lees: England and Scotland have exactly the same system; the only difference on the incapacity issue in Scotland was that research not involving drugs goes through a single designated committee rather than going through any of the general committees.

Professor Weissberg: It is difficult to know where to start. From the British Heart Foundation perspective, I guess there are two major roles that the BHF play traditionally. Let me just explain that the division of our spend is approximately £50–£55 million on research and about £15–£20 million on care and education. So the remit is to fund the very best of the fundamental research and clinical trials that are requested and required but, also, to plug the gaps in clinical care. As an example of that (and I mentioned heart failure earlier on) the Heart Foundation has funded, through the New Opportunities Fund, 155 nurses to look after patients with heart failure, because in effect hospitals do not have the resources to do it. If you have a nurse who can visit a patient at home and change the diuretic dose you can keep that patient out of hospital, whereas if you do not that patient ends up getting into end-stage heart failure and coming in as an emergency with all the risks that go with it. The organisation's spin on this is that we are interested in the fundamental research underpinning cardiovascular disease but, also, the clinical care that is required. I would echo the points made here by my colleagues that there are two aspects to improving health care. One is applying the very best of available

medicines and evidence-based medicines and evidence-based procedures, and I am afraid the UK is extremely poor at doing so. We have known for about 15 years now that thrombolycis, these clot-busting drugs, save lives in heart attacks and the quicker you give it the more effective it is. Only now, though, have we got to a position where patients are getting it within about 30 minutes of the onset of their symptoms. It takes a long time in our system for new evidence to be adopted and to be translated. I think in terms of trying to prevent morbidity in the elderly, one aspect—as has been said already—is applying best practice quickly and efficiently within our health system, and we have not been very good at doing that.

Q285 *Chairman:* Can you say why?

Professor Weissberg: Generally, cost, because all of the things you have heard about involve up-front costs. Again, we have all put forward economic arguments and mentioned "Is there a saving, ultimately, to be made?" The answer is yes, there is, but not to today's budget in that hospital. That is the way, I am afraid, the NHS looks at it; they are looking at this year's budget in this hospital: "If I keep a heart failure patient out of that bed somebody else's patient is going to fill it". So the bed is still filled, the work is still there, but in terms of future cost to the NHS there is a large saving, but we do not seem to have the flexibility to build that into the system. I think there has also been, if you like, an inherent caution, which has not necessarily always been bad in UK medicine, in that we do wait for the evidence to be pretty overwhelming before we apply it, and I think that is a benefit to the publicly-funded system; you cannot splash money around on new techniques and new drugs if you do not know that they work, but we need the clinical trials to show that they work and—more importantly—once the trial is over we need to implement that best practice very, very quickly. To pick up on one of the other things that was mentioned earlier on, which is imaging, imaging is becoming increasingly sophisticated. Time was, not so very long ago, if you had a stroke nobody wanted to image you, and speaking as a non-stroke specialist I think that is probably right. Nowadays, if you go to the right places, as has been suggested, and you get into the scanner very quickly you will have an image taken of where your stroke is and what is the vascular disease underlying it and, if you are luckier still, somebody will intervene on that and open up that blood vessel. However, there has been a leap of technology away from catheter based, x-ray based imaging which means inserting a tube into a vessel, infusing a dye and taking an x-ray picture—which was invasive, moderately dangerous, costly and required a lot of staff—to very slick, non-invasive techniques based on Magnetic Resonance Imaging, position emission tomography and CT scanning. As has been said, although most hospitals certainly have CT scanners now and eye scanners what they do not have is access, rapidly enough, for patients who need acute management; they tend to be used for the chronic condition, and even then you will wait, in some hospitals, six or nine months to have your back MRI image or a joint MRI image because of the backlog. I would echo what has been said about the implementation of what we already know. That would go a huge way towards offsetting some of the future problems that we have. As I said, from the point of the BHF, we are very interested in the pipeline of what might come along in the future and so we are particularly looking at strategies that might either prevent or deal better with disease that comes along. Another example which I have not mentioned are the ventricular-assist devices. These are mechanical pumps that can take over the work of the heart and have traditionally been used to tide patients over for transplantation. In other words, if a relatively young person with devastating heart failure has been deemed worthy of a transplant but there is no donor, a mechanical device is put in, which is basically a mechanical pump, which does the work of the heart until such time as the transplant can take place. These devices have been problematic because they cause complications, but they have reached a level of sophistication now where one can consider starting to put these devices into people with a view to sustaining them long-term and taking over the heart, and that is a technology which is advancing at quite a rate. I think, if you like, with ventricular-assist devices we are about where we were with pacemakers when I first started putting pacemakers in: they were the size of your fist, with wires about that size that you, somehow, had to manipulate under the skin into the heart, and now they are the size of half a matchbox with a very fine fibre which can be inserted in a matter of half-an-hour and the patient can go home the same day. I think the assist devices are liable to move in the same direction.

Q286 *Baroness Walmsley:* I would like to ask to what extent your priorities are recognised by government. Do you think there is a good link between science and policy development? Do you think things could be done any better and, if so, what would be the benefits?

Professor Weissberg: I will talk about cardiovascular rather than cerebrovascular and stroke, in that it has been a government target through the National Service Framework, and that is one of the reasons that the times, as I have already mentioned, in getting heart attack patients treated have come down because it has become a government priority, they

have put money behind it and so things have started to happen. If you like, it shows what can be done when the right impetus is put behind it. There are coalitions of funders for research: one, in particular, is the Cardiovascular Research Funders Forum, which is a coalition of the Department of Health, the BHF, the Wellcome Trust, the MRC, and the Stroke Association (I think that is probably it) who meet relatively regularly to discuss strategy and areas of research that are of importance. I think we have got a way to go yet to make sure that that then gets translated into implementation and funding but at least the infrastructure is there to do that. I think, from the cardiovascular point of view, we have been fairly lucky over the years. I think stroke has been, unfortunately, left somewhat behind. I do not know whether my colleagues would agree with that.

Professor Fentem: I think there are a number of points worth making as regards stroke. Stroke research has benefited from the NHS research and development programme, there is no doubt about that, and they enabled us to pick up some quite important projects in relation to rehabilitation. The other area which is rather important and which we have not touched on this afternoon is the question of research capacity. I came to see Lord Warner in December and Lord Warner said to me: "If I gave you £10 million would you know where to spend it?" The answer is that we would have a bit of difficulty in spending it in some of the areas which are our priorities, for the reason that stroke is quite a new discipline. As I said at the outset, 20 years ago nothing much was happening for stroke patients; stroke research is therefore relatively new, certainly compared with the research into heart disease. The result is that there is a capacity-building exercise that is needed in order to have the researchers around who were capable of undertaking this work. It is a great pleasure to be able to say that the NHS have, at last, picked that up. The Stroke Association is one of the strands of their support that they have given. We have had bursaries to help build research capacity for some years, but the NHS have now picked that up. Indeed, the level of support that was provided for such people was, I think, particularly generous, which is slightly surprising.

Q287 *Chairman:* It is not often we hear it said!

Professor Fentem: So far as the MRC are concerned, it is only 18 months since stroke was listed in their strategy. There was a meeting 18 months ago of their overall research strategy committee and at that committee it was agreed that stroke would appear in the strategy. It is not easy, either, to disentangle what portion of the brain sciences programme is relevant to stroke. So there is a sort of fairly artificial exercise which goes on, as reported in *Hansard* as to exactly how much money is spent on stroke research. The hard facts are, I think, that the Stroke Association spends about £2 million, the MRC probably about £4 million and over a period of time of perhaps 10 years, the NHS has spent £15 million. That is against the £100 million spent annually on cancer and larger sums of money that Peter Weissberg is now able to spend on heart disease. We are now a member of the Cardiovascular Funders' Forum but in the paper that I submitted, my Lord Chairman, I pointed out that I was a member of the Funders' Forum for Research in Ageing and Older People. That, I have to say, has been particularly disappointing. I hoped that that would be the research component of, if you like, the National Service Framework for Older People, but it did not prove to be that. Of course, the reason it did not work or has not worked so far is that there was not enough money on the table. We were a collection of very small charities: Help the Aged have about £5 million a year they spend, we have £2 million, and that is in contrast with the £100 million that the cancer charities brought to the table—maybe it is nearer £200 million now, I cannot remember. So there was no prospect that we would have some quick wins and make a big impact on research into ageing. That is a big disappointment. So I suppose, in summary, some good support may come from the NHS, particularly now with the National Stroke Clinical Research Network but not so good in relation, at least, to the Funders' Forum.

Professor Lees: I think it is right that we do not have all that many green shoots that are there, able to spend money. I can certainly find places to spend £10 million very easily. I think we are growing on stony ground—this is the problem—and the three things I would say we really need to do to translate that apparent policy of supporting stroke research into action are, first, to deal with the bureaucracy that we talked about—the red tape, the paperwork—second, to deal with that issue of incentives for multi-centre work (that is both remove the disincentive that if you are doing that you do not get points in the RAE, and add an incentive to the hospitals and the NHS system to encourage research), and, third, let us deal with the infrastructure. That involves two things. One will cost money, and that is putting in more in the way of imaging equipment and more in the way of radiologists and radiographers to run that equipment, but the second part need not cost money, and that is to say it will be government policy that every patient with stroke and every patient with heart attack will, when they come into hospital, be immediately diagnosed. So, for a heart attack patient, that may be that they get their ECG—done, and I think we would think it would be dreadful if you could not get a cardiograph done when you turned up at hospital with chest pain- and for a stroke patient it means an immediate scan. Right at the moment, the target is to get your CT scan within a couple of days—two days, for a condition where the brain is dying over hours.

Q288 *Baroness Walmsley:* If I may, my Lord Chairman, I have a little follow-up. All three of you gentlemen have talked in your response to my question about priorities about the structures and systems in place to set the priorities for research, with the exception, perhaps, of Professor Lees. I wonder if you can say something about the structures and systems that are in place to identify the priorities about implementation and best practice, and all those things. In your earlier answers you were lamenting the fact that a lot of the research does then not translate into better practice and systems to actually deliver the results of the research to the patient. Who decides now?

Professor Weissberg: In theory and in practice it is probably the National Institute of Clinical Excellence these days that decides. So once a new development is recognised out in the medical literature then it goes onto the agenda for NICE to adjudicate as to whether this is value for money within the NHS, and until that point is reached it is nigh-on impossible to introduce a new medical technique or system, even though the evidence is out there, because the funding is not there. The theory is, of course, if NICE approve it then the funding should be made available, but at a practical level we find in hospitals the money has to come out of a pot which is held in the Primary Care Trusts, and most of them are in the red. Even though we hear that NICE has said that such-and-such technology should be instituted across the board it has to be done at the financial disbenefit of that hospital. I will make one other point, though, which is going back to research in implementation: there is no doubt, in my mind, that the very best way to ensure best practice is adopted is to be doing research in that area. If you are doing research into stroke and acute thrombolycis you have to come up with a strategy to get your patients into that hospital to do that research within the minutes that you need. Once you have set that up and you have shown that it works, then generally speaking there is a moral imperative locally to make sure that you follow on. So one should not under-estimate the importance of clinical research in actually progressing clinical practice. It is no accident that the centres of clinical excellence are also the centres of research excellence because those are places that gather the patients up, that put them into research protocols, that brings them outside the rather turgid mechanism of the health service and into a research protocol which allows you to treat them quickly and get an answer. Even if you then have to wait for NICE to agree, it is pretty unusual for you, the local hospital that has discovered that treatment, not to carry on using it.

Q289 *Baroness Murphy:* Two things, if I may, following up that. One is, as Professor Weissberg pointed out, the National Service Framework on Cardiovascular Medicine has been very successful in concentrating the health service's mind on the right targets in that area. I wonder why, and perhaps Professor Lees and Professor Fentem might like to comment, the National Service Framework for Older People did not include best practice in relation to stroke. Yes, it has acute stroke units and good things in it but no targets were set and certainly not a very ambitious target.

Professor Lees: I am not sure I can answer that question, but if I can throw a question back to you: why was there not a National Service Framework on strokes specifically, given that it is the third leading cause of mortality and is a major medical cause of disability, etc, etc? I think stroke was put in as an after-thought to that. In England, just as in Scotland, we had stroke added to the cardiovascular disease document in much the same way; it is seen as the poor brother or sister.

Q290 *Baroness Murphy:* It is all wrapped up in things "elderly".

Professor Lees: Just tagged on at the end, yes.

Professor Fentem: I think we should say that Standard Five of the NSF for Older People has had its effect. I had made some notes on what I thought the links were. I have, for my sins, also served as a non-executive director of a PCT, and in the discussion there Standard Five of the NSF has certainly had its impact. One of the most important links has been the publication of the Royal College of Physicians' Guidelines on Stroke, which are evidence based and which have identified those areas in stroke across the clinical spectrum, from acute care to community care, where we have evidence and where we do not. It seems to me that that is a particularly valuable contribution (the recent edition 2004 has just been published), and that has had a tremendous impact on stroke care, and will continue to do so. May I just say, in support of Professor Weissberg, I welcomed John Reid's pronouncement that good research equates with good care, and good research saves lives. It has been demonstrated for cancer and we hope now that we might have the opportunity to demonstrate it for other conditions including stroke.

Q291 *Lord May of Oxford:* I want to pick up on something you have just said about the connection between basic, clinical research and the delivery of universally effective care based on that. I do realise that simply counting papers and things is not a reliable measure of the quality of work, and I do realise that there are differences in the quality of work in the different hospitals. Nonetheless, clinical research measured both by quality of papers and measured by relative expenditure on it by conventional methods, is something in which the UK is, for example, well ahead of Canada, which was the one that manages to put things better. Thirteen per cent of the world's clinical medical literature is produced by the UK. I realise there has been a certain amount of decline in this, and I repeat myself that I realise it is not the only measure, but I offer it back to you as something that casts a bit of a shadow over the statement that if you are really very, very good at doing research that means you will be very good at looking after the patients, because it seems to me that our failure is not a failure in the research as such but a failure in the effective delivery of it.

Professor Weissberg: Perhaps I can respond to that. I was not suggesting it was a failure of research, I was suggesting that if you are prosecuting good clinical research then that necessarily has an impact—

Q292 *Lord May of Oxford:* At the place where you are doing it. Therefore, I draw the conclusion, everyone has to be doing the basic research otherwise hospitals will not be doing a good job.

Professor Weissberg: I am not implying that. I said the centres of excellence that produce the research are doing the best clinical practice, by and large—not totally—and so what I was saying is that those centres that wish and are able to do the research need to be able to do it, and as we have heard there are big barriers to doing that. Going back to Lady Murphy's point about the impact of research, the NSF for Cardiovascular Disease was a somewhat easier nut to crack than, perhaps, many others because we had good evidence. So we could say we know that it saves lives to give aspirin, therefore that has to be one of the goals for the NSF. We know that streptokinase save lives, we know that ace inhibitors save lives and we know that statins save lives, and I would make the point that we know that because of studies done in the UK in our major centres (funded, I have to say, largely by the British Heart Foundation) that have added that dot to the I or cross to the T that says "Yes, this piece of evidence is incontrovertible, we must use it as best practice". It therefore went into the NSF and now the standard of care is vastly better for patients with cardiac disease than it was five to 10 years ago, but it is because we have that body of evidence which came out of the research that allowed us then to apply it. I think part of the problem with stroke has been—and, again, I am saying this not as a stroke specialist but, if you like, as a medical generalist—that even 10 years ago the GP would send the heart attack patient immediately to hospital because he felt they could do something for them, and the stroke patient would stay at home. The hospital was not seeing the immediate morbidity and problems associated with stroke in the way that we were as cardiologists in our coronary care units, and there is nothing like seeing a patient deteriorating in front of your eyes to stimulate you to want to do something about it. I think the problem with stroke has been that stroke patients have largely been left in the community and it is only now that we are starting to realise they are better cared for in hospital. As the pendulum swings towards bringing more and more stroke patients into hospital and sooner then I think the impetus and the whole research agenda will accelerate, and I think that is what feeds into the whole process.

Chairman: We have quite a number of questions we would like to pursue so I am quite keen to move on.

Q293 *Lord Turnberg:* Professor Weissberg, you very helpfully pointed out that the brain and the heart are pretty strong organs and if their blood supply was okay they would do all right, that you should not be worrying about them ageing and that the major problem, at the moment certainly and for a long time to come, is ensuring that the blood supply is okay and preventing atherosclerosis. This is all about preventing disease as against studying the basic biology of ageing. This may be a somewhat philosophical type of question but do you see somewhere in here the problem of doing basic research on ageing brains and ageing hearts irrespective of this disease-related deterioration due to vascular disease? Is this a silly thing to be thinking about now?

Professor Weissberg: No, it is not but it is quite a difficult thing to do in that it is difficult to get your hands on the organs that you want to study in that particular age group. That is why I mention imaging as being so important, because I think that with more investment in research the non-invasive imaging techniques are beginning to give us a handle on molecular mechanisms and cellular mechanisms in the brain and in the heart, and I think that will then unlock the ability to ask about the ageing process *per se* in the brain cells and in the myocardium. There certainly already is research going on into the association between atherosclerosis and vascular ageing. One of the prevalent theories at the moment is that a consequence of atherosclerosis, that is the plaque breaking down to cause a stroke or a heart attack, is the failure of the repair mechanism in the vascular wall; that there is a constant tension between the lipid causing inflammation leading to the plaque rupturing and the smooth muscle cells working as repairers keeping that plaque intact and stopping it breaking down, and there is clear evidence that the

cells from a plaque, the smooth muscle cells, are senescent. By that I mean if you try to make them grow and divide they do not do so, they have reached the end of their natural lifespan. There is molecular evidence now to show that as cells divide (it does not matter which cell you are talking about) the chromosomes get shorter and shorter and shorter with each division until there comes a point where the cell will no longer divide again, and some cancers occur because that shortening never takes place. There is now evidence coming out in cell biological literature that there may be, if you like, premature senescence at a cellular level. It is not quite the same thing as you are driving at in terms of ageing, but it is trying to get at the fundamental biology of ageing, if that is what you mean. I think there is quite a lot of mileage in that. The other example I would cite is something from my own research group's work, and that is Progeria Syndrome. These are these very unfortunate children that age extraordinarily rapidly and die, usually, at the age of 10 or thereabouts looking as if they are 80 or 90, but they die actually of vascular disease; it is that which causes them to die. It is not in the context of conventional risk factors for atherosclerosis—they do not have high lipids or anything like that—but they do have rampant atherosclerosis which kills them. The genetic cause of Progeria has just been identified as lamin mutations, and that has opened up a whole area of research. Lamin is a protein in the nuclear envelope which binds to a whole host of other proteins, and so that has opened up a whole area of cell biology and molecular biological research asking how do these proteins interact to prevent cells from becoming senescent under normal circumstances? Clearly, if you disrupt one of those proteins that cell becomes senescent very rapidly. So I think there are several indirect ways, if you like, into the biology of senescence or ageing, and I think that is already going on to an extent. Clearly, it is an important avenue of research if one wants to understand the natural process of ageing.

Q294 *Lord Turnberg:* Just as a follow-up on that, Professor Lees said we are going to die of one of either cancer, heart attack or stroke. I am not sure he is right because it is quite possible that in a number of years' time most of the common cancers will have been cured or prevented, and if we work on the vascular tree in the ageing process in the way you have described and the arteries remain patent and open and our hearts beat away nicely and our brains continue to function, it may be something else that kills us off. This is where the biology of ageing is going to be of importance.

Professor Lees: Or the lack of pension!

Q295 *Baroness Murphy:* The specific research you are talking about, looking at the cellular and molecular level in relation to the ageing phenomenon, has that been yet applied to the vascular system specifically? Do we know whether, as yet, that work has been done or is it still in the pipeline?

Professor Weissberg: It is being applied to the vascular system. There are groups around the country—my own group in Cambridge has certainly been doing some work on this and I know of about four or five other groups that are funded through the Heart Foundation—that do research on the phenomenon of vascular ageing as opposed to vascular disease progression.

Q296 *Baroness Murphy:* Are those two regarded as separate?

Professor Weissberg: Atherosclerosis is a disease associated with the ageing process but it is not unique to ageing, so it is not inevitable that as you get older you will get atherosclerosis nor is it inevitable that if you are young you will not get atherosclerosis. I think there is a distinction between the disease entity and vascular ageing. If one took atherosclerosis away— and of course it is very hard to do that in our society because pretty much everybody has got some of it— then you are talking about the haemodynamics of the stiff artery because there is no doubt that arteries get stiffer as they get older, and if the main conduit artery, the aorta, is stiff then it transmits much higher pressures to the tissues beyond and they can damage the tissues beyond—the brain, the kidney and the small vasculature—and I think we have been less good at getting a handle on that process. That is beginning to happen, again, partly through the new approaches to imaging and, also, I have to say, because it is no longer unfashionable to say "I am interested in physiology". There was a time, 10 years ago, when you had to be interested in molecules or cells to get any research funding at all, and if you said "I want to do more research on the haemadynamics of how a blood vessel behaves" you did not get funded. Fortunately, that pendulum is beginning to swing back now and we are starting to understand a bit more of the physiology—and we have got to because we are learning a lot about molecules and a lot about the cells but we have got to marry that with the physiology to be able to understand how it all works out. I think there is more work going on in that area.

Q297 *Lord Soulsby of Swaffham Prior:* We have heard from you gentlemen about heart disease and stroke and they are, clearly, seen to be priorities in the National Health Service and in the pharmaceutical industries. Is there sufficient co-ordination between clinical medicine and pharmaceutical companies in either the treatment of the conditions or the prevention, and if not how does one bring them together more effectively?

Professor Lees: I have worked with industry—not in industry but I have worked closely with them—and I think it is clear that industry has contributed enormously to the health service, and vice versa in terms of prevention. So that many of the drugs that have been developed, the statins and the anti-hypertensives and so on—vast numbers of drugs that have been looked at for preventative purposes in thrombin—were developed by industry, and industry benefited by getting the sales of these drugs, to the extent of enormous sums of money. But, I think actually there is still a huge barrier. As far as I can see there is no position where industry comes to the health service and says, "We want to work together to develop something". There is almost the opposite reaction; that if industry wants to work with clinicians to do a trial the health service puts barriers in the way by, for example, increasing the costs. If the Medical Research Council wants to run a trial in a particular hospital then the costs that are applied are those of doing the research itself, the added cost, plus, maybe, a little bit of overhead. If industry comes along, then every test that would have been done anyway in these patients is charged at as much as possible to the industrial company. So it is seen as a way of extracting money from industry to support the health service. Certainly there is nothing in the way of our research assessment exercise or the incentives for anybody to take part in industry-funded research; it is seen as being a bad thing to be doing. Yet, clearly, it is necessary; we have to work in partnership with industry. They very often have access to the compounds at a very early stage of development, they have access to groups elsewhere in the world who are willing to work with you; they can co-ordinate things, they have the facilities for dealing with the bureaucracy of getting compounds into different countries, and so on. So I think it is necessary that we work with them but I do not think we are doing it as well as we should do.

Q298 *Lord Mitchell:* It is quite startling to hear that and I just wonder how would you improve it if you could.

Professor Lees: The research networks that are being set up will help with that because they have been set up with an aim that they will encourage industry research. I think we also have to put something in the way of incentives in place for hospital managers to say "We want you to take part in this"; we have to put it in place with academics to say, "You will be given brownie points in the RAE, or whatever, which will be worth as much as taking part only in Medical Research Council-funded research". I think it is to do with sorting out incentives. Then, I think, we have got to go to industry and say, "Look, if we collaborate closely with you, if we give you the lower rate for conducting research in this country, we expect also to get the drugs sold to us at a lower rate". I think we can work in partnership happily.

Professor Fentem: I think the question is whether the present arrangements, in fact, are optimal. As Lord May will detect, we have been looking carefully in recent times at the Canadian stroke network. I think there are some features of the network that commend themselves. Whether it is too late to consider them for this country or not, I am not sure. The pharmaceutical companies actually contribute to the network, so the funding they put in the direction of research goes to the network and is not, therefore, distributed on the basis of contracts with individual clinical academic units, or whatever. That, it seems to me, has something to commend it and we need to move in that direction if we are going to make a real success of the clinical research networks.

Q299 Lord Soulsby of Swaffham Prior: I was going to come to the clinical networks. It does seem to me that the development of any molecule or any procedure is costly, extensive—10 years or more—and if the pharmaceutical industry is going to be charged for that then that is going to slow things down enormously. The network situation is going to help cure that, is it? Is it going to encourage pharmaceutical companies to come forward with more new molecules and new procedures than they would have done?

Professor Fentem: I think the question is how do we best engage them in the discussions? We are not at a stage yet where we can see clearly how that will be managed. Clearly, we have made a rather unsteady start to this because whereas the Government has made £100 million available for the next batch of research networks, the money that was discussed that would come from the OST to the MRC to support the research on those networks has not yet been forthcoming. So we may end up, on the present information, with networks but not with the funding for research programmes. A rescue bid could come from organisations like the pharmaceutical companies, obviously, and so we perhaps do need to work out exactly how we will engage with companies in organising the networks. These would be contracts, in the end, not with individual academic departments but with a network of departments.

Professor Weissberg: Can I just come in on that? It is an extraordinarily complex interaction between industry and academic and NHS research because,

inevitably, industry has a particular agenda, and that is that they want to sell their product, and they want to protect their product. One of the difficulties in trying to do research with industry—and I think it has been well-exemplified recently—is they are very nervous of you trying to do research on one of their products that they do not currently have a licence for, not because they are concerned that if you find that it works they are not going to make a lot of money (they would do) but because they are concerned that if you find something negative (and a good example of that is the inhibitors that were being trialled for bowel cancer and in so doing was the final nail in the coffin for their risk of causing heart disease) it makes industry very nervous of doing any further research, particularly outside their narrow remit if their product is selling well. So it is very difficult to persuade them to think laterally, if you like, with any of the products they have out there. I think we have to recognise that we do need to work with industry. They need us and we need them; it is a matter of coming up with a framework in which we are all comfortable. We are all, as researchers, a little bit nervous at the moment, under the current framework—which is not really a framework on how to interact with industry—as to how we will be perceived in terms of our interaction with that company. So there is a lot of work to be done to try to work out some ground rules there that are mutually satisfactory, but certainly industry needs us. I am sure it is no accident that the money for clinical research in this country has gone up after industry was saying "We cannot do clinical research in the UK and we will have to take it elsewhere." They recognise the need to do clinical research, preferably here, and we recognise the need for them to help us do it. It is a matter of coming up with a framework we are all comfortable with.

Chairman: We have, effectively, run out of time, and I am concerned that there might be a division bell ringing, in which case several Members of the Committee would have to go, but I would like to get two more questions on the table, perhaps, from Lord May and Lord Mitchell, with responses from Professor Lees—and if you wanted to amplify them thereafter that would be possible.

Lord May of Oxford: Very quickly, we have been talking about the current recent past—and may I say I completely agree that the research assessment exercise is in more ways than one inhibitory of collaborative research, and let us hope that that is one of the things that might be ameliorated—but looking beyond that, what are the things that you see if you look 10, 15, 20, 25 years ahead? What are the things that you may care to speculate on very briefly now, perhaps, that we might be looking forward to? In particular, you have touched on stem cells earlier but

I wonder what you think might be some of the longer term promises, given some of the things that have happened very recently.

Chairman: I wonder if we could have Lord Mitchell's question, and then perhaps you might make one response.

Q300 *Lord Mitchell:* Slightly different: it is referring to relationships with other disciplines. What opportunities do you see to develop links with complementary activity concerned with the aspects of ageing and those related to other disciplines? How successful have any efforts been to build such links? What problems have been encountered?

Professor Lees: Shall I start, perhaps, with Lord May's question? Very briefly, because I entirely support what Professor Weissberg said earlier. I think in the 10 or 15-year period we will have stem cells, but not just stem cells: there are drugs that are being developed, there are compounds being recognised now, which do seem to be able to switch back on the ability of neurones to re-grow, to encourage DENTRITE growth and to encourage them to start signalling to each other. It seems very likely that we will start work on these sorts of things over the next few years, but knowing how long it will take to get the right compound and to get these into clinical research practice, will be 10 or 15 years. I think there is a real possibility that we can encourage repair mechanisms in the brain.

Professor Weissberg: If I can pick up on the same theme, I think one of the reasons why it is crucially important we continue to do embryonic stem cell research in this country is not because I think that they are going to be providing a therapeutic tool themselves, but it is by studying those cells that we are going to understand the molecular mechanisms and molecular biology of tissue differentiation. Once you start to understand that then you can start tripping the switches by pharmacological means to induce a mature heart cell to start dividing again, which it would not normally do. It should be conceivable you can make it do that, it is just we do not understand the process. So I think tissue engineering and tissue repair is going to be the way over the next 20 years or so to deal with these "degenerative" diseases.

Professor Fentem: Picking something up right at the other extreme, if I may, Derek Wanless has focused on the importance of lifestyle factors in the development and progress of chronic disease. Older people are likely to be major beneficiaries, but we really do not how to deliver the messages effectively. We have always baulked at sustained interventions in this field—witness the physical activity taskforce and the obesity taskforce, which were dismantled in 1994 and which would have put us in place splendidly in relation to the problems that we now see out there. I

think a big challenge is going to be to implement Wanless. That will take 20 years.

Q301 *Chairman:* Indeed, when you see the word "taskforce" and the word "tsar" you worry it is going to be short-sighted and short-term.

Professor Fentem: Can I come to Lord Mitchell's question? I think there is undoubtedly scope for collaboration between the BHF (my colleague), Diabetes UK, Alzheimer's and Help the Aged. It may need some facilitating but there certainly is scope for that. I think the climate for collaboration is better than it has been. Some of it happens already, facilitated by the research group themselves. I can give you an example of the study by the European Prospective Investigation into Cancer (EPIC), which is a cancer study taking place currently, centred in Cambridge, working with a cohort of people in Norfolk. As I said, EPIC is based essentially on cancer and lifestyle factors in cancer, but that brings together Diabetes UK, the MRC, the cancer charities of course, and ourselves. So I think that those are the two mechanisms currently open to us. As charities we have got to sort ourselves out but, equally, provided we do not inhibit the teams of researchers that we support—and we do not—from going to multiple charities for their funding, quite a bit is possible. I could give some other examples but I think time prevents that.

Professor Weissberg: I presume that is what you meant by complementary activity, not complementary medicine?

Q302 *Lord Mitchell:* Yes.

Professor Weissberg: I think I would sound one slight note of caution, and that is that it is clear that we have limited resources, whether it be patients or whether it be research resources, but we certainly have a limited resource in terms of researchers in this country, and we do need to do something to address that. I was at a meeting this morning that is trying to do something about that. It is important, therefore, that we pool our resources and we have collaborations, and we talk to each other, but I would also just caution that if we over-regulate and if we over-formularise the way in which we do our research then we are going to stifle the slightly off-the-wall, entrepreneurial approach which, often, may lead to something which nobody has thought of. I think we must not lose sight of the fact that there must be some blue skies research in some of this; it must not all be directed at what we think is going to be the obvious answer; we need to have the flexibility to think laterally and take a punt at something which may not seem that obvious at this stage. I am just slightly worried, the way things are going, it is going to get harder and harder to do that.

Professor Lees: The other groups that I think we need to encourage collaboration with are the funding bodies in other countries. At the moment, it is possible that you can get funding for a multi-centre, multi-national study from one country's body—the NHMRC in Australia—and then struggle very hard to get the funding to do anything out-with that country. We should be able, I think, to agree that if the NIH in the United States funds a study then the MRC in the UK will fund its element of that study. There are individual examples where that is happening but there is not yet a system where one application would cover the whole world. I think it would be much better if we could, particularly for a condition like stroke where truly international research is the only way forward.

Chairman: Those last three comments sum-up a question I want to leave with you. All of you have stressed that there are inhibitions to the right kind of research, and indeed the development of clinical treatments. You have mentioned briefly the international dimension of this and how problematic that can be, for obvious reasons. You have mentioned red tape and paperwork, you have mentioned the current rules of the RAD and, dare I say, hospital managers. What I would be very interested to know—and if you are able to produce some examples, anonymously if necessary, that you could send to the Committee that would be helpful—is where the inhibitions come in. The red tape may be there for good reason but if it is obviously not for good reason, again, examples of why and how that is the case. Equally, if it is a matter of hospital managers and budgets for that single hospital, what kind of mechanisms could help override that in appropriate cases? I will leave you with that question and it would be very useful to have some either actual examples which can be quoted on the record, or, if they are anonymised examples, that is fine, we understand. Indeed, if it is a case of "Well, this is what would happen in the following circumstances", that is also going to be helpful. That being said, can I thank you very much indeed. This session has overrun: that is due to the stimulus you have provided for us, but we look forward to further input from you. Many thanks indeed.

Supplementary evidence by The Stroke Association

1. What emerging opportunities do you perceive for research on scientific aspects of heart disease and stroke over the next five to 10 years? And in the longer term (10–25 years)?

DELIVERY OF "PREVENTIVE" MEASURES

Derek Wanless has focussed on the importance of life style factors in the development and progress of chronic illness. Older people stand to be major beneficiaries of the change in emphasis that Wanless recommends. Whereas the benefits have been identified effective strategies for bringing about these benefits have not been defined.

Further advances in imaging and, through imaging, better classification of stroke by site and extent of anatomical damage.

Advances in evidence-based rehabilitation, re-training and the facilitation of recovery (plasticity) using adjuvant procedures.

Improved quality of evidence through the NSCRN—for therapeutic, surgical and rehabilitation procedures.

2. Although age is the single biggest risk factor for heart disease and stroke it seems that little attention is paid to underlying questions about how intrinsic ageing processes at the cell and molecular level contribute to the specific pathology that is seen in these conditions. Is this perception accurate?

The intrinsic ageing process is of limited relevance in this field. Less is known about the mechanisms of lacunar stroke and vascular dementia.

3. What opportunities do you see to develop links with complementary activity concerned with other aspects of ageing, particularly those based within other disciplines? How successful have any effort been to build such links? What problems have been encountered?

There is scope for collaboration with BHF, Diabetes UK, Alzheimer's Society and with Help the Aged to mention a few.

The small amount of research money available to The Stroke Association is an impediment. On the other hand there is in practice joint funding of strong research groups eg the Cambridge Stroke Group receive funding from BHF for their work on the imaging of carotid plaque. The European Prospective Investigation into

Cancer EPIC is an example of broad collaboration (MRC, CRC). The EPIC-Norfolk group at Cambridge (Prof K-T Khaw) The Norfolk cohort belongs to the infrastructure of a large prospective population study of approximately 25,000 men and women aged 45–79 years. It is examining the determinants of stroke incidence and mortality with particular emphasis on modifiable risk factors diet and physical activity, and biological mechanisms such as raised blood pressure, inflammation, haemostasis and glucose metabolism.

4. Do you think that the research councils and other research funding organisations give appropriate recognition to the importance of ageing ingeneral, and to cardiovascular system ageing in particular? If not, what actions do you think might remedy the situation?

The Research Councils face a dilemma. They are committed to supporting high quality research. Historically the restricted research capacity of ageing research *per se* has limited the growth of first class teams and the conception of first class projects. Fortunately cardiovascular research has had the wealth of the BHF behind it.

The Funders' Forum for Research in Ageing & Older People has not been a success thus far.

Small organisations have been expected to deliver the same quick wins which were delivered by the Cancer Funders' Forum.

5. How do you think the general public perceives the issues surrounding ageing of the cardiovascular system? Is enough effort being directed at engaging with the general public in this respect?

Witness the prospects for the implementation of Derek Wanless's proposals. We need acceptance of the message that stroke and CHD, and the changes which underlie them, are in large measure avoidable. Stroke and CHD are not inevitable accompaniments of ageing. We need to sustain prevention with evidence-based campaigns. Without more effective strategies for the prevention, treatment, and rehabilitation of stroke based upon good research, the cost of this disease can only increase.

NEW SURVEY REVEALS SEVERITY OF STROKE STILL WIDELY UNDERESTIMATED

Awareness of the gravity of stroke in UK is alarmingly low amongst both the general public and some health professionals.

TSA conducted a survey of 1,006 members of the general public, 200 General Practitioners and 75 Accident and Emergency Doctors from across the UK as part of The Stroke Association's Stroke Awareness Week, which ran from 4 to 10 October. The survey intended to ascertain levels of knowledge on stroke, treatment and prevention. Results demonstrate a lack of knowledge of the severity of stroke, particularly amongst some health professionals, women and young people.

Every year over 130,000 people in UK have a stroke. Results show that most people think stroke is a minor condition with 34 per cent of people estimating that there are only 50,000 people or less that have a stroke each year. Perhaps more alarming however, health professionals considerably underestimate the scale of stroke, with only 14 per cent of GPs and 28 per cent of A&E doctors accurately estimating the scale of the condition.

The number of women that have a stroke each year is also underestimated. Over 74,000 women have a first stroke each year. This is more than double other serious conditions such as breast cancer, which has 40,000 new cases each year. The survey found that 61 per cent of the general public believe serious conditions like breast cancer affect more women in the UK than stroke.

The serious consequences of stroke are equally misunderstood. Ninty-three per cent of women surveyed do not rate death as one of the most common consequences of stroke, despite the fact stroke is responsible for 13 per cent of all deaths in women.

March 2005

TUESDAY 25 JANUARY 2005

Present	Emerton, B	Soulsby of Swaffham Prior, L
	Hilton of Eggardon, B	Walmsley, B
	Sutherland of Houndwood, L	
	(Chairman)	

Memorandum by the Alzheimer's Society

INTRODUCTION

1. The Alzheimer's Society is the UK's leading care and research charity for people with dementia, their families and carers.

2. The Alzheimer's Society has over 25,000 members and works through a network of over 250 branches and support groups. It provides information and support for people with any form of dementia and their carers through its publications, helplines, website and local network. It advises professionals, runs quality care services and campaigns for improved health and social care and greater public understanding of dementia. **The Society funds an innovative programme of biomedical and social research in the areas of cause, cure and care.**

3. **For more information about the Society's research programme please go to www.qrd.alzheimers.org.uk**

4. Dementia affects over 750,000 people in the UK alone. Dementia is not a natural part of ageing but age is the most significant known risk factor. Over the age of 65, the risk of developing dementia doubles approximately every five years.

5. The Alzheimer's Society feels strongly that there is a funding crisis in research relating to key health issues for older people. This has led to a lack of stability in major research programmes and a "brain drain" of researchers to countries where funding and conditions of employment are more stable and rewarding. We see it as a priority to build capacity and increase funding and stability for promising new researchers. We view the best use of money to be direct support to research and the people doing it, rather than infrastructure and additional layers of management.

6. The number of people with dementia will increase as the population ages. It is estimated that by 2010 there will be about 870,000 people with dementia in the UK. The burden of illness created by dementia is huge compared to the amount of money that goes into researching the condition. The most common cause of dementia is Alzheimer's disease, which accounts for approximately half of the people with dementia followed by vascular disease, Lewy body dementia and a number of other diseases causing dementia.

7. It is essential that funding is directed into dementia research to step up the search for causes, a cure and the best way to care for people with Alzheimer's disease and other forms of dementia. Only with a better understanding of the causes of dementia will it be possible to identify appropriate preventative measures. Only with a clearer picture of how the diseases causing dementia progress and overlap will it be possible to develop effective interventions and only with an understanding of the complex pathology in later stages of dementia and the needs of people with dementia and their carers will it be possible to develop the best care.

PROMISING AVENUES FOR RESEARCH

8. There is increasing evidence that what is good for the heart is good for the brain. Epidemiological evidence suggests that as well as helping to keep the heart healthy, good diet and exercise can help to keep the brain healthy. It is especially interesting that two major heart disease risk factors—high blood pressure and high cholesterol—seem to be influential in dementia. Heart disease risk factors are highly modifiable either by lifestyle measures like diet and exercise, or by medication, or both. If these factors are important in dementia too, it may be that the same measures can be used to reduce the risk of dementia. It is therefore of particular note that a number of studies have now shown that people with high blood pressure in middle age run an increased risk of dementia in later life, and preliminary evidence indicates that treatments to lower high blood pressure may reduce the risk of dementia. Studies are also underway to determine the potential value of statins in reducing the risk of Alzheimer's disease.

9. There are numerous exciting developments utilising techniques for the early diagnosis of dementia in people "at risk". The availability of cholinesterase inhibitors as licensed treatments for Alzheimer's disease already emphasises the importance of early diagnosis to enable the best treatment to be provided for people with dementia. Early diagnosis will however become increasingly essential to optimal management as new and more effective treatments continue to emerge.

10. A number of exciting new research avenues for novel treatments have emerged from a better understanding of the molecular biology of Alzheimer's disease and an improving understanding of stem cell biology. The Alzheimer's Society is particularly excited by some of the stem cell developments and by research into a vaccine for Alzheimer's. A very limited trial of a vaccine in humans was stopped in 2002 due to adverse events in six per cent of the individuals. However the trial seemed to indicate that the build up of amyloid plaques was reversed in the brains of people with Alzheimer's disease who received the vaccination, and preliminary studies in animals and humans have begun to indicate that safer vaccination strategies are possible. The Alzheimer's Society strongly supports further research into the development of a vaccine for Alzheimer's disease.

11. The Alzheimer's Society feels however that it is important to recognise the broad range of biological and social research issues that are key to improving the quality of treatment, care and quality of life for people with Alzheimer's disease and other dementias. Reflecting this, we fund a portfolio of research that is both broad and exciting, ranging from studies determining whether neural stem cells can be redirected to parts of the brain that are affected by Alzheimer's disease to non-pharmacological interventions for behavioural symptoms. Substantial increases of funding are however essential if we are to really tackle these vital issues.

APPLICATION OF RESEARCH IN TECHNOLOGY AND DESIGN TO IMPROVE THE QUALITY OF LIFE OF OLDER PEOPLE

12. There have been interesting developments in assistive technology which can allow people with dementia to live more independently and remain in their own homes for longer than would otherwise be possible. An example of the technology is the "smart home", a home in which many of the appliances are linked electronically so that they can be customised in a way that will make daily life easier for the person with dementia.

13. Although we do therefore acknowledge that "smart technology" will have an increasing role to play in the care of people with Alzheimer's disease and other dementias, there are currently many more fundamental issues relating to quality of life, care and treatment that require research and towards which funding should be prioritised.

HOW EFFECTIVELY IS RESEARCH CO-ORDINATED IN THE PUBLIC, PRIVATE AND CHARITABLE SECTORS?

14. Whilst research councils and charities collaborate on specific studies a better mechanism to integrate more closely would be strongly welcomed. The Society is currently working with both the MRC and the Alzheimer's Research Trust (ART) on jointly funded projects.

15. An effective mechanism which led to a more integrated and co-ordinated structure would be extremely helpful and enable a more strategic development of research into ageing. However, it is important that the development of such a mechanism should not substantially increase "infrastructure" costs or redirect money from directly supporting researchers and research projects.

HAVE THE CORRECT PRIORITIES BEEN IDENTIFIED? ARE THERE ANY GAPS IN RESEARCH?

16. Currently, within the dementia field, research has concentrated mainly on Alzheimer's disease. This is heavily influenced by the pharmaceutical industry, which has less or no incentive to fund research into treatments for non-Alzheimer's dementia or interventions that are "non-pharmacological" or utilise "off-patent" agents. Treatment trials that are not funded by the pharmaceutical company are hence a major gap in dementia research. For example, the MRC is currently only funding one clinical trial in the area of dementia, and no trials investigating the treatment of non-Alzheimer dementias. This is extremely important, for example even very basic treatment questions regarding the use of aspirin or anti-hypertensive treatments in people with vascular dementia remain completely unanswered.

17. There should be input from consumers, who must be truly representative, in the setting of research priorities. We believe that the involvement of people with dementia and their carers will lead to better quality research and the priorities of the Society's research programme are set by our consumer panel. The Society's

award winning Quality Research in Dementia (QRD) programme is an active partnership between carers, people with dementia and the research community. The heart of the QRD is the QRD Advisory network: a network of 150 carers, former carers and people with dementia who play a full role in the research programme and help set priorities for our research programme.

Is there Sufficient Research Capability in the UK?

18. Large intervention and prevention trials and developing new treatments are extremely expensive and the resources to fund such work is painfully inadequate in the UK—substantially less funds have been available for specific trials and programmes of work in the last two to three years.

19. Proposed guidelines to develop research networks for Alzheimer's disease, stroke and diabetes, and established networks for cancer and mental health, will provide a slightly better infrastructure. However, in the absence of major funding for specific high priority research these networks are unlikely to address key issues or make a substantial difference. Again, it is vital that increases in funding go directly to research, rather than to layers of management or administration related to research, as this is what will have the real impact on reducing the burden of illness created by dementia and other conditions related to old age.

20. A concerted effort is required to increase capacity in research into ageing and age related diseases in the UK. The current situation requires there to be specific measures to encourage this type of research, such as capacity building grants from the MRC. The development of a lively and active research community, with an increased number of researchers, good support and networks, and stable, long term funding would attract new researchers into the field and encourage existing researchers to stay in the field and in the UK. This would have the result of progressing knowledge about the health related aspects of ageing much more than we can with the current situation.

21. The BBSRC "ERA" and "SAGE" funding schemes were good examples of productive initiatives on research into ageing, but we really need a more sustained and long term strategic approach that looks at specific illnesses related to age, like the diseases that cause dementia.

Is the Research Being Used to Inform Policy?

22. Currently there is a major problem translating research evidence into improved care and treatment. Perhaps the best examples of this problem include the difficulties of translating models of improved care into routine practice in nursing homes and changing the health of the nation based upon emerging understanding of disease risk factors. Setting standards and issuing guidance is an insufficient catalyst for change. Plans should also include action specific to older people, utilising the range of local resources, including those within regeneration programmes, and reflecting wider partnership working.

23. Substantially more effort and resource needs to be invested in implementing new evidence to promote health, care and treatment; and researching effective ways of enabling this implementation. Currently policy identifies some key areas, but does not go far enough to enable these issues to be tackled. To really make steps forward policy needs to move from tokenism to a strategically planned and adequately resourced commitment to implement change.

October 2004

Memorandum by Professor Carol Brayne

Introduction

This written contribution draws on experience as a lead principle investigator in longitudinal studies of older people over nearly two decades, as well as medical and public health training. I have consulted colleagues from the main study for which I am responsible, the MRC funded Cognitive Function and Ageing Study (MRC CFAS).

25 January 2005

KEY FINDINGS FROM MRC CFAS

We have reported from this multicentre study in England and Wales that:

— prevalence and incidence of disability, cognitive impairment and dementia rise exponentially after the age of 65;

— there is no down turn at the oldest age groups;

— there is variation across the centres in disability but not in dementia;

— pathology found in the brain after death at advanced age is found in both those who are cognitively impaired during life and those who are not and is mostly a mixture of vascular and Alzheimer's type;

— substantial proportions at each age, including the oldest age groups, report good health despite increasing health problems;

— very high proportions are demented in the period before death, particularly in the oldest age groups;

— potential genetic risk for Alzheimer's disease appears attenuated by the time most people reach old age probably because of the high background risk to the whole population.

The bibliography and design of CFAS are described in more detail at www-cfas.medschl.cam.ac.uk.

FRAMEWORK FOR ASSESSING POTENTIAL OF RESEARCH FINDINGS

It can be helpful to see research findings as fitting into a prevention framework. Each of these types of prevention has a different impact at the population level (from highly effective to minimal) but all are important.

Primary prevention (reducing "risk" exposure so that pathology does not develop). This type of prevention has the greatest potential yield if applied to populations. There are a great deal of observational data from epidemiological studies which suggest that certain types of lifestyle/opportunity (at all lifestages) are associated with less chronic disease and health active life expectancy. Bringing such results into feasible trials of intervention at appropriate level (individual, social network, community, high level policy) which generate sound data are far less common—and tend to be done at individual rather than community levels, lowering population impact.

The Wanless report has identified such public health research as an area for active development and this needs to be carefully encouraged—with a build up of the expertise necessary and an environment that facilitates research. Such research has to be built on firm disciplinary research, but then brought together into the complex intervention framework (well work up by the MRC). This type of research tends to take a long time and not result in multiple publications in high ranking journals—so needs positive nurturing. Current assessment and funding systems do not encourage such long term high risk investment for researchers, research groups, universities and funders. Some areas potentially important to health, but not traditionally researched as such, have been identified in the imminent ESRC call, but with limited funding and include the role of built environment (housing, transport, the way the built environment makes us active or inactive), intergenerational aspects, civic society, crime and disorder, accessibility and financial security. The new clinical networks being set up within the NHS for individual and groups of disorders have the potential to include only traditional therapeutic trials—it is important not to miss other types of intervention. Research which aims to investigate population behaviour at any age could have knock on effects for each cohort as future health is a function of current and past health.

Secondary prevention (early detection and alteration of natural history through early intervention). This has the potential to modify population health to some extent, if all the criteria necessary for screening are met. Not many interventions have been tested on older age groups, and this will continue to be an area of important research. The MRC has funded research into a trial of screening in the older population, which is now yielding results (which, importantly, can have negative findings as well as positive). Such trials have the same problems as interventions in primary prevention but their feasibility on a very large scale is proven, provided that populations can continue to be recruited through the primary care setting. The UK can provide amongst the best evidence internationally because of this ability to recruit from clearly defined populations.

Tertiary prevention (prevention of the consequences of disease once established). This type of research has the least potential impact on population health. There is insufficient follow-up on new and costly introductions of interventions, once short term trial evidence is released, such as the dementia treatment drugs, to see what real impact they have on the natural history of morbidity and ultimately mortality.

DEATH AND DYING

In the understandable concentration on healthy ageing and reduction of morbidity at given ages there has been less attention to the consequences of prevention earlier in life, and its impact on future populations reaching the oldest age groups. The relationship of changing health and wellbeing to survival, with quality of life and death has been less researched but is bound to receive increasing attention as the whole population ages. Dementia or severe cognitive impairment is very common in the period before death in the oldest age groups. This is unlikely to be prevented in the near future, if ever and we need to understand this stage of life too. A firmer foundation of research is needed to prepare for this societal change, including the frail stages of ageing not just "healthy active" life.

MODELLING POPULATION HEALTH

Work on modelling population health profiles including more detail in older age groups given changes in younger age cohorts is not highly developed and is an area of potential value. Although many are sceptical about the value of modelling it is valuable for policy assessment, particularly if carried out with sensitivity analyses and explicit discussion of uncertainty. This has been identified as an area by the Wanless report, and the MRC has asked HEIs to bid for dedicated doctoral studentships. Continuing support is needed to build up this area of expertise in the UK.

EVIDENCE BASE FROM COMPARATIVE STUDIES

Encouragement of a diversity of approaches to ageing research is sensible as each can reveal valuable insights which can be tested from a different angle in another (disease, system, lifestage, holistic, discipline based approaches, single and multidisciplinary), not least to provide sound evidence for modelling. Major gaps for which there are currently no large-scale research efforts are epidemiological studies examining variation in health across ethnic groups and cohorts in the oldest age groups. Such studies are most valuable if they have a robust population base and if they can have a set of more detailed biomedical and qualitative studies bolted on. MRC CFAS, amongst others, can provide a model for this type of approach, which can then be used to address biological questions (such as why rates of dementia might vary across populations) as well as policy questions (do we expect different patterns of ageing as our ethnic populations move into the older age groups, are future older people likely to be more healthy or less than now). These questions can only be explored with stable methodology and population sampling. The opportunity does exist but has not been taken up.

BARRIERS TO RESEARCH IN HUMAN POPULATIONS

There are now major barriers to research beyond achieving funding including the many levels of permission and engagement required to work with populations, from research governance structures (multiple within the NHS), ethical review and the legislative framework such that more time is spent in these processes than in the research itself.

September 2004

Examination of Witnesses

Witnesses: PROFESSOR CAROL BRAYNE, Professor of Public Health Medicine, Cambridge University, PROFESSOR CLIVE BALLARD, Director of Research, the Alzheimer's Society, and MRS LINDA KELLY, Chief Executive of the Parkinson's Disease Society, examined.

Q303 *Chairman:* Many thanks to you for coming and perhaps especially to Mrs Kelly because you are stepping in in the absence of Robert Meadowcroft and we appreciate that very much. May I also thank you and those whom you represent for the written evidence that has been submitted. That has also been very much appreciated and it is part of the record that we have. Perhaps I can say very briefly what this Committee is trying to do. We are about half-way through our deliberations. We are a Sub-Committee of the Science and Technology Select Committee and our intention is to produce a report probably before the summer recess. There are two main areas that we are focusing on. One is the medical/biological science of ageing and the issues that come up in that area, and the other is on assisted technology and again what can be done to improve the quality of life for those who are subject to the various vagaries of growing old. We do not have powers in the sense that we cannot tell the Government what to do, but we hope we can influence what they do. One of the issues we are looking at and we may well ask you about is whether or not the research strategy in UK plc is well balanced and covers the ground and whether there is enough collaboration and all that sort of thing. My colleagues all have names before them so I shall not go round the table, but we will all come in and ask questions of various kinds. It would be very useful when you start giving your first piece of evidence if you could just say for the record who you are and what your own organisation specifically does in this area. I will start with a very general question. I think it would be good to have your views on this for the record and also because there is not a complete understanding in the community at large. What are the differences and what are the similarities between Alzheimer's and other forms of dementia? Is it something that would be noticeable to the layperson? Is it something that you would regard as having a scientific basis for making that distinction? There is a whole series of implications. I wondered if I could ask each of you to say a little bit about that as we start and then we will follow through with the questions that we have in our minds. Professor Brayne?

Professor Brayne: I am Carol Brayne. I am Professor of Public Health Medicine at Cambridge University in the Department of Public Health and Primary Care and I have been working in ageing studies for the last 20 years, following up individuals largely aged 75 and over, seeing them at regular intervals and trying to get at the biology underpinning the changes that we see with age, most particularly brain ageing. I come at that question from a population perspective and not from a clinical perspective. What I can tell you is what we have seen over time, which is a decline in the general population aged 65 and over, accelerating after the age of 75 and over in fairly crude measures of cognition, but it is a distributional change, and within that clearly the bottom distribution are those that would be labelled as demented within the care service because one needs to have a cut-off point in order to be able to provide care and appropriate support to individuals. When one looks at the brains of these individuals across the whole spectrum one sees a mixture of pathology. There is vascular Alzheimer's and I am talking about really the very old population, so the 80-year olds and above who are most of the people to whom this kind of research applies. In our kind of population-based studies it would be difficult to differentiate between predominantly vascular and predominantly Alzheimer's, other than clearly if individuals have a stroke they are at much greater risk of having dementia and if they have Parkinson's disease also within the population they are also at greater risk of developing dementia.

Q304 *Chairman:* That is very helpful.

Professor Ballard: My name is Clive Ballard. I am Director of Research for the Alzheimer's Society and a Professor of Age Related Disorders at King's College London, although I am here predominantly representing the Alzheimer's Society who are the major charity representing people with dementia and their carers in the UK and who fund a research programme in that area. There are a lot of similarities but there are some important differences. I think the similarities are that all the late onset dementias lead to progressive and functional disability, all of which leads to much the same requirement in terms of support, care and treatment. I think there are important differences. The three most common conditions Carol has already mentioned, Alzheimer's disease, vascular dementia and dementia related to Parkinson's disease, and there are important symptom differences. For example, a lot of people with vascular dementia will have strokes and related disabilities. People with Parkinson's disease obviously have the motor symptoms of Parkinson's disease as well as the cognitive and functional problems. There are some very important differences. I think the most important difference of all comes when you consider treatment effects. For example, if somebody has a disability because of a large stroke, that is likely to be very different from somebody who has a general atrophy and shrinkage of the brain related to Alzheimer's disease. If you looked at somebody from the end of the room their disabilities might appear harmless, but what underlies them is very different and therefore the treatment need might be very different. The reason I think that is particularly important is that especially some of the non-Alzheimer's dementia, such as vascular dementia, have been particularly neglected and there are very, very few treatment studies in those areas.

Mrs Kelly: I am Linda Kelly, Chief Executive of the Parkinson's Society. We have two main charitable aims. The relevant one to you is that we promote research into cause, prevention and cure of Parkinson's. I represent people with Parkinson's and their families, and I think it is that wider remit that is quite important. Contrary to quite common general public opinion, Parkinson's does affect mental capacity. Most people think it is about movement and tremor, but in the population about 20 or 30 per cent of people with Parkinson's will get dementia. There have been some studies in the north of England and in the south where they have shown that if you live with Parkinson's for 20 or 25 years the likelihood that you will get some sort of cognitive impairment is up to 80 per cent, so it is actually real and important. I think there are differences between the dementias. I take Professor

Ballard's point, but I think the work on dementia and Alzheimer's has been where money has been put in. What we have found over the last two or three years is that agents who are not licensed for Parkinson's disease give clinical benefit and therapeutic gain and I think that is quite important. There are agents out there that could help many people but who are not licensed to do that. Dementia is actually an indicator of whether people go into care homes or not. I think it costs about £4,000 a year to treat someone with Parkinson's, and in a care home it is £20,000 plus. It is the rest of it that is important because if you can get people at home, they can be with their families, they tend to do much better and they actually tend to have better control of their symptoms. As soon as you put people in care homes they tend to deteriorate and you are lucky to see a GP or a registered nurse. I think dementia is not that well treated, it could be better treated and I think when you do treat it you can actually help people stay by and large in their home environment, if they are still able to do so.
Chairman: That is very helpful.

Q305 *Baroness Hilton of Eggardon:* I would like to pursue the generality of dementia and specific diseases. Do you think that all dementias will turn out to be specific diseases like Alzheimer's or do you think there is a decline with age which is a more generalised thing, or is it all in the end going to have specific labels?
Professor Ballard: I think that ageing in itself does not cause dementia, there have to be specific disease processes. I think in a large number of people, particularly in the older age groups, there is an overlap of these processes, so it might not be purely Alzheimer's disease or purely vascular dementia or purely Parkinson's disease, it might be a combination. For example, about 40 or 50 per cent of people who have Alzheimer's also have significant vascular disease in the brain, especially in the over-80s group. I think Carol mentioned that in population studies of that group when they overlap the pathology is very common and that is certainly the result of our own research findings on Alzheimer's as well.
Mrs Kelly: I think what is interesting is that there is what is called Lewy body Disease with dementia and there is Parkinson's Disease where they got dementia and currently the discussion is that these two conditions are a continuum. So I would support Clive's view on that.
Professor Brayne: What happens is that people come to see their clinicians and they become known for a particular area of interest. Secondary and tertiary referral centres is where progress comes from in a way because they gather together cases which have similar characteristics, for example early onset

dementia and that then becomes defined. Then you have some criteria that you can apply to the more general population and then you find this issue of it blurring out, that it is not as specific as it seemed from the clinical perspective or the very highly researched perspective. I would like to expand on what Clive said about dementia or cognitive decline not being part of ageing. The population data that we have shows that—obviously there are people who do extremely well for very prolonged periods and we all know people like that—there is this tremendous spread into the oldest age groups and none of the people in our own populations escape without some pathology in their brain by the time they die. This information has not been published yet, but our own data suggests that by the time people die the prevalence of severe cognitive impairment or dementia at the time or in the year before death is very high and the prevalence of dementia by the age of 85 plus is at least 25 per cent. So we are talking about, if it does not occur with age, a process which is extremely common with ageing.

Q306 *Baroness Hilton of Eggardon:* Of that 25 per cent, how many will be sufferers from Alzheimer's and how many will be suffering from vascular degeneration or Parkinson's?
Professor Brayne: They will have a mixture.

Q307 *Baroness Hilton of Eggardon:* So you cannot divide it up?
Professor Ballard: I think if you looked at what was believed clinically to be the predominant condition you would find probably about 50 to 60 per cent of the people would have Alzheimer's disease, 15 to 20 per cent would have vascular dementia, 15 to 20 per cent would have either dementia with Lewy bodies or Parkinson's dementia, and then there would be something like five per cent of people with rarer conditions. I would agree with Carol that although you can decide which are the predominant conditions, a lot of those individuals would have an overlap of the different pathologies.

Q308 *Lord Soulsby of Swaffham Prior:* From the population point of view is it possible to identify certain genetic groups, Alzheimer's in Iceland for example, that are more liable to develop these dementias than others?
Professor Brayne: In our population studies we attempt to replicate the genetics findings that come from the more specialised settings. The only gene that has come up as being a likely one at the population level rather than in very high risk families is really the Apolipoprotein E, it is of that particular type and in many studies E4 has been shown to be associated with increased risk. In the

bigger study which I have been associated with we have found that the risk is not as great as it appears from the other population studies, and this may be because we are looking at the older people with dementia and by that time the background risk of dementia has risen, so the genetic risk actually becomes less important.

Professor Ballard: I would agree with that. In terms of Alzheimer's disease and probably in terms of vascular dementia the Apolipoprotein E gene seems to be the most important. I think one reading of the literature which would support Carol's view is that that gene might be responsible for bringing forward the age of development of dementia rather than causing it *per se*.

Mrs Kelly: Some publications that have come out this month looking at genetic risks found a gene mutation that is actually in sporadic Parkinson's, and so at the minute they have seen it but do not know whether it leads to neurodegeneration, and that is the important question. There will be more work done in that field. The work was done in England, Italy or Spain and the US and the commonality of results was interesting.

Q309 *Chairman:* May I just follow up with a slightly more general question but building on what you have said, and it is something we run into all the time and we keep asking it ourselves. Is there a helpful difference to be drawn between what you might call the natural process of ageing and the diseases that cluster around the ageing process? We heard differing views on this when we were in Washington last week from the NIH people. It would be interesting to hear your own thoughts.

Professor Ballard: I think clearly there is a relationship, but the way that I would view it is that as people age, certain diseases become more frequent and they accumulate over time and therefore have a bigger influence on things. It is not ageing itself that causes the problems but the diseases that become more common with ageing. If you look at the age of a particular population then the risk of particular conditions will be higher, but that is because the risk of the underlying factors that contribute to those conditions become higher rather than that age itself causes the problems *per se*. I think there clearly is a close relationship, but it is really about understanding how these disease processes develop over time and with age, I think that is important rather than the age itself.

Professor Brayne: I think there is a huge blur between the normal ageing process with some decline and the very frail ageing, and that has been outlined from our own work as well as many other pieces of work. I am a lumper because I approach the problem form a population perspective. Splitting has allowed scientists to work on very specific areas

which are parts of the pathological process and identify different pathologies which contribute. If that had not happened, if people had just continued to say that this is all a mixture of things and it is all very highly age related even if not completely ageing itself, that would not have happened, that same focus and ability to make it an interesting scientific question and attract scientists and so on to do it.

Q310 *Baroness Walmsley:* Which is the more important factor, the genetic predisposition or age? Can you put proportions to it?

Professor Brayne: If you were in a family with one of the serious genetic mutations it would be the genes, but if it is in the general population I would say age is by far the strongest factor.

Professor Ballard: Age is clearly very strongly related, but I think it is about understanding why age is strongly related. If you look at risk factors for Alzheimer's disease other than genetic factors, for example high blood pressure in mid-life is a substantial risk factor for developing Alzheimer's disease in later life. There are also some environmental factors like dietary factors and things that have been suggested to be important. People who have had major head injuries in mid life or early life are at a three-fold risk. There are a lot of environmental factors that happen to people in early or mid life that greatly affect their risk of developing Alzheimer's disease in later life as well as the genetic factors.

Mrs Kelly: With Parkinson's disease you get people with young Parkinson's. I think it is useful to look at natural ageing and split it off from the condition because you can get clues then on how you might help people. We have just done some work on splitting age match controls in people with Parkinson's, and you can help people understand what is natural ageing and what is due to Parkinson's and perhaps focus treatments on that. With regard to percentages, genetics in Parkinson's is less than one per cent, it is tiny. On average it is when you are over 65 that you get Parkinson's, but one in 20 are under 40. It is a combination of genetic susceptibility but then you have to consider environmental factors and it might be things like Clive says, but it could be things like pesticides and living in rural areas. If you can understand what accelerates the ageing process in younger people that might help not only younger people but older people as well. So it is a slightly arbitrary split but I think it is quite a useful one from a Parkinson's perspective.

Q311 *Baroness Emerton:* Taking what has just been discussed and understanding that neurodegenerative diseases are clearly a very important part of the ageing process, how great do you think the overall impact is in terms of health, quality of life, social and economic participation? How is this impact changing as life-span continues to increase, and what are the main issues for scientific research? In what ways is your organisation (or your research community) addressing these issues? What are the highest priorities? What are the greatest scientific challenges?

Professor Brayne: The economic cost depends on which group of diseases you are looking at, but there is no doubt that the rarer disorders that occur, like Parkinson's disease, in economically active age groups. Early onset dementias and other major neurodegenerative diseases may not be overall costly in terms of the country, but are massively costly in terms of the individual and the community around them. The vast majority of the neurodegenerative disorders are happening in the older age groups where the economic impact of the individual is less because they are not in paid employment (although that may change if the pension age is abolished), and clearly they have a very major impact in terms of formal and informal caring to the societies around those individuals, and in terms of what needs to be set up in society to support those individuals. The CFAS study which I have been involved in along with Professor Bond from Newcastle, has an associated study—the resource implication study—in which he looked at formal and informal caring and he has produced a report, and there are some costings within that which estimate it in the millions. It depends on how you cost it, but there are figures out there. If it is helpful to the Committee I could provide that paper.

Q312 *Chairman:* That would be helpful.

Professor Brayne: The research community is addressing questions in terms of the biology of ageing and the biology of specific neurodegenerative diseases. Clive will comment on the Alzheimer's Society's very good attempt to generate biological and wider research, but I think there is a difficulty with the wider types of research. Most of the biological lab-based stuff is aimed at providing the bullet cure, and given the mixture of pathologies that we see in the older age groups I think it is very unlikely that that is going to make an impact on old age dementia, certainly in the near future and maybe in the longer-term. There is an importance in terms of trying to work across from the lab through to the population, and from my perspective it would be very good to see some sort of strategy, whether it be an NIA-type strategy or something else, to link these things up. It is not that people have not recognised it, the ESRC have, the BBSRC have and so have SPARK. There is a lot of interest and awareness but it is not quite all working together yet, and it is very difficult to get people working together on it. It is difficult to generate very good proposals which are clearly fundable. It is moving in the right direction.

Baroness Emerton: In time for the increasing age range that we are facing in life, says one who is particularly interested!

Q313 *Chairman:* We feel it quite consciously in this House! You can see the demography is advancing quite quickly.

Mrs Kelly: There are findings that Clive alluded to that should be underpinned by very robust research, and that research is very difficult to do. We would clearly like the research community to be doing it and that ought to be done within five or 10 years. The longer shot stuff, middle aged interventions, is going to be a much longer shot. We need a very robust research infrastructure to support that kind of long-term work.

Professor Ballard: I think that if we are not careful it could turn into a major crisis. There are about 700,000 people with dementia in the UK now, and looking at the projected population changes, that will be over a million before very long, and it will probably double by the middle of the next century, so that is an awful lot of people with dementia. Currently services and research addressing the issues are already very stretched, and if those numbers carry on increasing in that kind of way the condition will not be managed with current levels of resource or planning. Unless there is good strategic planning now it will become a crisis in 15 or 20 years' time. I think there are major issues to address. Going back to the cost, I think the CFAS study might well provide better costs, but in 1997 the Alzheimer's Society commissioned a report as part of their submission to NICE and that estimated a cost in the UK per annum of about £6 billion and that was probably an under-estimate because it was largely based on direct care costs and did not look at indirect costs such as the type of the carers involved in providing that care. It is a very, very substantial cost. It is also very high in terms of human cost. Obviously for somebody who has a dementia illness it impacts considerably on their functional capabilities, their independence, their autonomy and their quality of life. It is not impossible to provide somebody with severe dementia with a good quality of life, but sadly with the facilities that are available that is rarely the case. It is not impossible but generally it has a very major impact. If you look at carers, it also has a very major impact there. In a cross-section at any one time, as well as the subjective burden that carers might feel, about 50 per cent of carers would meet clinical criteria for depression and over a year of follow up about 80 per cent of carers would meet those kinds of criteria. So it is obviously having a very big impact on those individuals and it affects their physical health as well. People make more trips to their GP and are prescribed more medication and spend more time in hospital. There is a very big human cost to people with dementia and their carers.

Mrs Kelly: I would be slightly pushier than Clive about it. I think that the care structure in the UK has changed significantly. I think carers now, people with dementia, particularly the elderly, are very often elderly themselves, and I think being able to rely on a daughter and son or even grandchildren is not something you can do because most people have to work now, it is an economic need. As the incidence increases and more people live longer there is a great burden which a lot of people cannot cope with. Dementia often means that you will go into a care home and that is difficult. Care is very stretched in the UK and it is not going to be less stretched as we go forward. I do think there is an issue between balance of biological and cell science and translating it into clinical practice, I really do. I think it is true today and I do not think it may happen, I think it is happening now. That does not mean to say you want to get rid of the very good and high quality science we do, but it does need to translate into something and we would like to see a much more assertive stand on that. What are we doing? We did the analysis ourselves as we felt you have to do it yourself, you cannot complain if you are not doing it, and so we have asked our members what outputs they would want in research terms over five and 10 years to try and get some practical things we would like to see happening. We are just in the middle of that exercise and what is very interesting is that a lot of common things come up, so people are actually quite a lot in agreement.

Q314 *Baroness Emerton:* I think I am right in saying that there are in excess of six million informal carers caring for the elderly with dementia. I think you quoted, Professor Ballard, that 50 per cent are showing signs, so we are talking about three million people who might be showing signs of degeneration themselves.

Professor Ballard: I said certainly have depression.

Q315 *Baroness Emerton:* That is quite an important factor when we are considering the care pattern and the care provision.

Professor Ballard: Yes.

Q316 *Chairman:* Care in relation to the illnesses that you talk of is more intensive than in many other aspects of care.

Professor Ballard: One of the best books was actually called *The 36-Hour Day* and it was describing the care experience, and I think that is a very, very good description of it.

Q317 *Baroness Walmsley:* To what extent are your priorities recognised by Government departments? Do you feel there is a good link between science and policy in the field of neurodegenerative disease research? Could you say in what ways you think the situation could be improved and more could be done to develop links?

Professor Ballard: At the moment my personal opinion and the experience of the Alzheimer's Society as well is that I am not sure that policy and research do very well together at all. There has been a lot of rhetoric about so-called translational research in the last five years. I personally do not see very much evidence of a commitment to increasing funding or strategic planning to improve that. One of the things that has been mooted and is happening at the moment is the development of clinical research networks, one of which is being focused on Alzheimer's disease and will be developed, and that is very much an infrastructure predominantly for clinical trials which is very helpful, but that does not actually provide the support or funding for the actual trials that are happening, it is just an infrastructure for them. In addition, clinical trials, although extremely important, are only a modest proportion of the scientific work, both basic lab science and social science, that is needed in order to develop better care, better treatments and prevention. It worries me greatly that there is a lot of rhetoric without very much support to underpin them and that what support is available is focused on very narrow areas and does not recognise the breadth of work that is necessary in order to take the agenda forward. I think it particularly concerns me, if you look at what is happening to young scientists in the UK at the moment, that most promising PhD students are either moving to take up posts in industry or they are moving to the United States or other European countries because there are more secure patterns of funding and there are better ways of helping people to develop their careers. So in addition to funding specific projects and specific infrastructure it worries me greatly that if there is not the investment in research capacity to develop the world-class scientists of the future we will be left in a very sad situation.

Q318 *Chairman:* Is there evidence or is that an impressionistic picture of the movement of people? Have surveys been done recently?

Professor Ballard: There are surveys. I do not have those figures at my fingertips but I can get hold of some of that information. I think there is certainly a lot of evidence of reductions in more junior levels of scientists, more people going abroad and less available resources for those individuals who are in the developmental stages.

Q319 *Baroness Walmsley:* Can I ask the other two if they agree with that point of view and ask you all where you think the lead should be coming from to improve the situation?

Professor Brayne: When you say do we agree, do you mean specifically about the drain, the loss?

Q320 *Baroness Walmsley:* Yes.

Professor Brayne: I am not aware of any reports other than the general scientific reports about the migration because we have a lot of able folk coming in as well as we are recruiting scientists at PhD level and so on. What I have seen since the demise of the regional research and development is the lack of the NHS R&D work at the regional level, so you could bring junior scientists on, both medical and non-medical, in the local area and make them ready to compete in the national setting and put them through the system that way. That worked extremely well in the regions. It is the same argument we have had recently about the stellar research departments, that you cannot have a five star department unless you also have three and four star ones, you have to have the different football teams in order to generate the very top level. We saw that in action with our regional funding because then you could take the best of that bunch and put them forward for the MRC funding or the highly competitive funding. Could I just comment on the policy issue? Although I said that many of the councils are saying the right things and putting out bids in the right areas, that is always responsive mode, so they put out a call and then there are tenders and then the quality of the work and the area of the work is totally dependent on the community that already exists, but it does not fill in the gaps. It may continue excellence in certain areas and make that better. If we want to spread out across the areas we will have to have another approach, not this constant tendering because we have it from the NHS, we have it from all the councils and we have it to some extent from the charities as well. I think the scientific community is constantly in a position of having to bid again and again and again often for the same thing which you know would be valuable if it was done. It is a waste of scientific time to keep bidding. It will be done in the end because somebody will fund it.

Mrs Kelly: I would agree with Carol. I think that you have to have proactive as well as reactive calls for applications. I think the link from policy to research is actually quite weak at the moment from our perspective. There have been some quite nice examples in the last two or three years where they have got a group of scientists together and asked what they think are the key scientific questions and then they have looked at funding some of that work. If you do it this way you get better quality research.

Q321 *Baroness Walmsley:* When you say they have got groups of scientists together, who do you mean?

Mrs Kelly: We have done some of that. An example was with stem cell work, which is not quite ageing but perhaps relevant. Something like 4,000 articles were published in 2002 on what we could do. We put together a facilitator network and got everybody that we knew interested in the area to go and attend a conference and we asked them what they would like to do and then we tried to support the best idea there. The reasoning behind it is that you get people swapping ideas and you also get rid of things that are not viable, particularly in quickly emerging areas. We then got involved with the MRC and we asked the MRC if they would be interested in helping us do a conference and they did a stem cell conference. That does not negate the reactive applications at all, it has added to it and we do it in a rather modest way, but I think there is room for other groups to do that. It is very beneficial particularly in emerging areas where there is not that many scientists but people have come from a different angle.

Lord Soulsby of Swaffham Prior: When we were in Washington we saw some very active young groups. There was one group that our adviser knows very well and it is an Englishman who is in charge of it. He comes over here and he knows where to go to convince the people to go and tells a sad story of low salaries here, the difficulty with housing and so on and so forth. So the best people are going there. They are full of excitement as to what they are doing. How many will come back? I do not know. It is stimulating to see them and sad to know that it is taking place. I think there are some centres in this country where there is an exchange scheme and Cambridge is one of them.

Q322 *Chairman:* Happily, one of the young researchers I spoke to was coming to the Sanger Institute next month with similar excitement, wanting to see what is happening in this country.

Professor Brayne: Maybe one of the constructive things is greater encouragement of this exchange, like the MIT programme that we have from Cambridge which does encourage that. We have had people coming through our Masters programmes who do a couple of years with us and a couple of years in the States, so they are very familiar with both environments and then they can work quite easily across the Atlantic. It is very stimulating for all of us to have that kind of exchange.

Professor Ballard: Obviously one of the ways of trying to nurture promising younger scientists is through research fellowships and certainly the Alzheimer's Society supports those fellowships, as I am sure the Parkinson's Disease Society does and the research councils, but there are relatively few of them and particularly few in the area of neurodegeneration and so they become extremely competitive. Although it means that the people who are successful are usually extremely good quality, they are very limited in number and in terms of developing capacity that is probably not quite sufficient. Some of the initiatives, such as the ones that Carol mentioned at a regional level, used to be very helpful in supporting that kind of development, and that does not really exist any more.

Q323 *Chairman:* Why does it not exist now?

Professor Ballard: I am not sure. Carol might know the policy better than I do. I think what has happened more and more is a lot of funding has been given in slightly different ways, either to indirectly support trusts who are supporting research in other ways or as part of specific commissioning calls and I think those can be valuable in their own way, but there is a loss as part of that as well.

Q324 *Chairman:* And this is NHS money for research?

Professor Ballard: Yes.

Mrs Kelly: I think the reason is that people development *per se* is a judgement and people are trying to focus on that.

Chairman: We might have some witnesses from the NHS before us before too long.

Q325 *Baroness Walmsley:* Neurodegenerative diseases are clearly seen as priorities by the NHS and, of course, the pharmaceutical industries. Do you think there is sufficient co-ordination of effort between the two? Is the focus more on the treatment of problems as they arise or is the emphasis on prevention? Is the focus more on the one than the other or is the balance about right?

Mrs Kelly: I would slightly challenge the statement that they are seen as priorities by the NHS. I think if we really want to tackle it you have to take the person as a whole person. I think the silos of psychiatry and neurology are a very good example. In Parkinson's you can go to a neurologist, but if you had dementia you are meant to go to a psychiatrist and that seems to me not quite right. I would challenge whether they are a priority. I think the treatment of elements of neurodegenerative diseases are priorities but I think we need a whole person approach to it. I think the pharmaceutical industry has a wider remit and clearly might be able to comment even better than I can. They do early drug discovery and put products onto the market and I think that is really where they are. I am not sure the NHS and the pharmaceutical industry overlap that much in our area of expertise. With regard to prevention or treatment, if people could get the prevention of Parkinson's disease they would. I think if one could produce a vaccine that would be developed.

Q326 *Chairman:* Where is the funding going then?

Mrs Kelly: In the NHS?

Q327 *Chairman:* And the pharmaceutical companies. Is it really on treatments or on prevention?

Mrs Kelly: The biggest study we have done into Parkinson's disease is actually in surgery. Rather than leave it to the end stage, are you better to get it really early on and give people a better quality of life? It is a study costing about £10 million. It would be a very good use of money. In the pharmaceutical industry it tends to be cell death and ageing and general types of research like that and rarely in surgery, more in medication and different types of medication or existing medication and different uses.

Professor Ballard: I think the pharmaceutical industry has a very specific remit, which is to develop products that have a marketable value and they can be successful in developing several treatments which have moderate but important clinical benefits in terms of symptoms for people with predominantly Alzheimer's disease that the same treatment might help. I think that has been important but there are huge, huge gaps. For example, earlier I mentioned vascular dementia. You would expect, because of the studies into strokes, that things like aspirin, treatment with hypertension drugs, would be effective, but those studies do not exist because there is not an economic priority to drive those studies forward and nobody is funding them either. So there is a huge gap in the market. All the companies have been very helpful in developing symptomatic treatments, but they have left big gaps and it needs a better strategy if you are going to cover the breadth of people. Most of the effort is currently going in to developing drugs which might modify the disease caused and therefore there are several studies in progress at the moment that are looking at treatment approaches. There are a number of methodological issues around how you measure that in a clinical trial that are also being wrestled with in parallel. I think the prevention studies have not really had the same emphasis. There are epidemiological studies and case control studies that have compared people who have developed dementia and who have not and who have looked at lifestyle facts and things, but the level of evidence is fairly weak from a lot of those studies because there are so many complex factors to consider that can bias the apparent findings. Carol knows this area an awful lot better than I do. There are only a handful of actual properly controlled trials that are investigating those kinds of issues, and really there is a much bigger need to invest in those kind of prevention trials, but they are long-term trials that are expensive to fund and certainly from a pharmaceutical company point of view they wouldn't be a worthwhile economic investment. So it has to be part of an overall strategy of developing treatments.

Professor Brayne: The pharmaceutical companies by definition can only address real tertiary and secondary prevention, tertiary being when the disease is manifest and secondary being more related to screening. I think the pharmaceutical companies are paying a great deal of attention to the area which might be secondary prevention and they have given a lot of attention to this category which you may have heard called mild cognitive impairment. In the category mild cognitive impairment people have been shown to be at greater risk of developing dementia on follow up. However, for an individual it is not a terribly good predictor because, depending on the setting, between a third and a half might go on to develop dementia. However, if you put that against, say, hypertension, we do the same thing, we treat people who would not have gone on to have a stroke, but we treat the hypertension in order to treat the stroke. You need a very substantial amount of evidence to justify treating large sections of the population for a possible risk of conversion to dementia over time. Judging by the conferences, the pharmaceutical companies are really focusing in on this early stage dementia. The implications of that, where they have trial results, suggest that if they reduce that conversion to dementia even by a small percentage it would be really very substantial, because it would suggest that you could go out at the primary care level and identify individuals who might be at greater risk and start treatment, in which case you have a very large population to treat. I think we need to be very aware from the public health point of view that that is a very substantial cost on the horizon if there are positive trial results coming out. There are all sorts of issues to do with screening tests. I think the pharmaceutical industry is very focused on treatment, but they are pulling it into the normal range very much at the moment from my perspective and from our population distributions. If that were applied to the population then a huge section over the age of 80 and 85 plus would be eligible to receive such medication. On primary prevention, cigarette smoking is a good example of one which is probably a risk, it is almost certainly a risk factor for dementia and so the things that are going on at the moment in order to reduce exposure to cigarettes are likely to have a beneficial effect later on. Alcohol probably has an inverse relationship with a split projection and then a risk with it. There are things happening in the population which might tell us about prevention and the impact on the population later and this is perhaps where the White Paper on public health comes in. The area of public health and neurodegenerative disease could be economised by all the clinical research networks that Clive has mentioned because they are a little bit silo based, they come out through

the cancers, diabetes and so on, but public health has common factors which run right across. Ageing fits in with that agenda really, ie what is the appropriate action that we should take in terms of research and care across these wide areas, because individuals will have diabetes and dementia and possibly cancer and so on, but the clinical research networks are in silos. So I think there is quite a concern there. The evidence on real prevention of dementia from trials has been quite disappointing. The HRT trial for dementia was stopped because it appeared that the people on HRT had a greater risk of cognitive impairment and there was a lot of debate as to why that might be. The trials for primary prevention of dementia have not really thrown up anything very positive. There is some promising work on physical exercise and cognition, but these are studies which are extremely difficult to do and they really do need stable support to be able to do them. I would hope that that is the sort of thing where, because physical activity is coming out as a general exponent for good health, we should be able to make that agenda up through the public health initiatives. I do not know exactly what is happening there, but I understand there is going to be a co-ordination of public health research to try to make it more strategic. You may know more than I do on that.

Chairman: I suspect not.

Q328 *Baroness Hilton of Eggardon:* Do you have a social class correlation in relation to dementia and lifestyle from the point of view of better nourishment, perhaps more exercise?

Professor Brayne: It is very difficult to disentangle different effects. There does appear to be an education effect. There is a difficult issue there in relation to education or lifestyle and span of life. You might have a lower risk at a particular age, but whether or not you will die with dementia may be different because you live longer. There are two issues there.

Baroness Hilton of Eggardon: It catches us in the end!

Q329 *Baroness Walmsley:* We sometimes come up with bonus effects of things. You mentioned, for example, stopping smoking reduces pulmonary disease, but it has an effect in terms of dementia. There is quite a widespread prescribing of statins at the moment to keep cholesterol down, presumably to avoid vascular disease mainly. I heard that high cholesterol presupposes people to Alzheimer's as well. Could that be an unexpected benefit, this widespread prescribing of statins?

Professor Ballard: It could be, but it needs to be evaluated much more carefully. I have seen about five epidemiological studies looking at statins. You might have seen more. Most of them seem to indicate some potential reduction of risk. However, I always get worried when the results are not consistent. If you look at the different studies, some of them suggest it is all people with dementia; some suggest it is people with just certain types of dementia; some suggest it is only certain statins or that it is all statins or all lipid lowering agents. When you have that degree of inconsistency, it makes you a little worried about what the studies are really showing. There are two studies published that were placebo control trials which appeared to show no reduction of risk, although those trials were not predominantly looking at cognitive outcomes and they were in younger people so the statistical power of the studies was limited. Nonetheless, they do not provide much support for the hypothesis. What is required is a proper study in a higher risk group of individuals with proper end points that are cognitive. Going back to what Carol said about the HRT story, one of the possible explanations for the HRT and the statins might be that people who are of higher levels of education will generally look after themselves better, have a better diet; they will be more likely to go to their GP. If they are more likely to go to their GP for statins, they are probably also more likely to go to their GP for treatment of blood pressure, so there could be quite a lot of non-specific factors which are leading to an apparent reduction of risk in those individuals, which is why I think it needs to be examined carefully.

Q330 *Lord Soulsby of Swaffham Prior:* I have three questions which are all part of one another. The first one is crystal ball gazing. What do you perceive the opportunities are for research neurodegenerative diseases over the next five to 10 years in the short term and, in the longer term, over 10 to 25 years? What are the hopes and expectations?

Professor Ballard: The Alzheimer's Society is similar to the Parkinson's Disease Society. We look at research in care, cure and cause. I do not want to neglect the care area because there is enormously important work that has been done and needs to be done. One of the priorities for me and for members of the Alzheimer's Society is to implement what we know about how to provide good quality care into practice. What happens at the moment is that isolated research studies show that if you provide care in a particular way it can dramatically improve people's quality of life or reduce the need for sedative drugs and other things. Yet, when you look around the country, that practice is almost never implemented. In terms of care there are some huge issues. In terms of more biological type work, in the last few years we have developed so much better understanding of the molecular biology of Alzheimer's disease and other dementias that it has created tremendous new opportunities. There are now a whole number of different strategies for trying

to reduce the accumulation of amyloid protein in the brain, which is in the plaques in Alzheimer's disease. One of those is the Alzheimer vaccine which has been in the press quite a lot. There are a number of other approaches to tackling the same thing. There are also a number of approaches being developed to try and stop the development of tangles in nerve cells in Alzheimer's disease and again there are some agents in clinical trials at the moment. We heard mention of stem cells earlier. To me, one of the really exciting things in the last year or so is the fact that we all have these stem cells in our own adult brains and there is some evidence that they increase in response to stroke and to Alzheimer's disease. If we understood that process better, there might be possible opportunities to increase brain self-repair, for example. This is a personal view but in terms of the biological developments I would see the anti-amyloid approaches, particularly the vaccine and some of the approaches based on enhancing self-repair through stem cells as probably the most exciting things that are likely to lead to more substantive treatments in 10 years.

Mrs Kelly: Genetics and genetic mutations translating into clinical benefits. Use of stem cells or not is very exciting. Environment factors and their role, even things like pesticides etc. Pragmatism. We have talked a lot about having exercise, stopping smoking and that sort of thing. I do not think you have to wait for research to try and get people doing that. I would like to reinforce Clive's point. There is some very good treatment around, and if 100 per cent got the very good treatment it would move up the quality of care quite significantly. That is not to negate the fact that there have been breakthroughs, but there is some stuff out there which, if we implemented it better, could help a lot of people. The other thing is gene therapy and translating that into clinical benefit. That would be our list.

Professor Brayne: With the public health hat on and the epidemiology hat on, the exciting thing for us and the reason why I went into epidemiology was the ability to take the new biological findings and see what impact and meaning they had in the population setting, to take the likelies, the most exciting things and to test out the other areas of possible causation like pesticide exposure. Because of that background, I also have the caution which is that findings are likely to be less exciting. You put them in a setting and a context so it seems less exciting because you are immediately saying, "Yes, stem cells are exciting technology." When you think about it in relation to people with dementia who are aged 85–94, it may not be appropriate. We have to have a balance. Again, it comes back to the public health type of research, taking the novel science and trying to make it meaningful for populations and having a research base ready and waiting to translate that work. We have not had that research base ready and waiting to test things out and to translate the findings. I think it is possible to create that base possibly through the clinical research networks, by having proper, decent registers of patients, good information technology to be able to model what is going to happen in the populations in the immediate and the long term future, so that we can much more quickly move from good findings to meaning at the population level. At the moment it takes us many years. I do not think that is necessary. Epidemiology is an exciting population research to be able to translate those findings into meaningful results quickly.

Q331 *Lord Soulsby of Swaffham Prior:* At the molecular biological level, what are the animal models you can use for these various conditions?
Professor Ballard: There have been tremendous developments in that. Probably the most useful model that has been used to develop most of the drugs that are currently in clinical trials has been a so-called transgenic mouse model. These are various strains of mice that carry the genes that cause early onset familial Alzheimer's disease. As these mice get to about 12 or 18 months of age or even older if they can survive longer, they will start developing some of the pathologies. They are not perfect models of Alzheimer's disease because most of these mice will develop amyloid pathology which is the protein that develops in the plaques. They will not develop some of the other changes that happen in Alzheimer's disease. People are working on refining the models and trying to cross-breed different models but nevertheless, particularly as a lot of the drugs in current development are trying to target this particular protein amyloid, this does appear to be a very useful model for investigating those drugs. People have started in the last few years using fruit flies much more widely as well. For example, there was a very exciting study that came out last year looking at treatments to try and stop the development of tangles in nerve cells in fruit flies. Obviously, given the life length of fruit flies, it is much easier to do these studies over a quicker time period. I do not think that negates the need to then look at them in mammal models but it might give you an initial way of looking at it in a relatively cost-effective way before taking it on to the next stage of development.

Q332 *Lord Soulsby of Swaffham Prior:* With respect to animal models, are there any naturally occurring animal models in the restricted genetic populations of dogs and cats and wild animals?
Mrs Kelly: Not in Parkinson's disease. It does not occur except in humans. You are initiating it with chemicals which is why it is a limited model.

Professor Ballard: I think the transgenic models are the best models at the moment. There are certainly some strains of mice that, as they get older, seem to lose nerve cells in certain parts of the brain that we can investigate, but they are probably not quite such good models for Alzheimer's disease as the transgenic models.

Q333 *Lord Soulsby of Swaffham Prior:* You mentioned the complementary activity and social gerontology. How can one interact in a complementary way with the other sciences connected with ageing like gerontology for a better understanding of some of the dementias?
Professor Ballard: It tends to take strategic development. We mentioned developing partnerships. On an *ad hoc* basis, the Alzheimer's Society has tried to do that as well. As scientists, I think we all try and develop partnerships but it is very much about people you have met, what you see and information you have seen. It just requires a much more cohesive approach to try to put together people with different major areas of expertise in order to set up a proper strategic agenda. It is mainly about communication between different people with different expertise before you can really see how you can best put those expertises together.
Mrs Kelly: We have found it very difficult to do. Our only solution has been to get people together because it is so cross-disciplinary. You are trying to get people to look at a theme. Unless you physically get them in a room and say, "This is the subject for the day" we find we fail quite badly.
Professor Brayne: There are two models which can work. One is the complex intervention model. Essentially, it is project or theme based. In our own academic department, the diabetes model has worked extremely well with physical activity in high risk individuals to prevent the onset of diabetes. In that team developing those complex interventions, which is MRC funded, they have social scientists of varying backgrounds including psychometricians, psychologists and more sociologically orientated folk to bring in that whole set of disciplines; and the epidemiologists and the triallists and the primary care physicians and academics. That has taken about five years to gestate and get to its current very strong format. The other model which can work well is something like the CFAS study. It is totally dependent on secure, stable funding over a period of time. It is a sufficiently large study that we have been able to develop themes within the work. It straddles across from the molecular end, the work done on blood or brains or whatever, right through to the policy end and legal aspects of brain donation, for example, sociological aspects of brain donation. We have been able to support a very wide range of studies because of the core theme of an ageing population in

the research which has its own core focus. We can add on lots of different things as well and that has been very successful so we are bringing people together but it is around a study to collaborate.

Baroness Walmsley: I wondered what was the potential for the big NHS online medical records project for your sort of population studies?

Q334 Chairman: Assuming for the sake of argument that it works.

Professor Brayne: It is enormous. If the data is collected accurately by the professional carers, specialists and practitioners at the ground level and entered correctly, it has the potential to transform the work that we do because we would spend so much less time trying to create the populations. In one study I did recently, it was very, very hard to recruit cases and controls of Alzheimer's disease because of the data protection laws and the whole mass of legislation. Working straight through the NHS to case registers where people have already been asked whether they are opting in, in a generic sort of way, to being approached about research would make a huge difference.

Q335 Baroness Walmsley: How long do you think it will be before that happens?

Professor Brayne: I do not know. It has been in the offing. People have been trying with IT in the NHS for some time. The technology is a lot better now but I should think, at the earliest, it must be about 10 years.

Chairman: If you have any supplementary evidence or points to make on that, we would be very interested to receive them after the session.

Q336 Lord Soulsby of Swaffham Prior: Do you think the research councils and other research funding organisations give appropriate recognition to the importance of ageing in general and to neurodegenerative diseases in particular? If not, what actions do you think should be taken or could be recommended?

Mrs Kelly: No, I do not. One of the reasons is it is such a vast area. Perhaps it would be quite helpful to pick up on some key questions and try and move some key questions forward. Then, when we have success with that, get some more key questions. The benefits of that would be three fold. One, people could see something happening. Two, it gets exciting because you get expertise in the area. You do get people with a buzz. You get people wanting to move it forward. Also, you can get lots of stakeholders involved in that which I think again is very positive. One of the challenges of neurodegenerative disease in ageing is because it is so vast and it affects so many people. It is almost overwhelming. If you could narrow it down, it would help.

Q337 Lord Soulsby of Swaffham Prior: One of the things about neurological research seems to me that it is quite long term and it is not like material where you can do your experiment in a day and a half. It takes weeks. I am familiar with the spongiform encephalopathy research and you have to wait hundreds of days until you know something. That must put a lot of people off.

Mrs Kelly: I totally agree. I think it is not right. You could have a balance of some tangible outputs, even within three to five years. That would be perfectly reasonable and again would get a sense of energy. Once you get a sense of energy, it does make things happen. When you have people saying 10 or 20 years, it is a very long time away. That is not at all to negate big studies and properly controlled studies, but we should have specific ones for specific questions and try and get a little more energy into shorter term output studies that would benefit people. It would get some enthusiasm into it and get more people involved. It would attract funding and quality people. Research does have an element of fashion about it and therefore if you get things fashionable you attract people to you.

Professor Ballard: I agree with all of that. Although you might have some longer term objectives to develop something which could be a cure or substantially change pathology, when you are looking at research studies you obviously have milestones along the way, each of which will lead to significant output. At the moment, there have been so many developments in the last few years, it is an incredibly exciting area. The difficulty is one of capacity. I do not think there has been sufficient funding allocated to it, but it depends what people want to achieve. There is a natural tendency for the number of researchers researching an area to adjust so that it is equivalent to the funding that is available. What is happening in the UK more and more is that there is a modest number of very high quality groups that are researching the area and those groups will carry on researching the area and producing some high quality output. If as a country we want to be in a position where we are making a more substantial difference to research in these areas, the funding needs to be much broader than that. We should not just be encouraging a small number of elite groups to continue to pursue their research. It is really a decision about how much we feel the UK should be contributing to this area as a whole and also the priority put on the question. When we were talking about some of the numbers earlier, 750,000 people with dementia in the UK, that is an awful lot of people. If you consider that alongside something like cancer, for example, which is also a very important question, the magnitude of funding available for cancer research is many fold above that available for dementia research.

Q338 *Chairman:* Have you any figures that could illustrate that?

Professor Ballard: Not off the top of my head. I can provide some supplementary evidence.

Chairman: We would be very interested to see that.

Q339 *Baroness Walmsley:* Do you think it is because the people with these diseases are less vocal than the people with cancer?

Professor Ballard: I am sure that is true. It is one of the reasons why charities like the Alzheimer's Society and the Parkinson's Society have been very important. Certainly for Alzheimer's disease, it was not really until the late 1970s with the setting up of campaigning organisations that people had heard of Alzheimer's disease. It is not a new disease. It has been coming for a long time but nobody had heard of it until there was an organisation to campaign for it. Even now, because the people themselves often are not in a position to be vocal and therefore rely on other people to act on their behalf, they do not have the same kind of recognition and representation that other groups of people with serious illnesses have.

Professor Brayne: Some people have commented that the age group predominantly affected has an impact on whether something is discussed at length.

Mrs Kelly: There is another important thing that we should not forget. Truly, there has been a huge move forward in understanding of the brain, mapping of the genome and everything. Particularly over the last five or 10 years, things about brains have come up. Before, if you spoke to someone with Parkinson's, the future was very bleak, whereas now there is potential hope. That allows people to be more vocal. I think there is an age component but I also think there is an available opportunity component as well. From my perspective, it is a really important time to push it. There is opportunity out there and we might not want all of it in the UK but we should grasp some of it.

Q340 *Chairman:* That is one of the possibilities for this Committee. We can make recommendations and ensure at least that those who should hear them do

hear them. If you have further thoughts on this, we would be pleased to hear them.

Professor Brayne: This comes back to the very first question you asked about: is it useful to split Alzheimer's, vascular and so on. Clearly, the labelling of Alzheimer's disease has allowed these charitable efforts to succeed. It is exponential compared to how it was in the early 1970s and 1980s. It is enormously successful but it is still dwarfed by the success of the cancer charities. In the States, they raise a lot of money. It probably is not equivalent to cancer but there is a lot more money for Alzheimer's research. The only problem about it is the need to keep enfranchised those individuals who receive other types of diagnosis, where people say, "I am not sure if it is Alzheimer's or something else", or the vascular dementia groups, who feel sometimes almost excluded from the debate about Alzheimer's disease.

Professor Ballard: That is true. The Alzheimer's Society would recognise that as well. There has been a big campaign about vascular dementia that has recently started. It becomes a bit of a dilemma because, at one level, people now know what Alzheimer's disease is, so it is easy to talk about and people recognise it. I think it does lead to other people being neglected. If you look in the research literature, be that basic science or clinical trials, there is an incredible paucity of work looking at people with vascular dementia compared with those with Alzheimer's disease. Even within the Cinderella area of research, there is a Cinderella group within the Cinderella area.

Chairman: May I thank the three of you very much indeed for giving us of your time and expert opinions. Can I re-emphasise my invitation? If there are any points that occur to you following this discussion where you could provide more specific information, please let us know. Our process is that we will begin drafting within a few weeks so, if there is anything that you want to draw to our attention, the sooner the better. Once again, thank you very much for a very helpful session.

TUESDAY 1 FEBRUARY 2005

Present	Drayson, L	Oxburgh, L
	Emerton, B	Soulsby of Swaffham Prior, L
	Hilton of Eggardon, B	Sutherland of Houndwood, L
	Mitchell, L	(Chairman)
	Murphy, B	Walmsley, B

Examination of Witnesses

Witnesses: PROFESSOR ROSE ANNE KENNY, Head of the Falls and Syncope Unit, Royal Victoria Infirmary, Newcastle upon Tyne; MR MIKE BRACE, Chief Executive, Vision 2020 UK; PROFESSOR KAREN STEEL, Principal Investigator, Wellcome Trust Sanger Institute; and PROFESSOR DESMOND O'NEILL, Professor in Medical Gerontology, Trinity College Dublin, examined.

Q341 Chairman: May I say welcome and thank you very much for being willing to give us time and also for the written evidence with which some of you are associated that has come in. It is much valued and much appreciated. The work of the Committee is probably about halfway through. We have had panels of witnesses every week or two weeks since the autumn. We have visited the NIH and the National Institute on Aging in Washington and we have had a significant volume of written research. We hope that our report will be out in the early summer. The report carries no legislative power with it at all but what it can do, however, is stimulate those who have the capacity and power to make policy and point to where we are in the UK in terms of the development of the appropriate science and scientific abilities and comment, as I am sure we will, on research strategy, how the money is being spent, is it being well spent, is it being proportionately allocated, and all that sort of thing. This is the range of issues. Our two main areas of science have been, significantly, biological and medical aspects of ageing but also assistive technologies and the quality of life that we hope will be possible for those as we grow older who experience various forms of frailty. My name is Sutherland and I am Chairman of the Committee. My colleagues will introduce themselves as they raise questions and say who they are and, equally, if you would as you first speak introduce yourselves and perhaps indicate your background. Then we will happily move into the question and answer session. If at the end of that you believe there are issues that you would like to expand on we would be very happy to receive electronic or written additional comment. May I start with an initial question which in the end has to do with the question of whether as we grow older inevitably frailty of one form or another is our fate: sensory impairment, tendency to fall, difficulty coping with complex tasks, perhaps intellectual limitations, problems with driving, all sort of ways in which it seems to show itself. The broad question is is it inevitable that one or other or some of these befall

most of us or all of us and what therefore is the challenge from the changing demography and longevity becoming a much more common feature of life? If you would like to perhaps go along the table and just respond to the issue of whether frailty is inevitable, what does it do to our perception of longevity, and how are we coping? Professor O'Neill, do you want to start?

Professor O'Neill: My name is Professor Desmond O'Neill. I am a Professor of Medical Gerontology at Trinity College Dublin. I have a particular interest in older people, transport and driving. My answer to that would that frailty is less inevitable than it was. There is very good evidence from Manton's work and similar studies that disability has been dropping among older Americans, for example, at a rate of one and a half per cent a year, so the trajectory of the curve has been flattening. Whether this will be sustained with the younger generation is open to question but there are a number of interventional studies. For example, the observational studies of the Oxfordshire Stroke Project expected an extra one-third in the number of strokes in the Oxfordshire region and reported this year one-fifth less than had been in the previous study. So just as death and taxes are inevitable some frailty will be inevitable, but I think it is very important to get the message out to the public that frailty in old age is not always inevitable. With appropriate public health policies and indeed some of the secular changes, if we are going to be humble about that, this frailty can be deferred and that the period of frailty should be ever smaller.

Q342 Chairman: Fine. I should have reminded you that we are on air. We are not being broadcast at the moment but we might be so your comments may be noted by a wider audience than this one, especially if they are *sotto voce* as some of them are. Before we move along the table can I press you a little bit on that. We have been getting quite a number of folk who are in the statistics field saying that longevity is increasing but the quality of healthy long life is not increasing at the same rate, which seems to run a little counter to what you are saying, and we would be very interested in the relevant papers you mentioned.

Professor O'Neill: I would be delighted.

Professor Steel: I am Karen Steel. I work at the Wellcome Trust Sanger Institute which is near Cambridge, but for 25 years I worked for the MRC Institute of Hearing Research in Nottingham alongside colleagues who were working on clinical aspects of hearing. My particular research interest is in the genetics of deafness. That is why I am at the Sanger Institute and I have been there for about 18 months now. To your question, hearing impairment (which is my main interest) has long been viewed as an inevitable consequence of growing old among not only the medical profession but also the man in the street, and so very often people do not complain about it as much as they should as they are getting older, and indeed there is research that suggests that elderly people are much more reluctant to complain about a set level of hearing impairment compared to younger people. Thus the reporting is not adequate and the seeking of services is not adequate. My personal belief is that hearing impairment with age is not essential and is not necessary, but I have to say that is a belief rather than being based on firm evidence at the moment. This is the concept that drives my own research interests, that one day we will have enough information to be able to develop treatments, not just prosthetic devices which is what we have at the moment, hearing aids or cochlear implants, but one day we will be able to develop real treatments to prevent or slow down the onset of hearing loss with age. So that is my approach to the research in deafness.

Q343 *Chairman:* Can I ask you about the connection between that, which seems to have to do very much with the physical activity of hearing, and your background in genetics.

Professor Steel: I use genetics as a tool. Genetics is a tool, it gives you clues to the molecules involved in normal hearing processes and molecules that are dysfunctional when people start to lose their hearing. It is not research that is only ever going to be applicable to people who have a single gene defect and are born deaf. That is certainly not true. But a lot of the basic research we are doing at the moment is on those genes because those are very easy to detect, particularly using animal models, and most of this work can only be done with animal models. It is a tool. It has a much broader relevance because it tells you what biochemical pathways are involved in these processes. That information is relevant to everybody who is losing their hearing, which means most of us as we get older. It is not specifically related to single gene defects. We all have genes and those genes affect

all of us in different ways. So it is the underlying information that we need to have.

Chairman: That is very helpful.

Q344 *Lord Oxburgh:* Could I pursue that for one second. My name is Ron Oxburgh. I am not entirely clear whether you are saying that this is a natural process which you anticipate some time in the future we might be able to intervene to remedy, or whether you are actually implying that this is a disease which affects some and not others.

Professor Steel: That is a very interesting question. I think it is a philosophical question rather than a scientific question. I guess it is not natural for most of us to be living as long as we do nowadays. A lot of our daily life is not natural in any respect. So I suppose if you are talking about disease, yes, there are some cases where hearing impairment is clearly part of a disease process and maybe you could distinguish those cases from people who do preserve their hearing until fairly late in their lives, but I think they are just the ends of a spectrum and we should not just sit back and think it is inevitable. That is really the message I want to get over and if people think progressive hearing loss is inevitable then the research will not be done, because the will will not be there and the funding will not be there to do the research to develop treatments. So I do not think we should think of it as inevitable but, as I said, that is an item of faith.

Q345 *Lord Oxburgh:* I was not making any assumption about inevitability or otherwise, simply the observation that there is a syndrome of characteristics which people seem to acquire with advancing age, and loss of hearing is one of those.

Professor Steel: Can I make a comment on that. I think that hearing, like many other aspects of our life, is subject to some generic attacks that life throws at us, including everything that we do in life like working in noisy environments and eating and drinking and doing all the things we perhaps should not do quite so much of. I think that is inevitably going to affect not just hearing but other aspects of our ageing process, but I do not think progressive age-related hearing impairment is entirely due to those generic influences on our lives. There are going to be a lot of very specific factors that contribute towards progressive hearing impairment as we get older. Although things like cognitive decline can affect a lot of people (and cognitive decline probably does interact in some way that is not yet determined with hearing impairment) that does not necessarily mean that the two go alongside and at the same rate. The same with all the other senses as well. There are going to be some very specific factors—the variants of genes that we carry, for example, or environmental influences that specifically affect hearing—and other effects that are much more generic and affect lots of other functions as well.

Q346 *Chairman:* Professor Kenny?

Professor Kenny: I am Rose Anne Kenny. I am Professor of Geriatric Medicine in Newcastle at the Institute for Ageing and Health and Head of the Falls and Syncope, which is a blackout unit in Newcastle which is probably one of the biggest in Europe. So that is my expertise. I am going to take the discussion back just to clarify what is meant by frailty and what I understand by frailty if I could. Frailty is one of three things: the symptoms of frailty, as we understand it as clinicians, are fatigue, weakness, inability to mobilise; the signs are immobility, weight loss; and the consequences are decrease in functional activity, institutionalisation and death. That is what we mean by frailty. Very often it is confused with two other things—disability and co-morbidity (other illnesses). Whereas the prevalence of disability and co-morbidity is common in the frail person I have just described; it is not inevitable that people with co-mobility are frail or that those who have a disability are frail. Then if we come back to one of the signs of frailty which is weight loss and muscle mass loss and bone mass loss—sarcopenia—they are core to frailty and how we visualise a frail person. We know that we lose muscle mass at about one to two per cent a year; the bad news is once we hit 40. If you compare athletes in their 70s and non-athletes in their 70s, their rate of loss is the same but they start from a higher standard. We can actually influence that sort of loss by strengthening exercise programmes. We can rejuvenate muscle mass by a 15-year equivalent with a three-month exercise programme. So whereas there are physiological, age-related changes which we sometimes confuse with frailty, it is possible to influence those changes and possible, if we get in early enough, to raise the threshold at which we can influence those inevitable age-related changes.

Q347 *Chairman:* Mr Brace?

Mr Brace: I am Mike Brace. I am Chief Executive of Vision 2020 UK which is the UK branch, for want of a better word, of Vision 2020 which is a World Health Organization initiative with three basic aims: to decrease preventable blindness throughout the world; to get better professional support and better services for those where it is not avoidable; and really to raise public awareness on the whole issue to do with visual impairment. I co-ordinate the UK organisation which has now got 40 members across medical statutory organisations of visual impaired and the not-for-profit sector. I am not a researcher. I was blinded from a firework when I was ten so my interest is purely what is going to be around for me in the next few years. I have got quite a personal interest but also a professional one in terms of my work. For me, following from what the others have said, it is this whole thing about inevitability and it is also around managing expectations. If your expectation is frailty then I think the issue is that as your body starts to lose some of its functionality it is also then linked to what you expect to be able to do. Many visually impaired people—and we think there are about four and a quarter to four and a half million people with a significant sight loss and of that we reckon that 70 per cent are over 65 so it is a fairly significant issue for visual impairment and ageing—have an expectation that being old means "I cannot see and therefore I cannot do". For us that is one of the biggest single factors when you go into people's homes. They have an amazing level of ability left which is untapped, unused and unnurtured. If their physical deterioration is because they are not able to go and do the walks or do the things they had previously done, they have physical deterioration, but if they do the same on things like reading, stretching their mind, the using of computers, whatever, and if they think that is not possible when it is, then basically there is a loss of expectation of what life has to offer them. We think that very clearly links into a deterioration in their ability then to cope with the frailty or with the ageing process that is happening within them.

Chairman: Thank you very much. Baroness Walmsley?

Q348 *Baroness Walmsley:* When I was a little girl I was a voracious reader and I used to read under the bedclothes when I went to bed at night and my mother used to say to me, "You will ruin your eyes". I do not believe that is true and I do not think we are going to be faced by an epidemic of people who used to read under the bedclothes. However, we do have a younger generation who play music very loudly and I am of the generation that says, "You will ruin your ears"! What I want to know is, is that likely to present us with more of a problem of hearing impairment than we have had in the past, and are there any other life choices that people make that might present us with some of these sorts of difficulties in the future?

Professor Steel: I can comment on that. We all know very well that excess noise damages our hearing. Damage to our hearing is a one-way process because we are born with a set of sensory cells within our inner ear that are not replaced when they die, and any noise damage or any other sort of damage that damages them and makes those cells die leads to irreparable longer term damage. It is a one-way process basically and we never regenerate these sensory hair cells. The level of sound is obviously very important and the length of time of exposure is very important. People have looked very hard for evidence that using

Walkmans and other personal amplification systems does damage to hearing. There is actually limited evidence of that at the moment but then most of these are used by very young people and so their hearing is fairly robust and at a normal level, and some small amount of physical damage within the ear would not be noticed perceptually yet, but who knows what is going to happen in the future and whether those people will be more likely to be losing their hearing ability later on in life. I think we should take it seriously but certainly not put limiters on amplification devices because that would be a bit cruel to our youngsters. The other thing I would say is everybody varies. We already know of a number of different variants of genes that make certain individuals more susceptible to environmentally induced damage to their ears than other individuals, and so what might be true for one person and what might be a safe level of noise exposure for one person is not necessarily going to be the same for another person. We do need to be very careful. A lot of hearing impairment is an interaction between our genetics—our genome and the genes we carry and the variants of those genes that we carry—and the environment that we are exposed to. So I am not being alarmist but we should be careful about noise exposure.

Q349 *Baroness Hilton of Eggardon:* I am Jenny Hilton. I think quite a lot of my question has already been answered on hearing and vision but I wondered whether you could outline specifically the major causes of hearing loss. You have already talked about loss of hair cells, cochlear and so on. I think there is some evidence from heavy industry that exposure to heavy machinery does cause hearing loss. What other major causes of hearing loss are there? Also if I could couple that with loss of visual ability and ask what specifically produces failing sight in elderly people and what treatments are possible at present and in the future?

Professor Steel: Yes, in talking about age-related hearing impairment the true answer is that we know virtually nothing about the causes of hearing impairment as people get older. We know nothing at a molecular level and practically nothing at a cellular level but we do know some things that are important. For example, there are three independent studies now that have demonstrated that age-related hearing impairment has heritability of about 50 per cent. What that means is that about half of the hearing impairment is something to do with the variants of the genes we carry and the remaining half is probably due to environmental factors. Noise is almost inevitably going to be one of those, but we should not forget drugs, we should not forget infections as well because these can also affect hearing, and I suspect

that diet may have an effect. So we actually know very little. There is the start of some research going on but it is really very much at its early stages, and there is an awfully long way to go before we will fully understand the causes in an individual. The one other thing I should point out is that deafness, whether you are looking at childhood deafness or age-related hearing impairment, is very heterogeneous. There are lots of different causes. You can have ten people in the room all with the same level of hearing impairment and they can all have completely different reasons for their hearing impairment. So we do need to be very careful about generalising. This also means that diagnosis is critical because you cannot even start to think of treatments before you can diagnose because you may be treating the wrong thing, the wrong part of the inner ear, the wrong part of the process, so diagnostics are really important and there is virtually nothing that is being done at a physiological level of diagnostics. There is a little bit done on genetics but only in childhood deafness at the moment. Shall I move on to treatments?

Q350 *Chairman:* I wonder if Mr Brace wants to come in.

Mr Brace: In terms of vision, one of the key factors obviously is age-related macular degeneration and the complexities of there being a wet and a dry type of macular degeneration which has obviously created issues, because when certain treatments then become available like photo-dynamic therapy it is only applicable for certain aspects of age-related macular degeneration. You are one of the several thousand people out there and it is not appropriate for your expectation to be raised, because you think suddenly that there is a potential way of arresting your sight loss. Cataracts is obviously a significant issue and the recent Government initiative on cataracts has really been welcomed because there have been many thousands of people whose blindness or lack of sight has been reduced if not completely taken away by earlier operations for cataracts. The other two key areas are around early diagnosis of diabetic retinopathy so in terms of early treatment and understanding through diabetes how it affects the eye can obviously affect that quite significantly. The other one is glaucoma which is probably one of the most critical areas because if not diagnosed early it can be then quite critical. Those are probably the four key ones. There are obviously a number of congenital and other eye complaints but I think those are probably the four that feature most with the older or ageing population.

Q351 *Chairman:* Professor Steel, did you want to come back in on the treatment side?

Professor Steel: At the moment there are no treatments available. There are two prosthetic approaches. One is cochlear implants which are only suitable for severe or profound hearing impairment, so there is a limited population they will be helpful for. The other is hearing aids, and hearing aids are again limited in their usefulness because it is not just amplification that you need, it is more clarity, and again we know there is a real gap in the research on how to programme hearing aids to take account of the needs of individuals which includes their own specific requirements, how normal people process speech and other sounds that they need to understand, and also the ecology and the requirements of individual people. Hearing aids are very useful but nowhere near as useful as they should be and could be if we knew more about how to programme them. Treatment is something that I am very keen to work towards developing. I am thinking more of medical treatments so it is all fantasy at the moment, whatever you might read in the newspapers. I think that gene therapy in its simplest form is unlikely to be a useful approach for deafness. Approaches to try to trigger either introduced stem cells or native cells that are present within the inner ear to regenerate and reform the sensory epithelium within the inner ear are very useful approaches and those are some of the approaches that we will be using. A third one that is not often talked about is drug treatment. Drugs by definition are designed to get easy access to what is the very inaccessible structure of the inner ear. We could think about whether drugs could be used, for example, to regulate alternative genes that could do jobs that other genes are not doing properly or to trigger regeneration using drugs. These are all ideas but they are only glimmers in people's eyes at the moment. They are not available; there are no treatments available.

Q352 *Chairman:* Can I just follow up on the question of hearing aids. It sounds like a problem of technological research essentially, in which case can you give us some indication of the size of the market, if you like, because very often that is what drives technology?

Professor Steel: Yes, I can. In the UK there are probably getting on for nine million people who have a significant hearing impairment in one ear or the other. At least half of those, say four million, would definitely benefit from using a hearing aid. At the moment about 1.5 million people have a hearing aid but the use of those hearing aids is less than half so half of those people are not using the hearing aid for most of the time, and there is a very good reason for that; they are not much good. For some people they are fine but for others they are not doing the job they need to do so they end up in cupboards and drawers

not being used fully. That is a great shame and I think there really is a gap in research, not just on amplifying and amplifying particular frequencies but how can we code the sound that is coming in to give better frequency resolution and particularly better temporal resolution. A lot of our interpretation of sounds and understanding of speech and localising of sounds uses temporal qualities. When I say temporal I mean things that are changing within microseconds, not even milliseconds, and that is something that people normally take for granted. They can resolve microsecond differences in sounds when they come from different parts of the room but when you start to lose your hearing that is something that is lost and that is something that hearing aids at the moment are not reproducing very well, so there is a lot more research that needs to be done. This is basic research because the basic research needs to be done before it can be applied by hearing aid companies to develop the hearing aids to serve these purposes.

Chairman: That is very interesting. Lord Soulsby?

Q353 *Lord Soulsby of Swaffham Prior:* I could not do without wearing a hearing aid. I am Lord Soulsby. Can we turn to the issue of falling in older people. How well understood are the causes of falling and are falls mainly the result of generalised frailty or are there underlying issues such as diseases of the semi-circular canal and things like that? Also it is a question of balance which might come back to the semi-circular canal situation. What is the issue with ageing and frailty and falling?

Professor Kenny: Briefly putting it into context, in the UK 30 per cent of those over 65 will fall at least once a year and 40 per cent of those over 75 will fall at least twice a year. So it is a common problem. That is the first thing. It is also the commonest reason cited for admission to institutional care. That gives you both ends of the spectrum. For 40 per cent of admissions to nursing homes or residential homes in the UK the top reason cited is falls. Part of the first question around frailty and age-related physiological changes relates to falls because one of the best known, commonest and earliest identified risk factors for falls is muscle weakness, loss of muscle power, muscle strength and flexibility. Just to give you some feel for that, there was a recent study at the Royal Free which looked at muscle strength in males and females between 70 and 75 (so what I would consider "young" males and females) and it found that 50 per cent of females and 15 per cent of males were unable to mount a 30 cm step without holding on to a handrail. These are community-living people. It found that 80 per cent of females and half of men between 70 and 75 were not able to walk at a pace of three miles per hour. And 80 per cent of females and half of the men had limitation of their shoulder movement such that they could not comfortably wash their hair. So that is the sort of level of muscle strength impairment we are dealing with and that is one of the commonest causes of falls and why falls are such a common age-related problem. Then there are other risk factors such as the environment. They are self-evident things such as poor lighting, and that of course touches on the area of vision, and balance, which very frequently goes hand-in-hand with hearing impairment and about which we know very little. There are cardiovascular causes such as intermittent drops in blood pressure (which is particularly common now with the drive for aggressive treatment of high blood pressure and heart problems) and a slow heart rate or a fast heart rate. Those are the common causes of falls. A number of them are treatable. Most people who have recurrent falls have more than one risk factor. So the most successful treatment programmes are what we call multi-factorial where you target the top four or five risk factors for an individual. Despite all of that, at best, from the multi-factorial prevention studies, we would only reduce falls by 30 per cent. So there are lots of issues around falls and particularly recurrent falls that we do not understand completely on how these factors interplay. I think that is more or less your question.

Q354 *Lord Soulsby of Swaffham Prior:* But the consequence of a fall, apart from the distress, is maybe the fracture of a limb or damage to muscles. Very often it has been said that for women who fall and break the neck of their femur the chances of survival are low, due to the fact you get embolisms and other disastrous situations such as that when they have to go into hospital and have their femurs pinned and so on.
Professor Kenny: That is one factor. Again it is a spectrum of things. Almost half of women who have a neck of hip fracture never achieve their pre-fracture level of independence or ability for activities of daily living. That is a pretty remarkable figure. The mortality rates are improving with hip fracture. I am focusing on hip fracture because that is the expensive one and that is the one with the heaviest consequences. It is 20 per cent one year mortality now whereas it was about 35 per cent 10 years ago. So mortality rates from hip fracture surgery are improving. There are other important consequences like institutionalisation, social isolation, loss of independence, cognitive impairment and dementia as a result of the operative procedure, but also some of the causes of falls if they are due to intermittent low blood pressures can trigger neuro-degenerative processes—Alzheimer's and vascular dementia.

Q355 *Lord Soulsby of Swaffham Prior:* Maybe one of the reasons older people do fall is because they trip up as they tend to shuffle more rather than high step.
Professor Kenny: Yes and that comes back to muscle strength, muscle power and what we were saying earlier on about gait and balance and stability which increases in prevalence as we get older. That is back to our original point that you will lose muscle mass inevitably but if your starting point of muscle mass is at a fairly maximum threshold then the relative loss will be less apparent.

Q356 *Baroness Murphy:* I am Elaine Murphy and I am particularly interested to follow up on Lord Soulsby's question on falls. Going back to primary prevention and secondary prevention, I would be interested to hear what Professor Kenny and Professor O'Neill have to say about the emphasis on developing falls clinics, for example, of which I have visited many in the last year or two. I have become a bit sceptical about what it is I am seeing is happening and whether or not there is any evidence that actually they are making any difference. They are raising the tone of expectations and awareness amongst primary care physicians and that is an excellent thing, but are we actually doing any good? What is the role of treating falls?
Professor Kenny: I too am concerned. There is an agenda to have falls clinics up and running by April this year in the UK. The actual details of the falls clinics vary considerably from place to place and the breadth of assessment and intervention also varies such that in some facilities there is a single physiotherapy assessment or a very precursory nursing assessment, and it stops at that. That comes back to our original point, particularly in recurrent falls which are the ones most at risk of having fractures and institutionalisation ultimately, that there are multiple risk factors and there is evidence showing that targeting a single risk factor will not reduce significantly subsequent fall rates. It has to be a comprehensive assessment with multi-factorial interventions but even then we will still only reduce falls overall by 30 per cent, and the level of input to achieve that in terms of physiotherapy for example is a physiotherapy session weekly for three months in the first instance and that must be sustained, and that is in a research environment. Do we know whether or not falls clinics will make an impact on falls rates and ultimately fracture rates and institutionalisation in the UK? No.

Q357 *Baroness Murphy:* What is the mechanism? What is a physiotherapist doing? Is she altering the awareness of the proprioception of where one's limbs are and encouraging the practice of balance? What is going on?

Professor Kenny: What is recommended is first of all an initial assessment of where the major deficits are, but generically to answer your question, power exercises, strengthening exercises, flexibility and balance are all very important. It has to be those four components for it to be effective, in varying degrees for individuals.

Q358 *Baroness Murphy:* That is very helpful.

Mr Brace: I was going to add into that the pre-factors. The Pocklington Trust have done some research and certainly that has mentioned lighting in terms of the ability of people to see that little bit better to avoid the fall in the first place as a key aspect, but also so is contrast. That is where a lot of the social care assessments of people with visual impairment are looking. They are looking at lighting and contrast as being very key factors. The third element is poor design. Talking to an elderly person recently, they could not find a top-loading washing machine. They are all low-loading which means crouching or leaning forward which means a chance then of her feeling giddy. Trying to find a top-loading washing machine, something as simple as that, is a major difficulty that could affect a number of people. There are a number of other examples. The poor positioning of flexes and plugs on the floor rather than at waist height which means again you have got to get down on the floor to stick a plug in which potentially can add to the risk of a fall. So it is very simple things that are almost very practical things that could make a significant impact for those with a visual impairment who are then more likely to fall.

Q359 *Lord Mitchell:* My name is Parry Mitchell. I would like to ask a question on the subject of driving and really the most common reasons why an older person may have to stop driving. Of course related to that is by what criteria are these judgments made and by whom.

Professor O'Neill: The most common reason in the developed world is for health reasons and very often it is self regulated by older drivers, and all the evidence suggests that they possibly over-compensate here and withdraw from driving ahead of significant disability. All the crash data suggests that older drivers are the safest drivers and this is largely accounted for by strategic decisions on driving, limiting driving at night, for example, and in bad weather, and avoiding complex traffic situations, and by withdrawing prematurely from driving. There is major concern that this may be the key issue around driving but for the moment self-regulation seems to be effective certainly from a public health/safety point of view.

Q360 *Chairman:* On that I speak as someone who lives in the countryside where there are no buses. Is people withdrawing from driving earlier than they need going to be a major problem?

Professor O'Neill: This is a hugely important issue and clearly the balance has to be got right. One does not quite know what the secular trend will be in that those who are older drivers now have somewhat more restricted access. For example, we can see there was a jump of 600 per cent in older women drivers between 1965 and 1985 largely because of the entry of older entrants into the driving system, but everything points still to the fact that older people tend to be very sensible and there are concerns because not only are there issues around the provision of these services, but also public bus services as they stand may not be suitable for older people in terms of concerns about carrying shopping and concerns about safety. Indeed, one of the most important areas for future research will be assistive transportation of the Dial-a-Ride type which has been very successful for example in Portland Maine and has helped older drivers to graduate from driving into a supported environment.

Q361 *Lord Mitchell:* The driving age expires at 70. With that sort of age beginning to be on the horizon, it is something we all think about. Is that the right age given changes in demography and whatever? Does it need to be reviewed?

Professor O'Neill: There has been some very helpful research in the last few years suggesting that attention to age as some kind of parameter for safety is now a redundant and probably an ageist concept. The state in Australia that has no check whatsoever on older drivers is the state that has least accidents amongst older people, both pedestrians and in the car. In Scandinavia, the country that has no screening for older drivers has the highest level of transportation and the highest level of safety among older people. I think there is increasingly compelling evidence that we should be directing our attention elsewhere and this is an inheritance from perhaps an ageist view of older people with disability very much to the fore. This is probably why I started the piece I sent in with a La Rochefoucauld quote because people tended to concentrate on the *plus fou* and forget about the *plus sage*.

Q362 *Baroness Walmsley:* To what extent does frailty in any of these areas contribute to other health problems that might develop in older people, for example by limiting their activity and their social engagement? I do not know who wants to start on that one.

Mr Brace: I mentioned earlier on I think it is a very significant area. If the level of independence is lost because of either physical problems—for example, in the group I am looking at visual impairment—it may stop them in their lives from doing things they previously have done like walking, like reading, like knitting, a whole range of activities which have kept them in either a degree of physical or mental activity. The consequences of that are very often growing social isolation and therefore growing issues to do with care, to do with perception of the world, to do with potential mental health issues, because basically the rooms are around them all the time and there is no outlet for that. Many visually impaired people for instance, in common with other ageing people, do not want to go out at night so it is then linked to what is available during the daytime, that you have got accessible transport to, that then makes you feel welcome, and that can explain to you what is going on. Even down to joining a yoga class. If you do not know what the yoga exercises are and you need someone to continually show you what to do, that needs a bit of pre-planning which often does not exist so that puts you off and therefore you do not go.

Professor Steel: Can I comment on hearing. There is some research that has been done that suggests that social withdrawal is one of the tactics that people with deteriorating hearing use deliberately to avoid embarrassment, among other things. For about 35 per cent of the people that is their main tactic, and it is probably a lesser tactic for others in this study. So social withdrawal is a very significant consequence of progressive loss of hearing and everything that goes with that—not going out, not exercising so much because that involves going out, all of those social contacts that mean you are still part of the human race, and the psychological and in some cases psychiatric problems that do follow from social withdrawal, so it is an important issue.

Q363 *Baroness Walmsley:* Can I follow that up and ask is there a stigma attached to hearing impairment and is that one of the reasons why people do not report and do not want to wear a hearing aid because it tells the world that they are hearing impaired?

Professor Steel: I think there still is. Hearing aids are not fashion accessories in the way that glasses have become much more acceptable in every day life. It used to be that people did not like wearing glasses either but hearing aids have not quite got to that level yet and I think there is a still the common deaf and dumb association, which of course is far from the truth. So I think it is part of the people's expectations that they expect to lose their hearing as they get older, they do not complain about it as much as they should, and they do not go out and try to do something about it and get a suitable prosthetic

device like a hearing aid. I think there are a lot of social reasons for trying to make it more acceptable.

Q364 *Baroness Walmsley:* It sounds as if there is am amazing market to make fashionable hearing aids.

Mr Brace: I think some people accept the word old but they less accept the word disabled and therefore it is question of which is the worse stigma—being regarded as old or being regarded as disabled and for many the word disabled is still the worst of the two options.

Professor Steel: Walkmans are very common amongst the young and if we could get industry to develop one which looked just like a Walkman so that people looked as if they were using a Walkman.

Baroness Walmsley: Or a Bluetooth mobile phone.

Q365 *Chairman:* We look for the first diamond-studded hearing aid!

Professor Kenny: In the context of falls, one of the earliest consequences is fear of falling particularly if falls are unexplained, and that of course leads to isolation, loss of independence, and that leads to depression, and all of those feed in ultimately to this frailty cascade and an increase in fall rates.

Professor O'Neill: There are a number of studies now to show older people who have retired from driving are more prone to depression and feel socially isolated. I think this is important.

Q366 *Chairman:* I also have the next question which really follows on from that which is to what extent are the problems associated with frailty the result more of an inadequate environment than that of intrinsic deterioration? If the environment were suitably improved, could the problems be significantly reduced or delayed? Is there any reliable evidence about this?

Professor Steel: Yes, I think there is quite a lot that can be done to the environment. One of the main problems that people who are starting to lose their hearing have is understanding speech when there is a lot of background noise so there is quite a lot that can be done to reduce background noise. If that is traffic then double glazing helps. Having rooms which are designed with good acoustics (which often they are not and they have a lot of reverberation) reducing that reverberation by having lots of soft furnishings, for example, all of that helps. Also having bright lighting helps because a lot of people who are losing their hearing get a great deal of benefit from lip reading. They do not know they are doing it necessarily but they do get a lot from lip reading. You need bright light to be able to see people's lips and body language as well. There are a lot of things that people can do when they are in a listening situation either with a hearing impaired person or as a hearing impaired person themselves. There are a lot of tactics they can use. For example, introducing subjects so that people have an idea of the context before they start talking about a subject helps a lot. Speaking very clearly and facing the person, making sure you are in bright light, there are lots of strategies that can be used. There is a hearing tactics programme that the MRC Institute of Hearing Research developed a few years ago that was distributed quite widely. It has some very useful tips. Some of those tips are to do with environment so there is a lot that can be done.

Chairman: This is naughty but I cannot help it. Remembering the famous Granita Restaurant (or is it infamous?) where the great discussion took place between two senior politicians, it has terrible acoustics and there is not a piece of soft furnishing in the place, so perhaps the whole future of our political debate has been thus determined. I should not say things like that and I will pass back to Baroness Walmsley to be sensible.

Q367 *Lord Mitchell:* You mean one said "yes" and the other said "fine"?

Professor O'Neill: The issue of environment and frailty is hugely important and perhaps the area I would know particularly well would be around the older pedestrian. It is hugely clear from particularly the Netherlands that redesigning the traffic environment to facilitate older pedestrians results in quite a big drop in fatalities and serious injuries. We could design car safety features such as seat belts, which are designed for 30-year-old 70-kilogram adults rather than a frail older person, so there is more room for play. A very tangible area and a current one is perhaps sports utility vehicles. By allowing sports utility vehicles without a warning sticker, people may not be aware that their chance of killing an older pedestrian increases by over 70 per cent for a compact SUV and over 150 per cent for a large SUV. Again I think a simple issue about the environment, if you put a warning sticker then civic-minded drivers might be mindful of such warnings.

Q368 *Baroness Walmsley:* Mr Brace, do you have any comment about the environment?

Mr Brace: A number of areas. Some of it is not rocket science either, things like contrast. If you have got failing sight and you are trying to chase a white potato on a white plate on a white tablecloth it is not surprising that you run into difficulties, but if you have a blue plate and a white potato and a white tablecloth you can straightaway see where the plate is and where the potato is, so there are similar very simple things that could be done that would make life easier. My biggest issue really is in design. We are in danger of setting major issues for ourselves for the future because we are not thinking now. The 50-year-olds of today are probably the first semi computer literate generation. People like me who have started using computers 15 or 20 years ago and are struggling but are there and use them every day. In 20 years' time when the majority of vision impaired people are coming that will be the thing that they will want to continue to use, so it is inclusive design on a whole range of things, whether it be phones or screens you can easily read or have talking options, whether it be the way things are displayed in stations. Most people, whether they have got full sight or not, cannot read the indicator boards so increasingly you have got the embarrassment of asking someone where the next train is going from because the boards are too high and are in dot matrix print which half the people cannot see. It is silly things like that. A thing that affected me massively was the craze for touch pads on machinery so you did not have a button, you had a touch pad where you put your finger roughly near the area you wanted to locate and it would come up. If you are blind you cannot do that. Straightaway I am restricted about the range of products and the issues that I have. You cannot get instructions in any format that you can use easily. The list goes on. We need some sensible way forward. We are looking at design now of the internet access points. It is a major step forward to have text options and to have screens and everything for the internet that people can easily read. That will affect thousands of people in the future because it is those groups now that will be going blind in ten years' time but will still want to have internet access in a format that they can read.

Q369 *Baroness Walmsley:* Professor Kenny?

Professor Kenny: In the wider context of frailty the immediate environment impacts on fall rates in older persons. A person will often say that they tripped on their stone step going out in the garden or on a loose rug in the home, a grandchild's toy is common, lighting (and we have spoken about that) at the end of steep stairs, et cetera. In the wider environment, I think that our changing wider environment increases the chance of frailty in older persons by denying older persons access to local facilities, and enjoyable access to local facilities. My local post office has no seating and on a Thursday morning and Monday morning there are rows of older people standing. I am waiting for one to lose consciousness because I know half of them at least are on cardiovascular medication and they are standing for up to three quarters of a hour with no support. Simple little things like that about the local environment. That is the post offices that are still open. That is the local shops that are still open. Reducing all of those wider environmental access areas decreases mobility, increases social isolation, and increases depression. They are some of the factors which we know contribute to frailty in the original classification of the word which we discussed earlier. So the immediate environment is important but our wider environment is also very important. There is no evidence to support what I am saying to my knowledge.

Q370 *Baroness Walmsley:* Can I sweep up a question to all of you really based on what you have been saying. Clearly there is a lot that can be done and a lot of strategies that people can use if they have any of these frailties to help them continue their lives, apart from the re-opening of the post offices; we cannot do that. What do you think of the way in which we inform people about these things? How well do we do in terms of letting older people know what they can do to help themselves and what their families can do and how they can improve their environment to enable them to lead full lives even when they have these frailties?

Professor O'Neill: I think the answer is poorly, and again you could trail North America in this regard. If you go for example to a book shop in North America there are about 25 books on how to cope with and conquer the downsides of ageing and emphasising the positive sides, which is important. That has to be part of the issue because ageing is growth and loss at all ages, and in America people are better at bringing out the positive sides of ageing. I happen to be writing a book for the Irish market at the moment and just recently a book has come out in the *Daily Telegraph* which is very helpful in this regard. I think there are issues around people viewing old age disability as a stigma, and that has to be removed, but there is also a shortage of take-up of information. For example in the Dial-a-Ride area it is very important and the Department for Transport reports very low take-up of what is potentially a lifeline to people to prevent people unnecessarily staying on their own. The answer to your question is a very emphatic: a lot more could be done.

Q371 *Baroness Walmsley:* Such as what?

Professor O'Neill: I think the most important thing in terms of older people's advocacy is to start working with older people—and that includes government—with Bernard Isaac's motto in mind that "if you design for the old you include the young; if you design for the young you exclude the old." There are issues around terminology and I sometimes think if we used the phrase "us as we age" rather than "older people" it would not be some other constituency. It is through education campaigns trying to get people to develop a sense that this is us as we age.

Professor Kenny: I am going to do a Kirkwood on this. There are four reasons why we age: we do not have an inbuilt clock; 25 per cent of ageing is genes;

and the other two factors which influence ageing are damage and repair. The two latter ones we can influence and we can influence very simply by good nutrition, good lifestyle and exercise. I think that is a simple educational message that we need to get out early to people so that we counteract all of these triggering factors we have been talking about earlier which ultimately end in frailty.

Mr Brace: I think the information needs are varied and part of the issue then is how and in what formats do you deliver that information and to whom. I work with the visual impairment community and I think, by and large, we are a sight-orientated society. They reckon that most of our learning in the first ten years of our life comes from our sight and I think that continues in terms of people's focus on vision in terms of how you relate information, adverts, et cetera. Therefore, it does lead to quite a significant chunk of our population not having information and not having it in a format that they then could utilise. Some things are being done around that. For instance—again largely from the voluntary sector not from central-based services—there are information services linked to every eye clinic in the country. I think about 290 of the 400 clinics have got some form of information service, largely voluntary, where people who have had their diagnosis done and perhaps been told they have a vision impairment and there is nothing anyone can do are linked into people who (a) can listen to the trauma they have experienced and (b) can offer them some hope and some direction to say what is around, not that you can go and climb mountain and do wonderful sports but basic, simple things like a piece of plastic you can have to help you sign your name continually straight. Very basic stuff. Then linking them into a range of other activities, perhaps restoring things they have always done and do not think are possible. That information is crucial from people who can steer them through that. That is one practical thing that is being done and it is really quite crucial, but it is very haphazard and it is very limited. The other thing from a visual impairment point of view is that the rehabilitation services, the people who enable people to have a greater quality of life, are massively under-resourced. It is not just on funding but it is around the people around with the skill level and ability to assess to keep people supported and informed and able to exercise options. The last bit really is to whom? It is not just to the older people themselves. Unfortunately, with disability and frequently with the elderly, it is still working through a third party, it is still the family member, it is still the friend, it is still the carer whose perception has to be significantly changed and raised if they are going to be able to help the older person or disabled person to help themselves. That happens very clearly in care homes.

We have to try and ensure that the people with information a) have got it and b) can impart it to those that need it, and that includes family members very often.

Professor Steel: Could I finish off by discussing what Professor O'Neill pointed out, that design is really important. Also to mention that if you take the needs of the elderly into account when you are designing something it is a lot cheaper as an option than if you try to design something as an add-on. The telecommunications industry is a key example of that. It is very important that the needs of the elderly are taken into account right at the initial design stage not as an add-on later, on because it just does not happen or it is not cost-effective to do it at a later stage. With such major advances in telecommunications that are happening nowadays that is something that might be encouraged. I am not quite sure how.

Chairman: We are thinking about it, I have to say.

Q372 Baroness Emerton: Audrey Emerton. What you have just said has led nicely into the next question. Since frailty has many dimensions, there may be problems in demonstrating the cost effectiveness of specific interventions. Can you identify—and I think this is probably difficult—some examples that reveal how such interventions can be cost effective and what further research is needed?

Professor Steel: There is very little work that has been done in looking at the true cost of hearing impairment, if I could focus on that. Any assessment of cost benefit often focuses on mortality rather than morbidity and quality of life so it under-estimates the effects of loss of sensory abilities as you get older. There was a study in the United States in 1998 (and I think that is the latest and best costing that we have) that suggested that a child who is born with a hearing impairment actually costs $1 million (that is 1998 dollars) over their life time in terms of lost income, direct support, extra educational facilities that are needed, everything that goes with hearing impairment in a child. If you look at different ages of onset of hearing loss, then that cost goes down, until I think if you look at people who lose their hearing in their 70s then the cost was I think $43,000 which is still a very significant amount. That does not take into account any of the social aspects of their loss and the aspects of social withdrawal or any of the psychological impacts of social withdrawal that follow from that. That is just the pure cost—the cost of hearing aid provision and the loss of income. As you know, there are a lot of other costs that cannot be measured in pounds or dollars. That is really the best figure that we have. So if there was an intervention that can help reduce those costs at whatever stage that hearing impairment occurs, for example if it can be picked up earlier (and some interventions can be made earlier), then those costs are going to be reduced and benefits accrued, not only to the individual but also to society.

Professor Kenny: I am going to focus on fractured femur because that is expensive. Fractured femur costs in England about £2 billion per year. There is no evidence that falls clinics prevent fractured femurs, but we do know that 90 per cent of fractured femurs are due to a fall and we know falls interventions reduce falls. We assume that by running intensive falls intervention programmes we will reduce the cost of fractures. However, there are no UK studies which have examined that. I sat on a recent NICE panel for recommendations around falls preventions in the United Kingdom and despite the fact we had a health economist working avidly on this programme we were not able to come up with any recommendations in the context of costs for falls prevention.

Q373 Baroness Emerton: That is interesting because with the emphasis on risk assessment and risk management now, one would have thought perhaps—and let's just take uneven pavements, that is an incidence where there is a high level of falls. Would it not be a research project that one could do to look into the councils seeing that the pavements are improved and measuring what the level is of those that do suffer falls?

Professor Kenny: There was one observational study along those lines in Gateshead Newcastle which did show a reduction pre and post intervention in fall rates but not fracture rates after attending to local pavements, but it was not a randomised control trial, and there have not been any randomised control trials looking at the cost implications of fracture prevention in the context of falls prevention in the UK. There have in the US and we know that falls prevention is cheaper marginally by about ten per cent than the cost of hospitalisation as a consequence of falls, but not necessarily fractures.

Q374 Baroness Murphy: If we had been sitting here 15 years ago we would have been talking about HRT. Clearly that must have been an issue in the discussions of NICE in terms of the overall costs and benefits. Have we forgotten about HRT or has that just gone out of the window?

Professor Kenny: Some of us have not!

Q375 Baroness Murphy: Everybody is stopping it now. That was one of the cost-effective ways people thought fractures were going to be reduced. Is that a no-no now?

Professor Kenny: No, and addressing osteoporosis generally does reduce fracture rates but that is not the whole falls story.

Q376 *Baroness Murphy:* Sure.
Professor Kenny: 50 per cent of females will have an osteoporotic fracture at some stage in their life. The majority of hip fractures are due to falls.

Q377 *Baroness Emerton:* Professor O'Neill?
Professor O'Neill: There is evidence of effectiveness from early interventions for frailty. Cost-effectiveness is another matter. I would certainly hope that the deliberations of the Committee into this would support research into cost-effectiveness. The areas where we do see it are where the large pharmaceutical industry has an interest, for example around cholinesterase inhibitors and whether or not they delay your entry to nursing homes. It is equally important that that degree of fire power is brought to bear in the public arena as well. However, there would be some caveat in that when we come to health care and other policy decisions, cost is not always a factor and sometimes one wonders in areas around ageing whether people are made to run a little harder to produce cost effectiveness for certain interventions than they might be in other areas, for example cancer care or interventions for children, so there must be a little caveat there.
Mr Brace: I think it is that sort of broad sky. I know that there is some worldwide work being done now on the cost of blindness worldwide. We are looking at cost issues within the UK, but it primarily focuses on things like employment of the younger age group in terms of their ability to sustain employment and maintain family and maintain independence. In terms of older people, I think there is some work being done around the role of rehabilitation and timely intervention and early assessment of need and then provision of services around meeting some of that need, but it is very difficult to quantify. If you are talking about the provision of lighting costing X100 which at some stage down the line is a significant potential factor in avoiding a fall, I am not sure what the cost of admission into hospital would be for a fall but it is that more tenuous indirect way of quantifying cause and effect really.

Q378 *Lord Drayson:* I am Paul Drayson. I am interested in the way in which industry is or is not meeting the challenge that you have described. You have mentioned some very exciting opportunities for products to be improved, for example hearing aids, and research to improve the way information technology is going and so forth. Can you tell us how well you think industry is responding to this opportunity in areas such a sensory loss and frailty?
Professor Steel: The hearing aid industry is quite active. They obviously have a large market and they want to serve that community better but I think they are very dependent on the fundamental research

which is still being funded by a lot of organisations, particularly by charities, some from the Medical Research Council, some from places like the Scottish Office, RNID and Defeating Deafness. So I think fundamental research is something funders shy away from but the applied side they are much more interested in. I mentioned earlier that the importance is not just of supplying a hearing aid that can be programmed, but actually the whole process of choosing the right hearing aid and fitting it appropriately, and that is something that is very difficult, and that is what we do not know the rules for yet. Then there is also the follow-up to train the person to use it and make sure they have frequent follow-ups and are not just left to it because that is when they end up in the cupboard and not on the ear. That is not something that industry seems so interested in doing. They want to sell the hearing aid and that is fine. It is not just industry that needs to be involved in this; it is the National Health Service and the research community and funding for research that all needs to be in place in order to deliver a system that works, as best as a hearing aid ever can work.
Professor O'Neill: In the driving area there is a somewhat complex situation. I think in general companies have not woken up to the fact that there has been a change in the profile of their consumers. I remember running my first international conference on older drivers and one of the automobile manufacturers gave me a grant towards it but said, "Don't mention we are supporting an older drivers' conference." That was 10 years ago. I think that, unfortunately changes in safety for example, seem to be driven by lawsuits. Air bags and children in North America is an example of that. However, for those who research in this area to have better and smarter safety provisions for older people, when that class action lawsuit does come along there is an opportunity and I think it is important in terms of automotive science that people are working on areas of safety features that are more age specific. Also around the design of the fronts of cars and crumple zones for pedestrians. Again, unfortunately, the industry is not taking notice here and sadly it is only by way of class action lawsuit that this will happen. Ford have been mentioning a crash test dummy which is adapted towards ageing but in fact it is adapted more towards disability than ageing, so I think there is a huge opportunity for those involved in automotive design in the United Kingdom and there is a great potential to do better.
Mr Brace: I think I would probably put it into two areas really. I would call the first one proactive, and that is people thinking around the inclusive design programme, design for all, that then has particular application as you are getting older but you can still

1 February 2005   Professor Rose Anne Kenny, Mr Mike Brace, Professor Karen Steel
and Professor Desmond O'Neill

use things. Big button telephones, et cetera, were reintroduced because basically thousands upon thousands of people need that type of easily useable and seeable phones and dials. I think industry is very poor at the moment in waking up to the billions of pounds out there where potentially people will choose their product, and if it is ergonomically useable by them it means that it is a thing that they will treasure and use all the time. I think the reactive market is really the specialist groupings that have now tried to fill that gap, tried to invent more and more screen readers that you can plug into your telly that you can then use to run over your tin of peas to see the sell-by date or, indeed, whether it is peas at all. Lots of places are looking at that and are trying to make them at a level that is both useable and cost effective. The biggest problem with that is really cost. The development of some of the new technologies in terms of the numbers that are sold really does prohibit it from being within the reach of many thousands of people and that will increasingly be the older people's groups. If you are 55 now and are used to using your computer and then you want to have a screen reader fitted to your computer, which is something I use, you are talking between £800 and £1,000 just to get the additional software to enable you to carry on using your computer. That is a lot of money for something very basic and very simple that would enhance people's ability to continue a bit longer doing the things they are interested in.

Q379 Lord Mitchell: I find this remarkable and it does not make sense to me, to be honest. The market of people, shall we say, over the age of 70 is huge. We are getting to a stage now, particularly in the United States, where many of these people have an awful lot of money to spend. They no longer have children living at home or who have been gone a long time. I have asked this question before of other witnesses. I just do not understand why industry around the world is not seeing this as a massive market where they can make a huge amount of money. It just does not make sense to me. I have not got the answer. Maybe you have not got the answer. I just do not understand it.

Professor O'Neill: If I could just make one comment. The self-same automotive person who was sponsoring the conference but not sponsoring it said, we do have small section that looks at design for older people but very often our older people themselves have said what they want is what they perceive as a young man's car. There is still such a stigma around growing old that we have to try and beat. This is hugely important. People do not want something that is labelled as an older man's car. Some of the secular changes that have happened such as power steering, for example, and automatic gears

benefit everybody and are not clearly labelled as for older people. It is around the issue of universal design that Mr Brace was talking about and the issue of designing for older people and younger people at the same time. It is trying to eliminate the stigma. I suppose part of it is manufacturers are doing it and we are not aware of it but there is an issue.

Q380 Lord Drayson: I can see—and we have heard about that before—this stealth design effect where you do not mention the fact that you are taking into account the requirements of older people, but surely there are clear situations where products are needed for older people and, as Lord Mitchell has said, this is a very significant market? Is there something which in your experience you have picked up which prevents the development of the commercialisation of products? If we take that ageism point away about keeping it low profile while trying to take this on board, what is it that is preventing industry from recognising the opportunities here?

Professor Kenny: If I could address that in the context of falls. One of the issues with people who are falling is to know what is happening real time to that person and which of the risk factors is it? Is it their pre-perception, is it a sudden muscle weakness, is it balance, is it that their heart is going slower, is it that their blood pressure is dropping? The only real-time way we have of looking at that over a five, six or eight-week period is through heart rate monitoring. That is the only one we can detect. Part of the issue in the context of diagnostics and the older person is because of co-morbidity it makes the diagnostics much more difficult. It is a bigger challenge to industry to comprehend the number of risk factors and deal with all of those risk factors in a single tool. There are also issues around recall of events that older people have, therefore the technology has to be good and reliable and stand alone. There are issues about unwitnessed events. 70 per cent of falls or blackouts are not witnessed so you are very much reliant on your tool rather than your person or witnesses.

Professor Steel: I was going to address that question particularly in terms of medical approaches to hearing impairment. I think the reason that the big pharmaceutical companies are not actively pursuing this, even though it is a very large market, is that there is simply a dearth of basic fundamental research and knowledge in the area. You have to have a really good target if you are going to develop that and we just do not have that information. The research is very, very much at its early stages. When we do get to the stage where we have some good targets and good ideas of what is happening with sensory cells in the ear, what is happening with the whole ear, why is it not functioning any more, then I think we will have some clear molecular targets that drug companies will pick up and run with. Until the academic research gets to that stage, the drug companies are not interested; they are interested in the easier targets.

Q381 Baroness Murphy: I was going to ask a question very specifically on the co-ordination of research. Given what you have said about the very complex nature of age-related frailty and how research is funded in that area, is there sufficient co-ordination of research particularly from government, and what should be the role of government departments and the research councils in doing that co-ordination?

Professor Steel: That is a very interesting question and it sounds like there is an obvious answer to it but actually there is not an obvious answer to it. I think it depends on the different fields. The field of hearing research is a very small field. There are not very many people involved in it, particularly in the UK. We all know each other very well and we co-ordinate amongst ourselves. We all know exactly what everybody else is doing and who are the experts in each of the individual areas and we co-ordinate it ourselves. We do not need or want any control from the centre. That is my very clear message. For other research areas that is not the case. There are more people, there is more academic competition, there is more industrial competition and so maybe those are areas that would benefit. Maybe there is non-useful duplication of studies. Sometimes you do need to duplicate studies to verify them but sometimes it is not so useful. Maybe there are other areas that would benefit from more co-ordination but that is certainly not true in my area.

Q382 Baroness Murphy: I wonder if we could benefit from Professor O'Neill's experience in Eire. Is co-ordination of research in the Irish Republic any different? You have experienced both sides.

Professor O'Neill: I have to say I have to compliment the United Kingdom on the co-ordination that I see. For example, you have a co-ordination centre NCAR in Sheffield between the economic and social and medical. I have to say that many people in Continental Europe and Ireland are deeply envious of this attempt at co-ordination and the seminars I have attended there and spoken at were absolutely excellent. There are huge strengths here. My understanding is that this was a limited funding for a number of years so I would think a national centre for ageing research bringing together—because we do not talk medical any more—bio, psycho and social in terms of what we are doing would be very important. I also think that there are orphan areas. I think it is very important that this concept of joined-up government should apply to ageing as

well. On transportation and ageing for example, very often around the world departments of transport say it is a health and welfare issue and the health and welfare departments say it is a transportation issue, and it has a very small number of researchers because getting funding is very difficult. I would say the United Kingdom has very important elements in place and I am sure funding is never enough but it is a very important step. I think the establishment of large centres such as the one in Newcastle is certainly an inspiration to the people in the rest of Europe to bring people together from various disciplines.

Q383 Chairman: I am conscious that we ought to be stopping in a minute but I just wanted to try to amplify this point that has come up in the last ten or 15 minutes. I speak in ignorance and that may be the problem, but if you are thinking about hearing aids I know there is some magnificent research going on in speech recognition technology which I cannot but believe must be relevant to the sophistication of the machine that you put in your ear. There is the other side to it that you, Professor Steel, have properly stressed about what is happening in there and how much or how little we know about that. I wondered if there was a conversation between either the funding bodies or the researchers from these very different corners because of the sophistication of what they are doing this for, be it for security reasons or be it to stop us talking to other human beings and talking to machines instead, is there room for that bringing together and is it happening?

Professor Steel: There is always room for talking to each other but that is a very different thing. This is the sort of thing that happens at scientific meetings and this is why coming to scientific meetings is absolutely crucial so that you do keep in touch with other people. I should say speaking from the hearing research community, I was really talking about the international hearing research community. We have a lot of colleagues in the United States. I think it is true to say I know every team leader who is working in genetic deafness in the world personally and I have collaborated with many of them myself. It is a very small field. We also have very good links with the main charities that support hearing research—Defeating Deafness and RNID—in this country. There are very good communications amongst the UK hearing researchers. So, yes, there is always room for bringing all of these people together in the same room and letting them talk to each other. That is rather different to central control and saying these are the areas that must be researched and you are the one.

Q384 *Chairman:* I think you have made your view very plain on that but Professor Kenny wants to come in.

Professor Kenny: I would have taken a broader view of co-ordination of research. As we are talking it occurs to me that we have done very little in the falls field on the interplay between hearing and balance and falls, for example, and that is what I would mean by co-ordination of research—co-ordinating basic clinical and social science research. I think there are pockets who are doing it well but only pockets. An issue—and I know this has been addressed so I will be brief—is the fact that with the clinical training in geriatric medicine and other pressures, including R&E, there is a rapidly increasing decrease in the number of clinical academic geriatricians. There was a fall of something like 23 per cent in the last five years. If we are serious about co-ordinating those three major components in whatever research agenda it is, we have to be aware that for true translational research we need a strong clinical academic base and we are losing it. Unless we make an effort to try and recoup that loss we will have lost it.

Q385 *Chairman:* Part of the reason you are saying is research funding policy?

Professor Kenny: The research funding policy. Also there is a drive within the NHS to produce consultants very quickly. They do not now have to do research and there is not the incentive there. Research is becoming very much more difficult to deliver funding. It is becoming very much more difficult to achieve funding for clinical research. There is a "why bother?" attitude when they can get a consultant's job three years earlier.

Chairman: I know if Lord Soulsby were still here he would be asking about the MD PhD programme and what has happened to that which was one of the ways of driving the interaction between them. However, I will not ask that question because I think we ought to stop here because I know people have other commitments. As you can see, we have run a bit over time and that is because you have been so stimulating. We thank you very much for that indeed. If there are points—and I stress this again—where you feel I wish I had said that or why did they not ask this, do please feel free to contact Michael Collon our Clerk, or indeed Members, including Tom Kirkwood, our Specialist Adviser, to whom some of you may have privileged access. That would be very helpful, as has been this session, so thank you very much indeed.

TUESDAY 8 FEBRUARY 2005

Present | Drayson, L | Soulsby of Swaffham Prior, L
Finlay of Llandaff, B | Sutherland of Houndwood, L
Hilton of Eggardon, B | (Chairman)
May of Oxford, L | Turnberg, L
Murphy, B | Walmsley, B
Oxburgh, L

Memorandum by the Academy of Medical Sciences

INQUIRY INTO SCIENTIFIC ASPECTS OF AGEING

SUMMARY

1. The aim of biomedical research into ageing should be to improve the health and activity of people as they age. Extension of lifespan may well occur as a secondary consequence of improvement in health, but should not be seen as the primary goal. Life expectancy in industrialised societies has been increasing since the middle of the 19th century, with demographic figures showing no evidence for a slow-down.[1] An understanding of the factors that make for healthy, active ageing will therefore improve the quality of life for a large, and increasing section, of the population.

2. Research into ageing makes economic sense, as well as constituting a moral imperative. Clinical statistics show that health care expenditure does not necessarily depend on age, ie when disease strikes an older person, there is a higher rate of fatality and a shorter period of disability.[2] Prolonging healthy life will therefore, other things being equal, reduce the costs associated with long-term illness in later years. Research can also be expected to reduce the functional impact of conditions such as Alzheimer's disease, even if reducing the incidence proves more difficult. The widespread fear that enabling people to live longer by improving their health will result in an additional economic burden on health care is therefore not underpinned by evidence.

3. Research using short-lived model organisms has identified a range of interventions that can delay some of the manifestations of ageing in these species. Furthermore, advances in molecular biology, genetics and genomics increasingly show that principles established in model organisms can be translated across species. There are now unprecedented opportunities to increase our understanding of the intrinsic ageing process, how it constitutes a key risk factor for multiple diseases and how interventions might improve health and activity during ageing.

4. The UK is well positioned to contribute to, and exploit, the global explosion in ageing research. However, international comparisons, particularly with the United States, show that the volume of ageing research in the UK is low. UK research in this area is fragmented and structured in a way that neither takes full advantage of resources nor maximises translational benefit. In this response, we indicate realistic ways in which the UK research base could be harnessed to improve the health and well-being of older people, including:

   (a) A joined-up national programme that co-ordinates both funding and research strategy into healthy ageing. This should incorporate:

     — A concerted strategy of capacity-building, including Fellowships for clinical and basic scientists.

     — The creation of physical centres within which clinical and basic scientists can work together and share resources.

   (b) Improvements in clinical trials and population-based research through:

     — Improved use of the research opportunities presented by the NHS.

     — Increased inclusion of older people, of varying social and ethnic groups, in clinical trials and epidemiological studies.

     — Improved availability and detail of clinical trial data.

What are promising avenues for research? How will such research benefit older people and delay the onset of long-term illnesses and disabilities?

Basic Science

5. Genetics and genomics will continue to make substantial contributions to progress in ageing research. These are areas in which the UK is traditionally strong and are enhanced by the UK's role in the genome projects and the presence of world-class institutions such as the Sanger Centre. The establishment of BioBank will also bring great benefits to UK researchers, although its design has unfortunately not been optimised for ageing research, as it will exclude participants over the age of 65.

6. The fields of cell and molecular biology are also making great strides in UK ageing research. A recent example is the discovery that the shortening of telomeres at the ends of chromosomes acts as a marker for the biological (as opposed to chronological) age of individuals, and hence their vulnerability to a range of age-associated diseases. Physiological variation between individuals increases significantly with age, and the goals of "personalised medicine" might therefore bring particular benefits to older people in terms of enhancing efficacy while reducing adverse effects. Biomarkers that allow identification of patients who might most benefit from particular interventions are therefore of great value.

7. There has been a growing shift of focus to viewing ageing as a life long process, with significant determinants of later-life illness acting in adolescence, childhood and even *in utero*.[3] UK research into the early origins of patterns of ageing has led the world. Research should now be directed to the ways in which genes and the environment act at different stages in life to influence health during ageing.

8. The UK is particularly well positioned with regard to stem cell research. Less restrictive regulation will allow UK researchers to seize momentum and gain a global competitive advantage, notably in exploring potential novel treatments for the common degenerative disorders associated with ageing.

Population Research

9. Research in the fields of epidemiology, demography and population genetics greatly increase our understanding of the major determinants of healthy ageing. While the UK is strong in these fields, the potential for large-scale research of this kind has not yet been realised. The registration and record systems of the National Health Service have the potential to provide researchers with an extremely useful and powerful resource. Unfortunately, the quality of routine data generated by the NHS is relatively poor and has never matched the enormous research potential demonstrated by US patient databases such as Medicare. The value of record linkage methods was demonstrated by a group of Oxford researchers as long ago as the 1960s,[4] yet work in this area continues to be inhibited by a confusing regulatory framework and a great deal of bureaucracy.

10. Primary care based population research can evaluate data relating to individuals who may not currently be the recipients of healthcare. It is likely that future prospective cohort studies investigating environmental, genetic and disease interactions will also be based in a primary care setting.[5] It is therefore crucial that the potential contribution from community-based sites is better harnessed.

Clinical Trials

11 In order to achieve the maximum benefit for older people, it is important that older age groups are appropriately included in both epidemiological research and clinical trials, and that the range of individual variation is taken into account. Older people (and especially frail older people) are generally under-represented in clinical trials of treatments for which they are often the major consumers and from which they potentially have the most to gain. Outcomes from prescribing drugs for older people can differ greatly from those observed in trials of younger adults and unrepresentatively healthy older people.[6] It is often the case that the co-morbidities and poly-pharmacy that occur with greater frequency in older people exclude them from participation in trials. However, information on the effects of potential treatments on co-morbidities and interactions with other drugs is extremely important in order to inform pragmatic decision-making. The situation would be vastly improved by greater availability and detail of clinical trial data. Better access to this information would allow the sub-group analysis necessary to generate hypotheses about the determinants of responses in older people.[7]

Differences between the sexes, and between different social and ethnic groups in the UK

Gender Differences

12. Statistics show that women live about six years longer than men. Four of these six years can be accounted for by the failure of male mortality in middle age to fall at the same rate as women in the first half of the 20th century.[8] This has created a disproportionate number of widows suffering personal and economic hardship. Despite its widespread recognition, many aspects of the gender difference in longevity are not yet understood. For instance, why did the four-year difference emerge in the 20th century and why does it persist despite the convergence in lifestyles of men and women?

13. There is also an important difference between men and women in how ageing affects the reproductive system. Since many women today are choosing to start their families later, the impact of female reproductive senescence and menopause deserves particular attention.

Social and Ethnic Differences

14. Recent work implies that clear differences exist between social groups in the UK in their pattern of ageing. Of particular note is work that shows that psychological stress, including stress associated with work, may be a significant impairment to healthy ageing.[9] The biological mechanisms of this effect certainly merit further study.

15. With regard to ethnic differences, a recent Canadian study showed that, although the prevalence of heart disease varied greatly in the 52 countries examined, the actual causes of disease (eg hypertension, diabetes, smoking, alcohol, abnormal lipids) did not differ.[10] However, ethnic groups do show marked differences in ageing patterns, most likely through differences in interactions between genetic and environmental factors. As a paradigm of gene-lifestyle interaction, it is suspected that the "thrifty genes" postulated by J V Neal in 1962 may contribute to the high risk of diabetes and cardiovascular disease among some ethnic groups.[11]

16. Differences in the impact of risk factors on social and ethnic groups are important clues in understanding the nature of gene-lifestyle interactions. The diverse demographics of the UK provide particular opportunities for research in this area. It is therefore essential that the composition of populations chosen for both epidemiological research and clinical trials reflect this diversity, whenever conclusions are to be drawn about the population as a whole.

The application of research in technology and design to improve the quality of life of older people, including:

— Existing technologies which could be used to a greater extent to benefit older people.

— The development of new technologies.

17. Research into technologies to improve life for older people covers a broad range of social sciences, design and engineering disciplines. We will restrict our response to issues concerning biomedical technologies. This is an area where more clearly defined responsibility and co-ordination would make a real difference to older people and their carers. At a user level, older people with impairments often find it difficult to obtain objective advice about the availability and individual suitability of appropriate technologies. This work is often left to charities, whose local representatives may have difficulty keeping up to date with advances in technology.

18. On a clinical level, the input of technology for older people into clinical environments is not systematic and there is poor feedback from the needs of clinics into technological development. Much would be gained from the formal assessment of existing technologies, many of which lack evidence about their benefit or safety.[12] Similarly, the systematic evaluation of new and untested technological interventions would allow more effective prioritisation and targeting. Importantly, the results of such evidence-based assessments must be disseminated to practitioners, carers, patients and the wider public.

19. The lack of funding for "proof of concept" developments and the poor translation of technological interventions are symptoms of the wider crisis in experimental medicine in the UK. This activity is crucial in ensuring that the most appropriate diagnostic and therapeutic technologies are developed for the benefit of patients. The Academy report "Strengthening Clinical Research" calls for the establishment of a new paradigm for experimental medicine, involving improvements in infrastructure, careers, programme support and collaboration with industry.[5]

How effectively is research co-ordinated in the public, private and charitable sectors (including internationally)?

20. Research into ageing is poorly co-ordinated in the UK. At the level of individual institutions, it is clear that the implementation of the Research Assessment Exercise has had some unfortunate side-effects, particularly the discouragement of the collaborative, inter-disciplinary and translational approaches upon which ageing research depends. Much ageing research is also by its very nature long term, even for work with experimental animals, and this is often not recognised in traditional approaches to funding and research management.

21. The importance of research specifically directed to ageing has from time to time been recognised by individual research councils. However, these rather scattered, generally three-year, initiatives have been insufficient to make a substantial impact. A consistent, longer-term policy is needed. Attempts to co-ordinate publicly funded activities, including those of the research councils and the NHS, have been ineffective, almost to the point of invisibility. Better monitoring and evaluation of the outcomes of existing funding programmes is needed. In view of the potential for re-badging of existing research programmes, and in order to help align them with other scientific research on ageing, an external audit of the publicly funded portfolio of research into ageing would also be informative.

22. Many of the resources that are integral to ageing research, eg, colonies of ageing animals, tissue banks, fully phenotyped human population genetic data and so on, are simply too expensive and large scale to be supported by any individual institution. Co-ordinated access to an established network of shared resources would greatly improve the current situation.

23. The problems outlined here would be best tackled by a joined-up national programme that co-ordinates both funding and strategy for ageing research. Such a programme would replace and expand on existing research council and NHS programmes. This strategy would allow the identification of any gaps in the UK's ageing research portfolio and go some way to achieving an optimal use of resources in the field.

Have the correct priorities been identified? Are there any gaps in research?

24. With regard to research into age-associated diseases, there is little evidence that funding correlates well with the impact of diseases on health and well-being. This can be partially accounted for by the presence of large disease-specific research charities, whose combined focus does not correspond well to disease prevalence. While it is difficult for research councils to address this disparity through directed funding, there appears to be little transparency in the cost/benefit analyses applied to research council strategies when setting priorities for ageing relevant research.

25. The lack of good quality data about the diseases and disabilities affecting older people in the UK is also a major hindrance to appropriate priority setting. The resources available through the NHS have enormous potential to contribute to our understanding. However, as outlined earlier, NHS population research and database construction in this area is woefully inadequate.

Is there sufficient research capability in the UK?

26. There is under-capacity in ageing research in both clinical and basic science communities in the UK. The science of ageing is inherently multidisciplinary, with individual research projects often involving contributions from disciplines that have traditionally been viewed as separate. Both training and research are at their most effective when conducted in groups of collaborating principal investigators. Despite the success of some existing aging initiatives, few UK universities are getting on board. Incentives to enter and stay in ageing research and an increase in the number of collaborating groups working in the area are needed. Ageing research in the US has benefited from a strategy in which groups who were already carrying out world-class research were encouraged to shift their focus to issues related to ageing. This strategy might be usefully employed in the UK, where a world-class HIV research programme was nurtured by similar means.

27. Not all medical schools have an academic department for the medicine of ageing, and geriatrics is often seen as the "poor sister" to other medical specialities. It is notable that few trainee GPs go through a geriatric rotation, despite the vast majority of their patients being older. There is a negative feedback loop from the unpopularity of care of older people as a clinical speciality (fewer geriatrics house jobs chosen) and a lack of clinical academic attention. This leads to a significant question over the quality of clinical academics in this area. A concerted strategy of capacity-building is needed, for instance by creating high prestige, high value fellowships for clinical and basic scientists in ageing research. This kind of targeted approach is recommended

in the Academy report "The tenure-track clinician scientist: A new career pathway to promote recruitment into clinical academic medicine".[13]

28. In comparison with other clinical specialities, clinical gerontology appears to suffer from greater separation from its basic science counterparts. The development of relevant research programmes that are effectively translated into clinical practice requires greater interaction at all levels between scientists and clinicians. This would be best achieved by the creation of centres in which scientists and clinicians can work side by side, preferably within or very near the place where clinical practice takes place. The development of such centres should be a national priority.

Is the research being used to inform policy?

29. The Government is to be encouraged in its new initiative on public health. However, the potential impact of public health policies on healthy ageing has not been sufficiently emphasised. For instance, the impact of current trends in obesity and type II diabetes on the health of older people must be comprehensively assessed in order to inform robust policy.

30. When using evidence to inform policy, there must be improved recognition that, although observational and epidemiological studies may identify possible interventions, their efficacy and safety can only be determined by appropriately controlled clinical trials. It is essential that potential interventions are properly tested before they pass into general acceptance and use. Untested (and sometimes potentially dangerous) "anti-ageing" substances and practices are widely accessible and promoted in the UK. In the face of often poor quality media coverage of age-related health issues, advice to the public must be clear, unambiguous and derived from evidence-based research. The type of research that is currently reported under strategies of anti-ageing may actually discourage people from joining clinical trials and may even discourage academics and clinicians from entering the field.

31. However, the Academy welcomes recent Government interest in achieving a balance between individual and Governmental roles and responsibilities for health. Similarly, the interest of the House of Lords Select Committee on Science and Technology is very encouraging. Ensuring adequate resources and support for ageing research will in turn deliver the evidence upon which effective policy decisions can be made.

REFERENCES

[1] Wilmoth, JR. Demography of longevity: past, present, and future trends. *Exp Gerontol.* 2000; 35: 1111–29.

[2] Zweifel P, Felder S, Meiers M. Ageing of population and health care expenditure: a red herring? *Health Econ.* 1999; 8: 485–496.

[3] Barker DJP. The fetal origins of diseases in old age. *Europ J Clin Nutr* 1992; 46 (Suppl 3): S3–S9.

[4] Acheson ED. Oxford Record Linkage Study. A central file of morbidity and mortality records for a pilot population. *Br J Prev Soc Med* 1964; 18: 8–13.

[5] Academy of Medical Sciences (2003) Strengthening Clinical Research.

[6] Thiemann DR, Coresh J, Schulman SP, Gerstenblith G, Oetgen WJ, Powe NR. Lack of benefit for intravenous thrombolysis in patients with myocardial infarction who are older than 75 years. *Circulation* 2000; 101: 2239–2246.

[7] Rothwell PM, Warlow CP, on behalf of the European Carotid Surgery Trialists' Collaborative Group. Prediction of benefit from carotid endarterectomy in individual patients: a risk-modelling study. *Lancet* 1999; 353: 2105–2110.

[8] Grimley Evans J. A correct compassion. The medical response to an ageing society. *J Roy Coll Phys (Lond)* 1997; 31: 674–684.

[9] Marmot, M G Understanding social inequalities in health. *Perspect Biol Med.* 2003;46(3 Suppl): S9–23.

[10] Yusuf S *et al.* Effect of potentially modifiable risk factors associated with myocardial infarction in 52 countries (the INTERHEART study): case-control study. *Lancet* 2004; 364: 937–52.

[11] Neel JV. Diabetes mellitus: a "thrifty" genotype rendered detrimental by "progress"? Am J Hum Genet 1962; 14: 353–362.

[12] Academy of Medical Sciences (2004) Restoring neurological function: Putting the neurosciences to work in neurorehabilitation.

[13] Academy of Medical Sciences (2000) The tenure-track clinician scientist: A new career pathway to promote recruitment into clinical academic medicine.

October 2004

Memorandum submitted by Research Councils UK (RCUK)

INTRODUCTION

1. Research Councils UK (RCUK) is a strategic partnership that champions the research supported by the seven UK Research Councils. Through RCUK the Research Councils together with the Arts and Humanities Research Board (AHRB) are creating a common framework for research, training and knowledge transfer. Further details are available at www.rcuk.ac.uk.

2. This memorandum is submitted by RCUK on behalf of four of the Research Councils, and represents our independent views. It does not include or necessarily reflect the views of the Office of Science and Technology (OST). RCUK welcomes the opportunity to respond to this inquiry from the House of Lords Science and Technology Committee.

3. This memorandum provides evidence from RCUK in response to the main topics and questions identified by the Select Committee. Further details of the Councils' programmes, including recent research achievements, are contained in the Annexes:

Cross-Council Co-ordination Committee on Ageing—portfolio analysis	Annex 1
Biotechnology and Biological Sciences Research Council (BBSRC)	Annex 2
Engineering and Physical Sciences Research Council (EPSRC)	Annex 3
Economic and Social Research Council (ESRC)	Annex 4
Medical Research Council (MRC)	Annex 5

OVERVIEW

4. Ageing is a broad and complex field, and the term ageing encompasses both the ageing of individuals and the population, and the health and wellbeing of older people. Health and well-being are life-long processes, and the human body is constantly undergoing change. Growth and development in the early years merge into the changes of later life. The changes are very gradual and often difficult or impossible to detect except in retrospect. Ageing is a variable process, both between individuals and between different parts of the body. Ageing does not necessarily imply ill-health or loss of ability but rather an increase in risk. Thus old age is characterised by both variability and vulnerability.

5. The BBSRC, EPSRC, ESRC and MRC are key public sector funders in basic and applied research relevant to ageing (as a natural process), covering a broad remit, ranging from the molecular biology of ageing processes to the built and local environment, transport and the social and economic aspects of growing old. The Research Councils not only fund research specific to ageing, but also a considerable amount of relevant research into individual diseases, physiological systems, and technology.

6. In 2003, the four Councils carried out a portfolio analysis (based on 2002 data) across the breadth of the research they undertake, in order to highlight areas of overlap, identify areas of complementarity and any gaps, and thereby help the Councils work in a co-ordinated manner. Details of this analysis are in paragraphs 40–43 and Annex 1 below. The Councils are updating this portfolio analysis now for the Select Committee.

7. The Councils have funded research on ageing through their usual investigator-led mechanisms which use peer review to select projects to ensure high quality. The Councils have also had a number of single- or joint-Council Initiatives in this area:

— *Growing Older Programme* (GO)—ESRC led. GO was launched in 1998 and ended earlier this year. It consisted of 24 research projects totalling £3.5 million focussed on generating new knowledge on extending quality of life in old age (further details are given in Annex 4).

— *Innovative Health Technologies Programme* (IHTs)—ESRC led, MRC contribution; launched in 1999 the Programme aims to advance understanding of the current and future implications of innovative health technologies, the effects of which will be mediated by wider processes of social change. Innovative health technologies, such as new drugs, devices, procedures, hospital delivery systems and wider organisational and socio-technical change, present policymakers and the public with major new concerns and have the potential to impact significantly on the ageing process and the lives of older people. The programme funded 31 projects totalling approximately £5 million.

— *Brain Sciences Programme*—MRC (with BBSRC, EPSRC and CCLRC). This cross-Council programme, launched in 2003, is building capacity in multi-disciplinary approaches to neuroscience research. The MRC components include translation from basic to clinical research, with particular focus on clinical problems in mental ill-health and degenerative brain disorders.

— *Extend QUAlity Life*: EQUAL Initiative and EQUAL Network (EPSRC) with a total value of £8.5 million. The EQUAL Initiative was established in 1997 to address the needs of an ageing population and people with disabilities to help them achieve a more active life style, participate more fully and actively and avoid or alleviate the effects of disability. The Programme has been particularly active in promoting interdisciplinary engineering and design based research and its application. The EQUAL Network was established in 2001.

— *The Science of Ageing* (SAGE)—BBSRC; launched in 1998. SAGE focused on improving understanding of normal ageing, and had relevance to the Government's EQUAL Initiative in ageing. Applications were invited in any relevant area of research within the BBSRC remit. Twenty-nine grants with a total value of £5 million were awarded.

— *Experimental Research into Ageing* (ERA) BBSRC; launched in 2001 ERA covered work on normal ageing at the molecular, cellular, systems and behavioural levels. Applications were limited to three areas: (i) The genetics of normal ageing; (ii) Interventions in ageing; and (iii) Model systems. Twenty grants with a total value of £4.15 million were awarded.

— *Strategic Promotion of Ageing Research Capacity* (SPARC)—BBSRC and EPSRC; to be launched in late 2004. SPARC is a new programme arising from the activities of the Cross-Council Co-ordination Committee on Ageing Research. It is aimed at networking, building capacity within the ageing research communities of both Councils and to foster interdisciplinary working.

8. In addition, the Councils, led by ESRC, are shortly to launch a new cross-Council Research Programme— *The New Dynamics of Ageing* (NDA). This is a seven-year interdisciplinary £10 million plus research programme conceived by the Cross-Council Co-ordination Committee on Ageing Research (XCAR) (see paragraph 31, below).

9. The overall aim of the Programme is to advance understanding of the dynamics of ageing from an interdisciplinary perspective. Thus the central questions are: What are the new dynamics of ageing, what are the influences shaping them (biological, clinical, technological, social and behavioural) and how can their consequences be managed to achieve the maximum benefits for older people? It is essential to harness inputs from a wide range of disciplines to reveal the dynamic interplay between ageing individuals and their changing technological, social and physical environments—local, national and global—and to develop methods and means for overcoming the consequent constraints on the quality of life of older people. Research proposals will be invited in the following areas:

— Active ageing.

— Autonomy and Independence.

— Later life transitions.

— The oldest old.

— Resources for ageing.

— Locality, place and participation.

— The built and technological environment.

— The global dynamics of ageing.

10. The Programme will build on the work of the previous Research Councils' programmes on ageing and the National Collaboration on Ageing Research (NCAR). It has also been heavily influenced the Foresight Ageing Population Panel report "The Age Shift—Priorities for Action", and the European Forum on Population Ageing Research.

11. More details of the above initiatives are given in the supplementary Annexes.

12. The four Councils not only manage their own portfolios of research relevant to ageing, but also have been working closely together in this area through the Cross-Council Co-ordination Committee on Ageing Research (XCAR), established in 2000. Also, the Councils have played a leading role in bringing together other key groups on ageing research through the Funders' Forum for Research on Ageing and Older People (FFRAOP), for which MRC provides the secretariat. Details of these are in paragraphs 27–29, below.

THE BIOLOGICAL PROCESSES OF AGEING

What are the promising avenues for research? How will such research benefit older people and delay the onset of long-term illness and disabilities?

13. The biological process of ageing is influenced by genetic, nutritional, lifestyle and other factors, which in turn can be influenced by multiple factors including economic, social, and technological. All of these are promising avenues for research. There are not only gaps in knowledge about the factors affecting ageing, but also their interplay. The translation of research discoveries in basic biological processes to impact on the health and well-being of the population is a priority.

14. Many of the more common diseases, including cardiovascular disease, cancer, respiratory disease, and disease of the musculo-skeletal system become increasingly common in old age. Studies of these may not only lead to greater understanding of specific disease processes (and give clues as to what might then be done in the form of prevention or treatment), but may also throw light on the ageing process. Some examples of promising avenues are given below. Further details of some of these are in Annexes 2–5.

— Identification of genes involved with both common and rare diseases, and investigation of the biological mechanisms of ageing and diseases that manifest later in life, are all powerful starting points to guide the development of new and better diagnosis, treatment and prevention. A recent example of such an approach is the discovery by MRC-funded researchers of new evidence of a gene involved in the common form of Alzheimer's disease.

— BBSRC-funded studies of human fibroblasts taken from patients with a rare genetic disease Werner Syndrome have shown that transforming the cells to express telomerase resulted in extended lifespan, suggesting that inducing telomerase expression might be a possible therapeutic intervention in Werner Syndrome.

— The identification of a protein involved in a rare inherited eye disease is helping researchers at the MRC Human Genetics Unit to learn more about the mechanisms behind age-related macular degeneration, which is the major cause of blindness in people over 60.

— A team of BBSRC-supported scientists at Manchester Metropolitan University has shown that as we get older, our muscles re-organise themselves and become weaker. Our tendons compensate for this loss of strength by increasing their elasticity, but this places more pressure on our joints— making it harder for them to work properly and often leading to aches and pains. An understanding of this process led to further studies showing that a little light exercise can help maintain the muscle structure as people age. This helps joints to function properly, helping us react quickly should we slip and protects the joints should we fall.

— Good nutrition is a potentially powerful tool to delay or prevent the onset of age-related conditions, including cancer and osteoporosis. Evidence from the BBSRC-sponsored Institute of Food Research has shown that some food components, and gut fermentation products, can provide protection at various stages of cancer formation. Further studies may lead to better dietary recommendations and new dietary supplements for people, particularly older people, who may be more susceptible to gut cancers.

— MRC-supported researchers at the University of Cambridge have shown that supplements of Vitamin D reduced fractures by over a fifth in older people. Studies by the MRC's Resource Centre for Human Nutrition Research, Cambridge, are investigating the broader impact of diet on bone health.

— Alzheimer's disease and type 2 diabetes are among a number of disorders called amyloid diseases, which involve the abnormal folding of usually soluble proteins. A team at the National Amyloidosis Centre, Hammersmith, through MRC funding, have developed a drug that destabilises amyloid deposits, allowing them to be broken down. The new drug offers a new approach to treating a range of amyloid diseases.

— Humanised monoclonal antibodies offer exciting opportunities as the basis for potential treatments of a range of conditions that affect older people. A recent example is the launch of a new treatment for rheumatoid arthritis by a company spun out from the MRC Laboratory of Molecular Biology.

How are they affected by differences between the sexes, and between different social and ethnic groups in the UK?

15. There are many age-related variables which vary according to sex, or to social or ethnic group. One example is death rates from stroke which are significantly higher in men than women. Bone fracture rates are higher in women than in men. More older women than older men die in winter. Such differences may give clues as to causes, which may of course be biological (eg genetic, hormonal), lifestyle (eg nutritional), social, or in most cases probably some combination. When the causes are understood, it is possible to develop solutions. Much is already known about inequalities in health. What needs to be done to reduce such differences is a matter for policy-makers, as well as for all of us to take greater responsibility for our own health and well-being, as well as learning from future research on health behaviours and variations.

16. The most common disorders, including cancer and heart disease, are caused by a complex interplay between multiple genetic and environmental factors. Defining how genes and cells interact with other influences is vital in understanding the origins of health and disease, and to speed the development and testing of new drugs and treatment approaches. Unravelling the interactions between genes and environment is the long-term aim of the UK Biobank project. This is the world's most comprehensive population study of health and ill-health in middle age, jointly funded by the MRC, the Wellcome Trust, and the Department of Health. It will provide a vast amount of information about the relationships between genes, sex, lifestyle, health and disease.

17. The biological processes of ageing, including cognitive processes take place within particular social contexts and environments. There are complex interactions between biological processes and contextual and environmental factors which should not be ignored when looking at the ageing process. Physical, cultural, economic and social environments not only affect the ageing process, but can alter the perception of quality of life. The role social interaction plays in cognitive functioning and the availability of, and ability, to prepare nutritionally-balanced and healthy food, are just two examples of the interplay between social and biological factors affecting the ageing process.

18. Cognitive processes are a key area of overlap between the biological and social sciences. Social science informs the study of biological processes with, for example, understandings of social processes and contexts, perceptions of and reactions to cognitive decline, meanings of the experience of such decline, and insight into the contribution of social and cultural factors. Findings from a project within the ESRC's Growing Older programme "Quality of Life and Real Life Cognitive Functioning" have demonstrated a complex relationship between cognitive functioning and perceived quality of life. Most of the older people in the study expressed the view that keeping active and healthy, interested, reading, doing puzzles and socialising could help to prevent cognitive decline in old age and over half the participants deliberately engaged in specific activities to maintain good cognitive functioning. However, engagement in physical and social activities was not found to correlate with better performance on any tests of cognitive functioning. At the level of individual tests there was little evidence of an association between cognitive functioning and quality of life. However, self-rated cognitive functioning and better performance on "real world" problem solving tasks (but not "abstract" tasks) were significantly associated with higher self-ratings of quality of life. Those who reported their health as better also rated their quality of life as higher.

19. There is a growing body of evidence, particularly from the MRC's former Environmental Epidemiology Unit, that growth in fetal and early life affects people's health later on. Recent research on the MRC National Survey of Health and Development, a cohort of people born in 1946, has demonstrated that men with low birthweight who become overweight as adults, are at increased risk of osteoarthritis. BBSRC is currently inviting proposals aimed at characterising the nature of the effects of specific dietary imbalance during gestation on vascular function later in life.

20. The fields of social science, biology and medicine will be brought together to address problems such as these within the New Dynamics of Ageing programme.

THE APPLICATION OF RESEARCH IN TECHNOLOGY AND DESIGN TO IMPROVE THE QUALITY OF LIFE OF OLDER PEOPLE

21. The Research Councils have interpreted this heading to be focused on technologies and design aimed to help people maintain their independence and autonomy, rather than on technologies for the detection, prediction, diagnosis and treatment of age-related diseases, which could eventually lead to improved quality of life of older people. [Examples of the latter include stem cell research and tissue engineering, which could lead to the development of cell and tissue replacement/regeneration therapy for a diverse range of conditions ranging from Parkinson's disease, to replacement of "worn out" organs. It also includes research on prostheses, for which the Councils provide substantial funding].

EXISTING TECHNOLOGIES WHICH COULD BE USED TO A GREATER EXTENT TO BENEFIT OLDER PEOPLE

22. Areas where design principles and technologies have been applied include care and independence within the home environment, product and service provision for older consumers and accessibility within local environments. For example, researchers from the Bath Institute of Medical Engineering, funded through the EPSRC's EQUAL Initiative, are developing revolutionary new systems to help people with dementia to retain their independence and live safely in their own homes. Working with a housing association they have designed a range of prototype electronic devices to provide verbal reminders of potentially hazardous situations to the householder, such as taps left running or cookers left on. The systems are being demonstrated in a prototype "smart house" in Gloucester.

23. EPSRC supports two relevant consortia within its Sustainable Urban Environments (SUE) initiative: (i) "Urban sustainability within the 24-hour city" (Salford University) brings together experts from design, engineering, construction, urban planning and IT, to examine aspects of sustainability, from crime to accessibility and environmental sciences. (ii) "Accessibility and user needs in transport" (University of North London) will be examining effective socially-inclusive design and operation in urban transport.

24. The ESRC's Growing Older Programme represented the most extensive investigation so far into the factors determining quality of life in old age, including variations by gender and ethnicity. Part of the programme's work investigated the impact of technology on quality of life of older people. A project entitled "Transport and Ageing: Extending Quality of Life for Older People via Public and Private Transport", discovered that car ownership, access and travel (including by public transport) were associated with quality of life for older people. It also identified a number of significant barriers to the use of public transport such as personal security, cleanliness, inaudible announcements and lack of information. By contrast, car manufacturers were found to be thinking seriously about the ageing of the population and how to make car driving easier and safer for older people.

25. The ESRC-led Innovative Health Technologies Programme (outlined in paragraph 7) funded research which has examined the introduction, development and assessment of the Charnley hip-prosthesis focussing on the contributions of doctors, industrialists, health managers, patients and the media to the innovation process and the networks that link them. It has also explored perceptions of risk associated with concerns about infection, the viability of cement, quality control in materials and manufacture, and surgical operative conditions and procedures.

THE DEVELOPMENT OF NEW TECHNOLOGIES

26. Much research under this heading is funded by the Research Councils through their normal investigator-led mechanisms. However, highlighted here are some examples of themes within the New Dynamics of Ageing (NDA) Initiative where new technologies and design will be expected to have a major impact, including the design of the workplace pertinent to the needs of the older worker and the promotion of autonomy and independence within the home. With the predicted changes in demographics, inclusive design that meets the needs of the older worker is likely to become a priority for the future. The Initiative will address questions such as:

— How might the physical environment support the older worker, in terms of enabling devices and assistive technologies within the workplace?

— How can Information and Communications Technologies assist activity and extend working life and also increase independence within the home?

27. Another theme, originally supported through EQUAL and also now being taken forward through NDA, is design within the local and built environment. This will address questions such as:

— What aspects of the local environment enhance or diminish well-being in old age?

— What are the "active ageing" implications on public transport design?

— What are the implications for design of housing and the wider local environment?

How effectively is research co-ordinated in the public, private and charitable sectors (including internationally)?

28. The Research Councils have instigated and collaborated in a range of activities to facilitate and co-ordinate support and development of ageing research. Some specific activities have been highlighted in the preceding paragraphs, but the key groups are described below, highlighting both achievements and challenges.

The Funders' Forum for Research on Ageing and Older People (FFRAOP)

29. The FFRAOP was established in 2001 to extend the existing collaboration between the four Research Councils (BBSRC, EPSRC, ESRC, MRC) by bringing together the principal funders in age-related research, both public and private, to discuss matters of mutual interest and provide a platform to identify areas where a co-ordinated approach could make a greater impact. Its formal terms of reference are:

(i) To discuss and exchange information on current activities and future funding priorities.

(ii) To consider issues of mutual interest relating to all types of research from basic, clinical, social, and health and welfare programmes through to technology and design.

(iii) To identify areas that would benefit from joint working approaches.

(iv) To develop a joint strategy to disseminate the activities of the Forum.

30. The FFRAOP is a large and somewhat unwieldy body due to the nature of the field it covers. Despite their common focus on ageing, the principal funders constitute a very wide spectrum with different missions, which has inevitably created challenges. To date, it has mainly been a forum for discussion and exchange of views. The diversity of the FFRAOP distinguishes it from other Funders' Fora, such as those in the cancer and cardiovascular fields, which are able to make more of an impact because they are smaller and more tightly focussed. The Forum is currently reviewing its role.

Cross-Council Co-ordination Committee on Ageing Research (XCAR)

31. XCAR was established in 2000, with the key aims to encourage the development of research activities across the Research Council boundaries and to ensure that consideration of multidisciplinary research proposals are co-ordinated across the Councils. It has resulted in the establishment of the New Dynamics of Ageing cross-Council research programme, and the National Collaboration on Ageing Research (detailed in paragraphs 32–33, below).

The National Collaboration on Ageing Research (NCAR)

32. The NCAR was a three-year initiative launched with a major conference in November 2001 and funded via the Cross-Council Co-ordination Committee on Ageing Research. The key aim of NCAR is to stimulate interdisciplinary research in the field through workshops in key areas, networking and dissemination. The effectiveness of NCAR has recently been evaluated by an independent panel, which is due to report in the autumn.

33. NCAR has participated in the European Forum on Population Ageing Research (FORUM), an Accompanying Measure project funded under the European Framework Fifth Framework Programme (FP5), which shortly ends. NCAR is the coordinating partner for the European Research Area in Ageing (ERA-AGE), which was recently awarded under the European Commission's ERA-NET scheme. ERA-AGE aims to facilitate coordination of existing European ageing research programmes, promote interdisciplinary research activities between countries, support the production of European priorities for ageing research programmes, share good practice in coordination and management of ageing programmes, and to help break down the barriers between ageing research programmes and policy and practice.

8 February 2005

Public engagement

34. Where appropriate, Councils have developed a variety of mechanisms to take account of user needs in planning their research programmes. For example, the MRC has a subcommittee of Council, the "Advisory Group on Public Involvement" to foster consumer involvement in MRC research. For certain specific studies, particularly clinical trials, MRC includes patients' perspectives in designing the research and through membership of the Committees that oversee it.

35. A corner-stone of EPSRC's EQUAL Initiative was direct involvement of older people and disabled people, along with policy-makers and practitioners. Some examples are given in Annex 3.

36. The ESRC's Growing Older Programme has established extensive links with key user groups, including policy makers, organisations working in the ageing field and older people themselves. It has succeeded in giving voice to older people's own preferences, views and attitudes. ESRC Boards have policies on user engagement for all research. Users can range from people in business, government and the voluntary sector to the public more generally including those among whom social science research is carried out.

Have the correct priorities been identified? Are there any gaps in research?

37. Research priorities and gaps are identified by a number of mechanisms, including from within the scientific community, development of special initiatives through consultation, and at the level of the various cross-organisation committees.

38. Science-led. Here the mechanism is the standard one operated by the Research Councils. Scientists identify opportunities for research and submit proposals; the peer review process then selects those that are high quality and timely.

39. Specific Initiatives. In addition, the Research Councils' current or planned initiatives have focused on priorities and fill gaps. These include:

— BBSRC is in the process of announcing a new initiative to promote interdisciplinary interaction between biologists and chemists to identify small molecules that intervene in biological processes that will allow the details of the biological process to be understood in great detail.

— EPSRC EQUAL. It was agreed with stakeholders at an early stage that the EQUAL Initiative should be focus on the research and uptake of new design and technology by health and social services in a range of home and public environments. It was also agreed that end users should play an active role in all projects necessitating the development of new and highly successful methods of user involvement.

— NDA programme (detailed in paragraph 8 above). Key priority areas were identified through consultation with the broad ageing research communities, and will build on the ageing programmes of individual Research Councils.

XCAR/FFRAOP Research Portfolio analysis

40. A preliminary research portfolio analysis was undertaken by the Cross-Council Co-ordination Committee on Ageing Research (XCAR), and was based on the model used by the National Cancer Research Institute (NCRI). It was first undertaken in 2003, using data from 2002. Details of the portfolio analysis are given in Annex 1. A future goal is to include work funded through all members of the FFRAOP, ie including charities and the Health Departments, to enable broader co-ordinated working. Along the lines of the NCRI model, it is envisaged that the portfolio will be updated every three years; the next update is due in 2005.

41. The portfolio analysis carried out by the NCRI exemplifies the usefulness of such activities, and how charities and RCs can work together. The NCRI portfolio analysis led to the identification of gaps in research on lung cancer and preventative medicine, which has resulted in a £10 million joint investment to set up a National Prevention Research Initiative (NPRI).

42. The table below summarises the total Research Council spend in ageing-related research. The figures are the annualised spend of all relevant research programmes which were live on 31 July 2002.[1] The annualised spend of each research programme was calculated as the total cost divided by the duration.

---

[1] Figures for 2004 in the following memorandum by RCUK.

Research area	BBSRC	EPSRC	ESRC	MRC	Total RC
Total ageing portfolio (£m)	8.9	3.3	1.3	63.0	76.6

43. This preliminary analysis indicated a good spread of Research Council funding across most of the 10 areas. There was a predominance of support in research into the causes of, and influences on age-related diseases and disability, while the areas with least support were research into rehabilitation, and the delivery of effective and efficient health and social care for old and frail people. Both these also fall within the responsibilities of charities and Government Departments.

Is there sufficient research capability within the UK?

44. The Research Councils have several initiatives to build capacity in ageing research, both individually and jointly:

— SPARC: Strategic Promotion of Ageing Research Capacity (BBSRC and EPSRC), is specifically targeted at building capacity. This will be achieved through the support of small pump-priming projects and the organisation of a number of workshops which will specifically target parts of the ageing research community with the aim of bringing those (interdisciplinary) elements together, often for the first time.

— A central objective of the New Dynamics of Ageing Programme is to encourage and support the development of innovative interdisciplinary research groups and methods with the aim of helping to create a new generation of interdisciplinary researchers.

Is the research being used to inform policy?

45. This question may be best answered by policy-makers. Nevertheless, research provides a sound evidence base for policy and practice, and there are a number of mechanisms for helping (a) to ensure that research is planned with policy needs in mind, and (b) to encourage the take-up of research findings into policy and practice.

46. Many of the Research Council initiatives in ageing specifically recognise and address the need for research to inform policy and practice. EQUAL network—focuses on spreading information and linking scientists and practitioners. Aided policy development—input to housing policy, long-term care policy, telecare. Most of the 34 projects funded through the EQUAL Initiative relate to the needs of Government, other organisations and society in search of cost-effective approaches to improving the quality of life of older people.

47. A corner-stone of projects funded through the EQUAL Initiative has been the direct involvement of user groups and policy makers within academic research projects. Two examples of where EQUAL supported research has directly informed policy are:

(i) *Inclusive Design*: Inclusive design principles are increasingly being employed to ensure that commodities, services and all environments (eg home, workplace, local, transport) actively improve the quality of life of all people, particularly older people. Researchers at the Royal College of Art in London and the University of Cambridge were funded through the EQUAL Initiative to examine age and capability related factors in relation to industrial design. A major output of the project, known as "i~design", has been the establishment of a framework of principles and practical guidance for designers and manufacturers in the form of a book published by Springer-Verlag in 2003.

(ii) *Designing the external environment:* A publication aiming to improve the quality of life for older people, "Neighbourhoods for Life: a checklist of recommendations for designing dementia-friendly outdoor environments", is based on findings from a recently completed EQUAL project at Oxford Brookes University. The publication is a checklist of design recommendations to help housing associations create accessible outdoor environments that are easy for older people, particularly those with dementia, to use and enjoy. The publication was funded by a Housing Corporation grant and demonstrates the direct benefit of the engagement of user groups in such projects.

48. The New Dynamics of Ageing Programme aims, as one of its central objectives, to provide a sound evidence base for policy and practice (including the development of prototype systems, procedures and devices) so that research contributes to well-being and quality of life.

49. In order to translate basic biomedical research findings into improved health care, there is a need for organisations to work in partnership. This year the Government has commissioned the creation of a joint MRC/DH Health Delivery Group, to provide a more co-ordinated, strategic approach to building on their respective strengths for the purposes of translating basic and clinical research findings into benefits for patients, the economy, and knowledge transfer. Over the next few years the MRC, the Health Departments, medical charities, industry, patient groups, the Royal Medical Colleges and the Academy of Medical Sciences will be working together to set up and support clinical research networks and associated research programmes.

50. Input to Public Policy debates was a key theme of the ESRC Growing Older Programme. Links were established from the outset with officials from four Government Departments: the Department of Health, the (then) Department of Environment, Transport and the Regions, the Department for Education and Skills, and the Department for Work and Pensions. Inputs were made to important policy arenas and publications including the Cabinet Office report "*Winning the Generation Game*", the National Audit Office Inquiry on Older People's Services, and the Minister for Work and Pensions' Advisory Group.

Annex 1

CROSS-COUNCIL CO-ORDINATION COMMITTEE ON AGEING—PORTFOLIO ANALYSIS

INTRODUCTION

1. Particular issues arise in this type of analysis when looking at a field as broad and diverse as ageing, and some of these remain to be addressed. In contrast to the cancer field, there was not a set of existing, generally accepted, common definitions of scientific research into ageing and older people. Therefore the Research Councils agreed a set of definitions and terminology in order to divide the entire breadth of ageing-related research supported by the Research Councils into 10 categories, ranging from the molecular and cellular changes associated with basic biological processes of cell death, senescence and physiological ageing, to technologies and design to help older people maintain their independence and autonomy.

2. Research programmes supported by the four Research Councils were assigned to one of the following 10 categories:

(i)   The economics, psychology and sociology of ageing and the life-course.

(ii)   The economic, social and policy implications of an ageing population.

(iii)   Technologies and design to help people maintain their independence and autonomy (and the effects of those technologies).

(iv)   Technologies for the detection, prediction diagnosis and treatment of age related diseases (and the effects of those technologies).

(v)   The molecular and cellular changes associated with basic biological processes of cell death, senescence and physiological ageing.

(vi)   The causes of, and influences on age related diseases and disability.

(vii)   Prevention of breakdown in health and loss of independence in old age and of specific diseases and conditions which cause these.

(viii) Treatments for disease and the breakdown in health in older people.

(ix)   Rehabilitation strategies to improve and maintain function and restore independence.

(x)   The delivery of effective and efficient health and social care for old and frail people.

3. A particular challenge in the analysis was the need to take account of the fact that many research programmes relevant to ageing are multidisciplinary and multidimensional, including cutting across areas that may not appear to be immediately relevant to ageing. As yet, there are no adjustments in the analysis to take account of any fraction of research in a particular multidisciplinary programme that is not directly related to ageing. Consequently, the analysis <u>over-estimates</u> the actual spend directly attributed to age-related research.

4. The analysis parameters were:

— Research projects were only included if they were active on 31 July 2002.

— If a research project was relevant to ageing, it was included in the analysis as 100 per cent of its costs, even if the research was diverse, and ageing was only one aspect of it.

— Each research project was included in only one category, even if the research spanned more than one category.

— Spend was calculated as the total cost of the research project divided by its duration (termed annualised spend).

— Spend was quoted in two ways; (i) in millions of pounds; (ii) as a percentage of that Council's total spend in ageing research (in order to normalise the spend between Research Councils).

VISUAL PRESENTATION

5. The following two diagrams show, (i) the combined Research Council spend in ageing research, as the spend for each of the four Research Councils individually, as a proportion of each Council's total spend (Figure 2).

6. The spend is illustrated in the form of kite diagrams, as this type of presentation has proved useful in the portfolio analysis carried out by the National Cancer Research Institute (NCRI). In such kite diagrams, half of the spend is shown below the x-axes, and the other half above the axes.

Figure 1   Research Council Combined Spend in Ageing Research

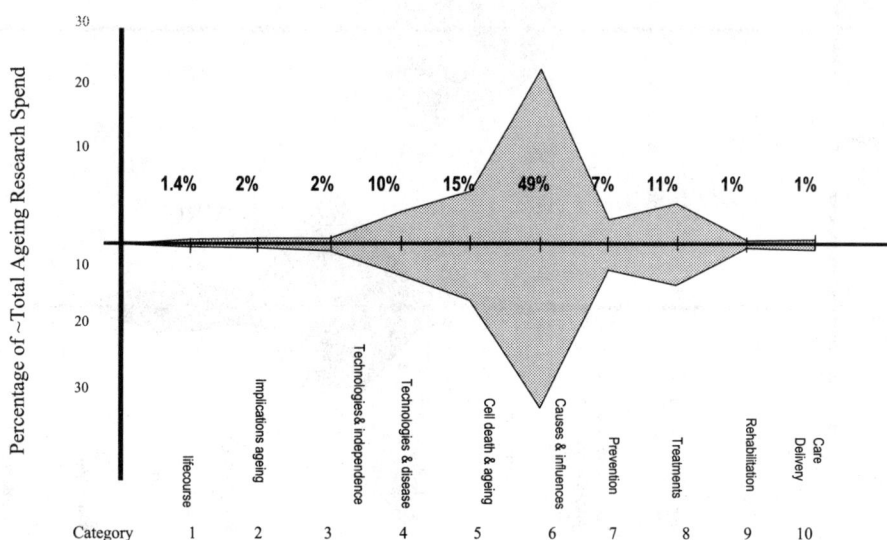

Figure 2   Individual Research Council Spend

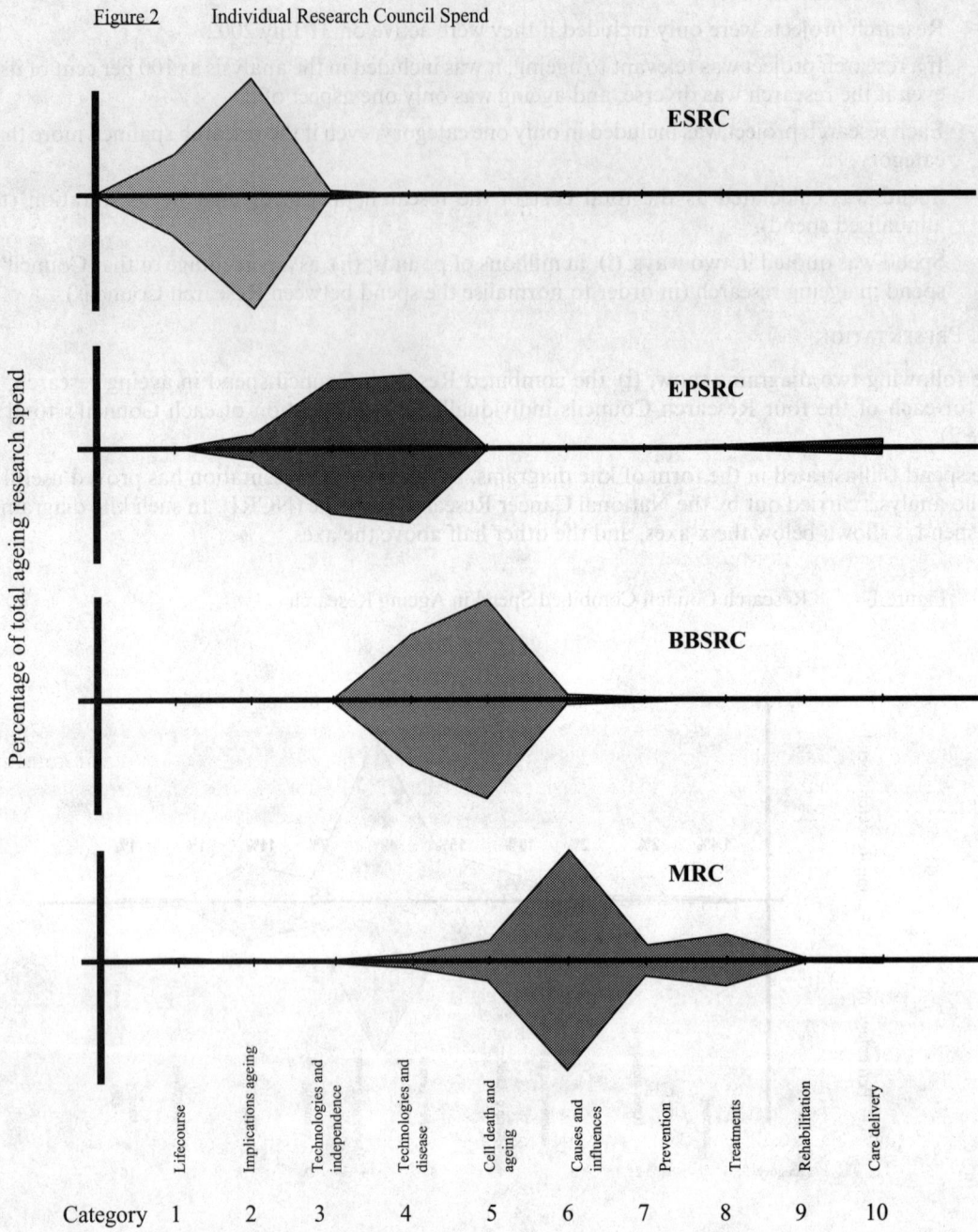

Note: all four diagrams are on the same scale.

Annex 2

Memorandum from The Biotechnology and Biological Sciences Research Council (BBSRC)

BBSRC SUPPORT FOR AGEING RESEARCH

1. BBSRC has been an active player in supporting ageing research over the period 1997–2004, funding a portfolio of research projects investigating the underlying biological processes of healthy ageing. In addition to supporting a number of research projects through its normal framework of research support (responsive mode and strategic grants to institutes), BBSRC has funded two initiatives:

2. The Science of Ageing (SAGE) launched in 1998 covering:

— cellular senescence: the mechanism of tissue damage and breakdown;

— biochemistry of stress, repair and accumulation of damage;

— ageing in biological systems, particularly neurosciences and immunology; and

— the ageing population and evolution: understanding the primary mechanisms of ageing and underlying genetic determinants of life span and reproduction potential.

3. Experimental Research into Ageing (ERA) launched in 2001 covering:

— the genetics of normal ageing;

— interventions in ageing: *including small molecule pharmacological agents, such as free radical scavenger*; and

— model systems.

4. These initiatives were designed to investigate and generate a greater understanding of the biochemistry, cell biology and genetics of the normal ageing process and to expand the capacity of the UK academic community in studying the fundamental biological science of ageing. Much of the research utilises model organisms from which it is expected that discoveries will be translated to the benefit of humans. These initiatives have been co-ordinated through BBSRC by a number of representatives in the UK ageing research community (BBSRC SAGE and ERA panels) to ensure projects are monitored for progress (by an annual workshop) and to ensure projects are achieving their objectives. BBSRC's advisory body (most recently the ERA Panel) has also been used to provide strategic advice about the future direction of BBSRC support for ageing research. BBSRC has appointed a representative from Help the Aged/ Research into Ageing as a member of the ERA Panel to enable better co-ordination with some representatives from the charity sector.

5. Recently BBSRC has supported a research project led by Professor Tom Kirkwood (Newcastle) titled BASIS (Biology of Ageing e-Science Integration and Simulation) through its Bioinformatics and e-Science Programme that seeks to develop a web-based modelling system to test and predict hypotheses in mechanisms of ageing that researchers in the community can down-load and use for themselves (see *Nature Reviews* (2003) 4 243–249 for work supported under SAGE leading to this project). Component parts of the project will include a "virtual ageing cell", "virtual ageing tissues" and eventually a "virtual ageing organism" to allow the development of predictive ageing research.

FUTURE BBSRC INVOLVEMENT IN AGEING RESEARCH: PRIORITIES AND GAPS

6. BBSRC will feature the support of ageing research under a new Strategy Panel called The Healthy Organism. This Panel will begin work at the end of 2004 and develop a number of plans including implementation of BBSRC's Strategic Plan objectives in Ageing research, following an analysis of the BBSRC ageing research portfolio. The BBSRC ERA Panel has identified one area likely to be of interest in the context of healthy ageing, the role of diet and nutrition throughout life and how appropriate diet and nutrition contributes to healthy ageing. In the context of research support mechanisms, the ERA Panel has identified that both research projects and training awards will be necessary to support future areas of research in ageing in order to maintain the research capacity in this field.

7. BBSRC is in the process of announcing a new £10 million initiative to promote the interdisciplinary interaction between biologists and chemists *Selective Chemical Intervention in Biological Systems* (SCIBS). This initiative will support work to allow the details of the biological process to be understood in great detail. Ageing is one area that will be highlighted: the process of healthy ageing is likely to be under the control of a number of different factors which may be amenable to detailed dissection through the use of small molecules

in this way. BBSRC is also collaborating with the Royal Society of Chemistry (RSC) to promote interactions between the disciplines in the "chemistry of ageing". An initial workshop was held in June 2004 and a further workshop is planned for January 2005.

Annex 3

Memorandum from The Engineering and Physical Sciences Research Council (EPSRC)

EPSRC INVESTMENT IN AGEING RESEARCH

1. EPSRC support for research focussed on the understanding and meeting the needs of older people has been made available both through standard responsive mode (investigator-led) mechanisms and targeted managed initiatives. Two key initiatives funded by the EPSRC are:

— The EQUAL (*Extending QUAlity Life*) Initiative.

— The EQUAL Network.

2. The EQUAL Initiative was established to address the needs of an ageing population and people with disabilities to help them achieve a better life style, participate more fully and actively and avoid or alleviate the effects of disability. EPSRC has funded projects through four calls within the EQUAL Initiative:

— EQUAL in the built environment (1997).

— EQUAL in the built environment and design for all (1998).

— Rehabilitation and design for all (1999).

— Prolonging independence in old age (2001).

3. Thirty-four projects with a total value of £5.4 million were funded through the first three calls of the EQUAL Initiative. Examples include:

— A multimedia reminiscence experience and conversation support for elderly people with memory loss (University of St Andrews and University of Dundee).

— Development of devices for use in a smart house for people with dementia (University of Bath).

— Development of a wheelchair virtual reality motion platform for use in evaluating wheelchair access (University of Strathclyde).

— Older users' perspectives on mobility—related, assistive technology research: an exploratory study (King's College London).

4. Five multidisciplinary consortia with a total value of £3.1 million were funded through the fourth call. Funding for all but one of these projects commenced in 2003. Funding for "Inclusive Design 2" commenced in 2004. The consortia are:

— SMART Rehabilitation: Technological applications for use in the home (Sheffield Hallam University).

— Supporting independence. New products, new practices, new communities (Imperial College).

— Inclusive design for getting outdoors (IDGO) (Edinburgh College of Art).

— Investigating enabling domestic environments for people with dementia (INDEPENDENT) (University of Liverpool).

— Inclusive Design 2: providing tools to improve quality of life for the wider population (University of Cambridge).

5. Through these projects, the EQUAL Initiative has served to integrate a wide spectrum of scientific, technological, economic and social activities—from fundamental molecular science (such as understanding the ageing process) through engineering (such as developing long range diagnostics, and improving housing design), to new patterns of work and leisure. The assembly of multidisciplinary teams and integration of academic researchers with user groups and policy makers has been a key feature of the EQUAL Initiative. This work will now be taken forward and expanded through a cross council programme, The New Dynamics of Ageing (NDA), involving BBSRC, EPSRC, ESRC and MRC (described in paragraph 8 of the main submission).

6. EPSRC has provided support of £60k for an "EQUAL Network" from October 2001 to September 2004. This is an interdisciplinary Network, with membership drawn from academia, industry, the voluntary sector and policy makers. A series of informative workshops have been organised by the Director of the Network, who has been particularly active in engaging directly with older people through the network to help shape the ageing research agenda. The work of the EQUAL Network will be expanded significantly through a new network, The Strategic Promotion of Ageing Research Capacity (SPARC) to be funded jointly by BBSRC and EPSRC.

7. Along with the managed activities, EPSRC also supports investigator-led high quality ageing research through responsive mode. EPSRC responsive mode expenditure in ageing research by financial year over the last five years (1999–2000, 2000–01, 2001–02, 2002–03 and 2003–04) amounts to £4.9 million[2] in total.

SPECIFIC COMMENTS

The biological processes of ageing.

What are the promising avenues for research? How will such research benefit older people and delay the onset of long-term illness and disabilities?

Differences between the sexes, and between different social and ethnic groups in the UK.

8. EPSRC support focuses on novel modelling and imaging techniques to enable faster and more accurate clinical intervention, for instance, in neurodegenerative diseases such as dementia. New ways of interpreting 3D images of the brain, such as recent work supported through responsive mode at the University of Manchester, has opened up the possibility of doctors being able to distinguish more easily between Alzheimer's and other degenerative brain diseases to enable faster and more accurate diagnosis.

9. There is an ongoing need to transform the large quantity of imaging and signal data into accessible and useful information for clinicians. This is being addressed by researchers in an EPSRC funded Interdisciplinary Research Collaboration, "From Medical Images and Signals to Clinical Information". Two of the clinical exemplars to be examined are (i) stroke and brain injury and (ii) from high dependency care to home monitoring.

10. EPSRC and BBSRC aim to build interdisciplinary collaboration within ageing research across the technological and biological interface through support for a new network, SPARC (Strategic Promotion of Ageing Research Capacity). This is discussed later in the context of "research capability".

The application of research in technology and design to improve the quality of life of older people.

Existing technologies which could be used to a greater extent to benefit older people.

The development of new technologies.

11. Engineers, designers and scientists play a central role in research leading to technologies and designs that enhance the quality of life of older people. In order to maximise impact and facilitate uptake, the EQUAL Initiative has ensured that social scientists, health and social service providers and policy makers engage actively with the scientific and engineering research communities.

12. Areas where design principles and technologies have been applied include care and independence within the home environment, product and service provision for older consumers and accessibility within local environments. For example, researchers from the Bath Institute of Medical Engineering funded through the EQUAL Initiative are developing revolutionary new systems to help people with dementia to retain their independence and live safely in their own homes. Working with a housing association they have designed a range of prototype electronic devices to provide verbal reminders of potentially hazardous situations to the householder, such as taps left running or cookers left on. The systems are currently being demonstrated in a prototype "smart house" in Gloucester.

---

[2] This amount is based on a search of the EPSRC grants database using the following keywords: ageing, assistive, dementia, rehabilitation, smart, telecare, telemedicine, stroke, "memory loss", elderly, "inclusive design". The results were refined to remove projects not directly attributable to ageing research. The grants selected do not include underpinning research also relevant to the quality of life of older people such as prosthetics and tissue engineering.

13. Two of the major consortia supported within EPSRC's Sustainable Urban Environment (SUE) initiative have some relevance to the accessibility needs of older people. "Urban sustainability within the 24 hour city" (Salford University) brings together experts from design, engineering, construction, urban planning and IT, to examine aspects of sustainability, from crime to accessibility and environmental sciences. Another SUE project, "Accessibility and user needs in transport" (University of North London) will be examining effective socially inclusive design and operation in urban transport.

How effectively is research co-ordinated in the public, private and charitable sectors (including internationally)?

14. EPSRC is engaged in the activities of the cross-Council Co-ordination Committee on Ageing Research (XCAR), detailed in the main submission paragraph 31, and is also co-sponsor of the National Collaboration on Ageing Research (NCAR), detailed in the main submission paragraphs 32–33.

15. The EQUAL Network does not co-ordinate research directly but has helped to link academics with organisations concerned with older people, such as charities, voluntary bodies, local authorities, housing associations and other representative groups. It has been particularly active in promoting interdisciplinary engineering and design based research and its application.

16. It is EPSRC's view that the EQUAL Initiative and EQUAL Network have been successful in establishing a multidisciplinary ageing research agenda and in actively engaging user groups and policy makers.

Have the correct priorities been identified? Are there any gaps in research?

This is discussed in the main submission.

Is there sufficient research capability within the UK?

17. To date 39 projects involving 33 universities have been funded through the EQUAL Initiative with a total value of £8.5 million. This constitutes a small but active community of researchers within ageing and disability research. EPRSC also provides support through responsive-mode on an ongoing basis.

18. To build on the success of the EQUAL Network, in autumn 2003 EPSRC with the Director explored the possibility of expanding the scope and remit of the Network. Through these discussions, the need to build capacity in ageing research was identified, either through the active support of young researchers or by attracting excellent researchers from other disciplines into ageing research with pump priming grants.

19. Following these considerations, interest was expressed by BBSRC in joining with EPSRC in supporting a proposal to build capacity within the ageing research communities of both councils and to foster interdisciplinary working across communities. The new grant, SPARC (Strategic Promotion of Ageing Research Capacity), is expected to be awarded within the next few months.

Is the research being used to inform policy?

20. A cornerstone of projects funded through the EQUAL Initiative has been the direct involvement of user groups and policy makers within academic research projects. Two examples of where EQUAL supported research has directly informed policy are Inclusive Design, and Designing the External Environment, as described in the RCUK text (paragraph 47).

Annex 4

Memorandum from The Economic and Social Research Council (ESRC)

1. The Economic and Social Research Council (ESRC) is the UK's leading research funding and training agency addressing economic and social concerns. ESRC has been active in support of ageing research through its responsive mode framework and through priority targeted investments, in particular, since 1998, the Growing Older Programme (GO).

2. This inquiry has chosen to focus on the biological processes of ageing and the application of research in technology and design to improve the life of older people; ESRC has focussed on this area within this Annex. However, the ESRC does support a much broader range of research on ageing in both responsive mode and

directive research that has implications for ageing. This work includes work on inequalities in health in an ageing population and the Simulating Social Policy in an Ageing Society (SAGE) Research Group.

3. The biological processes of ageing and the development and implementation of technology and design are areas where social science must, and does, contribute. The following are examples of key social science contributions; the social determinants of technological development and how social expectations of technology and design varies and how this affects use, the effect of technology and design on people's identities and an understanding of the role of social values. Does the use of design and technology differ by social context and any subsequent affect on social inequalities? Social science also contributes significantly to the contextualisation of biological difference between the sexes and different social groups (paragraphs 21 and 22 of the main text address these issues in more depth). It also has a key role to play in promoting and facilitating the involvement of users of technology and design.

4. There are two initiatives funded by ESRC which have particular relevance to this inquiry:

— The Growing Older (GO) Programme.

— The Innovative Health Technologies (IHTs) Programme.

5. These two programmes are outlined below. In addition to these two major programmes, there are examples of projects within other ESRC programmes which are of relevance to this inquiry. For example, work within the People at the Centre of Information Technology (PACCIT) Programme (a joint ESRC/EPSRC/LINK Programme) on the development of personal navigation aids on smartphones for people who experience difficulties travelling by foot, and work within the Science in Society Programme entitled "Boundary work, normal ageing, and brain pathology" which is aimed at understanding the ways that different constituencies work to define, organise and enact the boundaries between normal and abnormal cognitive ageing, and what this work tells us about social relations between older citizens and the biosciences, and their implications for cognitive citizenship. Both projects are currently in progress.

THE GROWING OLDER PROGRAMME

6. The Growing Older Programme was established in 1998 to pursue a broad-based multidisciplinary programme of research designed to generate new knowledge on extending quality life and to contribute to the development of policies and practices in the field. The GO Programme has resulted in a step-change in knowledge about quality of life in ageing. It has put some critically important topics and research methods onto the ageing research agenda and has been successful in researching and learning from older people's own attitudes, aspirations and preferences.

7. The programme covered six principle research topics: Defining and Measuring Quality of Life, Inequalities in Quality of Life, The Role of Technology and the Built Environment, Healthy and Productive Ageing, Family and Support Networks and, Participation and Activity in Later Life.

8. Twenty-four projects totalling £3.5 million were funded through the programme. Examples of projects within the Programme include:

— Quality of Life of the Healthy Older People: Residential Setting and Social Comparison Processes.

— Older Widow(er)s: Bereavement and Gender Effects on Lifestyle and Participation.

— Influences on Quality of Life in Early Old Age.

— Quality of Life and Social Support Among Older People from Different Ethnic Groups.

— Ethnic Inequalities in Quality of Life at Older Ages: Subjective and objective components.

— Older People in Deprived Neighbourhoods: Social Exclusion and Quality of Life in Old Age.

— Quality of Life and Real Life Cognitive Functioning.

9. The Programme has now reached its conclusion and is currently being evaluated. Major achievements of the Programme include:

— Very high quality social science that has broken new ground in the following ways; the first representative research in the UK on older people's own views on what contributes quality to their lives, the most extensive research so far on black and ethnic minority ageing, the first national study of loneliness for 50 years, a new approach to understanding quality of life as a dynamic concept, new tools for interviewing older people (including the very frail), new participative methods for older women from ethnic minorities, the first national study of grandparenting (replicated by ONS) and the development of a new instrument for measuring quality of life.

— The Programme has developed extensive links with user groups including policy makers, organisations working in the ageing field and older people themselves. Examples of those in contact with the Programme include Age Concern, Help the Aged, RNIB, National Pensioners Convention, Employers' Forum on Age, Greater London Forum for the Elderly, the MRC Consumer Liaison Group, the Community Fund, the National Director for Older People's Services, the Human Resources Directors' Forum and the House Builders' Federation.

— Examples of policy impact at project level include work with the Housing Corporation, the London Borough of London, the National Care Standards Commission, ODPM Social Exclusion Unit, Audit Commission and Scottish Executive. Key public sector organisations in the policy community have highlighted the importance of the GO Programme. For example the GO Programme has been used as an exemplar of policy-relevant research in the Office of Science and Technology, the Science and Engineering Base Group's paper to the Inter-ministerial Committee on Older People and in the NAO's report on the effectiveness of public services. Leading NGOs representing older people frequently use the GO Programme outputs in support of their campaigns. For example, in 2003, Age Concern England called on the government to adopt a strategic approach to meeting older people's needs based on the key determinants of quality of life identified by the Programme.

— The development of a major European dimension to the Programme including the EQUAL-AGE project designed to produce parallel information to GO from Germany, Italy, the Netherlands and Sweden.

THE INNOVATIVE HEALTH TECHNOLOGIES PROGRAMME

10. The Innovative Health Technologies (IHTs) Programme was established in 1999 with a main objective of advancing understanding of the interaction between innovative health technologies and wider changes in society. The Programme is not focussed on ageing but has obvious implications for the ageing process and on the social science contribution to the study of design and technology and the application of technology to biological processes.

11. The Programme covers the areas of Genetics, Informatics, Drugs and Enabling and Supporting Technologies. The programme encompassed 31 projects totalling £4.1 million of ESRC funding and £1.1 million of MRC funding. Examples of projects within the Programme are:

— Quality of Life as an Innovative Health Technology.

— The challenge of recent neurology to conceptions of mental and physical illness.

— IHTs at Women's midlife: Theory and diversity among women and "experts".

— Innovation, Assessment and the Hip Prosthesis.

— Technology and Natural Death: A study of older people.

12. Major achievements of the Programme within the remit of this inquiry include:

— The organisation of a workshop entitled *Ageing, Health Technologies and the Built Environment,* planned in collaboration with the ESRC's Growing Older Programme and the NHS Estates R&D Programme. The aim was to pool expertise to answer questions that each programme would find difficult to address individually. Relatively little is known about the link between the built environment and the use of clinical technologies or how this relationship varies by age. By exploring the ways these three dimensions come together in both clinical and non-clinical (such as domestic) settings, the workshop sought to identify new ideas for intervention and therapy, and new areas that need to be researched. The workshop addressed a number of important policy-related questions:

(i) Can we improve our understanding of the relationship between ageing, health technology and the environment at either end of the life course where a high level of health and wider social resources (such as housing and social care) are deployed? Will this enable a more strategic and targeted use of such resources?

(ii) How far can we derive lessons from research on the experience of ageing that can be transferred to the built and clinical environments?

(iii) How far can we redefine health care as social care as we deploy new technologies in non-clinical settings, and so reshape the experience and meaning of support for older people? What are the practical and optimal limits to this? NHS Estates have initiated this as a new area for research development and invited the Programme Director to contribute towards this. In addition, the different networks brought together for the meeting have been encouraged to submit new collaborative proposals to the New Dynamics of Ageing Programme.

— At a project level, one project has focussed on older peoples' understandings of technologies used in end of life care, this study has developed new methodologies for social science in a demanding and ethically sensitive field. The study highlights: the role that older people have in caring for the dying and their needs for support and training; information needs about issues of ethics, clinical practice and advance care planning; and the willingness of older research participants to discuss these matters and to enjoy the process of so doing. It draws together issues previously considered under the largely separate remits of palliative care and gerontology. It is being used to provide advice on palliative and end of life care, especially to nursing and medical practitioners and to voluntary sector organisations as they begin to assess the need for action in this field.

Annex 5

Memorandum from The Medical Research Council (MRC)

INTRODUCTION

1. MRC is the major public funder of research into ageing, supporting a broad portfolio of basic and clinical research on healthy ageing and on the causes, prevention and treatment of a wide range of conditions that affect the elderly. This includes:

— Fundamental processes of ageing.

— Epidemiology and health needs.

— Bone and joint diseases.

— Rehabilitation and support.

— Incontinence and prostate disorders.

— Vision and hearing.

— The brain and mental health.

2. In addition, the MRC supports a considerable amount of research in many of the diseases that become increasingly common as people get older, including:

— Cardiovascular Disease.

— Diabetes.

— Stroke.

— Cancer.

3. Furthermore, the MRC supports a wide range of other basic and clinical research that underpins research on ageing and older people, ranging from stems cells to magnetic resonance imaging.

PORTFOLIO ANALYSIS

4. The table below summarises the MRC's investment in research related to ageing, in the areas described above, and analysed according to the categories and parameters used for the Cross-Council portfolio analysis (Annex 1). In this, the spend is quoted as an annualised figure, in £k, for research programmes that were active on 31 July 2002. It is intended to update this analysis for spend in 2004. Support is largely through investigator-led proposals, with some managed initiatives.

Research category	1	2	3	4	5	6	7	8	9	10	Total
Spend (£k)	759	0	158	263	6,526	37,465	5,358	8,951	492	680	63,020

The research categories are:

(i) The economics, psychology and sociology of ageing and the life-course.

(ii) The economic, social and policy implications of an ageing population.

(iii) Technologies and design to help people maintain their independence and autonomy (and the effects of those technologies).

(iv) Technologies for the detection, prediction diagnosis and treatment of age related diseases (and the effects of those technologies).

(v) The molecular and cellular changes associated with basic biological processes of cell death, senescence and physiological ageing.

(vi) The causes of, and influences on age related diseases and disability.

(vii) Prevention of breakdown in health and loss of independence in old age and of specific diseases and conditions which cause these.

(viii) Treatments for disease and the breakdown in health in older people.

(ix) Rehabilitation strategies to improve and maintain function and restore independence.

(x) The delivery of effective and efficient health and social care for old and frail people.

SELECTED EXAMPLES OF MRC-SUPPORTED RESEARCH, INCLUDING RECENT SUCCESSES AND ONGOING RESEARCH

Alzheimer's disease and dementia

5. Alzheimer's disease gene/s within reach. A team of international scientists, led by Professor Mike Owen from the University of Wales College of Medicine, has discovered new evidence of a gene involved in the common form of Alzheimer's disease. Their study of 429 Welsh and American sibling pairs over the age of 65 with Alzheimer's found that around two thirds of pairs shared the same genetic characteristic on chromosome 10, revealing that there is at least one major gene for the disease nearby. Identifying the responsible gene, or genes, could in the longer term lead to new and better treatments for Alzheimer's.

Science 290, 2304–05, December 2000

6. Targeting amyloid disease. Alzheimer's and type 2 diabetes are among a number of disorders called amyloid diseases, which involve the abnormal folding of usually soluble proteins, leading to the build up of deposits that eventually destroy the tissue in the brain in Alzheimer's, or the pancreas in diabetes. A team led by Professor Mark Pepys at the National Amyloidosis Centre has developed a drug that destabilises amyloid deposits, allowing them to be broken down. The new drug offers a new approach to treating a range of amyloid diseases.

Nature 417, 231–3, May 2002

7. New dementia drug proves its worth. A disease called Dementia with Lewy bodies (DLB) is one of the major causes of dementia in old age. Changes seen in patients' brains suggest that they might be particularly responsive to new Alzheimer's disease drugs called cholinesterase inhibitors. Professor Ian McKeith and colleagues from the MRC/University Centre Development in Clinical Brain Ageing at Newcastle, with industrial support from Novartis, have conducted the first multicentre, placebo-controlled trial of the cholinesterase inhibitor rivastigmine. The drug produced significant improvements in the core clinical features of the disease, reducing hallucinations, delusions and agitation. This finding is leading to further trial studies and is already changing clinical practice as DLB patients are starting to receive the treatment.

Lancet 356, 2031–36, December 2000

8. MRC Cognitive Function and Ageing Study. This MRC/Department of Health study is investigating the extent of dementias and general cognitive decline in the population, how these conditions progress over time, and the degree of disability they cause.

Parkinson's disease

9. About 120,000 UK citizens currently live with Parkinson's disease. The residential care costs arising from immobility and cognitive difficulties are £400 million a year.

10. The MRC, the Parkinson's Disease Society and the Health Departments are funding a large national clinical trial, led by Professor Adrian Williams (Birmingham), to assess the long-term benefits of nerve stimulating implants for Parkinson's disease.

11. The MRC Clinical Sciences Centre Neurology Group is using the latest functional imaging techniques to look at how the brain controls movement, and what happens when this goes wrong in Parkinson's, Huntington's and motor neuron disease. Last year the group were the first to show that a nerve growth agent (called GDNF) can restore brain function and relieve disability in Parkinson's disease.

MRC Brain Sciences Programme

12. The Government SR2002 Spending Review allocated the MRC an additional £9.7 million specifically for Brain Sciences.

13. This programme aims to build capacity in multi-disciplinary approaches to basic, translational and clinical neuroscience research, with a particular focus on clinical problems in mental ill-health and degenerative brain disorders.

14. There have been two calls for proposals, in 2003 and June 2004, inviting two types of proposals; (i) high-risk/high-pay-off "pathfinder" awards, to act as a springboard for future research bids, particularly for researchers in the earlier stages of their career, and (ii) trial platforms to build capacity for future proposals for clinical trials in mental health. As an additional boost to the £4.7 million in the second call, the Department of Health for England is making £1 million available for applications that will create a springboard for future clinical, health service research and public health research into mental health.

Brain imaging

15. Inside the working brain. Scientists led by Professor Paul Matthews at Oxford University's Centre for Functional Magnetic Resonance Imaging of the Brain (fMRIB) have been using functional imaging to view changes in nerve activity in people who have sustained strokes or head injuries, and others with multiple sclerosis, schizophrenia and other problems affecting the brain and nervous system. Their work is helping increase understanding of how brain function is disrupted by disease or injury, and how the brain reorganises itself in response to damage. For example, work includes investigation of changes in movement-related brain activity in patients receiving rehabilitation therapy following stroke. In other work the team discovered that although the regions of the brain that anticipate pain are close to the areas that respond to pain, they are actually distinct, a discovery that could lead to new ways of managing conditions involving chronic pain, such as arthritis.

Proceedings of the National Academy of Science USA 97, 9281–6, August 2000

16. Dr Nick Fox, MRC Senior Research Fellow of the Dementia research Group, National Hospital for Neurology and Neurosurgery (London) is using the latest imaging techniques to look at the progression of brain changes in Alzheimer's disease.

Osteoporosis

17. One in three women, and one in 12 men aged over 50 will develop osteoporosis. Findings from the MRC Environmental Epidemiology Unit in Southampton, showing that elderly people who have had a broken bone have a greatly increased risk of further fractures, has led to a change in emphasis in osteoporosis prevention, influencing preventative guidelines issued by the Royal College of Physicians.

Osteoporosis International; 13: 624-629, August 2002

18. Other studies help define the role of diet in prevention. Professor Kay-Tee Khaw, University of Cambridge, showed that supplements of vitamin D reduced fractures by over a fifth in older people.

British Medical Journal, 326, 469–472, March 2003

19. Researchers at the MRC's Resource Centre for Human Nutrition Research, in Cambridge, are investigating the impact of a diet rich in fruit and vegetables on bone health.

Vision and Hearing

20. Deafness is the most common disability in older people, with half of all over-60s experiencing some hearing loss. MRC researchers in Cambridge have developed a new test designed to map more precise information about individual patterns of hearing loss. The test could lead to more accurate assessments of who would benefit from hearing aids or cochlear implantation.

British Journal of Audiology, 34, 205–224, 2000

21. MRC's new £12 million Auditory Brain initiative is investigating the role of the brain in hearing and communication. The research, which will be led by scientists at the MRC Institute of Hearing Research in Nottingham, will include studies of brain function, new methods to improve lip reading and the development of new treatments for people with cochlear implants. A key element of the work is a questionnaire to measure the impact of previously unrecognised aspects of hearing in everyday situations, such as the effect of background noise.

22. Professor Glyn Humphreys of the University of Birmingham has uncovered new information about visual extinction, a phenomenon affecting people who have suffered brain damage that impairs their brain's ability to process visual information. This additional knowledge could aid therapists involved in helping people to regain the ability to perform everyday tasks after suffering from stroke, head injury or a brain tumour.

Nature Neuroscience, 6, 82–89, 2003

Cardiovascular Disease

23. Benefits of cholesterol-lowering drugs. MRC funded research has shown that over a third of heart attacks and strokes, major causes of death and ill health worldwide, could be prevented if those at risk took drugs called statins, which lower cholesterol levels. The £21 million Heart Protection Study, the world's largest clinical trial of statins, followed 20,000 volunteers aged 40 to 80 over seven years. The study was funded by the MRC and the British Heart Foundation with the drug companies Merck & Co Inc. and Roche Vitamins. Its results have massive public health implications. The benefits of statins were found across the board, even in people who it was thought previously might not benefit, such as women, younger people, and people with low cholesterol, diabetes, narrowed arteries in the legs, or a history of stroke. If an extra 10 million high risk people worldwide took statins, it is estimated this would save 50,000 lives a year.

Lancet, 360, 23–33, July 2002

Prevention

24. Influenza vaccination in people over 75 years old. Recently-published MRC-funded research, undertaken at the London School of Hygiene and Tropical Medicine through the MRC's General Practice Research Framework, has shown that in people over 75 years old who had not been vaccinated against influenza, all-cause mortality was strongly associated with an index of influenza circulating in the population. The association was strongest for respiratory deaths, but was also present for cardiovascular deaths. In vaccinated people, there was no such association. There was thus a significant protective effect on mortality of vaccination against influenza. This finding shows that in very elderly people, vaccination against a disease which younger people can cope with saves lives.

BMJ, 329, 660–663, October 2004

Underpinning research

25. UK Biobank. Many disorders, including cancer, heart disease, diabetes and Alzheimer's disease are caused by complex interactions between genes, environment and lifestyle. Defining how cells and genes interact with external influences is vital to understanding the origins of health and disease. Using genetic information from DNA samples and the medical records of 500,000 volunteers aged 45–69, the study is the world's largest study of the role of nature and nurture in health and disease. Biobank data will help researchers to gain vital new insights into how to prevent and treat some of the major disorders that appear in later life. Biobank is a collaboration between the MRC, the Wellcome Trust, and the Department of Health (total investment of £61 million). The Scottish Executive has recently announced its intention to contribute £0.5 million.

26. Stem Cell Research. Stem cell research is one of the most exciting and potentially powerful new areas of science, offering new hope for some of the most devastating diseases of our time, such as heart disease, type one diabetes and degenerative brain diseases such as Parkinson's and Alzheimer's. Stem cell therapy promises to be able to replace irreparably damaged cells with healthy new ones.

27. The Government SR2002 Spending Review allocated £40 million across the Research Councils to take forward the UK Stem Cell Initiative. The MRC received £26 million, BBSRC received £10 million and ESRC £1.8 million. The EPSRC and the Particle Physics and Astronomy Research Council (PPARC) received small allocations to help develop key technologies. The MRC has taken the lead, working with other agencies, in developing a UK Stem Cell Initiative. National coordination is achieved via a UK Funders Coordinating Committee comprising relevant Research Councils and Charities plus the Regulatory Agencies, while

international coordination is achieved via a Policy Forum comprising 13 funding representatives from 12 countries with national stem cell initiatives.

28. A UK Stem Cell Bank has been established at the National Institute for Biological Standards and Control (NIBSC) in Hertfordshire, funded by the MRC (75 per cent) and BBSRC (25 per cent). The Bank will curate ethically sourced, quality controlled adult, fetal and embryonic stem cell lines and will be open to academics and industrialists from the UK and overseas.

29. The MRC has attracted leading international stem cell researchers to the UK and appointed Austin Smith (Edinburgh) an MRC Professor. A cadre of MRC stem cell studentships and fellowships are awarded annually, the latter being co-funded with other agencies.

30. New mouse lines provide important resource for disease research. Professor Steve Brown and colleagues from the MRC Mammalian Genetics Unit, in collaboration with Glaxo SmithKline, have used powerful genetic approaches to generate a large resource of mouse strains, many of which carry new genetic mutations. A comprehensive screen of the new strains, using a series of tests, has identified over 500 potential mouse models for a diverse range of human diseases including; osteoporosis, kidney failure, diabetes, abnormal cholesterol processing, spina-bifida, sight and hearing impairments. These models will help to identify gene defects causing human disease and further our understanding of how and why disease develops.

Nature Genetics 25, 440–43, August 2000

September 2004

Supplementary memorandum submitted by Research Councils UK (RCUK)

UPDATE

As highlighted in the original Research Councils UK (RCUK) submission to the House of Lords, it was intended to update the analysis of spend across the Research Councils from 2002 to 2004. This document provides the update, with cross reference to the original submission.

Paragraph 42

The table below summarises the total Research Council spend in ageing-related research. The figures are the annualised spend of all relevant research programmes which were live on 31 July 2004. The annualised spend of each research programme was calculated as the total cost divided by the duration.

Research area	BBSRC	EPSRC	ESRC	MRC	Total RC
Total ageing portfolio	£15.3 million	£6.5 million	£1.3 million	£128 million	£151.1 million

[refers to annex 1 of the previous submission, see p 205]

Figure 1
RESEARCH COUNCIL SPEND IN AGEING RESEARCH FOR RESEARCH PROJECTS THAT WERE ACTIVE ON 31 JULY 2004

Research Council Combined Spend in Ageing Research

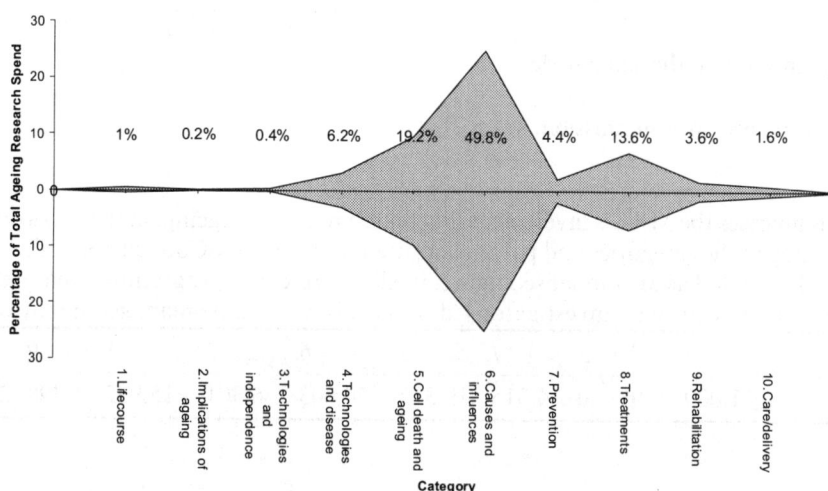

Annex 1

Figure 2

INDIVIDUAL RESEARCH COUNCIL SPEND

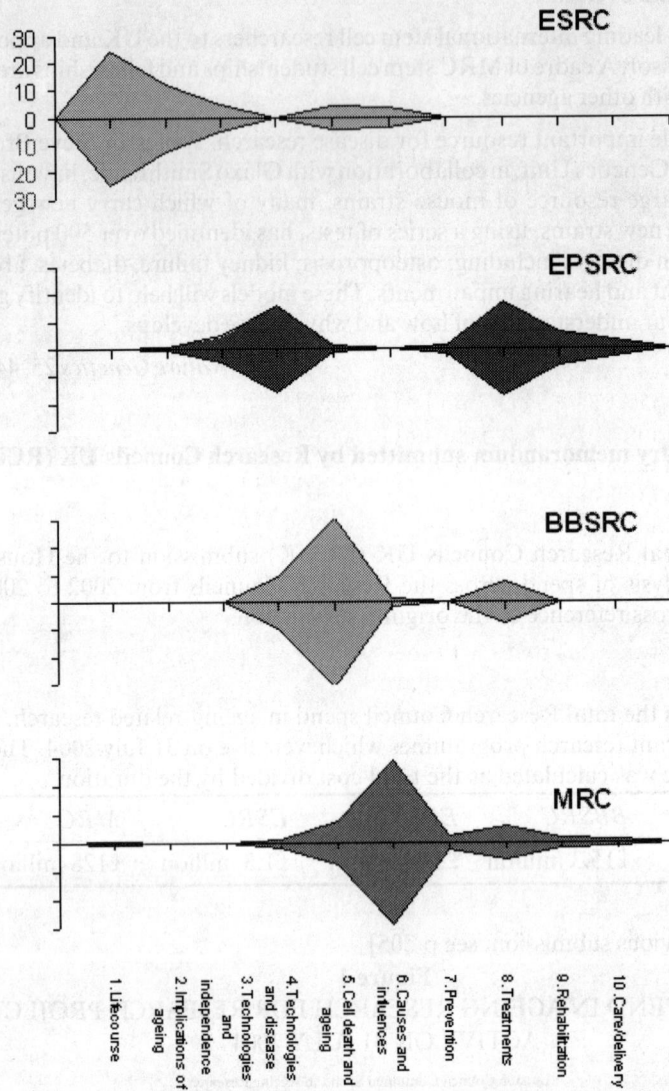

Note: all four diagrams are on the same scale.

[refers to annex 5 of the previous submission, see p 213]

PARAGRAPH 4

The table below summarises the MRC's investment in research related to ageing, in the areas described above, and analysed according to the categories and parameters used for the Cross-Council portfolio analysis (Annex 1). In this, the spend is quoted as an annualised figure, in £k, for research programmes that were active on 31 July 2004. Support is largely through investigator-led proposals, with some managed initiatives.

Research category	1	2	3	4	5	6	7	8	9	10	Total
Spend (£k)	1,000	0	0	4,315	19,332	74,603	6,301	15,932	4,498	2,064	128,045

February 2005

Examination of Witnesses

Witnesses: PROFESSOR LINDA PARTRIDGE FRS, Weldon Professor of Biometry, University College London (on behalf of the Academy of Medical Sciences and the BBSRC); PROFESSOR IAN DIAMOND, Chief Executive, ESRC; DR DIANA DUNSTAN, Director, Research Management Group, MRC; and DR ALISON WALL, Programme Manager, Infrastructure and Environment, EPSRC, examined.

Q386 *Chairman:* May I say welcome, and welcome again to some of you who have already been helping us in various ways, and many thanks for the written evidence which has been submitted which is immensely helpful for us. I shall not go round the table introducing my colleagues as we all have names in front of us. My name is Sutherland and you will know Tom Kirkwood who is our Scientific Adviser and Michael Collon who has been in touch with you to arrange the meeting and who is Clerk to the Committee. I think we should move straight on to the questions as there are a lot of very important issues here, but I would just say that if at the end you feel frustrated that there are things that we have not explored, you would be very much encouraged to drop us a line or email us, on reflection, should there be matters of some significance. Perhaps I can start with a fairly general question and you might just want to introduce yourselves and your responsibilities as perhaps each of you responds to this one. This is a question which has to do with the scientific aspects of ageing and one of the issues that keeps coming up in our discussions here and indeed in the USA when we went to the NIH and the NIA is the question of whether or not there is a useful distinction to be drawn between the impact of the diseases that cluster around ageing, but which are not necessarily associated only with older people, on the one hand, and what you do about them, which may be a quite distinctive process of ageing with various concomitants, which may well make one more vulnerable to these diseases of ageing, as they are sometimes called. Is such a distinction useful, but, more significantly for each of you, how does that work out if it either is or is not in the kind of research that you either participate in, or commission, or look for proposals in relation to much of your separate areas of responsibility?

Professor Diamond: Chairman, as you know, we range right across the research council spectrum. It is a truly interdisciplinary or multidisciplinary question, so if we go from the medical end through to biology through to the engineering and we will end with the social science. So Diana?

Dr Dunstan: I am Diana Dunstan. I am Director of Research Management at MRC. On the whole, I think MRC takes the view that ageing is a life-course event, as it were, that you start actually from the foetus and go right through, so we do not see that there is much benefit in drawing the distinction, as far as our research programme is concerned, that you

refer to. We work from the basic end to the clinical end and we look at all the stages of life. For example, we have got work on the early origins of adult disease which shows how life in the womb affects heart disease, for example, later on. We simply fund stuff that is good quality, that is relevant and regardless of the definition. I did ask our Board Chairmen which of your two definitions they would incline to and they inclined to the second bit, which is ageing as underpinning increasing vulnerability, but that does not really guide what the MRC does.

Q387 *Chairman:* And in the sense that what you focus on are various forms of the expression of vulnerability, diseases and so on?

Dr Dunstan: Yes, and the basic research at the other end. There is inevitably this grey area which may have been normal ageing, but it may shade over into disease, yes.

Professor Partridge: I am Linda Partridge and I am a Research Professor at University College London and I actually work on ageing, but I am also representing the BBSRC. I think they also would incline very much to your second definition, that what we are looking at is an underlying process of progressive loss of function that leads to increasing vulnerability to various diseases, but I think there are two things that are quite characteristic about their remit in that regard. The first is that they place considerable importance on the fact that there are interventions, both mutations in genes and environmental interventions like dietary restriction, that seem to be capable of delaying the impact of a very diverse range of ageing-related disease. This suggests that there is an underlying ageing process that can affect all these diseases simultaneously, and I think it is that which they are seeking to understand. The other important thing is the discovery that these interventions that seem to be capable of slowing down the impact of these ageing-related diseases and disabilities also seem to show evolutionary conservation, extraordinarily enough, so it means that we can use simple organisms, like yeast, nematode worms, fruit flies and mice to understand the ageing process in humans. I think those would be the two guiding points of the philosophy of the BBSRC.

Dr Wall: I am Programme Manager for the Infrastructure and Environment Programme within the Engineering and Physical Sciences Research Council. Just to put you in the picture, that is one of the three engineering programmes and particularly a managed activity that supports ageing research. This question for us is not really one we have spent time grappling with. We take a very practical view, so we are looking for science and technology to address particular problems, whether it is vision loss, mobility, dementia, and sometimes the research that we commission might be relevant to older people, but it will also have relevance to other disabilities, so I think we are looking at very practical solution-driven research.

Professor Diamond: I am the Chief Executive of the Economic and Social Research Council. I think the very nature of the questions demonstrates the multidisciplinarity of the areas that we are looking at now. For the ESRC, ageing is very much about growing older and, as you grow older, it is about enabling people to grow older gracefully, it is about enabling them to maximise the quality of their life as they grow older and in the way not only that older people, if you like, maximise their own quality of life, but the impact that older people have on other parts of society and issues, such as grandparenting. The role of grandparents and volunteering on the whole of society, I think, are critical issues as well as that link towards, if you like, the second definition of older mobility and the older old. There is a whole big spectrum now of the old and simply to try and lump the old together, I think, is not a sensible way to move forward. Finally, of course one of the great causes of ageing in this country is indeed not people living longer, but at the other end of the spectrum, childbearing, and that link is something that we really need to put into place when we look at one of the big questions that people ask when they talk about an ageing society, and that is pensions.

Q388 *Chairman:* Just a very practical point from our point of view, does what each of you have said make it more or less difficult to answer the question as to what proportion of research money is spent on ageing?

Professor Diamond: Very much. I think it would be fair to say that we have had the Growing Older programme, we are all extremely excited about the New Dynamics of Ageing programme that we are just about to start commissioning, and those are very much, if you like, directed programmes, but we also all in response mode have large amounts of research. Some of it is, for example, a piece on "the old" and others of it is just simply related to older people and some of the data-collection exercises are related to old people or having implications for old people while not directly specified there, so I think it is very difficult simply to put a figure on every piece of ageing research that is undertaken in the

research councils. What I can say very clearly is that for all of the research councils for whom it is appropriate, ageing is a vitally important priority and I am sure will remain a priority over the next few years for the research agenda.

Q389 *Chairman:* Does anybody want to add anything to that?

Professor Partridge: I think one needs to take a very detailed look at the portfolio of activities in order to be able to answer the question accurately. Things like tissue engineering and stem cells in the BBSRC remit would be obvious cases relevant to ageing-related diseases.

Q390 *Chairman:* The reason for pressing a little bit is that a question that has occurred to us is whether or not there is an appropriate percentage of the research budget going on the issues that surround now a very large, and increasingly large, percentage of the population. That is not the only criterion taken for research spend, but the question of appropriateness does come up and that is made more difficult if we cannot identify the areas.

Professor Diamond: Perhaps I might give a view and my colleagues will certainly, I am sure, have the opportunity to afterwards. The question should not be what proportion of the research budget should be spent on ageing; the question should be what are the research questions that it is deeply important for this country to answer and for which this country has comparative advantage in answering over and above those which are going to be answered anyway in the world and to make sure that we are doing that. That is why I said earlier that it is a priority of setting that research agenda, and identifying the research landscape that needs to be addressed is the critical issue.

Q391 *Chairman:* I take that point, but each of the areas of research represented in the country at large might say, "Well, that is our agenda of important questions", and it does not actually add up to an actual volume of cash available.

Professor Diamond: That is why we have to prioritise. The critical thing is to know what the agenda is and to be sure that you are at least prioritising within that agenda.

Q392 *Lord May of Oxford:* But that is the question you were asked, and you just said that you did not accept it because the question as to whether you think it is the right proportion is a statement about the assignment of priorities. If you just take your view and say that you made a list of the important questions and you are going to do this for everything, it might add up to a hell of a lot more money than is available.

Professor Diamond: I think I would have to say that the research base in this country across the entire science and engineering base would be able to spend much more than the money that is available, and it becomes a question of prioritising it across not only ageing, but across everything else, and we are going to have to be sure that if ageing is a priority area, then we are addressing those questions which are critical and important. I think it would be wrong *a priori* to say what that proportion should be.

Q393 *Lord Turnberg:* This may anticipate a later question, but I was struck by Professor Diamond's comment about the multidisciplinarity of research, and it obviously spreads right across the research councils. I know you have some mechanisms, but I just wonder how you understand the whole field across the research councils and how you begin to co-operate and co-ordinate what you fund in relation to what other research councils are funding. How well is that going?

Professor Diamond: I think very well. We have through Research Councils UK our Research Directors Group of which Dr Dunstan is a member. They certainly work to co-ordinate and link together important issues and to make sure that we are not, if you like, either (a) reinventing wheels, or (b) missing balls in areas where we wish to prioritise. We also are very clear in the way in which in response mode we deal with interdisciplinary research programmes, and we wrote last summer for the Council for Science and Technology a piece on how we dealt with interdisciplinary research projects and programmes, and I would be delighted to let the Committee have a copy of that, if that would be helpful, which would assure you of the way in which we peer-review and manage those things. Diana, I do not know if you want to talk about the RDG.

Dr Dunstan: We do talk about co-ordination of research at the Research Directors Group, but particularly in the field of ageing we have got a cross-council co-ordination group which was set up in 2000, I think, when we realised that we probably did not know enough about what each other was doing. It is partly for the exchange of information, it is partly that we have bound it together and actually, as Ian says, we have come out with the New Dynamics of Ageing programme which ESRC is leading, but of which we are all a part. One of the things we have done, which I guess relates back to your previous question about how much money we are spending, is actually look at our portfolios, and we sent it to you.

Q394 *Chairman:* Yes, we have received that.

Dr Dunstan: It is the kite diagrams. That was cribbing things from the way that we had looked at the council portfolios and it did seem in that case to throw up a lot of interesting gaps that needed to be filled. It has shown that there is a concentration, I think, in the research councils of investment in some areas and that other areas are relatively thin. What we would like to do now is to put that alongside what the charities fund and then see how well the whole field is covered through all the funding that is directed at this area, private and public sector.

Q395 *Lord Soulsby of Swaffham Prior:* I have a question arising from Professor Diamond's answer. He used the phrase "quality of life" and we have heard this phrase from many people giving evidence, so my question is, what is it and how do you measure it? Can it be quantified?

Professor Diamond: That is a very, very good question to which there are many, many answers. For example, one could define "quality of life" as being a life without serious disabling illness, and there is a huge literature which has enabled people to calculate what are called "disability-adjusted life years" and to see what the impact and the increase in those of either reducing disease or changing disease has been. I would argue that that is important and critical, but at the same time you need actually to talk to people about their mobility, their cognitive ability, their economic ability, a whole series of things, and to put together portfolios, if you like, or baskets of different indicators of quality of life to have a variable group of them. Now, some of that can be done in a quantitative way and has been done in a quantitative way and the ESRC has led on some of that work, and others of it are rather more qualitative, so the answer is yes, but it is again a multivariant set of indicators that you need and particular different indicators for the question that you are asking.

Q396 *Lord Soulsby of Swaffham Prior:* But the DALYs that you mentioned, are they possibly a useful measure of it?

Professor Diamond: I think DALYs have a lot of potential benefits because they do enable us to look over time and between different groups of people at the extent to which, if you like, disability is impacting, and the time of healthy life that the groups of people have. I think it is terribly important that we are able to do that and it has enabled us, for example, to be able to look at some of the sort of perceptions that people have of their future life and to show, as I am sure you have heard evidence of here before, that people actually will live rather longer than they expect to do and there are then clear implications for the quality of that extra time given the expectations they then might make about their financial provision. There are ways in which I think DALYs have many potential uses, and Dr Dunstan may like to add to them, but I would not say that they are the one and only indicator of quality of life by any manner of means.

Q397 Lord May of Oxford: I just have a very quick question which perhaps might best be done by written response. I thought this breakdown of pattern of spending was very interesting and potentially helpful, but I had a bit of difficulty with the categories which seemed to me, in my ignorance, to be a little confused and overlapping. I wonder if somebody could be so kind as to let us have a count of exactly what "life course through care delivery" meant and where they derive from, and, rather than trying to sort that out now, perhaps you could write to us.
Professor Diamond: Yes, we would be delighted.
Lord May of Oxford: It is a helpful thing.
Chairman: It is indeed.

Q398 Lord Soulsby of Swaffham Prior: If we can go on, I think the second and third questions are connected and in part you have answered them already, but could each person from the research councils describe the priority their research council attaches to the field of ageing and the science of ageing, and what specific action has been taken?
Dr Dunstan: The MRC has put in its 10-year vision document, which we published in 2003, ageing and the health of the elderly population as a priority, and for obvious demographic reasons we went to that. It is also one of about seven priorities in our current list and it will be addressed in our delivery plan, so it is up there. It has been decided by information coming up from the grassroots, being sifted by our research boards and being endorsed by our Council, so it is something that is really recognised within the MRC. I guess specific actions that we have taken are partly to be a partner in the New Dynamics of Ageing programme, but also to invest in other areas that might well be very relevant to this. For example, one thing which we have done recently is to support the appointment of a Professor of Gerontology at Oxford, a new one, and he is coming over to do particular work in stroke medicine and has been recruited from abroad and he, we think, will be a real catch for the UK, so that is just an example.
Professor Partridge: The BBSRC has had two research initiatives specifically devoted to the basic science of ageing, both of them for three years. The first started in 1998, SAGE, and committed just over

£5 million, and the second, ERA, in 2001 committed just over £4 million. They were looking at topics such as the genetics of ageing, molecular biology, cell biology, cell senescence, some chemical intervention and so on, and they were specifically directed to ageing research. There is also an initiative just starting at the moment called Selective Chemical Intervention in Biological Systems and this is looking for small molecules that interfere with various biological processes, and one of the priorities in that initiative is in ageing. Then very recently, as part of the delivery plan for Spending Round 2004, ageing has again come up as a priority at the BBSRC and there is going to be another initiative, with the priorities being set at present. BBSRC have set up a strategy board called The Healthy Organism, one subcomponent of which, which I am chairing, is looking after ageing and that is what will set the priorities for this new initiative. We also have a joint programme called SPARC with the EPSRC, which perhaps my colleague will speak about, which is fostering networking and small pump-priming grants for work in ageing.

Q399 Lord Soulsby of Swaffham Prior: When you use the word "priority", what does that mean? Does that mean a high level of priority?
Professor Partridge: The two initiatives that I mentioned first were solely for ageing research and there was nothing else on the agenda. The specific one on chemical intervention includes other topics, such as developmental biology, but the portfolio of topics that that committee is interested in are named, there are three of them, and one of them is ageing.
Dr Wall: This area is a high priority for EPSRC. In particular, we have a managed programme of activity which is our own Extended Quality of Life programme, EQUAL, and that has been running since 1997. We have commissioned 34 research projects worth £5.4 million which has covered areas, such as the built environment, design for all and rehabilitation. Then in 2003 we took a different tack in the programme and worked with the community to develop five multidisciplinary research consortia, funded with £3.1 million. A key theme all the way through EQUAL for us has been the involvement right at the start of the research process with users and with older people and a highlight for the EQUAL programme was funding the EQUAL Network, and you have already heard from Professor Peter Lansley at your seminar. We also pick up aspects of ageing from our major Sustainable Urban Environment programme, and that is covering, for example, design of the urban environment and user needs and transport. We have also mentioned the Strategic Promotion of Ageing

Research Capacity, which is a bit of a mouthful, and that is a successor to the EQUAL Network. It will have two strands in it, one being networking with the community and dissemination of the outputs, the other bringing newcomers into the area of ageing research and giving pump-priming funding. It is £1.3 million worth of funding from the EPSRC. Our major new activity is the New Dynamics of Ageing programme where we are putting up £5 million worth of funding with matched funding from the ESRC. I should not stop without saying that the other activity for us is our investigator-led route which is where proposals can come into EPSRC on any subject area at any time, and that door is always open to support high-quality ageing research.

Q400 *Chairman:* Do you get much through that door?

Dr Wall: Well, that is a very good question. We get a lot of underpinning research in the area of tissue engineering and biomedical engineering, but we are really missing the sort of assisted technology-type research proposals that we would support through programmes like EQUAL, and we would really like to see the community growing and using that investigator-led route as well.

Professor Diamond: From the ESRC, for a period of time since the mid- to late-1990s, ageing has been a critical area for the ESRC, and the Growing Older programme, which was recently evaluated as being outstanding, was our major vehicle at that time and that has led into the New Dynamics of Ageing programme. However, I would also say, as Alison just did, that we encourage response mode applications from researchers and we have had a number of those, not least, I think I should mention, £$\frac{1}{2}$ million of funding last year to research groups jointly from Michael Marmot's group at the University College and the Institute of Fiscal Studies which were looking to analyse data from the English Longitudinal Study of Ageing, which I think is going to be one of the really major resources in this area. We have also over the last four or five years funded a research group which has been led by Professor Paul Johnson and Professor Jane Falkingham from the London School of Economics and the University of Southampton which has been simulating an ageing society and looking at the social policy implications of an ageing society in the UK. Finally, I would just mention the investments that we have had in data which are ongoing, particularly our cohort data, and it is a fact of demographic life that some of the earlier birth cohorts are now really starting to become of an age—

Q401 *Lord Soulsby of Swaffham Prior:* We know, yes, we know!

Professor Diamond:—relevant to this area.

Q402 *Baroness Walmsley:* Could you say how successful have been the actions of your various research councils and how you measure that success? Could you also say what problems you have encountered and how you have addressed them? Finally, how do you disseminate the results of your research to the health professionals, to the Government and to the general public?

Dr Dunstan: As to how successful, there are some programmes that I think really have been successful. The Foetal Origins of Adult Disease was started, I guess, probably 15 years ago with work in Southampton and that has been followed on and is now, I think, accepted internationally as a viable hypothesis that has been proven, although there was a lot of scepticism when the MRC first started that work, and that has had a lot of investment over the years. Something which has taken rather less long was a trial of statins for lowering cholesterol and that has had a huge effect, and it has been very successful in that not only is it clear when people should be treated with statins, but now it is also clear that it is safe actually to buy them over the counter and that has been really taken up in policy and in practice. We also fund things like a trial that looked at community care of the elderly, which did not look as those that had community care from the primary care practitioners and those that did not because everyone does, but we looked at different methods of delivering it. In fact that showed that there was not much difference in benefit from the different ways of delivering it, but that actually a lot more effort needed to be put into ensuring that the elderly have sight tests, hearing tests and that the right kind of aids were offered to them, because very often they have a fairly severe deficit and they do not complain about them and it can really make a lot of difference to their lives actually if those are taken up. We try to disseminate the output through publications and we try to measure impact through better health and life years gain, that kind of thing, but the main problem that we have, apart from these relatively high-profile things that I have mentioned and some others, is implementation, and it is not simply something that relates to the elderly. Implementation of research results is a real issue for us. It is quite easy in some senses to get the pharmaceutical industry or the biotech industry to take things up, and I think within the MRC at least we have more or less got that worked out, but getting other things translated into practice and taken up is really extremely difficult. We are talking a lot with health departments, and recently I have been to Canada to talk to the Canadian Institute of Health Research and a foundation over there which focuses particularly on implementation, and I have come back with some really, I think, quite interesting ideas about how we might actually improve implementation.

Professor Partridge: I think we have judged the success of the various initiatives at the BBSRC in really rather similar ways. We have looked at research outputs obviously, but also one of the main aims of these programmes was to try and build capacity in the whole research area and to get new people involved. I could list a number of specific scientific achievements, if you would be interested and perhaps tell me at the end if you would, including some that have translated into clinical trials and specific exercise programmes and so on for the elderly, so there were a number of successes there.

Q403 *Baroness Walmsley:* Excuse me for stopping you, but could you tell us whether successful implementation is one of your criteria of success?

Professor Partridge: Yes, very much so. We are always very proud if something goes through to informing clinical practice or approaches to it, as in the exercise programme, so yes, that is something we would boast about as well as just pure science. The capacity-building I think we would judge simply as labs that were not previously engaged in ageing research having entered it as a result of those programmes and stayed in it, and there have been a number of such success stories. However, I think there have been a couple of problems. One has been trying to obtain follow-on funding for the groups that were involved in these programmes, whether for the first time or as new entrants, through the responsive mode committees in the BBSRC. These are the investigator-led approaches to the Council to obtain funding and there has been a very low success rate with those for ageing and we do not know why. It seems possible that the multidisciplinary nature of the ageing proposals does not appeal to committees that have specific expertise in biochemistry, structural biology or genetics because ageing is not confined to any one of those topics, but rather covers alot of different areas, so I think that is something we need to address in the Council. I think the other thing which has been something of a disappointment is the feed-through particularly into government departments, especially the Department of Health. I think ageing was last mentioned in our discussions with them in 2001 when we informed them about the ERA programme. We have talked to them about other things, stem cells, TSEs and so on, but not about ageing, so one of the things we have planned is a

very high-profile dissemination event at the beginning of next year when we shall bring together key people who might use our research to hear what we have been doing.

Q404 *Baroness Walmsley:* Will that be done through a seminar?

Professor Partridge: It will be done through a large invited workshop, yes, a one-day event.

Q405 *Lord Oxburgh:* Could I ask whether there will then be an account of this on your website or whether there will be a publication coming out of this?

Professor Partridge: There was certainly an idea that there would be a publicity document produced based on presentations at the workshop, and that could be translated into a website presence as well. I do not think we had thought of that, but we could do it.

Q406 *Lord Oxburgh:* When the Committee was in the United States, we were very impressed at the dissemination efforts that they put in. They struck us as particularly effective through reader-friendly documents, documents that could be read at different levels by different audiences, and I think we have not seen anything like that in the UK.

Professor Partridge: Yes, I think we could do a lot more.

Q407 *Chairman:* I was just going to ask on a related point, will, for example, this great event include people from the departments, such as the Department of Health, so civil servants and so on?

Professor Partridge: Yes, definitely. They would be one of our prime targets to make contact with. We want the policy-makers and the purse-holders.

Dr Wall: For our research grants we collect a final report within three months of them finishing and those final reports on the EQUAL programme have all been graded as good and two-thirds have tended to outstanding and better, so we know we have got some very good research outcomes, good publications and conference proceedings, but we also look at the relevance to beneficiaries and actually those projects tend to score highly on the relevance to beneficiaries. One of the other things we have particularly looked at is engaging users in the programme and we hope that by engaging them at the start of the research and having been engaged with the project all the way through, there will be a straightforward take-up route if the outcomes are successful. Just to give you an idea, the sort of users that we have engaged with projects are the RNIB, BT, Tesco, intriguingly, the Design Council, Age Concern and a number of city councils, so we hope they are all providing a route for rapid take-up of successful outcomes. A major dissemination activity for us has been the EQUAL Network where Professor Lansley has been organising a series of workshops which promote the outcomes of the research. One of them on transport, for example, was done jointly with the Department for Transport, one on safety of older workers in the workplace with the Health & Safety Executive, and they all involve users, practitioners and older people as well, so I think that has been a very good dissemination route for us. We know, and you have probably heard a lot of this from Peter directly, that some of the research is now being used to change building regulations, to give advice to housing associations, to change design guidelines and the Design Council now has a publicational website for training on design, so although the take-up of follow-on funding is still an issue for us, this is one area in the EPSRC where we have seen some rapid take-up of the outputs. We also provided our grants to the database for the Foundation for Assisted Technology in the hope that that would be another route for take-up as well.

Professor Diamond: If I may just pick that up for the ESRC, firstly, all our programmes, all our projects are evaluated formally for their academic content and I can report from our Growing Older programme, although the announcement has not formally been made yet, that a large proportion of them are actually outstanding, which did not surprise us because it has been a programme which has had a large impact and at the same time as worrying about the academic evaluation, we are deeply worried about the impact of our research. One of the things we are committed to is getting research into practice and that comes about in a number of ways: a strategic advisory committee, which included a number of stakeholders and users, both charities and government departments, which was part of the programme at all times; and through our concordats with the ODPM and the DWP where we talk about the results about ageing. In response to your point, Lord Oxburgh, there are two points I might mention. On a programme such as this, we have taken now a policy of having a media fellow for the Growing Older programme, Malcolm Dean, who is better known as the society editor of *The Guardian*, and part of his job was to write user-friendly or reader-friendly, for different levels, summaries of how research was pulled together, and he wrote a number of those and I would recommend them to you. We also run policy seminars where we get people, science writers, to engage with the researchers and to write high-level documents which give the research landscape and the policy implications, and we have one of those in

the area of pensions, which again I could let you have. Finally, I would draw your attention to the launch on 28 April of our new distributed ESRC *Society Today* electronic distribution which will, amongst many other things, have plain English summaries of every one of the research grants we have funded over the last three to four years, which will be accessible and easy, and we have a team of science writers at the moment making sure that they are finalised, as well as reviews of areas and accessibility to things and, for those who are interested in particular areas, regular email alerts to them of particular new pieces of research that are coming on board.

Q408 *Baroness Walmsley:* I wondered if the last two speakers have encountered any particular problems and, if so, have they been overcome?

Professor Diamond: One of the key areas if one is trying to get research into practice, I believe and the ESRC believes very strongly, is the absolute need to have ownership at the high level right at the beginning, and that is something that we are deeply committed to. Therefore, if we are intending to have a research programme which is going to lead to some policy, then we actually need to have the relevant, in this case, say, government departments or industry or the charity sector on board right at the beginning and being part of the development of the agenda and, therefore, part of the ongoing agenda so that the results that come out at the end are not suddenly results that appear from anywhere. That is one of the major, if you like, tricks that has to be addressed, I think, absolutely properly. The second thing is to make things reader-friendly. We put a lot of effort into media training for our programme directors and for our researchers because we are conscious that when you perhaps only have 20 minutes with a group of people, such as yourselves, in order to communicate some really quite high-level science, actually you have got to do it incredibly well and there is a skill in this media communication that many academics for very good reasons do not have, so we are deeply committed to that training.

Dr Wall: I agree with that completely. I would say that we do still have some problems of take-up and there are some projects that we funded in EQUAL which looked like brilliant ideas to us, and I was tracking one of them yesterday and it still has not been taken up, but we do not have an answer to that. They are struggling to get follow-on funding and the funding they need in order to take the ideas to the next level.

Q409 Baroness Walmsley: Are those at the stage where you are needing business input or are they at the stage where you need further research or policy change or what is it?

Dr Wall: I think some of them need business input, but actually the researchers will be looking for further research funding as well, so it is hard to say specifically.

Q410 Baroness Walmsley: Do you have any feeling for why businesses are not taking up some of these ideas?

Dr Wall: No, and, looking through our portfolio, we can see we have got a very strong representation from local authorities and from the charities, but not many businesses. There are some small IT companies, but much less than in all the rest of EPSRC's portfolio.

Q411 Chairman: We might be interested in some statistics on that if they could easily be put together.

Dr Wall: Yes, they could be.

Dr Dunstan: One of the suggestions that came from Canada was that we actually set up networks of what they call "knowledge brokers", and this is particularly for getting knowledge taken up in the Health Service, so these are people who understand the Health Service and they may be people that have come from the management side or they may be medical people. They know very well our research, what has been funded, what the output is and they go out there and try to sell it, try to get it taken up and, if it is not taken up, to understand why so that we can then feed that back in the loop afterwards. This has worked very well over there, so whether it is going to work over here, we do not know, but we intend to invest some money in it to try and see if it will take off here.

Q412 Lord Turnberg: I think to some extent my question has been answered, but I wonder if I could take you on a bit. As you know, this Committee is writing a report and making recommendations about what we should be doing in the field of research into ageing. You quite rightly, all of you, have shown us all your commendable activities and all the good things you are doing, and that is fine, and the report could simply applaud you and say that the garden is rosy, but I am not sure that would be terribly helpful. I wonder, therefore, if I could take you on a bit and ask you whether you can focus on the deficiencies and the failures. This is more difficult, I think, for you because obviously you want to demonstrate how good you are and you have done that pretty well, but I would like to hear more about where we should be doing more, where we can recommend that you, the research councils,

could do more, where you think you need to focus more effort and perhaps equally of course, if not more importantly, where we can recommend that the Government can do something.

Professor Diamond: While my colleagues are just preparing their thoughts, I might identify two areas which I think are incredibly important for this country if it is properly to address ageing research over the next few years. Firstly, it is a sad fact of life that many people who are researchers start off researching on some of our young people and as they get older in their demographic careers, they sort of hit ageing research a little later. I actually do not think that is ideal and we need to encourage a generation of young, junior researchers who find ageing an extremely exciting area. I think one of the evaluations from our ESRC Growing Older programme has been that there is a paucity of young, new researchers coming up.

Q413 Lord Turnberg: Do you have any idea of how to do it?

Professor Diamond: I think there are three things that we need to do. Firstly, we need to prioritise ageing research, broadly defined, for PhDs and to make sure that that is an attractive area. Secondly, I would submit that, working with the Government, it is very good to have joint research studentships which actually have policy relevance, and we at the ESRC have joint programmes, for example, with ODPM, and I think there are a huge number of potentials for that. I think that we also ought to continue to prioritise, and will continue to prioritise, ageing as an important area of research and that is for the research councils to do. The other area I was going to mention is that the infrastructure for studying ageing is critically important and data-collection on the elderly is not cheap. For example, I have seen quotes for a very large European study which the UK had the potential to be part of which was to collect large numbers of social and cognitive data on the elderly where the cost was going to be around about £100 an interview, so once you start multiplying that by the sorts of sample sizes that you need and maybe turning that into a longitudinal study, the numbers become very big very quickly. I think we have really to recognise that data infrastructure at this level is a large national resource and has to be funded as such if we are serious about it. Finally, the data are not simply social data, indeed they are not simply biological data and indeed they are not simply in some cases environmental data. We need to have the ability to merge data together and we need to be able, I would submit, to be able to merge in administrative data as well, and I know there are disclosure and confidentiality issues, but I do not believe they are

8 February 2005   Professor Linda Partridge, Professor Ian Diamond,
Dr Diana Dunstan and Dr Alison Wall

issues that cannot be overcome if we are serious about answering many of the research questions that are critical in this area.

Q414 *Lord Turnberg:* Do you think the human BioBank will help in that?
Professor Diamond: I think BioBank is an extremely useful and important potential research resource, but we need to be able to use it to its best ability.

Q415 *Lord Turnberg:* Will they be receptive to your ideas?
Dr Dunstan: BioBank will be very useful, I think, for ageing in the sense that it will throw light on the gene/environment interactions in diseases that appear in the ageing population. There are a number of other cohorts that Ian referred to before that need to be harvested, as it were, and we are working together between the research councils, the Wellcome Trust and the health departments to look at the cohorts so that we all know what is there, so that we can make the best use and work together on the future sweeps of them because they are very labour-intensive and very expensive, as Ian said, and we need to spend the money as best we can.
Professor Diamond: I have today been asked to chair that group and have accepted, so it will be a multidisciplinary group.
Dr Dunstan: I would also say that I agree with Ian about bringing the youngsters in to ageing research and it is not happening. I guess it is probably because for some reason certainly the basic sciences are not an obviously sexy area. I do not think we would offer studentships for ageing research particularly, but we have talked about whether we should be trying to attract people at first post-doc into this kind of research area. We think at a studentship level they probably need to learn skills in cell biology, statistics, epidemiology or whatever, and then maybe we should offer some carrots to go in at the first post-doc level, but that, I think, is the main drawback in basic research and indeed in clinical research, that you rarely see the really bright, young clinicians opting to go into geriatrics or gerontology. Some do, but very few relatively.

Q416 *Lord Turnberg:* I am a bit cynical about motives in researchers. They tend to go where the money is.
Dr Dunstan: Yes, but I think what we are saying is that with studentships people should be getting basic skills and then beyond that you can attract them with money.
Professor Diamond: Lord Turnberg, I would absolutely agree with you. I am quoted very often as saying that behavioural change in academics is very easy to engender; you simply throw money at

the problem. I think there is something to be said for that.

Q417 *Lord Turnberg:* It is not the entire problem.
Professor Diamond: No, it is not the entire problem. You have to have a really exciting area. It is actually very important to prioritise and to make money available because what you are often trying to do is to attract the very, very best researchers sometimes from a different, if you like, area so that, for example, one might be trying to try to get economists or psychologists in my area who have not worked on ageing before, but for whom the questions are really important and to get them to bring their transferable skills that they have taken elsewhere into a fresh area. I think that is terribly important for us going forward and some of the work that the Institute of Fiscal Studies is doing now is a really beautiful example of that.

Q418 *Lord Turnberg:* The sexy thing at the moment is to talk about research networks. Do you think we should be investing heavily in research networks in ageing?
Dr Dunstan: The Canadians would say that is a really good plan actually to have these virtual networks, and certainly over there they work terrifically well, but they have got networks that span the basic, if you like, experimental, nursing, translation and go through to the clinical and they really get some pull-through. There will be a kind of network, I think, established around the New Dynamics of Ageing programme, so we have been thinking whether in fact we need to establish complementary networks to go alongside those in the basic area, and yes, they would be helpful.
Professor Partridge: I just wanted to say something about interdisciplinarity, organisation of research and barriers to getting things done. There are various small rules that turn out to be major obstacles if one is trying to put together an interdisciplinary team, which is often what is needed for a research programme in ageing. For instance, BBSRC are not allowed to fund work on disease, so if you want to conduct a programme, for instance asking, "How is the underlying ageing process a predisposing factor for diseases?", there is straightaway a remit issue. There can also be issues over collaboration. For instance, people in MRC units cannot easily obtain joint funding with people funded through the EPSRC or BBSRC in a responsive mode. There are a number of such barriers which are a problem specifically for ageing research, I think, because of the need for interdisciplinarity. Another point is training. I think it is often most appropriate to train people in ageing research in the context of interdisciplinary teams

8 February 2005   Professor Linda Partridge, Professor Ian Diamond,
Dr Diana Dunstan and Dr Alison Wall

because they often need to learn about many different things. It is often very difficult for a young principal investigator to get going on their own in this field. I think you have to create centres and I think they have to be local centres, not virtual ones, where you have clinicians, translators and basic scientists working together as a group. That is the best context in which to train young scientists in ageing research. I think one inimical trend at the Research Council at the moment is the tendency to give what are called, I think, "research training accounts" to university departments, so that instead of awarding a studentship to somebody intending to undertake a PhD to look at a particular problem in a priority area for the research council, rather a large amount of money is passed to the department which then sets the priorities. That is going to make it more difficult to make this a priority area. The third point I would make is one which has been touched on already, which is that an audit of the kind of population data and other resources, such as ageing animal colonies we need as a nation for this kind of research would be very helpful, and some sort of co-ordination of the activities of funders to make sure that those resources are available would be wonderful.

Q419 Chairman: One of the things that we saw some evidence of in the National Institute on Aging in the USA was that whereas most of the senior researchers had started in another field, as Dr Dunstan was suggesting, and then had moved into, if you like, the exploration of the implication of that for ageing diseases and so on, it seemed to be the case that a number of younger people were actually beginning in the Institute on Aging and moving out into other areas, and we met some of those folks and some of them were coming to the UK to do PhDs, so I just wondered are we running behind the States, or are they running too far ahead, or is there evidence of this happening here where people might start with a focus of that kind and then move to broader molecular questions or whatever it is?
Professor Partridge: I certainly think in the US they are well ahead in creating these local centres where there is a group of people with a range of skills working to solve a common problem. Although they sometimes go and do other things afterwards, in terms of training scientists and sending them out into the wider world, they are leading us by a long way.
Dr Wall: First of all, perhaps I could just pick up the issue of the doctoral training accounts because EPSRC was the first research council to introduce those. We do have a lot of our funding through postgraduate training routed through the doctoral training accounts, but we also earmark part of those

accounts to particular research consortia so that we make sure that we are still getting studentships in high-priority areas, so we try to work a way round that. I would just pick up on a couple of the issues that I think are particularly challenging for us. The size of our community would be an issue for us too and we hope it is growing, but I think particularly for us we are not seeing a big push coming into the investigator-led research and there is a huge opportunity there for the research community to compete for more funding on the basis of excellent research, but those proposals just are not coming through the door. It is not that we have got a problem peer-reviewing them once they arrive, but they are not coming in in the first place. Another challenge I think would be one we picked up earlier which is involving business and a new theme for us in the New Dynamics of Ageing programme is older workers in the workplace, and perhaps that is a barrier to trying to get more business people involved in that and perhaps to bringing some real money to the table as well because the level of outside contributions to our research projects is, I think, lower in this area than many of the others across the Council.
Lord May of Oxford: We have been talking exclusively about UK themes and the next question is looking more widely. Obviously Britain is not the only place in which there is ageing research in elderly people, but there are, as we know, different patterns of survivorship and different patterns of survival after particular incidents and so on, but to what extent do the research councils deliberately interact, to what extent do you have an awareness of programmes in other countries, and to what extent do you interlink with them, particularly the US, as you just touched on? Are there examples of constructive results from this? What links do you maintain and, in order to move on to some of the other questions, just let me suggest, with respect, that we focus on the two councils that spend most of the money, namely Professor Partridge and Dr Dunstan.

Q420 Chairman: That is a good suggestion.
Professor Partridge: Certainly in many areas the BBSRC learns from what is going on abroad, particularly in the US, and often sends staff on specific site visits to see what they are doing. The BBSRC do not have formal contacts, for instance, with the NIA in the US. That is not peculiar to ageing, but it is true across the board. It is true in structural biology and other subjects, that they do not have formal links with overseas funding organisations, so the links are informal and tend to be based on those that occur between particular

principal investigators who know of cognate activities in other countries.

Dr Dunstan: From the MRC's point of view, we do talk regularly to Richard Suzman at the National Institute on Aging when he is over here or when one of us is over there, so I think we have got a fair picture of what each of us does. I have mentioned Canada already, and there are strong links between the Canadian Institute of Health Research and the MRC, again mostly an exchange of information. There is a group, the Heads of International Research Organisations, in the biomedical field and our Chief Executive belongs to that. That is NIH, Japan, Australia, virtually everyone that is anyone, and they have informal meetings twice a year and exchange a lot of information about what they are doing, and particularly focus on problems. At the moment they are talking about the design of animal experiments and whether we are all doing it as well as we might do, and global health issues, and of course ageing naturally is a factor in global health issues as well and that is one of the things that they are bringing out. I think we should not finish this topic without remembering the National Collaboration on Ageing Research and that one of its main outputs in a sense was that the Director of that is the co-ordinator of ERA-AGE (European Research Area in Ageing) which is actually bringing together centres of excellence in Europe in ageing research, so again we have got a reasonable picture of what the particular centres in Europe are doing.

Q421 Lord May of Oxford: Can I repeat the same question, Linda, wearing your other hat as Academy of Medical Sciences. Do they do anything explicit?
Professor Partridge: On ageing?

Q422 Lord May of Oxford: Yes.
Professor Partridge: Not as yet, no.

Q423 Lord May of Oxford: It could do something?
Professor Partridge: It is something they have the expertise to do, it would require resources obviously and the Academy does not have a great abundance of resources. Certainly they have the expertise and contacts to undertake such a thing, yes.

Q424 Lord May of Oxford: We have turned up some fascinating examples of differential success and treatments and so on which reflect on the underlying infrastructure.
Professor Partridge: That would be a very natural thing for them to do.

Q425 Lord Oxburgh: Coming back to this question of co-ordination, the fact is that a number of witnesses who have spoken to us already, particularly medical practitioners, have complained about the inadequacy of the co-ordination of research into ageing activities in this country. I think we just had a mention of the National Collaboration on Ageing Research, and there is the Cross-Council Co-ordination Committee, and the Funders Forum. What do you feel that these activities have contributed so far? Have they been successful? Have your Councils committed earmarked resources to them? How has this worked and what has the result been?
Dr Dunstan: I think we have talked about the Cross-Council Co-ordination Committee, we are working on things like the portfolio analysis. One of our programmes is then dubbed as the New Dynamics of Ageing Programme and, yes, we have all committed money to that. That is a success. The National Collaboration on Ageing Research did achieve some things but it was not as successful as we hoped and, indeed, the funding will not be continued beyond the end of the first tranche.

Q426 Lord Oxburgh: If I remember rightly there was an RCUK study into this, was there not?
Dr Dunstan: We had a proper review of it.

Q427 Lord Oxburgh: What was the outcome of that review?
Dr Dunstan: The outcome of the review was that we should not give another three years of funding.

Q428 Chairman: Should not?
Dr Dunstan: Should not. First of all, we established the links with Europe through Alan Walker, which I have mentioned, through ERA-AGE. Also the landscape had changed rather a lot since we set up the National Collaboration for Ageing Research so it was not quite as necessary as we felt it might be. They have not achieved as much, as we have all said, in directing or encouraging the community to send to the research councils really good multi-disciplinary applications, which was what we were looking for. The way they had approached it had not been as successful as we hoped.

Q429 Lord Oxburgh: Is that report published?
Dr Dunstan: It is available, certainly. We could send it to you. Would you like us to do that?

Q430 Lord Oxburgh: I think we would quite like that.
Dr Dunstan: We will send that. Do you want me to mention the Funders Forum?

Q431 Lord Oxburgh: Yes, by all means.

Dr Dunstan: Again, difficult. There are lots of funders fora across our biomedical research. There is a cardiovascular one, there is one on cancer, and they work. They are relatively focused in that sense. They have not got the spectrum of interests that the Funders Forum on Ageing Research has. The Funders Forum on Ageing Research was going, I guess, from the built environment and transport links right through medical research, basic research through to social sciences. It was a very wide spectrum of interests and quite difficult to pull it together. We tried to do it through setting up a business group that would devise ways that we could look at age across the spectrum. We have got some ideas now. We have got the funding in place now to appoint someone as a programme manager for doing it. It is the convention with funders fora that the chairmanship changes from the public sector and alternates with the private sector. It is about time for that to happen and we are hopeful that Help the Aged will take over as the Chairman. They are really very keen, there is a lot of enthusiasm and I am hopeful they will be able to bring it together a bit better.

Q432 Lord Oxburgh: Could you educate the Committee a little bit more on how these fora work? Are they information exchanges or do they plan research projects which different organisations might support?

Dr Dunstan: Usually they begin by being information exchanges.

Q433 Lord Oxburgh: Right.

Dr Dunstan: They usually do these portfolio analyses that we have talked about so you can identify what is being done, what needs to be done, what the gaps are and if you identify gaps then it is usual that there will be a consortium of funders from the Funders Forum who will jump in and say "We need to do something there. We will put money on the table. We will have a pot of money and we will jointly fund it." Par excellence in the cancer area, we have done that with lung cancer research, prevention and palliative care. Those were the areas which were found to be lacking. I would expect something of that kind to come out of an ageing programme if it gets up and running properly.

Q434 Chairman: Do you think it will?

Dr Dunstan: The enthusiasm of Help the Aged is such that if they do take on the chair I think it has a good chance.

Q435 Lord Oxburgh: Linda, how do you feel the BBSRC activities are co-ordinated?

Professor Partridge: With the other research councils specifically?

Q436 Lord Oxburgh: Yes.

Professor Partridge: In a somewhat ad hoc but generally successful way. I have mentioned the programme that we have going jointly with EPSRC, we have collaborated also with ESRC.

Q437 Lord Oxburgh: Do you have experience of the Funders Fora?

Professor Partridge: No, I do not. That is not something I have been involved with directly, nor with the interactions with the other research councils.

Q438 Lord Drayson: I would like to probe a bit further the links between research councils and Government departments. You have given us already a number of examples of links which you said have worked well. Can you give us some sense of it by comparing the enthusiasm of Government departments to ageing research as opposed to other research? Do you feel that the priority is reflected in the older priorities that you have? Can you give us some specific examples of problems you have encountered in these links?

Professor Diamond: ESRC has concordats with 15 different Government departments, including the Executives and Assemblies for Scotland, Wales and Northern Ireland. The importance to which ageing is placed depends clearly on the departments at one particular time. For example, in our concordat with the Treasury this year we had a big discussion on pensions. For example, in our concordat with the Scottish Executive last year we had a big discussion on some of the issues surrounding ageing and Scotland's population which has resulted subsequently in a jointly funded programme between ESRC and the Scottish Executive on Scotland's population, which includes a dimension on ageing. Within any Government department what we find are a set of priorities that they have, and ageing certainly has been part of our discussions with DWP and ODPM for whom, I have to say, it is very much a priority area.

Professor Partridge: I have mentioned BBSRC's main potential engagement in this regard which is with the Department of Health. I think we have been largely unsuccessful so far in drawing our research to their attention.

Dr Dunstan: We work closely with the Department of Health in England, Wales, Scotland and Northern Ireland. At the moment we have a joint committee with them, it is called the Joint Health Delivery Group, where we are showing to Government that we are working sufficiently closely together to make the best value of the public funds that are going into medical research. There are not really any huge difficulties, sometimes there are difficulties with setting up trials because the underpinning funding does not get to the right places in the NHS but that is largely being overcome now, it was at the start. I think we are all—and we are working together, as I said—trying to make implementation better, and that is something which we do see as a priority. We would all agree we are not doing it as well as we could, so we are trying to do that better. We have some links with the Department for Work and Pensions but that is largely on things like shift work and the health effects of that, which are not so much programmed to the elderly. We have got a concordat with the Department for International Development and that works really very smoothly, but we fund in Africa quite a lot of work, again on the early origins of disease, and work they are interested in. For example, children who have been born in the famine season seem to be less resistant to infections later in life and very often succumb completely to infections in middle age. That is something which is of interest to DfID in this particular area. On the whole, we do not have difficulty working with these particular government departments.

Q439 Baroness Finlay of Llandaff: I want to ask, you have listed departments which are principally based in England, I wondered whether your experience was that the devolved administrations and the devolution of health had made working with those devolved departments easier or more difficult?
Dr Dunstan: It has not been more difficult, but that is because we have got things like the Joint Health Delivery Group which everyone has signed up to and is really enthusiastic about. Also, we have got the UK Clinical Research Collaboration on which Scotland, Wales and Northern Ireland are represented. Everyone on the clinical side of things, biomedical side, is working very much more closely than they have done for a considerable length of time. You are asking me that question when things are going rather well, I think.

Q440 Lord Drayson: Focusing on the areas where you have experienced problems, and trying to home in on how you have addressed those and why you think they may have occurred, you mentioned, for example, not having spoken to DoH since 2001, do you have a sense as to why that is?
Professor Partridge: Yes, I think it is on both sides. I think we have not communicated clearly enough what the recent discoveries are and the fact that they have strong immediate implications which could feed into the health care. I think on the other side, on

the user side, there has been a failure to realise just how fast things have moved in basic science and how profound the implications of some of the findings are. There is a gap in understanding on the two sides of each other's activities, I think, and it is one that we need to narrow.

Q441 Lord Drayson: Is there a simple solution in your mind as to how that could be addressed quite rapidly?
Professor Partridge: Yes. I think the dissemination event that the BBSRC has in mind could be a good start but, also, this production of clear, simple, attractive explanations of what has been discovered and what it means could be very helpful.

Q442 Chairman: Just to clarify in my mind a little bit the implication of what you said there, a lack of understanding of the speed at which the basic research in your area and related areas is moving, I would have thought that has implications for the provision of health care and, indeed, the training of doctors, amongst others. Is that the sort of thing you have in mind?
Professor Partridge: Very much so, yes, and that is something the Academy of Medical Sciences has mentioned in their written evidence to you, that there is a great need for clinicians who are working with the elderly but who are well trained in the basic science. At the moment that does not seem to be happening in the context of training in geriatrics. It may be another way has to be found. Most practitioners in general medicine are seeing old people and perhaps that is the place to look for this kind of training.
Chairman: Indeed, the NHS spends a very high percentage of its money in that particular age group. We may well come back to the Academy in a moment. Lady Walmsley, do you want to ask a question?

Q443 Baroness Walmsley: Previous witnesses have identified a capacity problem to us and said there is a shortage of researchers of whatever age who are trained in the scientific aspects of ageing. Do you share that perception and, if so, what is your evidence for it and what measures have you put in place to do anything about it?
Professor Diamond: Very much, as I said earlier. The Growing Older programme evaluation, one of the key things which comes out of it is the small pool of available researchers. As I said earlier, we are talking about prioritising the research studentship programme and ageing as an area. I do think there are areas, particularly in economics of ageing and in psychological aspects of ageing, where there is a real need to develop a new cadre of researchers.

Diana has already mentioned the post-doc area, I think that is a key area. The other thing to do is simply to prioritise funding, and to make it very clear in prioritising funding that one is looking for exciting research questions which cross boundaries and bring to the party people who are extremely talented researchers but do not at this moment work on ageing. We have to work on that, and we will be working on that in the future.

Q444 Lord May of Oxford: Very quickly: it is a mixture of this and going right back to the beginning of something I was insufficiently alert about. These kite diagrams that we discussed earlier, I had not realised if you expressed the spending on ageing as a percentage of the research council portfolio, the MRC are spending a pretty big whack, and I think ESRC is a small amount, I realise it is only about one per cent of your budget, is it not, or less, £1.3 million a year. What is your total budget?
Professor Diamond: Our total budget this year is just over £100 million.

Q445 Lord May of Oxford: It is about one per cent of your budget. I find that astonishing, and it relates to the shortage of researchers. I would have thought the interplay between medical and BBSRC sorts of things and social dimensions was important. No wonder there is a shortage of research in some areas. Your initial non-quite engagement in the first question about priorities, could you expand on why you spend about one per cent on this area? Do you think that is right? That strikes me as jolly weird.
Professor Diamond: I think, as I said earlier, for ESRC the money that is spent reflects the need for a research programme, a growing older programme, and there is a commitment to spend a further £5 million. That commitment has been there and the funding is about to start. There is rather more than that going forward. That is the first point. Secondly, the data that has been given to you is the data simply on research projects, it does not include things like the infrastructure costs as well, I think that is important. The answer to your question, as I said earlier, is we need to be absolutely clear in our minds that the research priorities that we have are being addressed, and that we allocate appropriate money to make sure that is happening. As we move to a more responsive mode of funding, we need to make sure that we are attracting exciting researchers to come to us with exciting programmes. For example, the half a million pounds of funding to produce secondary analysis of the English longitudinal study of ageing does not appear in that data because the funding stream has only just started.

Professor Partridge: I think there are three things. If you are starting from the low base then there is a certain self-fulfilling element to it, so that is part of the explanation. It is like the early stages of an epidemic, it is very flat. I think, also, people trained in ageing research—as has been pointed out previously by our Chairman—do sometimes move on to do other things. I think that is because when a young investigator sets up their own lab for the first time in a research institute or a university, it can be easier to set up in something else which it is possible to do on one's own, which is generally not true with ageing research. I think the other really important factor is the general lack of basic and, indeed, clinical research in geriatrics. They are involved, mostly, with primary care, and people taking the MD/PhD kind of route into medicine tend to go into other areas. That is a big problem.

Q446 Chairman: Does anyone else want to comment on this?
Dr Dunstan: It is very hard to attract people into primary care research at all because the salaries which are available to academic primary care people, there is a huge disparity between those who are just in for the NHS. It is a really serious disincentive.

Q447 Chairman: Granted that in all of these areas the fact that you are starting from a low cohort base in itself causes a difficulty because who is training those who are coming up next, I think an equally important question, perhaps, is who is evaluating the research proposals which are coming up the system? Is it people who are trained in other areas basically and who work in other areas, or do you have the capacity to have peer reviewers who have some knowledge of this very important area?
Professor Partridge: I think that this is a very important question and the answer to it depends very much on the funding mode. For instance, at BBSRC when we set up SAGE and ERA, they were accompanied by specialist panels who were drawn in from all aspects of ageing and evaluated the proposals. There was a completely expert panel. When the researchers who have been funded in that mode then go into the responsive mode they are faced with a panel, often none of whom will know anything about ageing. Things become very difficult then.

Q448 Chairman: I did not quite want to put it that way.
Professor Partridge: It can happen.
Chairman: That was my fear.

Q449 *Baroness Finlay of Llandaff:* Having described the situation as it is, if you take a forward look, say five to 10 years, I wonder what you would view as the most important research areas within the field and what you are doing to ensure that these areas will be addressed effectively, because there may be a shift in current activities?

Professor Diamond: We have described already that the New Dynamics of Ageing programme is where we see over the next few years the critical area. Our colleagues described that and we put the major areas in our submission.

Dr Dunstan: The New Dynamics of Ageing programme is important for MRC too, but beyond that we have an overriding priority, I think, for clinical and translational research and, just underneath that, prevention research. Of course all of that is relevant to ageing. How we intend to take that forward generally is by keeping the budgets of our research boards level, without even getting any extra money that we get, and using all of our strategic money towards a clinical translation and preventative research. There is going to be a larger stream of money going into that area, some of which will be ageing research but not all.

Q450 *Baroness Finlay of Llandaff:* You just highlighted the problem of primary care, getting researchers into primary care.

Dr Dunstan: Yes.

Q451 *Baroness Finlay of Llandaff:* What are you doing, because the translational research will probably be most effective if it is delivered out in the community setting, and it may well involve primary care?

Dr Dunstan: We have been successful recently in appointing a new director to our primary care network, the General Practice Research Framework. It has taken a long time to find someone of the quality that we needed. We have now appointed him and he is working out how to use that as a translational network, so taking the research through to primary care that way. We have not had his proposals in yet but we are working with him to make sure they will do well when they do come in.

Q452 *Lord Oxburgh:* Forget networks and your dynamics programme, are there any burning questions, fundamental scientific questions, which your research council has identified and said "Really the world would be transformed" or "Care would be transformed" or "Understanding would be transformed" if we could tackle these?

Dr Dunstan: I guess gene/environment interactions are going to be hugely influential so we are setting up BioBank, which is a resource which people will use, we hope, to disentangle these. Those will influence the whole of the ageing process. The more we understand them, the more we can take the understanding into prevention or treatment and see which people can be treated with which particular approach. I guess that is an area that we are focusing on. The whole of the clinical research initiative is that now in a sense it is timely to take the human genome work through and use it. That is the emphasis MRC is giving.

Professor Partridge: BBSRC are in the process of formulating a policy in this area at the moment through their Healthy Organism panel. I think there are two things which have emerged already, one of which is diet and dietary restriction and health during ageing. How does dietary restriction work? How do the qualitative aspects of diet affect ageing style? I think that will be a priority area certainly. The other is the cellular and molecular basis of this increasing vulnerability to diseases. Certainly those will be two of the main priorities.

Chairman: Certainly dietary restriction was something we came across in the US as a very major issue.

Q453 *Lord May of Oxford:* Can I ask quickly: a more visionary view might be to say from the BBSRC point of view, given the surprisingly large number of genes that we share with other organisms—more than we thought—it will become even more important, and there will be even more interesting questions we can answer working on non-human things in the future, or do you think that is too visionary?

Professor Partridge: No, I think it is very much a plank in BBSRC funding policy in this area. We are funding, and will continue to fund, a great deal of work on model organisms for precisely that reason. The degree of conservation of mechanisms, including mechanisms for ageing, is astonishing.

Q454 *Lord Drayson:* I am interested in the industrial angle to this. You mentioned that industry is not engaging at the level you would like to see these areas of research. Which research programmes do you think industry could most helpfully get engaged in, and what are you doing to encourage industry to take these programmes up?

Dr Wall: I think there is a real opportunity to get more people involved in the New Dynamics of Ageing programme. The way we go about this, and a key aspect to the programme, will be building new research consortia. When we seek research consortia we not only invite expressions of interest from the university research community, we invite expressions of interest from the much wider stakeholder community as well, and then bring all the people together in a workshop and allow them to meet each other to discuss the research challenges, to network, to meet new collaborators. From that we have had considerable success in bringing new multi-disciplinary teams together with new users engaged as well.

Professor Diamond: It is terribly important, as I said earlier, we aim from the beginning to have partnerships. In the Growing Older programme that I described earlier every project was linked with a Government department because that programme was deeply involved in policy for Government. I would hope in the New Dynamics of Ageing programme that every project would be linked with an appropriate stakeholder. I think there are particular aspects here which will be very helpful if we are able to work with the strategic advisory panel, which includes business, to ensure that those stakeholders are engaged. I think it is critical we do that from the beginning.

Q455 *Chairman:* Time is going on, but I did want to ask just a bit about the Academy of Medical Sciences, this is Professor Partridge. In general, is there a contribution—it is not a funding body—that it can make in this area? Specifically, we noted with interest, and possibly a bit of disappointment, when we spoke to the British Geriatrics Society and the British Society of Gerontology and the British Society for Research on Ageing, they said they did not interact with each other all that much. That may be slightly overstating it, but that was the picture we got. We were more than a little surprised, I have to say, and I just wonder if the Academy of Medical

Sciences might be a locus for bringing these groups together?

Professor Partridge: I think that is a very good suggestion for something that they could do. The situation with the societies, I think, is one that is inevitable. They have their separate funding lines, their separate remits, their communities of members are quite different: one is primary social and behavioural, one is basically geriatricians and one is mainly basic and research-based clinical scientists. They are pursuing rather different goals and leading parallel lives, it is true, and I do not think anyone can be blamed for that.

Q456 *Chairman:* Like, one might say, the research councils if you opt to do something at that level, perhaps a bit further down the system.

Professor Partridge: I think certainly it would be possible for the Academy to identify the research active or the research sympathetic individuals within each of those societies, get them together, get them discussing common aims, possible inter-disciplinary programmes and eventually possibly even producing a new grouping from those individuals. I think that is something which could be achieved.

Chairman: I think we have run our full term of time. I would just emphasise, again, we would be very interested to receive from you further comments about matters, and we may address specific questions to you as a result of our discussion and your evidence. I think we have noted a number of matters that you will send material on, and they will be in the minutes that are circulated. We will look out for that. Lastly, we would hope to have our report out some time in the early summer, in other words before the main demise of summer overcomes all of us. If you have additional material, the sooner the better. May I thank you very much for giving us time and also for what you have submitted already.

Supplementary evidence by Research Councils UK (RCUK)

INTRODUCTION

1. Research Councils UK (RCUK) is a strategic partnership that champions the research, engineering and technology supported by the seven UK Research Councils. Through RCUK the Research Councils together with the Arts and Humanities Research Board (AHRB) are creating a common framework for research, training and knowledge transfer. Further details are available at www.rcuk.ac.uk

2. This memorandum sets out the RCUK response to the questions outlined in Sir Keith Peters' letter of 6 July 2004 to Research Council Chief Executives. It is submitted on behalf of all the Research Councils and AHRB, and represents their independent views. It does not include or necessarily reflect the views of the Office of Science and Technology (OST).

3. Our response comprises:

— RCUK views on the need to further encourage multidisciplinary research.

— Summary of current Research Council activities which foster multidisciplinary research, training and knowledge transfer.

— RCUK views on the barriers to multidisciplinary research and the changes needed to address these.

4. The annexes [not printed] provide further details.

Is there a need to further encourage multidisciplinary research?

5. As set out in the Government's "Science and Innovation Investment Framework 2004–2014"[3], strengthening multidisciplinary[4] research in the UK is a key challenge for all involved in the research base. RCUK believes that harnessing knowledge and skills across a wide range of disciplines, and providing the underpinning investment and research infrastructure is an essential element of delivering the Government's vision for making the UK the most attractive location in the world for science and innovation.

6. The use of multidisciplinary approaches provides the potential for innovative and paradigm-shifting research when those from different disciplines work together. RCUK believes that multidisciplinary research occurs optimally when the very best scientists from different disciplines are able to work together free from discipline or structural barriers. It is important to recognise that multidisciplinary research is undertaken both within Councils and between Councils. Each Research Council seeks to foster, where appropriate, multidisciplinary research either between disciplines central to their Councils' mission or by drawing on a wide range of disciplines to address a specific problem. Two examples are provided: firstly, the ESRC Centre on Economic Learning and Social Evolution which enables collaboration between economists and psychologists; and secondly, PPARC's work to discover the Higgs boson at the Large Hadron Collider at CERN, which required PPARC to pull together a team of truly excellent physicists, mathematicians, engineers and computing experts. Work between Councils has always existed but has had added impetus recently as described below. Furthermore, RCUK believes that novel, multidisciplinary approaches are needed to solve many, if not all of the big research challenges over the next 10–20 years[5].

7. As recognised in the Investment Framework, the key to a successful and productive research base is flexibility and maintaining a healthy balance between bottom-up responsive research and top-down strategic direction. Multidisciplinary research, like other forms of collaborative research, is therefore not an end in itself but a means for addressing outstanding and important issues, whether generated by talented researchers or strategically driven.

8. Strengthening the UK's multidisciplinary capability requires changes in institutional structures, in funding and training mechanisms, and most importantly to the cultural environment in which research is carried out. A key challenge is to grow the population of researchers who possess first rate specialist, analytical and transferable skills that enable them to work in multidisciplinary teams and outside of their traditional discipline areas. It is also noteworthy that some disciplinary boundaries run deeper than others because of different training, motives, language and career paths of those involved—such as the divide between clinical and non-clinical researchers in medical research, or between social scientists and "hard" sciences. To foster multidisciplinary research between researchers from such disciplines requires the development of trust and also career structures which reflect the different contexts of the research.

How are the Research Councils fostering multidisciplinary research?

9. There is strength in the diversity of the current Research Council system. The separate identities of each Council provide a strong focus for individual research and user communities. Within this model Councils have both individually and collectively sought to foster multidisciplinary approaches to research, training and knowledge transfer for many years. A mission-focus also provides a strong driver to look across disciplinary boundaries.

10. The creation of Research Councils UK in May 2002 added impetus to this activity by:

— providing Research Councils with a recognised forum in which to exchange information on research priorities and develop ideas about multidisciplinary activities;

---

[3] The section covering multidisciplinarity is paragraph 2.11; see: www.hm-treasury.gov.uk/media//FEE95/spend04_sciencedoc2-3090704.pdf

[4] *Multidisciplinary research* is defined as research requiring knowledge and/or expertise from two or more discrete fields in order to successfully deliver the objectives of the project or field of research. Throughout this document, this term is used in preference to *interdisciplinary research*, because it better conveys the nature of the joint working.

[5] RCUK Vision for Research, http://www.rcuk.ac.uk/documents/vision_final.pdf

— enabling the development and promulgation of joined-up strategies such as the RCUK Synthesis of Strategies and Vision for Research;

— facilitating an open, and collective approach to the development of major multidisciplinary proposals for Spending Reviews; and

— promoting best practice on the management and evaluation of multidisciplinary research.

11. Multidisciplinary models are increasingly necessary to tackle complex research challenges, whether developing our understanding of brain function, exploring the interactions between our environment and human society or investigating the behaviour of condensed matter at the nanoscale. Working in partnership with their academic communities, as well as other research funders and stakeholders including Government and the private sector, Research Councils have developed and implemented an extensive and successful portfolio of flexible funding mechanisms and approaches. Councils regularly review their policies and procedures as their research communities evolve and continually strive to eliminate any inadvertent organisational or procedural barriers to multidisciplinary working. The Councils will continue to share best practice in this respect, and will continue to work with other funders and stakeholders to remove barriers elsewhere.

Multidisciplinary research

12. The Research Councils promote multidisciplinary approaches by:

— working with researchers and users to identify key strategic challenges and problems—almost always cutting across established disciplines—and using top-down mechanisms to publicise, promote, or direct funding to, these areas;

— listening to individual researchers' views on the factors that influence their own aims, collaborations, and career paths, and reflecting these in policies and communications work;

— Formal Funders Forums (eg Environment Research Funders Forum, Forum for Research into Ageing and Older People) to ensure close coordination between Councils and other funders in key areas;

— using Research Council Institutes, or university research centres, to bring researchers together with clear multi-disciplinary goals, and long-term support, to help new ways of working develop;

— addressing any barriers to novel multidisciplinary approaches that peer review processes or grant schemes may produce;

— smoothing the path for funding and assessing multidisciplinary proposals that cut across Research Council boundaries; and

— promoting multidisciplinarity as a goal in international organisations—such as in decisions on EU Framework objectives.

13. Examples of such activities include:

— In 2000, a number of Councils undertook a programme of joint visits to leading UK universities to stimulate opportunities for closer working and the physical sciences and life sciences interface; identify factors which encourage or inhibit cross-disciplinary working; and explore ways of addressing these.

— Through RCUK, Councils are committed to consulting which each other on the development of their science visions and strategies and on the development of multidisciplinary proposals and initiatives.

— In November 2003 RCUK produced a "Synthesis of Strategies" which provides a comprehensive and simple overview of the portfolio of activities supported by the Research Councils, identifies issues of common interest, and focuses on the themes and areas where the Councils can add the greatest value by working together. In December 2003 RCUK produced a "Vision for Research", articulating the Councils' shared aspirations on the main research challenges of the next 10–20 years and the advances needed to deliver these challenges.

14. Over the past seven years (ie since the 1998 Comprehensive Spending Review) Councils have substantially increased their investments in major cross-cutting research initiatives, such that they now account for a significant proportion of Research Council activity. Flagship multidisciplinary programmes include (total commitment to date in brackets):

— basic technology (£104 million);

— e-Science (£213 million);

— genomics/post-genomics (£246 million);

— rural economy and land use (£20 million);

— sustainable energy economy (£28 million); and

— stem cells (£40 million).

Further information about these programmes can be found at Annex 1.

15. Research Councils also have a strong track record of supporting multidisciplinary research through Institutes, Interdisciplinary Research Collaborations (IRCs), and other university centres of excellence. Long term support can in itself be important in giving scientists confidence and time needed to build strong collaborative links, and tackle methodological and conceptual barriers to joint working. Centres and institutes can in addition give effective leadership and strategic commitment to developing new ways of tackling problems, and they can ensure access to the full range of equipment and skills needed for a broad approach to a problem. Examples of other multidisciplinary activities supported include:

— climate change research (Tyndall Centre for interdisciplinary research on climate change);

— life sciences-physical sciences interface activities;

— discipline hopping awards;

— nanotechnology interdisciplinary research collaboration;

— interdisciplinary programme on IT and society;

— innovative health technologies programme;

— systems biology centres;

— technology partnerships programme;

— detector development programme;

— high performance computing;

— CCLRC facilities;

— Human Frontier Science Programme; and

— Designing for the 21st Century.

16. Research Councils play an important role in advising on the research needed to deliver the policy objectives of the European Union Framework Programme. These objectives are largely multidisciplinary, focused on addressing such challenges as sustainable development, integrated manufacturing or global change. A feature of the funding instruments in the current Framework Programme is the focus on establishing consortia involving partners from different disciplines and different countries, via Integrated Projects. Research Councils fund the UK Research Office (UKRO) in Brussels to provide guidance and assistance to UK researchers wanting to participate in the Framework Programme, including practical help in proposal writing and in seeking partners for multidisciplinary proposals.

17. At an operational level, Councils regularly scrutinise and update their policies and procedures to ensure that there are no inadvertent organisational or policy barriers impeding the assessment and evaluation of multidisciplinary research proposals. In the last two years, the focus on harmonisation and convergence of appropriate administration functions has accelerated this process. Key developments include:

— In 2000, Research Councils agreed and published a joint statement on the peer review of research proposals at the interface of Councils' remits. As well as general statements of principle, this encouraged potential applicants to discuss multidisciplinary applications with Councils before submission, guaranteed that all Councils with a substantial interest in a proposal would be consulted in helping to assess the proposal, recognised the need for flexibility in peer review, and stated that the assessment process would be agreed between Councils to avoid double jeopardy.

— Programme Officers in the different Councils interact regularly to ensure that responsive mode applications do not "fall between the cracks". This means in practice regular dialogue between office staff, consequent discussion with applicants, mutual openness to RCUK partners peer review systems, and flexibility on financial arrangements.

— Councils have jointly developed a benchmarking process to support the continuous improvement and sharing of good practice within the Research Councils peer review processes. A rolling programme of assessment is being implemented.

— Implementation of the Councils Joint Electronic Submission system (JeS) has made it easier for those wishing to apply for funding for multidisciplinary research grants. For example:

  — JeS enables those developing proposals to share them securely with others within their own HEI or with potential collaborators in other HEIs or industry. It also enables Councils to simply exchange proposals for assessment.

  — Councils have agreed a set of common, core research grant terms and conditions.

  — Further developments under the overarching Councils Research Administration Programme will look at the improvement of peer review related activities, which will include Council wide electronic refereeing and a reviewer database, which will improve access to appropriate experts with multidisciplinary experience.

18. In the medium to longer term, Councils will benefit from evaluating the effectiveness of a range of different mechanisms for supporting and managing multidisciplinary research. Through RCUK, the Councils are continuing to share good practice on evaluation, for example organising cross-Council workshops on the evaluation of cross-Council programmes.

Multidisciplinary training

19. As identified above, increasing the number of researchers able to participate effectively in multidisciplinary research collaborations is a key challenge. Research Councils have developed a variety of flexible funding mechanisms to enable postgraduates to develop the skills needed to work in multidisciplinary teams.

20. The new funding provided under SR2004 to enable all Councils to increase the average duration of a PhD stipend to three and half years will also create greater flexibility and scope for pursing multidisciplinary training at postgraduate level, since longer periods of training can allow students to experience research environments in more than one discipline.

21. Research Council Doctoral Training Accounts (DTAs) offer universities significant flexibility in PhD training by awarding a block of funding rather than quotas of studentships. This flexibility includes the ability to support and facilitate multidisciplinary working by encouraging universities, departments and research groups to combine funds to create studentships at the interfaces between disciplines. The Roberts Review on the supply of people with SET skills stated that the DTA system represents a good way of achieving the flexibility needed in postgraduate training to acquire transferable skills. At present DTAs are supported by EPSRC, and BBSRC, with MRC moving to this mechanism from October. EPSRC and MRC have agreed to facilitate joint funding at the medical and physical sciences interface, and similar discussions will be held with BBSRC. Other Councils are taking alternative approaches to supporting multidisciplinary PhD training.

22. Effective research in a multidisciplinary field is facilitated by the interpersonal and management skills that transferable skills training provides. SR2002 provided an additional £17 million to enhance such skills training for Research Council students. The Research Councils are co-operating closely to create a co-ordinated mechanism to provide funds to individual universities and to monitor the strategies employed for their use.

23. The CASE studentship model can be used to support multidisciplinary training where the user partner works with an academic group in a different sector to import new thinking. Councils also fund specific multidisciplinary studentship awards. For example the ESRC/NERC scheme brings together social and environmental research, and the ESRC/MRC scheme (studentship and fellowships) addresses combined approaches in medical and social sciences. Multidisciplinary studentships are also awarded through a number of the multidisciplinary programmes listed above.

Innovation and knowledge transfer

24. Through RCUK, the Research Councils are increasingly working together on the knowledge transfer agenda. Working with industry and other users creates an extra drive for multidisciplinarity and can create both new problems and challenges. Councils are currently working to develop plans and goals to increase Councils' rate of KT and interactions with business by the end of 2004. This will be followed by the

development of an RCUK Knowledge Transfer Strategy. Examples of Research Councils knowledge transfer activities include:

— The Research Councils Business Plan competition, launched in November 2002, to help researchers develop their ideas for commercialisation by providing training and mentoring in business planning and entrepreneurial skills. The scheme also ran successfully in 2003 and a further call is planned for 2004–05.

— The Young Entrepreneurs Scheme, run by BBSRC, MRC & NERC provides training in entrepreneurial skills for postgraduate and postdoctoral bioscientists.

— Follow-On Fund: EPSRC, BBSRC & NERC are supporting an increase in the level of commercialisation of research outputs by providing funds to demonstrate the commercial potential of ideas arising from research supported by these Councils. The Fund will support activities essential to securing commercial opportunities such as licensing, seed or venture finance through further scientific or technical development.

— Research Council engagement in the DTI LINK scheme.

— Research Council support for Faraday Partnerships, promoting improved interaction between the UK research base and industry.

— Research Council and AHRB support for Knowledge Transfer Partnerships.

25. RCUK has made significant progress in engaging with business (via the Confederation of British Industry) and the Regional Development Agencies, and will continue to drive the evolution of these relationships as Councils begin to implement the recommendations from the Innovation and Lambert Reviews. The Research Councils are also engaging collectively as RCUK with OST and the DTI Innovation Group, contributing to the development of the Technology Strategy and delivery of the Technology Programme. Councils have collated baseline data across the whole spectrum of their knowledge transfer activities (ie co-operation in education and training; people and knowledge flow; collaborative research; and commercialisation) which has highlighted a wide range of multidisciplinary activities:

— in responsive and directive modes of grant funding;

— through programmes, Centres and Institutes; and

— by demonstrating substantial and wide ranging cross-sectoral engagement with users.

What do Research Councils feel are the main barriers to multidisciplinary research?

What changes could be set in place to encourage more multidisciplinary research?

26. Research Councils see the main barriers as:

— Pressures on time and to maintain a publication flow discourage university researchers from exploring new and challenging avenues.

— Career progression and the RAE tend to favour individual excellence rather than collective excellence.

— Cultural and communication barriers between disciplines.

— Conservatism in peer review by journals and funding committees, which is not actually as big a problem as:

— The perception that peer review is conservative and discipline-based, and the need for better communication and reassurance from funders.

— The need for some strengthening of incentives from funders to pursue challenging but important multidisciplinary areas—which is particularly difficult when Research Council funding is tight.

— Past and current difficulty in organising cross-organisational funding—Councils believe that this problem is now solved between the Research Councils, though there is still more work to be done to communicate this, and to improve co-ordination with other funders.

Further detail on these issues are given below.

Issues for Research Councils and other research funders

27. Research often produces the unexpected, so even with effective horizon scanning activities it is not always easy predict or identify emerging multidisciplinary opportunities. In addition, promising areas that offer potential solutions to multidisciplinary challenges often need to be rapidly exploited. One example of this is NERC's rapid engagement with the Japanese for access to the Earth Simulator, now actively engaged in a major international multidisciplinary research programme in Earth System Science. Such areas can be intrinsically high-risk/high reward and Research Councils recognise that there is a need for them to be able to respond rapidly to such challenges, providing, initially small scale funding to stimulate interest in multidisciplinary activities. Many Councils provide some funding for high-risk projects and Councils are exploring the effectiveness of mechanisms such as EPSRC's "sandpit events" and ESRC's Seminar Groups. It is also anticipated that some of the £70 million from the DGRC's strategic fund announced in SR2004 will be used to pump prime multidisciplinary activities.

28. Despite increasing investments by Research Councils and others, there are insufficient cross-disciplinary training opportunities at both undergraduate and postgraduate level (studentships and fellowships). At undergraduate level a more multidisciplinary approach needs to be integrated into courses and at postgraduate level more masters courses and PhDs need some cross-disciplinary component. IRCs and other Research Council multidisciplinary programmes or centres acting as a vehicle for multidisciplinary training, for example the Tyndall Centre for interdisciplinary work on climate change (NERC, ESRC, EPSRC).

29. At another level, the formation of partnerships between different funding agencies, including Research Councils, can sometimes be complicated and time-consuming due to the cultural and operational differences between these agencies. The substantial increase in volume of collaborative activity funded by the Councils demonstrates their commitment to eliminate completely any such barriers between individual Councils, and Councils will continue to work collectively and individually with other funders to address this issue.

30. In addition, the Councils and other funders need to do more to actively promote both the funding available for multidisciplinary research and training, and to showcase the successful outcomes from some of the major investments made in multidisciplinary research in recent years.

Peer Review processes

31. Effective peer review of proposals in innovative or emerging areas that cross disciplines continues to present a challenge for the Research Councils and other grant awarding bodies, both in the UK and internationally. In some cases, earmarked funding for specific activities can help to address conservatism in the peer review process, but the goal is to ensure that all Councils—and other funders—operate high quality peer review systems capable of assessing complex multidisciplinary proposals in a fair and transparent way.

32. Research Councils' have individually and collectively tackled concerns from their communities about lack of risk taking in peer review, narrow perspectives on academic discipline, failure to evaluate added value and double jeopardy in co-funded proposals. In addition to the actions outlined in earlier sections Councils have also:

— managed multidisciplinary peer review through multidisciplinary peer review committees in areas such as Engineering and Biological Systems and Biomolecular Sciences (BBSRC);

— replaced discipline based peer review committees with colleges of reviewers (EPSRC, ESRC & NERC). This approach is increasingly being adopted internationally with NSF and to some extent NIH establishing multidisciplinary research assessment panels; and

— invested time and effort in "educating" their reviewers in the assessment of multidisciplinary proposals to ensure that the benefits of joint working are recognised and assessed.

33. On a European scale Research Councils representatives on Framework Programme management committees have worked closely with the Commission in the development of its peer review mechanisms. In FP6 multidisciplinary peer review panels have been established and there has been a substantial increase in the use of external referee reports. However, the time taken between a funding decision and the award of a contract remains an issue to be addressed.

34. Despite these advances, it remains inevitable that the knowledge base of some parts of the peer review community will lag behind the scientific advances that catalyse ideas for multidisciplinary projects. Councils recognise that continual effort is needed to ensure that their reviewers adopt best practice when assessing multidisciplinary proposals.

35. In addition, there is a need for further exploration of the options for harmonisation and/or increased flexibility of peer review processes between the Research Councils and other sponsors of research. The challenge for Research Councils is maintaining the quality of the peer review process and the criteria of scientific excellence, whilst promoting multidisciplinary collaboration.

Research Assessment Exercise

36. There is a strong view among Research Councils that the Research Assessment Exercise (RAE) has previously undervalued multidisciplinary research[6]. Two elements of the RAE that are perceived to act as barriers are:

— the structure of RAE panels and Units of Assessment and discipline-based evaluation process; and

— the emphasis on publications as an evaluation factor, to the detriment of consideration of institutional strategies that would encompass such factors as multidisciplinary research.

37. Research Councils remain concerned that the proposed structure of disciplinary panels and sub-panels for the RAE in 2008 does not go far enough in encouraging multidisciplinary research and in providing for its assessment on equal terms with research in a single discipline. Research Councils will continue to work with the Funding Councils to try to ensure that multidisciplinary research is not disadvantaged in the RAE assessment.

38. The difficulty of knowing where to publish the results of multidisciplinary research and of getting papers into journals with high impact factors is another issue over which the RAE has a substantial influence. Given the significance of the RAE[7], it is less risky for researchers to focus on producing articles for publication in the mainstream literature of a traditional single discipline. There is also anecdotal evidence that it is generally more difficult to get multidisciplinary work published, since the publishing industry is largely discipline-based, and papers in cross-disciplinary journals, are often rated less highly than those in traditional journals. Publishing in newer journals with a multidisciplinary slant is a more risky proposition as these journals may have an as yet unproven citation impact and may not clearly map onto an RAE Unit of Assessment.

Structural issues in the HEI sector

39. RCUK believes that there needs to be cultural change within other funding bodies and the research community itself, so that there is greater recognition and acceptance of the importance of multidisciplinary working and the benefits it can yield. All parties in the research base need to be aware of the barriers to setting up and prosecuting multidisciplinary research, and to recognise their role in overcoming these.

40. The organisation of departments in universities usually follows the needs of undergraduate teaching, which, for most institutions, is their dominant source of income. The traditional management structure of a department (scheduling of teaching commitments, managing support staff, computing, libraries, budgets, premises etc) typically reflects the disciplinary nature of most undergraduate teaching. However, this sort of structure is not necessarily the most effective organisational model for the support of postgraduate training or multidisciplinary research. Many universities are already moving towards bigger and broader structures, eg faculties, particularly in the organisation of research.

41. In the past, Research Councils and universities have chosen to fund specific centres of excellence to bring together researchers from different disciplines into the same working space with the requisite facilities and support staff. Increasingly Councils are working in partnership with HEIs and other funders to explore more novel ways of establishing multidisciplinary capability in research intensive universities—for example through the creation of virtual centres (either individually or using a hub and spoke model) and Interdisciplinary Research Collaborations. It is important that these foci of multidisciplinary activities are embedded alongside, and linked closely with, strengths in existing disciplines. It is also recognised that such centres require visionary, dynamic leadership to drive them forward in a cohesive manner, as well as proper resourcing.

---

[6] RCUK has highlighted its concerns about multidisciplinarity in its response to the Funding Bodies' consultation on the RAE2008 Panel configuration and recruitment (May 2004); RCUK has also emphasised the importance of recognising multidisciplinary research in its submission to the House of Commons S&T Committee's follow-up inquiry into the Research Assessment Exercise (April 2004).

[7] Bearing in mind that, in addition to having a significant effect on the future resource of HEIs, the RAE is seen as dominating incentives, promotions and transfers between institutions in UK universities.

8 February 2005

42. These challenges are not faced by the UK alone. In the US the NSF and NIH consider the promotion of multidisciplinary research and training to be a major issue, particularly breaking down the silo approach to science implicit in the structure of their university departments. Several centres (both real and virtual) have been established, and Research Councils are continuing to liase with their US counterparts about the outcome of these initiatives.

European Union Framework Programmes

43. The structure, content and budget allocations in the Framework Programme are negotiated on a multinational basis. This means that although the Programme is inherently multidisciplinary, priorities or funding allocations may address challenges shared by only a few countries. For example, in the EU, a nuclear research programme remains yet some Member States have declared themselves nuclear-free, and research on fisheries or the marine/coastal environment is supported although some countries have no coastline or fishing industries. Stem cell research and related technologies are funded under FP6 but only by the narrowest of votes following significant opposition by several Member States. It is therefore essential that the UK continues to work with the Commission to ensure that UK multidisciplinary priorities are reflected in FP7 and can be effectively delivered through the available funding instruments, with minimal bureaucracy.

Networking and cultural issues

44. In addition to addressing concerns about the RAE and structural issues in the HEI sector, growing a research environment in which multidisciplinary activities can flourish requires action to stimulate engagement between researchers themselves. The establishment of teams with the necessary background and skills to undertake multidisciplinary research is often a challenging and time-consuming activity. Academics from different disciplines need to be brought together in such a way as to encourage them to explore and understand the mutual benefits of joint working. Potential collaborators need to be able to understand how participation in a multidisciplinary project or programme could benefit the core research interests of each of the participating groups. Although funding bodies, including the Research Councils, actively promote and sponsor networking between disciplines to encourage the formation and development of collaborations, there is also a need to address the broader lack of multidisciplinary networking opportunities—for instance major conferences are often run only for existing or established disciplines.

45. On an individual level there are many other constraints on academic time. Practical solutions might include freeing up more time for key individuals to pursue networking and communication activities by making greater use of fellowship schemes, buying out academics' time or the establishment of centres or hubs in universities (or groups of universities) where individuals from different departments can mix. Universities should also consider using multiple appointments in one research area spread across a number of departments, where the appointees are strongly encouraged (for instance by providing resource and/or postgraduate students) to collaborate in order to nucleate multidisciplinary research.

46. However, even if practical issues can be addressed there remains a range of cultural barriers that may prevent researchers from looking beyond traditional discipline interfaces. In some areas, researchers may struggle to speak the same language or understand the risks of working in different fields. Preconceptions about certain disciplines continue to persist. More needs to be done to determine and implement best practice to help researchers communicate more easily with each other and to challenge preconceptions.

47. It is generally more time consuming to plan, resource and undertake multidisciplinary activities, since all parties need to be involved in project planning and must be able to agree on a shared research agenda. Familiarisation with new technology or techniques must be built into project costs. A more sympathetic approach is needed in this regard from funders, but more importantly from departmental heads and research managers in HEIs. In addition, once a project is underway it may take time for participants to deepen their relative understanding of each others' specialisms and learn new methodological approaches or techniques. This can act as a disincentive to participation in multidisciplinary activities since it may result in a drop in an individual's publication rate and impact on their own promotional prospects as well as their Department's RAE score. Universities need to do more to ensure that there is effective support and career development for academic discipline hoppers.

48. Taken together with the driver of the RAE and the institutional barriers outlined above, these cultural issues act to perpetuate a largely mono-disciplinary approach within substantial parts of the academic sector. Significant efforts are required from funders from both halves of the dual support system, and especially from HEIs, to bring about a real cultural shift (starting at undergraduate level) so that a multidisciplinary approach to research becomes the norm.

March 2005

Supplementary evidence by Research Councils UK (RCUK)

INTRODUCTION

This written submission provides evidence from the four Research Councils in response to the questions identified by the Committee following the oral evidence session on 8 February 2005.

[Annexes with further information from the individual research councils are not printed]

JOINT RESEARCH COUNCIL RESPONSES

1. *The Committee asked for clarification of the categories used in the summary of expenditure*

The following is a list of the 10 categories used for the portfolio analysis (Annex 1, and paragraph 40–43, of the original written evidence submitted by the Research Councils UK), including examples of the types of areas of research encompassed within each category. These are examples rather than a completely comprehensive list. As highlighted in the original written evidence, the portfolio analysis carried out so far is only preliminary, and there are a number of limitations. For example, there are no adjustments yet for the fact that some research projects are relevant to two or more categories, and therefore projects were wholly ascribed to a single category. Furthermore there are no adjustments to take into account any fraction of research in a particular multidisciplinary programme that is not directly related to ageing, and consequently the analysis over-estimates the actual spend directly attributed to age-related research.

(1) The economics, psychology and sociology of ageing and the life-course.

— cognitive/psychological functioning;

— social groups/minority groups;

— culture/race;

— quality of life.

(2) The economic, social and policy implications of an ageing population.

— pensions and financial planning;

— working life;

— migration;

— social exclusion/inclusion;

— quality of life.

(3) Technologies and design to help people maintain their independence and autonomy (and the effects of those technologies).

— Assistive technology;

— Design of the built/outdoor environment;

— Smart homes/telecare research;

— Transport/mobility;

— ICTs/innovative health technologies;

— Way finding;

— Reminiscence aids;

— Inclusive design;

— Built environment;

— technology & behaviour.

(4) Technologies for the detection, prediction diagnosis and treatment of age related diseases (and the effects of those technologies).

— Medical Imaging (brain, bone, breast, lung etc);

— Tissue engineering;

— Wound healing;

— Medical implants;

— Marker discovery/development/evaluation/testing.

(5) The molecular and cellular changes associated with basic biological processes of cell death, senescence and physiological ageing.

— cell biology;

— telomere;

— apoptosis;

— cell cycle;

— brain ageing;

— systems ageing (organs).

(6) The causes of, and influences on age related diseases and disability.

— exogenous factors (diet, environment, activity);

— endogenous factors (genes,mproteins, receptors, cellular networks, metabolism, pathogenesis);

— gene interactions;

— Age related diseases includes:

(i)   cardiovascular, cerebrovascular;

(ii)   dermatological conditions (eg cancer, bunions, fungal, psoriasis);

(iii) endocrine and metabolic eg diabetes, thyroidism;

(iv)   foot disorders;

(v)   gastrointestinal diseases and disorders including hernia, incontinence celiac disease, ulcer etc;

(vi)   haematological disease and disorders;

(vii) infectious diseases inc TB, bacterial meningitis, bacterial gastroenteritis;

(viii) malnutrition and under nutrition;

(ix)   motor neurological diseases;

(x)   musculoskeletal problems;

(xi)   oral diseases and disorders;

(xii) prostate problems;

(xiii) respiratory disorders;

(xiv) vision and hearing;

(xv)   mental health problems, anxiety, depression, dementias.

(7) Prevention of breakdown in health and loss of independence in old age and of specific diseases and conditions which cause these.

— behavioural interventions;

— psychological intervention;

— vaccines;

— screening studies;

— imaging (screening);

— gene delivery (for prevention of disease);

— diet/nutrition;

— chemoprevention;

— surgical prevention.

(8) Treatments for disease and the breakdown in health in older people.
  — drugs/chemotherapy;
  — gene therapy;
  — recombinant antibody therapies;
  — tissue engineering;
  — cell replacement therapy (stem cells);
  — medical implants/tissue engineering;
  — surgery;
  — psychological intervention.

(9) Rehabilitation strategies to improve and maintain function and restore independence.
  — SMART technologies for rehabilitation;
  — Training techniques;
  — Functional/physiological rehabilitation psychological intervention;
  — quality of life.

(10) The delivery of effective and efficient health and social care for old and frail people.
  — Telecare;
  — Telemedicine;
  — Health services research;
  — Primary care research;
  — Quality of life;
  — Inequalities;
  — Evaluation of care;
  — efficacy of current care provision;
  — effect on carers (from social workers to family carers).

2. Each of the Research Councils referred to the New Dynamics of Ageing Programme in terms of which implied that this was a major step towards solution of the problems. Could each Council state: How the programme will be structured operationally?

The New Dynamics of Ageing Programme is organised along the lines of an ESRC managed Programme. However, for the Programme to run effectively all partners recognise the need for regular communication and pro-active collaboration on the programme. The Cross-Council Co-ordination Committee on Ageing Research (XCAR) will be used as a formal forum for communication about the programme, both between funding partners and between funding partners and the Programme Director, as well as addressing other Ageing issues.

On a day to day basis the Programme Director, Professor Alan Walker will manage the programme and its projects, reporting to ESRC, as the Council with single-point responsibility for the Director, and feeding back to the funding partners regularly. The management arrangements outlined under question 3 will be implemented, as with all ESRC programmes.

3. It was stated in evidence that NCAR was perceived to have underperformed, and that its funding had been or was to be discontinued. How is it thought that the New Dynamics of Ageing Programme will overcome the factors that led to NCAR falling below expectations?

The Research Councils carried out a review of NCAR during 2004 which indicated that NCAR had fallen below expectations in some but certainly not all areas of its remit. It should also be appreciated that NCAR was a networking activity and not a research programme (like NDA). The Research Councils are planning a number of steps to ensure that the performance of NDA will fully meet expectations in every area of its remit. The Research Councils will implement the following through ESRC which is managing the Programme and

Programme Director on behalf of the partner Councils. It is appropriate to point out that none of the managerial aspects described below for assessing progress for NDA were in place for NCAR.

The management procedures (below) are part of normal ESRC management mechanisms for a programme. The Programme Director (representing the Programme as a whole) will have the following formal management mechanisms.

Management mechanisms

(a) Troikas

The Programme will have a nominated Board Liaison member from the ESRC Strategic Research Board who will represent the Board to the Programme and vice versa. Twice yearly meetings will be held between the Programme Director, the Board Liaison Member and the Programme Case Officer. For the purposes of this cross-Council Programme, the main funding partner, EPSRC has been invited to attend troika meetings. Troikas offer an opportunity to strengthen the partnership between the ESRC Board, the Director and the Office, and to improve communication between all three parties. They also clarify the role of the Advisory Committee (see below) as support to the Director, within the framework of ESRC policy and practice.

A Troika meeting might typically cover the following issues:

— communication and Science in Society issues;

— knowledge transfer issues;

— developments in Research Council policy;

— recent and upcoming Programme activities;

— the Director's perspective on the progress of individual projects;

— monitoring performance against the Key Performance Indicators (see below) and, prior to that, discussion of what they should be;

— research highlights;

— impact highlights;

— upcoming or recent Reviews.

(b) Advisory Committee

The Programme Director will have an Advisory Committee to support and advise him throughout the life of the Programme. This will be made up of academics from across the range of disciplines and fields covered by the Programme and user members from appropriate fields, such as industry, the charity/voluntary sector, the private sector, government and policy makers. Research Council representatives will attend the Advisory Committee as observers.

(c) Key Performance Indicators (KPIs)

The Programme Director, in conjunction with the Board Liaison Member and office staff, will develop Key Performance Indicators against which the Programme can be monitored through Annual Reports and at troika meetings.

(d) Annual Reports to the Board

The Director will submit annual reports to the ESRC Strategic Research Board describing the progress made by the Programme over the last 12 months.

The role of XCAR

It has been agreed that the Cross Council Co-ordination Committee on Ageing Research (XCAR) will play a role in the feedback between Director and the Councils in addition to the formal management mechanisms outlined above. The Councils will use XCAR as a forum to discuss issues with the Programme Director and the discussion with the Research Council officers will become an item on the XCAR agenda on a regular basis:

the NDA will be a major item for XCAR to address at its meetings. The XCAR will implement a modus operandi whereby during 'Council business' both before and after the Programme Director arrives, members can raise concerns they may have which will form the basis of questions to Director which the Director will be able to address in both verbal and written form, as appropriate. The Research Councils will also make inputs to the design and organization of NDA workshops which will be used to encourage multidisciplinary research collaborations. These meetings will be carefully timed to coincide with the troika meetings.

April 2005

TUESDAY 8 MARCH 2005

Present	Broers, L	Hilton of Eggardon, B
	Drayson, L	Soulsby of Swaffham Prior, L
	Emerton, B	Sutherland of Houndwood, L (Chairman)
	Finlay of Llandaff, B	Turnberg, L

Memorandum by Robert Diamond

UNLOCKING THE VALUE OF THE OVER-50 CONSUMER[1]

ROBERT DIAMOND ARGUES THAT MARKETERS NEED TO THINK BEYOND AGE AND INCOME WHEN TARGETING THIS OFTEN-IGNORED MARKET

Marketing to the UK's over-50 customers is being heralded as a key industry trend for the first decade of the 21st century. The appeal is obvious, given the concentration of 80 per cent of assets, 60 per cent of savings and 40 per cent of disposable income within the 33 per cent of the UK population aged 50 +. The potential returns from tapping into this value are equally clear, and demonstrated in the US where dedicated 50 + marketing has been underway for over a decade.

The first challenge to unlocking 50 + value is in delivering effective targeting when age and income—the most common variables for market segmentation—are not clear indicators of true spending power. Meanwhile, as customers replace peer influences and aspiration with self-awareness and buying confidence, a more sophisticated approach to offer development is needed. Finally, as customers move into the unique position of time-rich media and marketing consumption (rather than time-starved), a more targeted view of communication is needed.

A SNAPSHOT OF THE UK OVER-50 MARKET

Much has been written about the demographic "time bomb" of the ageing UK population. However, many of the headlines hide the key messages that make the 50 + market so crucial for future brand sales.

A thorough investigation of the detailed dynamics within the over-50 market would take a paper in itself to explain. So, below is a summary of the situation in five key messages about the 50 + market.

1. Over-50s are the fastest-growing demographic group in the UK today:

    — 20 million people today, rising from 33 per cent to 44 per cent of the UK population in 20 years.

2. Fewer teens and young adults means more "empty nests", presenting a challenge for the process of long-term brand-building:

    — nearly half of European households have no one under 30.

3. UK wealth, savings and spending power is concentrated in the over-50s:

    — 50 + s hold 80 per cent of assets, 60 per cent of savings and 40 per cent of disposable income.

4. These trends make over-50s a key buying group in several sectors, in addition to their role as "parent-payer" for their children's spending:

    — 50 + s are the top buyers of new cars, holidays, IT equipment and fashion.

5. The need for actionable segmentation of the 50 + market is crucial, given that a significant number of over-50s are still less well off:

    — 40 per cent of UK pensioners are totally dependent on (meagre) state benefits.

A MARKET IGNORED?

Despite this demographic and economic certainty, many marketers seem to ignore—or misrepresent—the over-50 market. Some concerns are valid—for example that overtly appealing to a 50 + audience could alienate younger buyers (in the same way that the reverse is true). However, other perceptions are less well-founded—that long-established brand loyalties cannot be changed and 50 + s are unresponsive to modern

---

[1] Copyright Robert Diamond.

marketing. Is the UK marketing community—where only 10 per cent of Marketing Directors are 50+ and 80 per cent of agency staff are under 40—doing this market a disservice?

In an attempt to resolve what the real industry view on the over-50 opportunity is, we solicited the views of senior brand owners from a range of UK marketing departments. In summary, there is a widely-held appreciation of the 50+ opportunity but there are challenges in delivering against this, given current levels of customer insight.

These comments set an important tone for our exploration of the 50+ opportunity:

— that the ageing of the UK population presents more of an opportunity than a risk;

— that, generally, over-50s are less well understood than other segments of the market;

— that sensitivity is required towards 50+ customers when considering how the overall brand should be positioned (even if discrete 50+ targeting is not an option);

— and finally, that companies will need to tailor their offers, messages and channel choices in order to appeal to 50+ customers without alienating other buyer groups.

The prevailing "hype" around 50+ is clearly justified. The question is what to do about it.

IDENTIFYING VALUE WITHIN THE OVER-50 MARKET

The concept of 50+ targeting is nothing new. Most visibly in the UK, SAGA has been building relationships, mainly with the "older" end of the 50+ market, since the 1920s. However, the key change is that we are now seeing a significant element of the buyer base for "mainstream" brands (ie not dedicated to 50+) being made up of over-50s, who bring different expectations and experiences to their purchase decisions.

While the demographic trends do not materially affect the underlying economics of SAGA, the implications for "mainstream" brands managing a customer portfolio that includes over-50s are more fundamental. Ageing and changing household structures result in shifting product consumption patterns, different purchasing characteristics and expectations of customer service. In order to sustain and grow sales from existing customer bases, a shift in marketing approach is required.

THE CHALLENGE OF 50+ SEGMENTATION

Marketers looking to target discrete segments within the overall, mainstream market usually focus on two key discriminators: age (or broader lifestages) and household income. Given the need for fast and effective targeting tools, age is a logical shorthand for a customer's likely needs, behaviours and influences at certain times in life. Income is used as a proxy for potential value, either to the category or a specific brand.

Many observers, therefore, went ahead and applied an age-based approach to defining behaviours, needs and potential financial values within the 50+ market. Typically, the "Young Old" in their 50s today, are pictured as free-spirited, affluent and unconventional. The "Growing Old", aged 60-74, have been brought up with values influenced by post-war austerity and a firm belief in family values. Then there are the "Old Old", carrying the memories of the depression and frightened into staying behind locked doors by the threats of modern society. Using this model, marketers use broad homogenous segments (for example "Baby Boomers") and develop offers and creative to reflect this.

AGE AS A STATE OF MIND

In recent years, however, there is increasing evidence that age for over-50s is much more relative, becoming as much a state of mind as a state of body. Recent surveys suggest that three in four over-50s feel no more than 75 per cent of their chronological age. Given this, a more sympathetic view of ageing is needed, where physical age (what your birth certificate says), health age (how old your body feels), mental age (how old you feel) and lifestyle age (how old you act) are brought together to create a profile that is relevant and can be targeted. More about this challenge later.

At the same time as challenging age as a tool for 50+ selection, income also appears to bear little relevance in an environment where over-50s' spending power is often determined more by returns on assets rather than earned income. This point is illustrated by Figure 1, showing how (reported) income declines precipitously with age.

However, our experience tells a very different story. One of our automotive clients recently found that buyers of their new cars had an average income of £5,000 a year. However, buyers of used vehicles shared an average income band of £15–20,000—in other words, people who buy more expensive new cars are more likely to be living off asset-based income rather than still earning a regular wage.

This illustrates why a new approach is required that reflects an individual's real spending power, rather than a set of simple assumptions based on "regular" working income.

Figure 1
Income by age

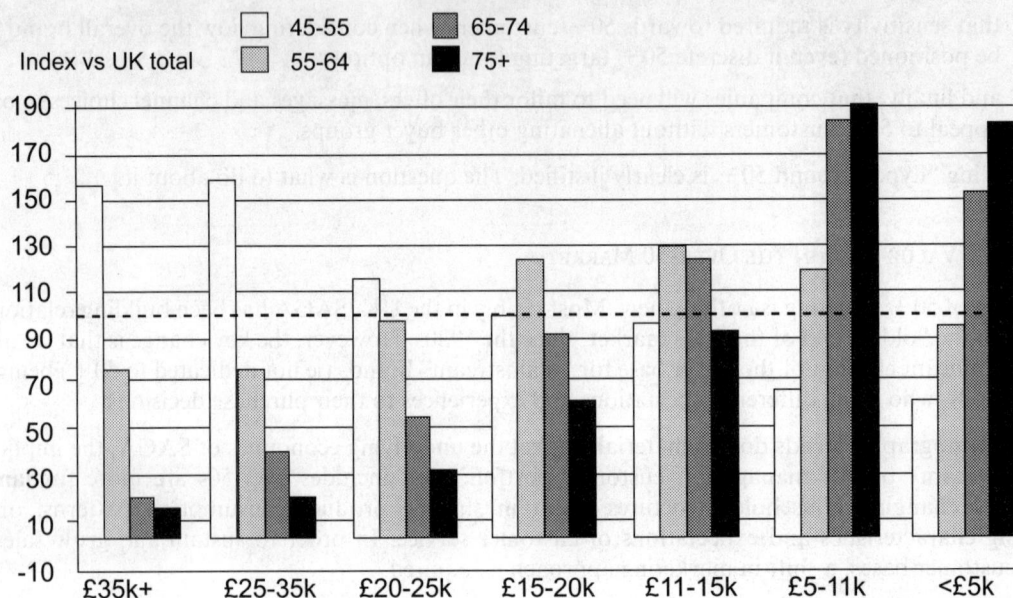

Source: TGI 2001

WHY START AT 50?

Our solution to this targeting challenge began with the insight that as people near 50, they face a number of fundamental life decisions that influence their personal (and spending) priorities. Three factors rise above others around age 50.

1. *Children leaving home*—by 50, 86 per cent of UK households have no one under 18 living there.

2. *Mortgages paid off*—by 50, 60 per cent of home owners have paid off their mortgage (for over 65-year-olds the figure rises to virtually 90 per cent).

3. *Planning for retirement*—although 68 per cent of UK households are still working between 50 and the legal age of retirement, financial planning for the years afterwards starts long before-hand.

A NEW TARGETING APPROACH

These three factors create a unique situation where—often for the first time ever—an individual's financial commitments on the mortgage, school fees and household items fall at a faster rate than the disposable income coming in from salary and interest on assets. This opens up a gap in uncommitted expenditure which we call an individual's "Financial Freedom". The degree of "freedom" will vary for each individual, reflecting the amount of money coming in and also what is required to cover the bills. Within this, the marketer's challenge is to attempt to target each individual according to their "Financial Freedom", then marry this with other considerations—such as how they spend their leisure time—in an attempt to marry spend potential with relevant interests that will drive a response to a marketing offer. Now we have an actionable approach that reflects age (as an entry criterion), but then moves beyond income to provide a precise and targetable measure of individual spending power.

To help define an individual's financial freedom, we have reached out to commercially-available databases that contain a comprehensive range of variables relating to lifestyle needs and behaviours. As a side-benefit, using commercial data also allows us to overlay the findings on to third-party rental lists to facilitate future customer prospecting.

While the specific insights and action plans resulting from our "Grey Matters" segmentation will vary by sector, overall key headlines include the following (Figure 2).

Figure 2
'Grey Matters' segmentation

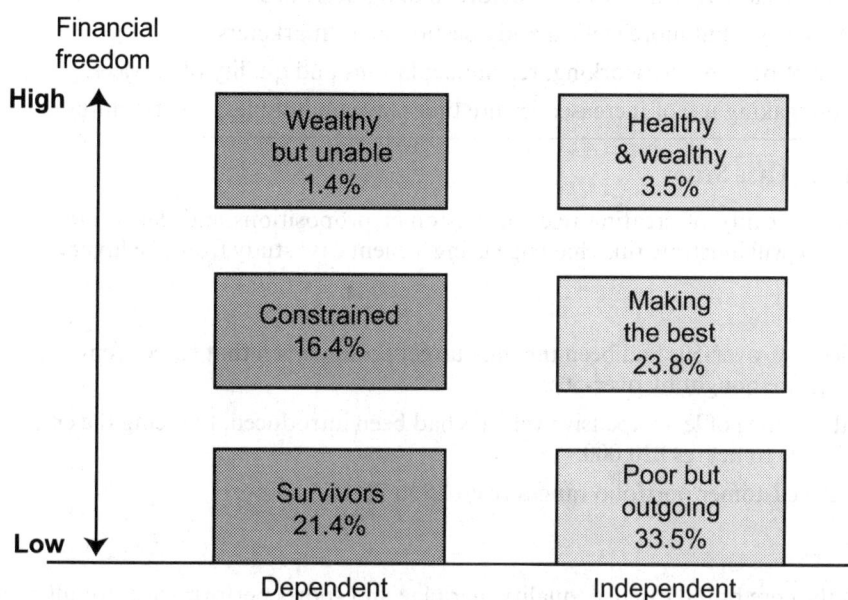

- The "classic" targeting group of wealthy, older individuals may be as small as 3.5 per cent of the UK's over-50 population (our "Healthy & Wealthy" segment).

- Of the 40 per cent of UK households that rely on state benefits for most or all of their income, nearly half also claim sickness or disability aid (our "Survivors").

- The "baby boomer" generation (which we call "Making the Best") are a formidable force, representing nearly a quarter of all UK over-50s.

To drive the development of relevant offers and messages to each segment, "pen portraits" are required that explain the needs and wants of each group. Using a combination of in-house material and commercial lifestyle databases (such as TGI and Claritas data as we have used here), we are able to demonstrate the different behaviours between segments.

As an example: "Healthy & Wealthy" are independently wealthy, likely to be retired (perhaps company directors). They may have second homes in the UK and Europe, they use charge cards rather than credit cards, enjoy a hectic social life (at home and out), fine wines and reading. They support charitable causes and drive luxury cars, and so on.

"Making the Best"—"baby boomers", many are still working, mortgages often remain (despite equity release), they carry multiple credit cards, enjoy DIY, gardening and betting, drive 4x4s and family cars, and eat at family-style restaurants.

(TGI, Claritas over-index versus UK population).

This approach may not be appropriate for all categories and brands. However, the overall approach—of moving beyond age and income as targeting variables—represents a fundamental shift for all marketers looking to unlock over-50 value. See box for a more general view of the age group, from qualitative research.

Qualitative research insights into the 50+ market

— More individual, less tribal.

— More experienced and confident in decision-making.

— Brought up in a verbal and written world rather than just visual.

— Educated to believe in the value of rational argument and product benefits.

— Predisposed to gathering information before making decisions.

— Marketing-savvy—but more cynical and questioning of marketers.

— Importance of personal networking, recommendations and quality of services.

— Focused on making use of increased leisure time through hobbies, sports, culture and learning.

Unlocking Value—Case Study

To ground us in the reality of creating relevant customer propositions and delivering these through cost-efficient channels, we will illustrate this challenge using a client case study from the luxury Automotive sector.

Client context

— Traditionally, over-50s had been the only target group, given that 65 per cent of all new luxury cars in the UK are bought by over-50s.

— Recently a range of less-expensive vehicles had been introduced, reducing the entry-level price from over £50,000 to nearer £20,000.

— Today the customer portfolio ranges from 25 to 75+.

Client objectives

— Retain the core brand essence (quality, heritage and sports performance) for all owners.

— Retain over-50s as a core buying group.

— Introduce a higher volume of younger buyers who will be managed up into more premium vehicles over time.

Our approach

— Insights into over-50 buyers.

— Media selection and targeting.

— Proposition development and delivery.

Our first step was to investigate whether purchase behaviour in the category varied with age. Without disclosing any of the client's proprietary findings, we can use an industry-standard after-sales survey (the New Car Buyers Study or NCBS) to demonstrate how car purchase behaviour evolves over time (Figure 3).

Figure 3
New Vehicle: reasons for purchase

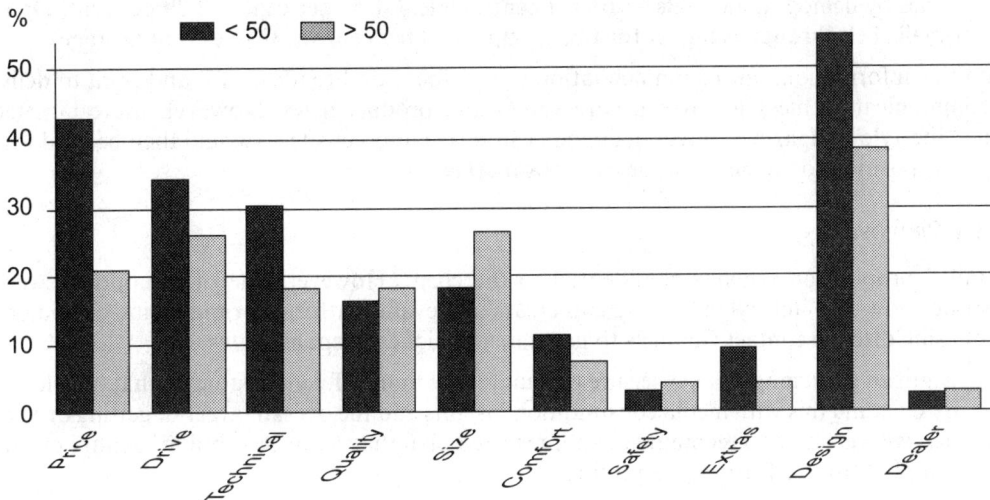

Source: NCBS 2002, half year survey

Design and price are the key reasons for under-50s choosing our particular vehicle. For over-50s, drive and size have become greater considerations. In addition, under-50s seem to score all factors more highly than their over-50 counterparts, suggesting stronger views about what they like and why. At the topline level, a different customer proposition (or slant on the product's benefits) may be needed for segments within each group.

NCBS data also demonstrate why "value" propositions need to be created relative to the buying group, given that over-50s buyers are significantly more likely to pay for their new car with cash rather than manufacturer or dealer credit.

MEDIA SELECTION AND TARGETING

When it comes to defining the most relevant "platforms" for communicating benefit messages and value offers, a key to understanding the over-50s market comes from understanding the use of leisure time. For family lifestage groups, you may be what you eat (as Tesco believes in its targeting). For teens, you may be what you wear (for Littlewoods). Alternatively you may be what you read (for WHSmith). For a significant proportion of over-50s it is often a case of "you are what you spend your free time on".

Going back to our "Grey Matters" segmentation and profiling tool, we helped this client find the different leisure interests of its target segments. For their traditional heartland buyer ("Wealthy & Healthy" in our matrix), we identified their media preferences to be:

— Newspapers—*Daily Telegraph, Daily Mail* and *Financial Times* are preferred titles.

For reference, Over 50s represent 33 per cent of the UK population but 49 per cent of newspaper readership. Most broadsheet (*Guardian, Independent, Times, Financial Times*) readership falls off with age but the *Telegraph* has exploited its unique position using a database of 400k subscription names to innovate new lifestyle clubs in wine, travel, fashion.

— Magazines—*English Heritage, Birds* (RSPB), *Amateur Gardening* and *Woman and Home* over-index for "Wealthy & Healthy" readers vs total population. Dedicated 50+ magazine titles (*Yours!, People's Friend, My Weekly,* etc) offer lower-than average cover prices—but with lower print quality as well.

SAGA's subs-based magazine stands out, delivering a 1.2 million monthly circulation as the bedrock of the Saga holiday and 50+ services offering.

— Television—viewership skews to BBC 1 and 2, with select Sky Sports programming mixed in. Over-65s are significantly more likely to watch news and factual programmes than 16–44s. However, many 50+s see themselves as portrayed negatively on television.

— Radio—listening focused on Classic FM, Heart and BBC Radio 2. 49 per cent of 55–64 year olds tuning in versus 82 per cent of 15–24s.

— Internet–"Wealthy & Healthy" usage, at an average 10 hours a month, is significantly ahead of average. 40 per cent of over-50s are Online, visiting more sites, more often and for longer. Usage varies by demographic: ABs = 61 per cent online, C1 51 per cent, C2 29 per cent, Ds 12 per cent. Email click-through is higher for this group (8–10 per cent vs. 3–5 per cent average).

Based on this information, our recommendation was to focus on broadcast TV and print to deliver a single brand communication message around core values and product news. However, more targeted media—including "lifestyle" magazines, direct mail and customised internet sites—would then be used for delivering a discrete proposition to segments of the over-50s market.

Customer Proposition

Our detailed proposition remains confidential to the client. However, one of the options we considered demonstrates how 50+ lifestyle targeting can create a relevant platform for managing customer loyalty (in this case) using discrete contact channels to generate the highest response rates.

Profiling identified gardening as a key leisure pursuit for the more affluent customers that our client was trying to retain. By blending this with media consumption insights and the overall target of getting drivers back into their vehicles, we were able to recommend an integrated plan that reinforced brand loyalty, product benefits and offered a platform for further prospecting.

In summary we proposed offering:

1. a short UK leisure break itinerary, taking in the finest gardens of Britain's stately homes;

2. our client to provide free admission using a Heritage pass;

3. providing a vehicle for response measurement and further data capture;

4. providing a commercial tie-in with the *Daily Telegraph's* lifestyle clubs matching premium hotel and restaurant deals in with the gardens itinerary.

5. leveraging our client's presence at special house-and-garden event days, to offer test drives to new customer prospects (marketed through advertorial coverage in SAGA's monthly magazine);

6. ability to plan and track your journey using a microsite on the brand's website. Look out for some news in Summer 2003!

Conclusions

Successful 50+ exploitation demands an alternative to the mainstream mass-marketing that many of these customers grew up with. Here is a group where value is highly concentrated within a minority of customers, who are more likely to be time-rich rather than time-starved, and whose responsiveness to marketing offers relies on personal relevance rather than peer pressure.

Not all businesses will find themselves needing to respond to the same degree, at the same time, or with the same level of sophistication. However, those that chose to ignore or misrepresent the over-50 opportunity will eventually find out that—sooner or later—their traditional customer base will have aged from under them.

May 2005

Examination of Witnesses

Witnesses: MR MERVYN KOHLER, Head of Public Affairs, Help the Aged, MR STEVEN SADLER, Technical Director, Tunstall Group Ltd, and MR ROBERT DIAMOND, Chief Executive, Diametric, examined.

Q457 *Chairman:* May I welcome you very warmly and thank you for giving us time and coming along to our question session this morning. Thank you also for the written evidence that your organisations have submitted; that has been very helpful and has been digested, and it is the basis of some of the discussion this morning. Can I point out to you that we are now being broadcast live on internet, so anything you say will not simply be taken down and used in evidence, but it is available to anyone watching this on internet. Equally, the discussion may be broadcast on the Parliamentary digital channel, and the microphones are quite sensitive. That being said, my colleagues all have name tags and I will not go around the table taking time to introduce them, they will introduce themselves as they ask questions. I would like to start with a fairly general question, but one that I think is central to the issues that we would like to talk about this morning; perhaps each of you might, in responding to this question if you want to, simply say who you are and which organisation you represent. The question I want to ask is the belief that we largely have, and it is reinforced in the media, that the older generation has very significant economic power now that perhaps it did not have in the previous decades. That being so, we have found—and this is one of the reasons for this session today—that there seems to be surprisingly little movement towards developing products specifically designed for this group of potential customers. You may or may not agree with that, but I would like you to reflect on it and say, if it is the case, why you think that is, and if it is not the case perhaps give us some of the evidence to the contrary. Mervyn Kohler, would you like to start?

Mr Kohler: Yes, thank you My Lord Chairman, I am Mervyn Kohler, the Head of Public Affairs at Help the Aged. The picture of a wealthier older society than we have ever seen before is a little bit unfair and it is certainly over-simplistic. Undoubtedly, the top 10 per cent—the top quintile perhaps—of our older population have got pretty high incomes. They have come from a background of reasonably good pension schemes—which actually delivered—and they have managed to build up a fair amount of capital savings, but for the other four-fifths we are looking at pretty staggering levels of subsistence. Barely half of our older population actually have an income large enough in order to pay income tax. We have got something like five million—again about half of our older population—now eligible for means-tested benefits of one kind or another, and those of course are only designed to provide people with subsistence income; ergo, quite a lot of our older population still remains, sadly, poor.

Q458 *Chairman:* For the others, is there an unwillingness amongst manufacturers or industries to look for products that would be welcome to them in marketing?

Mr Kohler: Yes, in general terms—and this is certainly what I would like to say to the Committee today—whilst there are a number of manufacturers and producers who obviously do market specifically to the older purchasers and therefore do a fair amount of market research there, in the general run of the provision of normal, everyday goods and services, the special needs of the older population tend to get overlooked, there is a trade-off with other age groups who are seen to be more accessible or interesting and so on and so forth. Take the ever diminishing size of mobile phones as an obvious example, there is huge consumer demand for small keyboards whereas the older population are struggling around trying to find out where the numbers are and that type of thing.

Mr Diamond: Robert Diamond, I am the founder and chief executive of Diametric, which is a marketing agency. We provide services to the large, national brand owners to help them in the effectiveness of their marketing, and three years ago we launched a unit of the company called Grey Matters to help mainstream brands understand and respond to the challenges of an ageing population. Our proposition is overtly commercial, we work on subjects that are of interest to mainstream brand owners, and I will be honest and say that our Grey Matters unit has struggled somewhat over the last three years to engage the large advertisers in the UK in a meaningful dialogue about the impact of an ageing population. The reasons for that are manifold, but I will focus on three specifically. The first is a genuine challenge around the idea of marketing to older people—when we talk about a mature audience we typically refer to over 45 or over 50, it is an arbitrary measure and I apologise in advance for that.

Q459 *Chairman:* Very arbitrary I would have said.

Mr Diamond: Fundamentally, there is a growing challenge that a distinct 50-plus mindset exists any longer, and there is some research that we presented prior to this meeting, recent research done by MORI, that shows that 88 per cent of 60–64 year olds said that the term "elderly" did not apply to them; 52 per cent of 75–80 year olds said the term did not apply to them. One reason, therefore, is that there is a genuine challenge about a distinct 50-plus mindset. The second reason is that if one thinks about the large advertisers and the marketers in the UK, they are often applying it to a heartland of rather stereotypically large families with children, and there is a genuine concern, I think, that by marketing their car or their computer or their food product overtly to an older audience, it has the potential to alienate the mainstream, and there is some evidence that that is taking place. The third reason I would point to is that marketing and marketers, it is a youth sport I am afraid; at 37 I am one of the old guard, which is rather disturbing, and again we have presented some evidence from the Institute of Practitioners of Advertising that suggested that 39 per cent of UK marketing directors are aged under 35 and only 10 per cent of marketing directors—these are the people who are spending the budgets—are aged over 50. Again, that leads to an environment which perpetuates and rewards youth and is rather cynical and critical of anyone over 35.

Q460 *Chairman:* Which leads me to wonder whether companies should not be required to have a non-executive board member with a particular remit in this area, but that is perhaps facetious.
Mr Diamond: An interesting idea.
Mr Sadler: Good morning, My Lord Chairman, my name is Steve Sadler and I am the Technical Director of Tunstall Group. Perhaps I could make two observations with regard to your question: one is that we actually design and manufacture products of various kinds for older people and vulnerable people, but even there, in that specific category, what we find is that the requirements of the products are often influenced by people other than the older people themselves, so it might be the buyer, it might be the intervening authority. If you look, for example, at today's telecare market, as it has been branded, which has developed from the old social alarm market, the vast majority of social alarms for community care were specified and had standards set for them by local authority procurers of one form or another—housing authorities and social services. In other words, if you have people making decisions and specifications on behalf of older people it does not necessarily get you the product that is right for the older person—sometimes it does, sometimes it does not, so there is that issue. The second point I would make is that in our industry we design and manufacture, but we also integrate other people's products. For example, my colleague made reference to mobile phones, cordless phones and so on, and what we find is that very, very rarely are those products targeted at older people specifically. My belief is that there is a very simple economic reason for that, that those suppliers optimise products for what they see as their core market initially, and that core market very often precludes the very young and the very old, it is looking at that central affluent age range, mobile phones being a prime example. It is almost not until you start to exhaust those core markets do people start to move into the adjacent markets as they would see it, and certainly we see it therefore as almost a timing effect as much as a lack of interest. Those varied products which are better suited to older people tend to appear later in the lifecycle of that type of technology. I offer those comments to you.

Q461 *Chairman:* If I could address both of you, Mr Diamond and Mr Sadler, the question that occurs to me is how much market research is done in respect of communities, and do you actually talk to older people as part of that market research, or do you just take the core market that you, Mr Sadler, were talking about—if people are affluent this is the kind of thing they will want, as distinct from affluent with certain digital skills or whatever?
Mr Sadler: If I could pick that one up first, for me there is quite a bit of research that goes on with the user base. Whilst various sessions and focus groups and other activities are run with older people we do see a dominant effect driven by the buyer and certainly, in our market, that has been driven by an intervening authority, usually a public sector person. I suspect that market still is rather skewed, therefore, in favour of the buyer rather than the end user.
Mr Diamond: From a marketing perspective the research is rather sadly self-selecting, in that one of the first things you do when placing research is choose which target group you wish to research amongst and then, by definition, you get a skewed result. In our experience we have been involved in two commercial initiatives by large manufacturing organisations; interestingly, both of them called Project Phoenix, completely independently of each other, which intimates people rising from the ashes, so in evolutionary terms rather the wrong way round I would have thought. In both those instances they actually went out and researched the needs of an older audience, and I think it is a trend that is becoming increasingly prevalent amongst brand organisations. Rather than looking at the opportunity of any ageing population, they are rather fearing the impact of an ageing population, so for one of the manufacturers they happened to be in the business of marketing deodorants and other personal care products, and one of the fascinating facts is that your need for anti-perspirants and deodorants diminishes over 50 which means, if that is your business, you are in trouble because your population base is ageing from beneath you. In that instance some organisations are making special efforts but, to be honest, the mainstream of their budgets is focused absolutely in the heartland of the buyer who, for many consumables, is perceived to be the rather stereotyped mother in her mid to late 30s with two children trailing around behind her in the

local supermarket, and that is who they research among.

Q462 *Lord Turnberg:* The question I was going to ask has been answered, at least in part. As I get older I find I am less and less interested in the advertisements that are around, and those that are I am less and less convinced by, so I suppose the older one is the less easy it is to convince someone through advertising that this is the thing they have to have, which must make it difficult for the advertising industry. I suppose the aged are fortunate in not being responsive quite so much to advertising, but nevertheless there are large numbers of products which should be available to the elderly, but I suspect there is a gap—I suppose that is why you have set up your grey group. What can be done? How can Mr Sadler sell his products better to an audience which is likely to be more critical of the gorgeous blue and red adverts?

Mr Diamond: We have spent quite a bit of time looking at this. Our starting premise is, fundamentally, that you have to educate the manufacturers of products and services as to the commercial opportunity available. Ours is a fairly simple business, which is that we are at the receiving end of other people's investment in marketing, therefore we have to be responsive to their needs and to the degree that we can educate them around where other marketing opportunities lie. We do not have a social agenda, ours is a purely commercial agenda. There is some fairly direct learning about marketing messages and propositions that resonate more with an older audience, and they are all rather warming: it is about presenting people with the facts in a clear and compelling manner, it is inviting individuals to make their own choices about which product is better than another product. Here too you get into a discussion about which medium you are using to communicate with, but it tends to be rather richer messages in terms of deeper content, so typically products that are marketed to older consumers tend to be presented in the print medium or in the radio medium rather than necessarily the fast soundbite and high cost of television, although the generalism does vary by product. Certainly, though, there are different cues which do appear to be relevant to older consumers when they are receiving marketing messages and making their own decisions based on them, and they are very different to the accepted ways of mainstream marketing and advertising.

Q463 *Lord Turnberg:* Is there a big gap there?
Mr Diamond: When I set up the Grey Matters unit I thought there was a huge gap, ands three years later and quite a bit of money down in investment I am not quite sure how big the gap is. Certainly, when we go round speaking to brand owners—and we work

across almost all consumer sectors that you can imagine, from technology to automotive, to consumer goods to travel retail—everybody nods and looks at the numbers and is academically interested about the ageing population, but they then go back and do what they have been doing before. As I say, the only brands that I think have responded in any major way have viewed the ageing population as a major commercial opportunity, or a major threat, and have therefore taken active steps to engage with older consumers.

Mr Kohler: May I add to that, please? I think there is something in the observation that the conventional way of getting messages across to the public seems to have less impact on the older population, and the examples I will give you are all from the public services. We still have something like two million pensioners in this country entitled to pension credit, which they are not claiming. There have been adverts on television, they have been written letters and all this kind of thing, yet for some reason or another—there is free money out there—people have not responded and have not claimed their benefit. You could say the same thing about a number of the programmes to improve people's heating systems and things of that nature; look at the resistance from the pensioner population to the withdrawal of pension books and their replacement with smart cards. There are still, probably, about a million people out there who have not got a bank account for their pension to be paid into. There is a gap, therefore, in terms of effective communications with older people which I think affects not just the commercial world but the world of Government as well.

Q464 *Chairman:* Mr Sadler, do you want to come in as well?
Mr Sadler: Just coming back to the point about who is making the decisions, if we look at how we could perhaps improve the marketing to older people, one way of course is to make sure that the proposition we are delivering is one that appeals directly to the end user. If you look at the example of the traditional social alarm market, which I have referred to already for our type of product, that was very much "This is a product that I am going to give you because you need it; it is not what you want, but I am making the decision that you need it." Those propositions have changed over time so if you look at today's telecare technology, it provides other things such as intruder monitoring, bogus callers, reminders to take your medication, in other words things that should appeal to you directly as an end user, you can make your own informed decision. So I think one issue is that we have got to make the proposition properly appeal to that older user. The other point that I feel quite strongly is the question of trust. We are talking very

generally about people with a great deal of experience behind them, they have seen these things come and go, have they got a perception that what is marketed and sold usually delivers the outcome they expect? Not always, so there is a question of trust there, and if I try and relate it to our own experience there is this issue of the channel by which that proposition gets to the end user. To give an example, if you take our products, you can send out lots of leaflets, you have television campaigns, but universally those have failed because they are alien to that older community; if the product is taken to that older person through a trusted channel, however, a local authority for example, someone they know, or with a strong brand name, or a blue chip company, that very often works. The example that springs to mind, is the work at West Lothian in Scotland where the council themselves were offering a product, technology and services—it happens to be our product but there are lots of others—to people over 60, and the take-up they have had is remarkable. They have 10,000 households with people over 60, and currently it has been taken up by about 1,700 people, so 17 per cent. Anyone in the commercial industry would be very pleased with that sort of take-up. My personal belief is that it is there because they have a good, strong council with a trusted record; a private sector company would not have achieved the same degree of success.

Chairman: That is very helpful, thank you. Lady Emerton.

Q465 Baroness Emerton: Thank you My Lord Chairman. Having listened to what has been said already it seems that there is, indeed, a problem of education, and I think Mr Diamond mentioned that it is education not only of the older people but also perhaps, dare I say it, of marketing managers and marketing personnel. Following the conversation we have had, can you identify any specific actions, for example the formation of a trade association, that might help to accelerate the development of companies' products and markets which would be targeted at the older consumers, who would be educated themselves towards those objects, because I think that point has been made in terms of the trust that is required by the older person.

Mr Diamond: If I understand your question correctly it relates to whether some form of education or some sort of trade body should be set up.

Q466 Baroness Emerton: Or both.

Mr Diamond: I had a note of it before we came in today, and I think it is a very interesting proposition. Without a doubt, this is a discussion topic which requires further debate and further education, both amongst consumers—who probably have debates on a daily basis with their friends about the irrelevance of advertising—and amongst the people who produce that advertising who rarely have the debate about where is the population going, where is the wealth within the population going, what is the impact of an ageing population on dependency in terms of a working population having to support an increasingly large base of retired people? Whether a trade body is the right way or not I genuinely do not know. I think the concept of more direct research and subsequent education amongst marketing practitioners has great merit. I certainly know that for Haymarket Conferences, which is one of the largest organisers of conferences for the marketing community, their annual Older Richer Wiser conference is consistently sold out and has the highest attendance of any of those commercial conferences. Clearly, therefore, people are looking for further information. There seems to be a gap though, which is the provision of information through conferences and trade bodies and then the take-up by commercial organisations in terms of drawing senior consumers into their commercial plans. It is interesting that you rather lightly suggested that potentially there could be a non-executive director involved in certain companies who actually champions certain cases; I think that is a very interesting proposition because I think that fundamentally when you look at the ageing of the population and some of the wealth statistics—and there seems to be some confusion or dispute over the wealth statistics—it does suggest that more people are getting older and most people have more money, certainly in terms of assets and retained saving, though it is less true in terms of disposable income. What does need to happen is that there needs to be a debate at board level within a lot of organisations, which need to challenge their marketing directors and their commercial teams on fundamentally are we almost following yesterday's business model and should we be considering where our industry is moving forward. The right platform for that I genuinely do not know, because it is quite a complex issue.

Q467 Baroness Emerton: Do you think it might be an issue that should be taken up in the basic educational programme of marketing?

Mr Diamond: I think so, absolutely, in as much as the stalwarts in the marketing community—and there used to be a lot of marketing training programmes—I started 17 years ago with Proctor & Gamble who are rather famous for their marketing programmes, and they taught an impressionable 21 year old how to market to housewives with children; I see no reason why they could not take the same individuals today and educate them about marketing to a 50 or 60 year old married couple, who have some money to spend and are very happy to invest in various products and services. I think it is just a fundamental lack of both awareness and also an increasing issue of what an ageing population really means in the UK.

Q468 Chairman: Or, alternatively, how to market to middle-aged children with older parents.

Mr Diamond: Absolutely, and I think that the dual dependency of looking after ageing parents and young children is an increasing reality, and I think that that could actually be the trigger that pushes this dialogue and discussion onto a broader spectrum.

Mr Kohler: My Lord Chairman, there is no particular rocket science involved in designing a world for older people; we are talking about issues to do with diminishing sight, diminishing hearing, diminishing strength, those sorts of issues, and there is information out there for manufacturers if they actually chose to use it. One of my favourite anecdotes is of the concept car which a Japanese manufacturer put together about 15 years ago, looking to the older driver of the future. This had features like a head-up holographic display on the windscreen so that you did not actually have to look down at the dashboard, and things like that, prismatic mirrors, swivel seats, radar-assisted parking, push-button handbrake, all these sorts of features. They never moved to market a car like that, presumably because they do not actually perceive at the moment that there is a purchaser base to make it worthwhile, but the answers are there.

Lord Turnberg: And a good seat, not one on the floor.

Lord Soulsby of Swaffham Prior: My Lord Chairman, this document we have just had, I am not going to infringe on any other questions if I pursue it?

Chairman: Pursue it, yes, indeed. This is the paper from Help the Aged.

Q469 Lord Soulsby of Swaffham Prior: Yes, I think so, it is about the designing and marketing of industrial and commercial products. Might I be bold enough to say that I do not think sufficient attention—indeed any attention in fact—is paid to some of the things that you have mentioned, Mr Kohler, like eyesight going, hearing going, strength going. So many things, like the instructions on packaging, are often in print that is unreadable unless you use a magnifying glass. There is far too much information, surely one can abbreviate that into a readable form for the older person. Pharmaceuticals in childproof bottles—you have to get a child to open it because some of the older people cannot do it, and so on. It does seem to me that no attention has been paid to people of 75 or 80 or over because it is the inability to use these very simple things that causes trouble to older people. One other grouse I have is that of young people on the telephone speaking far too rapidly so that you cannot understand what they are saying; there should be some instruction that if you are speaking to older people you should slow

down so that people can in fact understand what they are talking about.

Mr Kohler: You are absolutely right. It always staggers me that we see something like 40,000 people admitted to accident and emergency departments every year who have injured themselves trying to get into domestic packaging of one kind or another, using an inappropriate implement in an inappropriate way. There are all sorts of different trade-offs which do actually constrain the whole process. Pharmaceutical products, for example, come with pages and pages of small print because that is what they are required by law to actually produce and show what the product is exactly. In that pages and pages of script, the simple instruction about how you actually take the stuff probably gets, relatively speaking, lost. There are all these sorts of considerations; one of the food products which always causes a lot of concern is peanuts, when you really do have to have an applied skill to actually tear the foil at the top, but that is the best way of keeping a peanut fresh, so the peanut manufacturers to whom I have spoken tell me.

Q470 Chairman: Thank you very much. Do you want to come in, Mr Sadler?

Mr Sadler: Maybe we come full circle back to the point about the representation of the end user, whether you do it through awareness or the appropriate training. I would suggest that there are quite a few trade associations already out there and whilst I love your idea of having a non-executive in every single company representing the older person's interests, it might be quicker to target some of the trade associations and ensure that they are working to the right code of practice. My own organisation, for example, is party to such an association and I suspect even there they are not properly represented with an older person's representative.

Mr Diamond: One recent positive step in this direction has been, as I have observed through going around and seeing different brand manufacturers, the implementation of the recent Disabilities Discrimination Act, where people have, by law, been revisiting largely their websites. It is now quite common to go onto an internet site and you see a button saying "If you would like this in larger typeface, please click here." That concept, while it is extremely complex to implement through other media, whether it is packaging or the instructions on how to take a product, has narrowed which is that people should have choice, if they are visually impaired or if they would like to be, when on the telephone, treated in a certain way, and there should be provision for that to happen. The Disability Discrimination Act obviously is more regulation and we would much prefer a self-imposed way of working with organisations to recognise that some people do have difficulty in hearing and so on.

Q471 Lord Soulsby of Swaffham Prior: If I may come back for one moment, My Lord Chairman, you mentioned the internet and websites and computers, but not everybody has in fact got a computer and not every aged individual knows how to work a computer. The thing that would be adequate for a teenager or a 20 or 30 year old is no longer applicable for an older person; they are frightened of computers and it is no use saying go on the web and find it, because they (a) do not know it, or (b) do not have a computer to get on the web in the first place.

Mr Kohler: There is a hugely important point underlying what you have just highlighted there, and that is that as the majority of goods and services increasingly become marketed through the web and information is disseminated through the web and things like that, we do risk really marginalising a large chunk of our older population, and I think that is a serious concern across the whole of the social policy field.

Mr Sadler: It is very interesting, there was a large European study, going back probably three or four years now where all these issues about how we represent goods and information to older people were discussed—it was called Safe 21. The one point that sticks in my mind is the strong view that if you are trying to provide information and assistance to that older person living in their own property, you should be using familiar instruments around the home and, even at that stage, we were very much embedded in the internet but the recommendation was to use the television, use the telephone, use the informal carer coming to the door rather than some interesting but new technology. I think an interesting prospect that we might look at for the future is of that these things do converge, so when we turn off analogue TV broadcasting and we get complete digital broadcasting to the TV screen, you will have access to lots of information in context, which looks very much like a familiar instrument, where you can scale the text, you can change the representation on the screen. I think that should provide a very interesting challenge for exactly the problem we are talking about today.

Q472 Lord Broers: Unfortunately, I missed the visit to the Tunstall Group which I would have much enjoyed, but are you involved in that subject of simplifying the internet, for example? I am aware that there are several manufacturers in the world who are not so much targeting old people as targeting the Third World and just targeting the economics of the situation, so there will be a very simple internet access machine that is not a computer, you just turn it on and the internet comes up.

Mr Sadler: That is right.

Q473 Lord Broers: Then you turn it off and the internet goes away, so there are no clever computer skills required. Are you involved in that?

Mr Sadler: I think that is very much a key point of interest for our technology. If you look at where technology is today, the proposition has moved on from you must have an alarm to let us provide functionality that helps, and I have mentioned intruder, bogus callers and all these sorts of issues that are the very logical next step. Let me explain one particular issue: when you have done all these things it is largely about supporting independent living, taking away risk, helping to provide a safety net for living in your own home. The concern I have is that once you have done that, of course, you have often assisted in some form of social isolation because you have that person living in their home, often on their own, albeit trying to access information on health and social care. Video links to family members and so on is very strongly suggested to be the next step of the technology. To me the next step is very much more the interfacing of that telecare world to those normal instruments I talked about, and the obvious one is the television. Our interest is very much in linking that alarm world to this new set-top box world to provide social information and assistance on the TV screen. You can imagine a whole host of those services which we can only speculate about today, but will be delivered via that mechanism.

Q474 Lord Broers: I hope it will be very straightforward. The trouble is we fear and dread these extra set-top boxes, and we all know the most common item in our homes is the table full of remote controls, and nobody knows which one does what. I am a real advocate in this environment for a very simple, straightforward single interface, and if the internet could be provided as just another channel on the television set it would also perhaps be something that people could handle.

Mr Sadler: I agree with you entirely. The simplification is not just for the older generation either; all of us would benefit from easier access mechanisms to this information, and when it is presented on a TV screen you are not going to be interested in playing around with the mouse and all these technical issues you have with a PC, so inevitably the next steps will integrate and simplify products in that environment.

Lord Broers: My Lord Chairman, if I may also speak on a slightly different topic, I declare my interest as an old non-executive director of Vodaphone, and I would say that this phone problem is being tackled. Vodaphone is about to announce a product with nice big keys, that is just a phone and is not a camera and a golf swing machine and everything else you can imagine.

Chairman: Lord Turnberg wants to come in and then we must move on to Lord Drayson.

Q475 Lord Turnberg: Just one point, one of the drivers for all of this would be the commercial benefit to the companies, I suspect, but surely the company that produces an easily-opened packaged will have a commercial advantage over all the others that produce unopenable packaging. Cannot that message be got through? I am surprised companies do not do that, they could make it their point: our packets are dead easy to open.

Mr Kohler: Your statement is so self-evidently true it is hard to actually work out what is going on here. I suspect it does come down to trust. If we stay with the packaging work for a moment, a reasonably easy to open closure unit on a package of liquid, a fruit drink perhaps, or milk, something of that nature, costs a few marginal pennies but it is a highly competitive market where price is really important when it is sitting there on the supermarket shelf. Maybe that odd penny or two is our problem.

Lord Turnberg: I find that hard to believe.

Q476 Lord Drayson: I would like to probe this issue a bit further actually, because we have heard evidence from a number of sources about this failure by industry to meet what is clearly a growing demand caused by this accelerating demographic change towards an older population, so I really want to try and get to the bottom of why is industry failing to do this, because industry does not usually fail to meet a market opportunity. Is it because there is a failure of technology or is it a failure of marketing? You touched on this already, but I would like to probe it further: is it this lack of willingness or understanding or preparedness to actually understand this particular market sector, or is it a failure of design and technology to be able to develop products which as well as being effective for your 30-something family with young children is also easily-opened by someone in their 70s or 80s?

Mr Diamond: Can I attempt to answer that, certainly from a marketing perspective, and I am just going to draw on a paper which I authored last year with Professor Merlin Stone who is the IBM Professor of Relationship Marketing, which was called "Why Isn't Marketing Taking on the Over-50s Consumer?" We highlighted five reasons which I hope from a marketing perspective will answer that question. The background is that the big number that is quoted in the marketing community is that the over-50s consumers in the UK hold 80 per cent of all assets, 60 per cent of savings and represent 40 per cent of disposable income, so from a ruthlessly commercial perspective one would think that that makes them a very, very attractive proposition. We highlighted five potential reasons why marketing is not taking on the challenge—these are all hypothesis-based I should say. The first is a hypothesis that actually the wealth statistics hide the fact that the majority of accumulated wealth amongst the over-50s is very disproportionately held by a small number of the over-50s group—fundamentally it is held in illiquid assets, and when we talk about why are we not designing new consumer products packaging for an over-50s population, in almost every consumer product that you can think of the money is still with high volume, which tends to mean large family units, and that is one of the reasons why. It also suggests that if the majority of this wealth is locked up in property, in pension funds and so on, the wealth statistics might be somewhat misleading, and that in practice the 80 per cent of all wealth that is held by the over-50s cannot be easily accessed. The second reason—and I alluded to this earlier—is around the idea of an over-50's, a senior's mindset, no longer being valid. Everybody rolls out either Mick Jagger or Jack Nicholson as a role model—whoever thought that would happen—for describing the idea of you used to be a pre-50s, then you hit .50 and suddenly everything went downhill, and you certainly see a lot of research and verbatim quotes suggesting that is no longer the case. The third I have already alluded to, that appealing to the over-50s will alienate the mainstream, and certainly with the large budget brand owners we have had very open dialogues about if we are seen to have older consumers in our advertising, will that alienate younger consumers?

Q477 Lord Drayson: If I may just interrupt you there, what was going on with Dove then?

Mr Diamond: Dove is a very interesting example, and I should state that Unilever is one of my clients and we work with them on the question of targeting the over-50s consumers, and then also I, as Diametric, was quoted in *The Times* commenting on the Dove advertising campaign. They are being brave and they are being bold, and brave and bold sometimes lead to a marketing breakthrough in the commercial results, but often they do not. What Dove is seeking to do is differentiate itself from an extremely competitive marketplace by saying that, essentially—and I think this is a great comment on the beauty myth as we age—you should look the best that you can look, rather than if you are 60 you should try and look 20 or if your skin is this colour you should try and make it another colour. They are taking a fairly challenging approach and I am not party to their business results, I do not know whether it has been justified in terms of results. Interestingly, they have challenged a number of preconceptions about gender, about age, about physical shape and they have taken a very bold approach; personally, I like it but I do not know how the consumer at large has responded.

Chairman: It is very interesting, it is actually an Aristotlean approach rather than a Platonic one, but I dare say they had not thought of it in those terms. Aristotle: everything is good of its own kind, which is precisely what they were doing.

Baroness Hilton of Eggardon: They were not looking for the idea, were they?

Q478 *Lord Drayson:* Moving off the marketing issues then to the technological issues, how much is it a failure of attitude and vision of the engineers in designing new products? I am particularly thinking of the way in which technology is having a greater impact on all of our lives, so those who are 40-something and grew up with the use of personal computers are going to be much more computer-literate as a generation 15 years from now. How much work has been done on just how much more expensive it is to design a mobile phone, or a computer, or a car, which is as useable by someone who is 70 as it is by someone who is 30, so you do not necessarily market it as a car for the over 70s group, but you make sure that everyone from 17 to 70 can effectively use the car? Is it about the specification that is put to the engineers in terms of the type of group, or is there actually evidence that it is more expensive—you mentioned the problem about packaging—to develop a product which is as useable by that older population as it is by the more able, young?

Mr Sadler: Inevitably there is a mix of all those issues in there. Even if you look at our market—which is targeted largely at older people—if you look at the designers, they are still very much in the 30s age bracket and I see time and again errors of omission and commission on their part where they have not taken into account the use by older people. They continually have to be reminded to have the right interaction with the end users, to use the right specification to get back to the point about that particular market, so there is that side of it. The other thing we need to remember is that they tend to work primarily to the specifications that they are given, and then we come full circle back to the marketing element again, because certainly in all the industries I worked in in the UK and across Europe, the activity was very much driven to the specification of a market product manager, and if that market product manager has a particular belief in his core market, that will drive the outcome. Unless that person and his colleagues are aware of the adjacent markets and the different end users, they will not feature in the end product. At Tunstall we have deliberately targeted those end users, so maybe we are not as bad as some, but even there you can see those issues coming forward. For a general consumer product I can easily

see how that might come about, that you are not tailoring it to older people for example. Maybe one way to view this is if you look at the people involved in the chain of delivery of a new product, yes, you are a designer in your 30s, but as you move through the various management ranks, whilst you maybe retain some influence, by the time you have got a real appreciation of older people's needs through direct contact with your ageing parents or family members, you are not at the coalface any more, you are not the one writing the software or designing the piece of plastic. It relies on another mechanism, somehow you have to get that back into the design team, and there is a conscious effort to do that. It goes back to the point made earlier, that it is about awareness and training.

Q479 *Lord Drayson:* It is finding a mechanism whereby people can really use an in depth understanding of that more aged population, possibly because they are that generation themselves, and getting them engaged in the specification process and the design process of the product. You feel that that would lead to some positive change in the direction we want.

Mr Sadler: That is right. If you look at the guidance facing a designer today—including the people we use as well—the documentation and the guidance for older people and more vulnerable people and how you design for them is there, but you have to go and look for it because it is not mainstream education. If an engineer walked in off the street with his PhD, it is very unlikely that he will have faced the detailed user needs of some of those client groups, so he will have had the grounding, he knows how to design an electronic product, to write software and so on, but he will usually not have a detailed appreciation of what it means for a disabled user or an older person. It will take some initiative on the part of the company to do that and maybe that is where you need the non-executive influence or the trade association influence to instil that as a later phase of training and education.

Q480 *Baroness Hilton of Eggardon:* Just an aside on packaging, some packaging works well—fruit juice cartons are opened easily whereas milk cartons seem to fall to pieces when you pull back the plastic thing; nuts too, a lot of nut packets open easily—I am not a peanut eater—so there is a lot of variation. I would have thought that could be a selling point, that some people could be promoting the ease of opening their packaging perhaps, not just for the elderly but more generally perhaps, it is an irritant for us all. My question really is about the fact that promoting things for elderly people does not have the appeal and glamour that it has when promoting things for young people; do you think the Government should be doing more, either to provide information or to encourage initiatives and firms in this direction? Should there be more in the way of Government initiatives on this front? There are financial implications for Government of course.

Mr Kohler: I think we have simply got to find some tool somewhere that actually breaks the log-jam which we have been exploring over the last hour this morning, and we have somehow got to make the older population a little bit more aware of its own capacity to influence the marketplace as well. Many of the products aimed specifically at older people tend to have a kind of doom flavour about them, do they not, in the sense that you are marketing this because you, the purchaser, have a disability of some sort. We are all in denial about that, none of us actually want to say we are now old or disabled, we need help, and so on and so forth, so something has got to change. Somewhere it would be useful to be thinking of some sort of quality mark or something of that nature which could be attached to goods or services, such as the crystal mark that the Plain English Campaign have used—though I have not got a great deal of confidence in that, but energy efficiency ratings and things like that. There would then be some recognisable consumer message associated with that particular product which shows we actually thought about this in designing it for an older person.

Mr Diamond: If I could just build on that, I have experience of working and living in the US and there they have a consumer body known as the AARP or the American Association of Retired Persons, which operates as a commercial and almost quasi-political body in influencing manufacturers to listen to and be responsive to the needs of an ageing population. My perception is that they do a very good job and they have truly harnessed people power in using the power of their members, of which they have many in the US market. I sense in the UK we lack a single consumer body—rather ironically, outside of the listenership of Classic FM or the membership of Saga—we literally lack a harmonised consumer body that can go to manufacturers or service providers and put meaningful pressure on them. In terms of whether the Government should do something, I have to say that my preference would be for something which is more self-regulated within the industry. Within the marketing and advertising industry it happens to be the case that there are a number of effective bodies who are involved in self-regulation of the industry and I think those bodies could do a lot more than they do currently to educate, inform and guide their members.

Mr Sadler: I am not a marketeer, but if I could comment on a theme which seems to have a remarkable effect in terms of our sort of product, and that is about, if you like, humanising the story behind

the product and the marketing. We have had experience of lots of case studies—and I am thinking particularly of the Scottish council we referred to earlier—where they had older people who were allowed to live independently rather than moving to residential or nursing home care. It was not that they had a problem with nursing home care, of course, but a lot of people wanted to live independently. There were a number of case studies, but if I could mention one in particular, it was a case study of an older couple, the chap was in the early stages of a dementia condition and the lady had a mobility problem. Until that point the standard social care solution was going to be to separate that couple; they had effectively been joined at the hip for many years, they had survived two world wars and heaven knows how many grandchildren and offspring, they had this fantastically rich history behind them, yet our solution was going to be to separate them and move them. The point I am making is that the outcome meant they were able to live at home for three or four years longer together before they had to take another step. The reason I am mentioning that story is because we use that as a case study for designers, the same young designers that we have been talking about, who can be vulnerable to not capturing these needs. Some of the designers when we use this case study end up with tears in their eyes, so the point I am making is that if you can humanise those stories rather than a broader marketing message and show the rich history behind the end user, you can get quite a strong message across. If you can pick up those various success stories, roll them out and publicise them that might be one initiative we can take, but that one has such a powerful effect it sticks in my mind vividly.

Q481 *Lord Soulsby of Swaffham Prior:* Where is the United Kingdom in relation to other developed countries in terms of its progress towards helping aged people in developing products? Are there lacunae that we need to really identify and do something about or alternatively are we leading in certain areas that we should be very proud of? Where are we?

Mr Sadler: That is a good question. I have the luxury of sampling quite a few different countries because of the nature of our work, and you see a great deal of innovation in certain countries such as Holland and Japan and, to some extent, in the United States. My personal perception is in that in the sort of technology we are dealing with in terms of telecare and support in the home, the UK very much leads, which is fortunate for the UK, but there are examples where we do not. I am thinking there of telemedicine, monitoring of bodily vital signs and so on where there is some very new technology, and we are working to bring that into the UK and integrating the system rather than developing home-grown solutions. It is fairly patchy and broadly my perception is very much that we could benefit hugely from selective telecare components.

Q482 Lord Broers: Can I come back to the point about IT solutions, and then I would like to probe what Mr Diamond said about the American Association of Retired Persons because I link the two together. In terms of IT products, in this country there is a reluctance, a sort of fear, as Lord Soulsby was saying. In the States I would say it is otherwise, the grandparents are the experts and Florida is filled with people surfing the net—at least, that is my impression. Are there things we can learn over there about this, or have I had a false impression?

Mr Sadler: If you talk specifically about IT and internet access I think that is absolutely right. Whether that relates in some respects to distances in the United States I do not know, but if I cite one example, the success of telemedicine in the United States, it was very much driven by the physical separation of the cared-for person and the carer, doctor or whoever, so geography has an impact there. There has been the suggestion that that has been the cause of some of the interest in the internet because you have grandmother physically dislocated by some distance from other family members and so on. I do not know if I have answered your question, but I think that is one factor.

Q483 Chairman: I suppose one of the differences there is that geography intervenes in this country in that you are dealing with very small numbers, whereas in the States a very large proportion of the population live in dispersed situations.

Mr Sadler: It is a larger market than the UK.

Mr Diamond: That affects both the development and then also the selling and the marketing of a product, because obviously you can amortise your costs over a much greater universe. The only other comment I would make, having at the end of last year gone to speak at a conference in Palm Beach, Florida, which appears to be the spiritual home of the retired senior in America, is just about being inclusive. I think there is a perception that the American culture is more inclusive of an ageing population and certainly there is great provision made, both in Palm Beach but also in other areas as well, for elderly consumers in terms of how they shop and where they shop and so on. Again, how much of it is driven by the geographical size of the country or by the volume of consumers that manufacturers can then afford to invest in, I do not know, it needs further discussion.

Mr Kohler: Or indeed, as Lord Broers was suggesting, the part played by the American Association of Retired People who have succeeded in championing the older population in the United States and putting a very positive face on the idea of ageing in society. It is a matter of great regret and sadness that Help the Aged has been unable to emulate that percentage rate in the United States.

Q484 Baroness Emerton: This is a question on fundraising, particularly aimed at Help the Aged. Every charity is experiencing difficulty in fundraising, but I wonder, is the climate in relation to the older population making it more difficult in fundraising and are the public, in relation to the expectancy of a longer life, inclined to be more generous in their fundraising efforts or not?

Mr Kohler: No, I do not think they are. It is a fairly widely shared axiom in the charitable world that fundraising for children and animals is much easier than any other causes, and I am sure that fundraising for older people is fairly far down the track. We struggle, particularly, to get corporate sponsorship and fundraising from industry and commerce; the association for a company with an organisation representing older people is not yet seen to be particularly exciting, with one singular exception, which is British Gas, who recognised that their customer base was largely the older population and were quite happy therefore to build a link with Help the Aged, and there is a power company which has got a similar link with Age Concern. In terms of public appeal, I think older people do have a fairly low profile and low pulling power in charitable terms. In disaster situations such as on Boxing Day last year, one hears so much about the children who have been abandoned and things like that, and the media is not covering the older population who equally got involved in that way.

Lord Turnberg: I just wanted to ask a question relevant to what this Committee is about, which is the scientific aspects of ageing, and we are interested particularly in ensuring that good research is pursued into ageing, and also in ensuring that the fruits of research are applied. We have been discussing predominantly the application of what we know and how that can get out to the population we are talking about, but it seems that we need better drivers to ensure that the technological developments that we were hearing from Lord Drayson are put in place, and we need better drivers to ensure that those who can market these to the relevant audience are able to do so. What advice would you give us that we should put into our report that would help all of that? It was not on the list of questions, but really if we are to write a report we want to make a series of recommendations that will have an impact. I personally quite like the idea of following the American Association of Retired Persons as a lever, but what about others?

Q485 Chairman: This is your moment.

Mr Sadler: It is interesting to look at this because you can bring this full circle back to funding issue that we talked about, in the sense that the Government is already doing quite a bit. If you look, for example, at the issues on independent living where pipeline funding is there, that is a very good start to the process, but I think the issue that comes up time and time again is whether there is the facility to make sure we actually go ahead and deliver this? So where is the audit mechanism to make sure that with the £80 million of extra funding that has just been announced, at the end of the day we are not just priming the pump but are able to pipe the water, and I think you can cut that all the way across the elements we have been discussing today. For example, the awareness of engineers and training initiatives, you can take lots of one-off exercises and you can prime that funding for that technology and take the initiative of training, the point being that it is the continuity of much of this that matters, so that for future generations the training of engineers is on the agenda, to design for different end users. In the same way the marketers, when they do their training, need to understand the scope of the various market segments. I see these things quite often as one-off initiatives rather than as something that is embedded and learned. I think therefore that the continuity element is vital. If we take a prime example, there should be a recommendation on the audit process that follows up on the granting of funding we talked about earlier.

Mr Kohler: I think there is room for looking at the way in which we construct some of our education and training packages for people who are involved in this area of work. The point about the good news story that I will tell the Committee about is the design age unit down at the Royal College of Arts which has been running now for about 15 years or so, where the students are encouraged—not encouraged, they are pretty well compelled—to actually sit down with a group of older people to talk about the product they are thinking of designing so that they are able to get the feeling from the end user of what to put into the designing and thinking process behind it all. It must be possible to actually replicate models of good practice like that in a wider way.

Q486 Chairman: Interestingly, in the Royal College of Art it has been significantly supported by charitable donation rather than by public funds or industrial funds.

Mr Diamond: In a similar way we took a project to Central St Martin's School of Art and Design, which I think is one of the top art schools in the UK, and two years ago we held a competition there and we sponsored a place for individuals to reinterpret how marketing and advertising to an older consumer

might work, and we then commissioned an individual to develop some specific campaigns. Just coming back to your question about specific detail, I have a strong preference for education rather than legislation and I think that certainly in the community that I work in, within the marketing world, of which advertising is a subset, there are a number of existing trade bodies who I think could work more effectively to raise awareness of the facts, to raise aware of existing initiatives and existing organisations. One educational organisation that on a commercial basis I have been desperate to build a relationship with is the University of the Third Age, who I perceive from my parents and in-laws and am informed by the UTA themselves are almost building elements of what the AARP have successfully built in the US in terms of skills transfer, membership and so on. I think that precious few marketers—unless their parents are members—have ever thought about the rather crude but commercial opportunity of partnering with an organisation like the UTA, who themselves would need to be a little more open to commercial conversations than they have been in my experience. I think that is an opportunity where education coming through existing training bodies could be very beneficial.

Q487 Lord Drayson: I would just like to explore one aspect which we have not touched yet around entrepreneurship. In the context of Government policy, obviously successive Governments have put a lot of effort into encouraging young people to think about being self-employed and starting their own companies and so on. Do you think there is an argument to say that the Government should put similar efforts into encouraging older people, who perhaps have retired from a career in industry, to go into business as an entrepreneur and targeting this particular market, given that they will better understand their market, being of that age, but also research shows that people over 50 who start companies tend to be more successful than people under 50. I would be interested in your views on that.

Mr Kohler: I think it is certainly very true that the Government puts very little effort into the older population in relation to the world of work altogether. The number of re-training courses and things like that available to older people is pitifully small, which is why we still have this pretty large problem which the Government has been making much of over the last couple of months of the number of elderly people on incapacity benefit. They are unemployed, to all intents and purposes, not necessarily incapable of work, but there are not the schemes and the offers to encourage them back to the workforce. You are quite right, the dimension in which they would be coming back to the workforce would be as a self-employed individual, or setting up one's own business, but the support mechanisms are just not there from any publicly funded source of support.

Mr Diamond: It is a very interesting topic, and as an entrepreneur putting together my board non-executives at the moment, it is amazing how few people of my own generation feature on it. I think that clearly the experience that might have been gained in the work environment over a number of years should be allowed to flourish in an entrepreneurial way and, while I believe that entrepreneurialism really cannot be taught, it is something that people can grow up with and experience. In many ways it is about providing people with the opportunity to express their inherent and latent entrepreneurial nature without feeling that they are compromising whatever pension plans they have in place or whatever benefits they may be receiving. I think it is very, very powerful and while I am aware of Government initiatives to encourage entrepreneurialism amongst younger people—aware but not having experienced any of them—I think there is a profoundly interesting opportunity to provide a platform. Again I come back to the University of the Third Age, which I know only a limited amount about, but that has a non-commercial goal which almost performs against the entrepreneurial spirit, which is that we all have different skills and by sharing our skills we all have more boats and we all become more capable and talented. I do not think it would be a large step to apply that to a more commercial and entrepreneurial environment. It is very interesting.

Chairman: You should get them to read about Voltaire who, at the age of 74, made a killing in the Swiss watch market by spotting a gap in the market—an amazing story. However, we ought to stop now; it has been a very interesting session, very helpful, both your written comments and the discussion we have had which has been an excellent discussion. If there occur to you thoughts or answers to some of the questions that we have thrown out willy-nilly, where you think I would like to have said X or Y and I did not really think about Z, please do get in touch with us by e-mail or through the Clerk and give us the benefit of your thoughts, that would be much appreciated. In the meantime, many thanks.

Supplementary evidence by Robert Diamond and Professor Merlin Stone

WHY IS UK BUSINESS TAKING ON THE 50+ CONSUMERS?[2]

ABSTRACT

In this paper Robert Diamond, Founder and CEO of targeted marketing specialists Diametric and Merlin Stone, Business Research Leader of IBM UK Ltd and IBM Professor of Relationship Marketing at Bristol Business School explore the reasons for the apparent lack of take-up from UK business on the opportunity for profitable targeting of the UK's booming 50+ population.

50+ is the fastest-growing segment of the UK population, with 80 per cent of all personal financial assets and a significant proportion of spending power. Despite this, few businesses have developed products, services and marketing approaches tailored to the needs of this market. In this paper we explore five possible causes for this apparent lack of responsiveness, ranging from a possible "myth" concerning the 50+s wealth statistics through to the recruiting policies and prejudices of business marketing departments themselves. We conclude by asking whether in failing to respond, companies are exposing themselves to significant commercial risk—both from competitive brands who better meet the changing needs of UK consumers, and also from a never-before-seen level of consumer anger at businesses that continue to fail to reflect their interests.

WHY ALL THE FUSS ABOUT 50+?

"For the past hundred years, the real division was between the rich and poor. For the next hundred it will be between young and old"
Foundation for the Rights of Future Generations 2003

Statisticians would have us believe that a 50+ army is on the move. Across Western Europe, the post-war population bubble is approaching maturity and is changing the nature of demand for both public and private services. Within this picture the UK finds itself fitting neatly between "mature" Europe and the "youthful" US, with one of the youngest populations in Western Europe with fewer over 60s than Germany, France, Italy

---

[2] Copyright Robert Diamond

or Spain (*source: Eurostat 2002*). This means that while the European population is shrinking, from 270 million people to closer to 240 million over the next 20 years, the UK is expected to be stable at around 60 million people.

However, a stable UK population does not mean absence of change. Here are just a few of the facts.

Population

The 50+s are the fastest-growing demographic group in the UK today. They currently number 20 million people, expected to rise from 33 per cent to 44 per cent of the population over the next 20 years. Within this, the single largest segment 45–49 age group, currently representing 19 per cent of the total (*source: ONS*). Meanwhile the UK population aged under 40 is in absolute long-term decline, with 10–19 year olds falling by 9 per cent and 30–39s by 12 per cent over the next 20 years. As a result, "age dependency" has now become a fact of life—over the next 50 years the ratio of people over 64 to working age population is projected to grow from 25 per cent to 45 per cent (*Future Foundation*).

Wealth

Where it comes to money, the UK's wealth, savings and spending power is now heavily concentrated within 50+s. They hold 80 per cent of all assets and 60 per cent of savings, while over 75 per cent of all UK residents with assets worth over £50,000 are aged 50+ (*source: Quicksilver*). This group delivers 40 per cent of UK disposable income, making them a key buying group in high-profile sectors such as cars, holidays and IT. However the outlook is not all rosy. Many 50+s face an uncertain financial future—nearly 40 per cent of 50+s are dependent on State support for the majority of income. 52 per cent of Retirees say their pension pot is worth too little, with falling annuity rates and stock market returns the main reasons for others postponing their retirement (*source: Future Foundation*).

Household structures

The lack of business response to 50+ is all the more surprising when you consider the impact of population ageing on all aspects of family life. Families are starting later, with the average age for having a first child now 31, up from 28 a decade ago. One result is that a third of families with working parents still have children under 18 present at home (*source: BMRB/Mintel*). Over time this may influence how individuals form their brand preferences and transfer them on to others. At the same time 60 per cent of 50+s still have living parents, requiring them to cope with parents and grandchildren! (*source: Joseph Rowntree*) This increases the pressures on their time, and also may change the way they take their holidays and spend the rest of their leisure time.

Employment

Finally, with 70 per cent of men and 65 per cent of women now working past 50 there are 1.7 million more 50+s working over the past five years (*source: ONS Labour Force Survey 2002*). This increases their income, but also creates continued pressure on time-constrained older adults. It may change what happens as the economy's growth rate fluctuates, in terms of different regional and age patterns of unemployment or part-time working.

Actuaries have been considering the effect of these population trends for many years. As a result, planning for the long-term provision of state and private healthcare, pensions and other support vehicles is well-advanced (if not well prepared for!). However in contrast to this, few UK businesses have considered how the ageing population affects short-term demand: how could the big marketing budget holders—in food, household goods, technology, leisure, automotive etc—do more to respond to this emerging opportunity?

WHY ISN'T 50+ TARGETING TAKING OFF?

Despite these economic opportunities and evolving consumer needs, 50+ targeting lags in terms of the investment in innovation and marketing spend. A recent report estimated that as little as 5 per cent of advertising targets the 50+s, despite this age group being half of peak time TV audiences and dominating radio listening (*source: Help The Aged 2003*).

In looking for answers, we can begin with how leading global drinks player Interbrew sees the situation:

> *This (50 + s) important group is traditionally overlooked by advertisers in most fmcg categories—and beer is no exception. Traditional thinking in the media world is that people of this age are settled in their consumption habits so there is little point in targeting them with advertising unless it is for products aimed specifically at them such as Saga holidays. In the world of advertising, it seems nobody lives beyond 49!*

> *Despite the fact that adults 50 + account for 33 per cent of all on-trade drinkers, and around 50 per cent of ale volume, brewers often focus on advertising that reflects the lifestyle and attitudes of a certain age group, men aged 18–34, with particular emphasis on a trend-setting audience of 18–24-year-olds. But what about the remaining drinkers?*

> *Advertising is aimed at a younger audience because brewers are keen to recruit new drinkers and build brands among an emerging generation of drinkers as they establish their repertoire. In addition, over-50s are perceived as unreceptive to innovation and change, not easily influenced by advertising, they are not opinion-formers and ultimately they don't drink a high volume of beer.*

Interbrew Report "Targeting beers lost drinkers" 2003

Five reasons for lack of 50 + targeting

Why are 50 + s consumers not being targeted *even when* robust data exists that demonstrates their collective value to a category or brand? Given the hyper-competitive, mature markets that so many organisations are facing, this lack of commercial responsiveness may appear irresponsible (or certainly biased!). Clearly there is no single reason for this inactivity, but we would like to suggest five main drivers. Let's begin by issuing a challenge to the statisticians who talk of the mobilising "Grey army", by asking whether the level of spending power reported to exist within the 50 + s market *really* exists:

Challenge No 1—50 + s Spending Power is a Myth

We discussed above how 50 + s own the majority of assets and savings in the UK. This may suggest the single greatest challenge for targeting 50 + wealth—that the Mature market is essentially "asset rich" but "cash poor". On paper they hold £175 billion of UK wealth (*source: msn.co.uk 2003*) that could in theory be spent, but that the majority of this is locked up in housing and other long-term investments such as pensions.

Despite the increasing take-up of equity release schemes by older consumers, no-one knows how long the money will need to cover them for. With life expectancy at an all-time high—an average 76 for men, 81 for women (*in 2001*)—and still rising, people are more eager than ever to maintain their assets. Meanwhile, concerns over deficits in corporate pension schemes have heightened the need for individuals to provide for their own financial futures. On the health side, 7 million 50 + s now hold Private Medical Insurance cover given their concerns with state health provision.

The real winners from the post-war "wealth bubble" could therefore be in 20 or 30 years' time, when the inheritances from current affluent 50 + s pass on to their children (although the increasing longevity of their parents means that these children will inherit several years later than earlier generations). The implications for high-end asset management—and potentially for government actuaries involved in projecting future Inheritance Tax earnings—are likely to be significant.

In the meantime, expect more spending on "little luxuries" for self and others. The fact that 50 + s purchase 25 per cent of all children's toys and are the single biggest buyers of gifts at Christmas should come as no surprise—just a pleasure for the recipients!

Challenge No 2—The Idea of a Distinct "50 + " Mindset is No Longer Valid

> *"Sixty-six-year-old guys were never like us. Today, we have good nutrition and positive attitudes" Jack Nicholson in The Daily Telegraph Feb 2004.*

What it *means* to be 50 + has also changed. Perhaps there is no longer a clear need to innovate, target and communicate with consumers according to their age. A more relevant approach may be to talk to consumers based on shared values, attitudes and mindsets that cut across age boundaries:

> *"For some over-50s more self-focused, hedonistic attitudes will emerge as they imitate the lifestyles of the young". Already surveys suggested that they had similar alcohol consumption, TV, video and reading habits, and DIY and gardening interests, even if they listened to less music or engaged actively in sport"*
> Source: Guardian Unlimited

The key message here is to target individuals based on their self-perception, rather than your perception of them. Consider the following consumer evidence.

> When you use the term "the elderly", would you say this description includes you—88 per cent of 60–64s said no, and 52 per cent of 75–80 year olds said no" (*source: MFS PPP Healthcare*).

> "Do you feel 'young at heart'"—96 per cent of 60–64s said yes, 82 per cent of 75–80 year olds (*source: MORI 2002*).

Case Study—the growing consumption of "Better For You" foods

The trends influencing the development of the organic food sector affect consumers of all ages. They include increasing concern with genetically modified foods; concern over food safety and the environment; better and more informative food labeling; and the "macro" trends of a growing national problem with obesity; importance of physical appearance; changing household structures; and the changing role of women in the workplace.

However, these trends have influenced the 50 + s market particularly strongly. Specific trends influencing this sector include having less time-pressured lives (for some, though remember some are managing four generations), with less demand for convenience at the expense of health, and increasing awareness of the need to maintain healthy lifestyles, through diet and exercise. As a result, retailers have extended their organic offers; innovated new chilled and ambient ranges ("Better For You", "Free From", "Be Good To Yourself") and launched targeted "lifestyle clubs" (Tesco "Healthy Living")—without resorting to *age-related* targeting in any way.

Challenge No 3—Appealing to 50 + s Will Alienate the "Mainstream"

Another possible challenge to 50 + s targeting is that companies fear that by appealing to older consumers, they risk alienating younger brand buyers and future category entrants. It would be easy to revisit the Interbrew report earlier and add: *In addition, over-50s are perceived as unreceptive to innovation and change, not easily influenced by advertising, they are not opinion-formers . . .* **and being _seen_ to appeal to them could risk alienating essential younger audiences** (our addition).

However with today's average life expectancies, brands can safely expect 30 years of "lost" business if they ignore or alienate consumers once they pass age 50. At the same time given the number and sophistication of mature (ie, zero-growth) consumer markets, teenagers entering markets for the first time represent one of the few certainties for future growth. Therefore having maximum appeal to younger individuals is considered a key to future success. You may still conclude that you must not target older consumers seems churlish. Perhaps the real reason is that few businesses are comfortable with the idea of a genuinely segmented and targeted approach that allows you to appeal to *both* 30-somethings and 60-somethings? After all, who is the "mainstream" these days?

Challenge No 4—Marketing is a Youth Industry

"The new society will be a good deal more important than the new economy" Peter Drucker, The Economist 2003

One reason why businesses are afraid to appeal to 50 + may be the structure of their marketing departments and the services agencies that support them. Unlike other professional services sectors such as law or accounting, where experience is respected and charged out at a premium rate, marketing is staffed by (relatively) young personnel who create brands, advertising and direct marketing messages largely for people like themselves.

Consider the Institute of Practitioners of Advertising's data about the age profile of today's commercial marketers. For the marketing departments that create and manage brands, they indicated that:

— 39 per cent of Marketing Directors are aged under 35.

— Only 10 per cent of Marketing Directors are aged 50 + .

— 70 per cent of brand managers are under 35.

Meanwhile for the advertising, direct marketing and design agencies that support them:

— 82 per cent of people working in marketing agencies are under 40.

— 51 per cent are aged under 30.

— Of the 13,000 people in IPA member agencies, 776 are aged 50 + .

We are not suggesting that people who are outside a target segment cannot create compelling brand and marketing campaigns for that segment. It may be the pervasive culture of constant "new-ness" within marketing which is the real driver behind the interest in eternal youth and reluctance to market relevantly to a maturing population, even though it might be more profitable.

Challenge No 5—Older Consumers are Too Marketing-Savvy

Finally, there is the argument that businesses have tried (or are trying) to market to mature consumers, but that these individuals are too marketing-savvy to be seduced by targeted promises and propositions. Consider the environment in which today 50 + 's grew up in: the first televisions, the first television adverts, growth of the term "mass markets" and "mass marketing"; the first video recorders and even the first digital television. In 1960 there were three national newspapers, now they are eight. They were an estimated 40 titles on the average news stand then, now there are 400. At each stage, today's 50 + s have been at the forefront of media and marketing innovation that was later accepted as "mainstream".

So, mature consumers (especially aged to 60) are the first generation to grow up with mass marketing. Given this, it is reasonable to assume that they are also the first generation to become intolerant of and de-sensitised to the sheer number and type of marketing messages now being driven into the market.

CONCLUSIONS—IMPLICATIONS AND RISKS FOR UK BUSINESS

What does all this mean in practice? Certainly the risks for UK business go far beyond the possibility of upsetting existing customers. In the nearterm, businesses may find that their traditional customer base has simply aged from under them. Alternatively more sympathetic competitors could come up with more convincing ways of understanding, meeting and communicating their product or service benefits for older consumers. Over time the risks could grow to include:

— Failure to capture the full value of the Mature spend.

— Lack of a channel for listening to 50 + needs.

— Risk of creating 50 + "anarchists".

— Inefficient marketing spend.

— Long-term loss of market advantage.

— Sending a de-motivating message to their own staff—many of whom are 50 + or soon will be.

At a lower level, the implications for establishing and growing brands are equally significant:

— *Brands will be forced to take a customer portfolio approach*—up until now brands have looked to maximise the number of products and services they offer. From now on, expect them to focus in on specific target groups and then optimise—rather than maximise—the offers they deliver.

— *Customers will make themselves increasingly less available to market to*—savvy consumers will begin to opt out (both in a legal and an engagement sense) from traditional marketing. As the law courts move in their favour, expect more consumers to restrict their brand interactions to a limited number of brands and contact channels. For the owners of the databases that power these contacts, opted-in engaged consumers will be key to future success.

— *Brand-building will become more difficult*—a larger proportion of Mature marketing-savvy consumers will make it more difficult for traditional brand-builders to succeed. However this is not because they are unwilling to change brand preferences (as previously thought). Instead, they demand convincing reasons for change, not temporary reasons to switch brands.

— *There will be increasing frustration (and hostility) towards "inconsiderate" brands*—a lack of representation of their peers within modern media will give rise to a group of angry consumers. However unlike writing letters to their local newspaper or TV show, expect these people to actively—and visibly—campaign for fairer representation.

— *They are also increasingly cynical about the interests of "big business"*—as such they will resist all overt (and increasingly covert) attempts to win their custom.

Implications for (perhaps with sector examples eg retailing, telephony, financial services)
Market research and consumer insight (including databases)
Product policy
Branding
Marketing communications (use of particular media)
Distribution

April 2005

Supplementary evidence by Tunstall Group Ltd

BACKGROUND

1. Following the oral evidence given by Steve Sadler, Technical Director, Tunstall Group, at the sub-committee meeting on 8 March 2005, this supplementary submission is being sent at the suggestion of the sub-committee to emphasise two key points referred to in the meeting which we feel are worthy of further clarification. The two points concerned relate to:

— New evidence from the West Lothian Council telecare project.

— The need to ensure that new funding allocated to telecare in the 2004 Comprehensive Spending Review (£80 million over two years commencing April 2006) is spent as intended, so as to generate further evidence of the efficiency and effectiveness of telecare and to encourage mainstream deployment.

NEW EVIDENCE FROM THE WEST LOTHIAN COUNCIL TELECARE PROJECT

2. During his oral evidence Steve Sadler referred to the West Lothian Council Home Safety Service, where telecare equipment has been installed in 1,700 homes with residents aged 60 or over. This is to be further increased to 4,000 homes, with the long-term target to install similar equipment in all 10,000 homes in West Lothian with residents aged 60 or over. An academic audit study identified that over 3,000 hospital bed nights per annum were avoided through the use of this service at the point where there were 1,200 service users.

3. The cost of this West Lothian Home Safety Service is of the order of £250 per annum including telecare equipment, monitoring and response. Where home care services are also required (average 10 hours per week) then costs of £7,000 pa are typical. These care models compare favourably with the cost of residential care of £22,000 pa, whilst delivering choice and independence. There is preliminary evidence from West Lothian Council that up to 10 per cent of the clients using the Home Safety package would otherwise have entered residential care.

4. The West Lothian project is being independently evaluated by the University of Stirling. Their most recent report dated February 2005 concludes that the telecare technology has been well received by service users and informal carers. The findings suggest that independence and choice for older people are clearly supported.

NEW FUNDING FOR TELECARE

5. In the 2004 Comprehensive Spending Review the Chancellor announced new funding for telecare totalling £80 million over the two years commencing April 2006 to "keep up to 160,000 older people healthy, safe and independent in their own homes". This will be split as to £30 million in 2006–07 and £50 million in 2007–08, and is to be distributed to the 150 Councils with Social Services Responsibilities in England. The money is intended to be spent on telecare but is not ringfenced as such.

6. There must be a possibility therefore that, given the pressures on local authorities, the badged funding may not be spent as intended but diverted into other priorities. It is to be hoped therefore that the Government will do everything possible, through audit processes and other means, to ensure that the new funding is invested in the incremental provision of telecare as clearly intended by the Chancellor's statement. In this way further hard evidence can be collected about the efficacy and value for money of telecare to encourage mainstream deployment by Social Services and Primary Care Trusts. The aim must be for telecare to become a mainstream solution not reliant on pump priming funds.

RECOMMENDATION

7. Central Government should issue strong direction to Councils with Social Services Responsibilities in England to ensure that the new money allocated for telecare in the 2004 Comprehensive Spending Review should be spent as intended and not diverted by local authorities into other priorities.

March 2005

TUESDAY 8 MARCH 2005

Memorandum by Age Concern

1. INTRODUCTION

1.1 Age Concern England (the National Council on Ageing) brings together Age Concern Organisations working at a local level and 100 national bodies, including charities, professional bodies and representational groups with an interest in older people and ageing issues. Through our national information line, which receives 225,000 telephone and postal enquiries a year, and the information services offered by local Age Concern Organisations, we are in day to day contact with older people and their concerns.

1.2 Age Concern England includes the ActivAge Unit which has a number of programmes, including Ageing Well UK, Age Resource, an Intergenerational Network and support for volunteering. Ageing Well UK is a health promotion programme which aims to improve and maintain the health of older people. Its projects include the provision of health shops where mentors give advice on diet, nutrition and local health initiatives.

1.3 The Intergenerational Network brings together younger and older people, promoting mutual understanding and concern. It helps to tackle issues such as ageism between the generations, crime, social exclusion and disadvantage. An example is an original project set up by Age Concern in Warwickshire which has now been running for eight years. Volunteers offer support to targeted disadvantaged children. Citizenship courses are offered in schools exploring age, ageing and community relations to combat negative preconceptions between generations.

1.4 We welcome the opportunity to contribute to the Committee's inquiry into the benefits of technology and how it can be applied to improve the process of ageing. There are many excellent sources of information and expertise on Assistive Technology.[1] In this submission we seek to expand the issue to include older peoples' needs and rights to quality of life, independence and control—interpersonal contact, social life and purposeful social activity being fundamental components of what older people feel contribute to quality of life.

2. SUMMARY OF MAIN POINTS

— The main factors that promote long healthy life are well known but most depend on individuals' lifestyles; what is missing is knowledge of what affects choices and how to promote healthy lifestyles.

— Attitudes towards ageing and self-stereotypes are highly important factors in healthy ageing and this requires more research. Intergenerational contact is key to combating age-related prejudice.

— Involving end users (older people) at the early stages of setting research agendas or in early development stages will provide essential, valuable information to researchers and designers.

— An interdisciplinary approach to research, design and technology is required, particularly the integration of social science into the other disciplines. This would greatly aid better coordination of research.

— Current priorities include better funding for interdisciplinary and user-led research; synthesis and utilisation of existing knowledge and improving the links between research, policy and practice to improve quality of life for older people.

---

[1] Eg www.fastuk.org

3. THE BIOLOGICAL PROCESSES OF AGEING

3.1 Although there are links between ageing and the onset of illness, there is a large body of evidence to suggest that very few illnesses are inevitable consequences of ageing, and most are affected by individual behaviour and lifestyles. Ageing is a process which brings gains as well as losses, and recent research shows that attitudes towards the process of ageing, within individuals and within the wider social climate, are perhaps the most important indicators of how successful the ageing process will be.

3.2 The factors that promote good health and longevity in later life are:

— Physical activity—key in predicting independence and mortality in later life. Disability and infirmity may be largely the result of disuse of muscle rather than the inevitable process of ageing.[2]

— Having a social role and function—Long-term population-based studies[3] show that social and productive activities are as important as physical activity in reducing the likelihood of illness and institutionalisation. The mechanisms for these effects are unclear, participation in social activities in itself may reflect social competence and being in control of one's life; the benefits of physical activity may derive as much from incidental social and purposeful activity involved. Whatever the mechanism, the two factors are clearly related to better health and the delay of onset of illness.

— Good housing and living in a safe and pleasant neighbourhood.[4] A key issue in housing is fuel poverty, the UK has a particularly high number of energy inefficient houses. Other issues include the promotion of healthy, active ageing, eg by reducing the risk of falls at home.

— Neighbourhood issues such as crime and antisocial behaviour[3] (or the fear of them), or environmental concerns such as poor paving and litter which can lead to falls, can prevent older people from leaving their houses. This reduces opportunities for social interaction with family, friends, etc which then impacts on mental and physical health.

— Nutrition—barriers to healthy eating amongst older people include inadequate knowledge of appropriate diets, poor labelling of foods, and affordability and availability of healthy foods[3]. Age Concern is commissioning research from the London School of Hygiene and Tropical Medicine to identify and cost the minimum requirements for healthy life in older age. Part of this project will identify a healthy diet for older people and the income required to afford it.

— Absence of risk factors such as smoking and drinking to excess.

— Good mental health and well-being—which are affected by all the above factors.

3.3 These factors indicate that biological ageing is greatly affected by psychosocial and economic factors, which depend to some extent on people's choices and behaviour. Adopting healthy choices from a younger age is important, but changing behaviour in later life can also have significant effects on healthy ageing.

4. PROMISING AVENUES FOR RESEARCH

Ageism and stereotyping of ageing

4.1 Recent American research,[5] suggests that social stereotyping of ageing and the extent to which it is "internalised" by individuals can have significant effects on longevity. Out of a sample of 660 older people, follow-up showed that people with more positive self-perceptions of ageing, measured up to 23 years earlier, lived 7.5 years longer than those with less positive self-perception of ageing. This effect remained after age, gender, socioeconomic status, loneliness and even functional health were allowed for as confounding factors. This effect is greater than the physiological measures of low systolic blood pressure and cholesterol, and also greater than the independent contribution of lower body mass index, no history of smoking and a tendency to exercise.

4.2 The authors identify that, unlike race and gender stereotypes which people encounter while first developing group identities, people acquire age stereotypes several decades before they themselves become "old". Therefore they are most likely to accept stereotypes without question in earlier life and as they age, will

---

[2] "Effects of physical activity on health status in older adults", Annual Review of Health, 1992, reported in Choosing Health response.

[3] Age Concern, (unpubl), "Preventive Service for Older People: evidence from the research—Research Briefing No 6", February 2004, Research and Development Unit, Age Concern England, London.

[4] Age Concern (unpubl), "Age Concern's response to the Department of Health consultation, Choosing Health?", May 2004, Policy Unit, Age Concern England, London.

[5] Levy, B R, Slade, M D, *et al*, (2002), "Longevity Increased by Positive Self-Perceptions of Ageing", Journal of Personality and Social Psychology, 83, (2), 261–70.

be less able to challenge this stereotyping. Self-stereotypes can operate without older individual's awareness. The effects of this can be mitigated in some groups who can be shielded from stigmatising through, for example, positive intergenerational contact throughout the lifespan. There is evidence to suggest that older deaf people report more positive attitudes toward ageing than do hearing individuals. Older members of the deaf community tend to participate in intergenerational activities to a larger extent, in which they are given equal or higher status. This kind of intergenerational contact may be a source of "insulation" from mainstream negative stereotypes. Personality types may affect receptivity to stereotypes.

4.3 Research is now needed to explore this phenomenon further, including effects of multiple stereotyping on older people from minority groups, together with the factors which can help to mitigate the effects of society-wide denigration of ageing such as intergenerational contact.

The social psychology of ageing

4.4 More research needs to be done exploring social models of ageing. Better understanding of the psychology of prejudice and social stereotyping, and the impacts of these on older people's well-being, capabilities, performance at tasks and longevity would be useful for policy development in all areas affecting older people, particularly in health and social care, and employment, education and training.

Mental health in ageing

4.5 The potential to provide a cure or delay onset of dementia would have an enormous impact on the quality of older people's lives. In addition, depression is the most common psychiatric disorder in later life, 10–15 per cent of the population aged 65 years or over suffer from significant depressive symptoms. Age Concern and the Mental Health Foundation have launched a three-year Inquiry into mental health and well-being in later life. An initial part of this Inquiry has been a review of the literature and policy on the promotion of mental health and well-being.

Choosing health

4.6 Research is now needed on what affects lifestyle choices across the lifespan and into later life, and how people can be encouraged to adopt healthy choices. The role of technology in providing accurate information and supporting individuals to maintain healthy diet and activity regimes could be explored.

Diversity

4.7 A better understanding of diversity in the older population is required among researchers. The ESRC's Growing Older Programme,[6] which recently came to a close, highlights many important issues of diversity in the older population. Other important, key questions are: why do women live longer? What are the racial differences in ageing? Which are biological factors and which are cultural, lifestyle-related? Personality characteristics may also be important when it comes to attitudes towards own ageing, susceptibility to ageism, and differences in coping strategies.

Promising approaches to research

4.8 The breaking down of barriers between disciplines when it comes to addressing ageing issues in research is welcomed. Ageing is a process which is biological, but also psychological and social. Scientists and designers need to work with social scientists, psychologists and ergonomists to provide services and products which will be useful to older people. The objectives behind EPSRC's EQUAL (Extending Quality Life) initiative and the ESRC's new programme The New Dynamics of Ageing, are welcomed as approaches to interdisciplinary work.

4.9 Participatory approaches to research and development which involve the end user (in this case, older people) are badly required. It can be too easy to "over-technologise" problems and solutions, without considering the psychosocial aspects or needs of the user. We welcome the development of research bodies which are focussing on these new approaches which involve older people as equal partners in research, for

---

[6] ESRC, "Growing Older Programme—Project Summaries", Swindon: ESRC.

example the Cambridge Interdisciplinary Research Centre on Ageing (CIRCA). Features of CIRCA's research strategy are; an interdisciplinary approach, a life course perspective, emphasis on positive well-being and involvement of older people in setting the agenda.

5. Benefits to Older People and Delaying Onset of Long-Term Illnesses and Disabilities

5.1 As research from the Growing Older Programme and other studies confirms, the factors that sustain quality of life for older people (adequate income, living in a safe neighbourhood, practical services, having social roles and participating in voluntary and social activities) are also likely to improve health and physical functioning. These are identified by older people themselves as key aspects of their quality of life.

6. Differences Between the Sexes, Social Groups and Ethnic Groups in the UK

The ESRC Growing Older programme of research provide useful recent data on many aspects of diversity including gender differences; the impact of partnership status; differences between ethnic groups in terms of biological ageing; intersection of social status/other factors.

7. The Application of Research in Technology and Design

7.1 An interdisciplinary and participatory approach is key in the efforts of designers and technologists to improve the quality of life of older people. Social scientists and, in particular, older people themselves should be involved and consulted, as has been identified in the EQUAL initiative by EPSRC. In general, good design should be inclusive for all, and specific "assistive technologies" considered only when inclusive solutions are not possible.

7.2 There are many examples of high- and low-technologies which maintain independence and afford older people a greater level and sense of control over their lives. The important factors to consider are their usability, their acceptability to older people and the likely effects on their social functioning and sense of control over their lives.

Existing and new technologies

7.3 A recent report[7] explores the costs of providing assistive technology to enable older people to live independently compared with what might be required in terms of human care. It looks at the adaptation of buildings, including *Smart Home* technology whereby different devices interact and are controlled by a central computer; and at Assistive Technology (AT) where there is confusion about terminology, lack of information for users and for housing providers and staff, and a certain need for demystification of the concept. The report concluded:

— "There were considerable variations in AT provision between respondents.

— There is a need to listen to older people. They are quite clear about their needs, but very much less clear about what AT is there to help them, how they can access it and what they have to pay.

— Older people want to be able to control as many day-to-day routine activities as possible and AT can help them with this.

— Older people welcome AT when it addresses a FELT need.

— Older people have variable access to AT and therefore variable help from AT. They often have unmet needs.

— Installation of AT is not usually a problem, but the on-going reliable operation of the AT is essential."

---

[7] King's College London and the University of Reading (2004), "Introducing Assistive Technology into the Existing Homes of Older People: Feasibility, Acceptability, Costs and Outcomes", Institute of Gerontology, King's College, London.

8. How Effectively is Research Co-ordinated?

8.1 Research could be better coordinated for the benefit of older people. Although recent initiatives have begun to address the problem, coordination and true interdisciplinary research is still problematic. It is difficult to fund except through specific initiatives such as those mentioned above and the Research Assessment Exercise still does not specifically reward academic research bodies sufficiently for the considerable extra time and resources required to carry out work across disciplines.

8.2 If sufficient time, funding and commitment are not given to involving older people in research and development, initiatives to do so often fail. For example, EPSRC's EQUAL (Extending Quality Life) initiative set out to promote links between academics and organisations that provide or represent a service user perspective. This was thought to be a very positive approach. In practice, however Age Concern staff who attended initial meetings felt that user involvement was seen as an "add-on" within the programme, there was insufficient funding for participation of voluntary organisations representing users which was not part of the core research funds, and end users were not involved enough in the early stages of setting the research agenda, which was done by the groups of academics.

8.3 Involving end users (older people) requires considerable resources in terms of time, money and commitment on the part of researchers to hear the viewpoints being expressed by older people. Research funders are not always aware of or sympathetic to resources required, and researchers themselves do not always appreciate what it will mean to relinquish some control over their domain.

9. Have the Correct Priorities been Identified?

9.1 Initiatives toward greater collaboration between disciplines are welcomed. Further priorities would be:

— focusing on synthesis and dissemination of existing knowledge;

— prioritising a user-centred, interdisciplinary approach (which especially included social science) to new research or development of new design ideas;

— further exploring the link between research, policy and practice, facilitating a more "knowledge-based" approach to policy-making and putting more resource into applying the current knowledge from research into scientific and technological development;

— preventitive strategies to reduce or delay onset of illness;

— good design which is inclusive, specialist design only where it really is required.

9.2 As mentioned previously, the bio-medical model or disease model of ageing has received more research funding and academic interest than other models. For example we now have better evidence on what is likely to maintain good health throughout the life span, but very little information on how people make choices over their health-related behaviour and how to influence them to make better choices which emphasise positive well-being.

10. Is Research being Used to Inform Policy?

10.1 Research could be much better utilised within policy-making, particularly in the sphere of social science but also in other disciplines. Barriers to effective uptake of research information into policy making are complex and deep-rooted. The Australian experience[8] yields the following barriers to the utilisation of research to inform policy, which summaries UK experience also:

— "A complex bureaucratic and political environment, which may impact on the take-up of evidence-based research.

— Research can involve a lengthy process and the research and planning cycles need to be synchronised.

— Researcher's limited knowledge and understanding of the policy-making context means that research findings often have little impact on policy.

— The problem of information overload, translation of information and difficulties in accessing and sharing information. This raises the need to ensure that overload is minimised.

— Overcoming barriers to cross-governmental approaches to Evidence-Based Policy Making (EBPM).

---

[8] Bartlett, H and Findlay, R, (2003) "Linking the Ageing Research and Policy Agenda: towards a strategy for Queensland", University of Queensland Australasian Centre on Ageing.

— The absence of an overarching framework for EBPM and the need to strengthen the long-term strategic planning approach."

11. CONCLUSION

The potential for good, inclusive design to greatly improve lives is enormous but is balanced by the risk of increasing use of technology to socially isolate older people and result, paradoxically, in their feeling even less in control over their lives and environments. This needs to be carefully managed through holistic, interdisciplinary and user-led approaches.

September 2004

Memoranda by Help the Aged

Help the Aged warmly welcomes the opportunity to provide evidence to the House of Lords Select Committee inquiry on research on ageing. With the present global demographic trends, unprecedented numbers of older people are set to face the risks of disease, dependence and frailty. The issue of research on ageing is therefore of fundamental importance. We hope that the Committee's inquiry will serve to raise the national profile of research on ageing and will promote actions which will lead to practical benefits in the lives of older people.

Help the Aged is the only charity in the United Kingdom which dedicates its research portfolio exclusively to ageing. The charity invests some £2 to £3 million pounds per year in funding and supporting research. Through its special trust, *Research into Ageing*, we provide a range of studentships, fellowships and programme grants. Our biomedical research is of the highest quality, being published in leading academic journals and leading to practical outcomes which directly benefit the lives of older people. We commission high impact social research to support our policy base.

In addition to funding, Help the Aged forms strategic relationships with leading research organisations, such as the National Collaboration on Ageing Research, the Research Councils and government departments in order to influence both the magnitude and direction of research on ageing. Internationally, we have strong links with the UN, WHO, the International Association of Gerontology and the International Federation on Ageing, all of which have strong research interests.

Help the Aged (and *Research into Ageing*) publish a wide range of research reports and publications to disseminate important new findings to the practical benefit of older people.

SUMMARY OF RECOMMENDATIONS

Help the Aged calls on the government for:

— a clear statement making research on ageing a greater national priority.

— a "step-change" in funding levels for ageing research in the UK on a *per capita* scale of that of the USA. The current low order, inconsistent budget for research on ageing poses a real threat to the well being of older people. A stable, long-term regime of generous government funding must provide the basic research infrastructure to which charitable funding can contribute.

— the appointment of a "champion for ageing research" in a central government department, such as the Office of Science and Technology, to lead and direct a national research agenda on ageing.

— the development of mechanisms for building research capacity to invest in the career paths of researchers, including gerontology and geriatrics.

— emphasis to be given to the critical areas of cellular ageing biology (such as immunosenescence, molecular genetics, and replicative senescence) which not only provide vital new knowledge but which present the potential for the improvement of human health and well-being.

— funding of long term research to determine whether there is a compression or expansion of morbidity and the biological, and socio-economic impact of these changes.

— more research to identify the modifiable risk factors that contribute to healthy ageing and the effectiveness of early intervention programmes on healthy ageing. The interplay of environment with the organism (particularly genetics) must be the subject of further research.

— research to underpin preventative and treatment strategies of conditions that cause poor quality of life and dependence.

— tackling ageism to improve the public perception of the benefits of ageing research, to change attitudes to funding and to improve the involvement of older people in the research process.

— research to identify ageing differentials due to gender and ethnicity.

— greater involvement of older people and service providers in research agenda-setting to improve the delivery of tangible benefits to the older population from developments in science and technology.

— more research to provide a cost analysis of the preventative value of assistive technology to enable people to continue to live in their own homes.

— more translational research to ensure that research results enter into practice.

THE BIOLOGICAL PROCESSES OF AGEING

What are promising avenues for research? How will such research benefit older people and delay the onset of long-term illnesses and disabilities? What are the differences between the sexes, and between different social and ethnic groups in the UK?

The Challenge of an Ageing Population

Britain is an ageing society. The demographic trends that are taking place in the UK are widely recognised. For the first time, the number of people in the population aged over 65 exceeds those under the age of 16, as shown by the results of the 2002 census. The fastest growing sector of the population is the over-80s. In the next five years there will be a 10 per cent increase in this age group.[9] Globally there are similar trends. The proportion of the global population aged 65 and over in 1900 was 1 per cent (UK 5 per cent); in 2000 it was 7 per cent (UK 16 per cent); and by 2050 it is estimated to be 20 per cent, a figure the UK would reach in 2020. In Europe, 50 per cent of the population will be over 50 by 2030.[10] With these demographic trends, unprecedented numbers of older people are set to face the risks of disease, dependence and frailty. There are huge implications for the economy, for pension provision and for the costs of health and social care. The tremendous advances in biomedical, scientific and social research have improved our understanding of the ageing process, of age-related disease and of older people's experience of growing old. However, much remains to be done.

What are promising areas for research? How will such research benefit older people and delay the onset of long-term illnesses and disabilities?

There are four areas, in our estimation, which are of particular concern. They are: the biology of ageing, the determinants and status of healthy ageing; age-related disease and its prevention; and the effectiveness of treatments for older people.

Biology of Ageing

Ageing is a summary term for a set of processes that predisposes us to deterioration of health and ultimately death with the passage of time. It can be thought of as a group of processes (including physiological, genetic and environmental) that contribute to increasing risk of frailty, disability, morbidity and mortality. The challenge for the science of ageing is to identify such processes and develop preventative and treatment strategies to delay the morbidity and ultimately mortality that occurs with the passage of time.

As good health is vital for older people to live full and active lives, it is essential to know more about the general biological principles underlying the ageing of cells, organs and organisms. There are many promising areas of research within this area: teasing out the mechanisms of the increase in longevity and health expectancy and translating such mechanisms into interventions; understanding the gender differences that exist in response to caloric restriction, and the role of the insulin-IGF1 axis. The genetics of long-lived and short-lived species is also important to determine the contribution of "longevity" genes. Promising avenues of cellular and organ ageing research include immunosenescence (the failure of the immune system to respond effectively to infection with age) causing the death of around 4–5,000 older deaths each year from influenza (up to 20,000 in a 'flu epidemic) and many more deaths from subsequent conditions such as pneumonia. Studies on replicative senescence have the potential to bring clinical benefits in the future with strategies to block senescence and

[9] Office for National Statistics (2002). Census 2001: National report for England and Wales. London: HMSO (ISBN: 0116 216 689).

[10] Dean, M (2003). Growing Older in the 21st Century. EPSRC.

prevent oxidative damage. It is recommended that emphasis is given to the critical areas of cellular biology (such as immunosenescence, molecular genetics, and replicative senescence) which not only provide vital new knowledge but which present the potential for the improvement of human health and well-being.

Healthy Ageing

Life expectancy for UK citizens has been steadily increasing (approximately three months was added to life expectancy for each year of the last century) and while health expectancy (the number of years living in good health) has also been increasing, it is not clear to what extent the added years are experienced in good health.[11, 12, 13] There is a clear need for good reliable data to determine whether there is a compression or expansion of morbidity with the changing demographics and the biological, economic and social impact of these changes.

The science of ageing should be viewed as being wider than purely cellular changes, but viewed holistically as the wider factors contribute to morbidity and mortality. Lifestyle and environment contributes around 75 per cent of a person's chance of healthy ageing and longevity. The major indicator for health expectancies and life expectancy is socio-economic class with the greatest impact seen on health expectancies.[14] These inequalities in quality of life have been know for some time and should be urgently tackled at a political level. It is vital that these differences are explored further with longitudinal population studies and the environmental factors contributing healthy ageing identified and put into practice. Some of the modifiable risk factors are known: diet, exercise, smoking and can be the target of further governmental health promotion initiatives. These initiatives should take account of the data on health promotion in pregnancy, adolescence and throughout adulthood—ageing is not just about changes in middle age and beyond, many ageing processes start much early in life (bone loss starts in the third decade) and foetal health can contribute to these processes. More research is required to identify the modifiable risk factors that contribute to healthy ageing and the effectiveness of early intervention programmes on healthy ageing. The interplay of environment with the organism (particularly genetics) must be the subject of further research.

Age-related conditions

Preventing dependency, a key government issue,[15, 16] not only depends upon minimising the risk factors and understanding of the basic biological processes, but also on research delivering on the understanding of age-related conditions, the development of effective treatment strategies and specific preventative measures. Some of the major causes of death (heart disease, cancer, and lung disease) are relatively well funded; others are not, notably stroke. The day to day health concerns of many older people are often focused on the non-disease issues—their feet, eyes, ears and teeth—as well as the more general frailty associated with ageing such as muscle wasting and poor balance causing poor mobility, loss of independence and an increased susceptibility to falls. Major causes of dependency and poor quality of life eg sensory loss, bone and joint degeneration, cognitive decline, muscle wasting, falls, and incontinence are relatively poorly funded and require substantial investment.

Incontinence is a case in point where there is a small research base within the UK, poor understanding of the biological process, little in the way of effective treatment and research funding in response mode competitive manner is rarely available. Without special initiatives of ring-fenced funds (such as that initiated by Research into Ageing in 2000) little change can be expected to help the six million people in the UK with this disabling and distressing condition.

Research is desperately needed to underpin preventative and treatment strategies of conditions that cause poor quality of life and dependence.

Treatments for older people

Research opportunities do exist and are emerging to treat degenerative and debilitating conditions eg tissue engineering using stem cells and genetic engineering for the treatment of degenerative conditions, hormones in osteoporosis and cognitive decline. Major advances in biomedical, social, physical and behavioural research

[11] Fries, J F (1980). Ageing, natural death and the compression of morbidity. *N Engl Med J*, 303, 130-135.

[12] Manton, K G (1982). Changing concepts of morbidity and mortality in the elderly population. Milbank Mem Fund Q Social Health, 60, 183–244.

[13] Robine, J M and Michel, J P (2004). Looking forward to a general theory on population ageing. *J Gerontol,* 59A, 6, 590-597.

[14] Marmot M *et al* (2003). Health, wealth and lifestyles of the older population in England: *The 2002 English Longitudinal Study of Ageing*. London: Institute for Fiscal Studies.

[15] Department of Health (2001). The NHS Plan. London: HMSO8.

[16] Independent Inquiry into Inequalities in Health (1998) London: The Stationery Office.

8 March 2005

have improved health and functioning, and continue to reduce rates of disease for older people, although this impact has been uneven across the older population.[10] The representation of older people in pharmaceutical trials has improved with the new European Directive.[17] but there is still little funding available for the evaluation of clinical outcomes in trials involving interventions and treatment of older people.

Ageism affects attitudes to research on ageing at all levels. It influences both priorities and decision making in terms of funding and investment. Attitudes such as "incontinence and hearing loss are a normal part of ageing" are commonly experienced. Research activity is therefore low, the body of knowledge relatively poor, and hard fought for research funds hard to find. This vicious cycle needs to be broken. Similarly, the level of public awareness of the benefits of research on ageing, other than that in relation to specific diseases, appears to be poor. This particularly applies to research on healthy ageing which may not only prolong life but will improve its quality in the later years and have impact on public expenditure. Finally, there is a notable absence of the meaningful involvement of older people themselves in research, particularly in technology.[18] Ageism must be tackled to improve the public perception of the benefits of ageing research, to change attitudes to funding and to improve the involvement of older people in the research process.

What are the differences between the sexes, and between social and ethnic groups in the UK?

Gender differences have been identified in relation to response to caloric restriction[19] and in immunescenesence.[20] Ethnic differences clearly exist with demonstrable differences in longevity between countries.[21] The degree to which such ethnic differences can be attributable to genetic, socio-economic, nutritional, cultural or environmental factors is difficult to tease out,[22] but clearly all have a role to play. Help the Aged has well developed programmes working with the different ethnic communities and recognises the importance of inclusivity in this area. The scope for progress in identifying ageing differentials due to gender and ethnicity is large and warrants further investigation within identified priority areas of biological ageing.

RESEARCH IN TECHNOLOGY

The application of research in technology and design to improve the quality of life of older people, including: existing technologies which could be used to a greater extent to benefit older people; the development of new technologies

Introduction

Assistive technology (AT) has been defined very broadly as "any product or service designed to enable independence for disabled and older people".[23] With this in mind, it covers an extensive variety of aids, adaptations and supportive technologies including the following:

— Mobility aids, eg powered wheelchairs, stair lifts.

— Aids to daily living, eg accessible baths, showers or toilets.

— Environmental control systems, eg infra-red controls to allow the user to operate household equipment such as radios, TVs, light switches.

— Communication equipment, including accessible telephone equipment or videophones used for telemedicine.

— Security devices, eg community alarms to warn carers or other care services if anything is untoward.

— Smart Homes providing electronic or computer-controlled integration of assistive devices within the home.

— Beyond this, a range of more basic yet vital technologies aimed at assisting people to undertake activities of daily living. These include such aids as "jam-jar openers" and "stocking aids".

[17] *European Directive 2001/20/EC.* Official Journal of the European Communities L 121/34.

[18] Beresford, P (1992). Researching *Citizen-Involvement: A Collaborative or Colonising Enterprise?* in Barnes M & Wistow G (Eds) *Researching User Involvement* Nuffield Institute for Health, University of Leeds.

[19] Combs, T P *et al* (2003). Sexual Differentiation, Pregnancy, Calorie Restriction, and Aging Affect the Adipocyte-Specific Secretory Protein Adiponectin. *Diabetes* 52:268-276.

[20] Pawelec, G (2003). Immunosenescence and longevity. Biogerontology 4, 3, 167-170.

[21] Gavrilova, L A, and Gavrilova N S (2000). Validation of exceptional longevity: a book review. *Population and Development Review* 26, 40–41.

[22] Courtenay, W H *et al* (2003). Gender and ethnic differences in health beliefs and behaviours. J Health Psychol, 7, 5, 219-231.

[23] www.FASTuk.org

Priorities and gaps in research

Through the EQUAL programme the EPSRC has been the key government funder of research relating to design and AT over the past few years.[24] Within this successful programme there has been a real commitment to engage with users in delivering research which meets their needs—a progressive policy which should be developed upon.

Undertaking an assessment of research gaps and priorities would seem of little value unless there is greater and more transparent engagement with both older people in determining their priorites for technologies to support independence and those agencies responsible for providing and commissioning such technology. It remains the case that older people may not know what is available and those seeking to meet their needs don't always know what is wanted.[25] This is a real issue in that consumer demand must be one of the necessary elements of a successful introduction of services which should in turn inform the research agenda. Two key organisations, emPOWER and FAST (Foundation for Assistive Technology), are working to achieve a proactive approach to user involvement in this are. Help the Aged would greatly urge a more transparent process for agenda setting which begins from the perspective of older people.

Greater involvement of older people and service providers in research agenda-setting is recommended to improve the delivery of tangible benefits to the older population from developments in technology.

Barriers to transferring research into policy and practice

The translation of research into practice and policy remains a pressing concern. In their recent report,[26] the Audit Commission conclude that, in general, AT services in the UK are underdeveloped. As a result, new designs and technologies are not being transferred into practice. There may be a number of reasons for this.

The lack of integration and collaboration between agencies to deliver AT and the lack of professional training on and awareness of new technologies among service providers, including GPs, are certainly major obstacles.[27] Further, the question of budgets also complicates the picture—those agencies in the position to provide AT are not necessarily those that will benefit from them. For instance, Housing departments can use "housing supporting community alarms" but social services or health will reap the benefit. In addition, the capital costs relating to AT are not as much an issue as the revenue costs associated with providing staff who can deliver and train users to make use of AT.

Installation and user training of AT can be labour intensive and maybe off-putting for service providers with limited budgets. However, it is arguable that the longer term benefits of reduced interaction with the clients themselves should outweigh these costs. The Assistive Technology Forum argue that "a vicious circle exists where arguments for investment are undermined by a lack of evidence and effective evidence cannot be produced due to a lack of robust infrastructure". One of the problems is that devices are seldom offered as part of a support package with staff included. Successfully demonstrating the benefits of such technology is therefore problematic.

Whilst cost benefit analysis has taken place with some forms of assistive technology,[28] more research is needed to provide a cost analysis of its preventative value, in enabling older people to continue to live in their own homes. Generally, more translational research is required to ensure that research filters into practice.

Beyond this, there is a real need to ensure that older people are offered proper training and choice when accessing AT without which older people may be reluctant to make use of such technology. The shortage of Occupational Therapists and other health professionals with knowledge of AT creates delays in providing support to older people and is likely to reduce the time available to therapists to work with clients in providing appropriate AT.[29, 30] A Joseph Rowntree Foundation study[31] found that "*Age . . . [is] one of the strongest predictors of someone's interest in living in a smart home*". The most interested were aged 15–34—the "ambivalent" were more likely to include older people and the "uninterested" were most likely to be aged 55

[24] http://www.fp.rdg.ac.uk/equal/

[25] Technology for Living Forum UK: conference report. Help the Aged, 2000.

[26] Audit Commission, Fully Equipped: The Provision of Equipment Services to older or Disabled people by the NHS or Social Services in England and Wales, 2000, Audit Commission.

[27] Assistive Technology Forum: Position Paper—Summer 2004.

[28] Six month review of Seniorline calls: January–June 2001. London: Help the Aged, 2001. (Seniorline is a free phone line offering advice to around 100,000 older people and their families per year).

[29] Katbahvna *et al* (2002) Nothing Personal. London: Help the Aged.

[30] Market potential for smart homes, The. (Findings) Joseph Rowntree Foundation, 2000.

[31] With respect to old age: long term care—rights and responsibilities: a report by the Royal Commission on Long Term Care. (Volume 2) Stationery Office, 1999.

and over. Older people were the group most concerned about potential technical problems with the systems. Certainly the stigma of "disability" associated with the need to use special equipment[32] affects uptake of AT. Mainstreaming its benefits would seem to be vital in attempting to remove this stigma.

Strategic Issues

How effectively is research co-ordinated in the public, private and charitable sectors (including internationally)? Have the correct priorities been identified? Are there any gaps in research? Is there sufficient research capability in the UK? Is the research being used to inform policy?

Introduction

Between 2002 and 2004, Help the Aged played a leading role in the joint IAG/UN initiative "Research Agenda for the 21st Century". This initiative started with the Valencia Forum in 2002 and was followed by expert workshops in each of the four UN Regions (Cape Town, Barcelona, Santiago and Tokyo). An international comparison across the four UN Regions reveals three common strategic problems with ageing research which are applicable to the UK. They are: low relative investment; fragmentation and lack of capacity; and absence of strategic direction.

Investment

In terms of investment, the total Research and Development budget (all sectors) for the UK (2002–03) amounted to £18,817 million; government expenditure £2,841 million and accumulated research on ageing to less than £200 million, about 1 per cent of the total. Government funding for ageing research is principally in vested via four of the Research Councils. None of the Councils spends more than 5 per cent of their budget on ageing research. For example, in 2002–03, the EPSRC's total budget was £436.2 million with the "EQUAL" Programme worth £9 million, 0.7 per cent of the total. Not only so but the dedicated spend on ageing by the Research Councils appears to be decreasing.

In the 2002 Spending Review,[33] Government priorities were Genomics (£110 million); eScience (£98 million); and Basic Technology (£44 million). Ageing research was not identified as a priority and this holds true for the Spending Review 2004.[34] Ageing research was not mentioned in the Vision for UK Science, no research achievements in ageing science were mentioned and ageing research was not one of the six priority areas for Multidisciplinary Research.

The principal government departments with research budgets for ageing are the Department of Health (DH) and the Department of Work and Pensions (DWP). Help the Aged estimates that in 2002–03 on-going projects were worth £20.45 million (DH) and £3.57 million (DWP) with an annual expenditure of £4.80 million and £1.23 million respectively. These are relatively small amounts.

Charitable spending on ageing research for on-going projects in any one year resides at about £125 million (£124.26 in 2002–03). However, two important caveats must be made. It is very difficult to portion out the costs of research because much expenditure is age-related and is not necessarily categorised as "ageing research". For example, the AMRC does not categorise its research expenditure by "age" but many of its members, eg British Heart Foundation, Alzheimer's Society, etc fund research which is clearly age-related. Secondly, the high impact of charitable funding, which is often variable and insecure, depends on sustainable, high order, reliable central funding on which the UK research infrastructure is dependent.

In spite of the low order of spending, the UK compares well with Europe which under the 6th Framework Programme (FP6) does not currently identify ageing as a research theme, though €1,155 million are being spent on combating major diseases, some of which are age-related. Under FP5 only €190 million was spent directly on ageing research over four years (1998–2002) through Key Actions 1 and 6.[35]

However, the UK compares poorly with the USA which through the National Institute of Aging (NIA) combines high order strategic thinking with enviable levels of funding. NIA has a budget of $994 million in 2004–05, a rise of 44 per cent over the last five years ($688 million in 2000–01). Of this sum, at least $669 million

[32] HM Treasury (2002). Spending Review Whitepaper: Opportunity and Security for All. London: HMSO.

[33] HM Treasury (2004). Spending Review Whitepaper: Stability, security and opportunity for all. London: HMSO.

[34] http://www.europa.eu.int/comm/eurostat/

[35] National Institute on Ageing (2004). Report to Congress: FY 2005 Congressional Budget Justification. Washington DC: National Institutes of Health.

are being spent on Research Project Grants and a further 9 per cent on Institutional support.[36] The result is substantial progress in reducing illness and disability among older people in the USA and large reductions in projected healthcare costs.[37, 38]

A "step-change" in funding levels for ageing research in the UK is required on a per capita scale of that of the USA. Questions must be asked as to why the UK has persisted with a low order, inconsistent budget for research on ageing which poses a real threat to the well being of older people. Help the Aged, with others in the voluntary sector, will play its part in maintaining funding for research. However, it has to be recognised that a stable, long-term regime of generous government funding must provide the basic research infrastructure to which charitable funding can contribute.

Research Capacity

Research capacity building is an issue because of the generalised problem of the absence of a research career structure in the Universities and the way they are funded. Charitable expenditure on research in the universities went from £250 million in 1990–91 to £550 million in 2000–01 and much of this investment was targeted to support research capacity. At the present time, such capacity as exists is threatened by the absence of adequate funding and is tiny in relation to the scale of the UK problem. Between 2000 and 2004 the demand for funding at *Research into Ageing* rose from 100 to 250 applications per year and with funding levels constant, the rejection rate consequently rose to 1:31. High rejection rates threaten capacity and do not augur well for the maintenance and expansion of the research base. In our current Major Gifts Campaign, 32 proposals mostly of outstanding international merit, have been submitted. Each proposal required £10–15 million. Of the total fundable volume of £450 million, only one proposal will be funded. The remainder of the proposals are highly likely to be lost to UK science. Finally, charitable support for capacity building will not be helped by the government requirement for universities to move to a "full economic cost" model by 2005, though the government has provided some £90 million in 2007–08 in support of the voluntary sector (the Charity Research Support Scheme).[39]

The development of mechanisms for building research capacity is necessary to invest in the career paths of researchers, including providing opportunities for research training in gerontology and geriatrics.

Strategic Direction

There is no central organising body for ageing research in the UK. Ageing and age-related research is carried out independently in the universities with little strategic direction. The National Collaboration of Ageing Research (NCAR) was set up in 2001 and has been largely successful in promoting a cross-council model of research which has led to the inauguration of a new programme, the New Dynamics of Ageing. The Funders Forum on Ageing Research (FFOAR), a parallel development to NCAR, is a co-operative body made up of the Research Councils, six major charities and the Department of Health. It meets once per year to receive reports from its members and to make recommendations for research and development. It has advisory powers only and lacks the authority to direct a national agenda. There is no government department which takes the strategic lead on research into ageing.

In the USA, the NIA provides a high degree of strategic direction. It provides substantial funding for four major Extramural Programs (Biology of Aging; Behavioral and Social Research; Neuroscience and Neuropsychology of Aging; Geriatrics and Clinical Gerontology), Intramural Programs at a dedicated gerontology research centre, Conferences, Workshops & Meetings, Funding & Training and Scientific Resources.

In view of the profound demographic changes taking place in the UK, Help the Aged calls on the government for a clear statement making research on ageing a greater national priority.

There must be the appointment of a "champion for ageing research" in a central government department, such as the Office of Science and Technology to lead and direct a national research agenda on ageing. This appointment must combine strong leadership with budgetary control and must involve partnership working with existing bodies, such as NCAR and FFOAR to promote and co-ordinate research on ageing.

October 2004

---

[36] 2004 Task Force on Ageing Research Funding (2004). Meeting the needs of the 21st Century. Washington DC: Alliance for Ageing Research.

[37] Manton, K G and Gu, X (2001). Changes in the prevalence of chronic disability in the United States black and non-black population above age 65 from 1982 to 1999. Proc Natl Acad Sci USA, 98, 11, 6354-6359.

[38] HM Treasury (2004). Spending Review 2004: Science and innovation investment framework 2004-2014. London: HMSO.

Examination of Witnesses

Witnesses: DR JAMES GOODWIN, Head of Research, Help the Aged, DR IAN NOWELL, Innovation and Strategy Director, Age Concern England, and PROFESSOR ROBERT SOUHAMI, Director of Policy and Communication, Cancer Research UK, examined.

Q488 *Chairman:* Good afternoon and welcome to the Committee. Many thanks for taking the time to join us this afternoon. That is very much appreciated, as is also the written evidence with which you are associated either individually or on behalf of the organisations you represent. These written papers have been circulated and we have made good use of them, as you might discover in the process of the discussion to follow. You are now online and this is going out via the internet directly. Perhaps I can start with a general question and you can introduce yourselves at the same time. Can I ask about the research councils, because you see them and must watch them quite carefully as the alternative providers and, in some cases, the main providers of research money. They have spoken to us about the priority they say they attach to research on the scientific aspect of ageing. I wondered whether you had seen that priority in action. Are they attaching priority? Is the volume of research about right or at about the level you would expect to complement what you also are involved in? Are the research councils doing enough? Are there gaps or problems of coordination? This is just an opportunity to reflect on the volume of research starting initially with what the councils are responsible for and whether they are providing sufficient priority and drive.
Dr Goodwin: James Goodwin. I am Head of Research for Help the Aged, which is a large international charity which supports research into all aspect of ageing. We have good working relationships with all the research councils. We also have a formal relationship with the National Collaboration on Ageing Research which is funded by the research councils and with its successor, the New Dynamics of Ageing. We are very well placed to get a good perspective on the whole range of these services and across the four research councils which are researching ageing. Generally speaking, my view is that the funding levels for the research councils are low in comparison with the research councils' spending generally and also with international estimates of research. For example, my estimate of ageing research funded by the research councils is only about ten per cent of their total research. In some cases, it is as low as two per cent and in some cases—for example, the Medical Research Council—it is much higher than that. In terms of volume of funding, we consider it to be quite low. The central issue is not just funding at the present time but the fact that there has been no sustained core funding in the history of core funding for ageing over the last 30 years, which they have in the United States. If we

compare the research councils investment on ageing, they have a sustained budget for the last 30 years but the current budget is about $994 million. If we compare that with the £12 million going into the New Dynamics of Ageing, one can see straight away that there is quite a discrepancy there.

The Committee suspended from 3.44 pm to 3.54 pm for a division in the House

Q489 *Chairman:* In terms of what you said quite specifically I wanted to ask whether the National Collaboration on Ageing Research is a great loss. How do we know that the new organisation will do better what it was meant to do, because the research councils have pulled the financial plugs on this?
Dr Goodwin: When people ask me what are the main priorities for ageing research, my answer is not that it is academic priorities which we must decide in terms of where to go—for example, should there be research into pensions or technology in older people? They are more strategic and they would be the lack of investment in ageing research, the fragmentation in ageing research and the absence of strategic direction. The National Collaboration on Ageing Research provided some of their areas and in terms of its demise now those functions will be that much more difficult. The National Collaboration on Ageing Research did succeed in producing a multidisciplinary approach, although by many that is perceived to be a vehicle for the EPSRC, to promote their areas. That is not a view that I entirely share. In terms of what the research councils expect, they expect these days good discipline, good research in discipline and interdisciplinary research as well. Both have to be provided. Now that the NCAR has faded, we need to look at alternative bodies to provide strategic direction. That is one of the recommendations I made in my written evidence. At the moment, the only body to do that would be the Funders' Forum on ageing research of which Help the Aged of course is a leading member. In terms of gaps in ageing research, it appears to me from our international experience that where you have a high order of strategic direction the issue of gaps recedes to some extent. We also have to look at the relationship between gaps in research that we perceive and research capacity at present in the research universities. For example, if we identify a gap in the biology of ageing, there might not be the capacity in the universities in the first place by which to exploit that, so we need to identify that relationship. We need to consider deficiency of

funding so there may not necessarily be a gap. There might be a deficiency of funding in which we need to build capacity. Finally, it is method as well as area. We need to involve older people more in the research process itself and we need to think about translation aspects. In geriatric research, geriatric medicine, consultants now have had their training reduced and they therefore do not have to do any research. This is an issue that was raised by the European Academy of Medicine for Ageing. It appears to me that there are fewer and fewer academics involved in geriatric research and therefore that makes translation from evidence to practice that much more difficult. These are all general areas on gaps which we should consider before we identify some of the academic areas.

Dr Nowell: Ian Nowell from Age Concern England. I am responsible for a division within Age Concern which is innovation and strategy. Age Concern has a federal structure so in England we have over 400 independent Age Concerns. Our approach to research is somewhat different. Age Concern England plays a lead role on public policy in terms of ageing and older people. Our interest in research is very much along that public policy agenda. We are looking at research which is making an impact on policy and in terms of practice. Our interaction with the research councils is probably not as extensive in terms of Dr Goodwin's and Help the Aged's level of interaction. In terms of gaps, some of those gaps are about services that local Age Concerns are providing that are impacting on older people on a day to day basis. We are particularly interested in looking at the impact of preventative low level services. The gut feeling is that they are important. They do have an impact. It is producing sufficient evidence base to have an impact in terms of commissioning bodies and policy. There are areas where we are seeing big gaps. Age discrimination is now of particular interest. We are certainly looking at age related prejudice. We have done some work with the University of Kent. That whole area of stereotypes, the development and the impact seems to have a great deficiency in terms of research. Mental health is another area of particular interest to us which I think we highlighted in our written response to the Committee. We passionately support research into policy and practice. We support the interdisciplinary approach in terms of research and we very much welcome the New Dynamics of Ageing programme, building on the Growing Older programme, giving a real collaboration between the research councils and a real opportunity to have the different disciplines coming together in a way which will have an impact on older people.

Professor Souhami: Robert Souhami, Cancer Research, UK. Your original question was, were the research councils attaching priority to ageing research, and on that question I need to step slightly to one side because Cancer Research UK does not have an opinion on the funding of ageing research in its general sense. What we are concerned about obviously is cancer as a disease affecting the ageing population. If we look at the pattern of research into cancer as it affects an ageing population, both in terms of the therapeutics and the social aspects of cancer such as screening, quality of life and so on, the answer is clearly that both Cancer Research UK and its partners do not invest enough specifically into the questions of cancer as it affects an ageing population. The reasons for that are quite complex and you will probably want to explore them in a while. There is within the UK a very successful forum where the funding partners get together. That is the National Cancer Research Institute. In the National Cancer Research Institute, the major funders of cancer are sitting and discussing the questions of research priorities in cancer. Cancer Research UK is there, the Department of Health is there, the Medical Research Council, the Leukaemia Research Fund, Wellcome and so on. There is now a national forum for considering issues which relate to research priorities as they affect cancer. We have a pretty good idea of where those therapeutic and other priorities are. If you were to look at the generality of funding in cancer and say, "How much of that is specifically devoted towards therapeutic and other aspects of cancer as it affects an elderly population?" the answer is a very small proportion. If you were to look abroad, particularly to the US, to see whether cancer as a disease of the elderly is picked out as a specific area for focused research funding, you would find more in the US than in the UK or in other European countries.

Q490 Chairman: If my colleague, Lord May, were here I know he would want to ask two supplementaries. We have spoken about the quantity of research. What about the quality? Do you have any views about what is happening in this country? The additional supplementary is: if the quality is, however you assess it, high, low or indifferent, how is that measured and are there any relevant bibliometric measures?

Dr Goodwin: It is well recognised internationally, and Help the Aged has profound international collaborations in ageing research. Some of the best ageing research in the world is conducted in the United Kingdom. Without naming names, if you went to the United States they could pick out five or six leading researchers. That similarly applies to Europe. That is notwithstanding the fragmentation of ageing research in the United Kingdom. The kind of quality measures that we go for are those which are acceptable to the academic community in terms of high impact publications in peer review journals, the acquisition of national and international funding, awards of objective, academic merit and progress. The United Kingdom in those areas performs very well in terms of ageing research. What worries me greatly however is the sustainability of capacity in ageing research. That is exemplified by an exercise in which Help the Aged has just been engaged, which is to raise £20 million for a single ageing research project. We had 32 bids of outstanding international merit for those and we were only able to fund one. The combined worth of those was £420 million and £20 million leaves the other £400 million underfunded. There is good quality research in the United Kingdom, but it is the question of sustaining capacity with adequate funding and strategic direction.

Dr Nowell: It is not so much the quality of the research but how the research results are used. There is a great deficiency in terms of the dissemination of the results. In terms of the impact on practitioners and on organisations such as ourselves, we would welcome a far greater emphasis on more thought, more resources, in terms of the dissemination of the results that have been produced and the bringing together of different results to address the issues. The participation of older people and part of the quality is, how much impact is it having? How much are they engaged? How much are they valuing the research which is involving them in many instances?

Q491 *Lord Turnberg:* On the business of cancer research networks, there is a model for getting good research done in places where there are good researchers and applying it to practice, which is something you were talking about. Do you think that is a good model for research into ageing? Do you think it is a good model to apply or to try?

Professor Souhami: It is difficult to give a general answer. The cancer research networks specifically are dealing with therapeutic research. In so far as there is general therapeutic research to be done into problems of ageing, comorbidity and the way in which it is managed, yes, it has been a very successful model for cancer. Cancer has a curious advantage there though. It will be interesting to see how the other networks set up under the UKCRC umbrella fare. The curious advantage for cancer is that before the networks were set up it was already true that over 60 per cent of all the therapeutic trials in the United Kingdom were in the field of cancer. The reason why it has been the case for the last 40 or 50 years that cancer has been so concerned about therapeutics is because of the nature of cancer treatment. It is difficult, complicated, expensive and toxic treatment. There has always been a very strong desire amongst cancer clinical researchers to assess the value of what they do. That has been a very strong motivation for these networks working well. It is now the case in the UK that therapeutic research of that kind is

thoroughly embedded. I guess the answer to your question is, for cancer, for therapeutic research, it has been an excellent, palpably successful model. In so far as those things could be translated to research, therapeutic or other clinically related research questions in ageing, it is certainly a model to consider.

Q492 *Lord Soulsby of Swaffham Prior:* With respect to research capacity, what is the situation with respect to the flow of people like research students, post-doctorals, senior and junior fellowships in the field of cancer? Is it adequate?

The Committee suspended from 4.09 pm to 4.18 pm for a division in the House

Professor Souhami: Yes. The mechanism of flow is adequate. The numbers of people involved are not yet adequate, particularly in some shortage areas such as in radiation research and in surgical research into cancer and gynaecological research into cancer. I am talking about clinical research now. This is not a problem unique to cancer. The question of manpower shortage generally at the clinical level in therapeutic research in cancer is an important one and depends very much on the specialties one is talking about. As far as fundamental research in cancer is concerned, on the whole that works pretty well. I do not think at the moment there is a funding crisis which prevents people of real talent being able to be supported in the basic cellular pathology of cancer. I hope I do not sound complacent about this but at that level funding does not seem to be the problem. At the clinical end, there are problems in getting people through into high class clinical research.

Dr Goodwin: In terms of ageing research specifically, if I look across the portfolio of researchers in the United Kingdom, very few enter gerontology. Most of them train in other disciplines and they come to ageing after that. The special initiatives of the research councils have served to attract such individuals into research on ageing. For example, SAGE, ERA, EQUAL and so on. The aim from that therefore was that these researchers should become more senior and move into response funding. This has often proved difficult. Because we have stop/start funding of research in terms of ageing, it is very difficult to maintain a flow of research, undergraduates, graduates, post-doctoral fellows and so on. In four years, in spite of a huge effort from ourselves, we have funded 16 PhDs, 21 fellows and 12 large, post-doctoral programmes in excess of half a million each. That is indicative of the expense of this and the difficulty made by the absence of strategic coordination of funding.

Q493 Baroness Walmsley: Dr Goodwin and Dr Nowell, could you explain how your organisations promote research into the scientific aspects of ageing? Could you also say to whom your organisation is accountable and where the money comes from? Does it mainly come from individuals, from companies or from grant awarding bodies?

Dr Goodwin: We have four main priorities by which we promote research. They are by directly funding research, by influencing the direction of research nationally, by international collaborations and, fourthly, by promoting dissemination. In terms of funding, we fund between £3 million and £4 million a year in all issues of scientific ageing. We have just completed a £20 million major gift appeal which is going to the University of Edinburgh and we core fund the University of Oxford's Institute of Ageing. In terms of influencing, we have a formal working relationship with the National Collaboration on Ageing Research. We play a leading role in the Funders' Forum. We work closely with government departments, in particular the Department of Health, the Department of Work and Pensions, less so with the DTI Office of Science and Technology. We have many influences across members of the Department of Health and planning initiatives through Poverty Action in the DTI. Internationally, we are members of the Research Agenda Committee of the United Nations. We are consultant advisers to the International Association of Gerontology and the European Academy of Medicine for Ageing, and in the USA we have working relationships with the Alliance for Ageing Research and the American Federation of Ageing Research.

Dr Nowell: In terms of our approach to promoting research, it is partly commissioning research and that is to inform our public policy work, our development of services for older people through local Age Concerns. We very much look to influence the agenda of research through partnerships working for academic institutions and through some of the professional bodies, the British Society of Gerontology in particular, the BGS as well and other bodies. We also look to participate, disseminate and support conferences, working very closely with the BSG. We have been partnered jointly working with them to engage older people in their annual conference which we felt was important and is quite an interesting approach. We are also looking to develop and disseminate information about the experiences of older people themselves. We will commission work on the economic contribution that older people bring. It is not all doom and gloom. Older people make a very valuable contribution to their communities, both through paid employment and through a whole range of unpaid activities. In terms of accountability, for Age Concern England it is the National Council on Ageing. It brings together local Age Concerns, over 100 national bodies including Help the Aged, a member of our National Council on Ageing, but also professional bodies, retirement organisations and national bodies. That produces our board of trustees. On funding, our resources which are commissioning research that we are interested in, supporting the partnership work not particularly a huge amount of money and in effect that is part of our core budget. That would come through our fund raising, our trading activities, which would generate unrestricted income through which we will support those areas of activity. That is the overview.

Q494 Baroness Walmsley: What about companies? Do you not get any money from companies?

Dr Nowell: We will attract money from corporates in terms of developing. Say, for example, we have a strategy of technology in older people. That is very much about developing internet taster sessions through local Age Concerns. The money from Microsoft, Cable & Wireless, BT and other corporates will be used not for research in the classic sense. It will look at evaluation and what impact it is having. If that is constituting research, in that sense, yes, we will get some money from corporates but very much focused in Age Concern England on working with and supporting local Age Concerns.

Q495 Lord Drayson: You do not see any interest from companies doing applied research to better understand the use of their technologies, their products, for the older market place?

Dr Nowell: In terms of the interest in the market place and universal design, for example, the interest is not that huge. I do not think there is an awareness of what the opportunities are of engaging with the 50-plus population. We have established an Age Concern research service which is to get a better understanding through qualitative and quantitative tools of the aspirations, the attitudes, the needs and desires of the 50-plus population. I think the business world is incredibly slow in responding to those opportunities. We have a real battle because the digital divide is not a temporary feature. Once all the baby boomers come through, that is it. The impact on people who are not engaged is going to be so great in terms of services that the problem is far greater. In terms of numbers, we are not convinced that that challenge is going to go away, but the development of products designed for that 50-plus population, both hardware and software, is not impressive.

Q496 Baroness Finlay of Llandaff: This question is for Professor Souhami. It relates to cancers and their relationship to age and comorbidity. I would like to ask how much research CRUK is supporting on the problems associated with comorbidity. We know that life expectancy is going up. The incidence and prevalence of cancer are going up. We know that DNA damage is associated with ageing and liver disease. How much priority research that crosses the boundary or the non-boundary between the two is occurring, how much it is being supported?

Professor Souhami: Taking comorbidity first, I have given Mr Collon the statistics which back up what you are saying to show just how big the problem is in terms of the cancer problem in the over 70s and how that is going to grow. There are already 140,000 cancers occurring each year in the United Kingdom over the age of 70. There is no doubt that the relative survival diminishes greatly particularly in the over 80 age group. The issues of comorbidity, and the research done into it, are slightly complex. The way in which therapeutic trials are set up inside the United Kingdom, and indeed in other countries in the world, usually puts an upper limit to the age of inclusion in trials, simply because of the toxicity of some treatments. The question that you are interested in, though, is how many studies and how many therapeutic investigations are done specifically to put therapeutic questions which are applicable to an elderly population rather than the generality of cancer patients. The answer is very, very few, both in this country and in other countries. Partly that is an opportunity question, how many therapeutics one has which have low toxicity and where existing comorbidities will not be important for patients. There are not that many treatments that are out there that you can easily give to people who may have heart disease, diabetes or vascular disease. Just the same, that is not the complete explanation. Part of the explanation is simply that therapeutics of cancer in the elderly have not been a high priority in most developed countries in the world. Getting the age of inclusion into therapeutic trials up above 65 to 70 has been a slow process. Getting it from 70 up to 75 will also be a slow process as people have to adjust their mentality and think that there are trials which can be done which should include patients of this age. Much of the research that is being promoted in the US on therapeutics of cancer in the elderly is to ask exactly the questions that you are asking: what are the stumbling blocks which prevent the design and execution of therapeutic studies in an elderly population with cancer? Is it a question of comorbidity? Is it a question of late presentation? Is it a question of doctors and health care professionals who do not think about things in the right way? The truth is we do not know the answer to that in different settings. Within the UK, those questions are just as unanswered as they are in other populations. There is a big gap there.

Q497 *Baroness Finlay of Llandaff:* Given the large burden of disease which is there, what is CRUK doing about addressing that, because that burden is going to get greater over time?

Professor Souhami: Correct. At the moment, there is no concerted plan of any of the funding partners to alter the way in which therapeutic studies are being created and engendered inside the United Kingdom. In my view—and in the view of many people inside CRUK—it is not because of a cultural bias; it is simply that people have not placed this as the highest priority in their cancer therapeutics—the NCRI and the funding partners of the NCRI could well make this one of their priorities for considering research gaps inside the United Kingdom in exactly the same way as they have done with quality of life research in the United Kingdom in cancer, and radiation oncology research in the United Kingdom in cancer. There is an opportunity there for the funding agencies to reconsider the kinds of therapeutic questions they wish to see addressed. You put your finger on an extremely important point, in my judgment. You ask secondly about the question of the interface between the biology of cancer, the biology of ageing and DNA damage and repair. There one is on slightly stronger ground. The lifetime exposure to DNA damaging agents does not start or stop at a particular age so the question of DNA damage and the repair mechanisms that are responsible for keeping your DNA undamaged are applicable at whatever age you are looking at. The issues of whether or not there is a decreased efficiency in repairing DNA damage and the other cellular processes which are important in the emergence of a cancer as you get older are very under-funded in the UK, not because of an objection to funding such studies; it is simply a question of whether we have available model systems and scientists who are thinking about those problems in the UK. If you look across the Atlantic to the US, you find exactly the same problem. There is quite a difficulty in knowing whether or not there are separate problems to be addressed in cell biology of ageing with respect to cancer that are quite different in nature from the cancer problem generally. Although we do fund research directly applicable in cell biology of ageing and other cellular processes that are equally applicable to cancer and ageing, they are general cellular processes which are important generally to cancer rather than specifically because they are motivated towards an ageing population of cancer patients.

Dr Goodwin: If I could add some support to that argument, there are two issues related to your question on comorbidity. One is to better understand the ageing process. We know from research over the last 20 years that ageing is the biggest single risk factor for age related diseases. If we answer the question how does ageing predispose us towards disease, we can produce the mechanisms which will produce the interventions. Secondly, in terms of translational research, it comes back to the question of adequately trained and adequate numbers of geriatricians in research such that they understand the translatability of evidence into practice.

Q498 *Baroness Hilton of Eggardon:* If we could return to the organisations that support you and look at government departments, I wonder what your relationship is with various government departments. We have heard from them how they view this whole issue. Do you have good contacts? Are they receptive to your point of view, and what more could be done in this respect?

Dr Nowell: We have a range of good contacts with a range of government departments on topics which are of mutual interest, very much set by their policy agenda which often coincides with our policy agenda. In many instances, it is a positive process. There are challenges, particularly when there are cross-departmental initiatives. The joining up may be there with us but it is often missing within government. For example, the strategy for ageing which has been developed and is about to appear at any moment has been quite challenging for us to have a coherent input into that kind of process. Some of the experience we have had working very closely with the Department of Health, the Department for Work and Pensions has been very positive, and working with a number of other parts of government as well. The only bit that we have found a little more challenging is to look at where their research interests and agendas are before the commissioning stage. That we have with some departments but I do not think with sufficient.

Dr Goodwin: Relationships between government departments have improved considerably over the last number of years on the formal and the informal level. In terms of the formal level, we work closely with members of the Funders Forum in terms of clear discussions about the issues on the scientific agenda which we should be addressing to avoid duplication and over-investment or even under-investment. In terms of our special relationships, we work particularly closely with the Department of Health, the Department for Work and Pensions and, to a lesser extent, the Department of Trade and Industry. In terms of achieving the strategic levels of spending and the direction, that is a lot more difficult and somewhere where there is scope for improvement.

Dr Nowell: One area which is important is the interaction at a regional level with those regional bodies, the development agencies, assemblies and government offices. We have, with the English Regions Network, developed a dual region for all ages and if we are looking at the impact of changing demographics on regional strategies we have found that to be a very productive way of getting ageing onto agendas at regional and sub-regional level.

Q499 *Baroness Hilton of Eggardon:* There is no problem about access to government departments?

Dr Goodwin: We have always found them to be generally very responsive in terms of the information those government departments would like to have, in terms of the issues in the report in relation to older people and so on. That is a reciprocal arrangement as well because we like to discuss with the departments—and we do—what their priorities are for scientific research on ageing. That is something which we find increasingly easy.

Professor Souhami: As far as CRUK is concerned, all our money comes from the public. The science spend this year will be about £210 million. There is not a question of having to work with other people to raise money. There is an extremely important issue about how research fits in and whether research findings are then easily taken up by the National Health Service. One has to say that the relationships with the Department of Health and other government structures are very good. I would not like to have to deal with some of the problems they have to deal with. On the issue of availability of cancer treatments when they are new, have come forward and we take part in their development, it is always very important for us to make sure that organisations like NICE and so on are seeing the evidence for what it is. On the whole, there is plenty of opportunity to put your point of view. I do not think that presents a particular problem for us.

Q500 *Baroness Hilton of Eggardon:* They seem to make rather controversial decisions sometimes.

Professor Souhami: Yes, but controversial means that there are probably arguments on both sides and sometimes we would have pushed the argument more one way. I do not think there is a serious, fundamental problem in getting the evidence presented to people who wish to make decisions. You may have to argue about whether decisions are right but, to go back to your question, namely the relationships with other governmental departments, they are very good. I would like to stress the creation of the National Cancer Research Institute yet again, which may be something that the inquiry would be interested in. In my judgment, having been around in cancer research for a very long time, I think the creation of the National Cancer Research Institute has been one of the best things that the United Kingdom has done in terms of pulling together funding agencies around a common cause. What was really important there was that the Department of Health and the government injected a small but sufficient amount of cash into the National Cancer Research Network and the National Translation Cancer Research Network to lubricate the research process and its translation into therapeutics. It was not a huge amount of money, £20 million or so a year, but it was incredibly important in terms of getting the whole structure going. I have felt that this has been very helpful for cancer research and indeed the success of this led to some of the UK clinical research collaborations. These structures are important. They do push people forward. They do focus minds, in my judgment.

Dr Goodwin: It is interesting to note that there will be no analogous body in terms of ageing research and the reasons for that are partly historical, but are also because the nature of ageing research is eclectic and much more diffuse. The various bodies which fund research have widely differing interests. That, in many ways, means that it is more imperative that we have such an organisation and the strategic direction in order to do that, because if we do not have that, with funds attached to it, we are going to have the maintained fragmentation of ageing research in universities and research institutes which is going to make life very difficult, to see the kind of progress which we have seen of the paradigm of excellence which you have in the National Institute on Aging in the USA.

Q501 *Lord Turnberg:* You are an advocate of bringing it all together in a network of funders and organisations.

Dr Goodwin: You have to be cautious. I do not want to apply too much academic direction when the researchers themselves who are at the cutting edge of research are the people who decide the research questions. In terms of direction, if we look at the NIA, they have their four goals which they have maintained over the last five years and which have added greatly to the quality and direction.

Q502 *Lord Turnberg:* Cancer research networks do not have people telling them what research to follow so that would not come into it. It sounds as if that is not easy to do for some reason. Is that something to do with the organisations that are involved in this area, that they are not eagerly collaborating or cooperating? Should we in this Committee be saying something about that?

Dr Goodwin: There is a degree to which the research councils are collaborating in so far as the Funders Forum have all invested an interest in the New Dynamics of Ageing. What we do not have is a strategic umbrella of objectives which have been set, but in a sense there is ownership there and sustained, long term funding by which those goals can be followed. I do not think there is any absence of enthusiasm amongst the research councils themselves for research on ageing. What we need is somebody to bang some heads together and make sure that the funding, the infrastructure and the direction are there to promote the kind of excellence in research that we would like.

Q503 *Lord Turnberg:* It is not just the research councils, is it? There is research into ageing and other organisations.

Dr Goodwin: Yes. There is also the private sector. We have very good relationships with the private sector, with British Telecom, British Gas, Unilever and Pfizer. They come to us for advice on the directions in which older people as consumers of research would like to go. There needs to be full ownership of that institute. I would agree it is not just the research councils.

Q504 *Lord Turnberg:* I presume your organisations have reached a set of research priorities in the areas we are talking about. I would like to know a bit more about whether you have done that, how did you do it and how do you go about ensuring that your priorities are fulfilled?

Dr Goodwin: In terms of setting research priorities, we have very good relationships with the academic community. We core fund the Oxford Institute on Ageing. Equally, we support many researchers in many universities. We have a very good relationship with the directors of the five institutes of ageing. We have a research advisory council which consists of eminent academics and we have good relationships with the National Collaboration on Ageing Research and the Funders Forum. Also, we have a listening strategy which can inform our research process. Our research priorities fall into two areas, both strategic and academic. In terms of the strategic aims, there are three. One is to produce a statement for government as a national priority of ageing research and, with that, to increase the availability of funding. There needs to be a step change in funding to achieve the aims we want to see. We need greater strategic direction in order to defragment ageing research. That would be our strategic approach. In terms of our academic approach, I would remind the Committee that the UK government is a signatory to the International Plan for Ageing 2002, in two areas which were specified then as being of exceptional importance for the determinants of healthy ageing and basic, biological mechanisms of ageing. Both of those form part of our research priorities. In terms of Help the Aged, we have committed ourselves to the world ageing survey which is being carried out by the International Association of Gerontology. In terms of age-related disease prevention, two particular areas come to mind. One is cognitive decline and dementia. We fund work in both those areas. The NHS spends in excess of £14 million a year on dementia, and cognitive decline is very important to us. Another area for us is incontinence. It is a Cinderella area. Six million older people suffer from incontinence. It is an area in which there is low capacity. We have had a funding programme for that over the last two years, which is going on for another four years, in order to build capacity and quality of research. Fourthly, it is the effectiveness of treatment for older people about which we are especially concerned. Again, that is a translation issue in terms of how these findings get themselves into the lives of older people.

Dr Nowell: Our research priorities very much are corporate priorities. In that sense, we will commission research which reflects helping us achieve those priorities. All of them are very much outward facing in terms of looking at enhancing income in later life, tackling age discrimination. Sometimes there will be commissioning research; sometimes we will be developing a partnership relationship; sometimes it will be joint applications through case awards which, for us, seems to be a particularly helpful programme. An area that we have been looking at is developing links with the main research clusters so that we can engage with those clusters and enable local Age Concerns to play a more significant role on the research agenda at a local, sub-regional level. We look at the corporate priorities. They are determined by our board of trustees. They are informed by the views of older people and on that basis we will then commission and undertake our research strategy.

Q505 *Lord Turnberg:* How much money do you put into research each year?

Dr Goodwin: We spend about £4 million a year on the science of ageing and we have just launched a £20 million appeal which will be for the next five years.

Dr Nowell: Ours is much less significant than that. For our commissioning of research and our partnership work it is probably of the order of £200,000 or £300,000. We have significantly supported in addition to that Age Concern research services which initially has a third to half a million to pump prime over two years, and then we are looking for it to be self-sustaining.

Q506 *Lord Turnberg:* I wanted to ask CRUK a question. You mentioned that at the moment it has low priority in your organisation, the research of cancer in ageing. Do you have people in your organisation who have particular expertise in this area, either in those setting the policy or doing the work, and would it be helpful if we made such a recommendation to you?

Professor Souhami: In the current CRUK structure for setting research priorities, there is nobody whose specific academic research interest lies in cancer in an ageing population and the problems associated with it, either biologically or therapeutically. Would it be helpful to make a recommendation? It would certainly be something which the organisation would want to consider very seriously, yes, not just for Cancer Research UK but for the National Cancer

Research Institute as well. This is not a matter for CRUK alone, although we are obviously an important partner in NCRI. There is the MRC, the Department of Health and other people. The situation is that the only criterion for funding within CRUK is research excellence. There is no point in people applying to CRUK for funding bad science. We turn down 74 per cent of all requests for funding. 26 per cent get funded. The only criterion for funding is that your peers both at home and abroad think that this is good science. It is no good saying you want to do research into ageing if you do not have good people who are doing good science. It is just a waste of time and it raises a lot of false expectations. You have to be very careful about that. There is nothing special about ageing from that point of view. When I mentioned earlier the question of research into palliative care or the research into radiation oncology, the problem has been the shortage of expertise. It is the opportunity problem. You go right back to this issue of training and creating people who understand these things. There is nothing special about cancer in that respect. It is the same everywhere you look in biomedical research. It is not just a question of saying, "Let's do some research in ageing and ageing related to cancer"; it is a question of, "Let's do some first class research in that area." Within the organisation, we have a scientific executive board and the funding committees report to that in basic science, clinical science, translational science and population and behavioural science. The distribution of cash into those different areas is something that is constantly revised and updated. It is a continuing process inside the charity. Essentially, that is all we talk about when we are looking for opportunity, for new things coming forward, for deciding where technology opportunities lie. That is being quick on your feet really. If ageing research comes into that, the first thing it has to do is to show that it really can compete with other high quality science. If it is not good science, it will not compete with stuff that is good science.

Q507 *Chairman:* Whose responsibility is it to see that there is sufficient expertise for some of the major questions that may be left unattended just because there are not good scientists across the range?

Professor Souhami: Do you mean in cancer generally or in ageing?

Q508 *Chairman:* Across the range.

Professor Souhami: It is the responsibility of all the funding agencies to make sure that takes place. Big steps have been made in that with the question of considering medical and scientific careers and making them stable, which you have to do in the first instance, and then you have to influence what those careers are about by making funding opportunities available. You can lead the process up to a point. You can say, "There will be money in this domain if there are good ideas." That is about as far as a funding agency can go.

Dr Goodwin: I would reiterate that it is the absence of a sound career structure for scientists who wish to go into the ageing research area that is the big impediment to maintaining quality and quantity. Unless we have a sustained programme in scientific ageing of research funding, we are going to be in very difficult circumstances in 15 to 20 years' time when the current tranche of researchers are reaching the end of their careers.

Q509 *Chairman:* We see the problem; I am trying to establish whose responsibility it is.

Dr Goodwin: In my view, it is the responsibility of all the funding agencies. In terms of ageing, that is very much more diverse than in terms of cancer UK, but we all have responsibility for that. Someone has to take a lead in this.

Dr Nowell: I would come one step further back which is looking at the educational establishments as well in terms of ensuring that aspects of ageing, demography, are part of a whole range of processes, not just the professional courses for the medics and the related professional disciplines but for a much wider range of undergraduate and postgraduate courses. We do not make ageing exciting. We should be able to, because it is exciting. Even if you have the resources and the commitment of the research councils, if you do not get anyone interested and if you are not exciting the people who are going to be the cream in terms of the education system, it is not going to make a huge amount of difference.

Professor Souhami: Might I add a rider? At the time when Cancer Research UK was formed from the two previous charities, we decided to set up a training and career development board for precisely the reasons that you are alluding to, namely to make sure that we did not have gaps, as far as it was in our power to do that, in the training programmes of young laboratory scientists and young clinical scientists. That gave us quite a lot of strength in dealing with both universities, in making sure that job plans were right in universities, and in dealing with the Royal Colleges, in making sure that we were seeing things in the same way that the Royal Colleges were seeing them in terms of career structures, particularly in the case of clinical career structures. That focus on training and career development is actually an essential part of a funding agency's remit. Unless you make this a special activity which has its own financing and its own way of thinking about training and its own expertise, you lose it in a rather random process of funding.

Q510 *Lord Drayson:* We have heard from a number of witnesses to the inquiry of the prevalence of ageism within society and how negative attitudes to ageing make it more difficult to carry out scientific research in this area, and restrict the ability of industry to meet some of the demands that the ageing population sets. Is this something which you have experienced in your organisations and, if so, how do you overcome those problems?

Dr Nowell: To a certain extent, for us it is much very about age discrimination and ageism across society in that sense and it is one of our fundamental campaigning areas. In fact, tackling age discrimination is there, it is not just our responsibility, it is the responsibility of society and individuals at large. Certainly we would be looking to challenge some of the ideas that it is acceptable for older people to live in poverty, receive poor healthcare, be excluded and live miserable lives. That is part of the challenge for us, raising that awareness. At the moment it may well be necessary to raise it within the research communities as well in terms of we do not think they are necessarily excluded in terms of age discrimination and ageist attitudes. Our experience is that it is pretty endemic right across society. For us, that is part of it but also not only the campaigning, taking the opportunities that the Commission for Equality and Human Rights offer us all, for example, but also by promoting research into attitudes towards older people and old age and certainly in terms of looking at the stereotypes in this particular area that we are interested in. It is partly about campaigning and partly about promoting appropriate research and it is also developing and dissemination of information, as I think I have mentioned before, just highlighting that older people make huge contributions to our society. It would be very, very helpful and raising more awareness of that would be extremely positive.

Dr Goodwin: If I can add an interesting element to this issue. When we have been fund-raising within Help the Aged for ageing research, we have found this is not easy. Our fund raisers tell us that if they go to the general public for leukaemia or for childhood diseases the general public's hand goes into the pocket and a ten pound note comes out, but if you go to them for ageing research you have to have a convincing argument in order to engage their attention. What we have found is if you tie this to a condition of an age related disease, like Alzheimer's or osteoporosis, that is entirely more successful. The other problem we have met is that there is a widespread negative attitude to old age as to why we should be conducting research into ageing. Why should we conduct research into a process which is going to lead us to decrepitude and lack of independence? Therefore, there is a huge issue in terms of educating the general public as to the possibility of healthy ageing, not just the rectangularisation of the survival curve, so that we are all going to get that much older but also we need to compress morbidity so we live longer and die faster, in other words. I think once the general public appreciates that 60 is the new 40, that we are going to live healthier and we can compress morbidity, they will have a much more informed and much more productive attitude towards ageing research itself.

Q511 Lord Drayson: In respect of Cancer Research UK specifically, if you put more emphasis in your fund raising on the effects of cancer in the ageing population, would that have a negative impact on your ability to fund raise?

Professor Souhami: No, not at all. I do not think that would be a problem for us at all. Having foresight of that particular question did make me look at the images in the fund raising that Cancer UK uses, and whether or not we put our money where our mouth is, as it were. I think we are not too bad with that. The images do genuinely reflect most of British society, but whether the images and the fund raising reflect the proportions of British society which are going to get cancer is another matter. In talking to our fund raisers in advance of this meeting, because of that question, there was no sense at all in which they felt that saying "we wish to do research in cancer in the elderly" would be an adverse or a detrimental thing for the charity, not at all.

Chairman: Time marches on, but we have been interrupted a bit. I wonder if we can get two more questions in from Lord Broers and Lord Soulsby.

Lord Soulsby of Swaffham Prior: I think my question, my Lord Chairman, we have dealt with previously.

Q512 Lord Broers: This is to do with the way cancers present themselves, and do cancers of a particular type present in the same way regardless of age. Is the prognosis the same? For example, does cancer in an older person tend to be more or less aggressive and the therapies more or less effective?

Professor Souhami: I have given Mr Collon the statistics on that, which I photocopied so that the Committee could have those. If I can take the last bit first, there is no question that above the age of 70 the relative survival from cancers diminishes in the elderly compared with the decades below that. What is more, whereas the overall mortality of cancer in the United Kingdom has fallen by 13 per cent over the last decade, roughly one per cent a year, it has only fallen by about one to two per cent in the over-70s; in other words the advances in cancer mortality have not been equally distributed across the age range. The answer is the prognosis is worse.

Q513 Lord Turnberg: Do they die of cancer?

Professor Souhami: That is the next question. If you look at the data, this is relative survival after being diagnosed with cancer, so this is relative survival compared with the population of the same age. Having the diagnosis of cancer means that your survival is less compared with at an early age but the question is, is it the cancer that killed them or something else that then happens sociologically. Could it be that people did not want to give them the treatment they should have or, alternatively, if you have got cancer and then you get some other disease, do they not want to treat the other disease because you have got cancer. All of those things would increase your relative mortality from having a diagnosis of cancer. There are a lot of complicated questions in there. You go right back to the question of research here because if you want to disentangle that, that is quite a complicated thing to do. That is precisely the sort of sociological research that we need in order to understand the answer to the question that has just been posed to me. The second point that you made—going back in reverse order— was about whether cancer is specifically more aggressive in the elderly compared with a young patient. The answer is, not in general. Indeed, there are many examples of it being the reverse, of it being rather benign and slow growing in the elderly. Again, if you were to ask how much specific research on aggressivity, however defined, related to age in the particular tumour types that are common in the UK, there is very little to guide us on that. Such research as there is does not indicate that there is a global shift towards more aggressive cancer. The worst mortality probably lies not there but in other aspects of therapeutics in the elderly. As to your very first question, namely whether it presents in the same way regardless of age, on the whole, yes, it does but there is an interesting question, namely is an elderly patient's response to a symptom that you and I would regard as pretty serious the same as, say, in a younger age range. Again, there is now quite good evidence that the delays in diagnosis are more severe in the elderly and with detrimental effects. The reasons for those delays and the reasons why symptoms are overlooked are very complex, to do with people's prior understanding of what cancer means and that is a thing that may change as years go by. If you are talking about the population who are now aged 80 or above, their experience of cancer may have been formed a long way before, maybe 30 or 40 years ago. Again, the issues of presentation and going to your doctor in the elderly are extremely important issues. Clinically cancer presents in the same way, a breast cancer presents in the same way whether you are 80 or whether you are 60.

Chairman: We think there is going to be another division any minute, but I wonder if Lord Drayson could give us the last question.

Q514 Lord Drayson: This afternoon you touched on your view, as I noted here, that there are some differing interests within ageing research in the UK, and "fragmentation" was the word Dr Goodwin mentioned. What lessons do you think the success that Cancer Research UK has had could be applied to research for the ageing, in particular the excellent move the two cancer charities made in coming together? Without wanting to put Help the Aged and Age Concern on the spot, I wonder if you would comment on whether you think ageing research in the UK could learn from what has been done in cancer research, Professor.

Professor Souhami: I do not want to put people on the spot either.

Q515 Chairman: We do not mind, go ahead.

Professor Souhami: Again, I had forewarning of that question. When the merger was first put forward for Cancer Research Campaign and Imperial Cancer Research Fund, we looked at the portfolio of research that was funded by these two prior organisations. They were doing identical things. The two organisations were indistinguishable in the proportions of money they were spending on epidemiology, on social research, on basic biology or therapeutic research. There was not a scientific reason, or a structural reason, in terms of their objectives as to why these two charities should not merge. They funded the research in slightly different ways—one funded largely in response mode through universities, that was CRC, and the other largely through its own in-house organisations—but the principle behind it was the same. Once you had taken the step that you wanted to be a single charity there was not any logical reason why research should not continue in exactly the same way as it had done before. Had it been the case that one charity was funding entirely social or clinical research and the other basic research, I doubt if the union would have taken place because people would have seen that a lot of work would need to be done to make those two things compatible, but that was not the case. I think one has got to be very careful before believing that necessarily a union of charities always leads to success. The groundwork has to be done and the basis has to be correct.

Q516 Lord Drayson: What would you say are the top two benefits that have accrued?

Professor Souhami: That is relatively straightforward. The first has been that the public responded to it enormously favourably. One did not know that at the time, the merger was a character building exercise. It was not clear that it was not going to go seriously downwards but, with the benefit of hindsight, the public suddenly realised that there were two cancer charities and they did not really understand why

there were two, and now there was one in place, so that was very, very beneficial. I would like to give three benefits. Speaking personally, the second thing was it gave us much more clout with Government and universities and so on. If you want to get careers organised we are now a major funder of careers, you can talk to universities and stare Vice-Chancellors in the face and tell them what you want. The third benefit is the kind of research we are funding is extremely expensive in terms of kit, and both the two former charities on the world stage were too small to be funding in the way in which they wanted to fund. The funding is still too small actually but we are not as small as we were. If I can have three benefits, those would be the three.

Dr Goodwin: In terms of the charitable sector across the UK, there are more organisations involved in funding ageing research than Age Concern and Help the Aged. We have a Funders Forum of six charities, including the Wellcome Trust, and their interests are very diffuse because they do not only look at ageing. For example, the Nuffield Foundation funds some ageing but it has a substantial portfolio and, therefore, it is a member of the Funders Forum. As far as Help the Aged is concerned, we are members of the Association of Medical Research Charities which means that we fund high quality peer reviewed research in an academic sense in the science of ageing and older people, that is our focus, and also implement an international direction of research. I think Age Concern has a slightly different approach to research from that.

Dr Nowell: If I put myself on the spot that you may or may not have wished us to be, it seems to me that there is an issue in terms of merger and I think research is but one of the areas of interest. The bottom line basically is what is the benefit for older people. I think Professor Souhami has very clearly demonstrated that there will be benefits for the community at large by that particular merger. In terms of Help the Aged and Age Concern, there are benefits from having two national organisations that campaign. You have a bigger influence on putting ageing issues and older people on the agendas of a whole range of stakeholders. Also, you probably have a greater impact in terms of fund raising than if you have one merged organisation. I think it is actually the case that we do work together very effectively on a range of issues where it is of mutual interest. Elder abuse is but one, local forums, engaging older people in local communities, is another area. There are substantial differences. I think you have been hearing, hopefully quite clearly, that there is quite a different emphasis on why and how we do research which is complementary, it is not doing exactly the same thing in the same way. On the other bit in terms of areas which are very different, part of our research is looking at services delivered and developed by local Age Concerns for older people, direct services, whereas Help the Aged by and large does not undertake that area of activity, certainly nowhere near to the same extent. Both organisations have looked at the pros and cons of merger and we will continue to do so. It is on the public record that Age Concern England's trustees are willing to consider merger, so it is there. I do not regard it as being put on the spot. The research does complement each other and perhaps we can explore how we can develop that even more so.

Q517 *Lord Drayson:* Very briefly, Professor Souhami, you said the single best thing that has been done in the cancer research area is the creation of a National Cancer Research Institute. Is there an analogy here that the single best thing could be to create a national Age Research Institute?

Dr Goodwin: My view on that would be yes. If we look to both East and West, if we look to Europe there is even less investment there in terms of strategic development and funding research, and if we go in the other direction, and look at the United States, there are highly successful programmes, a high order of investment with good strategic direction. I think we can take the best of that and apply it to the British scenario and produce a substantial and more effective portfolio of peer reviewed research by that means.
Chairman: May I say we have beaten the next division to the conclusion of the answers. Thank you very much indeed. If there are additional points that you feel you either wish you had made or that occur to you afterwards, do not hesitate to email or write to the Clerk of the Committee or any one of us. Again, we much appreciated your written contributions. Thank you very much indeed.

Supplementary evidence by Help the Aged

EXTRACT FROM RESEARCH STRATEGY DOCUMENT

GOVERNMENT POLICY AND EXPENDITURE

Department of Trade and Industry

1. Apart from direct funding via the HEFCE, the Government exerts considerable influence on the Universities via the Research Councils, whose budget is controlled via the Office of Science and Technology (Department of Trade and Industry (DTI)). The aim of its research policy is to take the lead in providing new capital and enhanced research funding in order to restore, maintain and grow the infrastructure for research. The recommendations of the Government's Foresight Panel indicated that there were three primary areas into which funding should be channelled. These were Genomics, e-Science and the basic technologies. The science budget allocations for the three years 2001–02 to 2003–04 were announced in November 2000 (Spending Review 2000). The research vote was therefore transcribed into a funding formula to cover the period to the end of 2004 which added considerable extra spending to the baseline expenditure on research. These data are shown in Table 1.

Table 1

GOVERNMENT RESEARCH EXPENDITURE 2001–04 (OST Data)

(£M)	2001–02	2002–03	2003–04
Baseline	1,702	1,702	1,702
Additions	64	208	453
Total	1,766	1,910	2,155

2. The Government's priorities for research expenditure are reflected in the structure of the funding within each of the research councils. For example, in the Medical Research Council (MRC) £65 million of the extra funding has been awarded for genomics research and £8 million for health informatics, bioformatics and e-science. An allocation of £41 million was allocated to the Engineering and Physical Sciences Research Council (EPSRC) to fund basic research into new and developing technologies. This was a cross-Council allocation,

some of which was expected to feed across to areas relating to human health. A further £15 million cross-Council programme was established to tackle issues common to all Councils, eg IT provision such as SuperJANET. As part of the baseline expenditure, £675 million was provided for University research infrastructure (with an additional £225 million from the Wellcome Trust) as part of the Science Research Infrastructure Fund.

3. In the latest 2000 Spending Review, the Government has created a dedicated capital funding stream for the Universities amounting to a further £500 million per year by 2005–06. It has also doubled the OST budget for large families to £205 million per year by the same period.

Research Council Expenditure

4. There are four Research Councils who directly fund research into ageing issues. These Councils are the Medical Research Council (MRC), the Engineering and Physical Science Research Council (EPSRC), the Economic and Social Science Research Council (ESRC) and the Biology and Biotechnology Research Council (BBSRC). Their total levels of expenditure and their direct expenditure on research on ageing are shown in Table 2. The four councils are members of the Funders' Forum, a NCAR iniative to bring together all those bodies from the public and voluntary sectors who fund research on ageing. A preliminary analysis of the expenditure in Table 2 shows that only a small proportion of the total expenditure of the Research Councils is spent directly towards older people's issues. However, the inference that research into all issues relating to ageing is neglected may be fallcious, since a proportion of the work carried out in non-age specific areas may indirectly benefit older people. A good example would be research into those diseases which are associated with age but which do not exclusively affect older people, eg cancer. In any analysis of not only expenditure, but also the direction of research, the issue of identifying research related to ageing is problematic. For example, the Wellcome Trust does not categorise its research funding by age and is only able to approximate its expenditure on ageing research (*vide* Table 4).

Table 2

RESEARCH COUNCIL EXPENDITURE

DATA DRAWN FROM PUBLISHED SOURCES AS AT DECEMBER 2002

	Total Annual Budget (£m)		Older People's Programmes (£m)	Percentage of Total
BBSRC	213.9	SAGE	4.9	3.0%
		OTHER	11.9	
EPSRC	436.2	EQUAL	9.0	0.7%
ESRC	74.4	GOP	3.5	3.5%
MRC	349.6	HoE	54.9	5.5%
Total	1,074.1		84.2	2.8%

(SAGE = Science of Ageing (now replaced by ERA (Experimental Research on Ageing));

(EQUAL = Extending Quality of Life; GOP - Growing Older Programme; HoE = Health of the Elderly).

5. In the recent 2002 Spending Review, the Government has granted an additional £120 million per year to the Research Councils to contribute to the indirect costs of research. There is also a new investment of £100 million per year from 2002–03 to 2005–06 to provide increased stipends to PhD students and postdoctoral fellowship salaries.

Spending by other Government departments

6. In addition to research expenditure via the Research Councils, several Government departments have research budgets which are dedicated to older people's issues. Some of these departments are shown in Table 3. "Current projects" includes work that may have been proceeding for some time, eg longitudinal

studies. An interesting feature again is the relatively small amount of funding which is dedicated purely toward ageing research. For example, in the year 2002–03 the total R&D budget for the NHS was £540 million; direct expenditure on ageing research was *ca* £5 million.

Table 3

RESEARCH EXPENDITURE—GOVERNMENT DEPARTMENTS

DATA DRAWN FROM PUBLISHED SOURCES AS AT DECEMBER 2002

	Current Projects (£m)	Annual (£m) 2002–03
Department of Health (Older Peoples Services)	14.83 (n = 64)	2.50
Department of Health (NHS)	5.62 (n = 34)	2.30
Department of Work and Pensions	3.57 (n = 18)	1.23

Research spending by charities

7. The figures for research expenditure by other charities are shown in Table 4. The charities listed are all members of the Funder's Forum. It has not been possible to access all the required data from publicly available sources and even the Charities themselves could not provide some of these data accurately. For example, the Wellcome Trust does not categorise its research according to an age criterion, making expenditure estimates difficult. Therefore only a partial representation has been possible.

Table 4

RESEARCH EXPENDITURE ON AGEING—CHARITIES WITHIN THE FUNDER'S FORUM

Charity	Current Projects (£m)	Annual (£m)	(Total) £
Alzheimers Society	2.3	0.1	(0.1)
Anchor	NA	NA	
British Heart Foundation	1.4	NA	(40.4)
Joseph Rowntree Foundation	1.25	NA	
Nuffield	0.29	0.29	(5.22)
Research into Ageing	5.04	2.45	(2.45)
Stroke Association	5.98	NA	(0.44)
Wellcome Trust	108.00	NA	
Total	124.26	NA	

Figures in brackets represent total research expenditure per year. Data abstracted from published figures as at December 2002. "NA"—data "Not Available".

Gross domestic expenditure on research

8. The latest data on the UKs' gross domestic expenditure for R&D show the figures for 2001 and were released in March 2003. The data shown an annual increase of 5 per cent in real terms from 2000, to a figure

of £18.8 billion. The Office of National Statistics (ONS) differentiates between "sectors carrying out R&D" and "sources of funding". Expenditure by "sector of funding" for 2001, in real terms, was as follows:

Business Enterprise	46%	(£8,691 million)
Overseas Funding	18%	(£3,386 million)
Government	15%	(£2,841 million)
HE Funding Councils	8%	(£1,474 million)
Research Councils	7%	(£1,359 million)
Private Non-profit	5%	(£889 million)
Higher Education	1%	(£177 million)
	100%	£18,817 million

9. Therefore the OST expenditure for R&D in 2001 (at £1,766 million) represents 9.39 per cent of the total UK spend. It is likely that from the figures available, that only *circa* £200 million per year is spent directly on ageing research, making it a very small component of research expenditure nationally (ca 1 per cent).

The National Collaboration on Ageing Research

10. The National Collaboration on Ageing Research was launched in November 2001 following two national initiatives—the EQUAL initiative set up by the OST and a three year project—Age Net—developed by the Research Councils (funded through the OST's Foresight Challenge Competition). Its Director is Professor Alan Walker of the University of Sheffield.

11. The NCAR was launched in response to the driving factors of demographic change and the deficiencies of the UK research base. These deficiencies include a lack of multi-disciplinary research, poor collaboration and consultation between research funders and a lack of co-ordination between researchers and key end-user groups, not least of all older people themselves. The inclusion and empowerment of older people is an issue of increasing importance, exemplified by the notion of the "new politics of older age" and by the many models of older people's involvement which have been produced in recent years.

12. Therefore the main aims of the NCAR are set out as follows:

(a) To act as a link between initiatives and key research groups.

(b) To engage in a new Cross-council Approach.

(c) To increase the flow of research on ageing into the policy and practice communities.

(d) To provide a link to the major research centres in the EU.

13. There has been criticism that these laudable aims are yet to be fully achieved, and that there is no explicit aim to integrate older people into the research process. However, it must be said that the Collaboration would require more than its present level of staffing and financial resources to enable its full potential to be reached and that it has only been operating for 18 months.

Funders' Forum

14. The Funders' Forum is made up of the following bodies:

Research Councils—BBSRC, EPSRC, ESRC and MRC;

Voluntary Sector—Alzheimer's Society, British Heart Foundation, Help the Aged, Joseph Rowntree Foundation, Nuffield, Wellcome Trust;

Public Sector—Department of Health.

A summary of the research portfolios of the members is found in Annex B.

15. The Forum was intended to provide a platform to identify areas where joint working can make a greater impact and where the greatest gaps in research are. Its overall aim is to stimulate and facilitate multi-disciplinary working and develop research activities across the boundaries between research funders.

16. The Funders' Forum has been perceived as lacking leadership, coherence and unified and purposeful effort. Recently, discussions in the Forum have centred on the appointment of a National Institute of Ageing; integration of research in the NHS and the inclusion or representation of older people in the Forum.

17. The Research Councils are at an advantage in so far that they already have cross Council mechanisms for communication and strategy building (the Cross-council Co-ordination Committee, led by the MRC). The Charities in the Forum at present do not share such a mechanism and it is difficult to make an appreciation of what, if any, their shared position might be.

18. There also does not appear to be any integrated concentration of research direction emanating from the Forum, despite the members' position as leading funders of research. This situation does not compare well with the strategic direction found in The United States, where the National Institute of Ageing delivers a very sophisticated and informed leadership role, with an impressive budget and research portfolio.

19. Possible solutions to some of these problems include a proposition to fund a national centre of excellence of ageing research, either real (eg based on a University) or virtual; collaborations between the major University institutes of ageing in order to secure large European funding; a campaign for increased Government expenditure on ageing research; widening the collaboration of the Forum to include professional bodies, such as the British Geriatrics Society and the British Society of Gerontology.

Research on ageing in the UK

20. Consideration of the direction and extent of academic research on ageing (both pure and applied) is fundamental to the synthesis of an informed and correctly positioned research strategy. It appears that there is no centrally held information database on current research activity on ageing in the UK universities. A review of the current University research effort on ageing is clearly beyond the scope of this document. Indeed it is not clear if such a review has been carried out. However, the following synopsis of research activity has been derived from a search of the individual University websites based largely on the membership of Universities UK.

Universities UK—121 Members

Institutes of Ageing 7

Bristol, Cambridge, King's, Liverpool, Newcastle, Oxford, Sheffield

Research Groups or Centres 15

Aberdeen, Queens Belfast, Birmingham, Edinburgh, Keele, LSE, LUT, Manchester, Nottingham, Open, Reading, Stirling, Surrey, UNN

Research Programmes 12

Brighton, Brunel, Bath, Cardiff, Dundee, Imperial, Kent, Lancashire, Leeds, Leicester, LSHTM, Southampton, Teesside

21. From formal meetings with a number of University Vice-Chancellors, it appears that not only is there no centrally compiled record of current research on ageing in the UK but that often there is no accurate record of the on-going research within individual Universities. The NHS Strategic Reivew of Ageing (1999) was unable to compile a comprehensive complete and accurate record of ageing research in the UK. A database of current research on ageing would therefore appear to be a valuable asset to the development of a national strategic direction for research.

22. Research on ageing in the UK, within all areas including the Universities, the public sector and the private corporate sector appears to be fragmented and to lack strategic direction. This has been implicity recognised by the formation of the NCAR and the Funders' Forum and explicity by the NHS Strategic Review on Ageing and Age Associated Disease and Disability. Among the recommendations of the Review (1999) were:

(a) A directed strategy relevant to the health and social needs of the ageing population was necessary.

(b) A National Research Advisory Group should be set up to foster comprehensive research relevant to the health and wellbeing of older people, including a review of research priorities.

(c) A Network of Trusts should be set up with responsibility for carrying out commissioned tests of new interventions and services.

In relation to specific subject areas, further recommendations included:

(a) A review of the research priorities relevant to the health and wellbeing of older people.

(b) A regular review of assistive technology.

(c) Research on cost-effective means of influencing health behaviour in later life.

To date, it appears that few, if any, of the above recommendations have been actioned.

International developments

23. There is an international consensus on the agenda for ageing research. The document, entitled "The Research Agenda on Ageing for the 21st Century" was published following the Valencia Forum, which preceded the 2nd World Assembly in Madrid in June 2002. Developed by UN Programme on Ageing, with the support of the International Association of Gerontology, the Agenda was designed to support the implementation of the International Plan for Ageing. It identifies six major priorities for research and 10 critical research arenas. Specific research agendas for the UN Regions of the World are under development and will be published by the end of 2003.

24. The International strategy for Help the Aged was written in 2002 ("Older People Everywhere") and is currently under implementation. Its principal objectives are:

(a) Building a strong network of capable organisations through support to strengthening age-interested organisations world-wide;

(b) Supporting the most vulnerable groups through carefully targeted programmes;

(c) Raising awareness and commitment within the UK within critical audiences of policy makers, public and donors in the UK; and

(d) Delivering concrete results through new partnerships and collaboration with other organisations interested in similar issues, where there are opportunities for encouraging mutual learning and making an impact.

In implementing this programme there is an implicit concept of building the evidence base for informing HtA's activities, in partnership with Help Age International.

Conclusions

25. It is therefore suggested that the following conclusions may be drawn:

(a) Direct expenditure on research on ageing appears to be a small fraction of Government funded research expenditure and even smaller in relation to the total UK spend on R&D.

(b) The apparently low direct expenditure on ageing research is to some extent offset by the research on medical conditions which are associated with ageing.

(c) Biomedical expenditure far outweighs the sums spent on other areas of research on ageing.

(d) The principal areas of biomedical expenditure appear to be age-related cardiovascular conditions (eg heart disease and stroke); biology of ageing and mental function.

(e) In the social sciences, the main areas appear to be quality of life issues; family, kinship and support networks and healthy productive ageing.

(f) Some notable research "gaps" appear to be:

(i) modifiable risk factors for well-being and health (eg environmental factors, diet, stress, exercise, social participation, leisure, life style and recreation;

(ii) the economics of older age, including economic activity and ageing;

(iii) technology and the older user.

The research base on ageing in the UK is fragmented, lacks co-ordination and strategic direction.

INTERNATIONAL COMPARISONS

26. Government Science Investment Framework (2004–14) aims to increase R&D expenditure from 1.9 per cent to 2.5 per cent over the 10-year period. Average annual rate of R&D funding increases aimed at 5.8 per cent 2004–08. Over the 10-year period, average annual rate ALL SECTORS must be 5.75 per cent—a significant challenge. The following date compare the total R&D investment of Japan, the EU and the USA. These data should be compared to the figures for investment in science as a percentage of R&D, given previously in Table 4, for the UK only (maximum level—ca 0.4 per cent GDP).

Table 9

COMPARISON OF INVESTMENT IN R&D AS A PERCENTAGE OF GDP 2001

Source	GDP (€bn)	R&D %GDP	GBAORD %GDP	GBAORD (€bn)	% Private Sector of R&D
Japan	5,145	2.91	0.64	20.58	74
EU	8,524	1.92	0.73	62.22	66
USA	9,327	2.62	0.81	75.54	78

(Eurostate, 2003)

GBAORD—Government Appropriations or Outlay on R&D

Table 10

INVESTMENT IN R&D AS A PERCENTAGE OF GDP 2002 (HM TREASURY, 2004)

% of GDP	UK	France	Germany	USA
Business	1.24	1.37	1.73	1.87
Public Sector	0.62	0.83	0.78	0.80
TOTAL	1.86	2.20	2.51	2.67

USA—National Institute on Ageing (NIA)

27. Research programs supported by NIA (part of the National Institute of Health—NiH), include studies on the mechanisms of ageing, the processes of ageing, ageing and the nervous system, and ageing in relation to health and disease. NIA supports four extramural research programs:

> Biology of Ageing
>
> Behavioral and Social Research
>
> Neuroscience and Neuropsychology of Ageing
>
> Geriatrics and Clinical Gerontology

The Institute also has Intramural Programs with laboratory and clinical research conducted at the Gerontology Research Center and at NIA facilities in Bethesda, MD. It supports conferences, workshops and meetings plus funding and training of new investigators.

The Fiscal Year 2004 budget request for the NIA is $994,441,000 including AIDS, an increase of $36,785,000 and 3.8 per cent over the FY 2003 amended President's Budget Request.

NIH's highest priority is the funding of medical research through research projects grants (RPGs). Support for RPGs allows NIH to sustain the scientific momentum of investigator-initiated research while providing new research opportunities. In FY 2004, NIA will provide an aggregate average cost increase of 2.6 per cent for Research Project Grants. Also in FY 2004, NIA will fully fund 13 grants. NIA continues to support funding of AREA awards. Promises for advancement in medical research are dependent on maintaining the supply of new investigators with new ideas. In the Fiscal Year 2004 request, NIA will support 571 pre- and post-doctoral trainees in full-time training positions, the same number as in FY 2003. Stipend levels for NRSA trainees will increase by 4 per cent over Fiscal Year 2003 levels for predoctoral fellows, and from 4–1 per cent, based on years of experience, for post-doctoral fellows.

The Fiscal Year 2004 request includes funding for 67 research centres, 213 other research grants, including 181 clinical career awards, and 101 R&D contracts. Intramural Research receives a 3 per cent increase and Research Management and Support receive a 1.8 per cent increase over FY 2003.

EU—Research Programmes

28. The main, though not exclusive vehicle for EU spending on research has been through the Framework programmes. Figures for the levels of spending are as follows:

— Fourth Framework (FP4) €13.25 billion.

— Fifth Framework (FP5) €14.96 billion.

— Sixth Framework (FP6) €17.5 billion.

EU RESEARCH ON AGEING EXPENDITURE

29. Estimates for the proportion of these Framework programmes which have been spent on ageing research are as follows:

— Fourth Framework Programme 1994–98 (€13.25 billion);

   Biomedicine and health €157 million.

— Fifth Framework Programme 1998–2002 (€14.96 billion);

   Key Action 1 ("QoL") and Key Action 6 ("Ageing and Disability") €190 million.

— Sixth Framework Programme 2002–06 (€17.5 billion);

   Combating major diseases €1,155 million.

30. Assumptions have to be made that ageing related research areas are subsumed within the "biomedicine and health" and "major disease" categories (the data source (Eurostat) does not give these details).

CONCLUSIONS

31. International comparisons of research expenditure on ageing are difficult to make because of the absence of detailed data available from public sources and secondly because the data that are available are not or cannot be differentiated according to an age criterion. However the following conclusions can be made.

(a) Of the three economies under consideration (USA, EU, UK), the USA spends the most on ageing research in a highly strategic and well directed programme, via the NiA. For example, using data from 2001:

— Gross Expenditure on R&D: ca €244,000 million.

— Government Expenditure on R&D: ca €76,000 million.

— Government Research Expenditure on Ageing: ca €632 million.

In 2005–06 the NiA budget will increase substantially to an expenditure total of $1 billion per annum (€769 million).

(b) The UK's apparent spend on ageing research is far less than the USA, on a percentage GDP basis, or as a proportion of gross research expenditure, as the following 2001 data show:

— UK Gross Expenditure on R&D: ca €30,000 million.

— Government Expenditure on R&D: ca €3,000 million.

— Government Research Expenditure on Ageing: ca €300 million.

(€300 million = ca £200; estimates includes Research Councils ca £151 million; Government spending departments £6 million.)

(c) The EU apparently spends very little directly on ageing research (2001 data):

— EU Gross Expenditure on R&D: ca €164,000 million.

— EU Expenditure on R&D: ca €62,000 million.

—   EU Research Expenditure on Ageing: ca €200 million.

32. It is arguable that it is the gross expenditure that is the crucial factor, since one scientific breakthrough yielding a research outcome of substance (eg a new drug, therapy, intervention or finding which effectively alters practice or policy) benefits all members of society equally.

October 2003

Supplementary evidence by Cancer Research UK

CANCER IN THE OVER 70S IN THE UK

Incidence

—   Half (52%) of all cancers diagnosed each year in the UK are diagnosed in people over the age of 70.

—   Each year in the UK more than 140,000 people over 70 years are diagnosed with cancer.

—   The cancer incidence rate in people over 70 has increased by 3% over the last ten years (increased by 4% in the under 70s over the same period).

—   Cancers of the lung, bowel, prostate and breast account for more than half (55%) of cancers diagnosed in the over 70s in the UK.

	Persons—70 years and over	
	Number of new cases per annum	*% of all cases in the over 70s*
All malignant neoplasms excl NMSC	140,494	100
Lung	22,511	16
Colorectal	20,779	15
Prostate	19,129	14
Breast	14,170	10
Bladder	7,042	5
Stomach	5,996	4
Oesophagus	4,456	3
Pancreas	4,364	3
Non-Hodgkin's lymphoma	4,193	3
All leukaemias	3,517	3
Kidney	2,905	2
Head and neck	2,843	2
Ovary	2,831	2
All uterus	2,443	2
Melanoma	2,189	2
Multiple myeloma	2,128	2
Liver	1,490	1
Brain with central nervous system	1,353	1
Mesothelioma	1,086	1
Larynx	890	1

MORTALITY

—   Almost two thirds of deaths from cancer in the UK are in people over the age of 70.

—   Each year in the UK almost 100,000 people over the age of 70 die from cancer.

—   The cancer mortality rate in the over 70s has fallen by about 1.5% in the last 10 years (decreased by 13% in the under 70s).

8 March 2005

SURVIVAL

— Lung cancer five-year relative survival rates in patients under 50 are around 10-25% compared with less than 5% in patients over 70.

— Five-year relative survival rates for patients diagnosed with breast cancer in their 50s are around 85% compared with 60–70% in patients over 70.

— More than half of people diagnosed with bowel cancer before age 70 are successfully treated compared with fewer than 40% of those aged 80 +.

Table 1:

FIVE YEAR RELATIVE SURVIVAL BY SITE AND AGE AT DIAGNOSIS FOR PATIENTS DIAGNOSED IN eNGLAND AND wALES DURING 1996–99 AND FOLLOWED UP TO THE END OF 2001

		Age at diagnosis					
		15–39	*40–49*	*50–59*	*60–69*	*70–79*	*80–99*
		%	*%*	*%*	*%*	*%*	*%*
Bladder	men	90	84	77	70	62	48
	women	78	70	70	65	53	40
Breast	women	76	82	85	82	74	58
Cervix	women	83	73	60	48	36	22
Colon	men	61	54	50	50	47	40
	women	58	54	54	52	48	39
Lung	men	21	9	9	7	5	2
	women	28	13	11	8	4	1
Ovary	women	81	55	44	32	23	15
Prostate	men	76	58	75	77	68	48
Rectum	men	54	55	54	52	47	34
	women	60	61	62	58	49	36
Stomach	men	18	17	15	16	12	7
	women	19	22	20	19	14	
Testis	men	97	96	95	86	67	55
Uterus	women	77	81	85	78	67	45

POPULATION

— Currently around 12% of the population is over the age of 70, this has increased from 8% in 1970 and is set to increase to 16% by 2025.

— If current incidence rates remain the same the ageing population will result in an extra 100,000 cases of cancer being diagnosed annually by 2025, the vast majority of these cases will be in the over 70s.

March 2005

TUESDAY 22 MARCH 2005

Present	Drayson, L	Oxburgh, L
	Emerton, B	Soulsby of Swaffham Prior, L
	Hilton of Eggardon, B	Sutherland of Houndwood, L (Chairman)
	Murphy, B	Walmsley, B

Examination of Witnesses

Witnesses: LORD SAINSBURY OF TURVILLE, a Member of the House, Parliamentary Under-Secretary of State at DTI responsible for Science and Innovation, and CHARLOTTE ATKINS, a Member of the House of Commons, Parliamentary Under-Secretary of State, Department for Transport, examined.

Q518 Chairman: May I firstly welcome you; and secondly thank you all very much—we know you all have very busy diaries—for taking the time to come to meet the Committee. Needless to say, we think that this is an immensely important topic, and the Departments which you represent are at the centre of some of the most important parts of it. I have to remind you that there is a sound record taken of our discussion, which may be broadcast. We have a range of questions that we would like to cover in a comparatively short time and we know that there may be another division shortly, which raises its own problems. We all have names and rather than take time going around the table the nametags are out and perhaps we can do it that way. Could we start initially with OST and DTI and then move to Transport, if that is acceptable? Can I start with a reasonably general question about integrating research policy? The Department of Health of course has very significant responsibilities in this area, but nonetheless the Research Councils are all focused in the OST and by implication the DTI. Is there much coming together, meeting of minds and thinking through what the strategies are and how one might best develop them? And also thinking about the level of investment in research in this area, which has huge economic as well as other impacts?

Lord Sainsbury of Turville: There are in fact very close links between the Department of Health and the MRC, which is probably the most important department here. There has been a concordant between the MRC and Department of Health since 1981 and that was last updated in 2004. Also of course the Department of Health is very closely integrated into the decision making of the MRC through its membership on appropriate MRC boards and committees, including the MRC Health Services and Public Health Research Board, which is responsible for funding decisions and strategy development. We have made one big change of course recently, which is totally focused on this question of how do you get research out of Research Institutes into hospitals and particularly clinical trials, and that is the new MRC Department of Health Research Delivery Group, which is focused on this question of getting things out, particularly into clinical trials. We also of course now have very specific objectives for each of the Research Councils in terms of knowledge transfer. For example, the MRC's knowledge transfer objectives include increasing effectiveness of knowledge transfer from Research Council Institutes in line with the recommendations of the Baker Review of public sector research establishments and the National Audit Report on commercialisation of public sector science. So that is another dimension to this. Of course many of the Cross-Council Research Programmes have knowledge transfer objectives built into them. So those are the specific things. As far as ageing is concerned—and I think this is very important—we have two bodies which are concerned with coordination on ageing. The first is the Cross-Council Coordination Committee on Ageing Research, which was established in 2000, and also the Councils play a leading role in organising a Funders Forum for research on ageing and older people, of which MRC provides the Secretariat. So I think there is a great deal of coordination and also bringing in the people who can deliver.

Q519 Chairman: Just two points to follow up. I would be very interested to know how you think these coordinating bodies are doing; in other words, are the results there to show that they are actually functioning? And there is a very specific one because one of our witnesses at an earlier session suggested that BBSRC, who are clearly involved in some of the development research, seemed to think that they were out of the loop with regard to the Department of Health and they had not met with them for quite some time. So there may well be important areas of research—and indeed from our experience there clearly are—where there is no meeting of minds between what the Department of Health wants and what the BBSRC is doing.

Lord Sainsbury of Turville: I think that would take place through both the Coordinating Committee on Ageing Research and indeed the Funders Forum, so both these bodies would in fact be part of the loop, as well as in specific programmes where they are players in this, which do have these knowledge transfer objectives.

Chairman: Lord Oxburgh, would you like to complete that discussion?

Q520 Lord Oxburgh: Just to pursue that, it is one thing to have committees that meet, it is another thing to have them do something useful.

Lord Sainsbury of Turville: Yes.

Q521 Lord Oxburgh: Are you satisfied that there has been a positive outcome from these various coordinating bodies?

Lord Sainsbury of Turville: Yes. I think you can see this in the record. We have had a series of major programmes, first the EQUAL Programme and then The New Dynamics of Ageing Programme, which are clear programmes to bring together research in particular areas, which bring together different Research Councils and, as far as I am concerned, most importantly, are not talking-shops or networks but are actually programmes of money going into specific research. So from looking at the situation I am reasonably content with the mechanisms that are in place and are working. That is not to say that there are not some areas where coordination is not working, and if you feel that there are any areas where we are not performing as well as we should be because a particular bit of research has not been linked with another bit of research where it should be, then we would be more than happy to look at that and see what needs to be done.

Q522 Lord Oxburgh: As our Chairman said, a number of witnesses have brought to our attention coordination difficulties, and perhaps we could pursue those separately. But if one moved more to the OST area of responsibility, are you happy at the level of spend in the ageing area within the Research Councils? I know that the standard Research Council response to inquiries of that kind would be, "We do not have the applications to merit more money," but to some extent this is a chicken and egg situation, in which if the Research Councils indicate that this is an area of interest and there would be money attached to it the applications tend to be forthcoming.

Lord Sainsbury of Turville: I think the correct answer is that it is extremely difficult to make a judgment on that because it is very difficult to take it in any other way, because it is a very diverse field, and it seems to be very difficult to lump it together and say, "Is this enough, or not?" Because it is such a diverse area there are no statistics where you can say, "We are doing this, other countries are doing that." When you look at the statistics like that they are completely meaningless because the definitions are completely

different. So I do not think you get much by trying to do international comparisons. In any case, the real question is, is the money where we are dealing in stem cell research at the right level as compared to other areas within that field? I think when you lump it together you do not get any kind of real question and answer that helps you very much.

Q523 Lord Oxburgh: Whose responsibility would it be within OST to take an oversight view of the emphasis that the Research Councils are together putting on this interdisciplinary area?

Lord Sainsbury of Turville: This would be in different ways the Funders Forum, but perhaps, more importantly, the Coordinating Committee which would then report to the Strategic Committee of all the Research Councils. We can give you the figures of each individual Council.

Q524 Lord Oxburgh: I think we have those, thank you.

Lord Sainsbury of Turville: As you can see, it is quite difficult to add this together and say, "Is this the right figure or not?"

Q525 Lord Oxburgh: What is astonishing about those figures is the extraordinarily low ESRC figure, which I think as a proportion of budgets as well as an absolute figure is rather low. One would imagine that ageing would be rather higher on their agenda. I do not know if you have any comment on that?

Lord Sainsbury of Turville: No. I agree with you that *prima facie* you might say that this was too low, but we have had two programmes, EQUAL and now The New Dynamics of Ageing, both of which bring very much bring the social sciences into this. If you look at the sort of programmes, they look to me to be very sensible. But of course they do bring in areas of design and research and so on and the built environment, which do fall into other areas. But if you look at the EQUAL Programme, I think there were four calls. The first was on EQUAL in the Built Environment, then Design For All, Rehabilitation of Design For All and Prolonging Independence In Old Age, which is exactly the right kind of programme.

Q526 Lord Oxburgh: They are good names and I certainly know from direct experience that some of them have done good work, but with the rather limited resources available to them the question is: what have they achieved?

Lord Sainsbury of Turville: My sense is that within what they are trying to do they have achieved rather a lot. These are very specific programmes about how you design housing and other areas to cope with the problems of old people, and it seems to me they are right projects; I have never heard people say that they were not productive and useful. But again, if you have any evidence that they were not effective then that would be very interesting.

Q527 *Lord Oxburgh:* I think the question would be one of quantity rather than quality.
Lord Sainsbury of Turville: Right.

Q528 *Lord Oxburgh:* If we move on to this question of coordination, the NCAR was set up three years ago to coordinate this work and has been found to be ineffective. Are there lessons to be learned there?
Lord Sainsbury of Turville: I think the general feeling was that it had not been totally ineffective.

Q529 *Lord Oxburgh:* But hardly a recommendation for any group.
Lord Sainsbury of Turville: No, but it is not correct to say that it had totally failed. It did some good work. It was of course a network and in my mind there is a big distinction between networks which are just there to network, and networks which have funding attached to them and therefore can deliver programmes. What we have had is NCAR and we then had EQUAL, which was a network plus funding. We now have The New Dynamics of Ageing, which has rather taken over where EQUAL was as far as funding is concerned, and now we have the new network, which is the Strategic Promotion of Ageing Research Capacity, which is a network. So I think we are just doing it in a different way and there are both networks and funding mechanisms there to coordinate things.

Q530 *Baroness Murphy:* If I can come back to the Foresight Reviews in 1993–94 and up to 2001. They had a very strong emphasis on the need to deliver in this area, but so far all the evidence we have heard is that it is not happening, and we have heard yet again that coordination has not been very effective so far, although it may have done some good work. I wondered if you thought that a body along the lines of the US National Institute on Aging, which of course both funds extra-mural research and maintains its own research facilities, would be an appropriate kind of development in England to fund this sort of research, in England and Wales?
Lord Sainsbury of Turville: It seems to me that you have to make a choice with the Research Councils, which is that you can either split up the work in terms of structures, on the basis of discipline, or you could theoretically do it on the basis of problem areas. The decision in 1993 was to do it on the basis of discipline and I think as a whole, for a number of reasons, that is the right way to do it. Then where you have particular problem areas you coordinate by Committees or working parties or whatever the appropriate processes are. But the basic structure is on the basis of disciplines. If you said we should have

a National Institute on Aging I think you would immediately enter into the discussion, "Well, what about a National Institute for Youth, one for climate change, one for energy?" ie all the problem areas. You could do that but, as I said, my own preference would be that you keep it by disciplines because I think it is more necessary to do the integration within disciplines than to deal with the problems through processes. That would be, as a whole, my preference. The Americans have done it differently but that may be because they are under more political pressures to do so.

Q531 *Baroness Murphy:* Would you agree that so far, though, the way we have done it through disciplines has not enabled the focus that the OST itself has promoted in its Foresight Reviews?
Lord Sainsbury of Turville: I think that there is an important point here. I am not certain that the biggest problem is coordination. These are very different kinds of research and I think it is too easy to say that everything must be coordinated with everything. There are lots of things that you do not need coordination of, other than actually in a discipline sense. So I am not certain that the problem is coordination. There may be an issue that we are not doing enough in a particular area in terms of regenerative medicine or design for living for old people or mental health of old people, and I think that is something one always needs to keep an eye on. I am not certain that the problem is one of coordination because I am not certain you get anywhere by trying to coordinate stem cell research with, for example, designing houses for elderly people to live in.

Q532 *Chairman:* One of the things that we picked up when we did visit the National Institute on Aging is the issue of coordination because some projects clearly do require more than one expertise, and I agree with you that we have to find good mechanisms for doing that. The other point they made to us is that some longitudinal studies sometimes only have the drive behind them because they usually require both staying power and quite a lot of money if you have a dedicated research base for that type of longitudinal study, and that was one of the advantages we saw in the NIA, and just how we deal with that question in this country. Really quite expensive studies might well pay long-term benefits but we tend not to follow the projects funding.
Lord Sainsbury of Turville: I think you will find in various places, particularly ESRC, that there is very clear money which is dedicated to long-term projects which span a long time period because it is essential to get the database there, and if there was a real need for one then I cannot see any reason why that cannot be done within the current framework. I think The

New Dynamics of Ageing Project is a very good one, which is looking at many of those issues. If there was a need for the database it could certainly be organised through the current network.

Q533 *Baroness Hilton of Eggardon:* The problem seems to be not a matter of coordination but a problem of demarcation. We heard evidence from one of the Research Councils that looks at things at the basic cell level in ageing cells, and they said they were not allowed to look at whole organism sequences of their research, and it does seem to me that that is one of the difficulties, that you have this clear demarcation between various Research Councils and it is not so much a matter of coordination but a matter that some research ought to go on to looking at larger and larger units or whole organisms, which it does not. So it is no good having a committee which just gets people talking about what they are doing, but it is sometimes that some lines of research ought to go on and trespass into the areas of other Research Councils to make sense of it.
Lord Sainsbury of Turville: This would be the BBSRC, would it, which would say, "We cannot look at whole organisms"?
Baroness Hilton of Eggardon: That is what one of them said to us, that they were looking at the ageing process in individual cells but were unable to then extrapolate from that and look at the larger units of whole organisms.

Q534 *Chairman:* Not so much unable as the funding was not there to carry what was a linear progress of research from the cell to the organ.
Lord Sainsbury of Turville: It was not a restriction on the Research Council but it was a restriction on the Research Council's Strategic Research Programme?

Q535 *Baroness Hilton of Eggardon:* It was also a question of not treading on the feet of other researchers. There was some feeling that there were psychological inhibitors on moving into other fields.
Lord Sainsbury of Turville: But within that Research Council?

Q536 *Baroness Hilton of Eggardon:* Yes. They were not able to extrapolate from their basic research on cells into something of a larger scale.
Lord Sainsbury of Turville: I think that has to be a question of the management of the Research Council saying, "We want you to concentrate on *this*," and then other people concentrating on *that* and making the decision that that is the right way to do it, which may or may not be right.

Q537 *Baroness Hilton of Eggardon:* There might be other Research Councils who are very jealous of their particular provenance and do not want other people trespassing into their field, might there not?
Lord Sainsbury of Turville: I would be very interested to know which of those it is, because if it is a case of a Research Council cannot follow what would be a sensible research path because of the division between the Research Councils and that had been said to be a barrier, then I would very much like to know that because that is something that we should look at, to see if it is in any way holding up the research which is going on.

Q538 *Chairman:* I suppose we saw the line, as it was put to us, appearing between BBSRC and MRC, basically, and if we can give more specific information that would help.
Lord Sainsbury of Turville: We will be very interested to see that, to see that some arbitrary rule is not getting in the way of doing good research.

Q539 *Lord Oxburgh:* I think the point, turning back to the NIA for the moment, is that it clearly provided a focus to which people from different parts of the country looked when it came to ageing research, and it was also an organisation that dispersed funds for ageing research. So there was a coherence. It did not mean that that was the only research done on ageing because charities and other bodies do it, but that was a clear central focus. We are a small country and our efforts are pretty much dispersed around a number of different places. It seemed to us, it is fair to say, that its ability to not only do research in-house but to support a clearly focused programme of research grants, which made a coherent whole, really gave great strength to their programmes.
Lord Sainsbury of Turville: Could I just say that the problem you have with it is like all structural issues? You set up a National Institute on Ageing and then you find yourself two years later before another distinguished Select Committee saying, "Why are you not coordinating the research you are doing in Alzheimer's with this other excellent work going on in the Medical Research Council?" There are always these problems of what you coordinate with what, and I think you have to make a fundamental decision: do you do it by discipline or do you do it by problem area?
Lord Oxburgh: Let me say as someone who has lived with this in other areas, people who are working in single disciplines on what is a little bit of an off central theme for that discipline area tend to get looked at a bit oddly and feel to be a bit neglected and out on a limb in those single discipline departments. I recognise the problem you describe, obviously. But, given this problem of an ageing population is going to be one of the big social impacting events of the

coming decades, I think it is seriously worth considering whether it is not sufficiently important that it ought to be an exception to your rule.

Q540 *Chairman:* We are all very keen on this area, you will understand!

Lord Sainsbury of Turville: I think the fundamental issue is, are we doing enough research in this area in the different parts of it to really meet the need? That is the fundamental issue.

Q541 *Lord Oxburgh:* Do the bits add up to more than the whole?

Lord Sainsbury of Turville: Where it is important to bring them together. I do not think everything, as I have said, has to be coordinated with everything because we do not want to try to coordinate fundamental biology in with—

Q542 *Lord Oxburgh:* With zimmers.

Lord Sainsbury of Turville: Yes. So again I think the two questions are: is there any area where this coordination which should be taking place is not; and are there any areas that you see where you really feel that there are things we are doing on regenerative medicine, or whatever it is, is way out of line with what you think the opportunities are? Those are the two questions that would be helpful to us.

Q543 *Lord Soulsby of Swaffham Prior:* My Lord Chairman, I was going to bring up the point that Lord Oxburgh brought up, but I do not want to say too much about that, except with the intra-mural research programme in NIA my opinion was that they were getting more clinical research via the extra-mural programme than with intra-mural programme. One of the problems in this country is that it is difficult to get people to go into clinical research and one of the problems there is the Research Assessment Exercise. You get more brownie points by doing basic research, and the question comes up whether there should be any modification of the RAE to maybe take note of collaborative research between basic studies and clinical studies, because in various universities that I know people shy away from clinical research simply because they do not get the high ranking that they want.

Lord Sainsbury of Turville: My reading of the situation is that there is quite a major problem with clinical research, but the main reason for that is to do with the fact that we have never really looked at it and sat down and said: what is the sensible career path for people doing clinical research. We simply pile on top of each other the requirements of being a clinician and all the requirements of being a researcher, which means that people do not begin doing clinical research until they are in their 40s, and there is then

a very uncertain career path thereafter. We have identified this as a major problem and Mark Walport at the Wellcome Trust has been looking at that and has come up with some very sensible suggestions about how we form a proper career path for people doing clinical research, which will go a long way to improve it. So I think that is the main problem, but I agree that there is also a problem with the RAE. However, we can deal with this because this is about making certain that excellence in practice is included alongside excellence of theory. The main thing, I think, is just the careers path.

Q544 *Baroness Murphy:* The focus that a National Institute gives in the States for the development of research capacity and fellowships and development, just as we have seen developed by the Department of Health and the National Institute for Mental Health area here, has allowed a focus on development of that research capacity on which we have all had a lot of evidence that it is not very well developed in this country.

Lord Sainsbury of Turville: I think the issue here in looking at it is that we have had these quite substantial programmes and I do not think there has been any problem, when we have gone out to get a project within these areas, in finding good projects to do. So it has never been that we have put money aside for this and we have not had good enough projects; this is an area that when we go out we get very good projects. Again, it is quite difficult to say that there is a common issue here because it is very different kinds of research. As a whole I do not think there has been a particular problem of where in some areas you say we put money aside for this but we do not get good projects; in these programmes there have been very good projects.

Chairman: Baroness Hilton, do you want to come back in on that?

Baroness Hilton of Eggardon: No, I think most of my questions have been answered.

Chairman: Lord Drayson.

Q545 *Lord Drayson:* We have been quite struck by some of the witnesses talking about whether industry is responding to the perceived needs of an ageing population, and how industry does not seem able to take into account what is clearly a significant commercial opportunity and translate that into products which meet this growing population. Do you have any comment about what role the DTI could play in encouraging industry to accelerate activities in this area?

Lord Sainsbury of Turville: I think there is a role for the DTI and it is one that we are very much developing in line with the increased emphasis we have been putting on knowledge transfer. I have sat on a group called the Health Industry's Taskforce, which was a mirror to the one we did on the pharmaceutical industry, which is bringing together the National Health Service with the supply in industry and the DTI to improve communication between the two parties and the DTI. That group was chaired by Lord Warner and Sir Christopher O'Donnell. It has recently reported and it has made some very clear recommendations on how we get innovation. One area is getting the innovation taken up by the National Health Service in order to promote more innovation. The second area is through the New Technology Strategy, which we have in the DTI, and that very much covers health care as a key market area for the future. For example, one of the projects in April 2004 was that we had a competition and that was a consortium led by Oxford University and IBM on grid computing, which was how do you use the new techniques of grid computing to improve medical infomatics? So that is another way where we are getting the technology out of Research Councils into industry. We had other ones for basic computing, which interestingly has implications also for old people; and I think there was a project there, which is also about elderly people. So I think through these two mechanisms, one, using the National Health Service programmes to drive innovation in industry and, secondly, using the Technology Strategy and the collaboration of R & D, we can support industry taking forward novel techniques.

Q546 *Lord Drayson:* One aspect that was particularly striking is that there does not seem to be a whole lot of interest from industry in this area, and this was put to us because of the level of ageism in particular areas, reflecting the fact that a lot of people who are engaged in product design, people who might be marketing directors and so forth, tend to be in their 30s and 40s and who really do not have a clear appreciation of the developing needs of an ageing population. And that although the market opportunity is realised superficially, industry does not have the interest and the skills to bring these products to market. Do you think that is correct and, if so, is there a role for Government to do anything about it?
Lord Sainsbury of Turville: I think again we come back to the fact that one is dealing with very different kinds of industry, and if you are dealing with the pharmaceutical industry I would not think that that criticism could conceivably apply—or the biotech industry, for that matter. If you were looking at a question of design of equipment which could be used by old people, my own impression is simply—and this I know because of the Design Council—that there is a huge interest both in industry and among young designers to design equipment which, for example, old people can use. That is seen in design

schools and so on as a really challenging and interesting task. To what extent that gets taken up by industry I would not know the figures, but there is certainly a lot of enthusiasm. If you go to the Royal College of Art and look at their final years of design you will find there is cutlery designed for old people, chairs designed for old people and so on. It is seen as quite an interesting subject. Again, if you have any information which says that there is a whole category of equipment which is very much needed by old people, for which there is not any product even though we know how to design things, again I would be enormously interested to see if we could encourage people to look at it.
Lord Drayson: I think you are right that it is industry specific so the biotechnology industry and pharmaceutical industry is absolutely way up the curve on this, but in an area such as Information Technology and communication technology it has only been quite recently that people have been thinking about the purpose of mobile phones which can be used by people well into their 60s and 70s, and that reflects the way in which industry in these areas is not bringing these products into the market.

Q547 *Chairman:* I have seen some of the work in the Royal College of Art and I agree that it is very good work and they are lively young people who want to do this. But there is an example where I think this issue goes back to researchers needing to be brought together, which is where we started. We had somebody talking very well and helpfully about hearing problems which tend to increase with age and very good basic biomedical research going on there, but they seem not to have any contact at all with what is going on with chip technology and the technology of noise disaggregation and so on that is available in the world of electronics. Yet think what that could do for hearing aids, because I understand the main problem is that they cannot differentiate between different types of sounds. Such a bringing together, I suppose, is the sort of thing that the coordinating bodies ought to be looking at imaginatively because it could produce a new type of hearing aid that would have huge enabling prospects.
Lord Sainsbury of Turville: I think this is where you get down to the work of individual researchers. If the individual researcher working on this problem does not make that leap of imagination I doubt if you will get it any other way. I agree, that if there is really that kind of gap it might be something where we should say to the coordinating committees, "Try to see if you can put together projects which bring people together in this area."

Q548 *Chairman:* The imagination of the individual researcher is fairly critical, but of course the natural line they follow is the very interesting line that they are following and it is quite often something that comes in from the side that can produce a product or potential project.

Lord Sainsbury of Turville: Yes.

Chairman: And the structures do tend to reinforce their going down that line on a whole variety of issues we have raised this afternoon. Are there any other questions because we would like to move on to Transport?

Q549 *Baroness Walmsley:* Do you think they have the balance right between research which is promoted by, "Here is an interesting area, we think we can do more along this direction" and coming from completely the other direction with old people saying, "Here is a problem, can anybody do anything about it?"

Lord Sainsbury of Turville: I think this is always a key question. I think it slightly comes back to how you manage the different things. I think possibly we do need—not through the Research Councils because the Research Councils are focused on research excellence and driving the subject, and I think it is extremely difficult to give them a whole heap of new criteria and say that they should select projects because we think they are relevant or important—to make it very much into research excellence and one of the things of driving forward. As I say, we have other funding, particularly from Government Departments, all the technology strategy, which is very much mission driven. So it is driven by what people see to be the problems, whether it is industry saying, "We need this technology to get competitive advantage," or it is to solve a problem on energy research or a problem area or climate change, whatever it is. I think it would be an interesting question to ask whether we have enough research coming from the Government Departments who are responsible for this or the Department of Health in terms of mission research which says, for example, that hearing in old people is a major issue, are we putting enough money into just solving that kind of problem because it is a big social problem? That is obviously driven by what old people themselves see as their problem. I think that must come through other routes because it is always highly tangential to what Research Councils are supposed to do.

Q550 *Chairman:* If I may say so, I think that provides a very helpful bridge to Transport because I wanted to start by asking whether or not within the Department there is a comprehensive strategy that looks at increasing problems of isolation in old age, which very often has to do with inability to get around when people stop driving—for good reasons sometimes—and that does mean that the availability of public transport that is user friendly to that particular age group is very important. Is there an overall look at this or is it piecemeal?

Charlotte Atkins: Yes. You will be aware that we introduced local transport plans to empower local authorities to come up with a strategic plan for their own particular area, rather than going through this rather unseemly bidding process, whereby local authorities have produced a wish list and then expect the Department to fund it. So we are now moving into the second stage of that, second round of local transport plans, and within that, this coming year, we have focused on the need to introduce accessibility planning so that each local authority, when it produces its local transport plan, will have to look at the whole issue of accessibility. Therefore what they need to do is to assess the issues in their locality and particularly groups of people who are isolated in any way, also the location of services and such like, to ensure that transport, for instance, is then providing access to go to the doctor's surgery, to the leisure facility, to the shops and that sort of thing. I accept very much what you say, that there is a real problem for elderly people who have stopped driving in particular because they are not used to the public transport which is available. Where you get a number of people, very often women, for instance, who have never driven and have used public transport on a regular basis, I think there is much less of a problem there. Although there may an issue of accessibility because they know the pattern of public transport or are more *au fait* with where they can go to get information the isolation effect is less great. But I do think that when somebody has relied for many years—maybe going into 80s and 90s—on driving and then suddenly to be faced with losing that particular car or perhaps have been widowed or something of that order and have therefore relied on their partner to drive them around, that can be a real issue. That is one of the issues which we are getting local authorities to look at and requiring them to come up with those plans for the period of 2006 up to 2011.

Q551 *Chairman:* So these are blokes who have always driven to work and do not know where to get a number 17 bus or a bus at all!

Charlotte Atkins: Absolutely. They could jump on their bike, of course, which would do a huge amount for their heart condition and probably do a lot for their arthritis and everything else.

Q552 *Baroness Walmsley:* Very specifically on what you have been saying, is there any direct link between the authority that says, "Your eyesight is so bad now you cannot have a licence any more," and information about how else somebody can get around?

Charlotte Atkins: I do not think there is a direct link, but you are absolutely right in saying that.

Q553 *Baroness Walmsley:* There needs to be, does there not?

Charlotte Atkins: There certainly needs to be and we are certainly trying to provide that information. As you probably know, we have Transport Direct nowadays, which admittedly is accessed online, but which does provide a whole network of information about how journeys can be carried out, certainly by car but also by public transport. I think that is useful. It is clearly the case that we do have to provide more accessible information, and I do think that operators, whether they be bus companies or train companies, are trying to provide more information. We always have to improve more, clearly, but I do think that there is also a recognition that both buses and train vehicles of all sorts have to be accessible, so that anyone who does have an impairment, whether one to do with walking or one to do with visual or hearing impairment, then in that situation it is important that these companies do provide for a whole range of needs.

Q554 *Baroness Emerton:* I think in part you have answered the question which I was going to ask, but are there any measures that the Department are considering, for example to improve facilities for older people? Let us take, for example, travelling away for the weekend. Many older people find it difficult with their luggage and more recent trains do not have any facilities for luggage, particularly the line on which I travel, and there is nowhere to put the luggage, even on the rack, if you could reach the rack. It is this kind of needs assessment that possibly needs looking at in terms of what the older person requires in travelling on public transport.

Charlotte Atkins: I do think it is important that we look very carefully at the design of the rolling stock of our vehicles. As it happens the train I often travel on, a Pendolino, down the West Coast mainline—dare I mention it?—does have facilities for luggage on the ground and it does not require me to lift it up very high. But I think you are absolutely right in the sense that it is important to have those facilities; but also important for elderly people as well as people with buggies or luggage, to have easy access to the vehicles and that means obviously without having to step up and certainly being able to hang on to something like a handrail; to have something which, if you are visually impaired, you can see where the handrail is because of the different colours used, and so on. A whole range of things, which I think makes it easier to get on to the train. But of course things like steps at the station are a real issue and of course the other big issue is the bridge over the platform. There are a whole range of issues like that which do not just relate

to people who have an impairment, but who may be carrying children or luggage, whatever. We are now working towards making stations more accessible and they have already come under the Disability Discrimination Act in terms of step free access and so on, but also making reasonable provision for people who need that extra bit of help to use the train services and the bus services.

Q555 *Lord Soulsby of Swaffham Prior:* Just talking about transport, one of the discriminations against older people is travel insurance. Some travel insurance companies will not provide cover for driving motorcars for people aged 75 years and over. So many people that would go on the continent to drive around cannot do it any more. I am not sure that you can do anything about it—and I suffer from that problem—but it is a discrimination that assumes that because you are 75 years old you are no longer being considered as a safe driver.

Charlotte Atkins: In fact if you look at the evidence there is no reason for that because if you were to look at the numbers of accidents which could be put down to older age then, as far as I understand it, there is virtually no evidence. There is evidence that older people might find it more difficult at particularly complex junctions or particularly complex driving situations, but very often older people, unlike younger people, do in fact limit their driving often to more local areas if they feel that they are impaired in any way. I think there are other issues that the technology now and the adaptations now can provide with things like extra mirrors, maybe a swivel seat because very often for older drivers it is not so much driving but getting in and out of the car which is the difficulty, because you cannot bend because you have arthritis, or whatever. So I think it is very, very short-sighted of the insurance companies, but I have to say that insurance companies also aggravate much younger drivers at the other end of the scale and of course set the cost of that insurance at a level to be virtually prohibitive unless of course you have a parent who is willing to put the youngster on to their insurance, in which case you put off the evil day when you have to pay that very large price to insure yourself to drive. So I think it is both ends of the spectrum. I do think, however, that insurance companies are very short sighted because the evidence does not prove that older people are in any way a liability as far as driving is concerned, while they are fit to do so.

Q556 *Lord Soulsby of Swaffham Prior:* May I quote you?

Charlotte Atkins: You certainly can!

Q557 *Lord Drayson:* Continuing on that subject, we have heard evidence how other countries do not have a preset age for the expiry of their driving licence and interestingly these countries have a better accident rate. I wondered what the Department is thinking in this direction? We understand that the DVLA is looking at the whole area and considering a possible extension from 70 to 75 years of age. Would this Department consider not having a preset age at all?

Charlotte Atkins: Certainly the DVLA is looking at this whole area, and rightly so, because at the moment we have this limit of 70 whereby people have to assess whether they are fit to drive, and of course the renewal of the licence. Some countries have this 70 limit but others in fact, like Spain, have started looking at the age of drivers at 45, with regular extensions after that. I think that probably the Department will see that a limit at 75 plus would be worth keeping. I have to say that I do think from my own point of view, my own family situation when I had to persuade my mother to stop driving, it is quite reasonable to have an upper age limit at which drivers do have to consider whether they are fit to drive. I think it is a very different situation, particularly for the driver themselves, to assess whether they have deteriorated in any way in terms of their cognitive functions or indeed their ability to turn around and their vision and everything else, and I do think that it is quite difficult to make that assessment over time. Sometimes I think having an age—75, 70, whatever—when people have to consider the issues and make a judgment is quite useful. But it is something that the DVLA is going to be looking at and they expect to have this research completed by October this year.

Chairman: I know time is getting on but there is one question that we are keen to raise. Lord Oxburgh.

Q558 *Lord Oxburgh:* The Deputy Prime Minister has recently announced a significant expansion of housing in the southeast. May we properly assume that your Department is in contact with that Office—

Charlotte Atkins: Absolutely!

Q559 *Lord Oxburgh:* —to ensure that appropriate arrangements for the transport of the elderly, along with the transport of other age groups is in fact going on?

Charlotte Atkins: I do not think we particularly separate off the elderly as far as that is concerned. Clearly it is vital that growth areas have appropriate and accessible transport and certainly that is happening. There is a close cooperation between the Department of Transport and the Office of the Deputy Prime Minister.

Q560 *Lord Oxburgh:* But may I pick you up on what you said? That you have not taken the elderly as a particular area of concern—because we are in a time of change and the elderly faction of the population is significantly increasing and this means that transport arrangements that may have been satisfactory 20 years ago may not be satisfactory for the coming decades for which this housing will be relevant, and so maybe you do need to take another look at it.

Charlotte Atkins: What we are doing though is to make sure that public transport is in place when these housing developments are being developed. If you take as an example Fast Track, in Kent, which is a guided bus facility, which is being put in place before the houses are built so that when the houses do come on stream that is already in place, to encourage people to use public transport from the start, rather than automatically assuming that there will be a car parking space or enough car parking spaces in that housing development to cater for two or three cars per household. What we are trying to move towards is a much more integrated transport strategy so that people can use public transport and you do not have the scenario where you have housing developments built and then you ask the bus company to develop a route to that housing development and the bus company turns round and says, "The roads are too narrow to be used by our buses." So those sorts of issues, we are trying to work together as Departments to make sure that we do not fall into those mistakes.

Q561 *Lord Oxburgh:* To pick up a point you made earlier, are you ensuring that cycle ways are incorporated in this early planning stage too?

Charlotte Atkins: I have to say that we are doing a lot on the cycling agenda, and in fact I was speaking to a cycling conference just this morning because we have created a new body called Cycling England, which will be working very closely with the local authorities to expand both cycle routes and off road cycling and safer cycling, as well as reintroducing a national training scheme so that everybody can be suited for training.

Q562 *Lord Oxburgh:* That was not quite the question I asked, because cycle ways which are an afterthought are not satisfactory. Cycles ways which are put in at the time of your public transport can be a very different kettle of fish, for example those in Holland. My question is whether you are ensuring that this is taken into account right at the beginning?

Charlotte Atkins: We are certainly looking at that and as cycling minister I would want that to happen, and I will certainly take that back to the ODPM and my colleague who is dealing particularly with the funding. Time for cycling has definitely come and it is not just an issue of cycling for recreation, cycling for youngsters; it is something which everybody can enjoy and it is a very fast and effective and successful way of using transport.

Q563 *Chairman:* If I can push a little the elderly agenda because although Lord Oxburgh cycles madly not everyone over a certain age does! The needs are quite specific for that group and I am pressing again not simply that there is a transport policy which is integrated, which is marvellous and what we would want, but the practicalities and actually talking to older people about what these are; that the kerb and the bus can come close together, that there is not the problem of parked cars, that there is not the problem of narrow roads. These are the same problems for young mothers with pushchairs—or young fathers with pushchairs—but equally there are specific needs for older people, and we would particularly want to focus on designing the system *ab initio* to cover that.

Charlotte Atkins: Already 40 per cent of buses are accessible and it would be crazy having an accessible bus if you could not then access it from the kerb, and that obviously does require ensuring that cars are not parked at the point at which people want to board a bus. It does mean also having a bus lane in which cars cannot park and ensuring that buses get priority, like the Fast Track which I mentioned earlier, because I have to say there is no better way of encouraging car drivers to get out of their car than to see a bus speeding past them when they are sitting at a traffic jam. I do think it is the way forward, not just for elderly people but for everybody. I think if we encourage people to use public transport when they have a car then when people get older they are more able to access public transport when or if they decide no longer to drive.

Q564 *Baroness Walmsley:* Accessibility of course is very important, but do you think that the designers of buses and trains have really taken on board the fact that because of greater longevity there is an actual expansion of the numbers of older people in the population. I am going back to something you said

about the trains on the West Coast earlier on, because you might have noticed by my face that I did not really agree with you in terms of the availability of luggage space at a level at which older people can access it. What we are finding with the trains and the buses is that, yes, there may be a small amount of space where you do not have to lift up your case, but there is not enough of it and most of it is high up above the head and older people cannot reach it. The newer London buses do not seem to have any space at floor level for luggage, you have to lift it up to three or four feet above the ground and put it over the wheel arch. So that is no use at all for older people. It is the expansion of the numbers of older people that I think perhaps may not be taken into account in the provision of luggage space.

Charlotte Atkins: Well, that is a very important point which I will take back to our committee that looks at these issues. I think the other issue though is that now drivers of buses, for instance, are required by regulation to help elderly people and people with disabilities who need help and they are required to do that because I think that very often people are put off using public transport because of the attitude of the staff who are on those particular vehicles. I have to say that staff make all the difference to increasing the confidence of all people who travel by public transport, but particularly for women and people who are feeling vulnerable, and I do think that the attitude of staff can make a huge difference and is making a huge difference where staff are trained. I am pleased to say that many staff now are being trained and this is making a huge difference to people's enjoyment of public transport.

Q565 *Chairman:* Well, we ought to stop now. Thank you all very much indeed for your time and for your answers. If there are any specific points that you or your Department want to follow up, we will be very happy to receive them in writing and we look forward to your reaction to our report in due course.

Lord Sainsbury of Turville: We look forward to seeing your report too.

Examination of Witness

Witness: DR STEPHEN LADYMAN, a Member of the House of Commons, Parliamentary Under-Secretary of State, Department of Health, examined.

Q566 *Chairman:* Dr Ladyman, welcome and thank you very much for giving us your time; it is much appreciated. We have quite a range of questions we would like to go through and talk about, and I wonder if I can start by asking a question that is really based on the policy of the Department, a very good policy that as many people should continue to live in their own home as is possible because that is, by and large, where people want to live, be they well or unwell to a certain degree. It did occur to us that one of the implications of that is that there might well be a good case for increasing the amount of research on the kind of assistive technology that can be put into the home to make this more possible, free independent living and so on. I wondered if the Department had a view on this or has a policy on this specifically in relation to research.

Dr Ladyman: Well, before I answer that question, perhaps I can just say that my responsibilities in the Department are around the health and social care of older people. Lord Warner of course normally deals with research policy, so there may be some issues that you want to ask me about where I will have to write to you.

Q567 *Chairman:* Understood, and we appreciate your willingness to stand in because I know he was distracted by other duties.

Dr Ladyman: That is right. As far as assistive technology is concerned, I think you are absolutely right and I think technology has huge opportunity for helping people stay at home. We launched the Green Paper on adult social care on Monday, yesterday, and we made big play of the potential of assistive technology in that. Also, as you may know, we are spending £80 million over two years starting next year on helping to create pilots for local authorities to try and deploy this technology, so in a sense that £80 million, much of it, will be going on experimenting with the technologies. It will be applied studies rather than academic studies. The DTI is working very closely with the Department of Health and with the industry to try and help the industry to develop new tools and it is something where I think UK plc has actually got a bit of a lead on the rest of the world and there is a real opportunity for our country commercially as well as an opportunity for deploying the technology in support of older people and their care, so I entirely agree with you and, as opportunities are identified for us to help in that work, we will certainly want to take them.

Q568 *Chairman:* Well, that is very useful and perhaps when you do talk to Lord Warner about specific research initiatives which, not unreasonably,

you are not up to speed on, but he might be, we would be very interested to hear about those.

Dr Ladyman: I am sure we will come on to talking about this, but there are various funding streams going into research, so there is a huge opportunity there for deploying some of that money into technology, and of course the Engineering Research Council will have an interest in helping in this area. The £80 million preventative technology grants that we are making available to local councils, we are not kidding ourselves that that £80 million over two years is enough to deploy this technology, but that really is money for councils to see what works.

Q569 *Chairman:* To pilot it, yes.

Dr Ladyman: So it is essentially research-based funding.

Q570 *Lord Oxburgh:* I think probably the questions that I was going to ask would be among those that you might wish to answer by writing, but fundamentally your Department has the responsibility for older people and ageing. On the other hand, the OST has a significant research input in this area as well. I really have two questions. The first is whether you are satisfied with the co-ordination between what goes on in the research councils and what is supported out of the Department of Health's research budget, and whether that is indeed a coherent programme. Indeed, the second question is whether the level of that programme, whether the commitment of funds is sufficient to meet the needs that this increasingly large older population will put on the Health Service and if one can think about smart ways of doing things, whether it is looking after them physically in their environment or whether it is handling their conditions, it actually will be a matter of spending to save.

Dr Ladyman: Let's deal with the first part of your question. Yes, it is true that the money to the research councils comes through the Office of Science and Technology rather than through the Department of Health. The Department of Health has responsibility for co-ordinating research in respect to health issues and social care issues and, therefore, by definition, for the research around ageing. Now, we have a very, very strong relationship both with the Office of Science and Technology and the DTI of course and with the research councils, and we have concordats between the Department of Health with the Medical Research Council and with the Economic and Social Research Council. Therefore, in a sense you could distinguish between the two as being that the OST are responsible for sort of pay and rations, whereas research policy in respect of these issues is the responsibility of the Department of Health, and it seems to work quite well, so I do not think it would be necessarily beneficial if the Department of Health suddenly became responsible for passing money direct to the research councils and I think the existing arrangements do work reasonably well. Then we come to the wider question of whether we are getting the right co-ordination of research and making sure all the gaps are filled, and that is where the UK clinical research collaborative and the various networks come in. Of course they co-ordinate the Department of Health's research programmes across all health issues, but plugged into that collaborative is a funders' forum that we have created specifically around issues in relation to older people and ageing. That funders' forum includes representatives from the research councils, it includes representatives from the stakeholders and it is chaired for us by Help The Aged. It is very much part of the UKCRC network and it is that group which is responsible for making sure that all the areas where we need to be doing research are covered. Now, are there any gaps in the research? Well, yes, of course there are. Do we have to plug them all? That is probably a wider question. We are not the only country in the world that has an ageing population, so what we have to look at is where gaps emerge that nobody is looking at and the co-ordination has to be not just around UK research into ageing, but essentially around worldwide research into ageing and deciding where we need to prioritise our efforts. Can that be done better? Everything can be done better and that is why we have created the funders' forum to continue looking at this and trying to predict for us where we have these holes and where we need to move to fill them.

Q571 Lord Oxburgh: Do you happen to know to what extent the funders' forum is a meeting of officials or whether it is a meeting of researchers or authorities in the field or medics?
Dr Ladyman: I can write to you and give you precise details of that.

Q572 Lord Oxburgh: It makes quite a difference.
Dr Ladyman: Absolutely. My understanding is that it is a mix, but I will happily write to you and give you chapter and verse as to who sits around the table.

Q573 Baroness Murphy: I want to follow up Lord Oxburgh's question. We have heard that the research assessment exercise, which of course is within the Department's approach to university excellence in research, has had quite a major negative impact on the development of academic clinical gerontology and research into other aspects of ageing medicine, which has become part of a vicious cycle which has

led to the run-down of departments and it has had a knock-on effect on the development of care of the elderly services generally. I wondered if you had any comment on that. It has been said about other areas of course, like obstetrics and gynaecology and mental health too, but this is a particularly difficult area and I wondered if you had any comment on how the Department is tackling that or thinking about it.
Dr Ladyman: Clearly if there is evidence of any of the procedures and assessment processes that we go through having an adverse effect, then we are happy to look at them. In a sense, an assessment process of course is there to have an impact and to identify where things are not being done well enough and to redirect resources to where they can be better spent. I am not aware of the evidence for what you suggest, but I am happy to have that explored and drop you a line to tell you if we see any sign of it, but it is not something that has been brought to my attention certainly.

Q574 Baroness Murphy: Perhaps I could follow on from that, that some of us who visited the National Institute on Aging in Washington looked at the way they co-ordinate research both through providing funding and also by doing their own research intramurally. Do you think there might be any good reasons, as it were, for having such a similar body in this country?
Dr Ladyman: Well, we have looked at it very carefully and we have come to the conclusion that it would not be beneficial and the reason for that to a certain extent at least is the opportunity cost. If you create an institute of that standing, you have then got to create an infrastructure around it. It has got to have buildings, it has got to have an administrative overhead in terms of making sure it is able to deliver, and the cost of doing all of those things is a cost which you then cannot spend on research, so we have taken the view that a more informal network is more appropriate. We have experience in this country of working in this way in other fields of science with some considerable success, so that was where the thinking came from about creating the UKCRC and within it a national funders' forum to look at issues around ageing. We believe that we have the opportunity between those two to co-ordinate science at least as well as the NIA does in the States. If you create an institute of that type, undoubtedly it will do some good work, and I am sure the NIA does do some good work, but you have got to ask yourself, "Okay, but how much more work could have been done in a more dispersed way if we had had informal arrangements where we were not having to invest in an infrastructure?" We have come to the conclusion that that informal relationship and arrangement is the better one for the UK.

Q575 *Baroness Murphy:* Could I just remind you that the Department came to a different conclusion with mental health?

Dr Ladyman: Yes, but then you could argue that at least we have learnt from our experience.

Q576 *Chairman:* As a follow-on from that, inevitably if that is the line, fine, that is the policy, but the co-ordinating mechanisms have to be very, very good, better than average, and I have to say that we are getting a lot of messages from taking evidence that the co-ordination is not working as well. Even with the funders' forum, we have not had the picture of a dynamic agency out there in a changing world and the NCAR was wound up because it clearly was not functioning, and its successor body, as far as we know, has not after a year called for proposals. We are concerned about how good the links and the co-ordination are because, rightly, they are very, very important under the current policy.

Dr Ladyman: I think you are right and it partly recognises that the funders' forum needs to have that sort of dynamic role that you are talking about and we are working to try and ensure that it has that role. I guess there is a research project there in its own right to compare the informal arrangements that we are trying to implement with the formal arrangements that maybe the United States have got, and to those researchers who have come to you and said that they perceive problems in the British system, I challenge them to come up with scientific objectivity with evidence that actually it is any better in the United States or places where it has been centrally co-ordinated. We have not seen evidence to suggest that is the case. If we do see evidence that that is the case, I have no doubt that we will look again at our decision, but we have no evidence to that effect at this time.

Q577 *Lord Oxburgh:* But there is empirical evidence that quite a few people from this country had become dissatisfied with the system and gone to work in just the system we are talking about and we have met them.

Dr Ladyman: And I suspect if I searched, I could probably find some people from the States who are working over here.

Lord Soulsby of Swaffham Prior: Not many!

Q578 *Chairman:* But in fact that is a slightly different question which is comparing two systems, which are very important and will be part of what we try to focus on. If, having compared the two systems, you go in the direction of co-ordination, and this is the question I was asking, what ways is the Department following to ensure that the co-ordination is of the highest quality because the solid evidence time and time again has been—a very specific example, that

the Dynamics of Ageing initiative was announced a year ago and actually there is no evidence from the researchers that it is active. That is pretty solid, that it is not dynamic, so that is the kind of question that is put to us pretty regularly.

Dr Ladyman: Well, I will happily talk to Norman and drop you a line and give you further details, if that would be helpful.

Chairman: It would indeed.

Q579 *Lord Soulsby of Swaffham Prior:* Can we move on to some of the questions of clinical issues of older people. We were told by Professor Lees that mortality in the first 30 days after a stroke is about 30 per cent in this country compared with 15 per cent in Canada and there is evidence that brain scans after a stroke reduce fatalities and reduce health care costs merely because you know what to do when you have them. The Royal College of Physicians in March said that only 47 per cent of stroke patients were scanned within two days. I wonder why that is. Have you any reason for it?

Dr Ladyman: We recognised the deficiencies in the treatment of stroke when we wrote the National Service Framework for Older People, and we recognised that there were serious deficiencies in the infrastructure for treating people with stroke quickly and getting them to the right sort of environment. That is why we set a target to create a stroke unit in every hospital that is going to support people that have had a stroke. We have not achieved 100 per cent yet. I think the Royal College of Physicians' Sentinel Report suggested that we had reached about 82 per cent of hospitals with a stroke unit that meets all of their criteria. From memory, I think 91 per cent have met most of their criteria, but we need to get to 100 per cent and we need to get to a position where all accident and emergency departments are able to recognise stroke quickly, able to make sure that the right referrals are made, and able to make sure that the scans are being carried out, as we recommend, within 24 hours. It is of great sadness to me that we have not got there yet but getting from where we were to where we want to be is a long journey. All I can say is that we are determined to get to the end of the journey as quickly as we can.

Q580 *Lord Soulsby of Swaffham Prior:* Is this a matter of funding or more than that?

Dr Ladyman: I think it is more than that. In some places it may well be a matter of funding where funding has not been properly prioritised towards meeting the criteria of the National Service Framework for Older People and meeting the milestones we set in that document. In some areas it is a matter of training and a lack of understanding about what is required. Professor Philp, the National Director for Older People, is working very hard on trying to address both the mainstreaming of funding and the training and other issues.

Q581 *Baroness Walmsley:* It is all very well having a scanner in place but very often they stand idle when there is no technician trained to operate them. There is a lot of evidence that they are not working at capacity. So what is being done to build the staffing infrastructure that is needed to make these machines really earn their keep?

Dr Ladyman: We have in place a very comprehensive workforce strategy to try and attract people into these skilled positions. Unfortunately, we cannot magic skilled professionals overnight so we have to do a number of things. We have to encourage those who have left the profession to return and we have therefore a recruitment and retention policy in place. We have to train new technicians and we have increased the training places available to produce those people. We have to try and recruit from abroad and we are trying to do that as actively as we can. Also we have to make sure that the trusts themselves realise the importance of having these people in place in order to get full capacity from all their equipment and therefore are creating the vacancies for which people can apply to come and work. We are working on it at many different levels but we recognise the importance of it. Indeed, the Government is also committed in the NHS plan now to creating a situation where people who need operations and other procedures will not have to wait longer than 18 weeks from the beginning of a GP referral to actually getting their procedure. That will include all diagnostics. If we are going to meet that 18-week target the recruitment of professionals to operate scanners and make sure the scanners and other equipment is being used 24 hours a day seven days a week is going to be an absolutely key part of it. The Government entirely accepts that the recruitment of these professionals is essential and we are working on every level to try and achieve it.

Q582 *Baroness Emerton:* I think it is true to say that most elderly people attending an A&E department or admitted to hospital are following a fall and NICE have just reported that there have been no new case studies on the clinical and cost effectiveness of interventions aimed at preventing falls, and recommend that such trials be carried out as a research priority. Can you tell us what the Department is doing to take this recommendation forward? I know it is in the Service Framework but it is a very big issue.

Dr Ladyman: It is, and we have said that there should be a falls service in every community. We are working very hard to establish those falls services and the results that we have got so far are indicating that we are making significant progress. In addition to that,

we have what is called the Innovation Forum which is an initiative from the Office of the Deputy Prime Minister where councils who have achieved "excellent" status are being encouraged to come up with ideas for innovative working in their local communities. One of them, which is being led by Kent County Council, is a scheme to try and reduce emergency hospital admissions of older people by 20 per cent. There are 10 councils involved in that trial and a key part of all of it is to try and establish the benefits of preventative work with older people and in particular the benefits that can be achieved by having a successful falls service. I have been emphasising to all the councils in that innovation, because I am the sponsoring minister for that particular project, that the key thing they must produce is solid data that we can use to measure the success of what they have done so that people around the Health Service and around councils can say, "Okay, I can see on the basis of that data that if I invest X pounds in preventing older people getting ill or in preventing falls, the saving to me on my bottom line is going to be Y pounds, and therefore it is worth my while making that investment." Although that might not be the formal research project that perhaps NICE were thinking about, in practice it will provide much of the data that they are looking for.

Q583 *Baroness Emerton:* As best practice?

Dr Ladyman: Absolutely.

Q584 *Chairman:* Indeed, we have been looking at quite a number of areas in which that sort of distinction could apply, for example, the importance of diet from the earliest days right through.

Dr Ladyman: Absolutely.

Q585 *Chairman:* It is very difficult to establish "here is an old person who had a very good diet 40 or 50 years ago" or "here is an accident that was prevented".

Dr Ladyman: And, of course, we have to bear in mind that most of the people who are now the older frail are over 75 years old and that means their childhood was in the 1930s where diet was not as good as it is today. We can probably have a debate about that, I suppose!

Q586 *Chairman:* I thought I was one of the lucky ones brought up on a war time diet!

Dr Ladyman: Certainly I do not imagine that food was as easy to come by then as it is now. Diet and nutritional standards were less well understood. Poverty was far wider and far more severe than it is today. It is quite difficult coming up with concrete cohorts that you can use to measure these things. Having said that, I am sure that there are ways to do it and I do not think anybody doubts for one second that getting our children fed properly and having the right balance of vitamins and nutrients throughout their childhood is going to have a beneficial effect when you are older.

Q587 *Baroness Walmsley:* Can I take you back to something you were saying a few moments ago about the project led by Kent County Council. You were saying they have been told that they have to produce concrete evidence that if you invest so much there are so many savings. Are you also assessing the value of putting a certain amount of investment in where the savings are made out of somebody else's money silo? *Dr Ladyman:* Absolutely.

Q588 *Baroness Walmsley:* And how is that working? *Dr Ladyman:* Divine inspiration has just led me to understand that the Department of Health policy research programme includes a £2 million research programme on accidental injuries, so there is some work going on. We are absolutely looking at that and if you have a look at the Green Paper on adult social care, which I published yesterday, you will see that we quite specifically say that health and social care have got to start to work together in order to identify where savings in health might come about as a result of investment in social care and therefore the money might well need to come from health in order to pay for those investments. You are absolutely right and the Government has a very clear commitment to moving to a position where we are having those understandings.

Q589 *Chairman:* There has been recently, of course, a very interesting example involving NICE of the interaction between what affects health and what has social implications and that was the potential withdrawal of some prescribed treatment for Alzheimer's. The Department took a very clear line on this and I wondered if you would like to outline what the position is now? *Dr Ladyman:* The position is very clear. The National Institute for Clinical Excellence is independent of government. We cannot order them to change their decisions. We expect them to come up with objective, science-based recommendations to us. That is what they have done. Now the process they go through, of course, is to publish their interim guidance. They have published that advice for consultation. We as a Government are as entitled to comment on that as anybody else and we have this afternoon submitted our views on their consultation and we have asked a series of questions about the robustness of the advice that they have given. Our response has been put into the House of Commons' Library and I am happy to make sure that we get a copy to your Lordships as well. Basically what we have asked is a series of questions saying are you sure that you have looked at the wider implications of your decision? Have you looked at the wider implications of your decision on families and carers? Have you built in those costs as well to your calculations? There are a number of fairly robust points that we have made there about what we think they need to look at. In addition to that, in the two days which followed the consultation coming out I contacted the key lobby groups working with older people with dementia and also a number of experts working in this field and I made sure that they understood that they had this period of time in which to submit their evidence. Some of the experts that I spoke to, in particular from people like the Royal College of Psychiatrists, made it clear that not only did they want to submit more evidence on efficacy but they had serious doubts as well about the process that NICE undertook, in other words, the way they did their calculations. They believed there were errors in what NICE had done. We have made sure that the information from lobby groups and information from experts has gone into the consultation. We have put in our own questions to the consultation. The consultation closes today so the next stage then is for NICE to look at all of that evidence and then revise their guidance accordingly. In the meantime, the old guidance applies so nobody's treatment should be discontinued whilst we are waiting for NICE to produce its guidance. There is no point speculating as to what will happen after that guidance but just as I did say in the Commons at oral questions today, in the event that they come to the conclusion that these drugs do not work and therefore it is not worth giving them to anybody, any money saved that is not spent on these drugs I would expect to see being reinvested in other support for dementia sufferers and any other treatments that may be available that appear to be effective.

Q590 *Chairman:* That is very helpful. We understand the position you are in in dealing with an expert committee and so on but the process is critical. There is one last question that I think Lord Drayson would have wanted to ask. One of the things that we have been focusing on particularly in the area of assistive technology rather than drugs, although it applies there also, is the pull through of good research into the market-place. We have found that, by and large, the market-place is not all that interested or has not been putting a lot of effort into it, and that the fault is maybe in a variety of contexts. One of the issues that we did come across that is relevant here is that as a purchaser the NHS is clearly a major feature and if, for example, in the business of hearing aids, which is one of the things we came across, the NHS were to focus on what they thought the needs were that would be of great interest to the business sector and might be very effective. I wondered if there is a mechanism within the NHS for asking that kind of question, knowing that the secondary implication of the translation of research in one area into real products is one of the consequences?

Dr Ladyman: Yes, there is. The departmental research programme has three factors which motivate it. There is input from stakeholders telling us what they think needs to be looked at. There is input from scientists and experts telling us what new opportunities there may be that need to be explored. Then there is input from policy sections. So where Government or others have identified an area where we want to do better, then we can use our various mechanisms to influence research in those areas. That is one where I would put assistive technology. I think what we have done on assistive technology is a very good example of why the collaboration between us and the Office of Science and Technology actually works quite well because, of course, the DTI has a wider responsibility. It is not just interested in science; it is interested in UK plc; and it is interested in us developing companies that are world-class, leading edge and able to exploit market-places. The Department of Health and the Department of Trade and Industry together have identified assistive technology as being one of those areas. Just recently the Department of Trade and Industry organised a trip to Japan for leaders from this market-place, for representatives of the Department of Health, representatives of the industry and the technology sector, and representatives of the DTI and others, to look at the sort of things that are going on in Japan at the moment and the sort of ways technology could be deployed. About two weeks ago they had a wash-up session over in the Department of Trade and Industry building where I went and reiterated to the whole industry how important I see from a ministerial perspective the deployment of assistive technology and the opportunities that there are there. I made points, for example, like the importance of the industry identifying open standards for their technology so that if you or I one day are in the position of needing to purchase assistive technology we can buy the base station from one firm and later on add alarms and other equipment to it knowing that it is all going to work together. I pointed out to them, for example, that when the personal computer industry was going through its growing pains, the company that won, that set the standard for the rest of the world was not the one that said "we know best and we will keep our secrets to ourselves"; it was the company that said "we will publish our ideas as an open standard and encourage everybody else to make equipment that works with ours". That is essentially why we have the IBM personal computer on virtually every desk in the world today. I have been making those points to the industry, as have DTI, working with the industry to exploit this technology and

exploit the opportunity that we are giving them by investing a very substantial amount of money, £80 million over two years, and giving them sufficient notice that that £80 million is coming along so that they can be ready to make use of it when it is there. So the commercial opportunities as well as the health benefits are something that we are very much alive to and where the mechanisms that we use to influence these things in this country seem to be working well in our favour.

Q591 *Chairman:* I should say now that Lord Drayson is back I have been asking about the impact of the NHS as a purchasing agent on some of the issues that we have been looking at and about the interaction of the market and development of products. We have had a very interesting answer. I do not know if there is anything you want to add.

Dr Ladyman: Let me just add that the other example of digital hearing aids that you gave is also a very important one, where the NHS has transformed the market-place because when digital hearing aids first came out prices were quite often around the £1,000 mark but the NHS, by making a huge investment in digital hearing aids, has got the price down to at one stage I think we were getting them for £60 each.

Chairman: Keep it up!

Q592 *Lord Drayson:* We have heard from witnesses to the inquiry that there is quite a divergence in response by industry to the needs of the ageing population. You see examples in the health care industry of bio-tech and pharmaceutical industries which seem to be very aware and very much on the case, but in other areas we are picking up evidence of a little ageism in industry and a lack of understanding of the impact an ageing population is going to have, and a lack of know-how really as to how to incorporate that into new products that best suit their needs. Is that an impression which you also share? If so, what role, if any, is there for the Government to try and change this?

Dr Ladyman: I would not put the blame entirely on industry, to be frank with you. I think all of us in this country—and I include politicians, citizens, as well as industry—have not been quick enough to realise the demographic changes that we are going to go through over the next 50 years. Some of you may have heard me in recent speeches and certainly in yesterday's launch of the Green Paper talking about the fact that by 2050 we expect there to be about four times as many people needing care as there are today, and those people's care needs will be far more intensive than they are today. One of the points I have been making to those companies that might be able to develop assistive technologies is just to point out to them the huge opportunity that that presents for them. There are other areas as well. 70 per cent of us now are homeowners and we do not want to become renters when we retire and yet in terms of extra care housing it is the housing associations creating properties for let which at the moment are leading the extra care housing accommodation industry. I have been holding dinners with developers and with others, and in speeches and other meetings I have been making this point to them that there is a huge, huge, mega-billion pound industry out there in creating the sort of accommodation that older people want. Allowing them to buy it also has the advantage as a by-product that they can transfer some equity into their accommodation and we do not use the value of that equity when we are working out how much they should pay for their social care. So not only is it good socially but it a very good way of leaving something to the kids and not having the problems of all your money being used to pay for your social care costs. Yet at the moment the private sector is not getting into that extra care industry in anything like the numbers that I would like to see, so it is a matter of me continually having to remind them, working out what the barriers are, the Department having symposia with them and trying to work out what the problems are and removing those problems in order to try to get them working in this area. We are doing that on extra care housing. We are doing it on technology. We will do it on any other area that we come across. The one thing I would say about the technology area though is that it is probably not a good comparison to compare pharmaceutical companies with these technology companies. Before I became an MP I worked for the biggest of them, I worked for Pfizer. It is the biggest pharmaceutical company in the world. It is worth tens of billions of pounds. You cannot compare the response that an organisation of that size can make with the response that a small technology company capitalised at a couple of million pounds can make. You are not comparing apples with apples. So we should not be too hard on the technology companies.

Q593 *Chairman:* If I could take you up on that point because I think that is a fair point you make about the pharmaceutical companies. If you compare, for example, a small biotechnology company with 50 or 60 employees and their attitudes towards developing products for an ageing population with a computer software company of the same market capitalisation, the same age profile of the workforce, et cetera, you find chalk and cheese in terms of the attitude of the people in those companies towards developing those products. Bluntly, they do not think it is "cool" to develop products for that population. Is there something that we can do to try and shift those perceptions?

Dr Ladyman: I do not have any firm evidence that is the case but instinctively I can agree with you, because I can see from my own experience of working with some of these companies that there will be companies that have an almost ageist attitude to developing products for older people. What we as Government need to do is to keep telling them about the demographic changes to our society. If you are not selling to older people in a generation's time, you will not be selling to many people at all because that is the way our society will be. We keep having to get those messages over. We have to work hard with DTI and ourselves to position British industry to support older people and to exploit the market opportunities that they are going to offer in years to come. At the end of the day the commercial directors of those companies will do their sums and they will make them change.

Q594 *Baroness Emerton:* One of the witnesses we heard from emphasised the fact that most people that are involved in marketing are young people who are not interested in the older market at all, and in fact have not only no interest but no knowledge base. We wondered whether there was any way in which in the training of those going into marketing you could make them see that there are, just as you have been saying, great opportunities for the future in marketing for the older generation?
Dr Ladyman: I think that is a question that you would probably have to address to DTI ministers because I think you are getting more into their territory than mine, but as somebody who has an interest in this both as a British taxpayer and as somebody who in a few years' time will be reaching that category of being an older person, I entirely agree with you. I think we need to work hard at it. The way to deal with it is to make sure that they understand the commercial opportunity that there is out there. Older people have many advantages from the point of view of marketing. There are going to be a lot more of them. They have had a lifetime of work to save up some money so they have got some money to spend on your products. Those two things together, as I say, will speak to commercial directors in the years to come and I have no doubt that the commercial directors will change their companies to address that market.

Q595 *Baroness Walmsley:* Some of them have been able to save up a lot of money but there is a perception, and I think justified, that an awful lot of people do not have a lot of disposable income. Profit, of course, is cool, but I think there is a perception that there is not a lot of profit when you are trying to sell to a market-place that has not got a lot of money and where price is really very, very sensitive. Is there

anything that it is appropriate for the Department to do in that respect?
Dr Ladyman: Absolutely.

Q596 *Baroness Walmsley:* You are big purchasers.
Dr Ladyman: We are big purchasers and that is one of the reasons why we have started down this route of investing taxpayers' money in assistive technology, because if we left it to individuals to buy assistive technology and they could not afford to buy it, the result would therefore be they would have more accidents, end up in hospital and the taxpayer would pay even more for them. So it is far better for us to make investment in preventing people from becoming sick, and that is what we are intending to do. Of course we have people within the Department of Health who have an expertise in understanding the market-place and negotiating contracts with purchasers, and I can assure you—and I will not give publicly too much detail of what I have asked them to do—I have had meetings with those individuals and I have got them working on how we best can drive down the price of technologies using our investment and boosting the market-place.

Q597 *Chairman:* Clearly Japan was a good place to go to take evidence because they are further down the demographic change road than we are.
Dr Ladyman: Exactly, but interestingly one of the lessons that came back was that whereas we are focusing on assistive technology and the telecare market, preventative health, home alarms, that type of thing, the Japanese appear to be investing more in health-related technology. They are looking more at things like having a wrist strap that tells you when your blood pressure is going up or monitoring heart beat and those types of things, in other words predicting when you are about to have a medical emergency so that you can get into the A&E room before you have that medical emergency. They have gone down a different route than we have. We are at this time looking more at how we can do things like, for example, having alarms on your fridge door so if you do not open the fridge door sufficiently often somebody from the social care world will come round and find out and pressure sensors and fall sensors and those types of technology around the home. It is interesting that two different communities facing the same problem seem to have decided to try and address it in a different way. One of the things that we have to do, of course, is to put that together and hopefully British industry can be successful in both those market-places.

Q598 *Chairman:* Any written material you have or your officials could let us have on that would be very useful because it is an avenue that we have been exploring. I did not know about the mission to Japan and what lies behind it.
Dr Ladyman: I am happy to drop you a line to tell you about that.
Chairman: Can I say thank you very much indeed. It has been a very helpful session; we very much appreciate it. We look forward to you reacting to our report when we finally decide what to say.

Supplementary evidence from the Department of Health

You asked the Department of Health to provide the Sub Committee on Scientific Aspects of Ageing with an informed estimate on how UK research expenditure on ageing and age-related diseases compare with other countries, which undertake similar research.

The Department has approached a wide range of sources for the information requested, including DH funded research units which specialise in international comparative work, national research councils (MRC and ESRC) major international research funders such as the US National Institute of Ageing, the National Ageing Research Institute, Australia, the Canadian Institute of Health Research, and the European Research Network as well as the OECD and WHO. Despite these efforts, we have not been able to obtain reliable international comparisons of the costs of research on the health of older people. The reason for this is threefold:

(i)   Government departments do not appear systematically to collect expenditure data on "ageing"—research;

(ii) The definition of "research on ageing" varies from country to country and even between different research funders within countries. In particular, it varies in terms of the extent to which it contains and/or combines research on the biophysical process of ageing and that on the treatment and care of older people;

(iii) Some comparative data are available for research spend on specific conditions, such as stroke, CHD or cancer, which are particularly associated with ageing, but these conditions are not confined to older age groups and it is difficult to disentangle the proportion of research spend specifically targeted at older people.

We have been able to obtain limited comparative data on some of the "conditions associated with ageing", although the figures need to be treated with extreme caution, given the different ways in which they have been derived and collated.

Table 1   International comparison of research expenditure by disease type

Funding body		Year	Funding ($)	Funding (£M)
Cancer				
USA	National Cancer Institute (total budget)	FY 2004	4,735.9	2,461.6
Canada	Canadian Institute of Health Research	2003–04	94.0	40.5
Australia	National Health and Medical Research Council	2003	70.0	28.9
UK	DH and MRC	2002–03		211.2
Cardiovascular Disease				
USA	National heart, lung and blood Institute (total budget)	FY 2004	2,791.8	1,451.1
Canada	Canadian Institute of Health Research	2003–04	109.0	47.0
Australia	National Health and Medical Research Council	2003	45.0	18.5
UK	NHS (cardiovascular disease and stroke) and MRC (circulatory diseases)	2000–01		75.6

We understand that Help the Aged has provided the Committee with some information on estimated comparative spending on ageing research in their written evidence:

— USA Government Research Expenditure on Ageing: ca €632 million.

— UK Government Research Expenditure on Ageing: ca €300 million.

— EU Expenditure on Ageing: ca €200 million.

However, they also recognise that, because of the problems of definition the comparisons are not robust. In order to deliver a reliable response to the Committee's question, the Department would need to commission new empirical work.

Data is available from the OECD, which provides international comparisons on health expenditure per capita and age.

Table 2   Health expenditures and share of the population aged 65 and over

Country	Percentage of GDP spent on health 1998[c]	Ratio of health expenditure old/young[a,c]	Percentage of population over age 65 1998[d]	Estimated percentage of GDP spent on health for the elderly[b]
United States	13.6	3.8 (1)	12.4	4.8
Germany	10.5	2.7 (2)	15.9	3.5
France	9.6	3 (3)	15.7	3.4
Canada	9.5	4.9 (2)	12.4	3.9
Australia	8.3	4.0 (2)	12.1	2.9
United Kingdom	6.7	3.9 (3)	15.7	2.8

Notes: a. Health expenditure for the population aged 65 over health expenditure for the population aged 0-64.
b. This share is a first stage estimate, using the existing ratio and applying it to the 1998 expenditure.
c. OECD Health Data.
d. UN population statistics.
(1) 1995; (2) 1994; (3) 1993.

Source: ORGANISATION FOR ECONOMIC CO-OPERATION AND DEVELOPMENT, Healthy Ageing and Biotechnology, Policy Implications of New Research. 2002.

Total (public plus private) health spend as a percentage of gross domestic product (GDP) in the UK for this year 2004–05, is forecast at 8.3 per cent. The spending plans announced by the Chancellor mean that by 2007–08 we expect the UK share of GDP spent on health to be 9.2 per cent—well above the current European average.

March 2005

Supplementary evidence from the Department of Health

Annex A

FUNDERS' FORUM FOR RESEARCH ON AGEING AND OLDER PEOPLE AND COORDINATION OF CLINICAL RESEARCH ACTIVITY

The Funders' Forum was established in 2000. It is made up of senior representatives from the following organisations:

UK Health Departments

Office of Science and Technology

Economic and Social Research Council

Engineering and Physical Sciences Research Council

Biotechnology and Biological Sciences Research Council

Medical Research Council

Stroke Association

Alzheimer's Society

British Heart Foundation

Joseph Rowntree Foundation

Wellcome Trust

Help the Aged

Nuffield Foundation

The Forum last met in June 2003. For a time following that meeting, there was uncertainty about its future. That uncertainty has now been resolved: the Forum will be re-convened; a new Chairman has been appointed; and the UK Clinical Research Collaboration's (UKCRC) core team will provide day-to-day support of its work.

The organisation of the Funders' Forum by the UKCRC will ensure a coordinated approach to funding research and developing the research agenda.

The Department has pursued this strategy in respect of clinical research more generally. The UK Clinical Research Collaboration was set up in April 2004 as a partnership between government, the charity sector, the private sector, and the public. Its broad aim is to improve national health, increase national wealth, and enrich world knowledge by harnessing the clinical research potential of the NHS. The Collaboration will oversee the translation ofscientific advances into patient care and promote the growth in research activity, infrastructure and capacity needed to achieve this.

The funding to support this growth will be invested in the first instance in research networks covering mental health (a core component of the National Institute for Mental Health), children's medicines, diabetes, dementia and neurodegenerative diseases, and stroke. These networks are being modelled on the successful Cancer Research Network set up in 2001. Although not focused explicitly on ageing, they will cover many of the main conditions associated with ageing. Neurodegenerative diseases like Parkinson's, Alzheimer's and stroke, for example, disproportionately affect older people. The work of the networks will significantly advance our ability to understand and deal with these disabling diseases of old age.

The reinvigorated Funders' Forum, working from its UKCRC base, will involve key partners from the research councils and will continue to encourage interdisciplinary research. The Forum—chaired by Help the Aged—will bring together a wide range of relevant funders. A UKCRC based programme manager who will facilitate collaboration, information gathering and exchange will support its work.

In addition to information exchange, the function of the Forum will be to ensure greater coherence in the research commissioning process avoiding duplication and omission and identifying areas for joint funding. In so doing, it will help individual funding bodies such as DH to define its distinctive commissioning agenda.

Annex B

IMPACT OF THE RAE ON ACADEMIC CLINICAL GERONTOLOGY

1. The Government Department with responsibility for the Research Assessment Exercise (RAE) is the Department for Education and Skills. Following the outcome of the 2001 RAE, a review of research assessment was launched in June 2002. The review was owned by the four UK higher education funding bodies and led by Sir Gareth Roberts, President of Wolfson College, Oxford.

2. The Department of Health submitted the attached response to the public consultation that formed part of the review. The response did not refer to academic clinical gerontology specifically, but several of the points mentioned are relevant to this field.

3. The Department of Health has ongoing discussion with the Higher Education Funding Council for England (HEFCE) on issues including the RAE, in particular through the DH/HEFCE Strategic Alliance for Health and Social Care.

4. The Department of Health is encouraged by the efforts being made by the funding bodies to ensure that the 2008 RAE gives appropriate recognition to all types of research including applied research, practice-based research and interdisciplinary research.

JOINT FUNDING BODIES' REVIEW OF RESEARCH ASSESSMENT

Response from the Department of Health to the public consultation launched in September 2002

We welcome the opportunity to contribute to this consultation. The need for an assessment system that rewards science of the highest quality is beyond question and we endorse calls for greater discrimination at the top end of the quality spectrum. As well as encouraging cutting-edge basic science it is crucial that the value of applied research receives full recognition, and we are concerned that health-related research has been disadvantaged under past arrangements for research assessment. It is also vital that future assessment systems allow capacity to develop in areas of strategic national importance including nursing and public health. Our comments are detailed below and take into account views received from the other UK health administrations.

EXCELLENCE IN RESEARCH

At the core of the Research Assessment Exercise (RAE) rating scale has been the belief that high research quality equates to international excellence. This may hold good for cutting edge basic science, but may not be appropriate for applied research or research that aims to be relevant to the situation in one particular country (the UK). There is also an urgent need for clarity about the definition of "international excellence". We consider that this should be understood to refer to research of internationally competitive quality rather than implying international generalisability.

VALUE OF HEALTH RELATED RESEARCH

The 2001 RAE made some progress in addressing concerns that had been expressed previously about the handling of health-related research in the 1996 RAE. Greater recognition was given to the value to Health Departments and the NHS of systematic reviews, meta-analysis and other methodologies important in this field, and assessment by the relevant RAE Units confirmed that the overall quality of UK health-related research had increased significantly since the previous RAE.

However, limitations in the philosophy underlying Research Assessment remain and the impact has been to undervalue and discourage university participation in the national effort to translate research into better health and social care for the population.

PRIMARY RESEARCH

To substantiate the above statements it is necessary to consider first the structure of successful primary research in the field:

(i) It is almost always multidisciplinary;

(ii) It is almost always multi-institutional;

(iii) It is usually collaborative across research and service personnel.

The reasons are that projects often have to recruit sizeable numbers of patients in a particular diagnostic category, requiring participation of several or many service providers (eg hospitals or general practices), and have to call on a wide range of skills to deliver a comprehensive result (eg typically several clinical disciplines, medical statistics, health economics). The contributors to a single project may be university or NHS or research council employees, often with honorary contracts (either NHS or academic) in addition to their substantive contract. The RAE has taken a narrow view of the research contribution of individuals, which are then aggregated to the level of a single institution but no further. The result has been a disincentive to the development of those multidisciplinary and multi-site networks that are best fitted to tackle really substantial problems in health care.

The *content* of applied health research may also be judged harshly by the criterion of "pure intellectual quality" (para 6, consultation document) since it commonly represents an incremental application of more basic research to health care. It may therefore appear somewhat derivative and lacking in new insights. Nonetheless, it represents an essential step in realising the value of the "upstream" research investment upon which it draws. Conducting valid, ethical and informative research in sick human subjects poses intellectual challenges that are not encountered in the laboratory. It is essential that research assessment should be able to give credit for "value added to professional practice, applicability, and impact within and beyond the research community" (para 6), for example in the fields of public health, healthcare in acute and community settings, and in social care.

The NHS, by virtue of its size and concentration of services, offers the UK a leading international research position. Experience has shown that the UK can successfully undertake research at the cutting edge of technology that no other country has the infrastructure to support. An example is extra-corporeal membrane oxygenation (ECMO), a technique of respiratory support in intensive care. A landmark study in neonates funded by the Department of Health has influenced practice worldwide; a second study in adults is in progress.

SECONDARY RESEARCH

The randomised controlled trial (RCT) is the clinical paradigm of the laboratory experiment. Following its innovation by the UK Medical Research Council in 1948 it has been hugely influential as a research tool to assess the efficacy of all interventions in health care. The literature now contains well in excess of half a million published trials.

Much decision-making in health care, and in the commissioning of new research, requires a valid synthesis of the research that has already been done on the topic. This requires the technique of systematic review, which uses explicit search and inclusion criteria to ensure that the evidence synthesis is so far as possible protected from bias. The statistical technique of meta-analysis may be used where appropriate to combine validly quantitative data from a number of separate trials. The UK has been a leading contributor world-wide to the methodology of research synthesis (eg the NHS Centre for Reviews and Dissemination at the University of York; the Cochrane Collaboration, initially in Oxford and now in over 50 centres internationally). The UK also leads in applying systematic reviews to decision-making at the levels of national policy (eg by the National Institute for Clinical Excellence and the National Screening Committee), of regional/local health service commissioning and of individual patient care.

Systematic review is of particular relevance to healthcare because the published research base is so rich that decision-makers are faced with a "knowledge problem", and therefore systematic reviews are now an essential component of decision-making within healthcare. Systematic reviews and meta-analysis constitute "research" in that they create generalisable new knowledge from the valid synthesis of data from multiple primary studies. However, the research assessment may under-value them on the criterion of "pure intellectual quality" (though each is challenging to do validly), but they should be given recognition for their "value added to professional practice, applicability, and impact within and beyond the research community". Failure to give systematic reviews and meta-analysis that recognition is seriously undermining the willingness of universities to host such research, which in turn is threatening the availability of scientific expertise to support decision-making in healthcare.

22 March 2005

APPROACHES TO ASSESSMENT

In general, we consider that the 2001 RAE Units of Assessment (UoAs) functioned well and we would not wish expert review to be excluded from any future system of assessment. However, future arrangements for assessment must ensure consistency not only between UoAs (or whatever succeeds them), but also between expert assessors within Units. Decision-making must rest on calibrated judgements and thresholds must be consistent. To increase objectivity, some of the metrics listed in the consultation document (under Group 2: Algorithm) could be used in conjunction with expert review.

FREQUENCY OF ASSESSMENT

The burden of work and both the direct and opportunity costs of preparing a submission for assessment are considerable. This argues for fewer major assessments. There may also be merit in avoiding the strong cyclical patterning of research activity that has occurred in recent years under the RAE. Do all subjects have to be reviewed at the same time? The RAE has had a potentially dramatic effect on income every five years. It might be easier for institutions to have income fluctuating more frequently, but between more modest ranges.

RESEARCH ASSESSMENT AND MEDICAL SCHOOLS

While it is accepted that the RAE has improved the performance of science as a whole in the UK it is not at all clear whether it has benefited clinical medicine and indeed may have harmed it. Medical schools are obliged to educate and train their students broadly. In order to do this they must teach a wide range of specialities.

One change that might be beneficial would be to reduce the expectation that 100 per cent of academic staff in medical schools should ideally be "research active" to an international level. This has clearly been the expectation under the RAE, as maximum funding would come to a unit with a 5-star rating and over 95 per cent of its staff returned. If maximum funding was given for a return at a lesser level, for example 80 per cent, this would allow medical schools to take strategic decisions on what research they would undertake and who would undertake the research, and would take the pressure off those who undertake the many other vital roles in academic medicine.

We would also want future systems of research assessment to give equal weight to the contributions of all university-employed staff, irrespective of whether they are funded from HEFCE allocations or by the NHS.

NURSING AND ALLIED HEALTH PROFESSIONS

We have had mounting concerns that less well established disciplines such as nursing research or Allied Health Professions' (AHPs) work have been disadvantaged in a process where the quality standards have risen faster than such new subjects could be expected to keep up. This is discouraging at the personal level and financially damaging at the institutional one. This becomes even more pronounced since such new topics are frequently based in newer universities with only limited research resources.

The report of the joint HEFCE/DH task force on research in nursing and AHPs (November 2001) highlighted the underfunding in this field. In response to the report's recommendations, the Department is now funding researcher development and postdoctoral awards in nursing and AHPs. It is vital that future arrangements for research assessment make provision for the funding councils and universities to support the development of research capacity in emerging areas of strategic national importance including nursing and AHPs through, for example, a development fund. This also applies to other areas within the more established field of health services research.

IMPLICATIONS FOR PRE-REGISTRATION EDUCATION FOR PROFESSIONAL GROUPS

The Department would be concerned if any developments in research assessment deterred higher education institutions from seeking contracts for pre-registration education for professional groups in which research capacity is currently under-developed, and therefore high scores may not be achieved in assessment exercises.

HEALTH SCIENCES AS AN ENTITY

We see some merit in assessing all the UoAs related to clinical sciences together and aggregating the units to a greater or lesser extent. This could allow some of the special considerations pertaining to these subjects to be taken into account. In particular, there would be a need to nurture research capacity in certain disciplines critical to effective applied research (statistics, health economics) and promote emerging research capacity in other areas (nursing, AHPs).

April 2005

Written Evidence

Memorandum by the Biosciences Federation

INTRODUCTION

1. The Biosciences Federation was founded in 2002 in order to create a single authority within the life sciences that decision-makers are able to consult for opinion and information to assist the formulation of public policy. It brings together the strengths of 33 member organisations, including the Institute of Biology, which represents 45 additional affiliated societies (see Appendix). The organisations that have already joined the Biosciences Federation represent a cumulative membership of some 70,000 bioscientists and cover the whole spectrum from physiology and neuroscience, biochemistry and microbiology to ecology and agriculture. The Biosciences Federation is a registered charity (no 1103894).

2. This submission was informed in particular by a contribution from the British Society for Research on Ageing. As a consequence of the expertise on which the Federation was able to call, the submission focuses on how advances in the knowledge of biological processes of ageing can improve the quality of life of older people, rather than on developments in technology and design.

THE BIOLOGICAL PROCESS OF AGEING

3. Ageing is a normal biological process that is distinct from, but is a primary risk factor for, many late life degenerative diseases such as cancer and cardiovascular disease. The ageing process also imposes physiological deficits on the organism that are potent causes of the increased mortality and morbidity seen in the elderly population, including cognitive decline, decline in muscle and bone strength and balance, decreased efficiency of the immune system, sensory impairments, incontinence, and dermatological problems. Thus, as a result of damage and disordered function at the cell and tissue levels, ageing produces increased frailty of the whole organism. Evidence suggests that many of the degenerative effects of the process will be ameliorated through appropriate environmental interventions, including improved nutrition and other lifestyle changes such as avoiding UV exposure. Genetic therapies might also become more relevant in the future.

Promising avenues of research

4. A high priority for research should be to understand how ageing is a risk factor for multiple diseases. This requires a deep understanding of the basic processes of cell biology, including cell division and processes leading to cell death, and the mechanisms of continued control of gene expression. Research in simple organisms has identified genes that have an important influence on life span. Genetic research will open up new approaches to prolonging healthy life.

5. Work with model organisms is revealing that interventions such as dietary restriction and reduced signalling through the insulin/insulin-like growth factor pathway can extend lifespan and delay the onset of ageing-related pathologies. The organism is kept in a youthful state for longer, and the effect appears to be conserved across the animal kingdom. The challenge in future years is to understand how this pathway determines lifespan so that physiological insights obtained can be harnessed to improve human well-being.

6. Patients with a rare genetic disease, Werner's syndrome, show the accelerated development of many classical age-related diseases. The syndrome is now known to be caused by the premature accumulation of "senescent" cells. Future research will focus on determining the scale of the contribution that such cells make to normal ageing, and developing treatments aimed at preventing their degenerative effects.

7. UK research has demonstrated that a loss of the ability to produce new T cells is a significant cause of the failure of the immune system to fight off infection. This decline in T cell production can be prevented in several types of elderly mammal by treatment with the hormone interleukin 7 (IL-7). It has also been shown that changes in the neuroendocrine axis, primarily a decline in level of the hormone dehydroepiandrosterone (DHEA), predispose the elderly immune system to infection. The immune system is particularly vulnerable immediately after serious physical or emotional trauma such as a fall. Therapeutic intervention with IL-7 or DHEA could benefit older people within 5-10 years if suitably supported and translated into clinical practice.

8. The cognitive decline that accompanies normal ageing has a different etiology to that of senile dementia and remains poorly understood. Pharmaceutical companies have focused considerable research effort to developing medicines to treat senile dementia, but much less attention has been paid to the cognitive decline of ageing. What factors could counteract this? Is mental exercise as important as physical exercise in this regard? Could "smart drugs" help the elderly improve their mental performance? These are all important avenues for improving the well being of the population.

9. An important contributor to the reduced quality of life, and loss of independence, among the elderly is the decrease in muscle mass and reduced functional capacity of muscle. Because muscles lose their strength and bones their ability to heal, falls often lead to bone fracture, which can result in permanent immobility. Hip fracture is predisposed to by nutritional deficit, and is a major drain on the NHS and a social cost to the individuals concerned, and their families or other carers. Recent evidence has shown that community-based exercise training programmes in the healthy elderly and chronic age-related disease states can have profound effects in reversing muscle wasting and the accompanying functional deficit. Further work is required to elucidate the signalling events in muscle that result from exercise interventions.

Differences between sexes, and between different social and ethnic groups

10. Some differences would be expected between groups since longevity is recognised to be familial and to have a genetic predisposition. The sex hormones oestrogen and testosterone have important roles in the maintenance of effective skeletal muscle, while recent research has demonstrated that the immune system ages differently in men and women. The key organ responsible for the output of new T cells is the thymus, and this organ atrophies more rapidly in men than women. This appears to correlate with the increased rate of death from infection seen in elderly men, and the increased frequency of autoimmune diseases seen in elderly women. Ethnicity, environment and cultural practice are difficult to separate but all clearly influence ageing. Both diet (paragraph 5) and exercise (paragraph 9) affect ageing-related pathologies and a healthy lifestyle is more difficult for disadvantaged social groups to achieve.

THE APPLICATION OF RESEARCH IN TECHNOLOGY AND DESIGN TO IMPROVE QUALITY OF LIFE

11. More work is needed on materials used in joint prostheses to make the replacements last longer. Cross-disciplinary work in electronics and mechanics is required to develop robotics linking nerve function and muscle control. Functional electrical stimulation, that currently enables some stroke victims to be more mobile and hence less dependent, should be extended to facilitate upper body functions in the ageing.

CAPABILITY AND CAPACITY OF UK RESEARCH

How effectively is research coordinated?

12. National coordination to date has been largely ineffective at the research level, despite the creation of the National Collaboration on Ageing Research. There are two types of deficiencies: translating research discoveries made under the remit of one Research Council to clinical research sponsored by a second Research Council; and securing funding for work that currently falls between the remits of two Councils. BBSRC and EPSRC have had some success in integrating their research programmes with those of the major charities funding ageing research. The BBSRC's Experimental Research on Ageing programme, for instance, includes observers from the charity Research into Ageing. To achieve effective cooperation with this sector government must recognise that charities are mission focused and so only a small proportion of the available ageing research will be of value to any particular organisation, and that even an interested charity has only limited funds available for research.

13. To maximise the UK's return on international coordination requires recognition that (a) effective *national* coordination must be in place, (b) a national strategy for ageing research must have been agreed with the research community and underpinned with adequate resources, and (c) the international situation itself is highly dynamic so the UK must be opportunistic in finding partners. Within European Framework programmes there have been some notable triumphs for individual researchers, and some valuable networking activities have been undertaken (eg the IMAGINE network on immune ageing research in Europe). However, it is probably fair to say that the UK has not obtained full value from EU funding instruments. The impending requirement for UK institutions to secure the full economic cost of research currently threatens future UK involvement in European funding programmes.

14. At the community level, too, there is scope for translating the outcome of research much more effectively into clinical practice. Osteoporosis is a major cause of incapacity among the elderly, yet a recent EU report found that the UK has the lowest provision for bone densitometry of any member state. Likewise, vitamin D deficiency is known to be an important cause of skeletal morbidity in the elderly, and several studies have shown that giving vitamin D and calcium supplementation to elderly institutionalised individuals is associated with a significant reduction in the occurrence of fractures. Existing recommendations from expert groups including the Royal College of Physicians and the Committee on Medical Aspects of Food and Nutrition Policy remain largely unknown by the health professional community, and are yet to be translated into effective policy in spite of national service frameworks.

15. Attitudes of the elderly to lifestyle and nutrition impinge so much on the effectiveness of health promotion issues that any ambitions for an increased healthy life expectancy will require a good deal of effective, real-time communication between science researchers, health practitioners and customer representatives on such matters as target setting, resource allocation and modes of delivery.

Have the correct research priorities been identified?

16. Following the identification in 1994–95 of the ageing population as a Foresight priority area BBSRC has run two successive special initiatives, the Science of Ageing (SAGE) and Experimental Research on Ageing (ERA) programmes. The British Society for Research on Ageing considers that the areas selected for support under these programmes have captured much that basic biology has to offer in meeting the challenge posed by the ageing population.

17. However, at the awards stage of SAGE it became clear that the UK lacked a strong base in demographic analysis as applied to ageing research, and at that of ERA it was apparent that linkages between biological chemistry and gerontology could be usefully developed.

Is there sufficient research capability in the UK?

18. The Biosciences Federation is confident that the UK has sufficient research expertise to tackle all aspects of ageing research, but funding is a major problem. While the BBSRC programmes identified the right priorities, the mode of special initiative support made it difficult to sustain delivery of research in particular areas for longer than three years. Of the 28 SAGE principal investigators only 10 were able to progress their research subsequently under the ERA application criteria. This could allow gaps in UK research to develop. The capacity to conduct national research cannot be grown and sustained through this type of funding instrument. Some of the promising research highlighted in paragraphs 4-9 will require sustained investment over an extended time period. In general terms, ageing-related research receives only a fraction of the funding that goes into cancer and cardiovascular disease.

19. The largest US sponsor of ageing research, the National Institute on Ageing, has a budget four times the current *per capita* annual expenditure on biological ageing research in the UK. To match US *per capita* spending in the UK would require an additional annual investment of about £5 million per annum, which would support a research community of about 40-60 research groups working in all areas endorsed by SAGE and ERA. The multi-disciplinary nature of ageing research requires that this should be cross-Council funding.

Is the research being used to inform policy?

20. The Federation believes that research is not being used effectively to inform policy. There is no over-arching body taking responsibility for research specifically aimed at increasing or extending healthy life-span. The greatest missing element is a unifying research environment that brings all ideas together. The extreme complexity of the issues, and limited funding, mean that there is a requirement to prioritise approaches.

APPENDIX

MEMBER SOCIETIES OF THE BIOSCIENCES FEDERATION

Association for the Study of Animal Behaviour
Biochemical Society
British Association for Psychopharmacology
British Ecological Society
British Lichen Society
British Mycological Society

Genetics Society
Heads of University Biological Sciences
Heads of University Centres for Biomedical Science
Institute of Biology
Institute of Horticulture

British Neuroscience Association
British Pharmacological Society
British Society of Animal Science
British Society for Cell Biology
British Society for Developmental Biology
British Society for Immunology
British Society for Medical Mycology
British Society for Neuroendocrinology
British Society for Proteome Research
British Toxicological Society
Experimental Psychology Society

Laboratory Animal Science Association
Linnean Society
Nutrition Society
Physiological Society
Royal Microscopical Society
Society for Applied Microbiology
Society for Endocrinology
Society for Experimental Biology
Society for General Microbiology
Society for Reproduction and Fertility
UK Environmental Mutagen Society

Represented through the Institute of Biology

Anatomical Society of Great Britain & Ireland
Association for the Study of Animal Behaviour
Association of Applied Biologists
Association of Clinical Embryologists
Association of Clinical Microbiologists
Association of Veterinary Teachers and Research Workers
British Association for Cancer Research
British Association for Lung Research
British Association for Tissue Banking
British Biophysical Society
British Crop Protection Council
British Grassland Society
British Inflammation Research Association
British Marine Life Study Society
British Microcirculation Society
British Phycological Society
British Society for Allergy Environmental and Nutritional Medicine
British Society for Parasitology
British Society for Plant Pathology
British Society for Research on Ageing
British Society of Animal Science
British Society of Soil Science

Fisheries Society of the British Isles
Freshwater Biological Association
Galton Institute
Institute of Trichologists
International Association for Plant Tissue
International Biodeterioration and Biodegradation Society
Culture & Biotechnology
International Biometric Society
International Society for Applied Ethology
Marine Biological Association of the UK
Primate Society of Great Britain
PSI—Statisticians in the Pharmaceutical Industry
Royal Entomological Society
Royal Zoological Society of Scotland
Scottish Association for Marine Science
Society for Anaerobic Microbiology
Society for Low Temperature Biology
Society for the Study of Human Biology
Society of Academic & Research Surgery
Society of Cosmetic Scientists
Society of Pharmaceutical Medicine
UK Registry of Canine Behaviourists
Universities Federation for Animal Welfare

October 2004

Memorandum by The Bone and Tooth Society

1. BACKGROUND

Good health depends on physical activity. In turn, physical activity depends on healthy bones and joints. Without these, the health of our bodies is like a house built on sand. Physical activity has declined in all sections of the community and this has caused great concern because of the growing epidemic of obesity, diabetes and other adverse health effects. Counteracting the prevalent habit of sloth is rightly a major target for government and NGOs. But the barriers to achieving increased physical activity, particularly in older people have been neglected.

2. PERSPECTIVE ON HEALTHY AGEING

Older people suffer in increasing numbers from crippling disorders of their bones and joints. An international initiative, the "Bone & Joint Decade" is drawing attention to the need to devote resources to tackling this. The possibilities for community action based on existing knowledge should be exploited now. But there has been a lack of attention to the whole person in much of the current discussion. Thus, in focussing on avoiding diabetes, it is often forgotten that obesity is causally associated with degenerative osteo-arthritis, so that many obese diabetics are in great pain if they try to increase their physical activity. In these cases, the moment may have passed for effective action, which should have been taken before the development of the arthritis that typically begins in the 50s in such people.

3. MISINFORMATION LEADS TO INACTION: THE NEED FOR RESEARCH AND DISSEMINATION

Conversely, it is widely but mistakenly believed that obesity protects against osteoporotic fractures, so that expert advice about avoiding it can be conveniently ignored. There is thus a big job of education needed to optimise the achievement of good health in our "young old age". However, the knowledge base is completely inadequate. New research can show us how to achieve much better health than is now achievable. Rightly, research funding organisations are moving on from large basic projects such as sequencing the human genome to the task of connecting up our new basic knowledge with clinical and public health priorities.

4. THE ROLE OF THE BONE AND TOOTH SOCIETY

As a charity of 54 years standing whose objective is to foster research and education that provides just this form of connection as applied to the skeleton, the Bone & Tooth Society is not only the world's oldest organisation in this field, but one of its most influential and vigorous. We propose a more strategic approach to public research funding in support of the under-resourced research charities working in our area. We also wish to draw attention to the alarming shortage developing in clinical and basic scientists, which within 10 years will have a huge impact on what is achievable in all health-related fields if urgent action is not taken immediately. The Society has always been greatly interested in the application of the physical sciences in its field, on which it has been especially dependent for major advances.

5. THE PRESENT OPPORTUNITY

The government, admittedly with seemingly too tepid enthusiasm, has recently supported the development of more medical research that is directed towards translating the basic science advances of the last decades into clinical advances (UKCRC). What our Society feels strongly, based on our long-term experience, is that good clinical research translates equally as well into basic science advances as the reverse. The reverse in fact has become a mantra with which to damn clinical research. It is almost self evident to us that the study of disease shows us how to prioritise our basic science, and this is particularly clear if seen from an international perspective, based on experiences shared with international colleagues working in countries that have more successfully nurtured their translational and clinical research portfolios over the last two decades. The recent UKCRC initiative, in support of the Academy of Medical Sciences Report must be made the beginning of a sustained push to restore a balance that is sorely needed by the NHS as it struggles to find funds to treat too late what should have been prevented.

Another positive development is the growing prospect of a European Research Council. While this will clearly be focussed on larger multi-national research projects, it should be made to set a standard equally in restoring the quality of scientific peer review and in establishing strategic directions for most of our research effort, including ensuring translational relevance. The broad sourcing of scientific opinion will spread the task of scientific review beyond the present small UK circles of reviewers, where conflicts of interest have become difficult to either control or adjust for.

While there is clearly an important place for curiosity-driven research, often this forms an over-blown response to the difficulties of managing publicly-funded research that government, through neglect, places effectively into the control of their client base. University professors in charge of large departments collectively have to have various strong commitments to the *status quo*.

6. ACHIEVING HEALTHY BONES AND JOINTS: A FRESH START

One particular need in our field is for the better integration of science across disciplines. It is a nonsense that it is so difficult to get engineers, physicists and biologists to work with clinicians within the same grant-supporting system. To some extent, this is being addressed with discipline hopping awards, etc, but the real problem is that the cadre of scientific assessors frequently includes none who can take a broad and informed view of an application because none has a broad enough education, whether it be in physical sciences for medics and biologists or in biology for physical scientists. This sad, particularly British situation is in part the consequence of over-specialisation in schools and universities, with blinkering of the scientific horizon a lifelong consequence.

Secondly, there has to be a new approach to risk management of what is always a high-risk activity. It does not make sense to pour money into activities just because money was previously poured into them. This is to divert science funding to try to salvage opinions and reputations. Yet there are few safeguards. Future directions are too much in old hands or at the mercy of young opinions that are coloured by the culture of planned insecurity that has made of science an increasingly feudal and even fearful activity.

Without changing everything at once, it seems imperative that a large problem like the avoidance of forced immobility with its disastrous health and financial consequences should be thought through completely afresh. And if it became clear that barriers to interdisciplinary collaboration had to be broken down on something like a war footing for success to be likely, the necessary degree of energy follow through and commitment should be found from the very highest level of government to the bench and research ward. It is a long time ago, but the great medical research advances of WW2 driven by real energy and dedication translated into enormous numbers of lives saved in Korea and after, if not so spectacularly so in WW2 itself.

So far the Bone and Joint Decade has passed rather quietly. Sometimes it is rather too quiet just before bombs go off. Action now by the upper House might just be the stimulus that can convert years of life into years of healthy life, before we are all impoverished by the impossible task of sustaining too many old Britons in a miserable wheelchair or bed-bound half-life.

October 2004

Memorandum by The British Geriatrics Society (Scotland)

Following discussion at our recent Council meeting I have been asked to submit the following comments on behalf of BGS (Scotland):

BIOLOGICAL PROCESSES OF AGEING

A disproportionate quantity of research on genetics and molecular biology is being supported. Influences on lifestyle (exercise, nutrition, smoking etc) in later life are more promising areas of research, with the potential for immediate impact on peoples' lives, but such clinically-orientated research is not viewed as competitive by many funding councils.

A key determinant of quality of life in later life is health. As the presence of several chronic diseases is common in later life, better medical assessment, diagnosis and disease management are major influences. Concern is growing that initiatives such as intermediate care are depriving older people of access to such comprehensive geriatric assessment. There is overwhelming evidence that this approach is effective in enabling older people to remain independent for longer and to enjoy a better quality of life. Health services research on how to improve access to these cornerstones of medical/health care are urgently required.

APPLICATION OF RESEARCH IN TECHNOLOGY

Some technologies have the potential to be helpful in later life. The problem with many is expense and limited availability. The three main fears of old age are loneliness, "being a burden" and having to give up one's home to move into nursing home care. Strategies with the potential to modulate any or all of these would be welcomed.

RESEARCH CO-ORDINATION

The Charity, the Health Foundation, was a major funder of patient-orientated, clinical research. Unfortunately, it has shifted its focus away from older people. This now leaves Research into Ageing as the sole charitable funder of ageing research in the UK. There is no doubt that ageing research (and older people) is suffering as a consequence. There is major concern that major trials of therapies and pharmaceuticals still exclude "typical" older people. The mean age of participants in heart failure (a disease of old age) trials for example is 62 years, when the mean age of onset is 75 years. Arbitrary upper age limits of 70 or 75 years are still commonly applied to trials. This is not acceptable as most medicine are prescribed to older people.

Furthermore in contrast to the profile of most trial participants (male, middle aged, single pathology, otherwise fit and well, excellent compliance) the actual consumers of most medicine are female, over 75, suffering from multiple medical problems, receiving multiple different medicines, and compliance is sub optimal). This mismatch should be addressed.

September 2004

Supplementary evidence by the British Society for Research on Ageing, the British Geriatrics Society and the British Society of Gerontology[1]

BACKGROUND

The three learned societies representing professionals working in the field of gerontology (the BSRA, BSG and BGS) were all asked to give evidence to the House of Lords inquiry in to Scientific Aspects of Ageing on 12 October 2004. One of the questions raised by the select committee related to the links that existed between the three societies and other complementary organisations overseas. The accurate response was that links to international organisations were good, all three societies are members of the International Association of Gerontological and Geriatrics Societies (IAG) and the BSRA recently forged links with the American Association for Ageing Research, but there were no links currently between the three UK organisations. A consortium of representatives of the three societies (the BCCG) had existed in the recent past, but had ceased to meet essentially because it did not appear to have a useful aim or focus. As a result of the three chairs of the learned societies meeting at the House of Lords, it was agreed that a discussion should take place to identify points of common interest for the three societies, the form that any future collaboration should take and what were the possible benefits of any future joint activities for gerontological research in the UK. Subsequently a meeting was held by the chairs of the BSRA (Professor Janet Lord), BSG (Professor Chris Phillipson) and BGS (Professor Peter Crome) at Keele University on 15 March 2005.

OUTCOMES OF THE MEETING

All three chairs were keen to promote links between the three learned societies, but all agreed that these had to be useful and should help to meet the aims of each of their societies. Several potential future points of interaction emerged from the meeting:

— The three societies would collaborate to promote interdisciplinary training in gerontology, helping to meet the current gap in researchers able to work at the interface of social science, medical science and basic science in the field of ageing. In the short term this might be realised by an application to the joint research council funding initiative New Dynamics of Ageing for a PhD training network.

— Formation of a forum of the three societies (provisional name the Association of Gerontological Societies—AGES), that could act as a point of contact for policy makers influencing social, health and scientific research issues relating to old age in the UK and Europe. The forum would be publicised via links on the web sites of each of the societies and the secretariat for the forum would be based at the offices of the BGS.

— Communication between the societies to be improved, including cross-posting of society meetings and funding opportunities (especially those involving interdisciplinary projects) on each others web sites, creation of links directly to the other two societies web pages and an annual meeting of the chairs of the three societies.

— Setting up of a small workshop to improve the impact of the learned societies upon policy making in the UK. This meeting would not only discuss the current level of influence of the learned societies upon health, social and research strategies relating to ageing and the elderly, but will aim to identify which strategic issues each society feels need to be influenced by them in the coming years and what direction that policy should take. This meeting would include two to three members from each society together with representatives of Age concern and Help the Aged. The meeting will also create the programme for an interdisciplinary conference to review Gerontological Research in the UK and produce a Strategy Document to be made available to funding agencies, politicians and other interested parties. An application will be made to the SPARC initiative for the funding of the conference and the three learned societies will jointly fund the initial workshop to be held at Birmingham University in July 2005.

April 2005

---

[1] Supplementary to minutes of evidence 12th October 2004.

Memorandum by Dr S Brownsell and Professor M S Hawley

THE APPLICATION OF RESEARCH IN TECHNOLOGY AND DESIGN TO IMPROVE QOL

Assistive technology (AT) has the potential to play a vital role in helping older people to stay living at home in a more secure, safe and independent manner; which may reduce the speed of decline and need for future care and support. However, the evidence to support the widespread deployment of AT, and examples of research and development projects leading to service delivery changes is thin. Over many years Barnsley District General Hospital has been both supplying AT services to patients through its clinical engineering service, and also researching and developing the field.

It would appear that while the Government have been pro-active in developing policy (at least in some degree) to support AT, the evidence to support its widespread deployment can be sparse. There are also numerous examples of projects repeating previous work and being conducted without due attention to robust evaluation, if any evaluation has been conducted at all. Over recent years we have sought to contribute to a reliable evidence base and welcome this Committee on the scientific aspects of ageing.

1. THE ROLE OF ASSISTIVE TECHNOLOGY IN ADDRESSING THE NEEDS OF OLDER PEOPLE BOTH NOW AND IN THE FUTURE

This section summarises the results of an ongoing investigation into the role of AT in addressing the needs of older people both now and in the future. A formal literature review was conducted, seeking to identify the reasons why older people need increasing levels of care and support or move to more supportive environment, such as sheltered housing or residential care. A total of 2,037 papers were reviewed and 102 trigger factors or reasons identified.

While many trigger factors were evident in the literature, there appeared to be no ordering or ranking in terms of priority. In some ways this is perhaps surprising, as it would be assumed that planners and policy makers would require this information in order to target resources where the greatest returns may be observed. However, comparing one trigger factor against another is complex for three main reasons:

1. Trigger factors are often inter-related and it can be difficult to treat them in isolation;

2. Most of the trigger factors have been determined by qualitative investigations;

3. Studies vary in quality in terms of their approach, research rigour, and sample sizes.

In an attempt to prioritise the trigger factors local experts from housing, health, social care, voluntary services and carers representatives were invited to a stakeholder event. All of the trigger factors were randomly ordered and presented to participants who were asked to prioritise the trigger factors relative to how many older people require a change in the amount of care and support they receive as a consequence of that specific trigger factor. Group consensus for each individual trigger factor on a scale of one to five was required, with one indicating a very important trigger factor and five the least important. A total of 36 trigger factors were identified as being in the top three bands of importance and these are listed in Table 1 (in alphabetical order).

Table 1

FACTORS WHY OLDER PEOPLE NEED MORE CARE AND SUPPORT, AND THE ROLE OF AT

No	Trigger factor	No	Trigger factor	No	Trigger factor
1	A fear of falling.	13	Difficulty toileting/ continence management.	25	Needs assistance with personal care, hygiene needs, bathing, washing, dressing.
2	A major health event— such as support following a stroke or hip replacement.	14	Family, friends or neighbours can no longer provide support to maintain the person at home.	26	Occurrence of falls.
3	A perceived decline and concern for own health.	15	Family/caregiver stress.	27	Person feels isolated.

No	Trigger factor	No	Trigger factor	No	Trigger factor
4	A person feeling lonely.	16	Housework problematic (not including vacuuming).	28	Poor nutritional/dietary intake.
5	Abuse (physical or mental).	17	Inability to care for self at home.	29	Poorly maintained housing.
6	Bereavement, of a family member or friend.	18	Inability to cope with Independent Activities of Daily Living[2].	30	Presence of chronic disease (such as Parkinsons, heart problems).
7	Cognition impairment (such as dementia, confusion or memory loss).	19	Inadequate home care provision.	31	Recent onset of visual impairment.
8	Consequences of admission to hospital.	20	Managing pressure sores.	32	Requiring regular trips to hospital.
9	Depression, mental breakdown or deterioration.	21	Medication management—such as compliance problems.	33	Self perceived inability to manage alone or care for oneself.
10	Deteriorating physical functioning.	22	Mobility problems, getting around the house.	34	Self-management of health conditions (regulating insulin, dealing with the pain of arthritis).
11	Difficulty cooking for themselves.	23	Moving to be near relatives (on the advice of, or choosing to be nearer to relatives or friends).	35	Unsuitable accommodation.
12	Difficulty in managing stairs or steps.	24	Multiple minor longstanding illnesses.	36	Wound care—such as dressings, care of ulcers.

The role of AT

Having identified the trigger factors resulting in additional care and support the role AT can play in assisting, preventing, or minimising additional care and support were investigated under three headings, namely:

— Formal care services: Regular and ongoing intervention by care and support services, such as a carer, occupational therapist and so forth, not including training of AT;

— Current AT provision: Technologies that do not necessarily function without formal care services, but the main support is through technology. Such technology can assist, minimise or prevent a certain trigger factor and are commonly used by formal care and support services;

— Emerging AT: Technology to assist, prevent, or minimise the impact of a certain trigger factor. It is assumed that such technology could become part of current AT provision within five years.

Fig 1 presents each of the trigger factors of Table 1 using these three groupings above. Using this pictorial representation a number of findings are suggested.

[2] These relate to domestic tasks such as shopping, vacuuming, handling personal affairs.

FIGURE 1: THE POTENTIAL ROLE OF AT CURRENTLY AND IN THE FUTURE

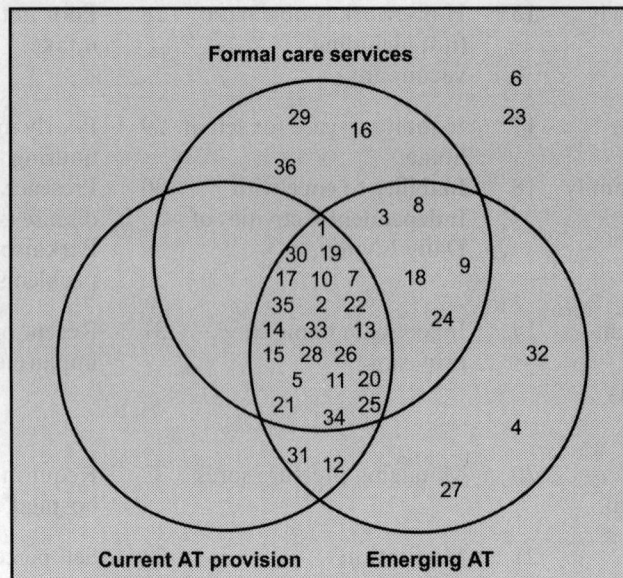

Formal care services and AT interaction

AT, when used appropriately, is a tool to assist the user, it is not necessarily the answer to all situations and neither should it be used as a last resort or in isolation of formal care services, but rather careful user centred assessment is important. Indeed Fig 2 suggests that 29 (81 per cent) of the trigger factors fall within the formal care services domain. Therefore, both now and in the future, at least to some extent, formal services are still likely to play a significant role in care provision. Fig 2 also indicates that 21 (58 per cent) of the trigger factors are in the central element consisting of all three domains. This suggests that AT has a role to play today, but that a greater role may be played in the future, but in all these situations the support of formal care services is required in combination with assistive technology. There is therefore a necessity to work with formal care services to ensure that the emerging technologies are appropriate not only to the older person, but to the professional user also.

AT cannot meet all of the trigger factors

Fig 1 suggests that 23 (64 per cent) of the trigger factors fall within the current AT provision domain, and an additional eight (22 per cent) in the emerging AT domain. In under five years AT may therefore be able to assist, prevent or minimise the impact of 86 per cent of the major trigger factors identified as resulting in more care and support for older people. However, AT is not the answer in isolation of formal care services nor can it assist in all of the trigger factors.

Emerging AT

For eight (22 per cent) of the trigger factors there is no current AT provision, but it is suggested that within five years AT could be deployed, where appropriate, as part of standard care provision. With five of these factors there is no current AT provision, but through formal care services in combination with emerging AT it is suggested that the impact of these factors can also be minimised. For example, the "Perceived decline and concern for own health", "Consequences of admission to hospital" and "Multiple minor longstanding illnesses" could be minimised by remote health monitoring where the technology monitors the health of the user and only calls for medical assistance when necessary, which should also reduce the likelihood of hospital admission.

The role of AT

Of the 36 most important trigger factors resulting in older people needing greater amounts of care and support AT can assist, prevent, or minimise the impact of 64 per cent of these trigger factors. Indeed, if the emerging AT proves successful and is in common use then AT can be utilised against 86 per cent of the trigger factors. It may be that if AT could be targeted specifically at the trigger factors as to why older people need increasing levels of care and support then this may "free up" staff time to be utilised effectively elsewhere. For example, by providing more personal services, or more one to two hours of home care services per week, and so forth.

Analysis of Table 1 suggests that 69 per cent of the trigger factors are included within health and physical aspects. This suggests that perhaps by focusing efforts on these areas we would be able to meet user needs better, help more people to stay living independently, while simultaneously reducing the demand for care and support needs.

2. FORGING SOLUTIONS FOR INDEPENDENT LIVING

We have enclosed a book, published in 2003 which is very relevant to this call. However we have attempted to provide a summary of the main points. Prof R Wootton, editor of the international journal of telemedicine and telecare commented that "this book draws together the evidence for the benefits of telecare systems and makes a powerful case for their introduction on a wide scale . . . as a source of information for healthcare planners and policy makers it will be invaluable." It covers three main areas, of which the later two will be highlighted here:

(a) The need for AT and telecare.

(b) The evidence.

(c) Implications and recommendations.

User views

The evidence section commences by focusing on the views of community alarm users towards AT. A face-to-face questionnaire was conducted with 176 community alarm users in the age range 56 to 91 with an average age of 76, living on a sheltered housing scheme in Birmingham. This represented an 89 per cent response rate and includes those both favouring and opposed to the introduction of advanced assistive technologies. The main findings were that:

— 77 per cent welcomed the prospect of automatic fall detection;

— 68 per cent welcomed lifestyle monitoring;

— 57 per cent welcomed medical monitoring; and

— 44 per cent welcome video conferencing.

In total 57 per cent of those interviewed were interested in at least three of the four, and 25 per cent interested in all four. Only 11 per cent of those interviewed were not interested in any.

Cost-effectiveness

The section continues by defining future systems that would be beneficial to users in the immediate (2nd generation system) or more long term. Based on this 2nd generation system a financial model was developed that adheres to the principles of health economics and compares the present system with the suggested 2nd generation system in the City of Birmingham with 11,500 users. In so doing it suggests the outcomes necessary by future systems if they are to be cost-effective.

Technically, the 2nd generation system is more advanced and consequently will be more expensive than the 1st generation system currently in place. The model suggests that at the start of the first year there would be £6.4 million outstanding. However, there are considerable operational savings compared to the present system and break-even is achieved during the 5th year of operation with a positive cash flow secured thereafter. Using a conservative approach, it is assumed that no interest is gained on finance after the initial loan has been repaid in which case, by the end of the system life cycle (year 10) the scenario suggests a return of the order of £8.3 million.

Sensitivity analysis reveals that the key areas are savings in the average duration of a hospital stay and the percentage of people in residential care. Changing these parameters by ± 50%, the best and worse case scenarios, suggests that the proposed 2nd generation system remains cost-effective (£0.5–£15 million).

One of the main findings was that to fully realise the benefits, a holistic approach involving collaboration across all imposed service boundaries is essential. The results of the analysis suggest that the savings appointed to the main providers are 4 per cent to housing, 47 per cent to the NHS and 49 per cent to residential care. It would seem appropriate that since the savings are appointed this way that the system is funded similarly.

Implications and recommendations

The impact of advanced telecare systems on human resources is a fundamental question which to date has been somewhat overlooked. The greater use of information and communications suggests an increased workload at the community alarm control centre for example. Modelling work suggests that at the control centre the proposed 2nd generation system actually reduces the number of calls by 57 per cent and the amount of time control centre operators are required to speak with callers by 55 per cent.

It is difficult to foresee the kind and extent of changes that could result if telecare were implemented on a large scale. AT and information and communication technologies clearly have considerable potential across many different aspects of social care. The implications for organisations and personnel are considerable. The divide between health, housing and social care will have to close for telecare to succeed and personnel will need to learn new skills and new ways of working.

It is evident that a greater degree of resources will be necessary in primary and social care and that a great reliance will be placed on computing and information access. However, perhaps the greatest implication is that, if successful, AT could assist many older and disabled people to live safely and independently in their own homes for longer. If this can be achieved, and there is evidence that such a system is wanted by users, is cost-effective and is deliverable, then the implications for service providers should be outweighed by the benefits that could be derived by introducing such systems.

The book concludes by making a number of recommendations that need to be addressed if AT is to flourish and provide users with greater levels of choice and the ability to improve their quality of life.

3. THE DEVELOPMENT OF NEW TECHNOLOGIES

The book provides a vision for future technologies based on the views of users and practitioners, technological developments, government direction, and the likely speed of organisational change. It also indicates the current level of progress/research being undertaken to meet these objectives. As such it provides an indication of where beneficial technologies should be developed over the next 15 years. A summary is provided here, but more in-depth detail can be found on pages 39–49.

2nd generation telecare systems (2003–05)

Overall, the 2nd generation telecare system provides greater support and monitoring than the present telecare equipment and removes the constraint of the user having to initiate a call for assistance. Automatic call generation and monitoring is provided through a number of new or emerging technologies, such as drug dispensers, automatic fall detection, or lifestyle monitoring. Each of the technologies included in the 2nd generation system can be provided on an individual basis so that a user may have a fall detection unit without a drug dispenser or lifestyle monitoring. The system is therefore truly plug-and-play or modular and able to address the particular "risks" of individual users. The intended users are the present community alarm users, while modules of the system may also benefit people in residential care or nursing homes. Details of the main components of this system are provided in the Appendix.

3rd generation telecare systems (2005–10)

It is envisaged that the elements in the previous generation will become more refined with time. The 3rd generation system is enhanced and made more flexible and responsive. Tasks that were previously carried out by staff but did not require contact with users are taken over by the system. This therefore enables staff to spend more time with users and provide a more caring environment. Details of the main components of this system are provided in the Appendix.

4th generation telecare systems (2010–20)

The focus of the previous generations was to monitor users and detect emergency situations. Attention was also given to prevention in respect to medical parameters, while the introduction of expert systems enabled the system to ensure that medication was prescribed correctly. The 4th generation system builds upon these previous generations by developing the system for both the user and provider.

For the user, intrusion is reduced with implanted sensors under the skin so the user no longer has to wear a pendant or similar device when in the home. When outside of this environment, the implanted sensors work in the same manner as the medical band module, communicating with the distance support module. Assistance with tasks of daily living enable users to stay independent in their own homes for longer, automatic robots conducting tasks such as cleaning. Medical professionals received support from expert systems in the 3rd generation system and developments in artificial intelligence will enable remote assessment. The Activities of Daily Living (ADL) has conventionally been used by social services in assessing older peoples need for long-term care, however this often annual "snap shot in time" assessment has often failed to assess the user as their needs change, especially relevant after hospital discharge. The 4th generation system addresses this deficiency by monitoring the user on a daily basis and automating the assessment (this could also be true for the single assessment process). Users can then be formally assessed after the system has indicated that intervention would be beneficial. This allows resources to be effectively targeted and truly allows for a preventative system, both in terms of the users health and their daily living. Details of the main components of this system are provided in the Appendix.

4. Overarching Considerations

Please note that the responses to the following sections are in relation to research and technology development in assistive technology and telecare for older people

4.1 *How effectively is research co-ordinated in the public, private and charitable sectors (including internationally)?*

There are bodies aimed at co-ordinating ageing-related research (the National Collaboration on Ageing Research—NCAR, and the Funders' Forum) but to date these appear to have had little impact on co-ordination in the field of assistive technology.

The New Dynamics of Ageing programme (led by Prof Alan Walker, University of Sheffield), has assistive technology as one of its priorities and is expected to lead to greater co-ordination of research in this field.

There is some current co-ordination in the public sector as a result of the existence of a small number of research funding programmes. An example of this is the Extending Quality Life (EQUAL) programme within the Engineering and Physical Sciences Research Council, where meetings have been held between some of the leading research groups in this field to decide upon priorities. As a result, a number of large multi-centre projects have been funded (see www.equal.ac.uk).

The European Union has no specific programme addressing older people's technology within Framework 6. There is, however, an e-inclusion sector within the IST (Information Society Technologies) programme, which may be funding current research on assistive technology. I am unaware of any means for co-ordination between this programme and UK programmes. It will be important to lobby for specific research into assistive technology for older and disabled people to be included within the EU Framework 7.

4.2 *Have the correct priorities been identified? Are there any gaps in research?*

Research into assistive and telecare technologies is still at a relatively low level and there are a great many gaps. Research and development is required across the board.

— Development of new assistive and telecare technologies

There is huge potential to apply existing and emerging technologies to the benefit of older people, especially information and communication technologies (ICTs), sensor technologies and signal and information processing technologies (eg speech recognition). Research is needed to analyse the needs of older people and to apply technologies to address these needs. Thus, research should be user- or application-led, as opposed to technology-led. Fig 2 shows the research process.

FIGURE 2: THE RESEARCH PROCESS INVOLVED IN THE DEVELOPMENT OF NEW ASSISTIVE AND TELECARE TECHNOLOGIES

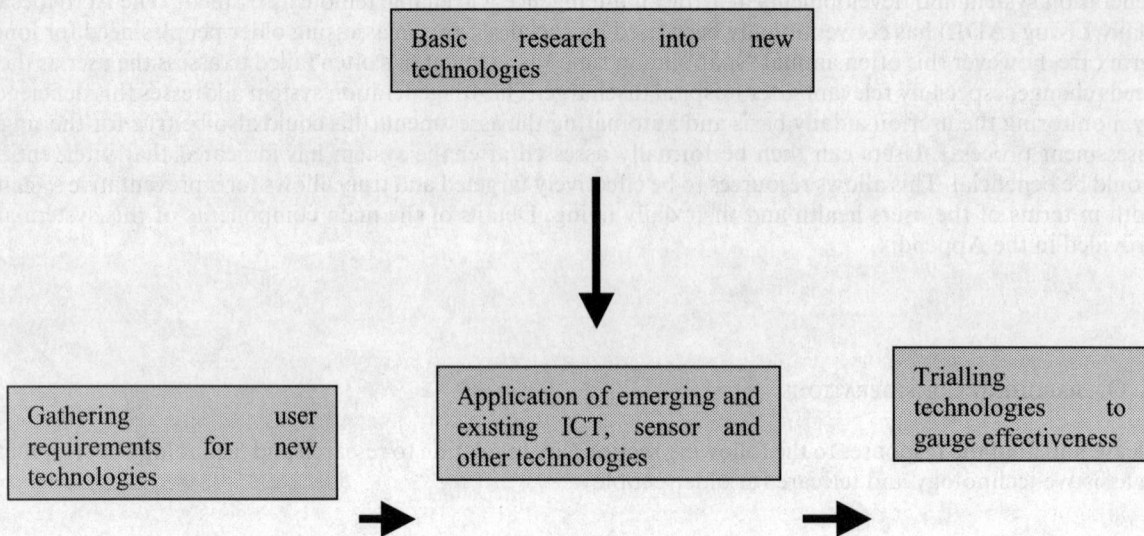

```
                    ┌─────────────────────────────────┐
                    │ Basic    research    into    new │
                    │ technologies                     │
                    └─────────────────────────────────┘
                                    │
                                    ▼
┌──────────────────────┐  ┌─────────────────────────┐  ┌─────────────────────────┐
│ Gathering       user │  │ Application of emerging  │  │ Trialling               │
│ requirements    for  │  │ and existing ICT, sensor │  │ technologies         to │
│ new technologies     │  │ and other technologies   │  │ gauge effectiveness     │
└──────────────────────┘  └─────────────────────────┘  └─────────────────────────┘
```

— Human factors involved in telecare design.

One of the main barriers to the effective utilization of assistive technologies and telecare is the interface, currently efforts have cantered around developing the basic technology rather than ensuring the appropriate interaction with the end users.

— User perspectives in telecare (eg acceptability, ethics etc)

There is little real understanding of user perspectives in relation to assistive technologies and telecare. Although studies have suggested that AT and telecare would be accepted by users, the acceptability of these types of technologies in general needs further research. One crucial factor in emerging concepts of monitoring technologies is its acceptability and ethical position. A consistent refrain in discussions with users over the deployment of monitoring technologies is that of "Big Brother", meaning the intrusive observation of people's everyday lives. Whilst it is anecdotally observed that people are willing to accept monitoring if they can see benefits to themselves, much more in depth study of the ethical aspects of monitoring is needed.

— Development of the most effective means of assessment for telecare

Within the field of telehealth there is an emerging robust evidence base for specific applications, such as tele-dermatology, but within AT and telecare such evidence is sparse. The recent Audit Commission report 2004, sought to add to the evidence but it may have over emphasised the case. Companies are also often heavily involved in the evaluation of their own products and this has, on occasion, resulted in the press publishing misleading articles of the benefits of interventions. This raises serious issues, for example care packages could be modified and a reduced number of support hours given in combination with the technology intervention. Based on the "evidence" from the manufacturers this may seem appropriate and is an appealing proposition, but if that evidence is fundamentally flawed and the technology does not work as well as suggested then this puts people at an increased level of risk. This is currently happening and it is suggested that only by external parties conducing robust research will this be addressed.

Current studies also tend to have questionable evaluations using questionnaires developed in house, which may have biased the result to be more positive than they actually are, rarely utilise control groups, and often allow recruits to self-select (thus only involving those people who are positive to the intervention). Large scale robust trials are therefore required, by independent organisations, that use accepted methodologies and research tools to learn the correct value of the emerging devices and seek to understand how different organisations and departments are required to work together. While a randomised control trial may not be the most appropriate method in all cases, research of a high standard is required. Such trials are desperately needed, and there are institutions in the UK that have the required AT and research knowledge but finance to conduct them is difficult to acquire.

— Assessment of efficacy, effectiveness and cost-effectiveness of telecare interventions

Evidence of the effectiveness of assistive technologies and telecare is sparse. There have been a large number of pilot projects in this field but little definitive evidence, largely because the pilots have been set up as service developments rather than research projects. Several cost models have been developed suggesting financial savings but these are based on assumptions of the performance of the intervention technology and there is limited support from trials that these assumptions are accurate. Research is needed to provide evidence to underpin the further deployment of these technologies. This can be seen as equivalent to the evidence that is crucial before the widespread introduction of new drugs and techniques into health care. The Health Technology Assessment programme and NICE should be more engaged with these technologies.

— Service delivery and organisation related to assistive technology and telecare services

There is little knowledge concerning the best way to organise and deliver services to support the effective deployment of assistive technologies and telecare. This evidence needs to be collected and information disseminated to service delivers. Specific attention needs to be given to how and who purchases assistive technology and telecare, who monitors the alert calls, what are the response protocols to respond to alert situations, who responds, and who pays for ongoing monitoring and call out costs. Many of these issues cross departments and the "glue" fitting the system together just isn't there.

4.3 *Is there sufficient research capability in the UK?*

Research into AT and telecare needs to span a wide range of disciplines, including:

— Engineering.

— Clinical disciplines.

— Social science.

— Information science.

— Cognitive science.

Research projects in this field, in the majority of cases, require multi-disciplinary input. This is a factor that has been recognized by EPSRC in the funding of EQUAL projects. Whilst there appears to be sufficient research capability within most of these disciplines to apply to the area, there are some gaps.

The expertise that is in short supply is at the interface between engineering and clinical/sociological disciplines. This can be illustrated with reference to Fig 2, showing the research process necessary to develop new technologies. Social/clinical researchers have the expertise to elicit user needs and user views (using largely qualitative but also quantitative research techniques). However, user views in relation to technology are often best researched by those who have knowledge and training in technology/engineering as well as training in social/clinical disciplines. This becomes even more apparent in the translation of user views into engineering requirements, where an in-depth understanding of the user is required alongside an in-depth understanding of the technology potential and limitations. This is also true at the other end of the process, where trials of the technology are carried out and user experiences and views here are invaluable in improving the usability and usefulness of technologies.

There is a need to train more people jointly in the engineering and clinical/social disciplines (this happens currently in Medical Physics/Clinical engineering/Bioengineering) and to support centres that are developing multi-disciplinary expertise combining these areas of expertise and developing methodologies for technology-related research across the disciplinary divide.

The commercial sector in AT and telecare is dominated by small companies, whose resources to deploy in R&D are very limited. As a result, there appears to be a low level of research and innovation in these companies in the UK. It is essential to encourage (through grants and other financial incentives) the AT and telecare commercial sector to work more closely with research centres in Universities and the NHS.

4.4 *Translating research into practice*

For AT and telecare to flourish it is vitally important for research to impact on policy and for service providers to embrace change. The lessons from other areas should be applied and these show success and speed of the adoption/diffusion process depends on (http://www.cmwf.org/publications/publications__show.htm?doc__id = 233248):

1. the roles of senior management and clinical leadership;

2. the generation of credible supportive data;

3. an infrastructure dedicated to translating the innovation from research into practice;

4. the extent to which changes in organizational culture are required;

5. and the amount of coordination needed across departments or disciplines.

The translation process also depends on the characteristics and resources of the adopting organisation, and on the degree to which people believe that the innovation responds to immediate and significant pressures in their environment.

The challenge is therefore to acquire the appropriate evidence base to provide credible supportive data which engages both senior management and providers at all levels so that change is driven from the top and truly embraced at a service level for the benefit of the people we are all trying to serve.

2ND GENERATION TELECARE SYSTEMS (2003–05)

Main features

Fall detection: A worn device to detect the presence of a fall and automatically instigate a call for assistance.

Fire detection: Detect the presence of fire, inform the user and if necessary to contact the control centre.

Gas detection: Gas levels should be monitored and the gas supply terminated if appropriate.

Temperature analysis: Analysis of room temperature and if necessary inform the user of a risk of hypothermia.

Water detection: Suspend the water supply if the bath, shower or sink overflows.

Incontinence monitoring: To indicate when incontinence pads need replacing.

Security: To provide a "panic button" at the front door and the other functions of a standard burglar alarm. Provide a record of when carers arrive and leave the residence. Allow authorised access to the users EPR[3] (Electronic Patient Record) and information services.

Drug dispenser: Dispenses the required drugs when required and reminds the user to take their medication if they forget.

Lifestyle monitoring: To detect changes in the lifestyle of the occupants(s) that may indicate assistance is required.

Medical monitoring: Stand alone equipment to measure the medical characteristics of users and facilitate a call for assistance if outside of allowable parameters.

Virtual consultations: Remote medical consultations with video conferencing technology, integrated with the medical monitoring stations.

Intelligent Home Alarm System (IHAS): This is the hub of the home based equipment and provides control to the various components of the home based technology; communicating with the user(s) and external organisations.

Electronic Patient Record (EPR): Contains all of the appropriate information regarding a particular user.

GP surgery: Provide medical assistance and video consultations.

Control centre: Provide support and act as a first point of call to users.

Hospital health services: Facilitate medical assistance and suspend and reinstate home care as necessary (information provided by updating the EPR)

---

[3] Further information on EPR's can be found at http://www.doh.gov.uk/ipu/whatnew/eprdefv3.htm

3RD GENERATION TELECARE SYSTEMS (2005–10)

Main features

Components of 2nd generation system: the previous modules are available in the 3rd generation system.

Lifestyle monitoring: identify the movements of users without having to use tagging, also measure the users gait and how often they climb stairs (if present).

Security: more developed burglar alarm and automatic recognition of user. Access to EPR for all professionals.

Weight detection: measures the users weight.

Drug dispenser: enable repeat prescription reminders and analysis of the medication held within the dispenser.

Medical band: provide 24-hour continuous medical monitoring for users wearing a medical bracelet or vest.

Distance support: communicate with the medical band and allow the user to call for assistance when away from the home.

Intelligent Home Alarm System (IHAS): the ability to track the user if they fail to return home at a specified time.

User control: provide verbal communication with the home based system.

Virtual GP/neighbourhood: provide remote physiotherapy and exercise schemes.

GP surgery: expert system to suggest to the GP what medication they should prescribe.

Pharmacist: enable paperless prescription.

EPR: store the users data.

Control centre: support for foreign languages and analysis of users EPR's to ensure that correct medication is being used.

Hospital Health Services: no change when compared to the role undertaken in the 2nd generation system.

4TH GENERATION TELECARE SYSTEMS (2010–20)

Main features

Components of 2nd and 3rd generation system: the previous modules are available in the 4th generation system.

Water detection: monitor the washing habits of the user.

Incontinence detection: detect the onset of incontinence.

Robotic assistance: provide mechanical assistance with vacuum cleaning, retrieving items from the floor and dressing.

Virtual GP/neighbourhood: the scanning of letters and forms that cause distress. Assistance being provided from friends or relatives, and ultimately the control centre or social services.

Implanted medical monitoring: implanted sensors measuring vital signs 24-hours a day.

Intelligent Home Alarm System (IHAS): route emergency fire calls directly to the fire brigade.

User control: the use of the mind to control electronic devices around the home.

Control centre: through an expert system, each users EPR is analysed under the automatic ADL assessment.

Memorandum by the Centre for Ageing and Public Health, London School of Hygiene and Tropical Medicine

RESEARCH INTO AGEING

1. At the same time that concerns about the implications of an ageing population rise higher on agendas, the pace of scientific study of the biological processes underlying ageing has been accelerating. Evidence submitted by others will doubtless provide a comprehensive picture. It seems that new knowledge is adding complexity to earlier rather simple ideas based on evolutionary arguments. We may certainly hope that advances in understanding of the basis of ageing at molecular and cellular levels will lead in due course to medical interventions that prolong life and reduce age-related illness. However, the timescale for practical outcomes seems likely to be medium to long term.

2. In the meantime, there is a substantial research agenda that will help generate the knowledge necessary (a) to intervene more effectively in the processes that lead to age-associated impairments of physical, sensory and cognitive functions and thence disability, and loss of capability, leading to dependence; and (b) to promote active, healthy ageing. This research agenda may be outlined as follows:

— Age-associated diseases, where the paradigm is the world-wide effort in academia and industry to understand the basis of Alzheimer's disease, with the aim of devising rational therapeutic interventions. Other major age-associated diseases which are the subject of substantial research effort are cardiovascular disease and cancer. On the other hand, diseases which have a big an impact on quality of life in old age without being life-threatening receive less attention, in particular osteoarthritis and loss of vision through macular degeneration.

— "Frailty" in older people designates the consequence of the co-existence of chronic conditions which are not capable of consideration as a single pathology, and which require long term and complex interventions, including rehabilitation. There is a need to move towards more evidence-based practice, based on sound evidence derived from multidisciplinary research.

— Healthy ageing, the phenomenon whereby many people manage to avoid ill health in old age (at least until near to death), requires close study to identify the determinants of this desirable state of affairs and the interventions—both medical and social—that will best promote this. The psychology of normal ageing needs to be better understood, not least on account of current expectations that as people live longer they will need to continue to work longer, raising questions about the maintenance of cognitive capabilities.

— Modifying the physical environment to reduce the disadvantage experienced by people with disabilities. Research is needed to underpin more inclusive approaches to design, as well as to devise better assistive technologies.

— Modifying the social environment to foster well-being and lessen the loss of capability experienced in old age, whether on account of physical and mental disability, poverty and loneliness. This includes the design and testing of interventions to promote health through strengthening social interaction and support.

— Improved modelling and forecasting of different states of health of the population, including in relation to different potential family support structures—important to clarify the implications of demographic trends and identify policy options.

3. Much of the research outlined above is carried out through the analysis of ageing in human populations, including both demographic analysis of Census and other official data, and epidemiological surveys and trials in sample populations. Topics that can be fruitfully investigated through a population-based approach include environmental and genetic risk factors for age-related diseases, and the efficacy and effectiveness of interventions designed to ameliorate ill health, disability and social disadvantage in later life. Population-based studies are important for the investigation of differences between men and women, and those in different ethnic and socio-economic groups; variations between populations—either geographically or temporally; understanding of cohort and life course influences; and forecasting and projection.

4. Understanding the processes involved in human ageing and tackling age-related ill heath requires that subjects be followed over considerable periods of time in what are known as longitudinal studies. Longitudinal studies require more commitment and administrative support than do the generality of biomedical and social science research.

5. One important recent initiative has been the establishment of the English Longitudinal Study of Ageing, the first fieldwork for which took place in 2002, involving a sample of 12,000 people over the age of 50 whose health, economic position and quality of life are to be followed as they age. It is noteworthy that half the

funding for the first five years' work is coming from the US National Institute for Aging, with the remainder from eight UK government departments. No UK Research Council is supporting this study. It will be important that the data collected in this study is made available to the research community if best value is to be obtained for the effort expended.

SUPPORT OF RESEARCH

6. Both ageing as a policy area and ageing research lack a single focus within government. Four research councils—MRC, ESRC, BBRC and EPSRC—are active in funding research on ageing and age-related matters. The latter three Research Councils have focused programmes of relevant research, whereas the MRC generally supports ageing research through its mainstream funding mechanisms (although it does on occasion co-fund research lead by other public bodies).

7. The Department of Health is active in funding relevant research through its Policy Research Programme, including work to support the National Service Framework for Older People. Other government departments also support research relevant to older people on an ad hoc basis, with the Department of Work and Pensions being prominent. European Union research funding under Framework Programme 5 supported a wide range of projects related to ageing, although this did not continue under the successor programme.

8. As regards voluntary sector support of ageing and related research, only "Research into Ageing", part of Help the Aged, addresses the range of biomedical opportunities, although its resources are relatively modest. More substantial research funding charities support work on age-related diseases that have historically cut people down in their prime, particularly cancer and cardiovascular disease. Conditions that detract from quality of life without causing death, such as arthritis and macular degeneration, have received far less support from voluntary sector funders and their donors. The Wellcome Trust is not currently focused on ageing as a research area, although programmes such as Health Consequences of Population change support relevant projects.

9. There have been some recent efforts to achieve greater cohesion of UK support for ageing research. The main players have established a Funders' Forum for Research on Ageing and Older People, and in addition a National Collaboration on Ageing Research has been set up (currently the subject of a formal evaluation). No doubt these bodies will submit evidence to the Committee. Our impression is that the Forum has had modest effect at best, although a new cross-Council research programme, led by ESRC, is promised. The Collaboration seems to have had too little resource to make a significant difference.

10. The UK arrangements for funding research relevant to an ageing population remain fragmented and arguably unfocused. This may be contrasted with the US National Institute of Aging: The point is not so much the size of its annual budget of one billion dollars. Rather, the NIA conducts and supports an extensive program of research on all aspects of ageing, from the basic cellular and molecular changes, through the prevention and treatment of common age-related conditions, to the behavioural and social aspects of growing older, including the demographic and economic implications of an ageing society. Thus the NIA covers the research agenda that is the responsibility in the UK of all the Research Councils and the Department of Health (excepting the design and technology research of the EPSRC). In consequence, the US has a far more coherent effort in the field than does the UK.

11. The National Institute for Aging exists because the US organises its biomedical research around diseases, rather than around research disciplines as in the UK. It would not be sensible to suggest wholesale reorganisation of our arrangements just to improve the support of ageing research. Nevertheless, the priorities, scale and balance of research on ageing in the UK should reflect national needs and scientific potential, not administrative mechanisms and institutional boundaries for the publicly funded support of research. Under present UK arrangements, there is no assurance that this is the case, nor is there adequate vision and leadership.

12. We respond next to the four questions posed in the Committee's Call for Evidence concerning research co-ordination, priorities, capability and the informing of policy.

13. First, as made clear above, we believe there is a lack of effective coordination of research, both within the public sector and across the public and voluntary sectors.

14. Second, to our knowledge, neither the Funder's Forum nor the National Collaboration have attempted a priority-setting exercise involving the whole research community, although the latter has held relevant seminars and has commissioned a bibliographic mapping exercise. Moreover, the MRC is unfocused in its approach to the support of ageing research. Accordingly, there can be no confidence that the present UK support for research adequately reflects national needs and scientific potential.

15. Third, the answer to the question of the adequacy of research capability must follow on from the answer to the previous question about priorities. In the area of population-base studies, longitudinal approaches are important for understanding relationships linked to ageing. Such studies require long term commitment to sustain the research infrastructure and support analysis.

16. Fourth, as regards research informing policy, the concept of an evidenced-based approach both to medicine and public health is now received wisdom, rightly so. However, a common problem as regards policy formulation is to generate timely evidence to influence decision making, failing which decisions are taken that turn out not to be supported by the research results when these eventually emerge. Government departments can find it difficult to commission research that might challenge current policy approaches. Hence there is a need for a strategic vision and leadership in research that can anticipate future policy requirements. In principle, UK Research Councils should be capable of doing this, but for the reasons outlined above, this is not happening for ageing research at present.

WORKING ON AGEING

Population Ageing: a global challenge

At the start of the 21st century, population ageing is an enormous challenge to the economic and social development of many countries in both developed and developing world. In 2020 the world population of elderly people will have trebled, with 700 million people aged 65 years and over. Although the highest proportions of older people in the population are currently observed in the most developed countries, the pace of demographic change in many developing countries is leading to rapid increases in the proportions and numbers of elderly people.

Projected growth in number of people aged 60+ (millions) 1990-2030

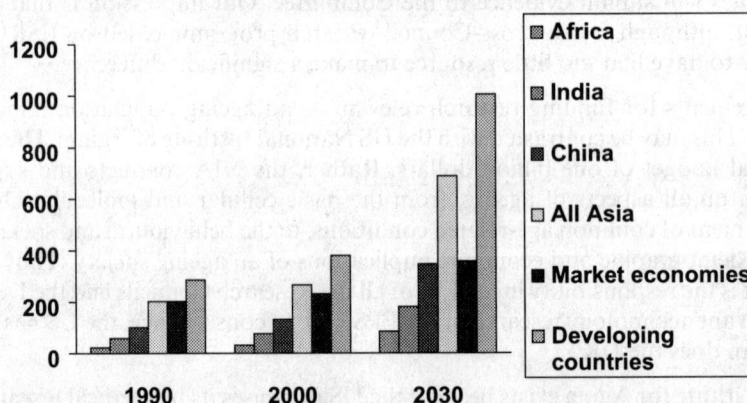

Public Health imperatives that result from the ageing of the population include: the need to identify strategies and interventions to improve the health and well being of elderly people; and the need to provide and deliver good quality health care to elderly people. Until relatively recently, opportunities for improving the health of elderly people have been limited: negative images of ageing and concepts that health promotion and disease prevention in old age are not worthwhile; and, until relatively recently, neglect by the research community of common problems of old age.

The Centre for Ageing and Public Health at LSHTM was formed in 1998 to bring together researchers across the School working in the area of ageing. Centre members come from a range of disciplines: epidemiology and statistical methods, demography, nutrition, social sciences, social policy, history, health promotion, health services research and health economics.

The main areas of research currently undertaken by centre members include:

— Demographic studies including international trends in population ageing, inter-generational exchange, socio-demographic life course and trends in disability and health expectancy.

— Epidemiological studies on age-related eye disease (cataracts, macular degeneration).

— Health services research, in particular the evaluation of health screening and of patient-based outcomes such as quality of life in chronic illness in older people, and methodological work to develop and validate new measures for use with older people.

— Nutrition ranging from nutritional influences on survival to evaluation of supplementation

— Housing and environmental influences on health of older people.

Most of this work is taking place in the UK and other developed countries but studies on nutrition and age related eye diseases are taking place in middle and low income countries. Research is funded from a variety of sources including the Medical Research Council, the Department of Health, the Economic and Science Research Council, UK Food Standards Agency, Health Technology Assessment, European Commission, Wellcome Trust UK, the British Heart Foundation, Age Concern, Pocklington Trust, Royal National Institute of the Blind. We place much emphasis on collaborations outside the School with researchers from numerous disciplines including clinical specialities especially geriatric medicine, ophthalmology, old age psychiatry; social gerontology, nutrition, housing, transport and the environment.

Below we present some recent findings from our research and information on new studies starting up.

Demographic studies

Understanding and disentangling the effects of demographic, socio-economic and policy change on family support both of and by older people has formed a strand of much collaborative work. The European Science Foundation network, *Family support of older people: determinants and consequences* led by a member of CAPH is drawing to the end of its work and will hold a concluding symposium as part of the International Sociological Association meeting in September 2004. Results show the strong influence of cultural and policy contexts on family support, rather than demographic ones alone and indeed the effects of demographic changes on potential family support are often misunderstood. Work by centre members in collaboration with demographers at LSE shows, for example, that in Britain in the next quarter century a higher proportion of elderly people are likely to have a surviving child than for any generation ever born. Projecting the implications of these trends into the future forms part of the work of an EU project in which School members are involved. Family history, family support and living arrangements are all important influences on health and health care use in later life. Work we have undertaken, for example, showed that marital status and social support in later life is strongly associated with psychological health, although factors such as smoking were more important when other domains of health were examined. Using the ONS Longitudinal Study centre members we also examined the effects of living arrangements and health of co-residents on where older people with cancer died. Among the population with cancer, as many lived alone as in the rest of the population of the same age so by 1991 half of all female cancer sufferers aged 80 and over lived alone. Compared with those living alone, older cancer sufferers who lived with a spouse who had no long term illness were two and half times as likely to die at home and twice as likely to die at home if they lived with a spouse who themselves had a long term illness. These findings have important implications for current initiatives to extend palliative care options and increase the proportion of terminally ill people able to die at home—if they so wish.

Epidemiological studies on age related eye disease

Age related macular degeneration is the major cause of vision loss in adults in developed countries. There are two sub-types of AMD—the more severe and visually impairing neovascular type and the atrophic type. The seven country EUREYE Study found that women had higher rates of both types than men (around two-fold increase). Smoking was a strong risk factor for both types but a history of diabetes or cardiovascular disease was associated with only the neovascular type. Little is known about the prevalence of this condition in developing countries. We have completed a feasibility study in North India which found that early signs of this condition were highly prevalent in the population and the rates for late disease were at least as common as in European populations. A large study is now underway investigating risk factors for both age related macular degeneration and cataract in the Indian population with a focus on biomass cooking fuels and dietary antioxidants.

Health Services Research

Evaluation of screening. The benefits of multidimensional assessment of older people in the community setting are controversial. Previous trials have been underpowered and inconsistent in their results. We conducted a large cluster randomised factorial trial to evaluate the benefits of different approaches to assessment and management of older people in the community. 106 general practices (from the MRC General Practice

Research Framework) and 33,000 patients aged over 75 years were recruited to the trial with response rates of 78 per cent. The main results of the trial published this year found no evidence of reductions in mortality, hospital or institutional admissions from an intensive in depth geriatric assessment in general practice, nor to management by a specialist geriatric service. There were small benefits on quality of life from hospital-based outpatient geriatric management. The evidence from the trial therefore suggests that caution is required before introducing routine assessment into the care of older people. The large size of the study and wealth of health data collected has also provided opportunities for add-on studies: a nutrition and physical activity assessment, additional data collection to determine the causes of vision impairment; a nested trial of screening for vision impairment; an investigation of factors influencing winter mortality using the mortality and health and socio-economic data from the study linked to local meteorological and infectious disease information including vaccine coverage. The results from these studies are described in more detail below.

The MRC Assessment Trial found that vision impairment was common in the older population and rose rapidly with increasing age from 10 per cent in those aged 75–84 to a quarter of those aged 85 and over. We found that over a half of vision impairment in the over 75s was due to remediable conditions: refractive error (32 per cent) or unoperated cataract (20 per cent). In 33 per cent the cause was age related macular degeneration. This suggests that screening for vision impairment should lead to better vision outcomes. However in the nested trial of vision impairment, visual acuity screening by the practice nurse only benefited a small proportion. Key explanations for the lack of effect identified were under-detection of uncorrected refractive error, only around half the recommendations for referral to an ophthalmologist resulted in referral by the general practitioners, and unwillingness by participants to self-refer to optometry services for further assessment, citing costs and lack of perceived need. These results are in agreement with other studies which have shown that despite the availability of free eyesight tests for older people, the uptake is partial, and the result is a serious burden of avoidable poor vision. We are now working on a feasibility study of a trial of optometry services in the general practice setting which may overcome the barriers identified in previous studies.

The influenza vaccine programme in elderly people is the start of a new public health strategy of adult vaccination in the UK. Equity in the delivery of the vaccine in epidemic years and in a future pandemic is a key ethical issue. We have used data from the MRC trial not usually available to examine more precisely population factors at individual and geographical level related to influenza vaccine uptake in older people. Uptake was 48 per cent in 1997 and did not increase substantially until 2000 when the uptake was a third higher at 63 per cent, the year in which national targets and payments to practices for each vaccine given to all over 65 year olds were introduced. Influenza vaccination was also lower with poorer neighbourhoods, personal socio-economic circumstances, and support than less poor. These differentials were not explained by higher uptake in those who were married, with underlying respiratory conditions, non-smokers and those without cognitive impairment or depression.

Although there is good randomised controlled trial evidence of the efficacy of the influenza vaccine in preventing morbidity in older people, mortality is too rare an endpoint for reduction to be well established. Further statistical methods were also developed from the MRC trial study data to assess vaccine effectiveness using observational data. Direct comparison of mortality in vaccinated and unvaccinated persons, which is the usual method, can suffer from confounding. They were avoided in favour of quantifying responses to circulating influenza in unvaccinated persons separately from vaccinated persons. A strong increase in mortality was seen in non-vaccinated in periods of high circulating influenza but in vaccinated persons there was no such association—strongly supporting an important protective effect of influenza vaccination in older people against death.

Evaluation of patient-based outcomes in chronic illness in older people. We have undertaken several studies to evaluate patient-based outcomes in a variety of chronic illnesses in older people. For example, as a follow-up to our original study of clinical outcomes, quality of life, health service use and costs in 221 older people on dialysis (North Thames Dialysis Study), we are now examining (i) changes in QOL over time, (ii) sociodemographic, clinical and dialysis-related predictors of QOL and (iii) predictors of poor outcome. We are also undertaking work to evaluate outcomes in polymyalgia rheumatica, a disease of older people. This prospective cohort study is assessing clinical outcomes and quality of life over a one-year period in a sample of 129 older people.

Methodological work to develop and validate new measures of outcome. Rigorous evaluation of health outcomes is the cornerstone of any successful health service. We have been been developing and validating patient-based measures of outcome (eg quality of life, symptoms, psychosocial outcomes) for use with older people. Our work with people with dementia, stroke aphasia, eye disease in India or who are in intensive care has provided the opportunity to develop innovative strategies to produce psychometrically rigorous measures for obtaining self-reports in difficult to assess populations (eg people with cognitive or sensory impairments). This work presents several new methodological challenges: How can we reliably elicit self-reports about health outcomes from people with dementia, aphasia or in intensive care instead of relying on proxy reports, which generally do not agree with people's own reports? What question format, framing and response scales are most appropriate for ensuring reliable and valid responses?

Nutrition

For a variety of physiological, psychological and social reasons older people are nutritionally vulnerable and frequently consume diets that are poor in both quality and quantity. This vulnerability often results in macronutrient and micronutrient under-nutrition among older people, and may be related to the onset and progression of degenerative disorders in later life. We have shown that vitamin C levels in those aged 75 and over were generally low and there was a inverse association between vitamin C levels and subsequent mortality. Plasma homocysteine levels were strongly positively associated with cardiovascular mortality in this age group. The lack of association between folate levels and mortality suggests that folate status in this population may have been sufficiently adequate to remove any negative effects of deficiency.

Polyunsaturated fatty acids, especially the omega-3 fatty acids derived from marine fish oils have been shown to be associated with a lower risk of coronary heart disease in a number of studies but there is less work on their role in other age related diseases. Recruitment is underway for OPAL (Older People and omega-3 Long-chain polyunsaturated fatty acids) which is a UK-based trial, evaluating the effect of fish oil supplementation on cognitive and retinal function in older people. We have obtained additional funding to carry out analyses on stored bloods in the EUREYE study to investigate the associations with omega-3 fatty acids and age related macular degeneration.

There remains much uncertainty about desirable levels of Body Mass Index (BMI) in older people and the usefulness of additional or alternative measures of body fat content or distribution. In two of our studies of older people we found that, in contrast to middle aged people, BMI in old age was inversely related to subsequent mortality. In the Whitehall study, men with the highest loss or highest gain in weight between middle and old age had the highest mortality while in the MRC Assessment Trial increasing waist hip ratio was associated with increased mortality, especially in women. These results suggest that, in old age, change in weight is a more useful indicator of risk than current weight and that a preferable measure to BMI of excess fat is waist hip ratio.

The Centre is also involved in research attempting to find cost-effective methods of preventing disease and loss of function in older people in Chile. A pilot study conducted in Santiago demonstrated that their was considerable self-targeting by older people in the uptake of a free micronutrient-dense nutritional supplement provided at health centres. The research also highlighted previously unknown manufacturing problems in ensuring the micronutrient content of the supplement which have subsequently been resolved

Housing and environmental influences on health

The UK has a large winter excess of mortality which is greatest in relative and absolute terms in the elderly. There have been few opportunities to examine the personal factors that pre-dispose to dying in winter. Using data from the MRC Trial of Assessment we found a small excess risk for women and for those with a self-reported history of respiratory illness. There was no evidence that other existing health problems or living circumstances or socio-economic deprivation of winter death.

The lack of socio-economic gradient in particular agrees with other studies from the UK and suggests that policies aimed at reducing winter death, such as fuel poverty relief, require reassessment in order to ensure appropriate targeting of those at risk from cold homes.

More detailed evidence on the effect of housing on the health of the elderly population and other vulnerable groups is also emerging from a national study of the health impact of England's home energy efficiency programme. Now in its final phases, this study is quantifying the changes associated with grant-funded energy efficiency improvements on the indoor environment, and the health and well-being of low income households. It includes an assessment, based on epidemiological modelling, of the impact of the scheme on winter mortality. Early results provide encouraging evidence about a number of health benefits of energy efficiency measures.

There is suggestive evidence that maintaining mobility is important to sustain the quality of life of older people. However, it is hard to assess which approaches are most effective. Working with colleagues at University College London and the University of Westminster, we are investigating how best to evaluate measures intended to enhance the mobilty of older and disabled people. This work is funded by the

Department for Transport and originates from a workshop arranged by the Centre. A particular task is to prepare draft guidance that the Department could issue to local authorities to assist them in the design and operation of the public realm in relation to the accessibility needs of older people.

Policy relevance of our work

Most of our research has direct policy relevance at both the national and international level and across various sectors such as health, transport and housing. Synthesizing evidence from a number of areas of public health research is particularly important for policy recommendation for older people. An example of this is an innovative project which aims to use modern health knowledge to define the requisites of healthy, community-living people aged 65+ years, and the minimal personal costs entailed. The project draws on the wide body of research from around the world that has given us consensual and generally accepted evidence on the major personal prerequisites for health and longevity in terms of nutrition, physical activity and psychosocial relations. The study, which is funded by Age Concern England, attempts to define the minimum costs for healthy living in relation to housing, diet and nutrition, physical activity, health and social care, transport, and other essentials. It should provide the first health-based assessment of required income for older people and a hence benchmark for government policy.

October 2004

Memorandum by Professor Roger Coleman and Dr John Clarkson

1. Research in Technology and Design to Improve the Quality of Life of Older People

1.1 While research into ageing itself is a well understood field, research needs with regard to design are less well undrestood, and in particular those aspects of design with the potential to extend active independence. The outcome of much research into ageing is in the form of medical, and to a lesser extent social interventions. These have much value, and have significantly contributed to longevity and demographic ageing. However, it is no coincidence that population ageing in the UK began with the industrial revolution and has advanced ever since. Design and engineering interventions have had significant impact on this picture, and an important future role.

1.2 The model below (fig 1) outlines the ways in which design can contribute to improving the life quality and extending the independence of older people. In the context of population ageing, significant benefits will flow from the effective implementation of design solutions in each of the domains indicated. Good, well-informed design, supported by appropriate research can push the boundaries of each of these domains and so effectively counteract design exclusion, moderate the impact of frailty and deter the onset of dependency.

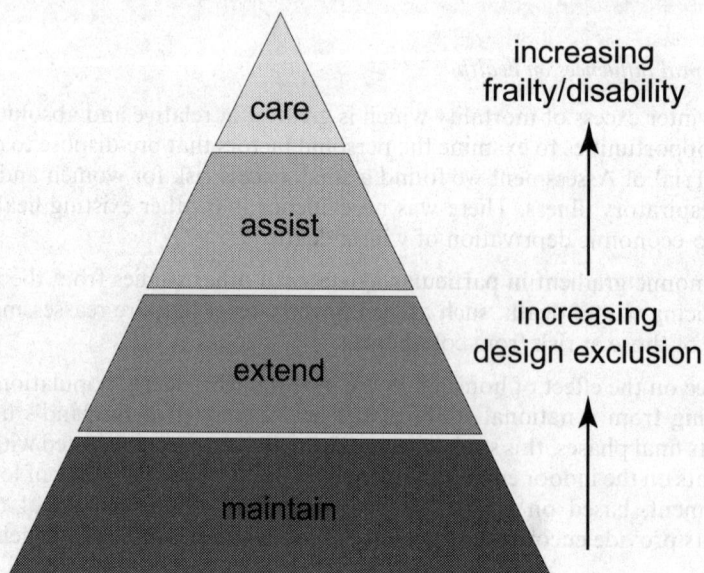

1.2.1 Ensuring that products and services, packaging and information meet the needs and support the lifestyles of the broadest majority of the population will counter design exclusion and thereby help to <u>maintain</u> active independence for longer among the ageing population.

1.2.2 Modular and customisable designs, in particular of interfaces to products, services and information, will further <u>extend</u> active independence significantly by making them accessible to those who currently are excluded by the design of core features.

1.2.3 Specialist products and interfaces, especially where they preserve dignity and do not stigmatise, isolate or otherwise alienate users will <u>assist</u> independence and social inclusion, in particular for disabled older people who may otherwise require institutional or home care.

1.2.4 Designs that facilitate <u>care</u>, in the home, and in institutions, that understand and support the needs of carers, and preserve the dignity of those cared for, will significantly enhance the life quality of the frailest and most severly disabled older people.

2. RESEARCH NEEDS FOR AGE-FRIENDLY DESIGN

2.1 Much work has gone into developing the concept of "inclusive design", and resources and methods to support it in practice, both in order to address population ageing, and to prepare industry for the Disability Discrimination Act, which becomes fully enforceable this month. In particular through the EPSRC EQUAL initiative and within the two i-design projects funded by the EPSRC. As a result a new British Standard BS7000-6 will be published later this year giving guidance for business and industry, on managing inclusive design. In addition, information resources for design, education and industry have been developed, along with policy document published by the Design Council.[1]

2.2 In the course of this work, important gaps in the knowledge base and other research needs have been identified, all of which amount to barriers to inclusive design, and its uptake by industry.

2.2.1 There is a lack of suitable and complete date on physical and mental capabilities and their distribution across the whole population. This makes it difficult to accurately assess the accessibility and suitability of designs, and impedes designers and engineers in ensuring that the products and services they design address the needs of the widest range of users.

2.2.2 There is a lack of research into the technical and practical aspects of mass customisation, and other design strategies that can adapt mainstream products, services and interfaces to individual users, be they in the home, the workplace, in public spaces, or part of transport systems. This makes it difficult for designers and engineers to ensure that people can live, work and travel independently for as long as possible.

2.2.3 There is a lack of date (in particular in formats accessible to designers) on the preferences and daily lives of older people, especially with reagard to their interaction with products and services. In addition, there is good evidence that products and services targeted at older people, and in particular assistive products, are rejected because they are insufficiently useable, or because the users perceive them as stigmatising.[2] This makes it difficult for designers and manufacturers to ensure the acceptibility and therefore the uptake of assistive products and technologies.

2.2.4 There is a lack of design relevant data on the needs of carers, both professionals and family members, in particular with regard to the devices and products they use in their work and the impact of these on their health, safety and wellbeing. This makes it difficult for designers to address such issues, and increases the likelihood of carers, and importantly older family members, suffering as a consequence.

2.2.5 There is a need for research funding directed at older user involvement in design, testing, evaluation and assessment of proposals and solutions at all stages of the development process, and in particular at the development of suitable research techniques and methodologies that can be integrated with commercial design processes. This would ensure that solutions are appropriate, accepted and cost effective in development and the market place, and assist designers and engineers in understanding the needs and lives of the people they are serving.

2.2.6 There is a need to involve designers (as well as older users) in research projects and programmes where the emphasis is on the development and application of technology, in particular in ICT, "Smart" housing and embedded intelligence, and the realm of assistive technology. This would help to ensure that the outcomes can be translated into appropriate and acceptable, user-friendly products and services, that can be manufactured, marketed and distributed effectively.

2.2.7 There is also a need for funding targeted specifically at "proof of concept" with suitable users, especially in the development of assistive and care products, and also in the other, broader domains, to ensure that only appropriate and acceptable products and services are delivered to the public. This would significantly improve the quality, usability and acceptability of supportive devices and devices that are currently rejected by end users. It would also facilitate the transfer of research from the academic to the commercial sphere.

3. Supporting Inclusive Design Research and Practice

3:1 *Item 2.2.1 above*

3.1.1 The authors of this submission are co-editors of two textbooks on inclusive design,[3, 4] and have contributed significantly to the international literature in the field. The major date set drawn on in these publications and currently available is the Disability Follow-up Survey (DFS[5]) commissioned by the Department of Social Security as a follow-up to the 1996–97 Family Resources Survey. Data from over 7,000 participants was collected, and the main focus was disability within the UK population. The date gathered related to activities of daily living (ADLs), such as climbing stairs, reading a newspaper, following a television programme, washing hands, but not product/service interactions.

3.1.2 Even with considerable interpretation, this data is not adequate to allow designers to make informed decisions about the numbers of people who will be able to interact with specific design feature, nor is it presented in formates that are readily accessible to designers and business decision makers. Other date sets are available, but not sufficient to fill this gap, if we are to support an ageing population with the minimum demand on care and welfare services there is a pressing need to gather new data on capabilities across the whole population, and in particular in regard to the physical, sensory, motion and cognitive skills required for interaction with products and services, in the home, at work and for mobility.

3.1.3 Gathering such data is probably beyond the scope of current research programmes, as a sample of 10,000 + would be required, and the structuring, analysing and presentation of the results of the survey will require careful design. Also the needs of key information-user groups will require investigation to ensure the maximum use of the results in engineering, design, business and education. The cost of such a survey is likely to be in the region of £2 million + .

3.1.4 This information is critical, not just for designers, but for business leaders to be able to understand the scale of the issue and recognise the business opportunities that represents. It will also have future value with regard to legislation and standards as it will provide the basis data for measuring design exclusion, and allow for rational decisions to be made with regard to the inclusivity of products and services. The availability of this data to UK businesses will help to put the UK in the forefront of design and industry responses to population ageing, and open up new market opportunities. It will also inform education from secondary level through to Continuing Professional Development in design, business studies and other related fields.

3.2 *Items 2.2.2–2.2.7 above*

3.2.1 Although these research priorities could be met through existing funding channels, they are unlikely to be addressed in a joined-up way outside a co-ordinated programme led by key agencies. The EPSRC EQUAL initiative has provided considerable impetus in this regard, but current national structure and proposals for supporting ageing research are insufficient and not focussed towards testing, evaluation, development and "proof of concept" inclusive design research. There is a need for more imaginative priorities and support mechanisms that recognise progress made in recent years and the distinctive perspectives and methodologies required by design research. Probably these would be best achieved by extending the remit of EPSRC's EQUAL initiative and creating new LINK or similar programmes devoted to inclusive design and supported by DoH, DTI, DfT and ODPM.

3.3 *Dissemination*

3.3.1 There is also a role for the Design Council, supported by the DTI, to focus and facilitate the transfer of knowledge and expertise to industry. To achieve this effectively, a better understanding is required of the industry barriers to appropriate design strategies. This in itself is a further research area with significant potential to impact on the life quality of older people, that could inform future government initiatives and help structure incentives to industry.

4. References

[1] Coleman R (2002) *Growing older; the new context for design,* Design Council, London.

[2] Yeates M., Bird D, *et al* (2000, updated 2002) *Fully equipped,* Audit Commission, Abingdon.

[3] Clarkson J, Coleman R, *et al* (2003) *Inclusive Design: design for the whole population,* Springer-Verlag, London.

[4] Keates S, Clarkson J (2003) *Countering Design Exclusion; and introduction to inclusive design,* Springer-Verlag, London.

[5] Grundy E, Ahlburg D, *et al* (1999) *Disability in Great Britain,* Department of Social Security, Corporate Document Services, London, UK.

October 2004

Memorandum by R Conrad, CBE

AGEING, SENSORY DEFICIT AND MINIATURISATION

1. This submission is concerned with the relationship between ageing, sensory deficit and the miniaturisation of technical devices.

2. Miniaturisation of technological devices makes increasing demands on certain sensory systems. In particular I refer here (a) to cutaneous sensation which includes discrimination of size, textures, shapes and (b) to proprioception including dexterity, manipulation of small objects and making fine adjustments to moving elements, detecting whether sufficient—or too much—force has been applied when the quantities involved may be minuscule. These sensory systems are likely to become ever more central in new technologies and which the design of devices must address. For that, reliable data are required.

3. Just as surely as do seeing and hearing, these sensory systems deteriorate with age with the attendant risk that older people will be unable or unwilling to use them. But whereas a great deal of quantitative data are already available for seeing and hearing they are seriously lacking for other sensory systems. There is an urgent need for epidemiological studies: to establish the capabilities of older people age-group by age-group. This will permit design characteristics and relevant sensory requirements to be matched. Only then will an ageing population be able to enjoy the benefits which new inventions will bring.

4. At present smaller and smaller devices are developed without reliable quantitative knowledge of the relevant sensory acuities of older people. Inevitably a growing proportion of the population will be excluded from participation or will require help. Knowing the level of deficit reached by different age-cohorts is essential to design. There is a fast growing need for something like a national data-bank.

5. A great deal is already known about, for example, the epidemiology of the sensory attribute of seeing. Thus it is now relative easy to define the minimum size of print needed for comfortable reading by people aged, say, 60–69; 70–79; 80–89 etc. This is, more or less, equally true for hearing. The important feature is not just that we know that people's vision deteriorates as they age, but that we know with some accuracy the amount of deficit for various age cohorts.

6. This submission is concerned with other sensory attributes which for the elderly are of comparable significance but for which this kind of epidemiological data is largely lacking. With respect to the subject of the Inquiry it is obvious to any old person that cutaneous sensation (is my finger actually in contact with a surface? Have I actually swallowed the small pill?) is of everyday importance. The same is true for proprioception; the exact knowledge of where one's limbs, especially fingers, are in space (is my finger solely on the correct button? Have I pressed the button hard enough?). Commonly, older people abandon using a device because it is "too fiddly."

7. Effectively applied, reliable data could minimises the number of people who might be excluded from using miniaturised devices, some of which could be of medical significance. At present these are designed largely by intuition or brief trials with available young people.

8. During the past century the study of sensory function has been a core feature of experimental psychology. This means that the necessary measuring procedures have been well honed in laboratories and are easily available. What is needed is wide-scale measurement with particular reference to older people. Clearly for this adequate funding would be essential.

9. No one doubts the importance of good design but all too often cost is a factor. The question becomes: for this much cost saving how many people are "disabled" because of loss of sensory acuity attributable to age? Population data to address the question is lacking. As the population ages, without appropriate design more and more people will be unable to make efficient and rewarding use of the smaller and smaller devices which seem certain to come.

October 2004

Memorandum by Professor Sir John Grimley Evans

The idea that some index of functional quality of life should be used to supplement mere longevity as an indicator of the success of health and social influences on ageing was first set out systematically in a WHO publication of 1984[1]. That report summarised a population-based perspective on later-life trajectories characterised by transitions from health active life into morbidity (ill health) on through disability to death. Most geratologists have since focused on disability rather than morbidity as the crucial transition, because it is disability and its associated loss of autonomy that older people fear, and which in turn leads to dependency with its cost implications for the health and social services. Moreover, much of modern medicine as applied to older people does not "cure" disease but relieves its symptoms and other effects and, in the best case, prolongs survival. People may still have the "disease" in a medical sense but it does not affect their quality of life. Such effects ought surely to register as success in prolonging disability-free life expectancy, rather than as failure in extending the duration of (irrelevant) "disease".

Health, especially self-rated health, is a slippery entity dependent on concepts and definitions of disease, exposure to medical diagnosis and therapy, and the various social factors that set the relative benefits and costs of declaring oneself as "unhealthy". There is also no necessary or direct link between states of health and functional capability or sense of autonomy. Disability, however, can be defined and assessed for research purposes. Admittedly, there have been some different approaches to the concept in the literature, and the WHO confused the issue some years ago with a somewhat idiosyncratic use of the term. None the less, the notion of disability defined by inability to perform some desired activity that it is reasonable and socially appropriate to want to do is a generally accepted tradition with a long history[2]. In essence, disability arises when there is an "ecological gap" between what a person can do and what his or her environment demands. There are disabling environments as well as disabled people.

I would urge the Committee to focus on disability-free life expectancy rather than healthy life expectancy as a measure of the well-being of an ageing population.

Although there is still debate over the details of the time trajectory it is now generally accepted that the prevalence of disability in later life has fallen in the United States since the 1980s[3]. As far as the UK is concerned, the informed view is that we simply do not know what is happening, but there is certainly no evidence that disability levels in later life are falling as in the USA. Researchers have done their best with the data from the General Household Survey but the Survey was not designed for the purpose and the self-reported data are subject to various forms of bias and distortion that can affect the evaluation of time trends. Self-reported data from questionnaires are not optimal for measuring the prevalence of disability in the population, and supplementary information from objective measures of functional abilities is required. There is extensive experience in the USA in the assessment of disability in the community that could be drawn on.

There can be no doubt that what has happened in the USA could be made to happen here through appropriate and co-ordinated health, social, and educational policy (see Table). It is therefore highly desirable that disability-free life expectancy in the general population should be monitored. The data could be used to assess the effectiveness of relevant government policies and provide a more secure basis for identifying current shortfalls and predicting future needs for health and social services.

There could be a perceived conflict of interest if the Department of Health, responsible for aspects of relevant policy, were to be charged also with the collection of data to be used for assessing the effectiveness of policy. While experienced researchers would need to be involved, the Office for National Statistics would be the most appropriate body to oversee the necessary repeated standardised surveys.

Table

APPROACHES TO LENGTHENING DISABILITY-FREE LIFE
EXPECTANCY[4]

Postponement as prevention*	Lifestyle
	Knowledge, opportunities, incentives
	Public health and medical care
Disability-reducing interventions	Surgical
	Medical
	Rehabilitation
Less disabling environments	Wealth distribution
	Housing
	Architecture and planning

*Because of age-associated loss of adaptability the older we are when struck by
a potentially disabling disease, such as stroke or coronary disease, the more likely
we are to die rapidly rather than linger in a disabled state.*

REFERENCES

[1] World Health Organisation Scientific Group on the Epidemiology of Ageing (1984). The uses of epidemiology in the study of the elderly. Technical Report Series No 706. Geneva: World Health Organisation.

[2] Verbrugge LM, Jette AM. The disablement process. Soc Sci Med 1994; 38: 1–14.

[3] Manton KG, Gu X (2001). Changes in the prevalence of chronic disability in the United States black and nonblack population above age 65 from 1982 to 1999. Proc Natl Acad Sci USA; 98: 6354–6359.

[4] Grimley Evans J (2003) Live longer, die faster: an attainable aim.
http://www.healthandage.com/PHome/gm = 20!gid2 = 2370

March 2005

Supplementary evidence from Professor Sir John Grimley Evans

1. The Committee asked Sir John Grimley Evans whether he could provide any figures on the proportion of NHS expenditure spent:

    (a) on those in the last six months of their lives (at whatever age);

    (b) on the 16 per cent over 65, other than the last six months of their lives; and

    (c) on those over 85 (again other than the last six months).

2. He replied that, with the caveat "other things being equal", the position was:

"In terms of healthcare costs the two significantly expensive things that happen to us are being born and dying. The increase in costs associated with final illness can be detected statistically as long as 15 years before the point of death but the main excess expenditure occurs in the last five years of life. The costs in the last five years of life do not derive from predictably futile treatment but from treatments doctors hope will be curative or palliative. With present levels of life expectancy most people experiencing what will prove to be their final illness are aged over 75. This can give the impression that high costs of health care are due to age rather than to being ill, and that any increase in numbers of older people due to lengthening of lifespan will increase NHS expenditure disproportionately. This is not so.

With present patterns of age-associated frailty, healthcare costs in the last five years of life rise at around 1 to 2 per cent per annum from the age of 65 to 80 and then fall. (There are no comparable data for younger ages available in the UK.) The increase from 65 to 80 represents the longer hospital stays and greater intensity of care necessary for frailer people. The fall after 80 is partly attributable to the withholding or withdrawing of treatment where a patient does not want it or doctors consider it not in the patient's best interest. It will also reflect the fact that the older people are when struck by severe illness, the shorter, on average, their survival.

But the 1 to 2 per cent per annum increase in costs with age from 65 to 80 is minute compared with a tenfold increase in costs over the last five years of life, an increase that will occur whatever the age of death. For this reason, further increase in lifespan in the UK will have negligible effect on overall healthcare costs. Indeed, if increase in longevity is associated with postponement of illness, and therefore shorter survival, costs might fall."

3. In reply to a further question on the comparative merits, and cost, of prevention as against cure, he replied:

"The relative merits of prevention and treatment were churned over in the heady days of coronary heart disease epidemiology 40 years ago, and no general solution emerged. While for a single specific condition (falls or stroke for example) prevention may be better in allowing individuals to avoid an unpleasant experience altogether, or, through the age-fatality effect to shorten its duration. But it does not follow that prevention is necessarily cheaper than treatment for two main reasons:

   (1) The cumulative lifetime costs of prevention may exceed the cost of treatment in terms both of economics and fiscal accountancy.

   (2) There is the problem of competing morbidity. As far as healthcare costs are concerned one might avoid sudden death from a heart attack in one's 50s (cheap) only to survive a stroke in one's 60s (pretty expensive) or suffer Alzheimer's disease in one's 70s (very expensive).

These arguments will be familiar to some people unsympathetic to the Committee's work, and, according to newspaper reports, have recently been taken out of the attic by health economists employed by an American tobacco company. Since the whole issue is both complex and unresolvable I would advise that to raise it at all would be to offer a hostage to Fortune and Distraction. There are good humanitarian reasons for improving the experience of ageing; there is no need to bring money into it!"

May 2005

Memorandum by Mrs Dorothy Morgan Evans

I suffer from progressive visual impairment due to macular degeneration. My experience during the past two years has demonstrated the difficulties arising from the fragmented nature of the services that are theoretically available to the visually handicapped and the consequent problems in accessing them. Responsibilities are split between statutory authorities (hospitals, social work), private practitioners (consultants, opticians) and voluntary bodies (RNIB, local blind welfare societies, societies devoted to specific visual handicaps eg macular disease, glaucoma). These agencies vary in competence and helpfulness.

The difficulty for people newly affected with visual difficulties is how to access the information needed to restore some semblance of normality and independence. What is needed is something more practical than pious invocation of more communication and cooperation between all concerned. From a personal point of view, a discussion with somebody knowledgeable about what is available and suitable at the point of diagnosis would have been of great benefit. As it was, my initial and only contact with the Social Work Department was to receive a bewildering number of forms (that I could not read) through the post, though admittedly the accompanying letter did offer me a chance to talk about my "feelings" which might have been helpful to some people. But my need was for information about how I could manage life without being able to write or read. And if there is any single definitive source of information I have still not found it. In fact, after two years of delving and ferreting about I am probably it! There are amazing devices available and my independence has been secured because I have one way or another discovered and bought them. But most of the information I managed to obtain eventually came from retailers of the equipment who were very helpful but are not perhaps the most disinterested of advisers.

Which brings me to another "what could be done" point. The necessary equipment is expensive. I depend mainly on three principal tools: an adaptation for my computer which enables me to enlarge and manipulate the screen; a CCTV which allows me to enlarge printed matter up to 16 times; and a sort of electronic telescope which can also be adjusted for reading. I have spent over £5,000 on these gadgets, which to me are as essential as is a wheelchair for those without physical mobility. There is one concession—articles exclusively for the use of the blind are not subject to VAT—but there are some grey areas where the VAT man argues that others could use the devices and so exemption could be withdrawn. In any case the fact remains that the equipment is costly and I wonder if it needs to be. For instance, the oversize keyboard I am using cost £164 (though I did manage to reclaim the VAT after a struggle). It has occurred to me that if the cost cannot be brought down to a more reasonable level could not some national scheme of renting the more expensive items be devised? No doubt the notion of providing physically handicapped people with their own mobility cars seemed equally far-fetched at one time.

I suppose that in the end it all comes down to what most afflicted people want to alleviate their various conditions—what do I need? where is it? how can I get it?

September 2004

Memorandum by the Independent Consortium

1. FOCUS OF THE SUBMISSION

This submission addresses the application of research in technology and design to improve the quality of life of older people, *with particular reference to people with dementia.*

2. EXISTING TECHNOLOGIES THAT COULD BE USED TO A GREATER EXTENT TO BENEFIT OLDER PEOPLE

Recent years have seen a rapid growth in research and development of new technologies to improve services and enhance the independence and quality of life of older people living at home. The actual and potential role of new technologies has been recognised in the National Service Framework for Older People (Dept of Health, 2001). A wide range of applications are being developed or are already in the marketplace, addressing both the direct and indirect support of frail and disabled people (Sixsmith 1998), for example: smart housing, client monitoring, teleconsultation, health and social care assessment, client records and care planning, client support (eg emergency response, counseling, information), health and social care information systems. However, the specific needs of older people with dementia have only been recently addressed and there remains considerable scope for research and development for this client group within a number of key areas (Judd *et al*, 1997; Sixsmith 2002; Orpwood 2002; Woolham and Frisby 2002a, 2002b; Bjoerneby *et al*, 1997):

— Supervision and surveillance. One of the major concerns in supporting cognitively impaired older people at home are the potential safety risks involved and the use of automatic alarms to highlight dangerous situations has received increasing attention from technologists and academics (cf Sixsmith 2000). For example, wandering behaviour may pose a significant risk for an individual as they may get lost or be unable to cope with the potential dangers of the outside world. However, restraint may be an undesirable or unethical option for people. Systems can be installed to determine whether a person has left a room or building and either use a prompt to discourage them from leaving or send a message to a carer or service provider if they do.

— Safety and security. The home environment can be a dangerous place for cognitively impaired people. For example, they may leave cookers and heaters unattended, while gas and electricity is potentially lethal if misused. "Smart housing" technologies may be particularly useful for people with dementia, automatically shutting off devices or allowing remote control by carers or service providers. Smart housing could also use sensors to control household appliances and devices, depending on movements and activities of person. Technologies that can provide such back-up whilst still empowering the person and not taking control away from them have been demonstrated (Orpwood 2002).

— Environmental control. Sensors for heating, cooling, ventilation, day and artificial lighting can automatically regulate comfort in the internal environment using systems that incorporate good energy management. In addition to passive controls it is recognised that it is important for autonomy and the sense of comfort for the individual to have the ability to actively control their environment, yet most available controls are not appropriate for older people with dementia. There is a need to develop better interfaces to enable people to regulate their own comfort.

— Carer support. Carer support is a key aspect of care in the community. Using telecommunications to carry out more routine tasks, such as shopping or going to the bank or post office, may provide them with more free time, relieving the "burden" of care. Access to information advice and counselling is also important. Smart house technology can also improve the quality of life of carers through ensuring careful monitoring of activities and alerting the carer only when necessary, eg allowing a carer to sleep secure in the knowledge that they will be woken if the person gets up and needs attention or reassurance.

— Reminder devices. New technology could also provide "reminder devices" to support independent living (European Commission, 1996; Woolham and Frisby, 2002a). These can provide cognitively impaired people with suitable decision support software to help in carrying out actions such as household activities, social participation, communication and vocational tasks.

3. THE DEVELOPMENT OF NEW TECHNOLOGIES

The development of technologies for people with dementia has generally focused on safety and security issues. However, there may be opportunities for more positive uses of technology to enhance quality of life. For example, Marshall (1997) suggests using technology to identify when a person is restless and bored and then initiate a familiar or enjoyable activity, such as playing familiar music or videos. Aromatherapy rooms could emit relaxing aromas to alleviate stress, while the use of telecommunications could help to reduce social isolation.

Research and development within assistive technologies needs to reflect the specific needs of cognitively impaired people as well as those people with physical impairments (eg mobility, sensory, motor, control and manipulation). For physically impaired people, the underlying basis for technological development and design is to remove the environmental barriers that turn a person's impairment into a disability. In contrast, cognitively impaired people may have impaired abilities to understand their environment, formulate plans, carry out actions, communicate or remember what they have done or where they are. This has a number of implications for the development and implementation of telecare for this client group. For example, people with physical disabilities can directly interact with assistive technology. Someone with arthritic hands can benefit enormously from taps that are turned on by simply moving their hand in front of an infra-red sensor. For someone with dementia such devices are confusing and inappropriate. Design engineers need to develop assistive technologies in a way that the user's interaction is the same as they have always used in the past. For example the taps in the Gloucester smart house for people with dementia (Orpwood 2002) look like traditional taps but actually just operate sensors that can monitor how far the user has turned them. The house is then able to control water to flow at the rate desired, or it can shut the tap off if the user leaves it running.

While it is accepted that technology can assist people with dementia there is also widespread concern about its potential misuse, and a fear that technologies designed for specific functions such as minimising risk can have a seriously negative impact on quality of life. It has been noted that there has been much greater take up of technologies that promote safety and the monitoring of health than those that support quality of life (Marshall 2001). Problems have been highlighted such as the potential erosion of privacy by the extension of telemedicine into the home environment, or the excessive restriction of the individual that can be concomitant with a safety and security culture. The potential for technologies to be a channel for ageism and the need for the user to be in control is recognised (Fisk 1999) and the challenge is to design technology interfaces that empower rather than restrict. There is a need for a better understanding of the dynamic between a range of technologies and their impact for good or ill on quality of life, to enable informed judgements to be made by specifiers and selectors of systems and devices for people with cognitive impairment.

It is important that the implementation and application of new technologies and related services are grounded in a thorough understanding of the individual within their social and care networks (Kitwood, 1997; Pieper and Riederer, 1998). The needs and abilities of the person may vary considerably. People in the early stages of dementia may be able to cope reasonably well with only limited care, while others may be require considerable help and support. Important individual factors to consider are level and stage of cognitive impairment, ability to carry out activities of daily living, problematic and emotional factors such as anxiety and tendency to "wander". The informal and formal care networks will also determine the kinds of technological interventions that are needed. Again this will vary from individual to individual, depending on factors such as availability of informal carer, physical proximity, carer network and capacity to provide care. The application of new technology needs to be tailored in order to complement the person's abilities and capacities and to provide help and support to care providers.

4. How Effectively is Research Co-ordinated in the Public, Private and Charitable Sectors (Including Internationally)?

The independent project comprises researchers at three universities and representatives from industry, social care and the voluntary sector. We are confident that the expertise within the group is adequate to take on a very challenging project, both conceptually and technically. However, the interdisciplinary nature of the project requires collaboration between several institutions and it is unlikely that a single institution would have all the relevant expertise.

5. Is There Sufficient Research Capability in the UK?

It should be noted that both UK and European research funding is restricted to home nationalities, making it difficult for other countries (eg USA and Japan) to participate in collaborative work, even when this is desirable.

6. Is the Research Being used to Inform Policy?

The Independent project addresses an important health and social care user group, with a prevalence of dementia of around 4–5 per cent of the over 65 population. The current Government has set a clear agenda to improve level and quality of services to support independent living within the community and the development of technologies is recognised as an important part of this process (DoH 2001). The following recent statements are also noted:

— *"By 2006 a further 100,000 people each year will be supported to live independently at home through extra intermediate and home care services" ("Delivering the NHS Plan—next steps on investment, next steps on reform"* April 2002).

— *"Improve the quality of life and independence of older people so that they can live at home wherever possible, by increasing by March 2006 the number of those supported intensively to live at home to 30 per cent of the total being supported by social services at home or in residential care."* (Priorities and Planning Framework for 2003–06 *"Improvement, expansion and reform: the next 3 years"*).

— *"Service capacity increased in other key services which support people at home so that in 2006: 30,000 more people a year receive care packages involving five hours or more a week of home care; 500,000 more pieces of community equipment are provided; there are 6,900 more extra care housing places. An increase of 6,000 in the number of people in care homes supported by councils over the three years to 2006."* (Priorities and Planning Framework for 2003–06 *"Improvement, expansion and reform: the next 3 years"*).

Current policy will require a change in the planning process, making it bottom up rather than top down and is implicitly looking for step change in achieving objectives. Plans are made locally but must meet these national targets that are "not negotiable". The implications of the policy and the demographics of increasingly older populations are that people with dementia will delay their entry into residential care and so methods of providing security, safety and support within the home for increased levels of dementia will be needed urgently. Equally, the eventual entry into residential care of patients with more severe dementia will affect the patient mix and the care needed in nursing and residential homes.

Exploitation of the outputs of R&D has been relatively limited. The emergence of new technologies within telecommunications, sensoring, artificial intelligence, robotics etc offer tremendous opportunities and, potentially, new technology could play a significant role in the delivery and support of community care services. However, the care industry has shown only limited signs of utilising new technology to improve products and services. New business and service models are required to allow technologies to be integrated within existing structures. Attention also needs to be paid to ethical issues and practical aspects such as installation and maintenance

7. References

Bjoerneby S (1997) The BESTA flats in Tonsberg. Using technology for people with dementia. Oslo, Human Factors Solutions.

Cooper, R G (1988) "Winning at New Products" pub Kogan Page. ISBN1-85091–769–8.

Department of Health (2001) National Service Framework for Older People. www.doh.gov.uk

European Commission (1996) Telematics Applications Programme, Disabled and Elderly Sector: Project Summaries. DGXIII–C5, Brussels.

Fisk, M (1999). Our Future Home: Housing and the Inclusion of Older People. London, Help the Aged.

Judd, S., M. Marshall, *et al* (1997). Design for Dementia. London, Hawker Publications Ltd.

Kitwood T, 1997 Dementia Reconsidered, Buckingham OU Press.

Marshall, M. (2001). "Dementia and technology. Inclusive Housing in an Ageing Society". In S M Peace and C Holland (Eds). Bristol, The Policy Press.

Orpwood, R (2002) "A 'smart' house to support the person with dementia". In Dementia Topics for the Millennium and Beyond, Ed S. Benson. Hawker, London. pp 87–90.

Pieper, R, Riederer, E (1998) Home care for the elderly with dementia. In Graafmans J, Taipale V, Charness N (eds) Gerontechnology: A Sustainable Investment in the Future. Amsterdam; IOS Press, 324–330.

Poulson D, Ashby M and Richardson S (1996) Userfit: A practical handbook on user-centred design for assistive technology. Loughborough: HUSAT.

Sixsmith, A J (1998) "Telecare at home". In Walker, A. (ed) European Home and Community Care 1998–99. London: Campden 141–142.

Sixsmith A (2000) "An evaluation of an intelligent home monitoring system". *Journal of Telemedicine and Telecare,* 6, 63–72.

Sixsmith A (2002) "New technology and the care of cognitively impaired older people". In Copeland J, Abou-Saleh M Blazer D (eds) Principles and Practice of Geriatric Psychiatry. Chichester: John Wiley and Sons.

Woolham, J and Frisby, B Building a Local Infrastructure that Supports the use of Assistive technology in Dementia Care. Research Policy & Planning 2002 Vol 20 No 1.

Woolham, J and Frisby B (2002) Using Technology in Dementia Care. In Dementia Topics for the Millenium and Beyond, ed S Benson. (Hawker: London p 91–94).

September 2004

Memorandum by Professor Peter Lansley

INTRODUCTION

Peter Lansley is Professor of Construction Management at the University of Reading. He has been closely involved with the development of the EPSRC EQUAL (Extending Quality Life) Initiative. He has chaired some of its awards panels and frequently acts as spokesperson for the Initiative. He is Director of the EQUAL Research Network which is concerned with promoting the contribution to improving the independence and quality of life of older people of design and engineering orientated interdisciplinary research.

The memorandum reviews some the features of the EQUAL Initiative and the organisation of research at national level and it offers some proposals for the future. It is informed by the experiences of the Network and the views of its members and supporters which include professionals, practitioners and older and disabled people as well as researchers. However this not an official account of the EQUAL Initiative. Rather it represents the perspective of those who have been closely involved with ensuring that it has had a clear focus on meeting the needs of older people.

THE VALUE OF DESIGN, ENGINEERING AND TECHNOLOGY RESEARCH

Recent research provides valuable support for the case that better design and application of both conventional and innovative technology can make a major contribution to improving the independence and quality of life of older people. The creation of more comfortable environments and of aids to living and recovery are valid areas for research.

Such research has been supported by a number of charities, some of which have a long-term commitment to improving living conditions for older and disabled people (for example, the Joseph Rowntree Foundation programme of work centred on Lifetime Homes, the work of the Thomas Pocklington Trust focused on visual impairment, and that of the RNIB in many areas including the design of the home). It has also received significant support from EPSRC, principally through its EQUAL Inititative. The success of these programmes gives a clear indication of both the positive outcomes which can be achieved and useful guidance on how to organise research to achieve maximum impact.

Given the range and magnitude of the issues faced by older and disabled people who may benefit from research there has been insufficient investment. However, since the research base is small and capacity for research is limited there is a need to consider how best to develop the research base and more generally how to organise ageing research, especially in the light of disappointing progress over the last three years.

THE EPSRC EQUAL INITIATIVE

EPSRC launched its EQUAL Initiative in 1997. This was focused on enhancing the independence and quality of life of older and disabled people through a programme of design, engineering and physical science orientated interdisciplinary research involving social, medical and health scientists as well as design, engineering and technology scientists. The programme required collaboration with intermediate organisations, such as housing providers, health and social services organisations, transport companies, and charities, and the direct involvement of older and disabled people in the individual projects constituting the programme. EQUAL has supported 39 projects ranging from very small one year feasibility studies with a value of £30,000, to large three year consortia projects with an award value of £650,000.

Most projects have considered how the environments of older and disabled people, and in some cases their carers, can be designed or modified to enhance well-being, independence and quality of life, but others have considered the enhancement of approaches to rehabilitation following illness or accident so as to enable the rapid return to home and, as far as possible, to normal daily routines. Although there has been a particular interest in the home environment including the devices and products used in the home, there has also been concern for care settings, public access buildings, urban environments and transport systems. Some projects have considered general aspects of ageing and disability whilst others have focused on specific aspects of physical impairment, sensory impairment (particularly vision and hearing), and cognitive impairment (especially dementia and stroke).

All projects have entailed the development of a detailed understanding of the way in which users interact with their environments, and their priorities and preferences. This has been a very necessary precursor to the gathering of data and creation of conceptual and operational models to enhance design information, improved design methodologies, better assistive technologies and innovative rehabilitation systems.

THE EQUAL PROJECTS

Those projects concerned with the home fall into two main categories. Building on the widespread success of community alarms and related systems, several projects have focused on the development of the smart home, advanced intelligent sensor systems, telecare and telemedicine. Other projects have been concerned with developing design guidance for new homes and yet others with the challenge of adapting existing homes so that older people can remain in them despite considerable infirmity. These have blended the perspectives of sociology, health care, design, technology and economics to provide important and compelling accounts of the options for policy makers, housing, health and social services organisations and for older people themselves. This work is able to make a sound economic as well as a quality of life case for the substitution of adaptations and assistive technology for traditional forms of care services. In some situations the savings could be considerable. A large proportion of the projects in all fields have a strong business or economic dimension reflecting their concern to meet the needs of government, other organisations and society to identify cost-effective approaches to enhancing independence and quality of life.

Projects concerned with infrastructure, transport systems and non-domestic buildings form two groups. Firstly, there have been those concerned with improving accessibility to buildings, transport systems and more generally the urban environment through better design and, secondly, projects concerned with developing navigation tools for people with specific impairments. Here again the integration of a range of disciplinary perspectives and exploitation of new technology have generated new practices, often with the potential to couple significantly improved independence with major cost savings.

The projects concerned with sensory and cognitive impairment have generated unique information about the needs of specific groups of people which is invaluable to designers, who previously have had little design guidance, and for health workers for example, Occupational Therapists, who have to match the needs of individuals with recommendations about how their homes might be adapted. Research with dementia patients is leading to systems which can afford them a greater degree of independence and confidence for longer whilst also supporting their carers. New technology has a role to play here but so too do new approaches to the design of care facilities. The work with stroke patients will contribute to improved recovery times and will enable some rehabilitation therapies to be home rather than hospital-based.

Inclusive design projects consider a wide range of conditions from normal ageing to ageing with multiple impairments. These are producing design data sets, advice, methodologies and technologies for design which are immensely attractive in terms of both innovative design processes and the resulting environments and products. Here there is much evidence to support the business and economic case for inclusive design especially when considering older people as consumers of products and services.

OUTCOMES

Just over half of the projects supported by the EPSRC EQUAL Initiative have been completed. The reminder will do so in the next two years. Many of their findings have been adopted by practitioners and policy makers, often within two years of project completion, and sometimes before they have been completed. Because the projects have involved collaboration with service providers and the involvement of older and disabled people, developments arising from the projects have been rapidly evaluated and refined. This has facilitated the further articulation of outcomes, especially where projects have produced state of the art and best practice guides, tool kits for professionals, demonstration systems, and devices and systems ready for application. Some of the outcomes have been of particular value to those who commission buildings, infrastructure and products, and to architects and designers who have to ensure that their designs are more inclusive of the needs of older and disabled people, and more generally the ageing population.

The research outcomes have also influenced, for example, the development of British Standards and building regulations, and the policies, practices and general outlook of key individuals within government organisations, such as the Housing Corporation, the Department for Transport, and the Disability Rights

Commission, even where they have called into question current policies and recommendations in relation to older people. At a more general level the findings have influenced expectations about how the built environment and everyday consumer products could and should be designed to accommodate the needs of older and disabled people. Similar comments apply to the findings arising from the rehabilitation projects. In particular these have raised expectations of what might be achieved through engineering and technology orientated research.

In addition the EQUAL Initiative has stimulated an enthusiasm amongst scientists from quite different fields for working closely together, and has highlighted the need to find further ways of working across scientific boundaries. For example, there is a need to understand in much more detail the implications of the biology of ageing, for instance, the variation in human biological functions, especially between ethnic groups. This is required not just to help designers accommodate particular impairments but also to aid health practitioners in the community to detect the onset of disabling conditions and to take appropriate action to arrest the rate of decline.

To summarise, the EQUAL Initiative has been particularly effective at identifying and supporting projects which, within a short space of time, have produced significant outputs for improving the quality of life of older and disabled people. Some of these outputs have already produced direct benefits. Others, through informing, for example, official standards and regulations, design procedures, and professional practice, will have a long term and systemic effect on the design and management of the built environment and consumer products, and on approaches to rehabilitation following illness or accident. Whilst modest, the approach taken by EPSRC to building research capacity and facilitating ageing research should be commended.

OTHER INITIATIVES

The EQUAL Initiative has run in parallel with other similar ageing related research programmes supported by large and small charities, housing and other organisations. Because some of these organisations are in a good position to ensure the application of their work, and many do so very successfully, they can create important expectations and standards of all research. A recent example is work carried out by RNIB Cymru and JMU Access Partnership on the design of housing to meet the needs of people with sight loss which is being incorporated into the requirements of grant funded Registered Social Landlords when they are building or adapting homes.

However, much of this other work is carried out in isolation and is rather *ad hoc*. For example, many organisations are presently involved with the development and application of home-based technologies in recognition of a major challenge for the quality of life of older people being that of supporting people in their own homes, especially people with dementia. There is a great deal of work needed here in bringing together these efforts if the aim is to develop cost-effective integrated services with good distribution networks, skilled installation personnel, and managers who are aware of the capabilities, cost effectiveness and limitation of new technologies.

BUILDING A COMMUNITY

In 1997 although there was a surprising number of university based research designers and engineers with some experience of ageing-related research, often gained through small-scale projects with charities or undertaken out of personal interest, there were very few experienced researchers in the areas to be covered by EQUAL. However, the Initiative was successful in attracting those with experience, as well as many newcomers from a broad range of disciplines within the physical, social, health and medical sciences. Probably because so many were new to the area, they were prepared for and relatively untroubled by many of the challenges of interdisciplinary user-orientated work. So, they quickly established new research methodologies which were to contribute to a new style of applied science. These new approaches deserve greater recognition for their effectiveness in the skilled business of involving users as active participants in the research process.

September 2004

Memorandum by Dr Frank Miskelly

INTRODUCTION

Developments in all areas of life usually entail embracing technology. The Zimmer Frame was arguably the greatest advance in elderly care in the 20th century. It is also a good example of an assistive technology. Electronic assistive technologies will identify the 21st century.

Recent developments in electronic and telecommunication technology are destined to make a significant contribution to elderly care both in institutions and in the community. Numerous electronic aids and devices have become available which improve patients' safety, security and ability to cope. Systems using advanced technology to support people at home could benefit both the patient and the care providers as it is generally accepted that care in the community is preferable to patients and usually less expensive than in institutions. Technological innovations working in partnership with the existing care system will change the future face of community care

NEW TECHNOLOGY AND PATIENT CARE

The successful introduction of a New Technology aid or device requires the following:

1. A device which successfully detects or prevents the clinical problem. The main clinical problems in older people are:

    (a) Falls.

    (b) Wandering.

    (c) Failure to Cope.

Numerous devices claim to alleviate these problems and our research is focussed on evaluating the benefits of the equipment in clinical practice. Many devices are designed for other purposes and then adapted to healthcare eg, prisoner tagging systems adapted to patients with dementia. Our experience is that the device does not always reliably perform what it claims.

2. An available infrastructure: Equipment will fail if it's usage requires the development of an infrastructure. The most successful method to introduce equipment systems is on an existing platform such as the Community Alarm System. The Community Alarm Service provides the monitoring and response arm of the system. It has developed an infra-structure of communications, data-bases, control centres and response networks which is well established in the United Kingdom and which has gained the confidence and trust of older people and professionals alike. The community alarm system provides an ideal framework for bolting on recent developments in electronic and telecommunication technology so future generations of the Community Alarm System are likely to form part of an integrated telecare system

3. Ethical Acceptability: In our research on Electronic Tracking and Tagging of older people with dementia a considerable barrier has been ethical or moral objections by patient interest groups to the use of equipment. These groups see the increasing use of technology as a substitute to high quality personal care. Our view is that technology is an additional safety feature which is utilised alongside the normal care package

4. Cost-effectiveness. Virtually no group is investigating this issue in the introduction and implementation of new technologies. There are several reasons for this. Firstly few groups are conducting proper systematic evaluations when equipment is introduced. Secondly, health economists are not always available.

THE "NEW TECHNOLOGY IN ELDERLY CARE PROJECT" (NTEC)

This Project is described briefly as it illustrates the type of equipment under development. The aim of this Project is to evaluate the benefits of modern aids and devices for older people living in institutions and the community. We focus on preventing or detecting:

    (a) Falls.

    (b) Wandering.

    (c) Failure to Cope.

in frail elderly living in hospitals, residential and nursing homes or their own homes.

The equipment is individually tailored to the needs of patients in their own home depending on the results of a "needs assessment." The Project is a joint venture between London Borough of Ealing, London Borough of Hammersmith & Fulham, Ealing Family Housing Association and Imperial College.

The aids and devices we have been evaluating include:

1. Video-monitoring system. This system allows people to see each other on their television at the same time as they speak on the telephone. It is useful where parents and offspring live some distance apart. For example, it allows a daughter in Kent to make a "virtual home visit" each day to her mother in Fulham which would be impossible by commuting

2. Electronic tagging. Alerts a carer when a person with dementia wanders outside a pre-defined area eg, a house. They can wander freely within the area. It allows the carer to perform the housework and only if the person tries to leave the house are they alerted.

3. Electronic tracking. Locates a person with dementia who has wandered off provided the person is carrying a GPS enabled mobile phone. This system can locate people anywhere in the country with an accuracy of five metres. It allows people with dementia to go out shopping and if they have not returned within an expected period we can locate them.

4. Computerised Fall Detection Systems. A camera attached to a computer continuously monitors the older person's living area. The computer uses pattern recognition analysis software to detect events such as falls and intruders. Any untoward event generates an alert at the Community Alarm Centre.

5. Bed monitors. Electronic devices which fit under the mattress and alert a carer or nurse when a patient vacates their bed. These devices prevent falls and accidents at night.

6. Chair monitors. Electronic devices which fit under the cushion and alert a carer or nurse when a patient vacates their chair. These devices prevent falls and accidents during the day.

7. Health monitors. Electronic devices which are worn on the wrist and alert a carer when the wearer has a fall, collapse or faint.

8. Fall detectors. Small bleep sized devices that fit to the belt and contain a mixture of accelerometers, impact meters or tilt meters to detect falls.

Some devices has shown substantial benefits in the care of older people while others have been less successful. Further evaluation is ongoing and new devices and technologies are being investigated.

NTEC EQUIPMENT EVALUATIONS

Sites	Bed Monitors	Chair Monitors	Video	Tagging	Tracking
Residential	X	X		X	
Nursing	X	X			
Sheltered	X	X			
Hospital	X	X			
Community			X	X	X

Why Is There A Need For Technology?

1. Demographics. The Western World is ageing, family sizes are smaller and the number of younger people to provide care is reducing. In future, some care functions will be automated using equipment rather than carers.

2. Healthcare costs. It can be more cost-effective to provide routine care for a client at home than in an institutional setting. Maintaining some people at home with care will only be possible with the assistance of technology

3. Quality of Life. People prefer to live at home close to their family and friends. Many people who may have entered a residential or nursing home following an accident or a bout of illness might be able to live independently in the comfort of their own homes if they were provided with a suitable level of technology support.

4. Telecare and Telemedicine can provide long-term monitoring of older people living in the community. Developing the use of technology in the community allows people to be treated and cared for at home rather than in hospital. The quality of care received at home is often better than in hospital. This isn't because hospital staff are less skilled or professional; rather, it is because the home environment is more conducive to good personal care.

Memorandum by The Queen Mother Research Centre for Information Technology to Support Older People

Although all technologies can impact on older people, this evidence will concentrate on Communications and Information Technology (C & IT).

1. SUMMARY

The applications of research in technology and design to improve the quality of life of older people

Information technology appears to have made an enormous impact on every aspect of society in the developed world. A more detailed examination of statistics, however, indicates that some groups are not benefiting from these advances. This situation has been referred to as the Digital Divide—the divide between those groups of people who benefit from Information Technology and those who do not or cannot access it. The Digital Divide has many causes, including economic disadvantage, but inappropriate software and human factors engineering has also played a major part in exacerbating the gap between those people who benefit greatly from computer technology and those who are excluded. It is this aspect of the application of the applications of research on which this submission will focus.

2. CURRENT INFORMATION TECHNOLOGY PRODUCTS

Much current information technology appears to have been designed by and for young men who are besotted by technology, and are more interested in playing with it, and exploring what the software can do, rather than achieving a particular goal.

Many older people and people and people with disabilities, however, lack the visual acuity, manual dexterity, and cognitive ability successfully to operate much modern technology. Many find the Windows environment, and the software associated with it, very confusing and difficult or impossible to use. Most mobile telephones require good vision and a high level of dexterity and video tape recorders are well known for providing many usability problems for older people.

In addition to the requirement for standard information technology products to be more usable by older people, the needs and wants of people who are in the "autumn" of their lives are not necessarily the same as those of younger people for whom these products have traditionally been designed, Specialised products are also needed which are designed to enhance independence and quality of life for older and disabled people.

Many people have developed very low expectations of older and disabled people's interest in and ability to use information technology products. A major cause of this, however, is government's and industry's lack of sensitivity to the particular needs and wants of older people and hence the inappropriate nature and poor usability of most products for older people. In general, the problem is not that older people are unwilling to use "new technology." The problem is that they are overwhelmed and frightened by the manifestations of technology which have been designed by people who do not understood the needs and abilities of older people.

3. THE POTENTIAL OF INFORMATION TECHNOLOGY PRODUCTS

3.1 Technology can make essential and non-essential services more accessible to disabled and elderly people who traditionally receive a poorer than average level of service, or may be excluded altogether from receiving these services due, for example to mobility visual or hearing problems. The services which are particularly relevant to older and disabled people include:

(a) Social communication—many older people suffer from social isolation , and appropriate electronic communication methods—mobile phones, email, chat rooms could provide substantial social and psychological support to isolated older people

(b) e-government—technology is increasingly being seen as a way of reducing costs and increasing efficiency of government, and at the same time a way of increasing participation in democracy by excluded or disaffected groups. On-line public information and electronic voting systems are examples of technologies that can enhance social inclusion.

(c) Support for the older workforce—there are good economic reasons for expanding the older workforce, but this can only be achieved if the workplace is appropriate for the older person.

(d) Healthcare—e-health applications can facilitate remote care and monitoring for disabled and elderly people, who may in any case need a higher than average level of care. At the same time, enhanced accessibility to on-line quality health information and decision support tools can lead to a more informed patient, who can as a result play an increasingly active role in their own care.

(e) Banking—on-line banking facilities can allow people to manage finances from home, reducing the need for a potentially difficult journey to a bank. Automatic teller machines (ATMs) allow direct and independent access at any time of the day to account information and cash, and increasingly offer additional banking-related facilities.

(f) Education—at a basic level, the Internet allows independent access to an enormous amount of information on a myriad of topics. Through e-learning applications, formal education, whether primary, secondary or tertiary may be made accessible to a wider section of society, and delivered in a way best suited to a learner with specific access needs.

(g) Commerce—through e-commerce web sites, independent access can be gained to on-line grocery stores, bookshops, clothing retailers; tickets for rail, bus, air or sea travel can be bought in advance. On-line auction services allow for an almost unimaginable variety of real—and virtual—products to be bought or sold.

(h) Dementia—although in its infancy research in the UK and the USA is beginning to show that information technology can provide support for people with dementia.

(i) Interactive television—this could provide a method for many older people to access services and information such as those listed above.

Other examples of applications of information technology for older people can be found in the Appendix.

3.2 It should be noted that a major user of government and e-health services are older and disabled people, and if the software provided for e-government is not usable by this group of people, it will have a very low up-take, and alternative manual systems will have to be in place, which will be expensive and inefficient. In addition lack of mobility and/or social isolation can mean that the introduction of usable web-based Banking Education and Commerce can make a much greater difference to the lives of older and disabled people than the rest of the population.

3.3 In addition usable web-based services could substantially reduce the social isolation of older people. This could be achieved, for example, by providing appropriate entertainment, by such technologies as mobile phones, interactive television, on-line chat rooms, and multi-user gaming environments. Currently, however, such technology is almost exclusively aimed at the younger age groups and able-bodied people. This results in increased exclusion of the people who who would most benefit most from improved access to web based services.

3.4 There is very little business software which takes into account the needs of older people, and the provision for disabled people is often less than adequate. This impacts negatively on the older worker, and the possibilities of extending active working life.

4. RESEARCH INFORMING POLICY

4.1 *Foresight Exercise—December 2000.*

In December 2000, the Ageing Panel of the DTI's Foresight programme reported to government. Appendix I contains extracts from their report (The Age Shift—Priorities for Action, DTI December 2000). This report calls for research programmes to be expanded, including the EPSRC EQUAL (extending the quality of active life) programme, and that "there should be manadory inclusivity during periods of rapid technological development (eg e-commerce)", and that "Government has a role to play as a promoter and exemplar of good practice."

It is not clear to this author that very much has changed since that document was produced. Unfortunately, unlike other Foresight Panels, the Ageing Population Panel was discontinued. The author has no evidence that the expertise on the Communications and Information Technology from the Ageing Population Panel has subsequently been used in the other Foresight panels which were continued.

The EQUAL project has continued, as recommended, and an EQUAL network has been formed of interested researchers. It is gratifying to note that there is to be an expansion of the EQUAL initiative involving other research councils. The percentage of the EPSRC and other research councils' budgets devoted to the C & IT needs of older people, however, is still miniscule compared with the percentage of the population who may benefit from such research. The vast majority of the research funding into ageing is focussed on drug and other medical interventions to alleviate the effects of old age.

4.2 *e-Government*

The current guidelines for UK Government Web sites published by the Office of the e-Envoy state the Government's policy as being that Web sites should be as accessible as possible.(Office of the e-Envoy "Guidelines for UK Government Web sites"). In the 2004 survey into the accessibility of UK web sites by the Disability Rights Commission (DRC), however, it was found that:

"81 per cent of web sites evaluated failed to satisfy even the most basic Web Accessibility Initiative Category": (DRC 2004, p37).

4.3 *Ofcom and Digital Television*

A major way in which C & IT will be provided to the public in the future is via digital television, and the access to programmes, will be via Electronic Programme Guides. It is satisfying to note that Ofcom has produced a Statement on Code on Electronic Programme Guides—26 July 2004, and a Code of Practice on Electronic Programme Guides. However this guide focuses only on certain groups of disabled people. Its General Principles refer to—"people with disabilities effecting their sight and hearing or both" —The main report has no mention whatsoever of older people, nor people with motoric and/or cognitive impairments which also effect significant numbers of older people. Indeed in the response to consultation comments (33) Ofcom states that it "sympathises with Age concerns view that EPG code should be extended to cover accessibility by people with dexterity and cognitive impairments, but this goes beyond the remit set by the Communications Act. By the same token we are not able to prescribe standards for remote controls". Both of these caveats provide a major shortfall in the requirements for many older people to successfully access and enjoy television—a situation which, if it continues, will severely compromise the possibilities of switching off analogue television (to which government is committed) exacerbated by older people being a major group not wishing to change to digital television.

In addition although the Independent Television Commission was for many years committed to and financially supported external long term research into the needs of older people, it is not clear that Ofcom intends to continue such long term research in the area of accessibility and usability of digital television for older viewers.

5. PRIORITIES AND GAPS IN RESEARCH

For the reasons adduced above, there needs to be substantially increased priority for information technology to be developed which is usable by and appropriate for older people and will extend the quality of their lives.

5.1 The key challenges for research in this area indicated by the foresight report were:

— To be customer led not technology driven.

— To design for inclusion taking into account the full range of user's needs and perceptions.

— To produce simple reliable systems.

— To design systems where the use of advanced technology is invisible in terms of both operation and cost.

5.2 The Disability Discrimination act tends to focus on young disabled people—whereas older people who are not "disabled" also require "reasonable adjustments if they are to be able to fully realise the benefits of information technology.

5.3 Similarly there is a major concentration on health care rather than social care, and this again is less appropriate for older people.

5.4 Old age is not a "health problem" which can be "cured". Barring sudden unexpected death, old people are likely to go through a period where they need support rather than aggressive medical interventions, and thus more emphasis needs to be placed on non-medical ways of improving quality of life—an area where information (and other) technologies can play a major part.

5.5 These are not trivial challenges, and major long term research is required to address these issues, as well as a commitment to apply the lessons learnt in research into government and industrial products and services. There are some isolated examples of good examples and practice, both in software and websites, but this is not widespread, and there is clear evidence of a lack of awareness in the need to develop accessible technology. At the same time levels of knowledge in effective inclusive design techniques are also disappointingly low. The constant appearance of new technologies also can increase the barriers to uptake by older and disabled people. [The most striking example from the history of computing is that before the windows environment was introduced many blind people were able to use computers both for work and leisure using speech synthesizers. The introduction of Windows, with at that stage no consideration of the needs of blind people, led to numbers of blind people being sacked because they could no longer use the companies computer systems. It was many years before Windows became accessible to blind people].

5.6 The major characteristics of older people in relation to their use of technology needs to be carefully mapped and subject to longitudinal studies which consider:

— The individual variability of physical, sensory, and cognitive functionality of people increases with increasing age.

— The rate of decline in that functionality (that begins to occur at a surprising early age) can increase significantly as people move into the "older" category.

— The more widely appearing problems with cognition, eg, dementia, memory dysfunction, the ability to learn new techniques.

— The effects of multiple minor (and sometimes major) impairments which can interact, at a human computer interaction level to produce a handicap that is greater than the effects of the individual impairments [Research into accessibility focused on single impairments will not always provide appropriate solutions].

— The significantly different needs and wants of older people due to the stage of their lives they have reached.

— How the environments in which older people live and work change their usable functionality—eg the need to use a walking frame, to avoid long periods of standing, or the need to wear warm gloves.

5.7 Long term studies are needed of how older people use technology and the relationship between their abilities and the requirements of new technology, including sensory motoric and cognitive performance and, importantly, combinations of these. These should include longitudinal studies about how older people's use of technology changes, for example with early introduction of support for dementia.

6. RESEARCH CAPABILITY

6.1 Research capability must be increased and this will only happen if more funds are focussed on it. In comparison with the resources available for medical and biochemical research, the funding available from governmental and charitable sources for technology to support older people is derisory, and relatively low compared to other technological strands, and there is little or no promise of long-term funding. There is also a lack of industrial support because, with one or two major exceptions, researching into the needs of older people is not seen as in the commercial interest of the company (despite all the publicity) and/or too expensive and/or they do not understand the needs of this group of consumers.

This means that "high flying" researchers are not attracted to the field. Researchers need to be encouraged to see the excitement of working in this field, and to be assured of the long term benefit of working in this important field.

Thus an EQUAL type initiative should be a permanent and expanding funding as part of EPSRC remit.

6.2 Centres of Excellence need to be set up with core funding to enable them to conduct innovative research without the constraints of constantly having to obtain funding for specific projects. Biochemical research has shown the effects of such core funding can have both on increasing the recruitment to the field but also to the innovations which are made, and similar initiatives are needed in research into technological support for older people.

7. RESEARCH CO-ORDINATION

There is some co-ordination of the research, such as the equal network, which could be built on, but the major challenge is increasing the quality and quantity of the research being done.

8. CONCLUSION

The appendix contains an overview of research at Dundee University and describes the UTOPIA project funded by the Scottish Higher Education Funding Council. UTOPIA is an acronym for "Usable Technology for older people: inclusive and appropriate". The search for this "utopia" would make a major contribution to improving older people's active life.

APPENDIX

Background to the submission and an example of current research activity:

Applied Computing at Dundee University is unique in the UK in having a large group (over 30 interdisciplinary researchers) who are researching into how C & IT can support older and disabled people. The University has also recently announced the Queen Mother Research Centre for Information Technology to support Older People. Most of the projects within the Centre are addressing specific requirements of older people, such as support for memory loss and dementia, detection of falling and other "dangerous" behaviour, lifestyle modelling, systems for non-speaking people, design of interfaces for older people, and most recently were the only non north American group to be funded as part of a joint Altzheimers Soc (USA) and Intel corporation research initiative. This project will investigate the use of digital television to assist carers of people with dementia by providing prompts for daily living.

UTOPIA (USABLE TECHNOLOGY FOR OLDER PEOPLE: INCLUSIVE AND APPROPRIATE)

This project includes a consortium of computing departments in the Universities of Dundee, which is the lead institution, Napier, Glasgow and Abertay Dundee. It is funded by the Scottish Higher Education Funding Council with the intention of assisting industry and commerce in exploiting the commercial opportunities opened up by these major demographic changes throughout the world.

The aim of the project was to raise the awareness of industry that the stereotype of an older person, who is both poor and technophobic, is not true for the majority of older people. In the developed world many older people have relatively large disposable incomes, and it is not they who are techophobic, but technololgy which has not been designed to take into account their needs. In the West, the "Baby Boomer" generation have a greater tendency than previous generations to be determined to get what they want and to spend money to obtain it. Thus there is a large market potential. There are also legislative requirements in many countries concerning access for people with disabilities. Approximately 50 per cent of those over 65 have a significant disability and the Disability Discrimination Legislation in the UK requires that "reasonable adjustments" are made so that people with disabilities can use equipment and access services. The US and other countries have similar legislation. Thus ignoring the needs of those older people with disabilities can leave a company open to legal challenge.

Although many older people have a significant disability, older people present a different challenge to designers than young disabled people. Information Technology for disabled people has tended to be focussed on young disabled people with a single disability. In contrast, older people all have multiple minor impairments of varying degrees—these will include, for example, poor eyesight hearing and memory, and increased stiffness in joints. Thus an older person's functionality may be reduced on a number of dimensions and this functionality will gradually decline as the person gets older. There is also a greater possibility of a sudden or rapid decline in functionality as people age. It is important to realise that, when using technology, these impairments can interact, thus the simple replacement of one modality (eg vision) for another (sound) may not be effective if the user has poor hearing as well as impaired sight. Finally, older people may have a different range of needs and wants than younger people. For example, they may be less inclined to set aside a long period of time to learn to use something of limited value to themselves than younger people.

C & IT products can be used to enhance the later stages of life in a number of ways. For the "fit" elderly, such systems can be used not only for providing a wide range leisure pursuits, but also technology which has been designed for the older user can be used significantly to extend economically active life. Whereas the frail elderly could use purpose designed C & IT equipment to reduce social isolation, to support memory and daily living. Such systems could also provide valuable support for the carers of frail older people, many of whom are elderly themselves. The UTOPIA project has developed a knowledge base, and substantial experience of working with older people and technology. Its aim is to disseminate this to developers, as well as to provide specialised services for those who wish to design C & IT systems for older people. To ensure that this advice is pragmatic, the project is grounded in a number of case studies examining particular aspects of design for older people. These case studies are:

— Artificial companions;

— Context aware Navigation Aids;

— Games technology;

— Messenger systems for help with technology.

— Older peoples' characteristics and their relationship with technology;

— Interface design; and

— Internet portals for the excluded.

Other projects within Applied Computing at Dundee University include:

— Computer Based Reminiscence, conversational support, and entertainment for people with dementia;

— Fall detection using video analysis;

— Gesture recognition for those who cannot use standard interfaces;

— Memory Aids using PDAs and mobile phones

— Accessibility of web sites

— Accessibility of "Accessibility options" for people with disabilities.

— Lifestyle modelling in a "smart house".

All this research has shown that, when designing for older people, it is essential that there is a primary focus on potential users of the technology. This, however, is often not straightforward, as, for example, one may be trying to obtain information about a technology of which the older person has no experience. We are thus examining innovative ways of interacting with users, and ways to ensure that designers have a real empathy with older users. We want to achieve a situation in which both older person and developer are both acting in a creative mode—which we call "mutual inspiration". We have thus gathered together a cohort of over 200 older people, both individuals and groups from day centres and residential homes who have a diversity of experience with technology, and a range of specific impairments (eg mobility, hearing, vision, speech problems, poor dexterity and memory). We have examined a range of ways in which older people can be encouraged to discuss requirements for novel C & IT systems, and evaluate prototype systems. These include questionnaires and focus groups, but also more innovative hands-on facilitated discussions and workshops and one-to-one in-home visits. We have also developed some very effective drama methods which use theatrical techniques, in collaboration with professional script writers and actors to facilitate discussion of further technology.

The aim of the UTOPIA project is to make an impact on the designers and developers of C & IT systems in Scotland.

— To raise awareness of the opportunities and challenges of an ageing population.

— To change attitudes of mind to what older people need and want from Information Technology.

— To provide a frameworks for checking accessibility, effectively and efficiently.

— To introduce a revised pragmatism which is sensitive to the needs and wants of older people without producing systems which are totally unsuitable for the rest of the population.

An important message from the project is:

— If you design for older and disabled people, you could be designing for everyone, but if you design for young fit people you will certainly exclude many.

This research will also form part of the recently announced Inclusive Design 2, EPSRC funded project with the Universities of Dundee, Cambridge, York and the Royal College of Art in collaboration with the Design Council.

September 2004

Memorandum by the Policy Research Institute on Ageing and Ethnicity

A. INTRODUCTION

1. PRIAE is the leading body specialising in ageing and ethnicity in the UK and across Europe. Established as an independent charity in 1998, the Institute seeks to improve health, social care and housing, income, pensions and, employment and quality of life for current and future generations of black and minority ethnic (BME) elders at the national and European level.

2. The Institute works with BME elders and age organisations, with clinical and non-clinical professionals and researchers, across sectors to influence, inform, develop and strengthen the knowledge base, capacity and practice in ageing and ethnicity.

3. PRIAE welcomes the opportunity to respond to the House of Lords Select Committee on Science and Technology call for evidence on the scientific aspects of ageing. This submission is based on the Institute's health specific national and European programmes in dementia; hospital care; diabetes and heart disease (all

funded by Department of Health) and the Minority Elderly Care (MEC) Report—empirical research undertaken as part of the EC Fifth Framework Research Programme. This research is highlighted for it is the largest research project in the area of ageing and ethnicity in the UK and across Europe, and a first for the European Commission in its 24 years of research framework funding. Relevant key findings from the Institute's research project are set out below. Due to its nature, related issues concerning BME elders and research enterprise and relevance are appropriately highlighted.

4. We set out first our key issues in research borne out of specific major developments highlighted above. This is then extended to cover the implications of our work and concerns for the future.

B. OVERVIEW OF RESEARCH AND DEVELOPMENTS IN HEALTH

1. The BME elder population once considered "too small to worry about by policymakers and planners" is now set to double, triple or quadruple in this and the next two decades.[5] This is in the context of historical underdevelopment of age and ethnicity, giving rise to the need for rapid progress, and is the primary reason for PRIAE's establishment.[6] It is in this regard that PRIAE has developed a range of health research and development programmes to remedy substantial gaps in our understanding of specific health conditions and influence changes in policy, research and practice.

2. We appreciate that the scope of this enquiry relates to scientific aspects of ageing rather than care and service provision. Our response is thus limited to this purpose though it is worth stating that pressures to make service provision appropriate and adequate is stimulating the need for improved scientific base in ageing and ethnicity: for example we know that through service usage, BME elders show a higher level of "earlier ageing". This is usually attributed to socio-economic considerations as well as approximating personal definition of old age to life expectancy of the country from which BME elders originate, usually lower than in the West. We know less about consequences of occupational concentrations in areas such as foundries, manufacturing, transport which the current generation of BME elders were employed in. Nor do we have sufficient understanding about the "migration" effect in the UK of BME elder women and men on their physical and mental health. This in turn has reduced the focus on behaviour patterns of BME elders, which may delay the onset of long-term and/or help manage better the conditions that they experience. The scientific knowledge base is poor in this regard as shown by PRIAE's own membership of Joseph Rowntree Foundation's Enquiry into Long Term Care.

3. The MEC research project The MEC research is designed and managed by PRIAE, begun in year 2001 and concluded in August 2004, with a launch of its findings to be held at the European Parliament on 9 December 2004. The MEC research project was undertaken concurrently in ten European countries: Bosnia-Herzegovina, Croatia, Finland, France, Germany, Hungary, the Netherlands, Spain and Switzerland and the UK. The project addresses the position of 26 different ethnic groups throughout Europe and includes both qualitative and quantitative research and aims to improve service provision in the field of health care and social care for BME elders. The research adopted a multi-disciplinary approach—with some 30 researchers across Europe from sociology, anthropology, social psychology, economics, gerontology, demography and management studies backgrounds.

4. The MEC Project uses a three-foci approach covering BME elders; health and social care professionals, managers and planners; and BME voluntary organisations. The research was conducted in West Yorkshire, London and Scotland with target Afro Caribbean, South Asian and Chinese/Vietnamese between 2003–04. All the interviews in the UK were conducted face to face and in the chosen language of the interviewee. Research Instrument was developed through critical incidents, focus groups and then adaptation of both clinical (Easy Care for example) and research instruments on health, together with SERVEQOL—a quality management tool for service specification. This necessitated the translation of research instruments into 7 different languages and the recruitment of fieldworkers with appropriate language skills. Few previous research projects on BME elders have been able to focus on all BME groups in the UK due to limitations in language.

5. The topics covered in the BME elders' survey Work Package 2 (WP2) include a wide range of demographic data, the socio-economic background of the participants; their legal status and migration history; their medical condition as well as various emotional/psychological attributes; their experiences with regard to racial harassment; their use and satisfaction with health and social care services; and their expectations and perceptions of health and social care services. The WP3 survey covers how mainstream providers design services for BME elders, the provision and use of health and social care services and service quality expectations, perceptions and the gap between these. The survey provides an extensive data set from health

---

4 Census 2001; References 1.

6 References 2.

and social care professionals and managers/planners and addresses whether BME elders have special health and social care needs and access problems and if so what the reasons for these are; measures used to encourage take-up of services by BME elders; resource issues and demand for services, collaboration in the design of services, service usage and target groups; and reasons for unmet service needs. In WP4 face to face interviews were conducted with 50 BME voluntary organisations in London, West Yorkshire and Scotland. The survey covers organisational characteristics; target BME groups and the needs of the elders; service provision; human and financial resources of the organisations; collaboration with others; attitudes towards mainstream provision and service quality expectations and perceptions. In some areas comparison of the results can be made across all three surveys.

6. The findings relevant to this Enquiry relate to health conditions which show that BME elders from seven ethnic groups face a range of health problems, for example:

— Afro-Caribbeans had a higher incidence of high blood pressure; compared to South Asians who had a higher incidence than the Chinese/Vietnamese.

— Afro-Caribbeans and South Asians had a higher incidence of diabetes than the Chinese/Vietnamese.

— Heart disease and lung/breathing conditions were highest amongst the South Asians.

— Osteoporosis and memory problems were highest amongst the Chinese/Vietnamese.

7. Full findings of the research will be released on 9 December 2004 at the launch at the European Parliament co-hosted by Claude Moraes MEP and Stephen Hughes MEP.

8. The purpose of MEC research was:

— To advance research in the area rather than be limited with small-scale studies which hitherto has been the experience to date in this area.

— To inform policy and planning and help direct appropriate investment in care and further research.

— To provide BME elders and organisations with sound knowledge base and tools, which they can use to influence nature of future work undertaken in the area, improving quality and funding.

— To use the research to produce specific actions from both clinical and non-clinical practice.

— To appreciate that ethnicity and age as important cross-sections can help majority older people with low incomes also (eg through research instruments developed and consequent practice which may arise from the findings).

— It is recognised in the health arena that BMEs have different health problems than the white British population. For example the differences with regard to diabetes are well known. Current research is attempting to identify the causal mechanisms leading to these differences. We believe the key issues are for the medical professional to understand the underlying causes of the differences in the incidence of certain medical conditions and then to address what can be done about it. There is a need to understand to what extent the differences between ethnic groups are unavoidable and what can be changed and improved over time. There may also be a strong case for more health education among certain BMEs.

9. The benefits of MEC research to the policymakers, planners, BME elders, organisations and research community is immense: we have quantitative data on health conditions and usage of services previously unavailable. The data is analysed with respect to age, gender and ethnicity allowing us to make specific deductions about prevalence of illnesses between these groups, and consequent responses leading to care considerations. This research was designed to inform policymakers on the direction of care based on the health experience of BME elders, and providers' response. From a research point of view, MEC research created 12 full time equivalent research posts for three years in ten countries. Fieldworkers were additionally employed. A majority of researchers had no experience of undertaking major research in ethnicity and age; where they had research experience in age, this was limited to qualitative work. In this way human and social capital has been produced; research instruments produced by PRIAE with partner comments, were applied in all countries and withstand rigorous statistical techniques. PRIAE conceptualised this research, designed it and led it at all stages with specific developments. This will be a first for a BME led body to engage in such a major research enterprise in age and ethnicity concerning health. The Enquiry asks for research capability: we have shown here that we have delivered a major and complex piece of research attracting personnel who could understand the proposal (earned the highest research rating in the theme of ageing) and implement it with use of appropriate techniques. At the end of this research phase, our main concern is how to sustain the personnel skilled up in the area and to maintain the engagement with our majority peers from gerontology to recognise the work. How funders see our work is essential to maintain the resource base for such research and supporting capacity within PRIAE.

10. CNEOPSA (Care Needs for Ethnic Older Persons with Alzheimers)—this research and development project from PRIAE established that dementia and ethnicity is on the agenda (Professor Marshall at the launch, 1998) and the research was described as "impressive and authoritative" by Health ministers (Rt Hon Paul Boateng MP 1998; Rt Hon John Hutton 1999).

11. PRIAE commissioned Dr Shah, a psycho-geriatrician and researcher and member of PRIAE's CNEOPSA working group recently, to outline assessment and diagnostic issues. We use an extract from this work (to be published by PRIAE)

Dementia is difficult to diagnose in BME elders (George & Young, 1991; Patel & Mirza, 2000a) because of issues listed in Table 5. A further issue is the paucity of suitable screening and diagnostic instruments for dementia in this group (Shah, 1998). Cognitive tests developed and standardised in one ethnic group may not be appropriate for another ethnic group because they are influenced by culture, education, language, literacy skills, numeracy skills, sensory impairments, unfamiliarity with test situations and anxiety (Shah *et al.*, 2004). Instruments measuring cognitive impairment developed for the English speaking indigenous population have been developed in a number of ethnic minority languages using a detailed translation and back-translation process and formal evaluation of psychometric properties (Shah *et al.*, 2004). The Mini-Mental State Examination (MMSE) (Folstein *et al.*, 1975) has been developed in several languages as listed in Table 6. The Hindi, Urdu, Punjabi, Bengali, Gujarati and Chinese versions are of particular relevance in the UK. The abbreviated Mental Test Score (Quereshi & Hodkinson, 1974) has been developed in several south Asian languages for use among Gujaratis and Pakistanis and in English for use among African Caribbeans in the UK (Rait et al., 1997, 2000a, 2000b). The MMSE, selected items from the CERAD neuropsychological test battery (Morris *et al.*, 1989), the CAMCOG component of the CAMDEX interview (Roth *et al.*, 1986) and clock drawing have been evaluated in elderly African Caribbean people (Richards & Brayne, 1996; Richards et al., 2000; Stewart *et al.*, 2001). Most instruments developed for BME elders are either cognitive screening instruments or those measuring severity of cognitive impairment; diagnostic instruments have not been formally evaluated for use with BME elders (our emphasis).

12. The implication of PRIAE's work in dementia is that while we have lifted the area where it is regarded as important and included in National Service Framework for Older People, appropriate instruments, prevalence rates, clinical and non-clinical understanding of how dementia (mental health generally) is expressed in behaviour, is yet to be developed.

13. "What works for us" R &D into CHD and Diabetes concerning BME elders—PRIAE project funded by R&D at DH. We include here an extract from our soon to be published work, prepared by Dr H.Waters in this project (led by Dr L.Fredli, S.Griffiths and M.Gabriel). Very little material has been found that connects the problems of elderhood per se with either of the two conditions reviewed here, though there are a number of studies that discuss the incidence of these two conditions among the communities. A large amount of research is being undertaken on these two conditions and ethnicity. None specifically examines the intersection of age, ethnicity and illness which is the focus here. Therefore, analysis of practice and health care interventions in our field has to be extrapolated from a number of sources, and not necessarily confined to those that are strictly academic.

14. It is worth pointing out that the higher incidence of CHD among South Asians was largely placed on the agenda by South Asians themselves. As in other areas of BME life, it was communities themselves which first began demanding that their specific problems be addressed. As early as 1985, the Confederation of Indian Organisations approached the Coronary Prevention Group concerning its anxiety over the high rates of CHD among Asians in Britain. The resulting report, Coronary Heart Disease and Asians in Britain raised many of the issues that are still being unravelled, but appears to be rarely cited.[65]

15. A number of studies have attempted to discover the clinical reasons for such a high incidence, and factors such as diet, lifestyle, metabolism and genetic predisposition have all been adduced.[7] Much large-scale clinical research remains to be done. For example, the incidence of hypertension—a risk factor implicated in CHD, itself a risk factor of diabetes—is higher among middle-aged south Asians (around 30 per cent) and African Caribbeans (around 25–35 per cent) than among the overall population (10 to 20 per cent).[8] Yet the incidence

[6] References 2.

[7] Coronary Prevention Group, *Coronary Heart Disease and Asians in Britain: a report prepared . . . for the Confederation of Indian Organisations* (London, CIO, 1986).

[8] See, eg, T. Knight, Z. Smith, J. A. Lockton, P. Sahota, A. Bedford, M. Toop, E. Kernohan and M.R. Baker, "Ethnic differences in risk markers for heart disease in Bradford and implications for preventive strategies", *Journal of Epidemiology and Community Health* (Vol. 47, 1993), pp. 89–95; Nada Lemic-Stojcevic, Ruth Dundas, Stephen Jenkins, Anthony Rudd and Charles Wolfe, "Preventable risk factors for coronary heart disease in stroke amongst ethnic groups in London", *Ethnicity and Health* (Vol. 6, no. 2, 2001), pp. 87–94.

of CHD is lower among African Caribbeans than the national average, while the incidence of stroke is higher.[9] One small scale survey, starting from the premise that differences in rates for the main cardiovascular risk factors are not substantial enough to account for the major differences in the incidence of CHD, surmised that worse "socio-economic circumstances (especially those associated with stress, such as that related to employment, income and housing)" among Asians may also be a factor.[10] The London Health Observatory has drawn attention to the "interaction between [health] risks" and "low income, unemployment, poor quality housing and low educational attainment" as "especially important in terms of differences in health between ethnic groups", with BME groups tending to have lower average incomes and higher unemployment.[11] Bardsley *et al* also call for more resources to be put into "Exploration of how differences in mortality by country of birth relate to socio-economic variables such as social class".[12] As we have already seen, BME elders, as pensioners, are among the poorest of an already poor social group—so the link between their health status and socio-economic status is not hard to discern, though it may be awkward to quantify and isolate in a rigorously academic way.

16. Similarly, it is difficult rigorously to quantify or isolate the factors underlying differential access for BME individuals to specialist services. Hence, material attempting to address this issue tends to fall outside the remit of the more purely academic literature reviews. Here, the expertise of PRIAE is important, in that, through its contact with BME elders at the receiving end of services, it can uncover the factors that may hinder them from getting appropriate care. More research has been done in the mental health field, relating to ethnicity, diagnosis and treatment, and discrepancies arising from discriminatory approaches, but little has been done in relation to other conditions. According to the London Health Observatory:

— out-patient attendance rates are lower for some ethnic minority groups

— . . . some evidence of inequity in specialist cardiac investigation services, especially for South Asian groups . . .

All these are factors will particularly impinge on BME elders, but, apart from PRIAE's work, their experience of medical and care services has not been examined.

CONCLUSION

(i) We have shown above that major research and development work that can enhance good health and delay onset of long term conditions for BME elders is in its infancy. There are major gaps, and where work is being done, including by PRIAE, insufficient recognition is being given to it. There is an appearance of much work being done, but this needs to be seen from the context of very low base line developments from which it has emerged.

(ii) PRIAE's own capacity to promote good research and undertake areas that it regards as important is curtailed by (a) how ageing and ethnicity is conceived by funders and researchers (b) by funding as a self-financing Institute.

(iii) Any research investment strategy, and we hope that the Committee's deliberations shall lead to this, is to be welcomed if it can increase the focus on ageing and ethnicity and consequent research and developments that can follow.

(iv) In late 2004 it is correct to summarise research in ageing and ethnicity as: Characteristic of BME elder research, development and practice is that it is patchy, piecemeal and ad hoc—where research in one area undertaken is seen as addressing "anything and everything you wanted to know about BME elders and condition x". In this sense, BME elder research and developments is reduced to a very narrow conception of what is appropriate in ageing and ethnicity (Patel 1999), thereby denying possibility of wide spread understanding the process of ageing (both biologically and socially) and its impact on BME elders and communities. It would be true to say that technological developments or clinical trials for specific areas concerning older people are not likely to include BME elders in the sample frame. If they do it is likely to be too small, rendering the justification made by PRIAE that

[9] V. Soni Raleigh, "Diabetes and hypertension in Britain's ethnic minorities: implications for the future of renal services", *British Medical Journal* (Vol. 314, no 7075, 1997, pp. 209-13, cited in Mohammed Memon and Farha Abbas, "Reducing health risks in ethnic communities" *Nursing Times* (Vol. 95, no. 27, 1999). pp. 49–51.

[10] LHO, "Black and minority ethnic populations", *op cit*, p 3; White, Carlin, Rankin and Adamson, *op. cit*;

[11] G Y H Lip, C Luscombe, M McCarry, I Malik and G Beevers, "Ethnic differences in public health awareness, health perceptions and physical exercise: implications for heart disease prevention", *Ethnicity and Health* (Vol. 1, no. 1, 1996), pp. 47–53, citing R. Williams, R Bhopal, and K. Hunt, "Coronary risk factors in a British Punjabi population: comparative profile of non-biochemical factors", *International Journal of Epidemiology* (Vol. 23, 1994), pp 28–37.

[12] Bardsley, Hamm, Lowdell, Morgan and Storkey, *op cit*, p 11.

unless we have dedicated research in ageing and ethnicity, the field will remain undeveloped with differential care as a consequence. That cannot be good when agendas' about social cohesion, inclusion, health equality and equity are promoted as policy measures.

REFERENCES

[1] Patel, N. (ed) (2003) Minority Elder Care in Europe—ten country profiles, MEC Research for the EC 5th Framework Research Programme, PRIAE.

[2] PRIAE report to the Royal Commission:
Patel, N. (1999) Perspectives on Black and Minority Ethnic Elders in the UK1 report commissioned by the Royal Commission on Long Term Care for the Elderly, research volume 1, HMSO.

[3] Dementia Matters: Ethnic Concerns (PRIAE-CNEOPSA Project), (1999).

October 2004

Memorandum by Dr Jane Preston, Dr Alan Hipkiss and Professor Robert Weale

CONTROLLING THE ONSET OF AGE-RELATED DYSFUNCTION AND CONSEQUENT PATHOLOGIES

1. It is a truism to say that in order to suppress deleterious age-related change we should remain young. This aphorism is applicable to studies at both cellular and molecular levels and we are beginning to understand quite clearly the biological reasons for the existence of ageing (Holliday 2004) and the underlying cellular and molecular processes. What is far less clear is how this understanding can be harnessed to improve human health and longevity. The merit in this approach is that by understanding the basic tenets of cell and molecular ageing, we have the potential to understand multiple age related diseases (Hayflick 2000), an approach that complements the more traditional disease focussed research process. This paper summarises promising areas of cellular and molecular research, and gaps in current knowledge of how to translate the *in vitro* studies into health benefits in later life.

CELLULAR AND MOLECULAR APPROACHES

2. *Oxidative stress*. The involvement of free radicals and reactive oxygen species in ageing and disease has been a popular avenue for research since the 1950s. Oxygen species are produced as a by-product of normal cell metabolism and also have specific functions as intracellular signals, but in excess produce oxidative stress, damaging all intracellular components, eventually leading to cell death. High free radical plasma load is correlated with poor cognitive function and reduced physical activity in men and women in their 80s (Maugeri *et al* 2004) and oxidative stress is implicated in a wide variety of health problems including neurodegeneration (Emerit *et al* 2004), vascular disease, muscle weakness and cancer. Interestingly, production of some reactive oxygen species is lower in women compared to men, which may help explain some of the differential in longevity. Thus, this avenue of research has enormous potential in the treatment of long-term illnesses.

3. Although it seems logical to expect that antioxidants (which reduce oxidative stress in experimental cell and molecular models) can prevent such oxidative damage, use of antioxidant vitamin supplements in a variety of combinations has been very disappointing in clinical trial (Tran 2001), with little or no positive outcome on disease progression. An explanation of the poor effect in human trials has been put forward by Lane (2003) and is based on the cell's need for a nominal level of oxidative stress to trigger gene responses to infection for example. Since intracellular detection of oxidative stress is essential, mechanisms have evolved to buffer exogenous antioxidants so that they do not dampen the desired response to infection. In the young this is a positive adaptation, but persists in old cells, even though by that time it would be desirable to reduce the, now damaging, oxidative load. He further suggests that excess antioxidants may be harmful since they would delay the resolution of infections and physiological stress. While there is no doubt that oxidative stress maintains a central place in understanding ageing, much more information is needed about the genetic and physiological regulation of endogenous intracellular antioxidants.

4. *Calorie restriction*. The only experimental approach consistently shown to improve health and longevity in animal models is calorie restriction—a reduction of up to 50 per cent of the calorie intake, while maintaining all other nutritional components. It is effective in delaying the onset of diabetes, CVD, muscle weakness, neuropathy in rats (Merry 2004) even in mild restriction studies (80 per cent of normal calories, Usuki *et al* 2004).

5. There is increasing evidence that the positive effects are a result of reduced oxidative stress due to slow production of free radicals by the mitochondria sub-cellular organelles (Lambert and Merry 2004). These positive effects are reversed by insulin (Lambert and Merry 2004) which increases production of reactive oxygen species by the mitochondria (Mahadev *et al* 2001). Insulin resistance and high blood insulin levels are common in older people, and characteristic of age-related Type 2 (non-insulin dependent) diabetes. Diabetes itself is a risk factor for Alzheimer's disease and CVD/stroke, so potential translation therapies from calorie restriction studies linking cellular oxidative stress and deleterious effects of insulin are great. This should include the effects of early life nutrition, from conception onward, since poor early nutrition and small weight at birth are major risk factors for diabetes, cardiovascular disease and stroke in later life (Barker 2003).

6. *Altered Proteins.* Ageing in humans, human cells in culture and in animal models is accompanied by intracellular accumulations of altered or aberrant protein forms. Age-related conditions such cataracts in the eye lens, amyloid plaque and tangles in Alzheimer's disease, Lewy bodies in Parkinson's disease and inclusion bodies in Huntingdons's disease and motor neurone disease (amyotrophic lateral sclerosis) provide exaggerated pathological examples of the same phenomenon (Bossy-Wetzel *et al* 2004, Ross and Poirier 2004).

7. Altered proteins of almost any origin, including those damaged by oxygen free-radicals, are normally selectively destroyed intracellularly by proteasomes, multicatalytic proteases which beak down proteins to their constituent parts (Grune *et al* 2004). It is important that the cell maintains sufficient proteasome activity to remove rapidly any altered proteins that are formed before they interact deleteriously with other cellular components (Luxford *et al* 2002, Morgan *et al* 2002). Compromised proteasome activity can also affect mitochondrial metabolism causing accumulation of dysfunctional mitochondria (Bota and Davies 2001), an increase in oxygen free-radical generation and formation of more altered proteins (Terman and Brunk 2004).

8. There is now convincing evidence to show that ageing generally is accompanied by a decline in proteasome activity (Caballero *et al* 2004), and that in many age-related pathologies this function is severely compromised in the relevant tissues (Keller *et al* 2004). Consequently, it is crucially important to study how the high proteasome activity of young cells is maintained, and determine the underlying causes of the age-related fall in this function. Caloric restriction in animals attenuates the decline in proteasome activity (Selsby *et al* 2004), which suggests that the system can be manipulated physiologically. It may, therefore, be possible to develop agents that mimic caloric restriction (CR mimetics) which help maintain proteasome activity at levels characteristic of the juvenile state. CR mimetics that maintain juvenile proteasome activity could therefore delay onset of those age-related pathologies where aberrant proteins accumulate.

9. *Replicative senescence.* As a concept, the idea that dividing cells have an inherent limit to their ability to replicate (Hayflick 1965) is a very attractive explanation of cellular ageing. There has been some criticism of the cell culture methods used to investigate and interpret this phenomenon (Rubin 2004) in particular that erosion of end regions of DNA, the telomeres, with each cell division function as a counting mechanism or "clock". Another interpretation is that telomere erosion is due to oxidative stress and replicative senescence is a stress response (von Zglinicki 2003). If we consider ageing to be a "function of rising intracellular oxidative stress rather than chronological time" (Lane 2003) the two interpretations become complementary and help explain the large variability in telomere loss within a cohort of the same age group.

10. Replicative senescence and the accompanying phenotypic changes to the cell, have been implicated in vascular disease, reduced skin healing and arthritis. A great strength of this line of research has been in understanding dysfunction of the immune system in later life. Correct function of the immune system is reliant on extremely rapid cell division to expand the population of T cells in response to infection. In later life, new naïve T cells produced by the thymus gland are reduced (Aspinall *et al* 2004), and as many as 50 per cent of the CD8 T cell pool (involved in response to viral infections) have shorter telomeres, reduced replicative potential (Effros 2004), and therefore reduced ability to respond to infection. Identification of these T cells may be a useful biomarker for ageing, since they correlate with osteoporosis and early mortality (Posnett *et al* 1999, Wikby *et al* 2002, Effros 2004). Recent research on the use of Interleukin-7 to stimulate the thymus gland in mice has shown increased T cell responsiveness (Aspinall *et al* 2004) and is a promising novel therapy.

BIOMARKERS AND LIFE EXPECTANCY

11. It is clear from the accumulated knowledge in biogerontology that ageing is not entirely chronologically determined; a rat is old at three years of age, while a three year old human is barely starting life. Although it is true that the risk of ill health increases with time, biogerontology would point to this being due to accumulation of cell and molecular damage. Research into valid and reliable biomarkers of senescence and longevity would help "unmask" the biological heterogeneity of the older population and identify areas for fruitful gerontological research. Discussing indices of a patient's state of health, Borkan and Norris (1980)

reported that, from a statistical point of view, a general practitioner's subjective assessment was very reliable. However, there have been numerous attempts to base estimates of life expectancy on a more objective basis. Borkan & Norris' results have been found to be incompatible with the data based on the application of the Seineur Protocol, a rigorous immunological study which led to the conclusion that appearances can be deceptive (Steinmann 1984; Lightart and al 1990).

12. Earlier authors had examined numerous human biological attributes as a function of age, but their results did not lead to any definition of biological, as distinct from calendar age. In several cases the choice of function was misguided. For example, Alex Comfort (1969) suggested the visual threshold and pupil diameter as suitable (but see Weale 1970). More recently, there have been suggestions as to what collection of functions might be useful (Jackson, Weale and Weale 2003). The number should be minimal, involve as little of the professional's and patient's time as possible, and involve as few invasive tests as possible. Subjective tests should be avoided. The choice of functions should demonstrably lead to a prediction of health and life expectancy. That this may be possible has been elaborated in Jackson & al's study.

13. The Medical Research Council is currently engaged in a longitudinal study, partly devoted to some of the above objectives. Unfortunately the starting age selected is near "mid-life", whereas a great deal of evidence suggests that functional decrement starts much earlier, in the 20s, if not at, or even before, birth (Weale 2004).

14. It thus seems appropriate to suggest that the study of biomarkers should form part of public health policy, because its results would be of use in the National Health Service, in pension arrangements, in matters relating to insurance, and in those relating to employment.

15. That said, it needs to be added that such data would be of little once-and-for-all value. Demographic and other population changes, skeletal growth, dietary influences, etc may influence the situation at any one time. Arrangements should be made for the creation of a monitoring agency, perhaps in analogy with the Health and Safety Executive, which would collect data at intervals of not more than every 10 years.

ARE THERE GAPS IN RESEARCH?

IS THERE SUFFICIENT RESEARCH CAPABILITY IN UK?

16. Some areas highlighted in this paper indicate gaps in our current knowledge and current methodologies.

17. *Longitudinal studies*; there is a fundamental need for longitudinal studies to help control for the cohort effects and increasing variability with age that masks the effects of biological ageing. The approach of the MRC is very welcome, however, we would strongly suggest that such studies begin with very early life (ideally conception or birth) and extend across the life course. "Snap-shot" comparisons of younger and older adults ignores the fact that all the changes described are occurring from the moment life begins; the only way to understand how "young" cells are capable of maintaining themselves more effectively than "old" cells is to study every life stage.

18. *Biomarkers of ageing*; ageing is not simply chronologically determined but due to accumulation of cell and molecular damage. Research into valid and reliable biomarkers would help identify those areas for fruitful research by reducing confounding factors in a heterogeneous older population.

19. *Cellular and molecular approaches*; although oxidative stress is well represented in biogerontological research, some fundamental questions about the control of oxidative stress remain to be answered before this can be translated in real health benefits, including the role of nutrition in early and adult life.

20. The study of proteasome function in removing aberrant proteins has potential for relatively rapid production of viable therapies for neurodegenerative diseases and is an area poorly represented in the UK.

21. In contrast, research on replicative senescence is well represented in the UK and is much further advanced in making the links between biogerontology and health benefits.

IS RESEARCH BEING USED TO INFORM POLICY?

22. There is a recognised tendency, both in the UK and internationally, for clinical and basic biomedical research to be compartmentalized into disease models or discipline specific approaches. Although this is being addressed by the BBSRC (for example the recent strategic area on nutrition and vascular disease throughout the life course), there is still considerable scope for greater collaboration between MRC and BBSRC; for example to fund basic exploratory biological research. In terms of health promotion policy, it is clear that nutritional and epidemiological evidence is being used currently to raise awareness of disease risk factors. It is less clear that biogerontological evidence is, or indeed can currently be, used to inform health promotion policy.

REFERENCES

Aspinall R, Henson S, Pido-Lopez J, Ngom PT (2004) Interleukin-7. An interleukin for rejuvenating the immune system. Annals of the New York Academy of Sciences 1019, 116–22.

Barker DJ (2003) Coronary heart disease: a disorder of growth. Hormone Research 59, suppl 1 35–41.

Borkan, G A & Norris, A H (1980). Assessment of biological age using a profile of physical parameters. Journals of Gerontology 35, 177–84.

Bossy-Wetzel E, Schwarzenbacher R, Lipton SA (2004) Molecular pathways to neurodegeneration. Nature Medicine 10, S2–9.

Bota DA, Davies KJA (2001) Protein degradation in mitochondria: implications for oxidative stress, aging and disease. Mitochondrion 1, 33–49.

Caballero M, Liton PB, Challa P, Epstein DL, Gonzalez P (2004) effects of donor age on proteosome activity and senescence in trabecular meshwork cells. Biochemical and Biophysical research Communications 323, 1048–54.

Comfort, A (1969) Test battery to measure aging rate in man. The Lancet ii,1411–1415.

Effros RB (2004) T cell replicative senescence. Annals of the New York Academy of Sciences 1019, 123–6.

Emerit J, Edeas M, Bricaire F (2004) Neurodegenerative diseases and oxidative stress. Biomedicine and Pharmacology 58, 39–46.

Grune T, Jung T, Merker K, Davies KJA (2004) decreased proteolysis caused by aggregates, inclusion bodies, plaques, lipofuscin, ceroid and "aggresomes" during oxidative stress, aging and disease. International Journal of Biochemistry and Cell Biology 36, 2519–30.

Hayflick L (1965) the limited in vitro lifetime of human diploid cell strains. Experimental Cell research 37, 614–36.

Hayflick L (2000) the illusion of cell immortality. British Journal of Cancer Research 83, 841–6.

Holliday R (2004) the multiple and irreversible causes of aging. Journals of Gerontology: Biological sciences 59A, 568–72.

Keller JN, Dimayuga E, Chen Q, Thorpe J, gee J, Ding Q (2004) Autophagy, proteasomes, lipofuscin and oxidative stress in the aging brain. International Journal of Biochemistry and Cell Biology 36, 2376–91.

Lambert AJ, Merry BJ (2004) effect of calorie restriction on mitochondrial reactive oxygen species production and bioenergetics: reversal by insulin. American Journal of Physiology 286, R71–9.

Lane N (2003) A unifying view of ageing and disease: the double-agent theory. Journal of theoretical Biology 225, 531–40.

Lightart GJ, Corberand JX, Geertzen HGM, Meinders AE, Knook DL, Hijmans W (1990) Necessity of the assessment of health status in human immunogerontological studies: evaluation of the Senieur Protocoll. Mechanisms of Aging and Development 55, 89–105.

Luxford C, dean RT, Dabies MJ (2002) induction of DNA damage by oxidised amino acids and proteins. Biogerontology 3, 95–102.

Mahadev K, Wu X, Zilbering A, Zhu L, Lawrence JT, Goldstein BJ (2001) Hydrogen peroxide generated during cellular insulin stimulation is integral to activation of the distal insulin cascade in 3T3-L1 adipocytes. Journal of Biological Chemistry 276, 48662–9.

Maugeri D, Santangelo A, Bonanno MR, Testai M, Abbate S, Lo Guidice F, Mamazza C, Puglisi N, Panebianco P (2004) Oxidative stress and aging: studies on an east-sicilian ultraoctagenarian population living in institutes or at home. Archives of Gerontology and Geriatrics, Supplement 9, 271–7.

Merry BJ (2004) Oxidative stress and mitochondrial function with ageing—the effects of calorie restriction. Aging Cell 3, 7–12.

Morgan PE, Dean RT, Davies MJ (2002) Inactivation of cellular enzymes by carbonyls and protein-bound glycation/glycoxidation products. Archives of Biochemistry and Biophysics 403, 259–69.

Posnett DN, Edinger JW, Manavalan JS (1999) Differentiation of human CD8 T cells: implications for in vivo persistence of CD8+ CD28- cytotoxic effector clones. Int immunology 11, 229–41.

Ross CA, Poirier MA (2004) Protein aggregation and neurodegenerative disease. Nature Medicine 10, S10–7.

Rubin H (2004) Promise and problems in relating cellular senescence in vitro to aging in vivo. Archives of Gerontology and Geriatrics 34, 275–86.

Selsby JT, Judge AR, Yimamai T, Leewenburgh C, Dodd SL (2004) Life long calories restriction increases heat shock proteins and proteasome activity in soleus muscles of Fisher 344 rats. Experimental Gerontology (in press).

Steinmann, G (1984). Admission criteria for immunogerontological studies in man: the Senieur Protocol. Mechanisms of Aging and Development 28, 47–55.

Terman A, Brunk UT (2004) Aging as a catabolic malfunction. International Journal of Biochemistry and Cell Biology 36, 2365–75.

Tran TL (2001) Antioxidant supplements to prevent heart disease. Real hope or empty hype? Postgraduate Medicine 109, 109–14.

Usuki F, Yasutake A, Umehara F, Higuchi I (2004) Beneficial effects of mild life-long dietary restriction on skeletal muscle: prevention of age-related mitochondrial damage, morphological changes and vulnerability to a chemical toxin. Acta Neuropathalogica 108, 1–9.

von Zglinicki T (2003) Replicative senescence and the art of counting. Experimental Gerontology 38, 1259–64.

Weale, R A (1970) The eye and measurement of ageing rate. The Lancet 2, 147.

Weale, R A (2004) Bio-repair mechanisms and longevity. Journals of Gerontology 59A, 449–54.

Wikby A, Johansson B, Olsson J (2002) Expansions of peripheral blood CD8 T-lymphocyte subpopulations and an association with cytomegalovirus seropositivity in the elderly. Experimental Gerontology 37, 445–53.

October 2004

Memorandum by QinetiQ

QinetiQ has undertaken considerable recent analysis of research data on the ageing process, specifically in the context of assessing the physical performance and potential of Service personnel as they age. We regard this research as having an important bearing on the population as a whole, and consequently on the Committee's area of inquiry. As a result of the studies, details of which are set out below, QinetiQ believes that further research is necessary in the following areas:

— *The effects of ageing on the physical performance of women.*

— *Ageing and task performance, concentrated on those tasks involving heavy loads on working memory, selective attention, information processing and rapid reactions to presented material.*

— *How and why attitudes and motivation change in the work place with increasing age.*

Introduction

The age structure of the European workforce is changing. The birth rate is falling, which means that from around 2011 onwards those in the age group 15–29 will represent a decreasing proportion of the population. By 2010, it is estimated that over 40 per cent of the working population will be aged 45 and over and by 2020 the modal value for working age will have increased from 35–39 to 50–54 years of age.

In 2003 QinetiQ undertook a study to review the research evidence that related the physical, cognitive and non-cognitive (psychological) factors associated with the ageing process to performance of military or analogous tasks[1]. The study also attempted to identify gaps in our current knowledge and identify strategic research that should be undertaken.

The approach adopted was to undertake separate reviews of the published literature on the effects of ageing on physical performance and the psychological effects of ageing on performance. This included the effects of ageing on cognitive performance, (ie thinking, decision making etc) and non-cognitive factors such as attitudes and motivation towards work.

Ageing and physical performance

"Physical Fitness" encompasses a variety of diverse factors, but can be described generally in terms of four component parts: strength, speed, endurance and flexibility. These can be measured in different ways but the ability to utilise oxygen is commonly used as a measure of "fitness" as high levels of this "aerobic capacity" are necessary for speed and endurance. A measure, known as $VO2_{max}$, (which is a measure of maximal aerobic power) is often regarded as the best indicator of general fitness.

Maximal aerobic power reaches a peak level at around 20 years of age, then declines throughout the rest of life at a rate of around 1 per cent each year.

However, this rate of decline can be reduced. Studies of endurance athletes have shown the effect of prolonged training on aerobic capacity well into later life. The decline appears to be more directly related to a reduction in the amount of training, rather than any factor directly related to the ageing process itself. Aerobic capacity appears related much more directly to activity levels than to age. The aerobic capacity of active individuals declines more slowly if they maintain a regular exercise programme. Sedentary individuals decline at a rapid rate during their 20s and 30s, followed by a slower rate of decline of their $VO2_{max}$ as they age further. It is likely that gradual increases in training levels could counteract the ageing process and allow an individual to maintain a constant level of aerobic fitness for many years.

Peak muscle strength is generally achieved between the ages of 20–30 years. It deteriorates from around the age of 30, but is subject to an increase in the rate of deterioration towards later middle age. The cause of this progressive loss of strength is an age-related loss of muscle mass, at an average rate of 0.5 per cent per year. A fall of 25 per cent in peak isometric force is usually observed between 30–65 years, but much of this loss will occur after 55 years of age. However, evidence from industry of older workers suffering strength-related problems is limited. It appears that reduced muscle function with increased age is not inevitable, and that resistance training can improve muscle recruitment and maintain, or even increase, muscle mass throughout life.

In 1999, the Research and Technology Organisation (RTO) of NATO held a symposium on the operational issues of ageing crewmembers, which investigated the case for a re-evaluation of age policies for military crewmembers and covered operational, psychological and physiological aspects[2]. Three significant conclusions were drawn:

— During these times of preventive medicine, health promotion and healthy lifestyles, *physiological age* of individuals appears to be more important than *chronological age* of groups;

— Knowledge, behaviour and experience seem to adequately compensate for ageing among crewmembers in military environments; and

— These factors, combined with new medical and surgical therapies, and technological advances (in equipment designs, etc) appear to justify seriously re-examining current age policies for military crewmembers.

Fitness and diversity

Men and women appear not to differ, in most respects, in the ageing process. Generally, women have a lower aerobic capacity, but some of this difference is attributable to societal norms that are gradually being eroded. Muscular strength is less in women, but specific training can lessen this difference. Major differences between men and women appear in the mid-50s, when a marked fall in muscular strength has been reported in women, but not in men. It is possible that this is brought about by hormonal changes, but that other factors such as cultural expectations may heighten this deterioration. More work may be required in this area. This study found no reported differences in the response to the ageing process by populations of different ethnicity.

Maintaining fitness

A study on the self-perception of fitness levels among fire-fighters showed no correlation between how fit personnel think they are and how fit they actually are. However, a supervised fitness programme restored aerobic capacity and strength levels in unfit fire fighters to the required levels, irrespective of age. A study of Finnish police officers showed that, whilst muscular strength declined over the 15 years of the study as the group aged, the absolute aerobic capacity of the officers remained constant. It concluded that the physical fitness of middle-aged police officers depended on the level of physical activity in young adulthood, and that age, in itself, was not related to reduced physical performance on the job. However, the sporadic nature of the high levels of physical performance associated with fire-fighting was shown to be insufficient to maintain a high enough training drive in itself (ie simply doing the job itself might not keep you fit enough to meet the demands it imposes).

Studies that have looked at older groups show that the response to a training stimulus appears to be unrelated to age, and that significant increases in aerobic capacity, strength and flexibility can be achieved in people well past normal working age.

Ageing and cognition

Psychologists generally consider two aspects of intelligence supported by experimental evidence: "fluid intelligence" and "crystallised intelligence". Fluid intelligence is held to be unaffected by experience (being largely determined by hereditary factors) and to depend on the integrity and efficiency of physiological and neurological functioning. Therefore, it is likely to be subject to decline from early adulthood onwards. Crystallised intelligence, in contrast, is a function of accumulated experience, knowledge and training, and is largely independent of fluid intelligence after early and middle adulthood. It can be expected to increase through adulthood into old age. Studies have shown that, on average, the older worker performs less well than their younger counterparts on tests of fluid intelligence. However, since the development of crystallised intelligence depends on the exercise of fluid intelligence, the rate of growth would be expected to diminish with age. Generally speaking, the pattern of susceptibility, or resistance, of intelligence sub-tests to the effects of ageing is in line with these hypotheses in that scores on sub-tests which appear to be primarily measuring crystallised intelligence are more stable with age than are sub-tests measuring fluid intelligence.

Specific cognitive abilities

Laboratory studies have shown that ageing affects performance on many information-processing tasks. These include: memory for previously presented material, divided attention, working memory, dual-task activities, and rapid reaction to presented information. The decrease in performance has been attributed to impairment of working memory, reduced processing speed or a combination of both. Although these decrements are strongly correlated with age throughout adulthood, they become more apparent after the age of 50 years.

Although early research suggests older workers have greater difficulty in learning new material, recent research has shown factors which can remove some or all of these difficulties so that there are little or no decrements associated with age. If the material to be learned is contextual, ie the environment supports the process, then older workers are just as adept at learning as their younger counterparts.

Additionally, if the learning is implicit in the task, ie unconscious learning, then little or no age decrements are found. For example, in a task involving planning the best route between two points on a map, older workers will later recognise presented place-names, on that map, just as well as younger workers do. This might indicate that working memory decrements are not as extensive as first suggested.

Many of the studies are open to criticism on methodological grounds. Although research has shown that the above decrements exist, they are quite small. Typically, the range of scores around the mode is much greater for older participants in this research than for younger participants. This means that any cited average score is less of an indication of any individual score among older people than among younger ones. That is, there is a large within group variation with, for example, many older people outperforming many younger ones.

Another point of note is that, by the very nature of this area of study, the majority of studies are cross sectional (ie comparisons are made between separate groups of individuals of particular age groups), not longitudinal (repeated studies undertaken on the same group of individuals at different ages). Those studies that have been longitudinal have produced results that show a less marked decline in cognitive ability as one ages.

Non-laboratory studies

If the measured outcomes of any test of cognition are actual work, or simulated work tasks, then age-related defects disappear. Although research into the cognitive effects of ageing goes back nearly 40 years, research upon how any age related cognitive decrements actually affect work performance has only begun in earnest within the last 10 years or so.

Most of these studies show that within middle adulthood work performance is rarely affected by age. In fact, older workers often show higher performance levels than their younger colleagues. This is not a total surprise given that older workers tend to be more experienced and so have much more crystallised job knowledge than do younger workers. It is likely that the older worker uses their wealth of expertise to develop more efficient "routines" to overcome any cognitive deficits they may experience.

Experience, usually measured by tenure, or length of service that is correlated with age, would be expected to counteract the effects of age on performance. Some studies of industrial and clerical jobs have shown that when length of service is controlled, age effects on performance disappear; conversely when age is controlled, the effects of experience remain. Experience is a stronger predictor of job performance than age.

Research into how older workers cope with training is an area of concern for the recruitment of older people. If experience is the mediator of age-related cognitive deficits, employers need to know how commercially viable the training of inexperienced older workers is. A great deal is known about the training procedures most appropriate for and acceptable to older workers. For example, older workers only show reduced ability to learn if the pace of learning is forced. Older workers also take longer to complete training, although if more time is given to learn, they can achieve the same level of attainment as their younger counterparts. This time limited deficit is not strictly an age-dependent feature. If the training course is intensive or difficult, then younger workers can be just as likely to show achievement decrements in post-training tests. It may be that the perceived workload in training can affect the effectiveness of the training as older trainees may feel they have to invest a lot more effort into achieving an accepted standard.

Non-cognitive factors

Research evidence in the field of personality and ageing is, at present, limited. Some studies suggest that older people score higher on scales of self-control, conscientiousness, tolerance, modesty, wellbeing and achievement via conformance, but lower on sociability, outgoingness, affiliativeness, extraversion, change orientation, conceptual thinking, and achieving via independence. Despite these findings, there is no evidence that any age differences within personality affect work performance.

It is possible that, even if the underlying personality does not change, as individuals age they conform to an age norm or that they become the stereotypical older person. The notion of an age norm seems odd, as it suggests that individuals take on age as an identity or role. Yet research suggests that this happens.

Research has identified both positive and negative stereotypes of older workers. Stereotypes can be overcome by direct experience with individual members of the group; however they guide initial behaviour and, thereby, shape subsequent interaction. Since it is a widely held stereotype that older workers are poor learners, they are less likely to gain access to training schemes and it is likely that the stereotype becomes a self-fulfilling prophecy.

Recently, this notion of age norms has been questioned. While there is broad agreement as to expectations of career achievements by certain ages, there is no clear indication that these expectations affect behaviour. There is no indication of sanctions being applied if one does not conform to the supposed norm.

However, like people at other stages in their lives, older people come to understand what is expected of them by looking for cues and role definitions provided by others. Age-related norms regarding matters such as when to retire may be general for a society or specific to an organisation. Such norms shape the way other employees, including supervisors, treat older workers and may lead to differences in the methods used to evaluate older and younger people and to the creation of "incentives" to retire. Despite stereotypes to the contrary, workers at midlife and beyond are capable of changing and adjusting to changes in their environments.

CONCLUSIONS

1. Differences within age groups, particularly older groups from middle adulthood to the sixth decade, are almost as great as those between younger and older groups. Therefore, generalising from mean performance levels for older groups could be misleading. The implication is that there will be older people who outperform those considerably younger and this is true for recruits as much as for job incumbents. Conversely, it is highly unlikely that there is a measure of physical performance, achievable by 30 year olds that will not be achievable by at least some people of twice this age.

2. Previously accepted age-related decrements in performance would appear to be related to lifestyle changes associated with ageing, rather than physical limitations.

3. It would be correct to state that ageing is associated with a decline in strength, endurance and reaction time. However, it appears that this is neither as steep as has been thought previously, nor as rooted in physiological origins as might be thought. Furthermore, as the majority of people—even those considered "fit" in comparison to their peers—are not achieving their maximal possible fitness level, there exists a reserve potential to utilise to counteract the ageing process.

4. Studies linking age and physical performance suggest that "Biological Age" rather than "Chronological Age" is a more satisfactory indicator of the ability to work at certain jobs.

5. Surprisingly, the age-related decline in physical fitness appears to be more related to expectation than to biology. As we age, we expect to be less fit, so we exercise less, worry less about weight gain, and attempt less demanding roles. This is culturally reinforced as others' perceptions of us get coloured by our age, so it becomes increasingly difficult to maintain the activity levels that would maintain the levels of fitness we had in our youth.

6. The evidence on physical performance suggests, for those already trained to the required standard, that with constant practice performance levels can be maintained to a fitness level of a VO2max figure of 45–50 ml/ kg up to 55 years and beyond. Some research suggests that even for physically demanding jobs normal professional activity might not be sufficient to maintain peak fitness requirements and therefore additional supplementary training may be required. Research with older groups suggests that response to physical training appears unrelated to age. This would suggest that, with training, older groups but below 55, could still regain physical fitness levels. However, the appropriate training regimes required to maintain and re-gain physical standards for older groups is an area that needs further research.

7. This study supports the recent conclusion by the US Rand Corporation[3] that "Age is a poor predictor of the decline of stamina, strength, reasoning and comprehension". Age has some effect on most, if not all human capacities, but our research indicates that age-deficits are not found to any significant degree until the sixth, seventh and eight decades. The studies examined suggest that for a typical working life (age 20 to 60 years), there is little evidence that older workers are incapable of performing equally well in *most* job situations, military and civil. Exceptions are likely to be related to some military jobs that require superior visual acuity, strength or reaction time.

8. Evidence from cognitive research shows that the results of laboratory studies do not hold in the work situation. There seem to be very few occupations that cannot be performed by job incumbents up to 55 years and beyond. Experience appears to compensate for what little performance decrement would be expected as a consequence of ageing. For some high level tasks, experience may be the most significant factor. A separate study into the relationship between length of service and experience being undertaken by QinetiQ as part of the MoD's Corporate Research Programme will be of relevance to this question.

9. However, for tasks that involve heavy loads on working memory, selective attention information processing and rapid reactions to presented materials, performance decrements might be much more susceptible to the effects of ageing.

10. In terms of physical and cognitive performance there appears to be no biological reason why most people should not perform effectively in a wide range of occupations, at least up until the sixth decade. The evidence from the research on non-cognitive factors indicates that evidence for personality changes as a result of ageing is flawed through the lack of longitudinal studies. There is no evidence that if personality changes that it has an influence on work performance. However, everyday observation suggests that behaviour appears to change with age.

11. Stereotypes of the older worker exist, some positive and some negative. Little evidence exists as to the validity of these assumptions. The concept of a norm has been suggested and there is some evidence that older people adopt behaviour congruent with expectations. It is also possible that some stereotypes become self-fulfilling. If the expectation is that older workers are more difficult to train then they may be offered fewer training opportunities. How expectations and motivation of the older working population are shaped and change over time is an area that requires substantial additional research. With recent political comment concerning the need to increase the age of retirement for economic reasons, this would appear long overdue.

REFERENCES

[1] Elshaw C,Kelm DM, Traynor ML Ageing and Military performance: Final Report. QinetiQ/KI/CHS/ CR031826 June 2003.

[2] RTO meeting Proceedings 33 (papers presented at the RTO Human Factors and Medicine Panel (HFM) Symposium, Toulon, France, 11–14 October 1999). RTO-MP-33.

[3] Goldich R L (1995). Military retirement and personnel management: Should active duty careers be lengthened? CRS Report for Congress. US Library of Congress.

October 2004

Memorandum by Professor Michael Rennie

I am Professor of Clinical Physiology at the University of Nottingham Graduate Entry Medical School in Derby. Previously from 1983 to October 2003 I was Professor of Physiology at the University of Dundee. I have approximately 30 years experience of human metabolic research, supported by major medical charities and the research councils; I have produced 210 papers in the refereed literature plus about 40 book chapters.

I would like to give evidence on the biological processes of ageing promising avenues for research, small benefits, effectiveness of research co-ordination, priorities, gaps and research capability in the UK and the use of the research to inform policy on the basis of current evidence.

BIOLOGICAL PROCESSES OF AGEING

1. *What are promising avenues for research?*

For any biological phenomenon the observed variation in the way that phenomenon presents itself is about 50 per cent due to environment and 50 per cent due to genetic pre-disposition. It seems likely that given a particular genetic pre-disposition, manipulation of lifestyle can help maintain physical and mental activity optimally into old age. Such broad brush statements are however little use in practical terms because we need to be able to make specific recommendation, for example in terms of diet (constituents, type, amount) and exercise (aerobic or resistance, amount). However, the evidence base upon which to make such recommendations is very poor. We really have very little understanding of what an optimal diet is for a healthy, active 70 year old woman in comparison with a healthy, active 80 year old woman or a 50 year old man. What recommendations should we be making about protein:energy ratios in the diet? Calcium intake? Zinc intake? Vitamin supplementation? Would it better for the healthy, elderly to do aerobic exercise or would they be better off doing resistance exercise as some of the emerging literature suggests? What are the benefits of changing lifestyle in the fifth decade? Is it a waste of time and should we be concentrating on optimising the health of our children in order to avoid not only obesity, which is a recognised problem, but osteoporosis and muscle wasting in later life?

All of these questions constitute promising lines of research which are important because they do not unnecessarily medicalize old age and certainly do not involve drug treatment. The problem with drug treatment for conditions associated with ageing is that so far none of the available drugs are particularly efficacious including drugs for osteoporosis which may make bones heavier but have very little effect in improving their toughness and resistance to fracture. Providing an evidence base for interventions which actually make a difference in increasing health during ageing is important because it is likely to be cheaper than the alternative, which are to use expensive drugs which we could not afford on a population basis. We must do the research to find out what works and disseminate the results among opinion formers, policy makers and the ageing population this is likely to have a much higher cost benefit ratio than, for example attempting to develop anti-ageing pharmaceuticals.

2. *Priorities*

I firmly believe that we need to do more research in human beings rather than concentrating on animal models of ageing. Let me give an example of an animal model of ageing which has produced a totally un-human like result. Muscle wasting, ("sarcopenia"), is a common consequence of ageing from the fifth decade onwards. We have recently carried out studies which have been published in preliminary form (Cuthbertson DJR, Babraj JA, Atherton, PA, Wackerhage H, Smith et al. The muscle of elderly men showed resistance to stimulation of myofibrillar proteins synthesis (MPS) by essential mineral acids (EAA a) as result of loss of capacity and sensitivity of protein synthetic machinery and altered nutrient signalling. FASEB (J 18. 2004) which show that muscle maintenance processes in the elderly are not as efficient as in the young because elderly people are unable to use of dietary protein as well as young subjects—they have what we call "amino acid resistance". This means that in a 24 hour cycle in which losses of muscle protein would in young people be replaced by meal stimulated processes there is a decrement of a few per cent which leads to loss of maintenance of muscle.

Recently, however, a paper has been published in the American Journal of Physiology dealing with a colony of very old rats. These rats are also sarcopenic but contrary to the behaviour of old human beings these rats show what amounts to an inflammatory response in which muscle protein turnover is revved up but with breakdown processes going faster than the synthetic processes. This picture is similar to that seen in rats, mice and other rodents in response to end stage wasting of muscle in many disease states. It is not a good model for human ageing.

Please note I am not arguing here for the application of old fashioned methods—we should be using the best available modern genomic and proteomic and metabolic approaches—but in people so far as possible.

3. *Gaps*

In my view there is insufficient drive to use modern methods of metabolic research in the elderly in the United Kingdom compared to, for example, the United States. There are certainly gaps in research concerning optimum nutrition and exercise patterns and these can only be answered by doing work in human beings rather than in animals. There are certainly insufficient research capability in the United Kingdom partly as a result of the Calman "reforms" which decimated clinical scientific research 10 years ago and because of the new managerial approach in the health service which has made it more difficult for junior hospital doctors to step off the training ladder to undertake clinical research fellowships. In addition there are only a handful of centres in the United Kingdom in which proper clinical scientific research concerning the elderly can be carried out with modern methods of metabolic investigation.

4. *Research co-ordination*

Research is poorly co-ordinated between the public, private and charitable sectors. For example although there is a research charity called Research into Ageing they are relatively cash poor and have to turn down many highly rated applications simply for this reason. There appears to be no co-ordination between the Medical Research Council and charities concerned with ageing and as far as I am aware there is no support for research into ageing from private sources. The BBSRC and its food and agriculture programme supports work on ageing but because of its strict remit which does not allow it to carry out research which can be classified as "medical" there seems to be no cross talk between the BBSRC and the MRC. Woe betide any applicant to the BBSRC who implies that the results may be used for example in the identification of new drug targets. This is obviously irrational.

5. *What should be done?*

First the research councils and the charities should sit down together and decide on research gaps, priorities and opportunities. They should then decide how much it would cost to fund the work and ask for bids in identified areas. The amount of resource required is likely to be of the order of £10 million per year for five years in the first instance.

Secondly, co-ordinated fund raising by a consortium of charities interested in ageing and research would be more efficient that the current hotch potch.

September 2004

Memorandum by the Royal Society

Biological Processes of Ageing

Ageing is a normal process of functional decline that is near universal in living organisms. In humans, ageing is the major risk factor for multiple age-associated diseases, including cancer, heart disease, neurodegeneration and diabetes.

Genetic research in short-lived simple organisms such as yeast, nematode worm, fruit fly, mouse has identified genes that have an important influence on life span as well as a range of interventions that can delay many of the manifestations of ageing and thus opens new approaches to prolonging healthy life. Furthermore, advances in molecular biology, genetics and genomics are increasingly showing that principles established in model organisms can be translated across species. This now leads to unprecedented opportunities to increase our understanding of the intrinsic ageing process, how it constitutes a risk factor for multiple diseases and how interventions might improve health and activity during ageing.

The brain also is a major avenue for research on the scientific processes of ageing. Cognitive decline, also known as normal cognitive ageing, results in aspects of memory, reasoning, speed of mental processing and executive functioning declining as people grow older. These can lead to a major loss of independence and quality of life. There is still not enough known about the phenotype of cognitive ageing: which mental processes deteriorate, when they do so, the brain basis of this change, and how the deterioration of mental processes correlate. There is still the lack of understanding of the biological basis for the 'common cause' hypothesis, the fact that age-related change in cognition is correlated with age-related changes in functions such as the senses, grip strength and lung function. In starting to find answers to these questions new ways have been developed to image the brain's white matter which allows hypotheses about cortical disconnection to be studied in relation to age-related cognitive change. In addition, much work also needs to be done to follow up ideas about oxidative damage as a basis for cognitive ageing and the many aspects of the genetic basis for cognitive ageing.

Stem cell research offers many opportunities for amelioration of age-associated decline and disease, and UK is particularly well placed to make progress in this area because it has one of the strongest regulatory systems in the world.

The UK is well positioned to contribute to and exploit these opportunities, although the current volume of research in this area is low compared with the United States. Using a combination of generic, theoretical and applied science, a balanced approach to the study of health during the later years of life can be achieved.

APPLICATION OF RESEARCH IN TECHNOLOGY AND DESIGN

Technologies such as artificial joint replacement, cardiac pacemaking and continence control are applications of technology that have had and will continue to have an impact on extending the quality of life. To achieve further advances work needs to continue on the development of new materials, electronics and mechanics. These applications should not be considered in isolation but in conjunction with standard technologies that exist to support independent living such as communication and mobility aids; and housing design and modification.

Below is a classification of the kinds of relevant technology with which the inquiry might be concerned:

— Low technology: Mobility aids (eg, canes, simple wheelchairs), vision devices (eg, magnifiers, large print), hearing devices (eg, assistive listening devices) and cognitive devices (eg, pill organisers).

— High technology: Computer applications, wireless technology, information technology, pervasive computing, wearable computers, sensors and home monitoring.

— Transportation: Older driver safety, the role of high and low technology in enabling mobility later in life, and alternative (to personal vehicles) transportation approaches.

— Home modifications and universal design: The environment, both through retrofitting and new construction for people as they age.

— Injury prevention: Falls, fire safety, poisons, pedestrian safety and other issues relating to safe environments in the home and in the community.

In addition to technologies that support independent living, consideration should be given to those technologies which, generally, involve "health care" interventions which counteract or compensate for the adverse effects of the natural ageing processes and enhance the quality of life. The overriding objective being to keep people healthy until they die. These interventions include:

— Disease prevention.

— Screening for diseases which meet appropriate criteria.

— Diagnostic technologies, particularly in relation to cognition and prognosis.

— Therapeutic procedures that extend quality life.

RESEARCH PRIORITIES

The UK has started to respond to the challenges presented by the issues of research into ageing through ageing-related initiatives by several of the UK research councils (BBSRC, EPSRC, ESRC, MRC). There have been some criticisms of the co-ordination of research into ageing but we hope that the launch of the National Collaboration on Ageing Research will start to bring these initiatives together. The many lines of inquiry in ageing research will require longer-term support. For example, in cognitive ageing there are requirements: for longer duration studies on cohorts of subjects, for organising researchers in large-enough multidisciplinary teams, and for a more co-ordinated approach to funding. Further consideration should be given to co-ordination between the work funded by the Research Councils and the National Health Service effort. This will go some way to improving the difficult translation of research from the laboratory to application in clinical practice.

Although we agree that aspects of future funding of pensions are, rightly, out of remit of this inquiry there are however economic considerations that the inquiry might need to embrace. For example, as the capabilities of "health care" technologies increase, so, generally, do their costs. The escalating expenditure during the last few weeks and days of life is often cited. In the case of the elderly, approaches such as the cost of the QUALY (quality-adjusted life year) will need to be refined to inform the opinion of society concerning resource allocation.

Should you wish any clarification or expansion of our views we would be happy to respond to any written queries and also to provide oral evidence to the Committee.

October 2004

Memorandum by The Royal Society of Edinburgh

THE SCIENTIFIC ASPECTS OF AGEING

1. The Royal Society of Edinburgh (RSE) is pleased to respond to the House of Lords Science and Technology Sub-Committee Inquiry into the Scientific Aspects of Ageing. This response has been compiled by the General Secretary, Professor Andrew Miller and the Research Officer, Dr Marc Rands, with the assistance of a number of Fellows with considerable experience in this area.

2. Biology, genetics and lifestyle all influence how a person ages, and a greater understanding of how these factors influence "healthy" ageing will allow us to begin to elucidate the aetiology of age-related disease. In this context, the Royal Society of Edinburgh is undertaking a range of activities in this area with the support of the Lloyds TSB Foundation for Scotland, and is supporting research and scholarly activities aimed at improving the quality of life of Scotland's ageing population.

3. The specific areas of the call for evidence are now addressed below:

THE BIOLOGICAL PROCESSES OF AGEING

What are promising avenues for research? How will such research benefit older people and delay the onset of long-term illnesses and disabilities?

Ageing Brain

4. The ageing brain is one of the most important avenues for research on the biological processes of ageing. Cognitive functions, like aspects of memory, reasoning, speed of mental processing, and executive functioning, tend to decline as people grow older. This applies even in people who do not have dementia or Mild Cognitive Impairment. Cognitive decline, including pathological and non-pathological aspects, is a major cause of lost independence for older people, a major factor in lowering quality of life, and is a huge financial burden on families and society.

5. NHS Scotland's Source Document "Risk Factors for Dementia and Cognitive Decline," issued in October 2003, and the USA's National Research Council report in 2000 on "The Aging Mind: Opportunities in Cognitive Research" identified neural health, cognition in context, and structure of the ageing mind as key areas for research on the ageing brain.

6. In particular, not enough is known about the phenotype of cognitive ageing. For example, which mental processes deteriorate, when they do so, the brain basis of this change, and how the deterioration of mental processes correlate. Too little is also known about why some people's functions deteriorate while others remain intact or even improve. Too little is known about the biological basis for the correlation between age-related change in cognition with age-related changes in functions such as the senses, grip strength, and lung function. Similarly, more needs to be known about whether cognitive decline is related to illnesses, either overt or subclinical pathology.

7. In addressing these issues, there are now new ways to image the brain's white matter, which allows hypotheses about cortical disconnection to be studied in relation to age-related cognitive change and to follow up ideas about oxidative damage as a basis for cognitive ageing. The genetic basis for cognitive ageing is also now possible with large-scale, fast-throughput genotyping, and telomere length can be studied as a correlate of cognitive ageing. There are, however, too few studies of endophenotypes of cognitive ageing, using experimental and psychophysical measures that can translate cognition into basic processes.

Gene-exercise interactions on bone health

8. Another important aspect that has changed over the last few decades is our increasingly sedentary lifestyle and the impact that this has had on "healthy" ageing. This is of particular importance in the musculoskeletal system. As we age it is inevitable that we lose bone strength and the outward manifestation of this age-related decline is frailty, falls and fractures as a result of osteoporosis. It is estimated that one in three women and one

in 12 men over the age of 50 will suffer an osteoporotic fracture with the resulting cost to the NHS and government of £1.7 billion per annum.

9. Physical activity has been shown to be an essential factor in bone health and the skeletal benefits of exercise can be demonstrated throughout our life cycle. Exercise can positively affect peak bone mass in children and adolescents, has been shown to help maintain or even modestly increase bone density in adulthood and can assist in minimizing age related bone loss in older adults. While the skeleton responds positively to mechanical loading by increasing bone mass and strength (functional adaptation) this response declines with age in both sexes. Not only is the loss of functional adaptation of bone a major aspect of the ageing process it is also highly variable between individuals suggesting a genetic contribution to the response. In fact understanding the interaction and the influence of environmental factors such as exercise on gene expression and function is one of the key areas that should be highlighted in our research effort. Understanding the cellular, biochemical and molecular basis of gene-exercise interactions is, therefore, essential to improving bone health and performance through exercise.

10. Despite the general belief in the importance of exercise to our health, the molecular and cellular structures/systems that contribute to the mechanostat in cells, particularly in the musculoskeletal system, remain unclear. This information would contribute to the design of pharmacological interventions to load related diseases or preventative strategies in health programmes and to our understanding of the mechanisms behind alteration of the sensitivity of this system during ageing and disease such as osteoporosis, osteoarthritis and Pagets disease. An understanding of the basic mechanism of the response to mechanical stimulation is also fundamental for repair and regenerative medicine. One area of research which has been highlighted in the Foresight Health Care 2020 report is tissue engineering with the long-term aim to treat age-related degenerative disease disorders. The development of engineered tissues *ex vivo* for transplantation will fail if we do not understand the components of the ageing process *in vivo* that lead to an impairment of the mechanosensor mechanism and hence disease in the elderly. We should, therefore, aim to increase the understanding of mechanically responsive cells using techniques at the interface between biology and engineering.

11. Large scale population based studies have provided clues to the likely impact of genetic status on the development of a number of age related disease of the musculoskeletal system. However they have largely failed to develop a clear idea of the genetic lesions involved at the level required to develop genetic screens to identify members of the population at risk. There is also need to focus on a functional genetics approach in order to identify genes with possible impact on the musculoskeletal health based on their known importance in the function of these tissues. Only with this information can the most useful data from the large population genetic studies be extracted.

THE APPLICATION OF RESEARCH IN TECHNOLOGY AND DESIGN TO IMPROVE THE QUALITY OF LIFE OF OLDER PEOPLE

Existing technologies which could be used to a greater extent to benefit older people

12. There are a number of existing technologies that could be used to a greater extent to benefit older people. For example, research could be undertaken into a "home hospital" for the elderly. An elderly person can find it difficult to go to the doctor or hospital but communication technology is available whereby he/she can do much by him/herself without directly taking up doctors' time or hospital facilities. For example, computer technology developed for the home office could be adapted for home medical care and with good communication channels a patient can use a digital thermometer which a doctor can "read", or carry out blood pressure measurements, and communicate with the doctor.

13. However, although maintenance of the elderly in their own homes is often the best option, the likely rise of IT support mechanisms and surveillance of old people in their homes (such as that that developed by SECOM in Japan) may lead to isolation and increasing mental problems. More specialists, psychologists and psychotherapists, community care workers and "friends" will, be required to maintain mental health and physical independence of elderly people.

The development of new technologies

14. As noted above, the loss of bone mass (10 per cent of loss of strength for each decade of years) with age is a major concern and leads to osteoporosis and fractures. New technologies are therefore needed for stimulating bone growth. New lightweight bio-compatible materials and techniques also need to be developed for improved implant/bone fittings that can enable secure extended life for these implants and reduce the need for revision surgery. In particular, new coating technology for implants is required, providing greater wear resistance, as well as biocompatibility.

How Effectively is Research Co-ordinated in the Public, Private and Charitable Sectors (Including Internationally)?

15. There has been a UK response to the challenge of the scientific aspects of ageing. Most of the research councils have had ageing-related initiatives, and the National Collaboration on Ageing Research has begun to bring some of these together. Ageing-related charities, such as Research into Ageing, National Osteoporosis Society and Arthritis Research Council, have also been supportive of research into the biological processes of ageing.

16. Cognitive ageing will, however, require longer-term support for cohorts of subjects, organising researchers in large-enough multidisciplinary teams, and a more co-ordinated approach to funding and a body such as the USA's National Institute on Ageing would help matters considerably.

Have the Correct Priorities been Identified? Are there any Gaps in Research?

17. In addition to the areas identified above, current research into Alzheimers, Parkinsonism, and like afflictions will be important, as will continuing research to find ways of preventing or curing the major degenerative diseases such as cancer and diabetes. Research over the past 50 years has also produced useful guidance in respect of diet and exercise and the avoidance of risk-producing habits such as smoking and some features of life-style. Some aspects of these, still need further well-planned research to confirm or modify current beliefs and there will be a need to examine the psychological barriers that prevent people following oft-repeated simple advice on healthy living.

Is there Sufficient Research Capability in the UK?

18. There are current difficulties in maintaining sufficiently large cohorts of people over time to explore cognitive ageing. There are some exceptions, such as the MRC's 1946 British Birth Cohort, which effectively has long-term funding, but some of the world-class cohorts that this country possesses are run on short-term grant support. In addition, there would be benefit in researchers on brain ageing being brought together in larger groups, a rare example of which has occurred in Newcastle.

Is the Research Being Used to Inform Policy?

19. An ageing population presents a massive health and financial burden, and research findings are being publicised and influencing policy, especially given the economic and social consequences for communities.

Additional Information

20. In responding to this inquiry the RSE would like to draw attention to the following Royal Society of Edinburgh responses which are of relevance to this subject: *The Ageing Population* (December 1999); *EQUAL (Extend Quality Life)* (January 2000) and *Healthcare in 2020* (September 2000).

October 2004

Memorandum by The Royal College of Physicians of Edinburgh

The Royal College of Physicians of Edinburgh is pleased to respond to the House of Lords Select Committee on Science and Technology's *Inquiry to Examine the Scientific Aspects of Ageing.*

The College welcomes this inquiry as one which is much needed. Indeed, hitherto there has been limited research in the field of age and ageing, and there is a concern amongst specialists in geriatric medicine that this is not viewed as a priority by the major bodies funding research in the UK. The demographic trends within the UK population indicate that a high priority in the allocation of research funds should be given to research proposals in this area.

There are, however, many promising avenues for research. These include aspects of brain function including the role of neuroprotective agents (which may maintain brain function); genetic studies to examine the ability of individual genes to accelerate or to protect against the ageing process; and studies of cardiovascular function in older people. There are excellent opportunities to study the impact of exercise and dietary modification on maintaining good health in later life. However, it is important to emphasise that older people have often been excluded from research studies carried out in the context of a number of medical subspecialties. The College strongly endorses the importance of research in this age group as being a priority, and that older people should not be excluded from such studies. We also suggest that there should be an attempt to facilitate greater of co-ordination of research than hitherto between the public, private and charitable sectors.

It should also be noted that the specialty of geriatric medicine has had great difficulty in making successful appointments to "academic" posts in the Universities. The lack of funding for research into ageing appears to have been a disincentive to talented researchers from entering the specialty. Conversely, the lack of academics in the specialty has meant that there has not been sufficient emphasis to force research into ageing higher up the priority list. A clear commitment to increase research into ageing may help the specialty to break out of this "chicken and egg" situation.

The College recognises that one particular problem has been the difficulty in distinguishing the effects of "ageing" from the effects of "disease". Most of the health problems and much of the disability experienced by older people are related to 'ill-health' rather than to the ageing process itself. The Inquiry may therefore find it difficult to focus specifically on ageing.

Current demographic trends raise important issues of how to care for the growing number of old people, but this has been allowed to dominate discussions to the virtual exclusion of a search for strategies which might improve their overall health. The negative tenor of analysis to date has been fuelled in part by a misunderstanding about health in old age. It is true that older people have in general poorer health status than younger people, and this is due in part to the higher rates of disease in old age. The incidence of heart disease, for example, increases with age, but this does not mean that ageing itself is a cause of heart disease. Nor does it mean that heart disease is inevitable in old age. The crucial distinction between the effects of age alone and the effects of disease do require to be reinforced in the minds of both the lay public and health professionals. Finally laying to rest the pervasive misconception that all the ills of old age are "just your age" would represent a major breakthrough for the health care of older people.

Evidence is beginning to emerge that, certainly for well educated, affluent older people, morbidity is already being compressed and that healthy ageing may be achievable for some. A landmark observational study from the University of Pennsylvania followed graduates from their early 40s to their mid 70s.[3] The study focused on the three potentially modifiable risk factors of cigarette smoking, body mass index and exercise patterns. For those with high health risks from these factors in their mid-60s there was both an earlier onset of disability and a greater level of cumulative disability, as well as more disability in the final year of life. In contrast, the age at onset of disability was postponed by more than five years in the low risk group. In this study, adopting low risk habits in later life was associated with not only an increase in lifespan, but also an increase in healthspan. The promise of healthy ageing resurfaced in recent longitudinal data on disability from the US showing that its older population are less disabled and less ill than had been predicted.[4] This unexpected finding may be due to a range of factors which include cohort effects, disability-reducing medical interventions and healthier lifestyles. It is telling that no equivalent data exist in the UK.

Physical activity is the major modifiable influence on health in old age. It is clear that regular physical activity—bodily movement that is produced by the contraction of skeletal muscle and that increases energy expended—is associated with a reduction in the risk of coronary heart disease, diabetes, cancer of the colon and several other chronic diseases. Exercise, a subset of physical activity, may be defined as planned, structured, repetitive movement done with the express purpose of improving or maintaining physical fitness. Demonstrating that exercise can be beneficial is less difficult than persuading people to be more physically active. Part of the problem is the common misconception that to reap health benefits, continuous, vigorous exercise (such as athletics, jogging or squash) is required. This notion has its origins in studies of the effects of endurance exercise training on maximal oxygen uptake in younger adult. This work produced a physical fitness recommendation of 20 to 60 minutes of endurance exercise at 60 per cent to 90 per cent of maximal heart rate, three or more times per week. This advice was so scientific, complex and prescriptive and set such an unattainable goal for sedentary and older people that many must have given up on exercise as a lost cause. However, a reassessment of the original evidence together with a growing body of new research has shown that the majority of health benefits can be gained by performing regular moderate intensity physical activities (the equivalent of brisk walking at three to four miles per hour for most healthy adults) outside of formal exercise programmes.[5,6,7] This good news for couch potatoes of all ages is particularly heartening for older people (who find it is much easier to adopt and maintain more modest activity levels), and it carries the added bonus that low to moderate intensity physical activities are more likely to be continued than high intensity activities.[8] It is therefore unfortunate that public health advice has failed to shake off the "high-tech" lycra-clad image of aerobic exercise and physical fitness, instead of embracing the broader concept of health and physical activity—which might include walking, dancing, bowling or gardening etc.[9]

Physical capacity peaks in young adulthood and then declines progressively decade by decade at a rate which varies from one individual to another. Part of this physical decline is due to ageing, and is not amenable to intervention. Even healthy ageing is associated with a striking loss of muscle mass and hence muscle strength; by the age of 80 approximately 50 per cent of muscle mass has gone. However, it is now appreciated that some age related changes that were once accepted to be solely the result of the ageing process are actually the result of disuse, and therefore potentially reversible. The practical importance of this is that an older person is often precariously close to the threshold at which a small decline in physical capacity will render basic everyday activities, like rising from an armchair, impossible. The small added loss of fitness which occurs in association with an episode of intercurrent illness may render even a previously healthy 80 year old immobile and dependent. However, there is substantial evidence that lost fitness can be regained with regular physical activity, even in extreme old age.[10] There are a host of other health benefits associated with regular physical activity in old age. Weight bearing exercise may slow the rate of bone loss in older women, balance exercise training makes falls less likely, and regular exercise may be helpful in major depression.[11,12,13]

The social benefits of group exercise activities in later life should not be underestimated in a population where social isolation and loneliness may be common. Clearly there are compelling reasons for old people to be physically active. However, if more old people are to have this opportunity, radical changes in attitude are required. Prevailing cultural expectations that pensioners should "put their feet up" must be challenged. Well-intentioned relatives who take over the household chores should be aware they may be depriving their elderly relative of their main physical activity of the week. Too often, the old person struggling with an aspect of self care in the community is simply provided with social support, when a more appropriate response would have been treatment to help regain the lost skill. The provision of inappropriate social services to old people may simply accelerate the rate at which physical abilities are lost, and low staffing levels in hospitals and homes are likely to create unnecessary dependence because pressure of time means that it is faster for staff to perform a task for the patient than to allow the person to perform it for him/herself.[14]

Technology is already being used to support older people to live in their own homes or in specially adapted "smart" housing. There is an increasing body of evidence of the benefits of such developments, although many of these advances have not been subjected to critical evaluation with randomised trials. It is a matter of regret that "specially" designed houses for older people are sometimes not suitable for disabled people in wheelchairs or who need walking aids. Architects need to be made more aware of these matters and the College strongly endorses the need for proper, randomised, controlled trials of these new technologies before they are implemented on a wide basis, at significant cost. Moreover, many existing technologies eg personal alarms, adapted furniture, the design of special housing, and sensory alarms, have the potential to be upgraded using more modern technology. Again, these should be subject to proper evaluation in appropriate trials.

A healthy old age depends heavily on luck, genetic and other factors which are not amenable to intervention. However, both lifestyle factors and nutrition in later life are crucial influences on healthspan and disability, and are potentially modifiable.[15] Additional disability free years in later life are precious to individuals and to society, but this prospect should not be overestimated. Disability may be postponed, but it will not be eliminated. Older people will still require longterm care, and many of the chronic disabling diseases of later life will still take their toll.[16] Unfortunately, older people are neglected by most health education campaigns. Older people require access to information about healthy lifestyles, the ability to appraise such information, and a sense of control over their own futures. It is also important to understand more about how and when such knowledge actually influences health behaviours: clinical research is required into incentives and opportunities which would motivate older people to adopt and maintain healthy lifestyles. Such changes are less likely to be achieved by exercise prescription schemes[17] than by turning our environment into a more attractive place in which to be physically active, with attention to personal safety, good street lighting and town planning. The ageing of the population is a success story, and although much debate has so far focused on how to care for the growing number of old people, an equally important target is how to maintain their health and to minimise disability.

REFERENCES

1 Shaw AB. Age as a basis for healthcare rationing: support for agist policies. Drugs Ageing 1996;9:403–05.

2 Fries JF. Ageing, natural death and the compression of morbidity. N Engl J Med 1980;303:130-35.

3 Vita AJ, Terry RB, Hubert HB, Fries JF. Ageing, health risks, and cumulative disability N Engl J Med 1998;338 (15):1035–41.

4 Manton KG, Corder L, Stallard E. Chronic disability trends in the elderly United States populations: 1982–1994. Proc Natl Acad Sci USA 1997;94:2593–2598.

5 Pate RR, Pratt M, Blair SN, Haskell WL, Macera CA, Bouchard C et al. Physical activity and public health. A recommendation from the Centres for Disease Control and Prevention and the American Colleges of Sports Medicine. JAMA 1995; 273:402–407.

6 Dunn AL, Marcus BH, Kampert JB, Garcia ME, Kohl HE, Blair SN. Comparison of lifestyle and structures interventions to increase physical activity and cardiorespiratory fitness: a randomized trial. JAMA 1999; 281: 327–334.

7 Andersen RE, Wadden TA, Bartlett SJ, Zemel B, Verde TJ, Franckowiak BS. Effects of lifestyle activity v. structured aerobic exercise in obese women: a randomized trial. JAMA 1999; 281:335–340.

8 Pollock ML. Prescribing exercise for fitness and adherence. In: Dishman RK, ed. Exercise Adherence. Champaign, Ill: Human Kinetics Publishers; 1988:259–277.

9 McMurdo MET. Exercise in old age: time to unwrap the cotton wool. Br J Sports Med 1999; 33:295–296.

10 Fiatarone MA, Marks EC, Ryan ND, Meredith CN, Lipsitz LA, Evans WJ. High-intensity strength training in nonagenarians. Effects on skeletal muscle. JAMA 1990;263:3029-34.

11 McMurdo MET, Mole PA, Paterson CR. BMJ 1997;314: 569.

12 Campbell AJ, Robertson MC, Gardner MM, Morton RN, Tilyard MW, Buchner DM. Randomised controlled trial of a general practice programme of home based exercises to prevent falls in elderly women. BMJ 1997;315: 1095–1069.

13 Blumenthal JA, Babyak MA, Moore KA, Craighead E, Herman S, Khatri P et al. Effects of exercise training on older patients with major depression. Arch Intern Med 1999;159:2349–2356.

14 Muir Gray JA, Bassey EJ, Young A. The risks of inactivity. In: Muir Gray JA, (ed). Prevention of Disease in The Elderly. Edinburgh London Melbourne and New York: Churchill Livingstone; 1985:78–94.

15 Allaire SH, LaValley MP, Evans SR, O'Connor GT, Kelly-Hayes M, Meenan RF et al. Evidence for decline in disability and improved health among persons aged 55 to 70 years: the Framingham Heart Study. Am.J Public Health 1999;89(11):1678–83.

16 Gordon M. Is the best yet to be? Lancet 1997; 350:1166–1167.

17 Harland J, White M, Drinkwater C, Chinn D, Farr L, Howel D. The Newcastle exercise project: a randomised controlled trial of methods to promote physical activity in primary care. BMJ 1999;319:828–832.

October 2004

Memorandum by Professor Aubrey Sheiham and Dr Georgios Tsakos

The questions addressed relate to how Science and Technology can help improve people's prospects of healthy and active life expectancy and whether Government policies are in place to achieve this.

ORAL HEALTH AND AGEING

The evidence we present is on how three aspects of research in technology relating to oral health can help improve people's prospects of healthy and active life expectancy. The first two aspects are related to how the mouth and teeth affect the health and quality of life and diet and nutrition of people in general and older people in particular. The third relates to the methods for assessing needs for dental care and oral health promotion.

1. *How the mouth and teeth affects health and quality of life and diet and nutrition of people in general and older people in particular*

The two main ways that the mouth and teeth affect the health and therefore the ageing process are:

1.1 The mouth contributes significantly to the quality of life. Quality of life is concerned with "the degree to which a person enjoys the important possibilities of life". A person's oral health status can affect them physically and psychologically and influence how people enjoy life; how they look, speak, chew, taste and enjoy food, socialise, as well as their self-esteem, self image and feelings of social well-being. Successful ageing is related to maintaining quality of life, which in turn is dependent on how well individuals can fulfil these performances. Normal oral functions such as chewing, speaking, laughing and appearance can be impaired by dental pain and discomfort, aesthetically displeasing teeth and loss of natural teeth. Social functions such as communication and aesthetics may be more important than biting and chewing and may be the main determinants in an individuals' subjective need for replacement of missing natural teeth and their feelings about the loss of teeth.

In a national study of randomly selected free living (753 persons) and institutionalised (202) subjects from the British National Diet and Nutrition Survey (NDNS) aged 65 years and over, the impact of oral status on 10 aspects of daily life was considerable; 17 per cent of free-living edentate older people reported having one or more severe oral related impact in the past six months. Considering that these impacts are "ultimate impacts" and not merely "intermediate impacts", then the effect of dental and oral disorders on quality of life is serious. Oral impacts levels were lowest in dentate subjects with the greatest number of teeth. For the dentate, the most common oral impacts were on eating and speaking. Impacts relating to emotional stability, sleeping, relaxing, carrying out physical activity and social contact were infrequent, but were severe when they did occur. Among those with an impact on eating, 25 per cent said it was severe and 42 per cent had the impact nearly every day or in a spell of three or more months. Oral impacts were more prevalent among the institution sample. The impacts were associated with the inability or difficulty to eat a range of 16 common foods. The impacts had large effects on whether people could not eat or eat with some difficulty a range of common foods such as sliced bread, cheese, roast potatoes, lettuce and apples. A strong significant relationship between having a socio-dental eating impact and perceived difficulty of eating was reported for almost all the 16 foods in dentate and all 16 foods in edentate subjects.

More edentate than dentate people had an oral impact. This reflects how badly fitting dentures affects oral health related quality of life among people with false teeth. Free-living dentate people with less than 11 natural teeth were more likely to have had an oral impact than those with 11 or more teeth. Eating related oral impacts were the most common impact reported by all groups. Speaking, emotional stability, sleeping, contact with people and smiling were also affected by oral impacts, although less frequently. This indicates that the quality of life of older people was fairly frequently and severely compromised by dental and oral disorders. In particular, the ability to eat several common types of foods was impaired.

1.2 Dental health status influences diet and nutrition. Oral health status is considered to be particularly important in older people and to influence their nutritional status. Tooth loss has been associated with nutritional deficiency. The presence of dentures and number of natural teeth are associated with masticatory efficiency and ability and being without natural teeth is related to being underweight. One of the most likely mechanisms by which impaired oral health may affect diet is that difficulty chewing causes dietary restrictions. Joshipura et al (1996) found that edentulous health professionals consumed fewer vegetables, less dietary fibre, and carotene and more cholesterol, saturated fats and calories than people with 25 or more teeth. Tooth loss was associated with a lower intake of hard-to-chew foods such as apples and carrots. Ranta et al (1988) found higher proportions of dentate people had eaten vegetables and fruit than their edentate counterparts. Studies which have analysed the effects of dental status on consumption of non-starch polysaccharides (dietary fibre) reported a reduction in intake with tooth loss (Moynihan et al 1994, Joshipura et al 1996). Older people have fewer natural teeth, and are also vulnerable to dietary restrictions for other reasons (disability, medical or social conditions). Tooth loss was associated with changes in foods preference and nutritional deficiency in older people (Chauncey, et al 1984, Brodeur et al 1993, Moynihan et al 1994, Krall 1998). The evidence generally available for elderly populations suggests that tooth loss alters food choice resulting in lower intakes for key nutrients such as iron and fibre. This evidence suggests that eating ability and masticatory efficiency are affected by oral health, and specifically by the number and distribution of natural teeth. Whether or not somebody reported that they had a problem with eating which impacted on their day to day life has been shown to be strongly related to difficulty eating certain foods (Smith and Sheiham 1979, Sheiham et al 1999). In the NDNS study about one in five dentate free-living British people aged 65 and over had difficulty eating raw carrots, apples, well done steak or nuts. More edentate subjects had difficulty eating than dentate. Foods such as nuts, apples and raw carrots could not be eaten easily by over half edentate people in institutions.

In random national samples of free-living British older subjects who had a dental examination, interview shown to be strongly related to difficulty eating certain foods (Smith and Sheiham 1979, Sheiham *et al* 1999). (NDNS) aged 65 years and over study, intakes of most nutrients were lower in edentate than dentate. Intake of non-starch polysaccharides, protein, calcium, non-haem iron, niacin, vitamin C were lower in edentate subjects. People with 21 or more teeth consumed more of most nutrients, particularly of non-starch polysaccharide. This relationship in intake was not apparent in the haemotological analysis. Plasma ascorbate and plasma retinol but not a number of key nutrients, were the only analytes associated with dental status.

An important finding in the NDNS study is that intake of non-starch polysaccharide (dietary fibre) was much higher in people with more teeth and significantly associated with the number of occluding pairs of posterior teeth. Intake of intrinsic and milk sugars, derived from foods such as fresh fruit and its derivatives, was also significantly associated with having more occluding pairs of natural teeth. Dietary fibre are an important component of diet, associated particularly with gastro-intestinal health, so the relationship with oral health in the elderly is of considerable importance, emphasizing the role that maintaining a functional natural dentition may have in improving the general health of the elderly.

The important conclusion from the national survey of older people is that dental status can have an impact on food choice and on the intake of key nutrients, and this can ultimately translate into variation in the blood levels of number of key nutrients, arguably, the most important of which is vitamin C

RESEARCH AND POLICY IMPLICATIONS

1.2.1 More research is needed to explore how the teeth and mouth affect ageing. There is a strong case for dentistry to concentrate more on psychological and social functioning, than on functional restoration, particularly for older people.

1.2.2 Traditional oral epidemiologic indicators do not tell us much about people's capacity to carry out desired roles and activities and whether people enjoy the important possibilities of life. Moreover, from the point of view of contemporary definitions of health, clinical measures used to define health status and needs in populations are subject to more serious limitations; they tell us nothing about the functioning of the oral cavity or the person as a whole, nor about subjectively perceived symptoms. Socio-dental indicators are measures of oral health-related quality of life and range from survival, through impairment, to function and perceptions. They measure the extent to which dental and oral disorders disrupt normal social-role functioning and bring about major changes in behaviour such as an inability to work, or undertake parental or household duties. They are subjective and their use should be complementary to the clinical measures of oral status and needs.

Recommendation: Socio-dental technology for assessing oral health-related quality of life should be developed to assess oral health related subjective impacts on quality of life and the impacts of the mouth on enjoying eating, and on diet and nutrition.

1.3 Assessing needs for dental care and oral health promotion. The purpose of needs assessment in health care is to assess unmet health and health care needs in a systematic manner and to gather the information required to bring about change beneficial to the health of the population. Health needs assessment is a systematic approach attempting to ensure that the health service uses its resources to improve the health of the population in the most efficient way. The concept of need is at the core of health care planning. Planning health services is, in turn, rooted in the ethical imperative to use resources appropriately. Needs assessment involves setting priorities on the basis of health needs that is taking into account the severity of illness and/or health care needs, which refers primarily to the capacity to benefit. A common assumption in the organisation and provision of health services, including dental health services, which is being challenged, is that the need for health care can be objectively determined by professionals. Now it is known that health care needs may be defined in other ways, because the definition of any given state of ill-health has become open to much wider interpretation than in the past. Health care needs now extend beyond a narrow clinical interpretation to issues like the impact of ill-health on individuals and on society, the degree of disability and dysfunction that ill-health brings, the perceptions and attitudes of patients themselves towards ill-health and the social origins of many common illnesses. These factors influence the utilisation of health services and, ultimately, the effectiveness of treatment. In this sense, they represent key concepts that should be seriously considered in the process of planning health care services so that resources are more rationally distributed by the ability to benefit. Because improving the quality of older people's lives is central to allocation of resources.

The concern with effectiveness and acceptability is central to any formulation of health care needs. Matthew's definition focuses on the "need for care", which should be distinct from "need for health". Health needs represent the distribution of particular forms of morbidity, as well as the distribution of those environmental, social and economic variables that influence health and illness. Therefore it is important to distinguish between the need for health and the need for health care. Health care is one way of dealing with the need for health. The need for health is perceived as relief from distress, discomfort, disability, handicap and the risk of mortality and morbidity (Acheson, 1978). With the growing demand for treatments based on evidence-based medicine, Matthew's definition has become widely accepted. Bradshaw (1972) constructed a taxonomy of need that incorporates those concepts and forms a sociological background that sets up a useful definitional framework. The main types of need are presented in Box 1 and their interrelation is pictured in Figure 1.

BOX 1 BRADSHAW'S TAXONOMY OF NEED: TYPES AND DEFINITIONS

Normative need:	Is that which the expert or professional, administrator or social scientist defines as need in any given situation
Perceived (felt) need:	This reflects the individual's own assessment of his or her requirement for health care.
Expressed need (demand):	This is felt need converted into action by seeking assistance

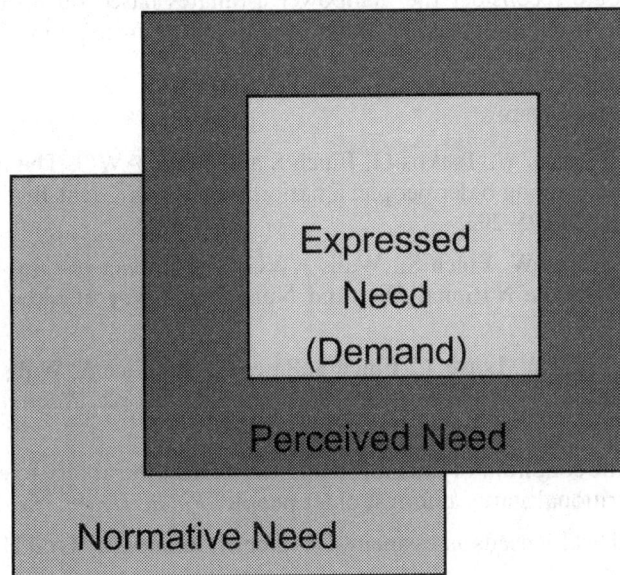

The relationship between Normative Need, Perceived (Felt) Need, and Expressed Need (Demand)

The shortcomings of the normative method of assessing need are:

(1) Lack of objectivity and reliability. Professional judgements in normative need are neither value-free nor objective. The so-called objective assessment often depends upon a consensus agreement from a number of subjective approaches. Therefore, objectivity cannot be regarded as a property of measures of normatively assessed health status and needs.

(2) Neglect of psychosocial aspects and quality of life concepts. The global definition of health (WHO, 1948) adopts a much wider perspective than that of normative need and incorporates the concepts of functional, psychological and social well-being. Nevertheless, the standard norm of measures of disease accepted by dentists is not always the norm in terms of functional or social requirements of people examined. Oral health problems, but not necessarily the specific pathological conditions, are related to a person's ability to carry out usual daily activities and affect the individual's personal comfort and quality of life. People's dental satisfaction bears little relation to the clinical assessment of oral conditions. The assessment of health by lay persons differs from that of professionals. Furthermore, there are differences in concepts of health and disease among lay people in different cultures. As a result, normative measures fail to assess the level of health-related quality of life.

(3) Lack of consideration for health behaviours and patient compliance. Normative criteria are insufficient for deciding treatment needs because they do not take into account the attitudes and behaviours of patients, which in turn have considerable influence on the effectiveness of treatments and improvement of oral health.

(4) Neglect of consumer rights. The need justified by purely professional assessment is questioned in terms of human or consumer rights. The clinical definition, based on the disease analogy, rarely coincides with consumer definitions.

(5) Unrealistic estimates for treatment planning. This is particularly important because the use of Normative needs, as illustrated in the latest Department of Health *Report of the Primary Care Dental Workforce Review*, February 2004.

There are comprehensive measures of dental needs that include the following elements:

A clinical dimension based upon sound concepts of the life history of the diseases; measures of social dysfunction; the perceived need of the individual; assessment of the propensity of the individual to take preventive action and the perceived barriers to prevention; a prescription of effective and acceptable treatments or cures; assessment of the skills and manpower required (Sheiham and Tsakos 2004). Such measures should be used instead of the inappropriate normative approach.

POLICY IMPLICATIONS:

Recommendation: Research on assessing dental needs sociodentally is not used to inform policy. The Department of Health should reconsider the manpower estimates based on normative need. That would encourage a more equitable distribution of care and more rational prioritisation of services.

SOME REFERENCES TO STUDIES CITED:

Sheiham A, Steele JG, Marcenes W, Tsakos G, Finch S and Walls AWG. The impact of dental and oral disorders on social well-being among older people; a national survey in Great Britain. *Community Dentistry and Oral Epidemiology* 2001: 29;195–203.

Sheiham A, Steele JG, Marcenes W, Finch S, Walls AWG. The Impact of Oral Health on Ability to Eat Certain Foods; Findings from the National Diet and Nutrition Survey of older people in Great Britain. *Geriodontology* 1999: 16; 11–20.

Sheiham A, Steele JG, Marcenes W, Lowe, C, Finch S, Bates CJ, Prentice A, Walls AWG.) The relationship among dental status, nutrient intake, and nutritional status in older people. *Journal of Dental Research* 2001: 80 (2); 408–413.

Sheiham A, Steele J Does the condition of the mouth and teeth affect the ability to eat certain foods, nutrient and dietary intake and nutritional status amongst older people? *Public Health Nutrition* 2001: 4(3); 797–803.

Sheiham A, Tsakos G Oral health needs assessment. Chapter in Community Oral Health, edit C Pine. Wright Publishers, Oxford, 2004.

Smith J M, Sheiham A How dental conditions handicap the elderly. *Community Dentistry Oral Epidemioogy*, 1979:7; 305–310

Srilapananan P, Sheiham A Assessing the difference between sociodental and normative approaches to assessing prosthetic dental treatment needs in dentate older people. *Geriodontology* 2001: 18; 25–34.

October 2004

Memorandum by the Society for Endocrinology

BIOLOGICAL PROCESSES AND AGEING

DHEA (dehydroepiandrosterone) is a steroid hormone produced by the human adrenal cortex. It is quite different from the other adrenal hormones for two reasons: first because most animal species do not produce DHEA so it is very much a "human hormone" and second, because of the striking changes in blood levels of DHEA through life. In childhood DHEA levels are low, then rise through adolescence and peak in the third decade of life. After this there is a steady decline in blood concentrations of DHEA, continuing into old age. Other adrenal steroids are produced at a relatively constant rate throughout life. It has also been shown that DHEA levels decrease in the presence of most chronic disease states, including diabetes, cancer, arthritis, heart disease etc.

These findings have led to the suggestion that DHEA is a hormone of youth and "wellness" and it has even been suggested that old age may be a condition of "DHEA deficiency". There have been a few studies looking at the effects of replacing DHEA, both in older people and in people with adrenal failure. It is clear from these studies that DHEA will not be a universal panacea for all the diseases of older age, but it is also clear that giving DHEA has significant beneficial effects on the overall quality of life. The improvements in quality of life are seen in ratings of well-being, anxiety, depression, and self esteem and occur three to four months after starting treatment.

The problem with carrying out studies on the effects of DHEA is that the pharmaceutical industry has no current interest in this hormone. DHEA and its active metabolites are all naturally occurring substances which have been well-characterised and crucially, do not offer the possibility of patentable products. This has caused a funding crisis in the area of DHEA clinical trials and much important research is therefore simply not possible. The most promising areas of research are: the use of long-term DHEA in older people, and the use of DHEA to treat anxiety disorders.

One way to stimulate interest from the pharmaceutical industry would be to characterise the DHEA receptor, which would lead to the development of novel drugs which interact with the receptor. There is a clear need for funding to be directed towards this basic science research which is directly relevant to human disease and ageing.

DHEA is inexpensive; it has few side effects when given in replacement doses. It has the potential to alleviate some of the health problems associated with ageing. However, non-commercial funding will be required to further our understanding of this hormone.

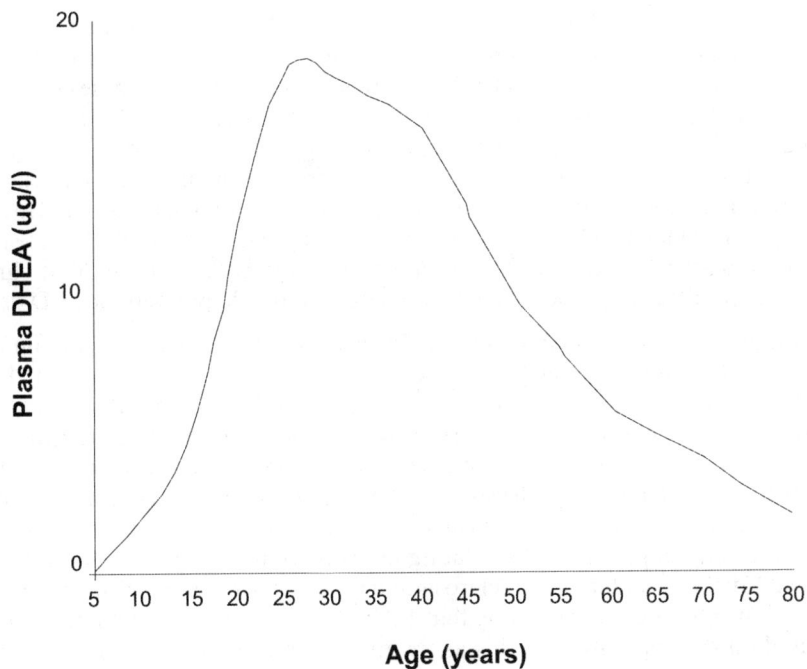

HORMONES, AGEING AND THE IMMUNE SYSTEM: DR MARTIN HEWISON AND DR WIEBKE ARLT, THE UNIVERSITY OF BIRMINGHAM

Ageing is associated with a decline in the production of several key hormones. The most notable example is of course the menopausal loss of ovarian oestrogen production in women leading to effects on osteoporosis, which are described elsewhere in this report. However, other hormones that decline with ageing include the pineal gland hormone melatonin, pituitary growth hormone release, adrenal dehydroepiandrosterone (DHEA), and vitamin D. Changes in these hormones are likely to have diverse clinical consequences but one specific aspect of physiology that has attracted much recent attention is the Immune System. Along with hormone loss, ageing is associated with a parallel decline in immunity, otherwise known as immunesenscence, suggesting an important link between endocrinology and immunology. Although the precise impact of age-related hormone loss on immune-related diseases (autoimmune disease, susceptibility to infection etc) has yet to be fully defined, there is a growing body of evidence suggesting that this is an important consideration in the elderly. Specific examples are outlined below.

ADRENAL STEROIDS

Adrenal hormone production comprises three steroids of major importance: the glucocorticoid cortisol, the mineralocorticoid aldosterone, and the androgen precursor dehydroepiandrosterone (DHEA). DHEA is distinct from cortisol and aldosterone in declining with advancing age. This age-associated secretion pattern is only seen in humans and higher non-human primates. Individual maximum concentrations of DHEA and its sulphate ester (DHEAS) are achieved during the third decade, followed by a steady decline with advancing age so that levels in the "oldest-olds" are only 10–20 per cent of those seen in young adults. This decline has been termed "adrenopause" in spite of the fact that secretion of other adrenal hormones such as glucocorticoids does not change considerably with age. Adrenopause is independent of menopause and occurs in both sexes as a gradual process at similar ages.

No specific receptors for DHEA have been reported so it is possible that it achieves its effects via metabolism to sex hormones. Nevertheless, DHEA has been linked to a variety of immune responses. For example, in a number of studies DHEA supplementation has been used to modify immune functions and alter the course of immunopathies. Most studies have been performed in patients with the autoimmune disease lupus (SLE). The concept of using DHEA in the treatment of SLE was based on the observation that women are more often affected and that circulating androgens and DHEA concentrations are low in patients with SLE. Moreover, androgen treatment can modify the disease progression in an animal model of SLE.

VITAMIN D

The active form of vitamin D, 1,25-dihydroxyvitamin D_3 ($1,25(OH)_2D_3$), is a pluripotent hormone which has properties that extend well beyond its established role in calcium homeostasis. Sufficient bioavailability of active vitamin D is dependent on regular exposure to light and dietary intake. These conditions are generally not met in elderly populations, in particular in Northern countries, which leads to relative vitamin D insufficiency with ageing, particularly in nursing home populations. The consequences of severe vitamin D deficiency with respect to calcium status and bone disease (rickets/osteomalacia) have been recognised for many years and the recent resurgence in this disease amongst some children has attracted much attention. The possible impact of sustained vitamin D insufficiency is less well-known but may affect a substantial proportion of the UK population, particularly the elderly. Several researchers have proposed that chronic exposure to low levels of vitamin D results in a distinct bone disease referred to as hypovitaminosis D osteopathy (HVO).

Another feature of vitamin D which may have significant health consequences is the immune modulatory actions of $1,25(OH)_2D_3$ this has been described at several levels including the regulation of T-cell proliferation and function and may influence a diversity of tissues with the skin and gastrointestinal tract being good examples. Furthermore, these effects of $1,25(OH)_2D_3$ involve mechanisms that are quite distinct from the renal/intestinal responses that are associated with classical calcium homeostasis. Dysregulated synthesis of $1,25(OH)_2D_3$ is a feature of inflammatory disease but there may also be altered immune function associated with vitamin D insufficiency which is an increasingly prevalent problem in particularly at more northerly latitudes, and within elderly populations. Circulating levels of vitamin D have been linked to autoimmune diseases such as type 1 diabetes and multiple sclerosis and other related disorders such as Crohn's disease. At a cellular level there is much evidence suggesting that $1,25(OH)_2D_3$ is a powerful immunosuppressive. Studies to date have focused on the application of this as treatment for autoimmune diseases and transplantation rejection but there is now growing awareness that vitamin D supplementation, particularly in the elderly, may also have considerable benefits in preventing immune disorders.

MELATONIN

Enzymatic conversion of serotonin by the serotonin-N-acetyltransferase (NAT) leads to the generation of melatonin. NAT expression is highest in the pineal gland and readily inhibited by light, with signal transduction from the retina via the hypothalamus to the pineal gland. This explains the diurnal rhythm of melatonin secretion with a maximum during night time hours (2–4 am). Intraindividual maximum levels are achieved during the first three years of life while young adults have 20 times lower levels. With ongoing ageing, melatonin secretion declines and the nightly peak level occurs one to two hours earlier.

The main physiological function of melatonin is the regulation of the diurnal rhythm. It has been shown that melatonin is a sleep-inducing hormone and age-related insomnia may be improved by timed administration of melatonin. Recent studies have shown that human leukocytes express NAT and synthesize. Furthermore, inhibition of this process led to alterations in the secretion of immune-active cytokines. This suggests a potential role for melatonin in immune regulation.

GROWTH HORMONE

Growth hormone (GH) is released from anterior pituitary somatotrope cells in a pulsatile fashion. GH release is stimulated by GHRH and inhibited by somatostatin, which are produced in the hypothalamus. Pituitary growth hormone (GH) production reaches its maximum around 20 years of age, but shows attenuation with age, both with regard to total secretion and to amplitudes of pulsatile release. Studies suggest that spontaneous GH secretion falls by around 14 per cent per decade of adult life. GH has been reported to have a variety of immunomodulatory effects *in vitro* but the *in vivo* significance of this is unclear particularly as many of the effects of GH may be indirect.

TESTOSTERONE AND THE AGEING MALE: DR COLIN JOHNSTON, WEST HERTFORDSHIRE TR

Testosterone deficiency in younger men is associated with a variety of symptoms including, diminished libido, erectile dysfunction, fatigue and decreased vitality, reduced muscle mass with increased central obesity, reduced bone density, decreased cognitive function, depression and anaemia. All or the majority of these symptoms can be improved/restored by testosterone replacement. Replacement therapy is now available using much more acceptable methods via patches, gels and gum pellets as well as the more traditional methods of injections or implants.

Blood levels of Testosterone including free or bioavailable Testosterone fall in the ageing male. Studies have also suggested an association between low testosterone and patients with diabetes and increased cardiovascular risk. Many of the symptoms of hypogonadism are similar to the "normal" ageing process inviting the question as to whether testosterone replacement could be beneficial for the elderly male, improving quality of life, cognitive function and reducing the risk of chronic disorders such as cardiovascular disease or osteoporosis.

Unfortunately testosterone therapy may be associated with significant risks to health. The increased risk of cardiovascular disease in males has been attributed to testosterone although there is no evidence to support this. Excessive replacement can be associated with increased red-cell mass and polycythaemia which might contribute to circulatory problems. It could be expected that the development of androgen dependent tumours especially the prostate might be increased but again there is no confirmatory evidence.

At present we know that there are a proportion of elderly men with detectable but low levels of testosterone especially when compared to the younger male. Many have symptoms compatible with testosterone deficiency but we have no evidence as to the risk/benefit of replacement therapy. This has resulted in recent position statements from both the US (United States National Academy of Science, Institute of Medicine) and the UK (Society for Endocrinology) urging caution before commencing treatment and emphasising the need for proper controlled trials. The UK would be in an excellent position to undertake such research. Such a trial would almost certainly not be funded by the pharmaceutical industry and will depend on central government funding such as the MRC.

SKELETAL DISEASES: DR PETER SELBY, UNIVERSITY OF MANCHESTER

A large number of skeletal diseases are associated with the ageing process. Although there is some research to inform many of these agendas a lot of this has been ignored by health policy makers and as a result of the morbidity and mortality associated with the skeletal disease in the elderly is substantial.

The primary skeletal problem associated with ageing is the occurrence of bone fractures. This has been known for many years. Furthermore it is generally accepted that the incidence of fracture is likely to increase over the coming years. This is predominantly the effect of an ageing population. In addition to their own problems of pain and immobility fractures are associated with a significant decrease in quality of life. Furthermore, vertebral fractures are associated with a significantly increased mortality. Following a fracture, in addition to the increased death rate, there is also significant evidence pointing to a loss of independence: only 50 per cent of people following hip fracture returned to previous level of independence. As a consequence the national health and personal social service costs of these fractures are substantial. It has been estimated these are currently in the region of £2 billion per year and that this figure is likely to increase with the passage of time.

Although there has been a significant research effort in the field of osteoporosis this has been predominantly driven by the needs of the pharmaceutical industry and issues not related to drug therapies have received much less high profile attention.

Although the prevention of falls on fractures was considered within the National Service Framework for older people this has not lead to major change in provision for the prevention and treatment of osteoporosis. Several topics around the field of osteoporosis are currently under review by the National Institute for Clinical

Excellence but current provision for osteoporosis is fragmentary. A recent EU report indicates that the United Kingdom has the lowest provision for bone densitometry (the means of diagnosing osteoporosis) of any of the member states. Although we understand the committee is not primarily considering health care issues it can be seen that this low level of provision indicates how poorly the results of research have been translated into practical provision within the United Kingdom.

Vitamin D

Vitamin D deficiency is a further important cause of skeletal morbidity in the elderly. It is now well established that for the healthy population even in temperate climates such as the United Kingdom the vast majority of vitamin D is formed within the body as the result of the action of sunlight on the skin. In the elderly population exposure to sunlight is reduced and therefore this source of vitamin D is less readily obtained. This presents a particular problem in institutionalised or housebound elderly. Low levels of vitamin D have been well documented to lead to muscle weakness together with softening of the bones (osteomalacia). The combination of these leads to an increased risk of fracture. Several studies have indicated that giving vitamin D and calcium supplementation to elderly institutionalised individuals is associated with a significant reduction in the occurrence of fractures. There is no public health policy guiding such supplementation in the United Kingdom even in high-risk institutionalised elderly patients. Again this shows a lack of willingness of the public health authorities to put lessons which had been learnt from clinical research into practice for the benefit of the elderly population.

An alternative approach to this problem would involve the fortification of certain foodstuffs with vitamin D. Although this is done some extent with spreading fats this is not undertaken in the United Kingdom to anything like the same extent as in other countries of Europe or the United States. The reasons for this are generally attributed to the possibility of over treatment leading to hypercalcaemia. However, in places where supplementation is routine this has only occurred rarely.

Paget's Disease

Paget's disease is a poorly understood condition which leads to a marked increase in turnover in discrete bones within the skeleton. As a result of this it can lead to, deformity, and fracture. It has recently been estimated that Paget's disease affects two percent of the population over the age of 55. The consequences of Paget's disease are less well understood. A large multicentre trial examined the effect of treatment of Paget's disease on specific endpoint such as fracture and arthritis is currently under way. This study (the Paget's prism study) is jointly funded by arc and the National association for the relief of Paget's disease. Little if any cognisance of the needs of patients with Paget's disease appears to be taken by those responsible for health care planning.

GROWTH HORMONE: DR ANDREW TOOGOOD, UNIVERSITY OF BIRMINGHAM

Growth hormone (GH) is produced by the anterior pituitary gland in a pulsatile fashion, with the majority being released during sleep, however the amount of GH released changes over the course of the human lifespan. GH release is maximal during puberty when it promotes linear growth, but thereafter secretion declines by approximately 14 per cent per decade of adult life. Although GH does have direct effects upon some tissues, many of its actions are mediated via insulin-like growth factor-I (IGF-I), a peptide produced predominantly in the liver. In parallel with GH, IGF-I levels also fall with increasing age. As a consequence of these changes, old age is a state of relative GH insufficiency, frequently referred to as the "somatopause".

In addition to changes in hormone secretion, the aging process results in adverse changes in body composition, particularly a decline in muscle mass and an increase in fat mass; bone mineral density declines and the risk of fracture increases; physical performance deteriorates and there is an increased risk of falls. Furthermore, ageing is associated with a worsening cardiovascular risk profile and increased morbidity and mortality from cardiovascular and cerebrovascular disease.

GH deficiency in younger adults causes similar changes to those outlined above associated with the ageing process, which has led to the suggestion that the elderly are GH deficient and would benefit from GH treatment. Randomised controlled studies have demonstrated modest benefits when GH has been used alone or in combination with exercise or sex steroids. Body composition improves, and there is some improvement in strength and exercise capacity. These data have provided the basis for the use of GH as an anti-ageing compound, particularly in the United States and increasingly in the United Kingdom, a practice not accepted by the mainstream endocrine community.

There is some evidence that treatment targeted at specific groups may improve function. One study of GH therapy given during the perioperative period to patients undergoing hip replacement increased the four-minute walking time compared to placebo. Such changes may improve recovery and reduce the time to independent living following similar operative procedures. Other groups where the benefits of the anabolic effects of GH are not known is in patients at risk of falls or those undergoing knee replacement surgery.

The benefits of GH treatment in the elderly are limited to changes in body composition and improvements in exercise capacity. These benefits are offset by a high frequency of side effects and concerns regarding the long-term safety of GH treatment in this age group. There are no long-term data that indicate whether the benefits are permanent or whether they extend the period of independent living. Furthermore there are no data that determine the cost effectiveness of GH treatment in healthy ageing adults. Future work must determine what is meant by the term somatopause; no single person or professional body to date has defined this clinical state or physiological process. Work is required to identify subject groups that will benefit from either short term or chronic GH treatment and what parameters should be assessed to demonstrate GH treatment is actually providing significant functional or health benefits. As the population ages and places increasing pressure on the Health Services small changes in functional ability may result in significant savings in bed occupancy and cost.

October 2004

Memorandum by Mr Frederic Stansfield

1. INTRODUCTION

1.1 This response is submitted on an individual basis. I am interested in ageing policy because I am a 52 year old man currently not working, but living with an elderly relative. My last position, some years ago, was as a Research Fellow in a new university, where my role included duties seeking to generate interdisciplinary research into aspects of the built environment. My own undergraduate degree is in Psychology and I have an MSc in Occupational Psychology, as a result of which I am specifically concerned about ageing related work issues, over and above the concern with issues relating to older people that arises from my personal situation. In between obtaining these degrees I worked as a systems analyst for a variety of public and private sector organisations. I also have interests relating to the History and Philosophy of Psychology, as well as in philosophy itself through participating in the activities of learned societies and other events relating to philosophy.

1.2 Your enquiry is specific to the scientific aspects of ageing, but the issues on this topic are highly interdisciplinary. Negative attitudes towards ageing are amongst the largest problems in the United Kingdom today, particularly in relation to employment, at a time when the proportion of older people in the population is greatly increasing. This is an issue that needs to be addressed by social scientific research, but new evidence from the biological and engineering sciences can help demonstrate the inappropriateness of current beliefs.

1.3 In this response I am taking ageing as a general issue without being very specific about particular age ranges. The age range of scientific interest will vary between research areas. In relation to the biological bases of ageing, it is important to have an understanding of human development over the whole duration of life. In relation to technology and design, many of the issues affecting the quality of life only seriously affect the very old. The age group between 50 and 65 has pressing needs in relation to economic and social science issues, but from the point of view of much science research the needs of this demographic group are not qualitatively different from those of younger adults.

2. THE BIOLOGICAL PROCESSES OF AGEING

2.1 It is clear that major advances are being made in relation to the biological processes of ageing, in particular because of the decoding of DNA and related advances in genetics. This is an area of research that is already very active in the United Kingdom and it is obvious that continued effort is justifiable in it.

2.2 In psychology, there was extensive behavioural research on ageing in the years following the Second World War. In relation to work issues, the Nuffield Foundation funded a long-term project at Cambridge University between 1946 and 1956 (Welford, 1958) and the Medical Research Council followed this by funding further work at Bristol and Liverpool Universities and University College London. More recently, this area of research has shared in the general expansion of university research.

2.3 A current need in psychology (leaving aside an important need for more research in the social psychology of ageing that perhaps falls outside the remit of the your committee) is to relate behavioural research and its application more closely to biological processes. I suspect that there is a lack of dissemination of advances in our knowledge of biological processes to applied psychology. One reason is that, as a rough approximation, the older universities in the United Kingdom (including Oxford and Cambridge) are the leaders in relation to biological psychology, but the main centres for applied psychology are in what were once known as "redbrick" universities and in universities with technological origins. Pressure for cheap research in small projects spread across institutions tends to favour further expansion of behavioural and observational research as opposed to innovative work requiring more laboratory facilities. Adoption of new techniques from biological psychology would be a major change of direction for psychology consultancies such as those involved in the recruitment and selection of workers.

2.4 From experience in my everyday life, more needs to be done in particular to research and/or disseminate knowledge relating to the effects of nutrition on the ageing process. In particular, my observation is that good food is crucial to maintaining an active life for the very elderly (eg those over approximately 85). There is not enough information to guide those concerned with shopping and catering for these senior citizens, not to speak of the need to change the priorities of those who provide woefully inadequate catering in hospitals and nursing homes. Not least, research is needed as to how to motivate the independent elderly to eat properly.

2.5 The scale and nature of current and likely discoveries in relation to the biological processes of ageing have major ethical implications, not least in relation to ethnicity. There is a need to invest in research on the philosophy of science in relation to biological processes and ageing, concerning methodological as well as ethical issues.

3. The Application of Research in Technology and Design to Improve the Quality of Life of Older People

3.1 In responding to your request for evidence relating to technology and design I am concentrating on issues relating to the built environment and transportation. This is not only because of my own career experience, but also reflects my opinion after being involved in the development of knowledge in several disciplines that the built environment should be a priority area for additional research.

3.2 Knowledge into specific equipment and aids for older people can often be gained from projects of manageable size. There tends to be support for such investigations because relevant charities provide resources and because business people who wish to be associated with a socially useful enterprise are glad to develop products. Substantial advances have been made: the equipment available today for the elderly and disabled is incomparably better than that a generation ago. Perhaps, however, one might mention hearing aids as a particular case where there is scope for advances based on new research.

3.3 In the behavioural sciences, research by applied psychologists into technology and design, whilst they would see it as within their remit, has been largely overtaken by ergonomists who concentrate more closely on experimental investigation, including behavioural and physiological issues. It is possible in relation to technology and design relating to equipment for the aged and for any other purpose that this leads to a concentration by researchers on physical equipment design rather than on wider issues as to its acceptability and use.

3.4 Given the widespread use of information technology in society today, there is an on-going need to commit resources for research on human-computer interaction involving people of different ages. For older people, attitudes towards computers are still often as much an issue as the actual usability of the hardware and software. However, United Kingdom research in this area needs to take into account the international scale on which the computing industry operates: the need is largely to attract major overseas companies in the industry to bring research on use of computers by older people to Britain.

3.5 In relation to the built environment, I would like to highlight four areas where additional large scale research is needed that would improve life in Britain for everybody, but in particular for older people. In each of these areas psychological issues are at least as important as narrow engineering and design ones if successful change is to be achieved. The areas are:

3.5.1 Accessible and available public transport. The United Kingdom has built up a transport system in which car use is essential outside major cities and highly desirable anywhere outside Central London. For the elderly this is a problem, not least because cars place cognitive demands upon their drivers for rapid responses, which is the type of skill that declines most with age. Replacement of motor car use is of course going to be needed for other reasons too including needs to avoid pollution and the depletion of oil reserves. Such replacement appears to be technically possible, but it is fiercely resisted largely for psychological reasons. People are by nature active, but in modern Britain they are largely, and inevitably, constrained to a largely passive role. People do not have access to cultivate the land outside their own gardens (where they have them). Manufacturing work has been largely overtaken by passive processing of information in service industries. This leaves driving a car as the main way many people have of controlling what happens in their physical environment, and they are not prepared to lose this power even if it results from technology that causes major problems for the elderly and other disadvantaged sections of the population. Research is needed not only to identify how to develop a transport system that will give older people freedom and mobility, but how to provide such a system that is also acceptable and preferable to those in the prime of life.

3.5.2 Britain has seen a revolution in retailing whereby small shops in local neighbourhoods or high-streets have been replaced by larger stores out-of-town or in shopping malls. The trouble is that many of the elderly cannot get to these new shops and even if they can these stores are too big to walk round (and the displays are at the wrong height if they are in wheelchairs). This problem is particularly serious for clothes where help with shopping or use of the Internet cannot compensate for visiting the shop. Exclusion of the elderly from shops has been made worse by the closure of post offices following changed pensions administration arrangements: for many old people a regular visit to the post office was a vital social activity. The research need is to identify shop arrangements that will maintain or increase the advantage of the new types of shops whilst making them usable and attractive to older people. (Incidentally, I was specifically asked by a relative to include this suggestion).

3.5.3 There is need for more research into housing design in relation to an ageing population, both in relation to the usability of ordinary dwellings by people as they age and to specialist housing provision for the elderly with special needs.

3.5.4 Good hospital provision is essential for an ageing population to have a healthy life, but there are inadequate arrangements in the United Kingdom for research into health care buildings. After the Second World War, when Britain's stock of hospitals was in a parlous condition, the Nuffield Foundation sponsored research into hospital design. This led to the development of professional expertise into hospital building needs retained largely within the NHS by dedicated professional staff. This knowledge resource has been adversely affected by the introduction of private competition into the provision of hospital buildings, which I witnessed in a small way whilst as a university researcher submitting unsuccessful bids for collaborative research in this field. All too often private designers are unaware of special hospital needs, often in details such as doorway design as much as the major functions to be provided by the building. External research facilities are in consequence needed to supplement and replace NHS resources in this area.

For the above list I have drawn on a mix everyday observation and career experience. Needless to say, study of the likely costs and benefits would be needed before commitments to major new research.

3.6 Built environment research relating to older people, and to people in general, would benefit by provision at a national level of a facility at which buildings could be prototyped indoors within a laboratory space for behavioural research.

3.7 Lack of able researchers is likely to be a problem for a research programme into buildings for older people. It might be addressed in part by recruiting researchers from the social sciences, where by contrast with built environment disciplines; surpluses of good graduates are being produced by the universities and where competing professional opportunities in private industry are fewer. In addition, I suggest later in this response (paragraph 4.7) that older people currently not working could be redeployed, after suitable training, into research.

4. POLICY AND STRATEGIC MANAGEMENT ISSUES

4.1 Research issues including the identification of priority areas and the allocation of funding is in my observation well co-ordinated between representatives of the civil service, universities and other research providers, public organisations and private organisations. The trouble is that they tend to talk to each other rather than the ordinary citizens who should ultimately benefit from applied research, particularly in relation to ageing issues. This is an issue notably for the age group between 50 and 65, many of whom, since they now longer work and are not yet of pensionable age, have little contact with the state or charities. In relation to those above 65, problems in identifying policy derive from a harsh class divide. On the one hand many senior citizens depend upon state benefits, and often receive services distributed by charities (who thereby acquire vested interests) using public money. On the other, old people on good pensions feel that distancing themselves from the state and charities (except as funders and organisers) is a way of maintaining their independence and status.

4.2 The large involvement of researchers themselves in the strategic management of United Kingdom research is amongst the reasons why funding tends to go to existing areas of research strength, and to be spread amongst many small projects. This is not so great an issue for research on the biological processes of ageing which falls within an existing area of research strength, but it is a problem that needs to be overcome for research in technology and design for older people, particularly in relation to the built environment issues indicated above in paragraph 3.5.

4.3 The United Kingdom spends approximately two per cent of its Gross National Income on research (I am basing this paragraph on data from the Office of National Statistics, 2004), which is substantially less than other developed countries. The answer to any question as to whether there is sufficient research capacity in the United Kingdom is therefore likely to be a resounding "No". However, the United Kingdom's research effort is skewed still further because of its concentration on certain areas, including defence, space research and health research. The Annual Abstract of Statistics (Table 20.4, page 320) shows that intramural expenditure by industry on civil research in 2001 was £3,562 million for the chemicals industry (which will include pharmaceutical research) and £30 million for the construction industry. These figures are astonishing given the importance of the construction industry for the United Kingdom economy, even if they are not strictly comparable, for instance because research undertaken by property owners into buildings may be recorded for their own industry sector rather than construction. The imbalance is not compensated for by central government funds. I have highlighted in this response the importance of construction related research for the ageing population. It has recently been reported to the House of Commons that United Kingdom output could be increased by £3 billion per year by employing ten per cent of those over 50 not in work who would like to work (National Audit Office, 2004). As a researcher over 50 and not working I cannot therefore believe that several £100 millions extra money per year (possibly even £1 billion) for research on ageing could not be found within the United Kingdom economy. This is the scale of investment needed to bring the construction industry up to the quality of our world-leading pharmaceuticals industry, and it could be targeted around built environment and transportation projects specifically benefiting older people, although not necessarily exclusively this age group.

4.4 I have made various suggestions for research within major research disciplines in this response. However, I do not think that one should worry too much about gaps in research. It would be better to address sufficient funds to research that will result in major improvements for specific large issues affecting the quality of life of older people than to spread money across many projects too small to be effectively applied.

4.5 The quality of the research capability in relation to the scientific aspects of ageing is as much a concern as the lack of such capability in relation to technology and design. In particular, the current suitability of universities for research in this area should be questioned. Universities cannot compete for the best staff in the areas of technology and design not only because of inadequate resources but also because of needs to maintain parity of pay and conditions between researchers and teachers in different disciplines. Many existing staff are "burned-out" through excessive workloads and lack of career development, setting aside issues relating to the great variations between the ability of university staff in different disciplines. Despite improvements in recent years, research management within higher education is often poor. Attempts to address these issues within universities are seriously hampered by resistance to change and by deeply in-grained organisational culture. If substantial additional funds are to be invested into scientific aspects of ageing, serious consideration should be given to using this money to set up a completely new research institution unencumbered by past history and commitments.

4.6 Research on ageing often benefits from complex statistical analysis because of the need to compare age groups either through by repeated observations or by comparisons of otherwise comparable sample populations. In addition, the ageing process results from many interacting causes, which have to be disentangled in the analysis of experiments. Lack of available researchers with the necessary mathematical and statistical skills is likely to be a problem that will need to be addressed, for instance in relation to research in the built environment.

4.7 The Research Assessment Exercise (RAE) is a disaster in general: I have pointed out in the *Times Higher Education Supplement* (Stansfield, 2004) that it is ageist as well as methodologically flawed. My complaint is but one amongst many. But the RAE is particularly disastrous for scientific research into ageing. Longitudinal research studying people over an extended period is essential for much research into ageing. The deadlines of the Research Assessment Exercise discourage such long-term studies. This periodic assessment of research also discourages large-scale research, both because this inevitably requires a longer-term commitment and because many universities press for a share of any available funds. In suggesting that a new institution should be created for research on ageing, I hope that this would enable the funds involved to be separated from those allocated and assessed by means of the RAE. The success of cognitive research on ageing financed over ten year periods in psychology in the early years after the Second World War shows from past experience the advantages of long-term funding.

4.8 More could and should be done to enable older people to carry out research into ageing themselves, not just be subjects for investigation. In making this observation I am thinking of people who could have previously carried out other work and who could be retrained to bring in fresh experience, not just existing academics. Given that a million people between 50 and 65 need to be found work (National Audit Office, 2004), research activity should at least employ its fair share of them. If 2 per cent of Gross National Income is spent on research, that implies 20,000 such new researchers, and productive use could be found for more.

4.9 Past research into scientific aspects of ageing has already had huge effects on the quality of life for elderly people. As just one example, the invention and improvement of artificial hips has enabled many thousands of old people who in the past would have been bed-ridden (and would soon have died) to live an active life. However, there are two major policy obstacles to the application of scientific research about ageing:

4.9.1 The attitudes of civil servants and others who define old age for policy making purposes in relation to retirement ages of 60 or 65, implicitly because of their financial interests. These dates were set roughly a century ago in relation to then expectations of life and the affordability of pension provisions. The psychological and biological evidence provides little if any justification for considering the mid-sixties as a major milestone in the ageing process: except in cases of illness declines in performance due to old age become significant at a considerably greater age. Yet retirement age is used as a dividing line for policy making in many areas across government, not just for matters specifically relating to pay and pensions.

4.9.2 Emphasis on short-term returns on investment in both public and private sectors of the economy. The financial returns on capital implied by prevailing interest rates, even at the comparatively low level of recent years, simply do not match the human life span. Decisions in relation to the scientific aspects of ageing need to be made in relation to needs predicted by demographic statistics and the time needed to carry out research ready for the time when there will be many more very old people. This should impose deadlines.

5. CONCLUSION

5.1 As a partial summary to this submission, the following is a selected list of suggestions made that would taken together form a programme of action:

(a) Substantial additional resources should be allocated to research on scientific aspects of ageing.

(b) Because of massive disparities in existing research effort, extra resources allocated should be concentrated particularly on investigation relating ageing to issues in the built environment and transportation.

(c) If built environment and transportation research receives additional funding; it should be concentrated on a small number of major topics, encompassing behavioural as well as technological research.

(d) If new large-scale research is instigated concerning the built environment, it should be carried out by a new institution with long-term funding.

(e) Investigators for research into scientific aspects of ageing should be found in part from the one million people aged between 50 and 65 who are not working and who would like to work.

REFERENCES

National Audit Office (2004) *Welfare to Work: Tackling the Barriers to the Employment of Older People.* Report by the Comptroller and Auditor General. HC 1026. Session 2003–04: 15 September 2004. Ordered to be printed by the House of Commons.

Office of National Statistics (1994) *Annual Abstract of Statistics.* 2004 edition. Number 140.

Stansfield. F. R. (2004) "RAE for the vain but not the old", Letter to the *Times Higher Education Supplement,* 28 May 2004, p 19.

Welford, A. T. (1958) *Ageing and Human Skill.* London: Oxford University Press for the Trustees of the Nuffield Foundation

September 2004

Memorandum by the Thomas Pocklington Trust

INTRODUCTION

Thomas Pocklington Trust is the leading specialist provider of housing and care for people with sight loss in the UK: www.pocklington-trust.org.uk. Pocklington also funds a research programme on the prevention, alleviation and cure of visual impairment, at present amounting to about £700,000 over three years. Formerly this programme was directed to basic medical research but, after an extensive policy review five years ago, is now focussed on social and public health research.

This submission of evidence to the Select Committee enquiry on scientific aspects of ageing is based on our experience in commissioning research in the visual impairment sector.

The Biological Processes of Ageing

Sight loss is very significant in later life: Around one in eight of people over 75 and one in three of people over 90 in the UK have serious sight loss, according to the most recent peer-reviewed study[1], funded by Pocklington. Much of this loss arises from correctable impairment eg refractive error[2].

A short literature search[3] commissioned by Pocklington from Kings College London in 1999 challenged the view that sight loss was an automatic consequence of ageing and pointed to the need for further research on prevention and cure of sight loss.

At this stage there was a singular lack of reliable social research on sight loss, as identified by other studies for the same policy review[3]. For example there were no studies in the DOH policy programme, and only one significant study in recent years on the JRF research programme.

However some progress has been made since. The needs of older people with sight loss has been the subject of a major study by UCL[4]. This has identified extensive need: sudden or worsening sight loss in later life was commonly reported by our interviewees to be a "devastating", "shattering", or "life- changing" event. The researchers also found that there can be a stoic acceptance that the social world necessarily contracts. People also felt that their social or basic human skills were diminishing: "I feel I want to scream just for human conversation".

Recent published research, funded by Pocklington with the London School of Hygiene and Tropical Medicine[1], has identified significant gender differences—older women are more likely than men to suffer sight loss, after adjusting for age differences.

The needs of people from ethnic minorities with sight loss have barely been studied in a rigorous way, as shown by another study commissioned for our policy review[5]: there have been a few studies since but none published in peer review journals, to our knowledge. Epidemiological links have been made between certain diseases involving sight loss eg diabetic retinopathy, macular disease, glaucoma, but much more research is needed. We, and the Housing Corporation, are at present funding a project by De Montfort University in Birmingham investigating how to improve access of ethnic minority people with sight loss to services, by building capacity in community groups.

There is no general cure for macular disease, which is the major eye condition in old age. The need for further medical research towards a cure is paramount. There is also a need for more work on prevention. There are promising emerging findings on links between dietary fats and macular disease and we are funding a study at the London School to take this evidence further, but more research is needed, and on other aspects of lifestyle and on possible risks with a variety of drug treatments.

Generally on biological aspects of ageing, although there are medical research units in major hospital/ university centres, the message appears to be that funding for eye research has diminished. A meeting is being held in the visual impairment sector in October to discuss what can be done, initiated by the voluntary sector, and hosted by Vision2020UK.

In September 2002 we held a joint workshop at the London School of Hygiene and Tropical Medicine to review the recent research on public health on people with sight loss: it was clear that there remained much to do, eg on screening in primary care, the role of the GP annual health check, and even the prevalence of specific eye conditions.

There appears from our perspective to be little coordination of research other than that led by the voluntary sector. If there is coordination elsewhere, we have not been engaged in that process. We are attempting to improve the way our own research is coordinated, as the charities develop better working partnerships.

The application of research in technology and design to improve the quality of life of older people

This is a key priority for people with sight loss, including older people, as technology can enable people to live fulfilled lives on a level playing field with their sighted contemporaries.

We have three areas of interest here:

— Lighting.

— The role of agencies in delivering technology including equipment to people with sight loss.

— Housing related assistive technology including telecare.

There are clearly many technologies which could be used to a greater extent to benefit older people. Many people with sight loss are not registered and so do not readily access low vision aids or other services.

Our recent research at the University at Reading[6] indicates that older people are not offered advice on lighting, even though it is clear that better lighting could improve their quality of life and their safety eg lighting on stairs could reduce the risk of falls, though more research is needed. This research is now being extended. Accordingly, we have begun to demonstrate that older people can be enabled to take part in activites they could not do previously, merely by access to better lighting eg play the piano, or watch TV. We are now assessing our own tenants in order to ensure they are provided with the best possible lighting—but what about the vast population of older people who do not have that specialist support? We have held a consultative meeting at the Institute of Directors in June, which brought together care professionals, Government policy makers, academic and charities to consider how best to progress research and development in this area. It is not being led from the public sector. There is much to do eg influence new building regulations, investigate the possible harmful effect of blue light, research the lighting needs of people with different eye conditions and pilot models of providing lighting advice. A summary report on that meeting will be available shortly.

We have briefly looked at how people with sight loss are accessing existing technologies, in studies on home improvement agencies services to people with sight loss, and on housing related assistive technology[7, 8, 9]. Owing to a lack of inclusive design and the reluctance of designers and manufacturers to produce for a specialist market, together with the isolation of many older people with sight loss, the evidence indicates that people are not getting access to advice or provision of techologies which could help their lives. The disciplines who would provide such advice ie Occupational Therapists and Rehabilitation Workers, are not technical experts, and in the case of the latter, have low training and status. These are national workforce issues.

We have held a seminar with the University of Reading and the EQUAL Network last Autumn to inform practitioners and the charitable and academic sector of these issues, and discuss how to progress. As a result, we have initiated an email newsletter through Vision2020UK on sight loss relevant research: this will be further developed. The EQUAL network provided a good means of raising these issues among a group who are not aware: generally we have found an astonishing lack of awareness and information among general policy makers and practitioners about the needs of people with sight loss and remedies.

This is all matched by a lack of research expertise amongst the academic community: very few social and public health researchers of high reputation have studied sight loss. There are few funders and those charities who fund such research are liable to be hampered by requirements of the new Research Governance Framework for social care research from the Department of Health.

We are a partner in an EQUAL4 Consortium project on Supporting Independence: New Products, New Practices, New Communities, about the implementation of technologies including telecare in homes of older people, for which we are providing one field site. It is surprising how few sources of financial support there has been for the implementation of the technology involved. Issues of consent and ethics are little understood. There is a cultural gap between engineers and social researchers, and much more mutual understanding is needed.

You ask whether the research is being used to inform policy. This is a difficult area for a research funder like ourselves. We try to ensure our research is published, and with partners hold workshops. However, like other charities, we have very limited management resources, and there are few obvious networks through which we can readily disseminate findings, apart from links to other sight loss charities and EQUAL Network. Neither NCAR nor the GO programme have majored on these areas. From our perspective, there appears to be a lack of leadership at National level on dissemination of research into policy and practice.

SUMMARY CONCLUSIONS

Sight loss has been, perhaps by its very nature, a relatively hidden issue in policy, research and practice. Although some progress has been made in the last few years, there remain huge areas where rigorous research is needed. There are issues about how far research has been coordinated, or linked with other research initiatives on older people. Neither has dissemination been facilitated. This appears to point to a lack of leadership in the UK on this topic.

Dr Angela McCullagh
Research Director

REFERENCES

[1] J R Evans, AE Fletcher, RPL Wormald *et al.* Prevalence of visual impairment in people aged 75 years and older in Britain: results from the MRC trial of assessment and management of older people in the community. Br J Ophthalmology 2002;86:795–800.

[2] JR Evans, AE Fletcher, RPL Wormald. Causes of visual impairment in people aged 75 years and older in Great Britain: an add-on study to the MRC Trial of Assessment and Management of Older People in the Community. Br J Ophthalmology. 2004;88: 365–370.

[3] In: Towards a New Research Policy: compiled by Dr Angela McCullagh, Pocklington, 2000. Available from Thomas Pocklington Trust, London.

[4] Housing and Support Needs of Older People with Visual Impairment—experiences and challenges. J Hanson, J Percival, R Zako and M Johnson, UCL and Bristol University. Pocklington Occasional Paper 1. 2003.

[5] Ethnic Minorities and Visual Impairment. A Research Review. MRD Johnson and MO Scase. Mary Seacole Research Centre, De Montfort University. Seacole Research Paper 1,2000.

[6] Lighting the Homes of People with Sight loss. G K Cook, L O'Neill, S Hill, University of Reading. Pocklington Occasional Paper No 4, 2003.

[7] The Effectiveness of Home Improvement Agencies to People with Sight Loss. J Rosser, E Laverick, K Croucher *et al.* Pocklington Occasional Paper No 5 (forthcoming), and Good Practice Guide. Foundations, University of York and Thomas Pocklington Trust, 2003.

[8] Helping People with Sight Loss in their Homes: Assistive Technology. K Ross, BRE. Pocklington Occasional Paper No 3, 2003.

[9] Independent Living for Visually Impaired People. The role of information and communications technologies in enabling new services. Report prepared for Thomas Pocklington Trust. J Barlow and R Curry.

September 2004

Memorandum by Professor Alan Walker, Dr Joanne Cook and Mr Peter Traynor

EUROPEAN RESEARCH PRIORITIES IN THE FIELD OF AGEING

This submission addresses the strategic questions posed by the Committee. It consists of a summary of the outcomes from a project spanning two and a half years that has been identifying the current gaps in ageing research across Europe and developing recommendations aimed at promoting better co-ordination of research in Europe, more cross-national collaboration and more interdisciplinary research.

INTRODUCTION

The European Forum on Population Ageing Research (FORUM) is an Accompanying Measure under the EU's Fifth Framework Programme. Drawing inspiration from the UK National Collaboration on Ageing Research (NCAR) FORUM was established in April 2002 to build upon the Research Directorate's efforts to enhance ageing research, by encouraging knowledge sharing, improving channels of communication, promoting broader European co-operation and raising the profile of European research on ageing. To achieve these objectives FORUM organised a number of events, including workshops, meetings and user consultations, which were attended by many key people in the field of ageing research in Europe, including scientists, policy makers, funders and user groups. The iterative process began with a series of three scientific workshops which focused on developing key ideas and recommendations regarding the future of ageing research, concentrating on the areas of Genetics, Longevity and Demography; Quality of Life; and Health and

Social Care. These draft recommendations were then considered at a meeting of the European Forum of research funders, then a user consultation conference and then again in a series of three more scientific workshops (a total of over 200 scientists have been involved in this work). Finally they were discussed, amended and approved by a second meeting of the European Forum in June 2004. The FORUM project concludes in December 2004 with a conference to present the final set of recommendations concerning European research on ageing.

Background to FORUM

— A major point of reference for this project is population ageing (Europe is the oldest region in the world) and the importance of responding to demographic changes in a pro-active and positive manner.

— The EU recognises the importance of co-ordination and information sharing in ageing research but, in contrast to the US, European ageing research currently lacks a co-ordinated approach.

— Scientists have been pushing for greater co-ordination for some time and continue to pursue cross-national and collaborative research on ageing and to argue that such research should be higher on the policy agenda.

— FORUM emerged from a recognition of these important issues and reflected the creation, in 2001, of a new collaborative structure on ageing research in the UK. The Key Action 6 on the Ageing Population and their Disabilities (under Framework Programme 5) created the opportunity for the project to obtain funding.

Objectives of FORUM

The FORUM project has five specific objectives:

— To promote European co-operation in ageing research.

— To develop synergies between national and international programmes.

— To improve channels of communication between Key Action 6 and national research efforts.

— To stimulate interdisciplinary research.

— To promote improved public awareness of ageing research.

Summary of recommendations

What follows is a short selection of some of the many recommendations generated by the FORUM process. The full list can be found in the final report of the project on the FORUM website at http://www.shef.ac.uk/ageingresearch. The recommendations command a high level of consensus among scientists, end user groups and national research funders and policy makers.

Key recommendations

These represent the top five priorities to emerge from the FORUM process:

— The recommendations from FORUM should be used to develop targeted funding for ageing research in Framework Programme 7.

— Major research and policy gains would be made from establishing a European Institute on Ageing to bring all disciplines on ageing together—this would provide the European identity that ageing research urgently needs to maximise its potential.

— Specific funding structures are needed to develop interdisciplinary and European research on ageing, research funding bodies/councils need to work together to provide funding incentives for this research and career structures need to be developed to enable and encourage researchers to take this direction.

— Involving users in research is essential and more research is needed on good practice and models of user involvement.

— Researchers in this field are ageing and there is a lack of new talent coming into ageing research—support structures need to be funded to attract new researchers.

Topic specific research priorities

A summary of the priorities under each of the three topics (quality of life; health and social care; genetics, longevity and demography) can be found in the appendix. The following are general priorities spanning the three topics.

— More focus should be given to comparative social policy and evaluating the efficacy of different welfare states and health care systems.

— More research on Europe's immensely diverse populations, and in particular how such diversity, of ethnicity, gender relations and migration patterns for instance, interacts with the ageing process.

— More studies of the interaction of environment and ageing, for instance the differences in the ageing process in rural and urban areas and the effect of residential versus the home environment on ageing and quality of life.

— Evaluating interventions—such as healthy and active ageing (including the ethics of such interventions).

— Transitions in older age, including changes in personal resources, family changes, retirement or continuing to work post-retirement.

— Research into older people as the providers as well as receivers of care and the various formal and information relationships involved in care.

— Agency in old age: older people's preferences and involvement in research and direct and indirect discrimination.

Research methods and approaches

— Increased funding is needed to develop the basic research tools for collaboration at a European level, including new comparative methodologies and databases, standardised instruments and greater co-ordination of data collection.

— European researchers need to work together to develop appropriate models and concepts, and to reach a consensus on the definition and measurement of concepts which would account for cross-cultural definitions whilst preserving context specific meanings.

— The diversity of ageing across Europe deserves greater recognition and exploration, as does the situation of different ethnic and migrant groups. More should be made of the richness of Europe's population, and there should be a focus on heterogeneity rather than simply looking for averages.

— Ageing research should be established as a discipline in its own right.

European collaboration

— An appropriate infrastructure needs to be developed at both the national and international levels to facilitate greater European collaboration. This should include the establishment or strengthening of national institutes of ageing, and the creation of a European institute or agency on ageing. Other developments could include dedicated journals, conferences and funding structures, better research training and a web based database of European ageing research.

— European networks on ageing research are needed to bring together scientists, user groups and older people to enable greater collaboration and dissemination of research on ageing. These networks need to be long term to build sustained collaboration. All stakeholders in ageing research also need to be included, not just researchers.

— Co-ordinating European collaboration on ageing would offer substantial benefits, including greater coherence in research and understanding across Europe, more opportunities for comparative analysis and policy and better use of Europe's high quality data in fields such as historical demographics, genetics and the care of older people.

— The recruitment and training of scholars, in particular promising young scholars, from different European countries needs to be promoted, to ensure optimal allocation of human capital and the build-up of efficient research teams and centres.

Interdisciplinary collaboration

— There is wide consensus among scientists that there should be a greater emphasis on interdisciplinary research in the field of ageing, but that this should not mean the dissolving of disciplinary identities. Indeed disciplinary identities should be maintained: the challenge is to develop synergy through research.

— Finding the necessary balance between the different disciplines requires a structure for better learning and understanding of different disciplines. There is a need for a common language and a role for the EU in creating a common database.

— Greater funding should be given to interdisciplinary centres, creating financial incentives to conduct interdisciplinary research and to educating, rewarding and developing appropriate career structures for interdisciplinary experts.

— Interdisciplinary research often falls between disciplinary funding bodies/research councils. There is a need for funding to go across disciplinary boundaries. Therefore, specific funding mechanisms are needed and the EU should play a role in facilitating this.

Involving the users of research

— Scientists are committed to involving users in research but acknowledged various difficulties including selecting who to involve and which projects such involvement would be suitable for.

— It was agreed that the formulation of a research agenda should involve a partnership model in which all stakeholders contribute to its development.

— A new methodology is needed in order to gain the maximum benefits from user involvement in research, and this should involve looking at existing examples of good practice and training for both researchers and users. If funders wish to encourage user involvement then the additional funds and time must be made available.

Policy recommendations

— Interdisciplinary, comparative cross-national and longitudinal research are difficult, time consuming and expensive but they are extremely necessary. Research funders must provide for this if they want the advances in knowledge that this research can bring.

— There should be a focus on demonstrating how research on ageing can contribute to people's lives and government policy, and the public should be convinced of the value of ageing research.

— Experiences of good practice for the effective dissemination of European research need to be developed and facilitated. This aspect of research often takes place when funding has expired and little resources are available for this critical stage of the research work. An additional funded phase for dissemination is needed in national and European funding programmes.

— The links between research findings and policy need to be developed. Currently the value of research is lost because of inadequate dissemination and the failure to carry through research findings into policy impact.

— Research findings should reach as large an audience as possible, including policy-makers. There is an important role for NGOs to play in translating findings into more understandable information and policy recommendations. For NGOs to carry out this task properly they must be funded.

— National funding bodies must support the future of ageing research and in order to do so effectively, ageing research has to be seen as a priority for research funding across Europe. The EU has an important facilitating, accompanying and co-ordinating role to play, for example, through networks and Framework funding.

— Each national funding body should have a commitment to fund a programme of research on ageing or at the very least a collection of co-ordinated projects. Otherwise the absence of this leads to exclusion from networks such as ERA-NET.

— All scientists and user groups agreed that the EU has a fundamental role to play in supporting, encouraging and if necessary obliging national governments to organise at least some form of "national agenda on ageing research". Without such measures the co-ordination of research on ageing will never reach the organised levels it receives in the US and this could damage the competitive advantage of European research in this field.

CONCLUSION

The aim of the FORUM project was to bring together the different groups active in the field of ageing research in Europe: scientists, research funders and user groups, to share knowledge and good practice and to identify the key priorities for European research in this field. The project has been very successful in bringing these groups together and has generated a great deal of enthusiasm among scientists. FORUM has gathered a wealth of valuable knowledge on interdisciplinary research and priorities for future research in this field. This knowledge will be shared at the final conference of the FORUM project, in Brussels in December and through the website and newsletters. However, whilst FORUM is drawing to a close, it is essential that those involved in the various aspects of ageing research take forward what has been learnt and work together to promote cross national and interdisciplinary collaboration. The ultimate aim of this endeavour, like all research on ageing, must be to extend the quality of older people's lives.

NEXT STEP

ERA-AGE Project

At the first meeting of the European Forum in March 2003, participants asked the FORUM team to develop an ERA-NET Co-ordination Action proposal to the EU's Sixth Framework Programme. This application was successful. The European Research Area on Population Ageing Research (ERA-AGE) began on 1 March 2004 and runs for four years. The groundwork for this project has been the European FORUM project, and the priorities developed by the FORUM process will be used to inform the work of ERA-AGE.

ERA-AGE is a consortium of nine partner countries and five associate partnerships, the aim of which is to create the framework for a European research area in the field of population ageing research, enabling research funders to work together more effectively and therefore gain maximum added value from national investments in this field. For more information please see the ERA AGE website (www.shef.ac.uk/era-age).

October 2004

APPENDIX

PRIORITIES FOR RESEARCH ON AGEING IN THREE AREAS

Research priorities and knowledge gaps	Area specific recommendations for European research
1. QUALITY OF LIFE Health resources	
(1) Aspects of prevention, rehabilitation and disease management in health care systems and their effects on health behaviour and QoL.	(1) Reviews are needed of existing conceptual and empirical research to prepare for comparative collaboration.
(2) QoL of older people with chronic disease.	(2) Preparation for comparative research is needed which involves reviewing policy, health systems, societal structures and cultures.
(3) Inequalities in health.	
(4) Historical shifts, generational differences and the changing role of the health care system.	
(5) Effects of migration and ability of health care systems to take into account the multi-cultural background of users.	
Personal resources, social participation and support networks	
(1) Research on policy and the role of the welfare state in shaping standards of living and quality of life.	Same as adjacent and comparative studies should be recommended as they help us to avoid ethnocentric biases in the definitions and perceptions of what is a good life.
(2) Comparisons between rural and urban populations of older people.	
(3) Housing and the impact of the person-environment relationship more generally for quality of life.	
(4) Issues of diversity, risk and marginality—especially minority ethnic groups and older migrants within Europe.	
(5) Interation of the resources of older people and personal coping and adaptation to risks and barriers.	
(6) Issues of empowerment and citizenship alongside the importance of advocacy and the continuance of ageist stereotypes.	
(7) Life course trajectories, family change and intergenerational relationships, including new family forms and the risks of social isolation.	
(8) Mental (and physical) activity and social participation.	
(9) Relationships between formal and informal care systems and the role of older people as caregivers needs further research.	
(10) Developing the implicit theory of quality of life.	
(11) Quality of life of vulnerable groups such as the frail and those with dementia and developing concepts and models that may help us study and monitor welfare among such groups.	
(12) Objective living conditions, and how they are subjectively perceived and adapted to.	

	Research priorities and knowledge gaps	Area specific recommendations for European research
Socio-demographic and economic resources	(1) Diversity needs to be emphasised more including the causal factors of inequalities between countries and social groups and the extent to which these factors are universal. (2) Changing gendered life course trajectories. (3) More comparative knowledge on people in residential versus people living at home. (4) Need to focus more on the economic position of future older people—income how income needs, levels and perceptions change as people age, the impact of wealth and inheritance. (5) Retirement and transitions in older age, expectations of, support for, incentives to continue to work. (6) Do classic inequalities remain or new ones emerge and is the gap between rich and poor older people polarising or converging?	Same as adjacent box.
Environmental resources	(1) The environment from micro to macro needs to be analysed as an important component of QoL. (2) 3-D framework for including the environment in QoL—bringing together individual, psychological and social and environmental. (3) Understanding the importance of indoor and outdoor space. (4) More research on people living at home, in particular people with dementia. (5) Older people with learning difficulties are ageing in place. (6) Intergenerational issues of segregation/integration in public places and the spatiality of ageing. (7) More evaluations of practical environmental measures.	Same as adjacent box and research on environmental variables should be core to QoL.
2. HEALTH AND SOCIAL CARE Effective interventions in health	(1) More research is needed that investigates the effectiveness of interventions in health and social care systems. (2) The whole age range should be studied. Very few studies exist on the "oldest old". (3) Focus on preventative-curative-palliative aspects of intervention. (4) The ethics of intervention needs examining. (5) Before and after measures should be studied. (6) Focus on physical diseases.	(1) Research on the feasibility of transferring interventions across to other cultures and learning more about cultural concepts/context. (2) Studying the impact of interventions on a more diverse population and making cross-cultural comparisons.

	Research priorities and knowledge gaps	Area specific recommendations for European research
Access to services and e-health and e-care	(1) The adjustment process of the evolution of technology to human development need taking into consideration. (2) The response and adaptation of specific groups of the individual population to technology can be diverse and refined measures will be needed. (3) Research needs to consider and mainstream a multi-level quality of care aiming first at the quality of life of the patient. (4) Basic research is needed on e-health and e-care to assess efficiency, ethical guidelines, impact and the interaction of these services with other services. (5) Analysis and policy follow-up is needed on the standardisation process and quality of e-health and e-care benefiting the older and oldest old patients. (6) Research on the long-term differences between profit and non-profit health services. (7) Examine cooperative structures developing between care professionals and caregiver households.	(1) European Study on the emerging development, access and ethical issues around e-health and e-care services. (2) A macro-sociological comparative study is needed on the determinants in European welfare states for care policy design, development and implementation.
Epidemiology and populations studies	(1) Urgent need for a European longitudinal study. Ideally this should involve as much of Europe as possible and receive long-term funding. (2) Review existing longitudinal studies to develop and standardise concepts, models and methodologies. (3) Develop longitudinal surveys on special problems and to identify the level and quality of health and social care in Europe. (4) Address the issue of "healthy ageing" and preventative strategies in old age. (5) Develop more healthy ageing indicators.	(1) Establish a large scale European longitudinal study.
Socio-economic and cultural factors shaping care needs	(1) Comparative, phenomenological, multi-dimensional and cross-paradigmatic research is needed at the national and European levels. (2) A critical evaluation of research on care, care reforms and policies—to re-orientate research at the frontline of care, formal and informal care. (3) Research needs to focus on social care which has become neglected. (4) Focus on the diversity of needs and developing a greater understanding of the cultural diversity of the ageing population. (5) Outline and criteria management—developing quality and efficiency concepts and measures. (6) Focus on care management—including values, quality and performance.	(1) European Observatory on Ageing and Care of Older Persons—to include, European Research Centre on Ageing and Care.

	Research priorities and knowledge gaps	Area specific recommendations for European research
3. GENETICS, LONGEVITY AND DEMOGRAPHY Genetics	(1) The phenotype "longevity" needs defining more objectively, possibly from a biochemical and physiological point of view. (2) The growth of genomics and proteomics is revealing the important role of genetic variability in modulating the quality of ageing in humans. This offers a fantastic opportunity to assemble genotypic specific risk profiles. A multi-disciplinary approach would be required to plan the research and interpret the data. (3) The development of stem cell technology has provided the opportunity for the study of the relationship between different biological levels; molecular, cellular, organ, systemic to be explored in more depth. This opportunity should be exploited. (4) It is important to exploit different approaches, including familial studies, twin studies and population studies by using complementary tools.	
Longevity	(1) Headlines could help to identify key areas of research, like the frailty syndrome, in order to ascertain when people start to go down the curve of functioning. (2) More focus should be given to what happens before mortality, why people survive with co-morbidity in very old age and what can be changed by which interventions. (3) The relationship between diseases and longevity should be examined in order to better define which genes to study. (4) Research on stem cells has provided a great opportunity to move from molecular and cellular level to organ and system level study, for instance in "repairing medicine", ageing functions as a very effective model for the study of most diseases.	
Demography	(1) The two key priorities of ageing research should be to provide: (i) A better understanding of the determinants of healthy ageing and longevity; (ii) Policy relevant research on the social, economic and health consequences of an ageing population. (2) While there is substantial data on ageing across a range of topics, a number of areas have been identified where date is lacking, including different aspects of retirement—disparities in healthy ageing, eg in relation to gender, class, race and culture, and also across regional and national boundaries, differences in living arrangements and the consequences of these differences on ageing. (3) The discipline of demography needs strengthening to develop: surveys of European wide demographics—cross-national and comparable data, more data on the demographics of ageing; biological/social data and national statistical data. (4) Demography is not only about the length of life (mortality) but also about the quality of life (eg healthy life expectancy) research could benefit from a greater focus on this issue.	

Memorandum by Professor Robert Weale

With an increasingly ageing population, and the Government's continuous exhortations for public transport to be used, it would seem that transport facilities should become even more user-friendly than they are.

1. The directions and bus numbers at the front of buses do not seem to be presented as clearly as they might. They are not always illuminated when necessary, and, even in daylight, their legibility is often below par, especially if an older person's eyesight is not as young as it used to be.

2. It is a matter of common observation that bus drivers frequently fail to drive as near to the kerb as is desirable. This may be due to vehicle obstruction, but, alternatively, to oversight. It also needs to be said that a close approach of the vehicle to the kerb is only a palliative; often there remains quite an effort for the ageing passenger to overcome in boarding the vehicle. Once inside a public transport vehicle, s/he may find that the four (?) seats reserved for him/her are frequently occupied by younger posteriors, not always willing to vacate the seats or, perhaps, failing to understand English. A pictorial enjoinder might conceivably help.

3. Although cabs are not, strictly speaking, part of a public transport system, they provide a useful supplement. Entering and leaving cabs appears to be a nightmare for some older persons. This may be due to the (excessive?) space left between the passenger seats and the dividing wall, designed, no doubt, to accommodate luggage or parcels. In differently designed cabs, they could be placed in a boot.

4. Train carriages may present problems when the platform is not level with the floor of the carriage or on bends. Curved platforms could be eliminated, if, as is the case in Japan (and now on some stations of the Jubilee Line), trains were programmed to stop within a a few centimetres of prearranged marks. Possible gaps could be bridged to ensure safety. There is also a case to be made for the provision of hand grips inside the carriages so that the elderly may steady themselves when the train is in motion, and there is no other means of support.

5. The existence of boarding steps for aircraft would seem to be an anachronism, especially when they are coupled to the difficulties offered by steps leading from waiting areas to the tarmac.

6. Insufficient consideration appears to be given in general to the legibility of instructions and direction in general. There is, of course, enormous competition from commercial advertisers, and it may be the case that, however hard public transport authorities may be trying to convey a message, commerce is going to prevail. However, that stage has not been reached. The shape of letters, their contrast, and their positions often leave a lot to be desired as regards elderly readers. To be specific, blue and violet may be found in colour combinations rendering the information offered of little use.

7. There is a case to be made for information in all waiting areas being made to attract attention by flashing at the start of a period needed for an older person to reach the target (train, plane, coach) indicated. This would not only be helpful but might also be useful in combating visual commercial competition.

September 2004

Memorandum by the Wellcome Trust

INTRODUCTION

1. The Wellcome Trust is pleased to be given the opportunity to respond to the House of Lords Select Committee on Science and Technology on the subject of *Scientific Aspects of Ageing*, and welcomes the setting up of the Sub-Committee to consider how science and technology can help an ageing population live a healthier and more active life.

2. The Trust is aware that medical advances and demographic transitions are having radical effects on population ageing. The estimated increase in world population over 65 years of age to 1.2 billion by 2025[13] presents a major public health challenge, especially for low and middle income countries that are also struggling with the double burden of disease—infectious and non-infectious diseases. In some developed countries the proportion of older persons is approaching 20 per cent, partly as a result of low fertility rates but also because of longevity. However, with advancing age comes adverse health and a debate on research and technology, as well as a public health approach to help improve people's prospect of a healthy and active life expectancy is opportune.

---

[13] WHO World Health Report, 1998, UN Population Division, World Population Prospects (The 1994 Revision).

SUMMARY

3. A significant proportion of the research funded by the Wellcome Trust is directly or indirectly related to ageing. Using a broad set of key words to define ageing related research we estimate the Trust has funded approximately £547 million of research in this area from 1994 to 2004: 16 per cent of the total research funded by the Trust in this period.

4. However, in its main programmes, the Trust has never given a specific priority to ageing related research so this funding reflects those research grants that have been awarded in competition with a wide range of other disciplines and in all likelihood will have many overlaps with them.

5. Therefore, in undertaking the work to complete this response, we found that there is a wide range of research that is related to ageing but a sub-set of this might be more narrowly focussed on, for example, conditions that affect the elderly. In order to discuss priorities and the co-ordination of funding it will be important to have a more focussed definition of the area. With regard to cancer, this is one of the tasks that the National Cancer Research Institute (NCRI) undertook when deciding on how to discuss prioritisation in that area. This model might be an appropriate one for the Committee to consider with regard to ageing research.

6. However, discussions with a limited number of Trust-funded scientists have highlighted specific areas that might benefit from greater attention. For example there appears to be a need for multidisciplinary teams in universities, bringing public health, clinical gerontologists and biological researchers together. This approach, together with wider use of medical care technology, could assist an ageing population live a healthier and more active life.

ABOUT THE WELLCOME TRUST

7. The Wellcome Trust is an independent, biomedical research-funding charity established under the will of Sir Henry Wellcome in 1936. Its mission is to foster and promote research with the aim of improving human and animal health.

8. In the financial year ended 30 September 2003, the Trust's total charitable expenditure was over £500 million, the majority of which was to fund research in the UK.

SCIENTIFIC ASPECTS OF AGEING—RESPONSE FROM THE WELLCOME TRUST

9. The Trust does not have a special initiative on ageing research but it does fund research in many biomedical areas that are related, directly or indirectly, to ageing. For an insight into funding in these areas, we searched our databases for keywords and subject areas that cover some of the main diseases and disorders normally associated with advancing age. In addition to "ageing" or "longevity", cognitive function, joint diseases, stroke, cell biology and cell cycle are amongst the areas searched (see Annex 1); in total the Trust funded grants in the region of £547 million over the decade 1994–2004, representing about 16 per cent of the total funding portfolio. In addition, substantial investment has been made in medical imaging technology, infrastructure support, and genomic analysis of ageing bringing the total to £877 million (26 per cent) over the same period.

10. For the majority of the research that it supports the Trust operates a responsive mode funding mechanism. However, in addition to this there are a number of strategic initiatives that have been launched and those which relate to ageing have been listed below.

11. *The Health Consequences of Population Change Programme* (http://www.wellcome.ac.uk/hcpc). This five-year initiative was launched in 2001 and established a £65 million fund to support several key areas aimed at research into the effects of demographic shifts and socio-economic changes on public health in the developing world including the ageing population.

12. *The Cognitive Systems Foresight Project* (http://www.wellcome.ac.uk/en/l/biosfgunkste.html). This is an area of multidisciplinary research highlighted by the Trust for funding, jointly with the UK Research Councils. Cognitive systems are natural or artificial information processing systems, including those responsible for perception, reasoning, decision-making, communication and action. Cognitive systems research is therefore an area that could have implications for assisting ageing and frail populations.

13. *The UK Biobank* (http://www.ukbiobank.ac.uk). The Trust is a major funder (together with the MRC and the Department of Health) of the UK Biobank, which will be the world's largest resource (500,000 individuals, between the ages of 45 and 69) for the study of the role of genes and the environment (or nature and nurture) in health and disease. Many diseases and disorders of old age (cancer, cardiovascular, diabetes, Alzheimer's, joint diseases, cognition/dementia, and quality of life) will form the basis of this resource to uncover the genetic

and environmental factors that lead to these conditions. This combination of information from participants will create a powerful resource for biomedical researchers. It will enable them to improve our understanding of the biology of disease and develop improved diagnostic tools, prevention strategies and tailor made treatments for disorders that appear with advancing age. The pilot phase of volunteer recruitment is about to commence and will take five years to complete.

14. The concept of prospective longitudinal studies is to have the baseline measures in place, including biological samples, before the onset of disease. The primary goal is to provide research to enable the application of genomics technologies for patient management and intervention strategies rather than therapy.

15. As mentioned above the Trust has not previously highlighted ageing research as a specific priority and so we felt it was not appropriate for us to answer some of the specific questions regarding how ageing research is co-ordinated or prioritised. However, it is hoped the following general comments, arising from consultations with a limited number of Trust-funded scientists, will be useful to the inquiry:

— In general, basic research into disease mechanisms should be supplemented with a broader public health agenda to provide health protection and healthier lifestyle promotion together with primary/ secondary prevention. A broader evidence base is needed since the number of older people participating in clinical trials is not representative of their number in the population. Since life expectancy is closely linked with social class, more research into social factors (such as access to health care, education) and the underlying reasons for this link is probably needed, but for which there is limited funding.

— Elucidating the role of genes and non-genetic factors (for example, environment, diet, exercise); research into disease mechanisms, pathogenesis and ageing mechanism(s)—for example, cell senescence, neuronal cell death, the role of telomerase, proteomic research/technology, are promising areas given the advances in genomic research and technology.

— Research into dementia (Alzheimer's, Parkinson's as examples), and motor neuron disorder, and model systems such as mutations in fruit flies (*Drosophila*) and worms (*C. elegans*) could provide molecular models into human ageing, which have not been fully exploited.

— The use of non-human primates to understand cognitive functions and test treatments for dementia is likely to increase. There are alternatives which could be used such as transgenic rodents genetically modified to have human-like nervous systems. However, the development of these models and in vitro (non-animal) alternatives could benefit from more targeted funding.

— While stem cell research (or therapeutic cloning) is a relatively young area and such therapies appear distant, the benefits could be high for future generations. The UK now leads in this burgeoning field given the recent ruling by the Human Fertilisation and Embryology Authority to allow scientists to clone human embryos. In this regard research using embryonic stem cells, understanding their differentiation and maintenance, in particular neuronal stem cells, could be exploited for research into cognitive function.

— Public health aspects of diet and exercise have an impact on healthy ageing. The World Health Organisation has been advocating a "life course approach" (http://www.who.int/hpr/ageing/index.htm) to reduce disability and delaying the onset of chronic diseases by the promotion of a healthy lifestyle, avoiding or reducing risk factors associated with some of the most common disabilities.

— Calorific restriction using animal modes could provide insights into the role of metabolic processes in ageing.

— Loss of muscle strength, bone loss and joint diseases; new technologies, such as tissue engineering, could focus on wound healing—especially bone fractures resulting from falls and accidents.

— In the field of population genomics, there is a high degree of international co-operation through EU initiatives and other organizations, eg the Public Population Project in Genomics (P3G, see http://www.p3gconsortium.org) which is an organization that aims to foster collaboration between researchers.

— Research into an ageing population covers basic, medical and social sciences. Capacity building for a multidisciplinary approach is needed and researchers should take advantage of existing networks, such as P3G, to establish collaborations and multidisciplinary teams.

— A recent study (http://www.wellcome.ac.uk/en/1/awtpub.html) commissioned by the Wellcome Trust on Public Health Sciences: Challenges and opportunities, concluded that a national strategy is urgently needed to foster research into major public health problems in the UK. It is likely that research into ageing populations will fall within this category.

Wellcome Trust funding in key research areas related to ageing. Data was obtained by searching for the indicated keyword/phrase over the period 1994-2004.

	Number of awards	£ awarded (millions)
Ageing, longevity	224	52.51
Mental health (Alzheimer's, dementia)	250	66.13
Antioxidants, free radical damage	53	4.87
Apoptosis, cell cycle, cell death, senescence	355	61.98
Joint and bone diseases (arthritis, osteoporosis)	185	43.70
Cancer	100	62.42
Demography	189	34.32
Diet, vitamins	99	13.82
Geriatric medicine	12	1.71
Hearing	4	0.59
Exercise	30	2.40
Stem cell	165	45.16
Stroke	155	47.12
Vision	564	110.23
Total:	2,385	546.97
Percentage of total funding (1994–2004):		16.20

Supplementary evidence from the Wellcome Trust

Further to your email of 26 January 2005, asking the Trust to supplement our written evidence to the House of Lords Select Committee on Science and Technology regarding "Scientific Aspects of Ageing", please find below some more detailed explanation of how we arrived at the figures provided.

As we discussed prior to submitting our evidence, the Trust funds a wide range of research that could be related to ageing, with a sub-set more narrowly focused on, for example, conditions that affect the elderly, but awards are not made through a specific scheme.

In paragraph 3 of our evidence, we estimated that approximately £877 million of the research funded by the Wellcome Trust over the last 10 years is directly or indirectly related to ageing, using our broadest definition of ageing-related research.

In our evidence we gave a break-down of some Trust funding in key research areas related to ageing in Annex 1. A total of £52.51 million is specifically related to "ageing or longevity" research, as these words appear either in the title of a grant or are specified in classification fields. The way this search was performed means that a grant cannot be "double counted", even where it can trigger more than one of the keywords.

VISION

The relatively large amount of funding that you note went to vision research shown in Annex 1 can be in part explained by the fact that the Trust supported five buildings. A total of £31 million was awarded through the Joint Infrastructure Fund[14] (JIF) and a subsequent similar scheme, for buildings to conduct research into neuroscience and vision, some of which may be related to scientific aspects of ageing.

The Trust also ran a specific Vision Research Fellowship scheme between 1994 and 1998, which funded 17 Fellows at a total cost of £2.4 million. However not all of the funding shown as relating to vision will be specific to ageing.

[14] JIF was a £750 million partnership between the Wellcome Trust, the Office of Science and Technology, and the Higher Education Funding Council for England. Buildings in Sussex, London, Belfast and Newcastle were supported for research into neuroscience and vision.

HEALTH CONSEQUENCES OF POPULATION CHANGE

A more targeted public health approach to ageing populations is incorporated within the Wellcome Trust's Health Consequences of Population Change Programme.[15] This is a five-year initiative which focuses on research into the health impact of shifts in population structure and dynamics in the developing world. One of five key research themes relates to demographic transitions, particularly public health issues of ageing populations where this poses a new set of problems for public health in the developing world.

The Trust has funded a number of grants in the area including a major award to a Centre of Excellence in Population Research in Costa Rica, along with others, some of which have been highlighted in the Wellcome Trust Annual Review 2004 (enclosed, see page 44). So far 13 awards have been made in the area of "Ageing or Longevity", totalling £2.1 million and these awards are included under the total for "Ageing or Longevity" shown in Annex 1.

February 2005

Annex 1

WELLCOME TRUST FUNDING IN KEY RESEARCH AREAS RELATED TO AGEING[16]

	Number of awards	*£ awarded (millions)*
Ageing, longevity	224	52.51
Mental health (Alzheimer's, dementia)	250	66.13
Antioxidants, free radical damage	53	4.87
Apoptosis, cell cycle, cell death, senescence	355	61.98
Joint and bone diseases (arthritis, osteoporosis)	185	43.70
Cancer	100	62.42
Demography	189	34.32
Diet, vitamins	99	13.82
Geriatric medicine	12	1.71
Hearing	4	0.59
Exercise	30	2.40
Stem cell	165	45.16
Stroke	155	47.12
Vision	564	110.23
Total:	**2,385**	**546.97**
% of total funding (1994–2004):		**16.2**

[15] The programme is funded from 2001–06. See our website, http://www.wellcome.ac.uk/node2143.html.

[16] Using our broadest definition of ageing-related research, approximately £877 million of the research funded by the Wellcome Trust over the last 10 years is directly or indirectly related to ageing. This table shows the result of more specific searches, using the key words shown above. The search was conducted such a way that a grant can not be counted more than once, even if it triggered more than one of the keywords/phrases. We have not attempted to combine "Ageing or Longevity" with any of other key word listed in this table. Data was obtained by searching for the indicated keyword/phrase over the period 1994–2004.

ISBN 0-10-400728-1